CRYPTIC
CROSSWORD
CLUEFINDER

CRYPTIC CROSSWORD CLUEFINDER

A DICTIONARY OF CROSSWORD CLUES

J.A.Coleman

Macquarie
Regional Libra

ARCTURUS

Arcturus Publishing Limited
26/27 Bickels Yard
151–153 Bermondsey Street
London SE1 3HA

Published in association with
foulsham
W. Foulsham & Co. Ltd,
The Publishing House, Bennetts Close, Cippenham,
Slough, Berkshire SL1 5AP, England

ISBN 0-572-03097-5

This edition printed in 2005

Copyright © 2005 Arcturus Publishing Limited

British Library Cataloguing-in-Publication Data: a catalogue record for this
book is available from the British Library

Printed in India

INTRODUCTION

Thousands of crossword clues are published every day of the year and it would be an impossible task to cover even a fraction of this output in one dictionary. However, it is possible to recognise the general patterns used by compilers and such recognition is the first step on the road to solving a clue.

Typically, a clue in a cryptic crossword will contain a direct clue which is sufficient to provide the answer if you can recognise it, plus one or more indirect clues which will also provide the answer but may need to be manipulated for that purpose, and one or more pointers which will indicate how the indirect clues should be manipulated to provide the answer. An example might be **Carmen, perhaps, breaks into surgery(9)**. We could be looking for a solution for 'Carmen' (or 'carmen') or for a word meaning 'surgery' but since it is only 'perhaps Carmen' we should expect the direct clue to be 'surgery'. This might tell you the answer (OPERATION) but, if not, you can look at the indirect clue 'Carmen' (OPERA) and the pointer 'breaks' which invites you to rearrange the second indirect clue 'into' to form the anagram - TION, giving the same result.

The components of indirect clues are listed below:

Abbreviations - recognised ones such as SS for (steam)ship or 'compiler's language' forms such as NS for North Sea

Anagrams - letters, usually from given words, re-arranged to form another word, so that '*shattered* [arm]' becomes MAR or RAM

Articles such as 'a' and 'an', printed in the clue, may be used as part of the solution, but may be overlooked because they are so common; this includes foreign versions such as 'der', 'la', etc so that 'Continental articles' can be UNDER

Cockney expressions such as 'apples and pears' (STAIRS) and words from which the initial 'h' has been dropped so that '*Cockney* headgear' becomes (h)AT

Colloquialisms or careless speech such as 'ain't' or ''otter'

Compound words which should be read as two separate words so that 'legend' becomes 'leg' and 'end' meaning FOOT

Derived words are words derived from words given in the clue - as distinct from the given words themselves - so that, for example, SHE can be derived from the word 'female' given in the clue

Foreign words quite often appear, often combined with English words, so that '*French*man' requires HOMME

Given words are words printed in the clue which are sometimes used, as printed, in the solution, particularly in the case of Articles and Small words

Hidden words - words forming part of given words such as CHIN which can be found hidden in 'Fren/ch in/sults'

Homophones - words which sound the same as words given in the clue but which have different spelling and meaning as, for instance, WAIT and WEIGHT

Numbers, particularly Roman numerals, which are often used to represent letters, with C(100), D(500), L(50) and M(1000) standing for 'many'

Oblique descriptions are elaborately-worded or punning clues designed to disguise the required synonym rather as Churchill's 'terminological inexactitude' meant a plain old-fashioned LIE

Old words - obsolete and archaic words are used in crosswords, even though banned in other word games, so that 'the old' means YE

One of a class - here the clue gives a general class (eg: dog) and you are required to provide a particular example (eg: SETTER) or you may be given 'setter' as the particular specimen requiring the general class DOG

Opposite/negative clues require a solution which is the reverse of a given or derived word, so that 'face up' would yield BACK DOWN and 'not over' is more likely to mean UNDER than 'unfinished'

Part words - the clue may be so worded as to require the use of part of a given or derived word, so that 'some pepper' might mean PEP or PER

Poetic words - words used mainly by writers such as Spenser, Shakespeare, etc, so that 'poets' guild' might be GYELD

Proper nouns, including personal names, are sometimes used, often as the first word of the clue, so that the capital letter does not immediately indicate the use of a proper noun.

Quotations from literature, the Bible, the classics, history, etc often appear, sometimes unfairly, in that there are no indirect clues to give the solution to those unfamiliar with the quotation.

Rhymes - the solution in such cases is a word which rhymes with an indirect clue, so that 'her. . .' might require CUR, SIR, PURR, etc

Selected letters - letters from given words may be retained, so that 'initially my eye' gives ME, or they may be omitted so that '*decapitated* (w)omen' becomes OMEN

Singulars and plurals - a 'singular' word may be half of another singular word, such as SING-SING, which has two identical parts, and 'plural words' may require the repeated use of a singular word such as IS to give ISIS

Small words - insignificant given words such as 'at', 'on', etc which, like articles, can easily be overlooked; 'pass on' may give COLON rather than 'hand over' or 'die'

Split words - any word may be split to allow another word to be written inside so that 'put *in* de-ed' becomes DEPUTED and, using abbreviations in the same way, 'highest *in* ship' give STOPS

Stuttered words - an indication that you need to double the stuttered letter so that 'a *stuttering peal*' becomes APPEAL

Synonyms are words having the same meaning but spelt differently and in some cases more than two meanings may be used; eg: 'able to', 'chimney', 'container' and 'prison' would all be satisfied with CAN

Any of these components can be combined to form the solution by adding words or parts, including words or parts within others, omitting parts of words or letters, reversing words or parts, substituting words or letters for others, or by using combinations of these devices such as writing part of one word backwards inside another. How you are to use these various components will be indicated by the pointers provided, which may be as devious as the clues themselves.

In this book you will find examples of all these various forms together with many tips and hints. In some cases the solution is not a recognisable word but the example is there to illustrate a point and the letters of the suggested solution can form part of a required answer. Some words have a number of entries, each relating to a different use and identified by a superscript number. When looking up a particular word, it is worth while checking all entries; 'the first . . . T' will be found under the entry dealing with uses of 'the' itself, whereas 'the first ball . . . B' is under the entry that deals with 'the' in its normal role as an article attached to a noun.

All the above formed the introduction to the original *Cluefinder* which was published in 1995 by Cassells. Since that date, additional material has been added, increasing the size of the book by some 60%. This is that book, *Cryptic Crossword Cluefinder*, which may perhaps prove to be 60% more useful than its parent.

KEY

The following list gives details of the symbols, etc used above and in the following pages:

anagram	[cat]
any word included or omitted	*
beginnings	IGN-
direct clue	<u>cat</u>
endings	-ING
examples	•
hidden word	/cat/
implied-additions	(on)
-inclusions	(in)
letter replaced	\c\at
pointers	*out*
selected letters-omitted	(a)
-retained	<u>a</u>
word-split for inclusion	B-ED
-used in Down clue	(D)
-written backwards-across	<
-down	∧

The list of words printed in bold at the head of each section gives words for which that letter can be used as an abbreviation. Compilers' versions, as distinct from normal usage, are given in italics.

A

Academician, accepted, ace, ack, acre, active, adult, advanced, afternoon, aleph, alpha, alto, amateur, America, ampere, an, ana, ane, angström, annus, ante, answer, are, argon, associate, atomic, atto-, Austria, *ay, aye,* before (ante), blood group, bomb, effect, electric current, examination, film, fifty, five hundred, five thousand, *first character,* first-class, first letter, *high class,* it, key, level, mass number, note, nucleon number, one, paper, road, string, *top grade, top mark,* un, vitamin, year (annus)

---

a¹

as 'a' – English:

a	AN, I, ONE, UNIT
a *deficient*	omit A
a *dialect*	HE, IT, SHE, THEY
a *follower*	B
a *for example*	VOWEL
a *loss*	omit A
a *missing*	omit A
a turn to . . .	AUTO

a²

as 'a' – other languages:

a *Continental* . . .	UN, UNE
a *French* . . .	UN, UNE
• a *French* composer	UNRAVEL
• a *French* dressing	UNROBING
• a *French* pirate	UNHOOK
a *German* . . .	EIN
a *Greek* . . .	ALPHA
a *Hebrew* . . .	ALEPH
a *Parisian* . .	UN, UNE
a *Scottish* . . .	ANE
a *Spanish* . . .	UN, UNA, UNO
an *Italian* . . .	UN, UNA, UNO

a³

as an inclusion:

• a *break in* the se–t	SEAT
• be–t *about* a . . .	BEAT
• colour *including* a . . .	READ, TAINT
• fl–y *around* a . . .	FLAY
• me–t *round* a . . .	MEAT

a⁴

as a 'prefix':

• A50	–AL
• a 2p . . .	APP–
• a 50-50 . . .	ALL
• a bank	ADRIFT
• a billow	AWAVE
• a bit of money	–AL
• a boat	ASS

• a book	ANT
• a border	AHEM
• a bounder, Scot	ACADIAN
• a cat	ATOM
• a Celt	ASCOT
• a cereal	ACORN
• a character here, *say*	ACARDIA
• a chimney	ALUM
• a church	ACE
• a church feature	ASPIRE
• a cleaner	ACHAR
• a climbing plant	AVINE
• a colliery	AMINE
• a competitor, *say*	ARRIVAL
• a container	AJAR
• a container like this	ACANTHUS
• a cricket club	ACC–
• a cricketer you are, *say*	ABATURE
• a decoy	ALLURE
• a defender	ABACK
• a deficiency	ALACK
• a desire	AITCH, ALONG
• a disguise	AVAIL
• a doctor in front	AMBLED
• a drink	APORT
• a drink	ARUM
• a drunken father, *say*	APATITE
• a drupe, *say*	APLUMB
• a face cover, *say*	AVAIL
• a faint beat	APPULSE
• a fall	ATRIP
• a feast	ASPREAD
• a few, *say*	SUM
• a fiddle	AGUE
• a fight	ABOUT
• a fine fellow	AGENT
• a fish	ACHAR
• a fish	AGAR, AIDE
• a flower	AROSE
• a foot	AFT

Anag [cat]; Any *; Begin IGN–; Endings –ING; eg •; Hidden /cat/; Implied add (on); Implied in (in); Letter replaced \c\at; Omit (a); Pointers *out*; Retain a̱; Split B_ED; Down (D); Backwards <or ^

• a foot ailment	ACORN
• a four	AFORESAID
• a friend	AMATE
• a frock, *say*	ADDRESS
• a fruit, *say*	APLOMB, APPEAR
• a funeral vigil	AWAKE
• a gambler	ABETTER
• a game point	APOLOGIST
• a general	ALEE
• a giant	AGOG
• a girl	AMISS
• a girl might, *say*	ADAMITE
• a girl severed, *say*	ANICUT
• a goddess	AMUSE
• a grating	ARACK
• a harbour	APORT
• a <u>head</u>*start*	AH
• a horse	AMOUNT
• a hundredweight	ACTON
• a husk	APOD
• a journey	ATRIP
• a jump	ABOUND
• a labyrinth	AMAZE
• a large drink, *say*	ABIGAIL
• a large meal	ABIGEAT
• a large quantity, *say*	ALLOT
• a leader	ACID
• a leader-worker	ABEYANT
• a learner	–AL
• a legume, *say*	APPULSE
• a light touch, *say*	ATICAL
• a lightweight	ACT
• a lightweight, *say*	ANNOUNCE
• a line	–ARY
• a lintel, *say*	ABEAM
• a little porcelain, *say*	SUMMING
• a load, *say*	AWAIT
• a loose woman	ABROAD
• a loud tale	AFFABLE
• a married . . .	AWED
• a mask, *say*	AVAIL
• a match	ABOUT
• a measure	AFOOT
• a meeting place	AVENUE
• a member	AMP
• a method	AWAY
• a method, *say*	AWEIGH
• a minor road	ABROAD
• a mole, *say*	APPEAR
• a mother	ADAM
• a mother-worker	ADAMANT
• a mountain range	AURAL
• a niece is, *say*	ANESIS
• a noble, *say*	ACCOUNT, APPEAR
• a Norseman, *say*	JOCKEY, RIDER
• a Northern . . .	AN
• a note	ADO, ALA, ARE, ATE
• a note	ATONE
• a number take exercise, *say*	TENDRIL
• a pace	ASTRIDE
• a pamphlet, *say*	ATTRACT
• a paper handkerchief, *say*	ATISHOO
• a parrot performing	APOLLYON
• a party circle	ADORING
• a path, *say*	AWEIGH
• a pause, *say*	ARREST
• a pick-me-up, *say*	ATONIC
• a pig, *say*	ABHOR
• a peer, *say*	ASHORE
• a pilaster, *say*	APPEAR
• a pit	AMINE
• a plague	AT EASE
• a ploy	ATACTIC
• a poem	ANODE, AVERSE
• a poet	ANDANTE
• a Pole scoffed	APOSTATE
• a policeman	ACOP
• a priesthood, *say*	ACCURACY
• a prison	ASTIR
• a prize	ATROPHY
• a profit	AGAIN
• a promontory	AHEAD
• a quiet man	APRON
• a quiet sitter	APPOSER
• a raid, *say*	ARRAYED
• a ray, *say*	ABEAM
• a reason, *say*	AGROUND
• a religious heretic	APIARIAN
• a rendezvous	AVENUE
• a reward	ATROPHY
• a right	ALIEN
• a ring, *say*	APPEAL
• a river	ANILE
• a road	AWAY
• a road to the hill	AVIATOR
• a row, *say*	ALIGN
• a rule, *say*	ARRAIGN
• a ruler, *say*	ACHING
• a sailor, *say*	ATTAR
• a saint, *say*	APPAL
• a sanctimonious heretic	APIARIAN
• a savage . . .	ACCRUAL
• a screw	AWARDER
• a service	AMASS, ARAF
• a sex, *say*	AGENDA
• a share	ARATION
• a shelf, *say*	ALLEGE
• a ship	AHOY, ASS
• a silly tax	ADUMBRATE
• a singer	AWAIT
• a sitter, *say*	APPOSER
• a sixpence	AVID
• a skin, *say*	APPEAL
• a soft fruit	APPEACH

Anag [cat]; Any *; Begin IGN–; Endings –ING; eg •; Hidden /cat/; Implied add (on); Implied in (in);

- a sound — ATONE
- a sound, *say* — ANNOYS
- a spanner — ABRIDGE
- a spell in this place, *say* — APHASIA
- a spirit — ARUM
- a stain, *say* — ATTAINT
- a step — APACE
- a step — ASTRIDE
- a stone fruit, *say* — APPEACH
- a strong group — AFFORCE
- a stud — ASTABLE
- a stye — ABOIL
- a superior — ABETTER
- a tax — ATOLL
- a team, *say* — ASIDE
- a tenet, *say* — ADRIFT
- a valley, *say* — AVAIL
- a very quiet dog — APPROVER
- a vice — AGREED
- a wager — ABET, ALPHABET
- a wanderer, *say* — AROMA
- a warden — ARRANGER
- a waterpipe — AMAIN
- a weight — ACT
- a wicked fellow — ABADDON
- a woman (US) — ABROAD
- a writer — ASCRIBE
- a Yugoslav, *say* — ACERB

and
- a leopard — ANNOUNCE
- a poem — ANODE
- a poet — ANDANTE
- a twitch — ANTIC
- a weight — ANNOUNCE

and
- leave *after* a . . . — AGO
- man *behind* a . . . — AGENT
- obliged to *follow* a . . . — ABOUND

and
- an angry insect, *say* — ACROSTIC
- an opening — AGATE
- an urge — AITCH

(*see also* an)

a⁵
as a 'suffix':
- a boy *and* a . . . — ERICA
- feature article — CHINA
- fish *with* a . . . — CODA
- one *joining* a . . . — PERSONA
- barrel *having* a . . . — TUNA

a⁶
a bit of ca/ke en/closed — KEEN
a little m/an tic/ked . . . — ANTIC
a shure of he/r est/ate — REST

A
AA man — AARON, ARCHIE
AA gun — ARCHIE

AAA — DASHBOARD
abandon¹
indicating omission:
abandon a . . . — omit A
abandon daughter — omit D
abandon husband — omit H
abandon one . . . — omit A or I
abandon ship — omit SS
abandon son — omit S
abandon wife — omit W
abandon * — omit *
- sen(try) *abandons* attempt — SEN
abandoned by * — omit *
- cab(le) *abandoned by* the *French* — CAB
quietly *abandons* . . . — omit P
abandon²
abandon fight — SCRAP
abandon sin — SHE-DEVIL
abandoned [claim] — MALIC
abandons colours — MAROONS
abandons trenches — DITCHES
[dance] *with abandon* — CANED
abbess/abbot/abbey — ABB
abbreviate
abbreviate boo(k) — BOO
abbreviated period — TIM(e)
abbreviation of par(t) — PAR
abdicated — ABD
Abel — ADAMSON
aberration
aberrant [tones] — NOTES, ONSET, SETON
aberration of [mental] . . . — LAMENT
ablative — ABL
able
able seaman — AB
able-bodied seaman, *say* — WHOLESALER
able to be [used] — DUES, SUED
(*see also* sailor)
abnormal
abnormal [lump] — PLUM
abnormally [low] — OWL
aboard
aboard — (in) S–S
- work *aboard* — SOPS
aboard — incl SS
- Ma–e *aboard* — MASSE
aboard — ON
- lady's *aboard* — HERON
aboard ket/ch ar/riving . . . — CHAR
(*see also* on⁶)
abolish
abolish a . . . — omit A
abolish * — omit *
- fa(the)r *abolishes* the . . . — FAR
- franc *abolished* in (F)inland — INLAND
abominable
abominable snowman — YETI

Letter replaced \c\at; Omit (a); Pointers *out*; Retain a̲; Split B_ED; Down (D); Backwards <or ^

abominable [taste]	TEATS, TESTA
abominably [evil]	LIVE
abort	
aborted [sea trip]	TRAIPSE
abortive [try, Pa]	PARTY
about¹	
about (=approximately)	
about	C
• about a boy	CALF, CANDY
	CANTON, CERIC
• about a girl	CANNA, CLASS
• about a member	CAMP
• about an old king	CLEAR
• about an old ship	CARGO
• about fifty	CL–
• about right	CR–
• about this *Latin* . . .	CHIC
• about time	CAGE
• about *to be removed*	omit C
• about *to leave*	omit C
• about *twice*	CRE–
about	CA
• about 500	CAD
• about about	CARE
• about *about*<	AC
• about about about *about*	CAREER
• about right	CAR, CART
• about time	CAT
• about *twice*	CARE
• about *to be removed*	omit CA
• about to get up	CAROUSE
• about *to leave*	omit CA
about	CIRC(A)
• about East	CIRCE
• about the *French* . . .	CIRCLE
• about you and me	CIRCUS
about²	
about (=concerning)	
about	RE
• about a boy	REASON
• about *about*<	ER
• about fifty	REL–
• about money	RECENT
• about now	REPRESENT
• about over	REPAST
• about poetry	REVERSE
• about some quarters	REPARTEE
• about sea	REMAIN
• about tax	RECESS
• about *to be removed*	omit RE
• about *to leave*	omit RE
• about *twice*	CARE, CRE–
• I *take* about . . .	IRE
• leave about . . .	GORE
• snake, one about . . .	ASPIRE
about *retirement*<	–ER
about *to return*<	–ER

about *to rise*(D)^	–ER
(*see also* touching)	
about³	
indicating inclusion:	
about a . . .	incl A
about a hundred	incl C, AC
about fifty	incl L
about five	incl V
about four	incl IV
about nine	incl IX
about one	incl A, I
about right	incl R, RT
about six	incl VI
about ten	incl X
about time	incl T
about turn	incl U
about *	incl *
• talk *about* scabies	CHITCHAT
about⁴	
other uses:	
about face<	LAID
about [now]	OWN, WON
about time<	ARE, EMIT
about turn	U
about turn at . . .<	TA
enthusiastic *about*<	DAM
above	
above	SUP(RA)
above(D)	(*see* over³)
above ten	ELEVEN, TENT
above zero	NOTICE(D)
Abrahamville	LINCOLN
abridge	
abridged	ABD
abridged boo(k)	BOO
abridged st(or)y	STY
abroad	
abroad [in gold] . . .	DOLING
abroad	
indicating use of a	
foreign language:	
• *Continental* house	CASA, MAISON
• *cross-channel* bridge	PONT
• go *abroad*	ALLER
• *overseas* contract	APPALTO
• walk *on the Continent*	MARCHER
• work *overseas*	LAVORO, TRAVAIL
[travel] *abroad*	VARLET
(*see also* continent, cross⁴, foreign)	
absent	
absence of	NO
–approval	NOOK
–friend	NOPAL
–hooter	NONOSE
–males	NOMEN
–medicine	NODOSE
–stomach	NOTUM

–wickedness	NOVICE
absent	AWOL
absent king	omit K, R
absent worker	OFFHAND
absent *	omit *
• ap(pal) *absent* friend	AP
absentee	omit EE
an *absent* . . .	omit AN
absolute	
absolute	ABS
absolutely transparent	SHEER
absorb	
absorb eggs, *say*	SUCCEED
absorb oxygen	incl O
absorbed in *	incl in *
• saint *absorbed in* music	ASTIR
absorbing a . . .	incl A
absorbing *	incl *
• music *absorbing* saint	ASTIR
absorbs mu/ch I li/ke	CHILI
abstainer	RECHABITE, TT
abstract	
abstract	ABS
abstract a . . .	omit A
abstract form	REMOVE
abstract money	omit L
abstract *	omit *
• Greek so *abstracted*	(ɒo)CRATES
absurd	
absurd [idea]	AIDE
absurdly [used]	DUSE, SUED
abuse	
abuse [slave]	SALVE, VALES
abused [animal]	LAMINA
abusing [dogs]	GODS
academic	
academic	MA, PROF
academic appointment	CHAIR
academic stream	CAM, ISIS
academician	A, ARA, PRA, RA
academy	RA, RADA
accept	
acceptable	OK, ON, U
accepted	A, INSET, U
accepted by t/he m/ajority	HEM
accepted by *	incl in *
• we are *accepted by* group	SWEET
accepting a . . .	incl A
accepting *	incl *
• b–at *accepting* nothing	BOAT
accident	
accident	HAP
accident in [plane]	PANEL
accidentally [spilt]	SPLIT
after accident [rider] . . .	DRIER
accommodate	
accommodated by *	incl in *

• girl *accommodated by* a–n..	AMAIN
accommodating a . . .	incl A
accommodating *	incl *
• Ab–e *accommodating* us	ABUSE
accommodating ma/ny, ala/s	NYALA
accommodation rented	FLATLET
accompany	
accompanying	WITH
–gangster	WITHAL
–woman	WITHER
–you, *say*	WITHE, WITHY
accompanying page	ATTENDANT
accompanied by	incl AND
• Henry *accompanied by* son	HANDS
accomplished	
accomplished actors	OVERCAST
accomplished country girl	DONEGAL
accomplished explorer	OVERCOOK
accomplished, *say*	VERST
according	
according to	
–art	SA
–law	SEC LEG
–nature	SN
–rule	SEC REG
–value	AD VAL(OREM)
according to some (=dialect)	
• *according to some*, swift . . .	WIGHT
• information *according to some*	WITTING
accordingly legal	SOLICIT
account	
account	AC(C), ACCT, BILL
account clerk	BILLPOSTER
account for	
–cutlery	SPOONBILL
–footwear	SHOEBILL
–instrument	HORNBILL
account outstanding	BILLOWED
	BILLOWING
accountant	AC, ACA, CA, FCA
accountants	CAS, SAA
• accountant's girl	CASSANDRA
• accountant's note	CASE
accurate	
accurate imitator	DEAD PARROT
accurate shot	(ANNIE) OAKLEY, TELL
accurately (=to the letter)	
• absolutely *accurately*	DEAD LETTER
ace	A, EXPERT, I, NOI–
	ONE, PRO, WINNER
	(*see also* expert)
achievement quotient	AQ
acid test	PH
acknowledge	
acknowledge worker	AVOWANT
acknowledged debts	–IOUS
acknowledgement	ROGER

Letter replaced \c\at; Omit (a); Pointers *out*; Retain a̲; Split B_ED; Down (D); Backwards <or ^

acoustic

acoustic wave	WAIVE
acoustics, *say*	ECOSYSTEM
acquire leverage	PURCHASE
acre	A

across

across (=a cross)	X
• across fish	X-RAY
• get monkey across	APEX
• put the man across	HEX
across the Channel (=in French)	
• swim *across the Channel*	NAGER
• bridge *across the Channel*	PONT
• fly *across the Channel*	MOUCHE
• *across the Channel*, men . . .	HOMMES
	(*see also* abroad)
across	TRANS–
across a street	SAT
across the Atlantic	–TOUS
fl–y *across* a . . .	FLAY
run *across*<	NUR

act[1]

[act]	WILDCAT
[act] *peculiarly*	CAT
[acted] *strangely*	CADET
	(*see also* indeed)

act[2]

act	BILL, TAKE APART
act	
–fraudulently	BEACON
–gallantly	BENIGHT
–impishly	BEDEVIL
–legally	PROSECUTE, SUE
–like	
a dog *say*	BEAKER
a stone *say*	BEJEWEL
–more rashly	BEWILDER
–of	
union	MARRIAGE, WEDDING
war	DORA
act as	
–consumer	EAT
–publisher	BEADMAN
–ruler	BEAKING
–sentry	BEGUARD
–sentry, *say*	BEGGARRED, BEGHARD
–starter, *say*	SAGO
–swindler	BEACON
–telephone	BEARING
acting	ON
acting as	QUA
–a pig	QUAHOG
–monarch	QUAKING
acts collectively	DRAMA, PLAY

activate

activate [plot]	POLT
activated [a model] . . .	LOAMED

active

active	A, ACT
• active people	AMEN
• active railway	ALINE
• not active	NOTA
active Communist	LIVERED
active [life]	FILE
[great] *activity*	GRATE
[stride] *actively*	DIREST

actor

actor	PLAYER, TREE
actor's remuneration	PART PAYMENT
actors	EQUITY, RADA
actors on tour	CASTAWAY
[actors] *on tour*	CROATS
actors' wages	CASTRATE
actuaries	FA
acute lamentation	KEEN

Adam

Adam	FIRST MAN, FIRST MATE
Adam (and Eve)	BELIEVE
Adam's ale	WATER
Adam's first wife	LILITH
Adam's wine	WATER
Adam*son*	ABEL, CAIN, SETH

adapt

adaptable [sort]	TORS
adaptation of [recent] . . .	CENTRE
adapted [an old] . . .	NODAL
adapting [another's] . . .	SHERATON

add

add	
–garnish	ATTACH
–it on, *say*	SUMMON
–it up, *say*	SUMMIT
–letters, *say*	COUNTESSES
add	
–an ode	ANODE
–pound *to* fee	FEEL
–weight *to* dreadful . . .	DIRECT
added weight	EXTRACT

additional

additional	
–award	BAR
–additional message	PS
–additional postscript	PPS
additional	MORE
–beer, *say*	MORALE
–directions, *say*	MOREEN
–donkeys, *say*	MORASSES
–Scotsman, *say*	MORMON
additional	EXTRA
–parties, *say*	EXTRADOS
–weight	EXTRACT
additional premium	AP

address

address in America	GETTYSBURG

Anag [cat]; Any *; Begin IGN–; Endings –ING; eg •; Hidden /cat/; Implied add (on); Implied in (in);

address			DRAKE, HOOD, NELSON
indicating mode of address:		Admiral of the Fleet	AF
ambassador's address	HE, EXCELLENCY	**admire**	
archdeacon's address	(VEN)ERABLE	admirer, *say*	SUTOR
bishop's address	GRACE	**admit**[1]	
cardinal's address	EMINENCE	admitted	IN
–old	MOST ILLUSTRIOUS	• admitted dog	INCUR
dean's address	VERY REV(EREND)	• admitted group	INSECT, INCULT
duke's address	GRACE	• admitted *to* hospital	INWARD
earl's address	LORD	admitting	AM
judge's address	LORD	• admitting essayist	AMELIA
king's address	MAJESTY	• admitting girl	AMRITA
knight's address	SIR	• admitting one ship	AMISS
magistrate's address	HONOUR	admitting	IM–
mayor's address	WORSHIP	• admitting journalists	IMPRESS
member's address	HON(OURABLE)	• admitting two	IMPAIR
pope's address	HOLINESS	• admitting working	IMPLYING
prince's address	HIGHNESS	and	
queen's address	MAJESTY	• I am an attendant	IMPAGE
teacher's address	MISS, SIR	• I am out of date	IMPASSE
vicar's address	REV(EREND)	• I am wan	IMPALE
	(*see also* previous)	admitting	IAM
address		• admission of age	IAMAGED
indicating place of residence:		• admitting vehicle	IAMBUS
ambassador's address	EMBASSY	• admitting wind	IAMBISE
clergyman's address	MANSE, PARSONAGE,	• I am second-class	IAMB
	RECTORY, VICARAGE	admit	OWN
monk's address	FRIARY, MONASTERY,	• admit queen	OWNER
	PRIORY	• many admit . . .	MOWN
PM's address	NUMBER TEN,	• transport company admits . . .	BROWNS
	DOWNING STREET	*admitted by* mo/st ar/my . . .	STAR
Pope's address	VATICAN	*admitting* tha/t he n/ever . . .	THEN
adherent	BUR(R), FAN	(*see also* claim, confess, declare)	
adjective	ADJ	**admit**[2]	
adjoin		indicating inclusion:	
adjoining (=ad – joining other		*admitted by* *	incl in *
words or letters)		• men *admitted by* wrong . . .	TORMENT
• ad*joining* m–e	MADE	*admitting* a . . .	incl A
• ad*joining* s–ly . . .	SADLY	*admitting* nothing	incl O
• ad*joining* student and		*admitting* *	incl *
the *German* . . .	LADDER	• wrong, *admitting* men . . .	TORMENT
adjourned	ADJ	**adopt**	
adjust		adopt children	TAKE ISSUE
adjust harmony	TUNE	*adopted by* *	incl in *
adjustable [seat is] . . .	SIESTA	• daughter *adopted by* Ma–e	MADE
adjustable spanner	DRAWBRIDGE	*adopting* a . . .	incl A
adjusted [Kit's] . . .	SKIT	*adopting* *	incl *
adjusting [strap]	PARTS, SPRAT, TRAPS	• Ma–e *adopting* daughter	MADE
adjustment	ADJ	**adore**	
adjustment [let us] . . .	TUSSLE	adore Communist	LOVERED
Adjutant-general	AG	adore, *say*	A DOOR
adman	PRO	**adrift**	
administer	MANAGE, RUN	*adrift* [in the] . . .	THINE
administer, *say*	MANEGE	[came] *adrift*	ACME, MACE
admiral		[ship] *adrift*	HIPS, PISH
admiral	ADM	**adult**	
	BUTTERFLY	adult	A

Letter replaced \c\at; Omit (a); Pointers *out*; Retain a̲; Split B_ED; Down (D); Backwards <or ^

• adult people	ΛMEN
adult film	X
adult worker, *say*	MATURANT
adulterate	
adulterate [wines]	SINEW, SWINE
adulteration of [meat]	MATE, TAME, TEAM
advance	
advance	SUB
• advance for fruit	SUBLIME
• advance *to* position	SUBSTATION
• advance with *German*	SUBMIT
advance, *say*	COMMON
advanced	A
advanced fast	LENT
advantage	VAN
advent	ADV
adventure	
adventurous girl	ALICE
adventurous [girl in] . . .	RULING
adverb	ADV
adverse	
adverse	ANTHONY
adversely affected rats<	STAR
adversely affected [rats]	ARTS, STAR
	TARS
advertise	
advertise	AIR
• advertise room	AIRSPACE
• advertise sportswear	AIRSTRIP
• advertises tours	AIRSTRIPS
advertisement	AD, BILL, PLUG
	POSTER, PUFF
	(*see also* notice)
advise	
advice centre	CAB
ad*vice centre*	VI
advise, *say*	COUNCIL
advisor	CABMAN
advocate	ADV
advocates	BAR
Aero Club	AC
aeroplane	JET, MIG, etc
affect	
affect [large] . . .	LAGER, REGAL
affected [animal]	LAMINA, MANILA
affected settlement	CAMP
affecting [lots] . . .	SLOT
affectionate	
affectionate	FOND
• boy	FONDLES
• relative, *say*	FONDANT
• worker	FONDANT
affectionate	KIND
• boy	KINDLES
• Communist	KINDRED
afflict	
afflicted [by a lone] . . .	BALONEY

affliction [she 'ad] . . .	HEADS, SHADE
afloat	(in) S–S
aforesaid	
aforesaid	DITTO, DO
a*foresaid*	A FOUR
African	
African capital	RAND
African capital	A
African *flower*	ZAMBESI
African heathland	MOOR
African lives	BERBERIS
African *leader*	A
African, *say*	CREW
after	
after	POST
• after a time	POSTAGE
• after some hesitation	POSTER
• after teacher	POSTMASTER
• after the fruit	POSTDATE
• after the Italian . . .	POSTIL
• after the river . . .	POSTURE
after²	
indicating one word written	
after another word or letter:	
• *after* all the *old return<*	ALLEY
• *after* he married	HEM, HEWED
• *after* mid*night I'll . . .	GILL
• almost ful(l) *after*taste	TASTEFUL
• dine *after* noon	NEAT
• many *after* the . . .	THEM
• not so much *after*care	CARELESS
• Scot *after*guard	GUARDIAN
• space *after*ward	WARDROOM
after³	
other uses:	
after accident [men are] . . .	MEANER
after all	LAST, REARMOST, STERNMOST
	TAIL-END CHARLIE
	TAIL-ENDER
after all	(in) EN–D
after analysis [it was] . . .	WAIST, WAITS
after dark, *say*	TONITE
after date	AD
after death	PM
after five, *say*	SEX
after me, *say*	FAH
after midnight	AM, –IAM
after one, *say*	TO(O)
after opening	omit 1st letter
• *after opening* wine	(t)OKAY, (g)RAVES
after seven, *say*	ATE, AIT, EYOT
after reform [it was] . . .	WAIST, WAITS
after retirement	(in) B–ED, (in) C–OT
• bird, *after retirement* . . .	BOWLED
• *after retirement*, learner . . .	CLOT
after retreat, ogre< . . .	ERGO
after review [army] . . .	MARY, MYRA

after tax	NET(T)
after the style of	ALA
after the start	omit 1st letter
• *after the start of* bad weather	(w)INTER
• (l)eaves *after the start*	EAVES
after three, *say*	FOR(E)
after twelve	PM
afterlife	
afterlife, *say*	WENDED
afternoon	
afternoon	A, EXAM, PM
*after*noon	after AM
• *quiet afternoon*	AMP
*after*noon	after N
• a quiet *afternoon*	NAP
afternoon service	TEA-SET
afterthought	PS
again	RE
against	
against	CON
• against dogs	CONCURS
• against poetry	CONVERSE
• against the edge	CONVERGE
against	V
• against drink	VALE
• against one and . . .	VIAND
• against the current	VAMPS
against, *say*	AUNTIE
age	
age of	
–building	HALLAGE
–building, *say*	HAULAGE
–vehicle, *say*	CABBAGE, CARRIAGE
–vessel, *say*	PANNAGE
age *of backwardness*<	ARE, EGA
age of womanhood, *say*	GESTATING
aged	AE, AET
aged head	OLDNESS
aged judge	REFOLD
agent	
agent	AGT
agent	BOND
• agent's boss	M
agent	REP
• agent *has* a bit	REPORT
• agent *has* a chimney	REPLUM
• agent *with* paintings	REPART
agent	SPY
• agent is aware, *say*	SPINOSE
agile	
agile [animal]	LAMINA, MANILA
agility of [apes]	PEAS
agitate	
agitate	STIR
• agitate Communist	STIRRED
• agitate prison	STIR
• agitate, *say*	STIRRUP
agitated [waters]	WASTER
agitatedly [paces]	CAPES, SPACE
agitation of [men at] . . .	MEANT
agree	
agree *with* directors	SIDEBOARD
agree total	TALLY
agreed	ATONE
agreement	AY, AYE, YEA
–Franco–German	OUIJA
–French	OUI
–German	JA
–Italian	SI
–Russian	DA
–Spanish	SI
agreement in writing	CORRESPONDENCE
agreement, *say*	PACKED
aggravate	
aggravate [parent]	ENTRAP
[it was] aggravating	WAIST
aggressive	
aggressive	
–American	DOUGHBOY, GI
–Frenchman	SOLDAT
–German	SOLDAT
–Italian	SOLDATO
–Spaniard	SOLDADO
aggressor's weapon	HAWKSBILL
(*see also* belligerent)	
agriculture	
agriculture	AGR, EARTHWORK
agricultural collection	FLOCK, HERD
	STABLE
agricultural policy	CAP
ahead	
ahead <u>w</u>ith	W
<u>went</u> *ahead*	W
aide-de-camp	ADC
ail	
ail, *say*	ALE, BEER
ailing [king is] . . .	SKIING
what ails [thee, Ms] . . .	THEMES
aimless	
aimless [stroll]	TROLLS
[saunter] *aimlessly*	NATURES
ain't	
ain't, *say*	ARNOT
air	
air *and* sea	GAS-MAIN
[air]-*conditioned*	RIA
air controllers	CAA
air expeller	COUGHER
air expeller *say*	COFFER
air filter	STRAIN
Air Force	
–flew	RAFFLED
–in front, *say*	RAFFLED
–instruments	ANEMOMETERS

Letter replaced \c\at; Omit (a); Pointers *out*; Retain <u>a</u>; Split B_ED; Down (D); Backwards <or ^

air-hose	WINDSOCK	**alert runners**	WAKEFIELD
air passage	FLIGHT	**alfresco party**	OUTDO
ai_r terminal_	R	**algebra**	ALG
Air Traffic Control	ATC	**alias**	
air traffic control	AILERON, ELEVATOR,	alias	AKA
	JOYSTICK, RUDDER	_alias_ [given to] . . .	VETOING
Air Training Corps	ATC	**alien**	
air trip	WINDFALL	alien	ET
airborne	(in) F–LIGHT	• alien deity	ETHEL
• a number airborne	FANLIGHT	• alien roué	CADET
airborne nanny	FLYING BUTTRESS	• offer alien . . .	BIDET
airborne policeman	BLUEBOTTLE	alien (=foreign)	
aircraft compartment, _say_	BOMBAY	• _alien_ ship	BATEAU
aircraftsman	AC, ERK, LAC	• _alien_ soldiers	SOLDATEN
	COMPOSER, VERDI et al	• _alien_ woman	DONNA
airman	FO, PO	**all[1]**	
airway	LARYNX, THROAT, WINDPIPE	_after_ all	begin with ALL
in the air	(in) SK–Y	• cure _after_ all	ALLHEAL
• _air_sick	SKILLY	• unknown _after_ all	ALLY
air transport	CARRIAGE	all-_embracing_	incl ALL
aired beforehand	PREVENTED	• sh–ow all-_embracing_ . . .	SHALLOW
airy fairy	BLITHE SPIRIT	all _finished_	L
airline[1]		all _gone_	omit ALL
airline	BA	• m(all)ow all _gone_	MOW
• airline fashion	BATON	all _in_	incl ALL
• airline girl	BASAL, BALASS	• sh–ow all _in_ . . .	SHALLOW
• airline study	BACON	• s–ow _includes_ all . . .	SALLOW
• airline toilet	BALOO	al(l) _not finished_	AL
airline	BAC	all _out_	omit ALL
• airline above . . .	BACON	all round	'ALLO
• airline delicacy	BACCATE	all _round_<	LLA
• to airline company	TOBACCO	all _round_	AL–L
airline	BEA	• go al–l _round_	ALGOL
• airline, a _French_ one	BEAUNE	_almost_ al(l)	AL
• airline buildings	BEASTIES	**all[2]**	
• airline students	BE-ALL	other uses:	
• airline study	BEACON	all _and_ part	WHOLESOME
airline	TWA	_all but_ a . . .	omit A
• airline in . . .	TWAIN	_all but_ one	omit A, I
• airline not known	TWANK	all dead	OLIVE
• airline unknown	TWAY	all-[English]	SHINGLE
airline[2]		all off	NOON
airline	GAS PIPE, ISOBAR	all out	GENERAL STRIKE
airline dessert	PIE IN THE SKY	_all over the place_ [I went]	TWINE
airli_ne terminal_	E	all right	NONE LEFT, OK(AY)
airlines	LYRICS	all round	EIGHTEEN HOLES
aisle		_all round_	
aisle, _say_	ILL, ISLE	• one with wa–ter _all round_	WAITER
Albert		all-round achievement	HOME RUN, HOMER
Albert	WATCH-CHAIN	all round(er)	BALL, BAND, BELT
Albert's place	HALL		DRAKE, FRANCIS, MAGELLAN
alcoholic state	DT(S)		O, ORB, SPHERE
alderman	ALD	all, _say_	AWL, HOLE
Alderney	GBA	All Souls	NOBODY
ale		all types	FO(U)NT
ale, _say_	AIL, BIER	all women	NOMEN, OMEN
aleph	A	all wrong, _say_	NORITE

Anag [cat]; Any *; Begin IGN–; Endings –ING; eg •; Hidden /cat/; Implied add (on); Implied in (in);

allow		• alternative cereal	ORRICE
allow	LET	• alternative cut	ORLOP
• allow Henry	LETHAL	• alternative energy	ORE
• Malcolm allowed . . .	MALLET	• alternative entrance	OR-GATE
alloy		• alternative note	ORC, ORE
alloy of [iron]	NOIR	• alternative piece	ORBIT
[silver] *alloy*	LIVERS, SLIVER	• alternative timber	ORDEAL, ORPINE
allude		• alternative trade	ORDEAL
allude to, *say*	REEFER	and	
almost¹		• alternative coins	DORP, LORD
almost al(l)	AL	• alternative letters	BORN, CORD, FORM,
almost all gone	–GON, ONE		HORN, WORD etc
almost crazy	CRACKER(s)	• alternative directions	NORE, SORE,
almost dressed	ROBIN(g)		WORE, WORN
almost fully-developed	ADUL(t)	and	
almost left	POR(t)	• alternative *to* decay	ROTOR
almost lose sight	GOBLIN(d)	• choose alternative	ELECTOR
almost pointless	NEEDLES(s)	• man *with* alternative . . .	MANOR
almost succeed	DOWEL(l)	• out-of-date alternative	PASTOR
almost the finest . . .	THEBES(t)	• fellow *with* alternative . . .	DONOR
almost unnecessary	NEEDLES(s)	*alternative solution to* [clue]	LUCE
almost wholly bad	BA, AD	alternative technology	AT
almost²		*alternative* [to her] . . .	OTHER, THROE
almost fal/l ove/r	LOVE	**altitude**	
almost left	NEAR	altitude	ALT
almost the last of t͟he , , ,	H	altitude, *say*	HIGHT
almost the last of the wi͟ne	N	**alto**	ALT
aloft		**alumnus**	OB
aloft, sailor . . .(D)^	BA, RAT	**always**	
go *aloft*(D)^	OG	always	AY, AYE, EVER
alone		• learner always . . .	LAY
alone, *say*	A LOAN, SOUL	• always *in* the way	RAYED
alongside	HYPOTENUSE	• always *in debt*	REVERED
alpha	A	always	FORAY
Alpine		**amalgamate**	
Alpine Club	AC	*amalgamate* [ores]	ROES, SORE
[Alpine] *resort*	NEPALI	*amalgamating* [teams]	MATES, STEAM
also		*amalgamation of* [parties]	PASTIER
also	AND	**amateur**	
• also alter, *say*	ANDVARI	amateur	A
• also lift, *say*	ANDRASE	amateur	HAM
• also metal	ANDIRON	• amateur bandsman	(RADIO) HAM
also known as	AKA, ALIAS	• amateur lost blood	HAMBLED
altar	REV COUNTER	• amateur town, *say*	HAMBURG
alter		amateur	LAY
alter [a trend]	RANTED	• amateur circles	LAIC, LAITY
alter dress	SHIFT	• amateur cricket side	LAY OFF
alter, *say*	ALTAR	• quiet amateur	PLAY
alteration to [route]	OUTER, OUTRE	amateur's department	DIY
alter	RATEL	**amazing**	
alternate		*amazed* [by a] . . .	BAY
alternate	ALT	*Amazing* [Grace]	CAGER
alter[nate]	NEAT	*amazing* [thing]	NIGHT
alternate time intervals	TM, IE	**ambassador**	
alternating current	AC	ambassador	HE
alternative		• ambassador attending	HEAT
alternative	OR	• ambassador speaks	HEADDRESSES

Letter replaced \c\at; Omit (a); Pointers *out*; Retain a͟; Split B_ED; Down (D); Backwards <or ^

• ambassador's residence	HEADDRESS
ambiguous	
ambiguous [words]	SWORD
ambiguously [said]	DAIS
ambition	
ambition at the age of	
–three, *say*	BEFORE
–eight	BENIGN
–nine, *say*	BEATEN
ambivalent	
ambivalence [over] . . .	ROVE
ambivalent [male]	LAME, MEAL
ambivalent person	NOYES
amend	
amend [speech]	CHEEPS
amended [later]	ALTER
amendment of [law]	AWL
America(n)[1]	
American	AM
• American employed	AMUSED
• American in charge	
can . . .	AMICABLE
• American shrub	AMBUSH
• American woman	AMRITA
American	AMER
• American church	AMERCE
• American in Germany	AMERIND
American	US
• American can . . .	USABLE
• American journalist	USED
○ American period	USAGE
• American woman	USHER
and	
• American beauty queen	MISSUS
• American sailors	TARSUS
• American school period	TERMINUS
• born American	BUS
• round America	–OUS
• this *Latin*-American	HOCUS
and	
• American *in* Abe's . . .	ABUSES
• American *in* acid test	PUSH
• American *in* me	MUSE
and	
• *in* America	U–S
American[2]	
American address	GETTYSBURG
American banker	MISSISSIPPI, etc
American capital	DOLLAR
American *capital*	A
American citizen	STATESMAN
American doctrine	MONROE
American drag	YANK
American exclamation	OGEE
American *flower*	MISSISSIPPI, etc
American *leader*	A
American saloon	SEDAN
American sports pitch	SCREWBALL
American tug	YANK
amid	
amid t/he w/aves	HEW
amidship	(in) S–S
amid *	incl in *
• many *amid* trees	FIRMS
* *amid*	incl *
• I *am amid* breakers	WAIVES
amiss	
[goes] *amiss*	EGOS
[went] *amiss*	NEWT
ammunition supplier	MAGAZINE,
	ROUNDSMAN
among	
among Berbers	MIDRIFFS
among peopl/e at a	
ble/ak . . .	EATABLE
among *	incl in *
• she *is among* ma–d . . .	MASHED
* *among*	incl *
• is *among* engineers	RISE
amount	
amount of metrication	LITRE
amount of metri/cat/ion	CAT
ampere	A
amphibian	
amphibian, *say*	TOED
amphibian leg	NEWTON
amphibian working	NEWTON
amputate	
amputate feet	DOCKYARD
amputate fee(t)	FEE
amputate th(e) . . .	TH
amputation of to(e)	TO
amplitude modulation	AM
amusing	
amusing detour	DIVERSION
amusing fellow	FUNGUS
amusing fellow, *say*	FUNGI
amusing, *say*	HUMERUS
an	
an	A
–abscess	ABOIL
–assignation, *say*	ATTRIST
–attic	ALOFT
–empty space	AVOID
–entrance	AGATE
–entrance, *say*	ADORE
–incursion, *say*	ARRAYED
–infection, *say*	ATTAINT
–insect, *say*	ATTIC
–interval, *say*	ARREST
–Italian leader, *say*	ADDUCE
–objection	ABUT
–ocean	AMAIN
–opening	AGAT

Anag [cat]; Any *; Begin IGN–; Endings –ING; eg •; Hidden /cat/; Implied add (on); Implied in (in);

–orchestra	ALSO	angel	BACKER
–orchestra playing	ABANDON		MICHAEL, RAPHAEL et al
–ulcer	ABOIL	**anger**	
–upright state	APICAL	anger, *say*	BHYLE, CALLER, COLLAR
–urge	AITCH	angry	*(see separate entry)*
an *absent*	omit AN	**angle**	
• a dog *with* an *absent*	SP(an)IEL	angle	FISH
an *Italian* . . .	UNA, UNO	• angle iron	FISH CLUB, FISH-PRESS
an *uprising*(D)^	NA	angle	L
	(see also a)	**Anglican worship**	CE
anaesthetic		**Anglo-**	
anaesthetic	NUMBER	Anglo-American	EAM
anaesthetic, *say*	EITHER	Anglo-French waters	SEAMER
analysis		Anglo-Saxon	AS
analyse failure	BREAKDOWN	**angry**	
analysed [ores]	EROS, ROES, SORE	*angrily* [throw]	WORTH
analysis of [soil]	OILS, SILO	angry	CROSS
analyst's bike, *say*	PSYCHICAL	• angry allusion	CROSS-REFERENCE
anarchist		• angry European, *say*	CROSS-CHECK
anarchist	RED		CROSS CHEQUE
• anarchist dead, *say*	REDDED	• angry lawyers	CROSSBAR
• anarchist lair	REDDEN	• angry man CROSS-PARTY, GEORGE CROSS	
• anarchist ring	REDO	• angry wound	CROSSCUT
	(see also communist)	angry	HOT
ancestral tree	ELDER	• angry footballer	HOTSPUR
anchor-worm	FLUKE	• angry soldiers	HOTFOOT
ancient		angry	SORE
ancient	ANC, FLAG	• angry man, *say*	SORAL, SORDES, SORTED
ancient	AGED	• angry saint	SOREST
• ancient mother	DAMAGED	• angry soldiers	FOOTSORE
• ancient orchestra	BANDAGED	*angry* [lion]	LOIN, NOIL
ancient		angry motorist	HORNBLOWER
indicating old words:		[pace] *angrily*	CAPE
• *ancient* goat	GATE	**angström**	A
• *ancient* friend	INGLE	**animal[1]**	
• *ancient* poet-laureate	ARCH-POET	animal	
	(see also old[3])	–attacks say	BULRUSHES
ancient city	TROY, UR	–club	PIG–IRON
ancient hunter	OLD TIMER	–cunning	ASSART
Ancient Mariner	NOAH, SHELLBACK	–devoured	BULLATE
ancient, *say*	ANTIC	–family	DOGSKIN
ancient times	BC	–fastener, *say*	BULLOCK
ancient vessel	ARK	–fodder	CATHAY
ancient weapon	PISTOL	–fur	CATNAP
and		–got up	DOG–ROSE
and *French* . . .	ET	–*has* a right . . .	ASSART
and *German* . . .	UND	–joint	DOGSHIP
and not	NOR	–king	WOLFER
and *Roman* . . .	ET	–painting	ASSART
and *without* a . . .	(a)ND	–sees	OX–EYES
ane	A, I	–sleeps	BULLDOZES
anent	ON, RE	–speculator	STAG
	(see about[2])	–talk	YAK
anew		–torment	BADGER
[made] *anew*	DAME, EDAM, MEAD	–trail	DOG, PIGTAIL
[men hope] *anew*	PHENOME	–trap	PIGGIN
		–with	

mother	DOGMA	**answer**	
nothing on	RATOON	answer	ANS
–would wander, *say*	HIPPODROME	• answer *back<*	SNA–
animals mounted	CATSUP	• one answer	–IANS
animal's teacher, *say*	COWSHED	answer	KEY
animal²		• answer letter	KEY-NOTE
[Animal] *Crackers*	LAMINA, MANILA	• answer telephone	KEY-RING
Animal Farm	RANCH, STUD	answer	LIGHT
animal feet, *say*	PAUSE	• answer head	LIGHTNESS
animal friend, *say*	BRUTALLY	• teacher *with* the answer	HEADLIGHT
animal group, *say*	HEARD	• team answer	SIDELIGHT
animal rescuer	NOAH	**ante**	A
animal, *say*	BARE, HOARSE,	**antelope**	
	LAMA, LAM	antelope	BUCK
	LINKS, STERE, WHORES,	• antelope has been, *say*	BUCKBEAN
	YEW, YOU	• antelope is warm	BUCKSHOT
animal *sound*	BRUIT	• antelope *with* sheep	BUCKRAM
animal's home	INSTALL	• antelope's family	BUCKSKIN
animate		antelope	DOE
animated [scene I] . . .	NIECES	• antelope's family	DOESKIN
animation of [animal]	LAMINA, MANILA	• *old* does	DOTH
[spoke] *animatedly*	POKES	antelope, *say*	KNEW, NEW
Anitra		antelopes, *say*	NEWS
[Anitra's] *Dance*	ARTISAN	**anti-**	
Annie Oakley	MISFIRING	anti-aircraft	AA, ARCHIE
announce		anti-aircraft fire	UPSHOT
announce their . . .	THERE	anti-American	NOUS
announce you and me, *say*	STATUS	anti-ballistic missile	ABM
announcement of time	THYME	anti-tetanus serum	ATS
annoy		**anticipate**	
annoy informer	NARK	anticipate no share	EXPECTORATION
annoying habit	HAIR SHIRT	anticipating	(in) HOP–E
annual		**antiquarian**	FAS, SAS
annual	PA	**any**	
• annual camp	PATENT	any other business	AOB
• annual payment	PARENT	any, *say*	NE
• annual right	PART	*any* [sort]	ORTS, TORS
• annual *return<*	AP	[any] *sort*	NAY
annual meeting	AGM	anybody	ALL, ONE
anoint		*anyhow* [I am] . . .	AIM, AMI
anoint, *say*	ANNEAL	*any*[thing]	NIGHT
anonymous		anyway	
anonymous	AN	indicating a palindrome:	
• *anonymous* queen	ANER	• *anyway*, a flop	DUD
anonymous	omit N	• father *anyway* . . .	DAD, POP
• *anonymous* ma(n)	MA	*anyway* [let us] . . .	LUTES
another		*in* any *case*	AN–Y
another form of male . . .	LAME, MEAL	**aorist**	AOR
another husband	SECOND MATE	**apart**	
another order for [lamb]	BALM	*apart* [from] . . .	FORM
another order [given to] . . .	VETOING	*apart from* a . . .	omit A
another order given to [army]	MARY, MYRA	*apart from* a new . . .	omit AN
another shape [I drew]	WEIRD	*apart from* the front	omit 1st letter
another spell of weather	W(H)ETHER	*apart from* the leader	omit 1st letter
another way of		*apart from* name	omit N
putting [things]	NIGHTS	*apart from* *	omit *
another way to [put] . . .	TUP	• fa(the)r *apart from* the . . .	FAR

Anag [cat]; Any *; Begin IGN–; Endings –ING; eg •; Hidden /cat/; Implied add (on); Implied in (in);

[tear] *apart*	RATE, TARE
apiary	
apiary, *say*	APRE
apogee	APO
apoplectic	
apoplectic [general]	ENLARGE
apoplectically [rave]	AVER
apostle	
apostle, *say*	LOOK, MARC
appal	
appalling [thing]	NIGHT
appallingly [made]	DAME, EDAM, MEAD
apparent	
apparent, *say*	APP
apparent in t/he w/ay . . .	HEW
apparently	APP
apparently not	KNOT
appeal	
appeal	IT
appeal	O
• appeal for fish, *say*	OBLIQUE
• appeal for insects, *say*	OBESE, OBIS
• appeal for money	OGIVE
• appeal to cog	OPINION
• appeal to costume, *say*	OLIVARY
• appeal to friends	OPALS
• appeal to girl, *say*	ODORINE
• appeal to governor	OBEY
• appeal to Kenneth, *say*	OAKEN
• appeal to make	OCREATE
• appeal to make, *say*	OCHREATE
• appeal to male sex	OMEN
• appeal to purchase, *say*	OCELLUS
• appeal to sailor	ORATING
• appeal to vendor, *say*	OCELLAR
appeal	SA, SOS
appealing	CUTE
appear	
appear smaller, *say*	SEAMLESS
appear [untidy]	NUDITY
appearance in tw/ice ni/ghtly...	ICENI
appeared injured	BLED
appeared loud	TURNED UP
appears in . . .	incl *
• it *appears in* an opening	AGITATE
appears in We/st End s/how	STENDS
appears to be weak	WEEK
appears to be [worse]	SWORE
appears to have so/me tal/l...	METAL
apple	
apple *core*	P
apple juice, *say*	SIDER
apple *peel*	AE
apple picker	EVE
apple tree	OAK
apples (and pears)	STAIRS
apply	

apply conditioning	BRAINWASH
apportion	
apportion [blame]	MABEL
apportionment of [shares]	SHEARS
appreciate	
appreciate	DIG
• appreciate it	DIGIT
• appreciates lodgings	DIGS
appreciate	GROW
• appreciate new	GROWN
• appreciate trousers	GROW-BAGS
apprehend	
apprehend a . . .	incl A
apprehend *	incl *
• police *apprehended* husband	CHOPS
apprehended by *	incl in *
• husband *apprehended* by police	CHOPS
apprentice	
apprentice	APP, L
apprentice cook	DEVIL
	(*see also* learner)
appropriate	
appropriate the lady's,	
say	KNICKERS
appropriate title	NICKNAME
approve	
approval	OK(AY)
approve wine	PASSPORT
approx	C, CA, CIRC
	SOME
	(*see* about[1])
APRE	APIARY
April	
April *1st*	A
April 1st	MARCH-PAST
apron	
apron manufacturer	STAGE MANAGER
apron producer	FIG-TREE
aquiver	
aquiver [over sin]	VERSION
[he's] *aquiver*	SHE
Arab	
Arab	AR
• Arab adversary	ARRIVAL
• Arab girl	ARENA, ARGAL
• Arab *on* camel	ARRIDING
• Arab torture	ARRACK
and	
• Arab *in* Maine	MARE
• man *embracing* Arab	DARES
• soldiers *surround* Arab	RARE
Arab	HORSE
• Arab drama	HORSE OPERA, HORSEPLAY
• Arab fight	HORSE BOX
• Arab money	HORSE BRASS
Arab chieftain, *say*	CHIC, SHAKE
Arab's cry	NEIGH, WHINNY

Arab's cry, *say*	NAY, WINNIE	• argumentative oarsman	ROWER
Arabia	UAR	• quiet argument	PROW
arable land	LEA, LEY	• th(e) *short* argument	THROW
Aramaic	SYRIAC	**aright**	AR, ART
arbitrary		**Arion's rescuer**	DOLPHIN
arbitrary [rules]	LURES	**arise**	
[demand] *arbitrarily*	DAMNED	*arise*, Sir . . .(D)^	RIS–
arch		*arising* as an . . .(D)^	NASA
arch	CHIEF	*arising from* [a new] . . .	WANE, WEAN
• chief method	ARCHWAY	*arising from* se/a dept/ths	ADEPT
• chief queen	ARCHER	may *arise*(D)^	YAM
∘ novice chief	LARCH	**aristocrat**	
archaeopteryx	EARLY BIRD	aristocratic	U
archaic	ARCH	aristocrat's carriage	TUMBREL, TUMBRIL
	(*see also* old³)	**arm**	
archangel	GABRIEL, MICHAEL et al	arm-lock	(HALF-)NELSON
	RECORDING HEAD	arm rest	SLING
archbishop	ABP	[arm]-*twisting*	MAR, RAM
	CANTUAR, EBOR, LAMBETH	[arm]-*wrestling*	MAR, RAM
	LANG, LAUD et al	armed female	BRITANNIA
archdeacon	VEN	armed timer	WRISTWATCH
arched flyover	RAINBOW, VIADUCT	armless female	VENUS
archer	CUPID, EROS	arms limitation	STRAIT JACKET
	HOOD, TELL	**Armenian**	ARM, HAIKH
architect		**armour**	
architect	PLANGENT	armour-*plated*	(in) M–AIL
architect	ADAM, WREN, WRIGHT et al	armour, *say*	MALE
• architect *and* worker	ADAMANT	**army**	
• architect, honoured	WRENCH	army	TA
• high-flying architect	WRIGHT	• army advanced	TALENT
architect's office	DRAWING-ROOM	• army engineer	TARE
architecture	ARCH	• army man	TAKEN, TALES
Arctic animal	POLAR BEAR, POLECAT	• army family, *say*	TAKE-IN
ardent		• army leader	TAKING
ardent, *say*	EAGRE	• army minstrel	TABARD
arduous		• army team	TAXI
arduous [task 'e] . . .	SKATE	and	
[slog] *arduously*	LOGS	• Dad's Army	PASTA
are		• farewell to army	VALETA
are, *say*	R	• fight an army	SPARTA
are (metric)	A	army chaplain	HCF, OCF
are not	ANT	army command	ATTENTION, SHUN
are you *and* I *said* . . .	RUI–	army dentists	RADC
are spotted, *say*	ARSINE	army doctors	RAMC
area		army entertainer	HOST
area	A	army group devoured	UNITATE
• area *behind* fish	CODA	army jumper	PARATROOPER
• area *in front of church*	ACE, ARC	army MC	HOST
• area *to* left	AL(T)	army paymasters	RAPC
• area *to* right	ALIEN, AR(T)	army rations	WARFARE
• area transport	ABUSES	army, *say*	HOAST
argentine		army teachers	RAEC
argentine	SILVER	army technicians	REME
Argentine cast	INGOT	army vets	RAVC
argonaut	JASON		(*see also* reserve, soldier)
argument		**around**[1]	
argument	ROW	meaning: about	

Anag [cat]; Any *; Begin IGN–; Endings –ING; eg •; Hidden /cat/; Implied add (on); Implied in (in);

approximately			
roughly, etc	(*see* about¹)		

around²

around (=a round)	O
• around *following* doctor	VETO
• around *in* ho–t . . .	HOOT
• around *on* soldiers . . .	OMEN
around [town]	WONT
around a . . .	incl A
around *	incl *
• run *around* one . . .	RUIN
run *around*<	NUR

arrange

arrange board	PLAN TABLE, PLANTABLE
arrange, *say*	MARTIAL
arrange [table]	BLATE, BLEAT
arranged	ARR
arranged [a new] . . .	WANE, WEAN
arranged rose	GOT UP
arrangement of locks	COIFFURE, HAIR-DO
arrangement of roses	BOUQUET, POSY
arrangement of [roses]	SORES
[secret] *arrangement*	RESECT

arrest

arrest a . . .	incl A
arrest one group	CO-PILOT
arrest head	COP
arrest suspect	APPREHEND
arrest *	incl *
• police *arrest* king	CORPS
arrested by ¶	incl in *
• king *arrested by* police	CORPS
arrested, *say*	COPT

arrive

arrival	AR, ARR
arrive	AR, ARR
arriv*ed finally*	D
arrived frequently, *say*	CAMELOT
arrived *with* an artist	CAMERA

arrow

| arrow*head* | A |
| arrow-maker | FLETCHER |

ars | RR

arsenal

| Arsenal's journal | MAGAZINE |
| Arsenal's shots | GUNFIRE |

arsonist's case | MATCHBOX

art

art class	GENRE
art committee	DRAWING-BOARD
[art] *form*	RAT, TAR
[Art] *Nouveau*	RAT, TAR
art of potter	ONEUPMANSHIP
art school, *say*	SLAYED
artful place	MUSEUM, STUDIO
artless	NORA
[art]*work*	RAT, TAR

| arty, *say* | RT |

artery

| artery, *say* | JUGGLER |

Arthur's place | CAMELOT

article

article	ART
English article	A, AN, IT, THE
• article *on* poetry	AVERSE
	ANODE
• article *in* church	CITE
• artist *has* article . . .	RATHE
French article	LE, LA, LES, UN, UNE
French/English articles	LATHE
French/German articles	UNDER
German article	DAS, DER, DIE, EIN, EINE
Italian article	IL, LA, LE, UNA, UNO
Spanish article	EL, LA, LAS, LO
	LOS, UNA, UNO
Spanish/Italian articles	ELLA

articulate

articulation of bone	BEAUNE
articulated aloud	ALLOWED
articulated one . . .	WON
articulated lorry	LAURIE

artificial

artificial	ART
artificial diamond	SHAMROCK
artificial flowers	CANALS
artificial stone	SHAMROCK
artificial [stone]	NOTES, ONSET
	SETON, TONES

artillery | ART(Y), HA, HAC, RA

artisan

| artisan, *say* | RIGHT, RITE, WRITE |

artist

artist	ARA
• artist-fellow	ARAF
• artist-graduate	ARABA
• artist is English	ARISE
artist	PRA
• artist I exalt	PRAISING
• artist not known	PRANK
• artist unknown	PRAY
artist	RA
• artist ran	RASPED
• artist wearing a jacket	RAINCOAT
• artist *with* complaint	RAGOUT, RASORES
• Cockney artist	RAINBOW
and	
• horse artist	COBRA
• male artist	HERA
• police artist	COPRA
artist	CLAUDE, ETTY, LELY et al
artist, *say*	–TITION
artist, *Turner*<	REWARD
artist's board, *say*	PALATE
	(*see also* painter)

Letter replaced \c\at; Omit (a); Pointers *out*; Retain a; Split B_ED; Down (D); Backwards <or ^

as

as	AS
• as an indication	ASSIGN
• as below	ASUNDER
• as quiet	ASP
as	LIKE
• as a baby	CHILDLIKE
• as divine . . .	GODLIKE
• as Edward	LIKENED
as	QUA
• as king	QUAKING
• as light	QUAVERY
• as unknown	QUAY
and	
• like a building	QUASHED
• like a caravan	QUATRAIN
• like the *Italian*	QUAIL
as	SO
• as below	SOUNDER
• as deep, *say*	SOLO
• as far, *say*	SOFA
• as thick, *say*	SOTHIC
as a [rule]	LURE
as above	US, UT SUPRA
as arranged, [Alsatians] . . .	ASSAILANT
as before	
indicating an old word:	
• roast, *as before*	ROST
• *as before*, in another	
way	OTHERGATES, OTHERGUESS
as if he would	HEED
as if some on . . .	SUMMON
as far as I'm concerned	TOME
as it happens	LIVE
as it turns out [her top] . . .	POTHER
as said	UT DICT(UM)
as said by a . . .	BUYER
as stated, he'll . . .	HEAL, HEEL
as the poet said	(*see* poetic)
as the writer put it	SIC, STET
as you like it	AYLI
as you say, we'll . . .	WEAL, WHEEL
ash dispenser	ETNA etc VOLCANO

Asian

Asian	E
• Asian study	EDEN
• Asian treaty	EPACT
• faint Asian . . .	DIME
Asian (in East)	INE
• Asian training	INEPT
• fellow *with* Asian . . .	FINE
• swindle Asian	CONINE
Asian adder	INDIAN SUMMER
Asian *flower*	MEKONG etc
A̲sian *leader*	A

ask

ask	BEG
• ask a person	BEGONE
• ask Barnaby	BEGRUDGE
• ask for fish	BEGGAR
• ask in	BEGIN
ask for . . .	FORE, FOUR
asked aloud	ALLOWED
asking for tea	FORTY

askew

askew, *say*	RILEY
[goes] *askew*	EGOS
[it was] *askew*	WAIST, WAITS
[went] *askew*	NEWT

asleep | OUT

asparagus

asparagus tip	SPEARHEAD
asparagus *tips*	AS

aspect

aspect, *say*	GUYS

asphyxiate

asphyxiate	GAS
• asphyxiate family	GASKIN
• asphyxiate lad, *say*	GAS-BUOY

aspiration

aspiration	H
aspirations	HH

assail

assail, *say*	COURSE, JIB, SHEET
	SPINNAKER etc
assail a number, *say*	PELTATE

assassin

assassin	BOOTH, OSWALD
assassinate	KILL
• assassinate Edward	KILLED, KILTED
• assassinate ruler	KILLER
• assassinate that man, *say*	KHILIM

assault

assault course	PUNCH LINE
assault man	MUGGENT
assault, *say*	SAILOR

assemble

a rum *assembly*	ARUM
assembled [ratings]	STARING
assembly [line]	LIEN, NEIL, NILE
assembly, *say*	COUNSEL
[General] *Assembly*	ENLARGE

assign

assign [blame]	AMBLE, MABEL
assign property	ATTRIBUTE

assimilate

assimilate a rum	ARUM
assimilate a . . .	incl A
assimilate *	incl *
• companion *assimilates* rum	CRUMB
assimilated by *	incl in *
• rum *assimilated by*	
companion	CRUMB
assistant	ASST

associate	A
associate fellow	AF
associate member	AM
associate of Bacon	EGGS
associate of drunk	DISORDERLY
associated with tart, *say*	HOARD, HORDE
association	ASS(N)
assort	
assorted [nuts]	STUN, TUNS
assortment of [hooks]	SHOOK
assume	
assume	DON
assume a . . .	incl A
assume *	incl *
• P–a *assumes* it . . .	PITA
assume, *say*	HARROGATE
assume title	DON
assumed by *	incl in *
• it *is assumed by* P–a . . .	PITA
assure	
assurance company	PRU
assured, *say*	CONFIDANT(E)
astern	
astern was . . . <	SAW
follow *astern*<	GOD
astray	
astray [in the] . . .	THINE
[doesn't go] *astray*	STEGODON
[went] *astray*	NEWT
astride	
girl *astride* a horse	JACOBEAN
pa–ge *astride* a donkey	PASSAGE
astronaut's pub	SPACE-BAR
astronomical unit	AU
astute	
[astute] *move*	STATUE
astutely [I sold] . . .	SOLID
asylum	CRANKCASE
at¹	AT
at first	A
at *first*	start with AT
• male at *first*	ATMAN
at first sight	S
at *heart*	incl AT
• h–e at *heart*	HATE
at *last*	end with AT
• shape at *last*	FORMAT
at last	T
(a)t *losing* a . . .	T
at one on	–ATION
at one point	ATE, ATS
at *the back*	T
at *the back*	end with AT
• be at *the back*	BEAT
at *the beginning*	A
at *the beginning*	start with AT
• pamphlet at *the beginning*	ATTRACT

at *the bottom*(D)^	T
at *the centre*	incl AT
• at *the centre of the* Civil Service . . .	CATS
at *the end*	T
at *the* end	ATE
at *the end* . . .	end with AT
• flourished at *the end* . . .	FLAT
at *the front*	A
at *the front*	start with AT
• tear at *the front*	ATRIP
at *the middle*	incl AT
• we *with* her at	
the middle	WEATHER
at *the rear*	T
at *the* rear	ATE
at *the rear*	end with AT
• about at *the rear*	CAT
at *the start*	A
at *the start*	start with AT
• one at *the start*	ATONE
at²	
indicating origins:	
at Cardiff Arms Park (=Welsh)	
• fervour at *Cardiff Arms Park*	HWYL
at Hampden Park (=Scottish)	
• game at *St Andrews*	GOWF
at Longchamps (=French)	
• horse at *Longchamps*	CHEVAL
at sea (=nautical expression)	
• behind *at sea*	ABAFT, ASTERN
• change course *at sea*	TACK
• stop *at sea*	AVAST, BELAY
at³	
other uses:	
at cross purposes	VOTING
at fault [when] . . .	HEWN
at first	incl –IST
• *almost* pur(r) at first	PURIST
at first sight	S
at heart s/he w/was . . .	HEW
at heart *	incl *
• young *at heart*	INCUBUS
at home	IN, (in) N–EST
at last, winter . . .	R
at odds [over] . . .	ROVE
at one time	(*see* old)
at pleasure	AD LIB(ITUM)
at random, [cast] . . .	CATS, SCAT
at rest	(in) B–ED, (in) C–OT
at sea [all the] . . .	LETHAL
at suit of	ATS
at the bottom of(D)	
• about *at the bottom of*	
the river	PORE
at the bottom of the . . .(D)	E
at the double	(in) HAST–E
at the end	AD FINIT(UM)

at the finish	(in) EN–D
at the heart of *	incl in *
• one *at the heart of* he–r . . .	HEIR
at the heart of a/ny ala/rm system	NYALA
at the outset she told youth	STY
at the place	AD LOC(UM)
at the police-station	OFF-BEAT
at the wicket	BATTING, IN
at this place	AHL
at this word	AHV
at university	UP
at war	(in) AC–TION, INACTION
at what place?, *say*	WARE, WEAR
	WEIGHER
at what time?, *say*	WEN
at work	(in) HAR–NESS, INFIRM
at work, [boredom] . . .	BEDROOM
[ship] *at sea*	HIPS, PISH
* *at first*	start with *
• detectives ran *at first*	RANCID
* *at heart*	incl *
• sick *at heart*	SILLY
• wax is *at heart*	CERISE
* *at last*	end with *
• credit one *at last* . . .	CRONE
* *at the beginning*	start with *
• sweet, not *at the beginning*	NOTICE
* *at the end*	end with *
• quiet in *the end*	SHIN
* *at the middle*	incl *
• be *at the middle*	ABED, ABET
ate	
ate *about* . . .	A–TE
• ate *about* 51 . . .	ALITE
ate *up* (D)^	DEF–, ETA
ate bird	BITTERN
ate, *say*	AIT, EIGHT, EYOT
ate tea, *say*	EIGHTY
ate twice, *say*	PECTATE
Athenian	TIMON
athlete	
athlete	BLUE
• athlete understands, *say*	BLUENOSE
athletic team	ALLOA, CHARLTON
Atlantic	POND
atmosphere	ATM
atom	
atomic	A
atomic number	Z
atomised [town]	WONT
atomising [spray]	PRAYS
attach	
attached to a . . .	incl A
• *attached to* a stake	ABET, BETA
• stake *attached to* a . . .	ABET, BETA
attached to *	incl *
• animal *attached to* her . . .	RATHER

attack	
attack	GOAT
• attack animals	GOATHERD
• attack fish	GOATLING
attack equipment	CLOBBER
attack spirits	MUGGINS
attack worker	ASSAILANT
attacking bat	DRACULA
attend	
attend	BEAT
attend	SERVE
• attend Scotsman, *say*	SERVIAN
• attend worker, *say*	SERVANT
attendant	PAGE
• attendant insect	PAGEANT
• attendant worker	PAGEANT
attending	AT
• attending ceremony, *say*	ATTRITE
• attending cricket match	ATTEST
• attending robbery	ATHEIST
• attending trial	ATTEST
attending lesson	(in) FOR–M, INFORM
attorney	ATT
Attorney-General	AG
attract	
attract	DRAW
• attract fish	DRAWLING
• attract game	DRAWBRIDGE
attractive	CUTE, DISHY
attractive	WITHDRAW
• attractive artist	DRAWER
• attractive artwork	DRAWING
attractive bar	MAGNET
attractive binding	ENGAGING
attractive girl	BELLE, CUTIE, DISH
	DOLLY, PEACH, STUNNER
attractive instrument	GLAMORGAN
attractive rock	LODESTONE
attractive strip	MAGNETIC TAPE
au pair	FOREIGN EXCHANGE
auction	
auction, *say*	SAIL
audio-	
audible beat	BEET, TIC
audible pause	PAWS
audibly weak	WEEK, FEINT
audience hears a noise	ANNOYS
audio frequency	AF
audio-visual	AV
auditor adds	ADZE
auditors	EARS, SAA
augmentative	AUG
August	AUG
aunt	
Auntie Jennifer, *say*	ANTIGEN
aunt's pain	AGONY
aureole	HEADLIGHT, O

Anag [cat]; Any *; Begin IGN–; Endings –ING; eg •; Hidden /cat/; Implied add (on); Implied in (in);

Australia

Australia	AUS, DOWN UNDER, OZ
Australian *capital*	A
Australian *flower*	DARLING etc
Australian *leader*	A

author

author	STERNE, WELLS et al
author, *say*	REITER
author's *opening* . . .	A
author's place	WELLS
author's statement, *say*	IRITE

authorise

authorisation	OK(AY)
authorise embargo	SANCTION
authorise penalty	SANCTION
Authorised Version	AV

autobiography

autobiography	CV
autobiographical subject	I, ME

automatic

automatic data processing	ADP
automatic pilot	GEORGE
automatic, *say*	HANDGUN

autumn

autumn	FALL
• autumn trip	FALL
• wet autumn	RAINFALL, WATERFALL

available

available in [shop]	HOPS, POSH
available in so/me sh/ops	MESH

avenue	AV(E)

average

average	AVE(R)
• about average	CAVE(R)
• average state	AVER
• right average	RAVE(R)
average	MEAN
• average period	MEANTIME
• average square	MEANT
• the *Camptown* average	DEMEAN
average	MED
• army *has* average . . .	TAMED
• "Average", I state	MEDICAL
• average man	MEDAL
average	PAR
• average man	PARED, PARIAN, PARTED
• average ruler	PARKING
• average sum	PARAMOUNT
average entertainment	FAIR
average, *say*	MIEN

avert

aversion therapy, *say*	COUNTERPANE
averted [crash]	CHARS

Avogadro's number	N

avoid[1]

avoid	DUCK
• avoid fish	DUCKLING
• avoid payment	DUCKBILL
avoid city	DODGE
avoid container	SKIP
avoid surgery	BYPASS
avoid talons, *say*	ESCAPE CLAUSE
avoided issue	CHILDLESS
avoids carrier	SLIPSHOD

avoid[2]

indicating omission:

avoid a . . .	omit A
avoid drug	omit E
avoid extremes of (h)ea(t)	EA
avoid one not drinking	omit TT
avoid publicity	omit AD
avoid students	omit LL, LS
avoid *	omit *
• mon(k)ey *avoids* king	MONEY
I'd *avoided*	omit ID

Avonville	BATH

award

award	CH
• award a member	CHAMP, CHARM
• each award . . .	PERCH
award	MEDAL
• award *to* star	MEDALLION
award	OBE
• award *to* animal	OBELION
• award *to* man	OBERON
• royal award	ROBE
award	OM
• award all . . .	OMAN
• h–e *grabs* award	HOME
	(*see also* honour, order)

away

away (=a way)	–ARD
• away *with* our . . .	ARDOUR
• many away	CARD, LARD
• away *in* h–er . . .	HARDER
away (=a way)	–AST
• away *in* sea	MASTED
• Away *with* king!	ASTER
• many away	CAST, LAST
away	OUT
• away in Greece	OUTING
• Away *with* work!	OUTPOST
• many away	CLOUT, LOUT
away result	OFFEND
away south	omit S
away with a . . .	omit A
away *	omit *
miles *away*	omit M

awful

awful display of [art]	TAR
awful [part]	PRAT, TRAP
awful people, *say*	DIATRIBE
awful weight	DIRECT
awfully [tired]	TRIED

Letter replaced \c\at; Omit (a); Pointers *out*; Retain a̲; Split B_ED; Down (D); Backwards <or ^

awkward		[pole]-*axed*	LOPE
awkward angle	OBTUSE	**axiom**	AX
awkward [sort]	ORTS, ROTS, TORS	**ay**	
[I creep] *awkwardly*	PIERCE	ay(e)	A, I
axe		ay(e)s	AS, IS
axed [a fir]	FAIR	**azimuth**	AZ

B

a follower, Bach, bachelor, baron, bass, bay, bed-bug, *bee*, Beethoven, bel, Belgium, beta, beth, billion, binary, bishop, black, blessed, bloodgroup, *bloody*, book, born, boron, bowled, boy, Brahms, breadth, Britain, British, *inferior*, key, magnetic flux, note, *paper*, *road*, *second*, *second-class*, second letter, three hundred, three thousand, vitamin

B	
B-	BLESS
B9	BENIGN
B10	BEATEN
B minor	BLESS
B minus	BLESS
B row	BRACKET
babe	RUTH
baby	
baby bird	STORK
baby-carriage	GESTATION
baby slept	KIDNAPPED
Babylonian	URGENT
bachelor	
bachelor	B
• bachelor *has* study	BLAIR
• bachelor *is French*	BEST
• strike bachelor	LAMB
bachelor	BA
• bachelor *has* study	BACON
• bachelor *with* jolly . . .	BARM
• strange bachelor	RUMBA
bachelor of	
–Arts	AB, BA
–Civil Law	BCL
–Commerce	BCOM(M)
–Dental Surgery	BDS
–Divinity	BD
–Education	BED, EDB
–Engineering	BAI, BE, BENG
–Law	BL, LLB
–Letters	BL
–Literature	BLITT
–Medicine	BM, MB
–Music	BMUS
–Philosophy	PHB
–Science	BS, BSC, SCB
–Surgery	BCH, BS, CHB
Bach's works	S
back¹	
indicating reversal:	
back again<	ER

back-cloth<	ERIC, MINED
back door<	ROOD
back-drop<	PROD
back-end of year<	CED
back entry<	ROOD
back-flow<	WOLF
back-heel<	TAR
back line<	KNAR
back number<	NET, ON
back pay<	YAP
back room<	MOOR
back street<	DR, TS
back stretch<	EMIT
back to . . .<	OT
back to front bat<	TAB
back trouble<	LIA
back-up<	PU
back-up may . . .<	YAM
back way<	DR, TS, YAW
back way in<	NI
back-yard<	DRAY
*back*bite<	PIN, WANG
*back*fall<	PROD
*back*firing guns<	SNUG
*back*hand<	RAT
*back*ing horse<	RECAP
*back*saw<	WAS
*back*side<	IX, NO
*back*sliding VIPs<	SPIV
*back*spin<	NIPS
*back*stop<	POTS
*back*tracking deer<	REED
*back*water<	LOOP
pay *back*<	YAP
back²	
back	BET
• back leg	BETON
back	REAR
• back China	REARMING
• back number	REARM
• back row of violins	REARGUES
• back to sea	REARMED

Letter replaced \c\at; Omit (a); Pointers *out*; Retain a; Split B_ED; Down (D); Backwards <or ^

back biter	MOLAR, WISDOM TOOTH	bad speller	MAGICIAN, WARLOCK
back bite<u>r</u>	R		WITCH, WIZARD
back down	FACE UP	bad spelling	CHARMING
back dow<u>n</u>	N	bad tempered man	CROSSPIECE
back end of yea<u>r</u>	R	*badly affected* [by a] . . .	BAY
back in front	RUMPLED	*badly constructed* [table]	BLATE, BLEAT
back number	EPIDURAL, SPINAL	*badly designed* [town]	WONT
back numbe<u>r</u>	R	badly *missed*	omit ILL
back of beyon<u>d</u>	D	• badly *missed* fr(ill)y . . .	FRY
back of lorry	TAILBOARD	*badly* [organised]	GRANDIOSE
back of lorr<u>y</u>	Y	*badly* organised [trips]	SPIRT, SPRIT
back of neck	NAPE		STRIP
back of nec<u>k</u>	K	*badly treated* [men at] . . .	MEANT
back of truck h<u>e</u> ra<u>n</u>	KEN	*badly written* [letters]	SETTLER
back row	REARRANGE	[gone] *bad*	–GEON
back ro<u>w</u>	W	**badger**	
back seat	SADDLE	badger bait	TEASE
back sea<u>t</u>	T	badger's home in front	SETTLED
back to front	RUMPLED	**Badminton performer**	SHOW-JUMPER
back track	PASTRY	**baffle**	
back trac<u>k</u>	K	*baffle* [noises]	ESSOIN
backing hors<u>e</u>	E	*baffled* [by her] . . .	HERBY
backmarker in rac<u>e</u>	E	*bafflement of* [all the] . . .	LETHAL
*back*sid<u>e</u>	E	**bag**	
backward		bag	DOROTHY
backward<	DRAW	bag clasp	CATCH
backward boy<	NOD, NOR et al	bag of lettuce, *say*	SACCOS
	DAL, NOS, YOB	*bags* a . . .	incl A
backward glance<	KEEP	*bags* *	incl *
backward island<	ABLE	• m–an *bags* a duck	MOAN
backward school-boys<	SLIP-UP	baggage control	GRIP, PIMP
backward-looking boy<	NOD, NOR et al	*bagged by* *	incl in *
	DAL, NOS, YOB	• duck *bagged by* m–an	MOAN
bad		baggy	KNEED
bad	OFF	baggy, *say*	KNEAD, NEED
• bad finish	OFFEND	bagman	GLADSTONE
• bad season	OFFSPRING	**Bahamas**	BS
• bad worker	OFFHAND	*in the* Bahamas	B–S
bad actor	HAM	**bail**	
bad [actor]	CROAT	[bail] *out*	BALI
bad *back*<	DAB, LIVE	bailiff, *say*	BAY-LEAF, CAESAR
bad feeling	ILLNESS	bailsman	WICKET-KEEPER
bad fish	RANKLING	[can bail] *out*	CALIBAN
bad *French*	MAL	**baker**	SUNBATHER
• bad *French* relatives	MALKIN	**balance**	BAL
• bad *French* ruler	MALAGA	balance, *say*	WAY
• bad *French* sweet	MALICE	balance sheet	BS
and		balanced, *say*	WADE
• for bad *French* . . .	FORMAL	**bald**	
• neither bad *French* . . .	NORMAL	bald	DISTRESSED, UNLOCKED
• the *German with* bad *French*	DERMAL	bald, *say*	AIRLESS, HEIRLESS
bad hand	SCRAWL, SCRIBBLE	<u>b</u>ald-*headed*	B
bad ignition	ARSON	bald patch	O
bad man	CHRONICLES	• doctor *has* bald patch	VETO
bad mark	CROSS, SCAR	**bale**	
bad spell	CHARM	bale	BL

Anag [cat]; Any *; Begin IGN–; Endings –ING; eg •; Hidden /cat/; Implied add (on); Implied in (in);

[bale] *out*	ABLE, ELBA	• hat-band	CAPO
in bales	B–LS	• string band	BO, CO, DO, GO
ball		band leader	CONDUCTOR, ROBIN HOOD
ball	O	<u>b</u>and *leader*	B
• ball-bearing	ONE(S), –OSE	band, *say*	BANNED
	OWE(S), OWN(S)	(b)and *without a leader*	AND
• ball-boy	OLEO, OVAL	bands of rock *and* stone	STRATAGEM
• ball *on* the green	OVERT	**bandy**	
• ball-point	OE, ON, OS, OW	*bandied about* [names]	MANES, MEANS
• ball-points	ONE(S), OWN(S)	*bandy* [legs]	GELS
ball	YORKER	bandy words	BOW-LEGGED
ball-game, *say*	CROAKY	*bandy* [words]	SWORD
ballpoint manufacturer,		**bang**	
say	PENOLOGIST	bang-like	POPISH
Baltic		bang on	CORRECT, RIGHT
Baltic journalist	LAPPED	bang *on* time	REPORTAGE
Baltic queen	LETTER	banger	FIREWORK, TNT
ban			SAUSAGE
ban a . . .	omit A	**banish**	
ban beauty, *say*	BARBEL	*banish* a . . .	omit A
ban bishopric, *say*	BARELY	*banish* king	omit K, R
ban box, *say*	BANK-RATE	*banish* *	omit *
ban colour	BARRED	• *banish* wife *from* (W)ales	ALES
ban Communist	BARRED	**banjo**	BARMAID
ban firm	BANCO	**bank**	
ban first-<u>b</u>orn	omit B	bank	BK
ban gambling, *say*	BARBETTES	bank attacker	ALLIGATOR, CROCODILE
ban gangster	BANAL	bank go-between	FERRYMAN, RIVER
ban on lake, *say*	BARMIER	Bank of Scotland	BRAE
ban		ba<u>n</u>k rate	BR
–one building	BANISHED	banker	RIVER
–one colour	BARITONE	• English banker	THAMES etc
ban private eye, *say*	BARDIC	• French banker	SEINE etc
ban profits	BARGAIN	• German banker	RHINE etc
ban song, *say*	BANDITTI		(*see also* flower, river)
ban sweetheart	BANJO	banker's statement	IDEAL
ban wire, *say*	BANKABLE	banking	BKG
ban woman, *say*	BANSHEE	*banks* of <u>river</u>	RR
ban *	omit *	**baptise**	
• *ban* learner *from* c(l)ub	CUB	baptise child	CALL-GIRL
banned, *say*	BAND	baptised	BAP(T)
banned girl, *say*	BANDANNA	Baptist	BAP(T)
banned service	BARDLET	**bar**	
banned woman	BRIDE	bar	SILKS
bans weeder	BAR-SHOE	*bar closing*	omit last letter
parking *banned*	omit P	• *bar closing* tim(e)	TIM
parking *banned* in A(p)ril	ARIL	bar fees	COUNTERCHARGES
	(*see also* bar)	bar gangster	BANAL
banana		bar on letter	BARONESS
<u>banana</u> *skin*	BA	*bar opening*	omit 1st letter
banana *split*	BAN, ANA	• *bar* opening (h)ours	OURS
bananas	CRAZY, MAD, NUTS	bar ornament	GRACE NOTE
bananas [I sold]	SOLID		MORDENT, TRILL
band		bar profits	BARGAIN
band	O	bar purchase	LEVERAGE
• band *together with* archdeacons	OVENS	barmaid	BANJO, HEBE, PORTIA

Letter replaced \c\at; Omit (a); Pointers *out*; Retain <u>a</u>; Split B_ED; Down (D); Backwards <or ^

barman	BARRISTER, COUNSEL	barristers	BAR
	GANYMEDE	**barter**	
barred fight, *say*	BANDBOX	barter hawk	SELL
barred Scot	BANDIAN	barter vehicle	TRUCK
barred the *old*, *say*	BANDAGED	**base**	
	(*see also* ban)	base abandoned	FOOTLOOSE
Barbados	BS	base fellow	FOOTMAN
in Barbados	B–S	*base of* tree(D)	E
barbarian		base, *say*	LO, VIAL
barbarian	HUN	basic, *say*	ALIMENTARY
barbaric [rite]	TIER, TIRE	basic subject(s)	R(R)
barbarous [Huns]	SHUN	nava̱l *base*(D)	L
barbecue		**bashful**	
barbecue	OUTDO	bashful head	SHYNESS
barbecues, *say*	GRILSE	ba̱shful *head*	B
bard	WILL	**Basil**	
bare		basil	HERB
bare (=with nothing on)		• Basil's book	HERBAL
• bare arm	LIMBO	Basil	BRUSH
• bare tree	MAYO	**basking**	
	(*see also* naked)	bask, *say*	PYRENEAN
bare	OUT OF GEAR	basking	(in) SU–N
bare, *say*	BEAR, CARRY, DELIVER	**basket**	
	GRIZZLY, POOH	basket	BKT
bare skin, *with* nothing on	BUFFOON	basket-maker	OSIER, WICKER
bareback rider	GODIVA	basketry	RUSH JOB
barefaced	NONOSE	**bass**	
barely frozen	JUSTICE	bass	B
barely seen	NAKED, NUDE	bass note, *say*	DEEP SEA
barely true	JUST	**bat**	
barer	LESSON	bat	CRICKET CLUB
bargain		bats	(*see separate entry*)
bargain	SNIP	batsman	OPENER
bargain crop	SNIP	ba̱tsman's *first* run	BR
bargain price	SONG	batsman's position	INCREASE,
baritone	BAR		STANCE
bark		batter	(*see separate entry*)
bark	BK, WOOF, WOW	batting	IN, INCREASE
bark of tree	BAY	batting side	INSET, OFF, ON, ONSET
barker, *say*	COFFER	**bathe**	
barker's pitch	DOGSTAR	bathe queen	WASHER
barn		**bats**	
[barn]*storm*	BRAN	bats	CRAZY, MAD, NUTS
demolish [barn]	BRAN	*bats* [can see]	SEANCE
baron		*batty* [idea]	AIDE
baron	BN	**battalion**	BAT(T), BN
Baron Munchausen, *say*	LIKING	**batter**	
baronet	BART, BT	batter	EYELID
baroque		*batter* [wives]	VIEWS
baroque [art]	RAT, TAR	battered cooker	STOVE
baroquely [coiled]	DOCILE	*battered* [crate]	CATER, REACT
barrel		*battering* [ram]	ARM, MAR
barrel	BL	**battery**	
in barrels	B–LS	battery	BAT(T)
barrister		battery-powered warship	GUNBOAT
barrister	SILK		

Anag [cat]; Any *; Begin IGN–; Endings –ING; eg •; Hidden /cat/; Implied add (on); Implied in (in);

battle

battle	WAR
• battle *at* sea	WARMER
• battle casualties, *say*	WARDED
• battle circuit	WARRING
• battle-gear	WARDRESS
• battle has started	WARISON
• battle rations	WARFARE
• battle shout	WARRANT
• battle study	WARDEN
battle	WATERLOO etc
battle call	ENGAGEMENT RING
battle-dress	BALACLAVA
battle scene	ACTION PAINTING
battle station	WATERLOO
battlefield	ACRE
[great] *battles*	GRATE
battling [over] . . .	ROVE

bay

bay	B
• bay tree	BASH
bay, *say*	BITE, BYTE
bayleaf, *say*	BAILIFF
BBC	AUNTIE, BEEB
b-bird	BEAGLE, BOWL
BD	
BD, *say*	BEADY

be

be fastened, *say*	BETIDE
be drunk	BELIT
be female	BEHEN
be *heard*	BEE
be keeper	HAVE, OWN
be my telephone, *say*	BEMIRING
be pierced, *say*	BEHOLD
be positive	LIVE
be prepared	BP
be quick	EXIST, LIVE
be sullen at this point	SULKIER
being smart	PERSONABLE

beach

beach artist	SANDRA
beach fibre	STRAND
beach, *say*	SURE
Beachy Head	B

bead

bead counter	ABACUS
beady, *say*	BD

beam

beam-arm	RAY-GUN
beam, *say*	MANTLE
beams, *say*	RAISE

bear

bear	BRUIN, POOH, RUSSIAN
bear in front, *say*	POOLED
bear company	STAND FIRM

bear punishment	STICK
bear, *say*	BARE, NAKED, NUDE
	OUT OF GEAR, UNDRESSED GRISLY
bear twin	POOH-POOH
bear up	THE GREAT BEAR, URSA MAJOR
	URSA MINOR
bear *up*(D)^	HOOP
bear wine	PORT
bears scorn	POOH-POOH
bears suffer	HASLET
<u>bear</u>skin	BR

bearing

bearing	AIR
• bearing left	AIRPORT
• bearing wine	AIRPORT
• strong bearing	FAIR
bearing	N, S, E, W
• bearing poems	NODES
• bearing wine	SHOCK
• bearing flower	EASTER
• bearing one each	WIPER
	(*see* also directions)
bearing	DEMEANOUR
bearing a . . .	incl A
bearing, *say*	MEAN
bearing *	incl *
• ship *bearing* German . . .	SHUNS
borne by *	incl in *
• German *borne by* ship	SHUNS

beastly

beastly driver	SHEEPDOG, TOAD
beastly fighter	GLADIATOR, PICADOR
	TOREADOR, TORERO
beastly lot	ZOO
beastly man	CENTAUR, SATYR
beastly mother	DAM, MARE
beastly overheads	ANTLERS, HORNS

beat

beat	PIP
• beat Edward	PIPED
• Beat it!	PIPIT
• beat queen	PIPER
beat	TAN
• beat fellow	TANGENT
• beat Nicholas, *say*	TANNIC
• beat ruler	TANKING
beat [all the] . . .	LETHAL
beat bottom	WORST
beat cloth	WORSTED
beat favourite	WHIPPET
beat player	BATTER
beat seed	PULSE
beat time	TEMPO
beat tramp	LAYABOUT
beat *up*(D)^	GOLF, MAL
beat up [sorbet]	STROBE

Letter replaced \c\at; Omit (a); Pointers *out*; Retain <u>a</u>; Split B_ED; Down (D); Backwards <or ^

beaten club	FLAT-IRON
beaten [silver]	LIVERS, SLIVER
beater	CONDUCTOR
	HEADMASTER, TANNER
	HEART, PACEMAKER, PULSE
beau	ADONIS, DANDY
beautiful	
beautiful blonde	FAIR
beautiful country	FAIRGROUND
beauty queen	MISSUS
because	AS, COS, FOR, SINCE
become	
become angry, *say*	CERED
become calm	ENDANGER
become embarrassed	GORED
become father	BEDAD
become fit	GETABLE
become less civilised	BEWILDER
become older	PASSAGE
become quiet	GOSH
become [quiet]	QUITE
become solvent	ENDOWING
become tense, *say*	TITAN
become taller	STRETCH ONE'S LEGS
becomes [tired]	TRIED
becomes warm	GET SHOT
becoming respectable	PROPER
bed	
bed	COT, GARDEN, PLOT
bed factory	PLANT
bed maker	GARDENER
bed makers	PLANTS, ROSES etc
bed of nails	QUICK
bed of nails(D)	S
bed, *say*	LAIR
bedfellow	PROCRUSTES
*bed*head	B
bedridden	(in) BE–D, (in)B–ED
• *bedridden*	BILLED
• *bedridden* king	BRED
bedridden	(in) CO–T, (in) C–OT
• son *is bedridden*	COST
• *bedridden* learner	CLOT
bedridden (=laid up)(D)^	DIAL
bedroom	DORMITORY, WARD
bedsitter	OYSTER
bedspread	MULCH
[bed]*spread*	DEB
bedevil	
bedevil [his] . . .	–ISH
bedevilled [by a] . . .	BAY
bedlam	
Bedlam [in the] . . .	THINE
[like] *Bedlam*	KIEL
bedraggled	
bedraggled [mare]	REAM

[it was] *bedraggled*	WAIST
bee	
bee	B
bee *in* bonnet	B, FIRST LETTER
beekeeper	HIVE
beekeeper, *say*	HAVE, OWN
bees	BB, BS
beef	
beef consultant	OMBUDSMAN
beef entrée	CARPENTRY
beef *entrée*	B
beef not available	BULLY OFF
beer	
beer container	BELLY, STOMACH
beer *container*	DALEK, WALER, WHALES
beer, *say*	AIL, BIER, LAAGER
beer strike	WALLOP
beer with fish	ALEGAR
beer *with* head	STOUTNESS
Beethoven	
Beethoven quartet	BEET, HOVE, OVEN
Beethoven's *finish*	OVEN, VEN
Beethoven's *Third*	E
beetle	
beetle	OVERHANG, PROJECT
beetle design	PROJECT
wings of beetle	BE
befog	
befogged	(in) M–IST
• a king *is befogged*	MARIST
• Ron *loses* his head *when befogged*	MONIST
before	
before	A, AN, ANTE, BEF, ER, OR
before	ERE
• before transport	EREBUS
• before the children	EREMITES
• before the court	ERECT
before	PRE
• before *and* after	PRELATE
• before Herb, *say*	PRESAGE
before Christ	AC, BC
before delivery	ANTE-NATAL
before five, *say*	FOR(E)
before nine, *say*	AIT, ATE, EYOT
before noon	AM
before noon	in front of N
• see *before* noon	SEEN
before the bench	UP
before the day	AD
before three, *say*	TO(O)
before twelve	AM
*before*hand	in front of L, LT, R, RT
• appeared *before*hand	CAMEL
• me *before*hand	MELT
• contribute *before*hand	GIVER
• he *has* one *before*hand	HEART

Anag [cat]; Any *; Begin IGN–; Endings –ING; eg •; Hidden /cat/; Implied add (on); Implied in (in);

befuddle
befuddled [by a gin] . . .   BAYING
befuddling [wines]   SINEW, SWINE
beg
beg, *say*   PREY
begged, *say*   PREYED
begin
[begin] *afresh*   BINGE
begin to ẹat   E
begin ṯo eat   TEAT
begin to fight   SET-TO
beginning
beginning   A, ALPHA
beginning   PARTI–
 • beginning *with* friend   PARTIALLY
 • beginning *by*
 breaking [into]   PARTITION
beginning *in* Greece   ALPHA
beginning *in* Israel   ALEPH
beginning of April   MARCH-PAST
beginning of Ạpril   A
beginning of last . . .   L
beginning *of* last month   DEC(I)–
beginning of play   ACTI–, KICK-OFF
beginning of p̲lay   P
beginning of the . . .   T
beginning of ṯime   T
beginning will, *say*   STARTLE
(m)eat beginning *to go off*   EAT
begone
begone   omit BE
 • Begone! Begone!   GONE
 • Begone, (b)rid(e)   RID
begotten
begotten [in anger]   EARNING, NEARING
[woe]-*begotten*   OWE
behead
behead   omit 1st letter
 • *behead* (g)oats   OATS, (b)UTTERS
 • *beheaded* (t)he (b)ad
 (a)long . . .   HEADLONG
 • *beheaded* (w)omen   OMEN
behind
behind
indicating one word written
after another word or letter:
 • daughter *behind the* times   AGED
 • directions *behind*hand   TARES
 • girl *behind* the lines   BREVE
 • man *behind*hand   HANDED
 • put directions *behind* tree   ASHEN
behind bars   (in) C–AGE, (in) PE–N
behind family   BUMKIN
behind the times   PASSE
behold
be*holding*   incl in B–E

 • be*holding* a saint   BASTE
 • be*holding* clear . . .   BRIDE
 • be*holding* notice   BADE
being
being drawn   UNDERTOW
being human   ERRING
being human, *say*   HERRING
Belgian   LIEGEMAN
belittle
belittle country   FRANC(e)
belittle countrymen   IRIS(h)
belligerent
belligerent American   GI
belligerent poet   MARTIAL
                           (*see also* aggressive)
bellringer   CAMPANOLOGIST
                                    CLAPPER
belong
belong   LIVELONG
belonging in Fir/st Ar/my   STAR
belonging to the pub/lic e/nemy   LICE
belonging to you, *say*   YORE
below
below   ASUNDER
below
indicating one word
written under another:
 • live *below* soldier(D)   GIBE
below forty   FOR, FORT
below freezing   OFFICE
below seven   SIX
below (s)even   EVEN
belt
belt *up*(D)^   MAL
bemuse
bemuse [all the] . . .,   LETHAL
bemused [by all] . . .   BALLY
bend
bend   S, U, Z
bend a knee   KNEEL
bend a [knee]   KEEN
bend *before* hill   TURNPIKE
bend fastener   BUCKLE
bend oar   SWEEP
bend piece   ARCHBISHOP
bend [rules]   LURES
bender   ELBOW, JOINT, KNEE
bending [low]   OWL
bent into [shape]   HEAPS, PHASE
bent [nail]   ANIL, LAIN
bent striker, *say*   CURLICUE
beneath
beneath   UNDER
 • beneath fish   UNDERLING
 • beneath mammal   UNDERSEAL
 • beneath trees   UNDERSTAND

Letter replaced \c\at; Omit (a); Pointers *out*; Retain a̲; Split B_ED; Down (D); Backwards <or ^

benevolent Communist	KINDRED
Benjamin	
Benjamin is working	BENISON
Benjamin is complete, *say*	BENZOLE
bent	(*see* bend)
bequeath	
bequeath it, *say*	WILLET
bequeath *to* alien	WILLET
bequeath *to* Edward, *say*	WILTED
Berlin division	WALL
berserk	
berserk [slayer]	LAYERS, RELAYS
[goes] *berserk*	EGOS
berth	WATER-BED
beset	
beset a . . .	incl A
beset *	incl *
• runner's *besetting* sin	COSINES
beset by *	incl in *
• king *beset by* wo–e	WOKE, WORE
beside	
father *beside* himself	PAPA
man *beside* himself	TOM-TOM
mother *beside* herself	MAMA
soldier *beside* himself	GIGI
besiege	
besieged by *	incl in *
• island *besieged by* engineers	RISE
besieged Lady	SMITH
besieging *	incl *
• engineers *besieging* island	RISE
besotted	(in) LO–VE
bespatter	
bespatter [door]	ROOD
bespattered [car she] . . .	SEARCH
bespectacled	
bespectacled	incl in O–O
• *bespectacled* bishop *in* right . . .	ROBOT
• *bespectacled* king *in* the Merchant Navy	MORON
bespoke	
bespoke [T-shirt]	THIRST
best	
best	WORST
best china	CHUM, MATE, SOULMATE
best club	ACE
best diamond	ACE, ICE CREAM
best man	CHAMPION, WINNER
best parliamentarian	WHIP
best part of the . . .	TH
best part of the meat	EAT
[best] *possible*	BETS
best spade	ACE
best suit	TRUMPS
best time	PLUMAGE

best type	ELITE
best writing	FIRST HAND
bet	
bet frequently, *say*	OFFENBACH
bet in Germany	BACKING
bet *on* a fight	LAYABOUT
betting levy, *say*	SYNTAX
beta	B
betray	
betray disciple	FINGERMARK
betray store	SHOP
better	
better	GAMBLER, PUNTER
better bed	LAYER
better half	RIB, WIFE
better *half*	BET, TER
better sportsman	GAMBLER, PUNTER
better teacher	MASTER
better workman	FITTER
between	
between bends	S–S
between ol/d and y/oung	DANDY
between the sheets	(in) B–ED, (in) C–OT
between us	U–S
bewilder	
bewildered [men at] . . .	MEANT
bewildering [speed I] . . .	ESPIED
[I am] *bewildered*	AIM
beyond	
beyond reason	OTT, OVER THE TOP
beyond the mouth	omit 1st letter
• river *beyond the mouth*	(h)UMBER (o)USE, (t)RENT etc
beyond the river	PASTURE
bias	
bias in [test]	SETT
biased [umpire]	IMPURE
bible	
bible	AV, BIB, NT, OT, RV
• bible queen	AVER
• bible records	BIBLISTS
• nothing *in* the Bible	NOT
• bible-woman	OTHER
• last word *about* the Bible	CURVE
bible classes	RE, RI
big¹	BIG
big-*hearted*	I
big-*end*	G
Big *Top*(D)	B
big*head*	B
big*mouth*	B
big²	
big	OS
• big flower	OSIRIS
• big sheep	OSRAM
• big-time girl	OSMOSIS

Anag [cat]; Any *; Begin IGN–; Endings –ING; eg •; Hidden /cat/; Implied add (on); Implied in (in);

and		bill	AD
• very large bird	OSTEAL	• Bill *is in* front	FACADE
• very large vehicle	OSCAR	• Bill *is on* time	ADAGE
• very large victim	OSPREY	• bill it	ADIT
and		**bill²**	
• big-*hearted* flower	HOSTA	bill of exchange	BE
• big-*hearted* M–oe	MOOSE	bill of lading	BL
• th–e big-*hearted*	THOSE	bill of parcels	BP
big³		bill of sale	BS
Big Bang time	REPORTAGE	bill payable	BP
big banger	TNT	bill receivable	BREC
Big Ben	NEVIS	Bill's companion	BEN, COO
big build-up	SKYSCRAPER, TOWER	**billow**	
big drinker	FISH	billow, *say*	WAIVE
big fiddle	CELLO	billowing	OVERDUE ACCOUNT
big fight	BATTLE	*billowing* [robes]	BOERS, BORES, SOBER
big game	FINAL	[sails] *billowing*	SILAS
big guns	RA	**biochemical oxygen demand**	BOD
big issue	GRANDCHILD(REN)	**biography**	BIOG, LIFE
big landlords	BLOCK LETTERS	**biology**	BIOL
big letter	ENLARGE, LARGESSE	biology class(es)	TAXON(TAXA)
big lie	ONER	**bird**	
big luminary	SUN	bird	COCK, CROW, TERN, TIT etc
big man	BEN, FATAL	• bird *and* animal	TITMOUSE
big match, *say*	FATTEST	• bird *and* fish	REELING, TITLING
big noise	BOOM, VIP	• bird ate . . .	HAWKBIT, TERNATE, TITBIT
big *noise*	GRATE	• bird-boy	RUFFIAN
big officer	MAJOR	• bird complaint	GROUSE
big picture	CLOSE-UP	• bird disease	THRUSH
big race	GIANTS, TITANS	• bird-dog	COCKTAIL, HARRIER
	MARATHON	• bird exists	MARTINIS
big, *say*	GRATE	• bird expired, *say*	CROWDED, REEDED
big ship	LARGESS	• bird flying, *say*	TITUP
big sum	IMPOUNDS	• bird follows	DOVETAILS
big timer	BEN	• bird food	PIE
big toes, *say*	POLICIES	• bird helps, *say*	COCKADES
big way	M, MI	• bird in front	COCKLED, REELED,
bigger area, *say*	MOORLAND		RUFFLED, TITLED
bigger offer, *say*	MORBID	• bird is cooked, *say*	DUCK-SHOT
bike		• bird joint, *say*	COCKNEY
bike riders, *say*	CYCLAMEN	• bird nuts	CUCKOO
bikini		• bird painter	WHISTLER
bikini	ATOLL	• bird pecks	MOABITES
bikini top	BRA	• bird-ring	MAGPIE
bikini *top*(D)	B	• bird ruler	REEKING
bilabial		• bird, *say*	TURN, WIDER
bi-labial, *say*	TULIPS	• bird speed	TITRATE
bilingual		• bird-table, *say*	TURNTABLE
bilingual agreement	OUIJA	• bird-talk	CHAT
bilingual articles	ELLA, LATHE, UNDER	• bird trap	CROWNET
bill¹		• bird *under* vehicle (D)	CAROUSEL
bill	AC	• bird walking	CROWFOOT
• Bill Hill	ACTOR	• bird will, *say*	TITTLE
• Bill Price	ACCOST	• birdman	COCKED, COCKLES, RUFFIAN,
• Bill *with* another man	ACED, ACERIC,		TERNAL, TITHE, TITLES
	ACHE, ACRON, ACTED	• birds arrive, *say*	COXCOMB

• bird's difficulties	KNOTS	bits of paper	CONFETTI
• bird's perch	CROWBAR	*bit out of* so/me re/d . . .	MERE
• bird's recreation	HOBBY	*bits out of* a/n ap/ple	NAP
• birdshot	SNIPE	bitty, *say*	BITE
• birdsong	PENCHANT	**bitch**	DOGMA
• blackbird	BEAGLE, BOWL, BROOK	**bite**	
bird	PRISON	bit her, *say*	BITTER, NIPTER
bird fancier	CAT	bite *back<*	GNAT, PANS, PIN
bird house	HAREM	bite biscuit	SNAP
bird noise, *say*	CHEAP	*bite out of* a/n ap/ple	NAP
bird sanctuary	NEST	biting cold	NIPPY
bird settling down	NESTLING	biting pastry	TART
bird watcher	EAGLE EYE, GAOLER	**bitter**	
	JAILER, SCREW, WARDER	bitter	BEER
bird's nest	CLUTCH HOUSING	bitt<u>er</u> *end*	R
birth		bitter fish, *say*	RILING
birthday	PRESENT DAY	bitter fluid, *say*	BHYLE
birthplace	BED, BP, NATAL	bitter-money	SOURDOUGH
biscuit man	GARIBALDI	bitter prostitute	TART
bishop		bitter, *say*	BIT HER, NIPTER
bishop	B, BP, RR	bitter turnover	TART
	ABBA, ANSELM, ODO	**bizarre**	
bishop's chair, *say*	THROWN	*bizarre* [affair]	RAFFIA
bishop's letters	RR	*bizarrely* [robed man]	DOBERMAN
bissextile	BIS	**black**	
bisexuals	HEBRIDES	black	B
bit		• a black deed	ABACTION
a bit pale	PAL(e), WHIT(e)	• a black mark	ABSTAIN
bit ahead	CRUMBLED	• a black tree	ABASH
bit her, *say*	BITTER, NIPTER	and	
bit of a bloomer	PETAL, SEPAL etc	• black cat	BOUNCE
bit of a boob	NIPPLE	• Black Death	BEND
bit of a habit	MONKSHOOD	• black hole	BO
bit of a laugh	HO	• black fish	BANGLE, BROACH
bit of <u>c</u>haracter	C	• black rage	BANGER
bit of character	SERIF	• blackball	BO
bit of <u>c</u>rest	C	• blackbird	BEAGLE, BOWL, BROOK
bit of crest	PARTRIDGE	• blackspots	BRASH
bit of <u>f</u>ish	F	and	
bit of fish	FIN	• black<u>head</u>	B
bit of <u>f</u>un	F	• black*out*	omit B
bit of fun	JAPE, JOKE, LARK	black	DARK
bit of <u>l</u>itter	L	• black fish	DARKLING
bit of l/it/ter	IT	• black queen	DARKER
bit of litter	KITTEN, PIGLET, PUP(PY)	• blackhead	DARKNESS
bit of luck	L, LU	black	JET
bit of luc/k I sh/all . . .	KISH	• black art	JETCRAFT
bit of <u>p</u>aper	P	• black convict	JET LAG
bit of paper	ARTICLE, FEATURE, LEADER	• black cravats	JETTIES
bit of <u>p</u>ig	P	• black fashion	JETTON
bit of pig	BACON, RASHER	• black dog	JET-SETTER
bit of <u>p</u>ride	P	• Black *has* much weight	JETTON
bit of p/rid/e	RID	• black sheep	RAMJET
bit of pride	LION CUB	• black Uncle	JETSAM
bi(t) *short*	BI	• black weight	JETTON
bits of <u>p</u>aper	PA	• Blackburn	JET STREAM

Anag [cat]; Any *; Begin IGN–; Endings –ING; eg •; Hidden /cat/; Implied add (on); Implied in (in);

• blackish offspring, *say*	JETTISON
black	PITCH
• black hose	PITCH PIPES
• black journalist	PITCHED
• black king	PITCHER
black	TAR
• Black *and* Tan	TARTAN
• black glue	TARGUM
• black sailor	TAR, TARTAR
• black salt	TAR, TARTAR
black and blue	DIRTY
black and white players	PIANISTS
black art	NECROMANCY, NIGROMANCY
Black Beauty	DARK HORSE, NIGHTMARE
black belt	DAN
black country	JAPAN
black gold	OIL
black lead	OTHELLO
black mole ˙	JETTY
black note	FLAT, SHARP
black paint brush	SABLE
black sailor	COALTAR
black stuff	COAL, OIL, TAR
black suit	C, S
blade	
blade, *say*	VAIN, VEIN
blame	RAP
blanket coverage	BEDSPREAD, DUVET,
	EIDERDOWN, SHEET
blast	
blast of [air]	IRA, RIA
blast rocks, *say*	CURSORES
blast swan, *say*	DAMPEN
blasted [pest]	PETS, STEP
blazing	
blazing [fire]	RIFE
blazing [row]	WOR
[guns] *blazing*	GNUS, SNUG, SUNG
blemish	
blemish	SCAR
• blemish *on* metropolis	SCARCITY
• blemish *on* female	SCARF
• circular blemish	OSCAR
blend	
blend here, *say*	NEEDIER
blend it, *say*	WISKET, WHISKET
blend of [teas]	EATS, SATE, SEAT
blend, *say*	KNEED, NEED
blended [wines]	SINEW, SWINE
blending [into sea]	ESTONIA
blending into th/e land/scape	ELAND
blessed	
blessed	B
blessed one	DONOR, GIVER, SAINT, TAKER
blessed sacrament	BS
Blessed Virgin (Mary)	BV(M)

blind	
blind [dates]	SATED
blind (man)	VENETIAN
blind gangster	HOOD
blind mic(e)	MIC
blissful state	IGNORANCE
Blithe Spirit	AIRY FAIRY, (SKY) LARK
blitz	
blitz [town]	WONT
blitz[krieg]	GRIKE
blizzard	
blizzard [in Ayr]	RAINY
[in a] *blizzard*	AIN
[rode] *in a blizzard*	DOER
blob	O
block	
block a view	DAMASCENE
block shoe	CLOG
block *	incl in *
• stone *blocking* river	TASTY
block flooring, *say*	PARKY
blocked by *	incl *
• river *blocked by* stone	TASTY
blockbuster	SCULPTOR
blockhouse	IGLOO
blood	
blood count	DRACULA
blood factor	RH
blood letter	MOSQUITO
blood money	ERIC
blood pump, *say*	HART
blood sucker	BAT, LEECH, VAMPIRE
blood-sucking grasshopper	CRICKET BAT
bloodgroup	A, AB, B, O
	FAMILY, KIN
bloody	B
• bloody cheek	BLIP
• bloody fool	BASS
• bloody wet	BRAINY
bloody	RARE
• bloody diocese, *say*	RARELY
• bloody king	RARER
• bloody saint	RAREST
bloody	RED
• bloody battle	REDACTION
• bloody, *say*	READY
• English *in* bloody . . .	REED
• lawyer *has* blood . . .	DARED
bloody channel	AORTA, ARTERY, VEIN
bloody channel, *say*	VAIN, VANE
bloody fool	BF
bloody scarce	RARE
bloody tube	AORTA, ARTERY, VEIN
bloody tube, *say*	VAIN, VANE
bloom	
bloomer	FLOWER

Letter replaced \c\at; Omit (a); Pointers *out*; Retain a̲; Split B_ED; Down (D); Backwards <or ^

blooming	OUT	board game	GOSPORT
blooming female	IRIS, ROSE et al	board meeting	CHESS MATCH
	(*see also* flower¹)		DINNER PARTY
blow		board member	CHESS PIECE, PAWN etc
blow	ONER, WIND		DIRECTOR
blow apart [outer] . . .	OUTRE	• board-members' dance	PAWNSHOP
blow at this point, say	WINDIER	• board-member's joint	DIRECTORSHIP
blow open [door]	ODOR, ROOD	Board of . . .	
blow-pipe	OCARINA, WHISTLE etc	–Control	BC
blow *to the ear*	GAEL	–Education	BE
blow up	DYNAMITE	–Trade	BOT
	EXAGGERATE	board, *say*	BORED, DRILLED
	UPPERCUT		WEARIED
blow *up*(D)^	PAR	board weight	PLANKTON
blow up building	PUMPHOUSE	*boarded by* a . . .	incl A
blow up [dam]	MAD	*boarded by* *	incl *
blow ill, *say*	TOOTLE	• bri–g *boarded by* number . . .	BRING
blower	TELEPHONE, WIND	boarder	PG
blowing about [in the] . . .	THINE	*boarding* *	incl in *
blowing up [a ship]	APHIS	• number *boarding* bri–g	BRING
blown [about]	U-BOAT	boards	STAGE
blown about [by a] . . .	BAY	• boards train	STAGECOACH(ES)
blue		**boast**	
blue	DOWN, OFF COLOUR, SAD	boast *about*<	GARB
	SPEND	boastful relation	TALL STORY
blue-blooded boys	REGAL, ROYAL	boasting	AM, IAM, IM
blue-blooded line	VEIN	(*see also* admit, claim, confess, declare)	
blue film	ANGEL, MAX	boasting	SNAKE-BITE
blue fish, *say*	BLUE-EYED, SADDLING	**boat**	TUB
blue flower	DANUBE, NILE	boat builder	ARKWRIGHT, NOAH
blue jumper	ATHLETE		SHIPWRIGHT
blue pencil wielder, *say*	CENSER, SENSOR	boat in front	SCOWLED
blue ships	NAVY	boat propeller	GONDOLIER, OARSMAN
blue water	DANUBE, NILE		ROWER, SAIL
blues	CAMBRIDGE, OXFORD	boat, *say*	WAILER, WALER
blues rhythm	STROKE	boat shelter	DUGOUT
bluestocking	MALADY	boat strike	SMACK
bluff king	HAL	boater	STRAW
blunder		boatman	JEROME, KERN
blunder [made] . . .	DAME, EDAM, MEAD	book boats	VOLCANOES
blundering [steps]	PESTS	**bob**	
blunt point	ROUNDHEAD	bob	S
blur		Bob's producer	BELLRINGER
blurred [letters]	SETTLER		CAMPANOLOGIST
[saw it] *in a blur*	WAIST, WAITS	*short of* a bob	omit S
blush		**body**	
blush	GORED	body-builder	STEROID
blushing	RED	body odour	BO
BMA dance	MEDICINE BALL	body support	BIER, BONE, SPINE
Boadicea's people	ICENI	body support, *say*	BEAUNE, BEER
boar		bodyshop worker	EMBALMER
boar, *say*	CARRIED, DELIVERED	bodywork decay	CARROT
	BORE, DRILL	**bogged down**	(in) FE–N, (in) MAR–SH
	EAGRE		(in) MU–D
board		**bogus**	
board	BD, DIRECTORS	bogus journalist	SHAMED

Anag [cat]; Any *; Begin IGN–; Endings –ING; eg •; Hidden /cat/; Implied add (on); Implied in (in);

bogus [priest]	RIPEST, STRIPE	• books *about<* . . .	TO
[claimed] *bogus* . . .	DECIMAL, MEDICAL	Books *I & III*	BO
Bohemian	BOH	book-store	RESERVE
boil	FURUNCLE	handbook	MANUAL
boil beer	WALLOP	**book²**	
boil [beer at] . . .	BERATE	indicating character in	
boiled [over]	ROVE	or title of novel, etc:	
boiler-fuel overlord, *say*	COKING	• *booked*	
	COAKING	–3	MEN IN A BOAT
boiling point	BP	–4	JUST MEN
boiling *point*	B	–5	FAMOUS
boiling [point]	PINTO	–7	PILLARS (OF WISDOM)
boiling [swede]	SEWED, WEEDS	–10	LITTLE INDIANS
boisterous		–39	STEPS
boisterous [gale]	GAEL	• *booked* as thief	(ARTFUL) DODGER
[throw] *boisterously*	WORTH	• *booked* captain . . .	AHAB, HORNBLOWER
bond	SPY		NEMO
bond lover	SCRIPOPHILE	• *booked* Finn	HUCKLEBERRY
Bond's boss	M	• *booked* traveller	GULLIVER
Bond's club	STICK	• *booked* woman	SHE
bondsman	ERNIE	**boor**	
bone		boor, *say*	BOAR, BORE
bone	T		EAGRE
• a bone	AT	boorish, *say*	RUED
• girl *with* bone	SUET	**boot**	
bone, *say*	BEAUNE, WINE	boot unavailable	KICK-OFF
bonehead	SKULL	boots	(SAM) WELLER
*bone*head	B	**Booth**	ASSASSIN
[bone]*shaking*	EBON	**boozy**	
bony digit, *say*	BONITO	*boozy* [male]	LAME, MEAL
bony impediment	GAUNTLET	[man is] *on the booze*	MAINS
book¹		**border**	
book	B, BK, LIB, TOME	border dispute	HEDGEROW
Book *I*	B	border *flower*	RIO GRANDE, TWEED etc
book	VOL	border poet	SIDEBURNS
• book boats	VOLCANOES	border restriction	LIMIT
• book insect	VOLANT	border security	HEMLOCK
• book worker	VOLANT	*borders of* Hungary	HY
book cover	COPYRIGHT	*borders of* the . . .	TE
book *covers*	BK	*(see also* **boundary***)*	
book-*ends*	BK	**bore**	
book matches	NOVELTIES	bore ape	DRILL
book production	GENESIS	bore cloth	DRILL
book reviewer	AUDITOR	bore, *say*	BOAR, BOOR
book turns	ACTS		EAGRE
bookcase	SATCHEL	bored, *say*	BOARD, MANAGEMENT
bookmaker	AMOS, JOB, EZRA, etc	boring	DRY
	AUTHOR(ESS), EDITOR	• boring advertisement	DRYAD
bookmaker's work	NOVEL	• boring head	DRYNESS
bookkeeper	LIBRARIAN	• boring holes	DRY CELLS
bookmaker	PAPER	• boring period	DRYAD
books	BB	• boring publicity	DRYAD
books	NT, OT	boring drink	GIMLET
• about books	CANT, RENT	boring group, *say*	DULCET
• about books	COT	boring job	WELL-TO-DO
• books *about* . . .	N–T, O–T	boring part	BIT, DRILL

Letter replaced \c\at; Omit (a); Pointers *out*; Retain a̲; Split B_ED; Down (D); Backwards <or ^

born

born	B
• born a monarch	BAKING
• born *and* bred	BRAISED
• born fool	BASS
born	N
• born in New York	NINNY
born	NAT
• born right on . . .	NATRON
born	NE, NEE
• born at hospital	NEATH
• born dead, *say*	NEEDED
born fool	GOD'S APE
born free	DELIVERED
[Born] *Free*	BRNO
born *in France*	NE(E)

borne

borne by al/l oth/er . . .	LOTH
borne, *say*	BORN, BOURNE

borough

borough	BOR

bosom

bosom	BUST
• bosom in front	BUSTLED
• bosom will, *say*	BUSTLE
• monarch *has* no bosom	ROBUST

boss

boss	NOI–
• boss *has* a few . . .	NOISOME
• boss *is given* directions	NOISE(S)
boss	STUD
• boss expired, *say*	STUDIED
• boss *has* ten . . .	STUDIO
• boss *has* debts	STUDIOUS
• boss I love	STUDIO
boss of	
–British Airways	BAKING
–MI6, *say*	SPIKING

botany

botany	BOT

botch

botched [task Ed] . . .	SKATED
botching [all the] . . .	LETHAL

both

both directions	
indicating a palindrome:	
• flat *in both directions*	LEVEL
both ends of the . . .	TE
both ends of the candle	CE
both sides	LR, RL
• copper *on both sides*	CURL
• girl *in both sides*	LEVER, REVEL
both sides	
indicating an inclusion:	
• river *on both sides of* road	TARDY
both ways	
indicating a palindrome:	
• look *both ways*	PEEP
both ways	
indicating reversal:	
• played *both ways*	STRAD

bother

[a bit] of *bother*	BAIT
bother [about] . . .	U-BOAT
bothering to [write a] . . .	WAITER

bottle

bottle	BOT, NERVE
bottle fruit	GOURD
bottle-*opener*	B
bottle-party	PINTADO
bottle-*top*(D)	B
bottled	(in) VI–AL
bottled spirit	GENIE
bottling a . . .	incl A
bottling *	incl *
• wa–s *bottling* in . . .	WAINS
bottling premises	CHATEAU
* *bottled*	incl *
• drink *bottled in* the outskirts of souk	STEAK

bottom

bottom gear	KNICKERS, PANTS
bottom of all the big . . .(D)	LEG
bottom of foot	SOLE
bottom of foot(D)	T
mug, *bottom up*(D)^	GUM

bought

bought	BT, BOT

bounce

bouncer	BALL
bouncing [babe]	ABBE

bound

bound	BD
bounding [over]	ROVE
bounds of possibility	PY

boundary

boundary	FOUR, IV, SIX, VI
• boundary out of date	FOUR SQUARE
boundaries of Surrey	SY
boundaries of the . . .	TE
boundary dispute	HEDGEROW
boundary restriction	LIMIT
boundary trees	LIMES
(*see also* border)	

bounder

bounder	CAD
• bounder expires	CADDIES
• bounder states . . .	CADAVERS

bovine

bovine cheek	COWSLIP, OXLIP
bovine part	COWSLIP, OXLIP
bovine part, *say*	COWSHED

bow

Bow (=Cockney)	
• Bowman's (h)ouse	OUSE

Anag [cat]; Any *; Begin IGN–; Endings –ING; eg •; Hidden /cat/; Implied add (on); Implied in (in);

	(*see also* Cockney)
bow of liner	L
bow-legged bird, *say*	BANDICOOT
bowed woman	VIOLA
bowman	ARCHER, CUPID, EROS, TELL
	CELLIST, VIOLINIST
	COCKNEY
bows	FIDDLESTICKS
bow of ship	PROW
bow of ship	S
bows of ship	SH
bows in front	PROWLED
bowtie	CABLE, HAWSER, PAINTER
bowl	
bowl this way, *say*	SOBOLE
bowled	B
bowled out	omit B
• (b)elatedly *bowled out*	ELATEDLY
bowler	DRAKE
bowling	ON, TOM
bowls rent	YORKSHIRE
box	
box-kite	CRATE
box, *say*	KRAIT
box, see	SPARELY
boxed	(in) CR–ATE
boxed in by *	incl in *
• is *boxed in by* r–ing	RISING
boxer	ALI, CLAY
boxer	DOG
• *boxer's* supporter	DOG-LEG
boxer	PUG(ILIST)
• *boxer understands, say*	PUG-NOSE
boxers	ABA, WBA, WBC
boxer's diary	SCRAPBOOK
boxing a . . .	incl A
boxing belt	CROSS, HOOK, LEFT
	RIGHT, SWING, UPPERCUT
boxing champion	SPARKING
Boxing Club	ABA
Boxing Day duo	TURTLE DOVES
boxing, *say*	PHAETON
boxing venue, *say*	SQUARING
boxing *	incl *
• r–ing-*boxing* is . . .	RISING
boy	
affectionate boy	FONDLES
boy	B, LAD, SON
boy *and* girl	BENGAL, LEONORA
	PATELLA, PATINA, REGINA
	REGNANCY, VICUNA
	THEOSOPHY
	(*see also* girl and boy)
boy *and* a girl	LENA
boy editor	TIMED
boy-friend	NORMALLY, REGALLY

	ROYALLY
	(*see also* friend)
boy gets up, *say*	SUNRISES
boy *has* support, *say*	ALGEBRA
boy *meets* maiden	ANTONYM
boy *on* one side, *say*	REGICIDE
boy, *say*	SUNNI, SUNNY
boy scoffed	MALATE
boy *with* trophy	SIDCUP
boy wipes up, *say*	SUNDRIES
boy-worker	PAGEANT
bra	
bra	FALSIE
bra-burning ceremony, *say*	FALSIFIER
brace of peacock	STRUT
bracket	
bracket a . . .	incl A
bracket *	incl *
• gunners *bracket* carrier	RHODA
bracketed by *	incl in *
• carrier *bracketed by* gunners	RHODA
braggart	PISTOL
brain	
brain treatment	ECG
[brain] *treatment*	BAIRN
brainy case	CRANIUM, HEAD, SKULL
branch	
branch	BR
branch deposit	BIRDLIME
branch office	BO
brand	
brand, *say*	MARC, MARQUE
branding-iron statement, *say*	ICIER
brandish	
brandish	CEREAL, OATMEAL
brandish roller	WAVE
brandish, *say*	WAIVE, WEALD
brandy	
brandy and soda	BANDS
brandy, *say*	MARK, MARQUE
in brandy and soda	B–S
brass	
brass animal	RHINO
brass band	MONEY-BELT
brass rubber	ALADDIN
brave	
brave	INDIAN, REDSKIN
brave child	PAPOOSE
brave fellow, *say*	MANDARIN
brave group	INDIAN CLUB, TRIBE
brave wife	SQUAW
brave opponent	PALEFACE
brave, *say*	BOWLED
brave set-up	TOTEM POLE
Brazil(ian)	
Brazil	NUT

Letter replaced \c\at; Omit (a); Pointers *out*; Retain <u>a</u>; Split B_ED; Down (D); Backwards <or ^

Brazilian	BR	*break open*	incl *
• Brazilian drunk	BROILED	• English master *breaks*	
• Brazilian wears spectacles		*open* cr–ate	CREMATE
at church	BROOCH	*breaks* *	incl in *
• Brazilian with different . . .	BROTHER	• war *breaks* flier	BEWARE
Brazilian	BRA	*broken by a . . .*	incl A
• Brazilian square	BRAT	*broken by* *	incl *
• Brazilian *with* the *Italian* . . .	BRAIL	• flier *broken by* war	BEWARE
• company *has* Brazilian...	COBRA	*broken into by a . . .*	incl A
Brazilian *flower*	AMAZON	*broken into by* *	incl *
Brazilian *leader*	B	• sh–op *broken into by* all	SHALLOP
Brazilian steps	SAMBA	**break³**	
breach		indicating omission:	
breach *	include in *	*break end off* shove(l)	SHOVE
• I breach he–er	HEIR	*break ends off* (s)hove(l)	HOVE
breach [wall of] . . .	FALLOW	*break ends off* bran(ch)	BRAN
breaching [wall by a] . . .	WALLABY	*break head off* (f)lower	LOWER
bread		*break tip off* (s)pear	PEAR
[bread] *crumbs*	BARED, DEBAR	**break⁴**	
bread *crusts*	BD	other uses:	
bread round	DOORSTEP	break	HOL, WE
bread, *say*	DOE, DOH	*break of* day	D
	BRED, REARED	break point	SNAPS
breadmaker	FINANCIER, FLOUR	break the ice	DEFROST
slice of bread	BR	break vessel	CRACKPOT
breadth	B	breakdown specialist	ANALYST
break¹			COUNSELLOR, PSYCHIATRIST
indicating anagram:			SHRINK
break down [result]	ULSTER	*breaking into* sa/fe at/ night	FEAT
break [into] . . .	–TION	broken romance	SERIAL
break [into a] . . .	–ATION	broken statue	BUST
break out of [Broadmoor]	BOARDROOM	short break	HOL, WE
break [plate]	PETAL		*(see also* broke)
break up [town]	WONT	**breakfast**	
break [the law]	WEALTH	*break*[fast]	FATS
break the [law]	AWL	breakfast (cereal)	BRANDISH
break[down]	WOND–	breakfast food, *say*	SERIAL
breakdown of [law]	AWL	**breakwater**	
break[fast]	FATS	breakwater, *say*	GROIN
breaking [rules]	LURES	*break*[waters]	WASTER
[*break*]*out*	BAKER, BRAKE	**breast**	
break[out]	TOU	breast-fed rodent	TITMOUSE
breakout [last]	SLAT	breast feeding	TITRATION
breakthrough [in art]	TRAIN	**breather**	
broken down [van I] . . .	IVAN, VAIN	breather	GILL, LUNG
broken [leg]	GEL, –GLE	breathing space	PORE
broken [romance]	CREMONA	**bred**	
broken up [by a] . . .	BAY	bred, *say*	BREAD, DOE, DOH, DOUGH
broken[hearted]	EARTHED, RED HEAT	**breed**	
brokenly [I moan] . . .	NAOMI	breed aliens	HATCHETS
[code]-*breaking*	CO–ED, DECO	breed fish, *say*	RAISE
[horse]-*breaking*	SHORE	breed it, *say*	HATCHET
break²		breeding dogs, *say*	PUPATION, PUPPETRY
indicating inclusion:		**brew**	
break into *	incl in *	*brew of* [ale]	LEA
• all *break into* sh–op	SHALLOP	*brewed* [tea]	ATE

Anag [cat]; Any *; Begin IGN–; Endings –ING; eg •; Hidden /cat/; Implied add (on); Implied in (in);

brewing [ales]	LEAS, SALE, SEAL	*bring back* new<	WEN
brews, *say*	BRUISE	*bring in* a	incl A
[trouble] *brewing*	BOULTER	*bring in* *	incl *
bribe(ry)	PALM-OIL	• pun–t *brings in* girl	PUNDIT
brick		• Bill *brought in* the *French* . . .	LACE
brick carrier	HOD, STRETCHER	*bring round* a . . .	incl A
brickmaker	CLAY	*bring round* *	incl *
bride		• king *brought round* the . . .	LEATHER
bridal train	HONEYMOON EXPRESS	*bring up* boy(D)^	YOB
Bride*shead*	B	bring up sentry	REARGUARD
bridle-path, *say*	AISLE	brings in rent	ISLET
bridge		*brought about by* [a new] . . .	WANE, WEAN
bridge	BR	brought forward	BF
• bridge *has* different . . .	BROTHER	*brought round* [his pal]	PHIALS
• bridge in East	BRINE	brought together	ATI, ATONE
• bridge that is . . .	BRIE	*brought up* [a lot] . . .(D)^	TOLA
bridge	SPAN	**Britain**	B, BR, GB
• bridge champion	SPANKING	**British**	
• bridge *enclosing* one . . .	SPAIN	British	B
• bridge that is long	SPANIEL	• British are good horsemen	BRIDEWELL
bridge builder, *say*	ARCHAEOLOGIST	• British nationality	BRACE
bridge game	PONTOON	• British weather	BRAIN
bridge opponents	NE, NW, SE, SW	British	BR
bridge partners	EW, NS, SN, WE	• British and *French*	BRET
bridge player, *say*	CARDIOLOGIST	• British fish	BRANGLE, BRIDE
bridge players	E, N, S, W	• British landlord	BROWNER
Bridg*end*	G	• British philosopher	BRAYER
bridge*head*	B	• British service women	BRATS
bridle	(*see* bride)	• British state	BRAVER
brief		• British tree	DRASH
brief		British	
indicating abbreviation:		–Academy	BA
• *brief* manuscript	MS	–Airways	BA
• *brief* period	MIN, MO, HR, SEC	–America	BA
• *brief* reply	ANS	–Association	BA
brief agreement	COMPACT	–Columbia	BC
brief attire	LAW SUIT	–Empire Medal	BEM
brief-case	SHORT SUIT	–Home Stores	BHS
brief farewell	SOLON(g)	–Institute of	
brief flutter	SHORT WAVE	Management	BIM
brief season	SHORTFALL	Radiology	BIR
brief trip	SHORTFALL	–Legion	BL
brief*case*	BF	–Library	BL
briefly writ(e)	WRIT	–Medical Journal	BMJ
brig	BR	–Museum	BM
brigade		–Library	BML
brigade	BDE	–Optical Association	BOA
brigade-major	BM	–Oxygen Company	BOC
bright		–Petroleum	BP
bright boy	RAY	–Pharmacopoeia	BP
bright land	WEST	–Pharmaceutical Codex	BPC
brightly coloured	(in) R–ED, RED	–Printing Corporation	BPC
brilliant champion	STARCH	–Rail	BR
brimstone	S, SULPHUR	–Red Cross Society	RCS
bring		–Road Services	BRS
bring about [a new] . . .	WANE, WEAN	–Shipbuilders	BS

–Standards (Institution)	BS(I)
–Steel (Corporation)	BS(C)
–Sugar Corporation	BSC
–Summer Time	BST
–Thermal Unit	BT(H)U
–United Provident Association	BUPA
British capital	STERLING
British *capital*	B
British company	BL
British country	
music	GOD SAVE THE QUEEN
	NATIONAL ANTHEM
British *flower*	SEVERN, THAMES etc
British Honduras	BH
British *leader*	B
broach	
broach *	incl in *
• I *broach* h–er . . .	HEIR
• barrel *broached by* a . . .	TUAN
broad	
Broad Street	LARGEST, WIDEST
broader, *say*	WHIDAH, WHYDAH
broadcast	
[broad]*cast*	BOARD
broadcast [news]	WENS
broadcast news	GNUS
broadcast race	RELAY
broadcast [race]	ACER, ACRE, CARE
broadcast, *say*	SEW, SEWN, SO
broadcast seed again, *say*	RECEDED
broadcast twice, *say*	SO-SO
broadcaster	SOWER
broadcasting organisation	AUNTIE, BEEB
broadcasting, *say*	SEWING
[live] *broadcast*	EVIL, VILE
[outside] *broadcast*	TEDIOUS
Broadmoor	CRANK CASE
broke	
broke	NOCENT
broken sculpture	BUST
	(*see also* break)
broker	UNCLE
bronchitic	
bronchitic, *say*	COFFER
bronchitic lungs	ANCIENT LIGHTS
broth	
broth [made in] . . .	MAIDEN
broth of a [boy]	YOB
[stale] *broth*	LEATS, STEAL
	TALES, TEALS
brother	
brother	BILLY, BR, BRO
brotherhood	COWL
brought	(*see* bring)
brown	
brown	BR

• brown and . . .	BRAND
• Brown drunk	BROILED
• brown insect	BRANT
brown	TAN
• brown hats	CAPSTAN
• brown man	TANGENT
• brown potassium	TANK
brown bread	TOAST
brown schoolboy	TOM
browned off	SUNBURNED, TANNED
browse	
browse, *say*	BROWS, GREYS
bruise	
bruise, *say*	BREWS, WAIL, WHALE
	WHEAL, WHEEL
brush	BASIL, SAGE
bubble	
bubbling [stream]	MASTER, REMAST
bubbly [girl in] . . .	RILING
buckle	
buckled [post]	POTS, SPOT, STOP, TOPS
buckles, [gold pair]	PRODIGAL
buckling [down 'e] . . .	OWNED
budding	
budding of (f)lowers	LOWERS
budding writer	PE(n)
Buenos Aires	BA
buffet	
buffet [car]	ARC
buffeting [gale]	GAEL
buggy type	BACTERIOLOGIST
build	
builder	JACK, JERRY
builders of	
[Kew longed]	KNOWLEDGE
building	BDG
building area, *say*	HALLIARD, HALLYARD
building at this point, *say*	HAULIER
building charges	HALLIONS
building [Ma used]	MEDUSA
builds [town]	WONT
built of [stone]	NOTES, ONSET, TONES
built-up [shoe]	HOES, HOSE
[empire]-*building*	PREMIER
[master]-*builder*	REMAST, STREAM
bulk	
bulk of grain	GRA, RAIN
bulk service	MASS
*bulk*head	B
bull	
*bull*head	B
bully	COWER, FLASHMAN, HECTOR
bully	OXY–
bully beef	WARFARE
bully prince	HECTOR
bulletin	LOADED, SHOT

Anag [cat]; Any *; Begin IGN–; Endings –ING; eg •; Hidden /cat/; Implied add (on); Implied in (in);

bum

bum-boat	TRAMP
bum-[boats]	SABOT
bum rap	SPANKING
bum [steer]	RESET

bump

bump into attendant	RAMPAGE
bumpy [lane]	LEAN
bumpy [ride]	DIRE

bunch

bunch of fives	FIST
bunch of keys	ACE, AGE, BAD, GAB
	AGED, BADE, CAFE, DEAF,
	EDGE, EGAD, FACE
	DEFACE, FACADE

bundle

bundle of [papers]	SAPPER
bundle [was tied]	WAISTED
bundled up [in rags]	RASING

bungle

bungle [each] . . .	ACHE
bungling [all the] . . .	LETHAL

bunker	WARDEN
bunter	BILLY, GOAT, SANDSTONE
buoyant actress	MAE WEST
Burlington House	RA

Burmese

Burmese	SHAN
• Burmese tea, *say*	SHANTY

burn

burn church	SCARCE, SEARCH
<u>burn</u> *both ends*	BN
burn fish	CHAR
burn fuel	CHARCOAL
burn planes, *say*	GLOWING
burn, *say*	FLAIR
burn them, *say*	SERUM
burn vehicle, *say*	GLOBOSE, GLOBOUS
burned incense, *say*	SENSED
burning	(in) FI–RE
burning desire	ARSON, PYROMANIA
burning issue	FIRE-ENGINE
burning land	ALIGHT
burning ring	FLAMINGO
burnt bones, *say*	BEAU NASH

burst

burst [into] . . .	–TION
burst [into a] . . .	–ATION
burst [into tears]	STATIONER
burst into *	incl in *
• he *bursts into* mas–s	MASHES
burst [open]	NOPE, PEON
bursting [vein]	VINE

Burundi

Burundi	RU
capital of Burundi	B

leader of Burundi	B

bury

buried	INTOMB
buried in /a gar/den	AGAR
bury	INTER
• bury Edward	INTERNED
• bury girl	INTERVAL
• bury *up to* the knees, *say*	INTERNEES
bury a . . .	incl A
bury *	incl *
• *bury* saint in ha–y	HASTY
burying *	incl in *
• ha–y *burying* saint	HASTY

bush

bushman	TOPIARIST
bushwhacker	TOPIARIST

bushel	BU, BUS(H)

business

business	ADO
• business about . . .	ADORE
• business exercise	ADOPT
• business *with* the Navy	ADORN
business	BIZ
business	CO
• Brown on business . . .	BRONCO
• business event	COINCIDENT
• business friend	COPAL
• business support	COBRA
• business woman	COW
• businessman	CODAN, CODON,
	CODES, COGENT
business	FIRM
• a loud business	AFFIRM
• in business *with* a line . . .	INFIRMARY
• study business	CONFIRM
business area	EC, SHOPFLOOR
business	
subscription	YOURS FAITHFULLY

busybody	ANT

bust

bust [bust]	BUTS, STUB
[bust] *bust*	BUTS, STUB
bust in [marble]	RAMBLE
bust up [over] . . .	ROVE
busted [gut]	TUG
bust, *say*	KISSED

but

but *French* . . .	MAIS
but *once*	SED

butcher

butcher [cows]	SCOW
butcher's complaint	BEEF
butcher's (hook)	LOOK, SEE
butchery of [tribe]	BITER, TIBER
[lamb] butchered	BALM
butler	JEEVES, RAB, RHET

Letter replaced \c\at; Omit (a); Pointers *out*; Retain <u>a</u>; Split B_ED; Down (D); Backwards <or ^

butt

butt in(to) *	incl in *
• I *butted into* he–r . . .	HEIR
butter	GOAT, RAM
butter-paper	RAMPAGE(S)
butter-*up*(D)^	MAR
buttress	NANNY-GOAT

buy

buy dog, *say*	BIKER
buy parts for radio, *say*	BIVALVES
buy *sound* . . .	BY(E)
buyer's option	BO

buzz

buzzed, *say*	WORD
buzzer	BEE, FLY

by

by	PER
• by a boy	PERSON
• by cutting	PERSEVERANCE
• by *returning*<	REP
• by *turning over*<	REP
by (=times)	X
• nothing by . . .	OX
by accident [spilt] . . .	SPLIT
by all accounts might . . .	MITE
by arrangement [I went] . . .	TWINE
by canopy	ATTESTER
by ear, Handel . . .	HANDLE
by *half*	B, Y
by loch (=Scottish)	
• *by loch*, one . . .	ANE
• church *by loch*	KIRK
by [means] . . .	MANES, NAMES
by means of, *say*	THREW

by mistake [I went] . . .	TWINE
by name	SC
by no means al(l)	AL
by-pass	COLOSTOMY, ILEOSTOMY
by-passed by *	incl in *
• city *by-passed by* r–ing	RELYING
by-passing a . . .	incl A
by-passing *	incl *
• r–ing *by-passing* city	RELYING
by proxy	PP
by, *say*	BUY, BYE
by the ears I'll . . .	AISLE, ISLE
by the mouth were . . .	WHIRR
by the river, *say*	DECIDE
by the sound of her . . .	OFFER
by the sound of it	BUY, BYE
by the way	ROADSIDE
by the way	incl RD or ST
• the man, *by the way*	HERD
• a Red, *by the way*	STARED
• the *French, by* the way	LAST, LEST
by the way	incl N, S, E, W
	incl RD, ST
by turning [over]	ROVE
by using [miracles]	RECLAIMS
by word of mouth passed	PAST
eaten *by mouth*	ETON

bye

bye	B
bye-bye	BB

Byzantine

Byzantine [art is] . . .	STAIR
Byzantine *capital*	B
Byzantine *leader*	B

C

about, approximately, Caesarian, calorie, canine, cape, caput, capacitance, carat, carbon, cargo, castle, Catholic, caught, cedi, cee, Celsius, cent, centi-, centigrade, centime, century, chapter, Charles, circa, city, cloudy, club, clef, cold, college, colony, colt, common time, complex numbers, compliance, computer language, Conservative, constant, contralto, copyright, coulomb, Cuba, cubic, electrical capacitance, horizon, hundred, hundred thousand, key, *lot,* **many,** note, *number,* **roughly, san,** *sea, see,* **social class, speed of light, spring, tap, third grade, vitamin**

cab	
cab, *say*	HANDSOME
cabs, *say*	TAXES
cabbage	
cabbage, *say*	KAIL
cabinet	
cabinet enquiry	CASE STUDY
cabinet-maker	ADAM, CHIPPENDALE
	HEPPLEWHITE, SHERATON
	EBENISTE
	KINGWOOD, ROSEWOOD,
	SATINWOOD
	PRIME MINISTER
Caesar	
Caesar's (=Latin or Roman)	
• *Caesar's* clemency	LATIN QUARTER
• *Caesar's* cloak	TOGA
cage	
cage seagull	MEW
caged in *	incl in *
• cat *caged in* pen	SCATTY
cagey, *say*	KG
caging a . . .	incl A
caging *	incl *
• pen *caging* a cat	SCATTY
cagy, *say*	KG
cake	
cake	BUN
• cake container, *say*	BUNKAGE
• cake firm	BUNCO
• cake particle	BUNION
cake burner	ALFRED
Cakesville	ECCLES
calamity	
calamitous [drop]	PROD
calamity [when] . . .	HEWN
[it was] *calamitous*	WAIST
Caledonian	

Caledonian (=Scottish)	
• *Caledonian* oxen	OWSEN
• fat *Caledonian*	FOZY
	(*see also* Scottish)
calf	
calf	CF, STOCKING FILLER
calf, *perhaps*	NEW JERSEY
calfskin	LOWER CASE
California	
Californian city	LA
Californian tree, *say*	RED-WUD
call	
call *about*	R–ING
call *about*<	BUD, –ETIC
call at pub	BARRING
call *back*<	BUD, –ETIC
callboy	RINGED
call for prayer	COLLECT
call from Tom	MIAOW
call from Queen	MIAOW
call *on* debtor	YELLOWER
call round	RING
call *round*	R–ING
call *to* grub	RINGWORM
call to prayer, *say*	NEIL
call *up*	TALLY-HO, YOICKS
call *up*(D)^	BUD, –ETIC
called, *say*	SIGHTED, SITED
called cops	COPSE
called in a . . .	incl A
called in *	incl *
• Le–n *called in* doctor	LEMON
called into question [all the]...	LETHAL
callgirl	CALLUNA
calling for . . .	FORE, FOUR
calm	
calm down	ENDANGER
calm, *say*	PIECE

Letter replaced \c\at; Omit (a); Pointers *out*; Retain a̲; Split B_ED; Down (D); Backwards <or ^

calorie	CAL	*can't keep* *	omit *
Cambodia		• fat(her) *can't keep* her	FAT
Cambodia	KA	*can't spell* too *well*	TO, TU–, TWO
capital of Cambodia	C	*can't spell* too well	TOWEL
leader of Cambodia	C	**Canada**	CDN
Cambridge university	HARVARD	**Canadian**	
came		Canadian Air Force	RCAF
came here by boat, *say*	ROE-DEER	Canadian *capital*	C
	ROWDIER	Canadian *flower*	ST LAWRENCE etc
came here on a horse, *say*	ROE-DEER	Canadian *leader*	C
	ROWDIER	Canadian National Railway	CNR
came to a point, *say*	PIQUED	Canadian navy	RCN
	(*see also* come)	Canadian Pacific Railway	CPR
camouflage		Canadian police force	MOUNTIES, RCMP
camouflaged [tanks]	STANK	Canadian Royal Academy	CRA
camouflaging [guns]	GNUS, SNUG	Canadian sailors	RCN
[desert] *camouflage*	RESTED	Canadian soldiers	CEF
camp		**Canary Islands**	E
camp child	STALAGMITE	**cancel**	
camp helper	AIDE	cancel	omit DO
camping	(in) T–ENT, INTENT	• *cancel* door	OR
camping holiday	INTENT	cancel score	SCRATCH
campanologist		cancelled	incl O
campanologist, *say*	WRINGER	• *cancelled* match	OWED
	YOUTH HOSTELLER	• *cancelled* race	ORAN
can¹		• *cancelled* soldiers' . . .	OMEN
can	–ABLE	**candela**	CD
can be prosecuted	ISSUABLE	**candle**	
• can I?	AMIABLE	candle point	TAPER
can	MAY	candlemaker	STEARIN, TALLOW, WAX
• can a European . . . ?	MAYPOLE	candlepower	CP
• can cough	MAYHEM	**canine**	
• this can, *say*	DISMAY	canine affliction	TOOTHACHE
can	TIN	canine letter	R
• can sell, *say*	TINSEL	canine racer	LAPDOG
• can state	TINCAL	**cannibal**	
• cans will, *say*	TINSEL	cannibal, *say*	MASSETER
can²		*cannibalised* [cars]	ARCS, SCAR
can be heard coughing	COFFIN	*cannibalising* [parts]	SPRAT, TRAPS
can be [leased]	SEALED	**canon**	CAN
can be said aloud	ALLOWED	**canoodle**	
can be said to . . .	TOO, TWO, TU–	canoodle	BILL (AND COO)
can be said to be . . .	TUBE	• canoodle with Chinese	
can become [angry]	RANGY	gang, *say*	BILTONG
can he, *say*	CANNY	canoodle	NECK
can opener	PRISON GATE	• canoodle with sailor, *say*	NECTAR
c̲an *opener*	C	canoodle	SPOON
canned	(in) CA–N, (in) T–IN	• canoodle twice	SPOONBILL
• no *tinned* . . .	CANON	**can't**	(*see* can, unable)
• *canned* beef	TOXIN	**cant**	TINT
canned	BLIND (DRUNK), TIGHT		(*see* can, unable)
• canned fruit	BLIND DATE	**canter**	
• liquid canned	WATERTIGHT	*cantered* [into] . . .	–TION
can't	TINT	*cantering* [horse]	SHORE
can't keep a . . .	omit A	**canto**	CAN
can't keep quiet	omit P	**canvas**	
• do(p)e *can't keep* quiet	DOE	canvas	PAINTING

Anag [cat]; Any *; Begin IGN–; Endings –ING; eg •; Hidden /cat/; Implied add (on); Implied in (in);

canvas support	EASEL
canvassed area	CAMP SITE
canvassed views	LANDSCAPES, SEASCAPES
	TOWNSCAPES etc

cap

cap	HAT
• cap colour	HATRED
• cap fit	HATABLE
capless (m)ale(D)	ALE
capped	BLUE, INTERNATIONAL
capability	BROWN
cape	C, HORN
Capek's play	RUR
caper	
caper, *say*	ANTIQUE

capital[1]

capital	AI
• capital fish	AILING
• capital money	AID, AIL
• capital *return*<	–IA
• *raise* capital(D)^	–IA
capital (=first letter)	
• *capital loss* in (S)pain	PAIN
• *capital of* Spain	S
• *capital punishment*	
for (s)entry	ENTRY
• state *capital*	S
capital *missing*	omit 1st letter
• capital *missing*	
from (t)ill	ILL
capital *withdrawn*	omit 1st letter
• capital *withdrawn*	
from (B)erne	ERNE

capital[2]

capital	HEAD
capital cover	HAT, HAIR, SCALP
capital flat	TEMPLE
capital improvement	HAIR-DO
	PERM(ANENT WAVE)
capital investment	HEADDRESS
capital issue	BEARD, HAIR, WHISKERS

capital[3]

capital (=chief city)	
capital authority	GLC
capital footwear	WELLINGTON
capital players	LSO
capital type	BERLINER, LONDONER
	NEW YORKER, PARISIAN, ROMAN

capital[4]

other uses:	
Capital Gains Tax	CGT
capital letter	ENLARGE, LARGESSE
capital letters	TOPAZ
capital punishment	FINE, STOCKS
Capital Transfer Tax	CTT

capricious

[act] *capriciously*	CAT

capricious [mood]	DOOM
capriciously [makes] . . .	KAMES

capsize

capsized [ship]	HIPS, PISH
capsized vessel<	TOP
[it was] *capsizing*	WAIST

captain

captain	CID, OLD MAN
captain	SKIP(PER)
• captain with sailor	SKIPJACK
captain's place	BRIDGE

captivate

captivate a . . .	incl A
captivate *	incl *
• ma–n *captivates* one . . .	MAIN
captivated by gent/le har/mony	LEHAR
captivated by *	incl in *
• one *captivated by* ma–n	MAIN

captive

captive	incl in *
• no–ted *captive* bird	NOMINATED
captive	(in) C–AGE, (in) GA–OL

capture

capture	BAG
• capture animal, *say*	BAGASSE
• capture the Tube	BAGPIPE
• *press* captures . . .	PAPER BAGS
capture king	SECURER
captured, *say*	COPT
captured by *	incl in *
• queen *captured by* PM	PERM
captured in larg/e vil/la	EVIL
captures a . . .	incl A
captures, *say*	COPSE
captures *	incl *
• PM *captures* queen	PERM

car

car	AUTO
• car dealer	AUTOCHANGER
• car driver	AUTOPILOT
• car indicator	AUTOCUE
• cars in front	AUTO-SLED
car	GT
• nothing *in* car	GOT
car	MINI
• car *on* motorway	MINIM
• cars go	MINISTRY
car	RR
• girl *in* car	RADAR
car club	AA, RAC
car driver	PETROL
car key, *say*	KHAKI
car lifter	JACK
car rug	AUTOMAT
car salesman's technique	AUTO-SUGGESTION
car-test	MOT
(c)ar *won't start*	AR

Letter replaced \c\at; Omit (a); Pointers *out*; Retain <u>a</u>; Split B_ED; Down (D); Backwards <or ^

carat	CAR, CT	• carried Portuguese noble	BOREDOM
carbon		• carried, *say*	BOAR
carbon	C	carried by	ON
• carbon copy	CAPE	• carried by Scot	–ONIAN
• carbon-dating	CAGING	• club carried by . . .	BATON
• carbon fibre	CHAIR	carried on	
• remains of carbon	CASH	–in error, *say*	SINDON
card		–snogging, *say*	NEKTON
card	A, ACE, J, K, Q	carried, *say*	BORN, BOURNE, WARN
card	CHARACTER	*carried by* (D)	
• card player	CHARACTER ACTOR	• mother *carried by* boy	DAMSON
card	DENRY MACHIN	*carried by* mo/st ar/tists	STAR
card game, *say*	PEAKY, PICKET, WIST	*carried by* *	incl in *
card player	DECKHAND	• log *carried by* ship	SLOGS
card players	NEWS, SEWN, WENS	*carried out* [a test]	TASTE
cards	HAND, TALON	carried papers	PIPE-DREAM
cardinal		*carries*(D)	
cardinal	CARD, RED, WOLSEY	• boy *carries* mother	DAMSON
cardinal point	EMINENCE	*carries* a . . .	incl A
cardinal points	NEWS, SEWN, WENS	*carries* cross	incl X
cardiograph	TICKER TAPE	carries on	
care		–signalling	WAVESON
care of	CO	–staunching	STEMSON
care for, *say*	WRECK	carries sailor, *say*	LODESTAR
[care] *free*	ACER, ACRE, RACE	*carries* *	incl *
careless bonds	CASUALTIES	• ship *carries* log	SLOGS
careless (h)ost	OST	carry	BEAR
careless [metering]	REGIMENT	• carry money	BEARD
carelessly [done]	NODE	*carry back in* a/erop/lane<	PORE
carer, *say*	WRECKER	*carry* money	incl L, P
cares, *say*	REX, WRECKS	• carry money *in* s–ack	SLACK
[rank] *carelessness*	KNAR, NARK	• he *carries* money	HEP
career		carry on	
career people	RACE	–diving	PLUNGEON
careering [over]	ROVE	–fighting, *say*	PUNCHEON
careers [about]	U-BOAT	–playing	BATON
[cars] *careered*	ARCS, SCAR	–pushing	SURGEON
cargo boats	MN	–*say*	CARRION
Caribbean islands	WI	–teasing, *say*	RIBBON
carpenter		carry revolver	CARTWHEEL
carpenter	CHIPPY	*carry* round	incl O
carpenter's mate	WALRUS	carry, *say*	BARE, WARE
carpentry	CARP	carrying hose	STOCKING
carpet	REPRIMAND	**cart**	
carriage		[cart]*wheels*	–CRAT
carriage, *say* ACNE, FIGHTING, HANDSOME		[he's] *in the cart*	SHE
carriage paid	CP	**Cartesian**	
carried	(*see* carry)	[Cartesian] *formula*	ASCERTAIN
carrier		**cartoon fish**	STRIPLING
carrier	BARKIS, BR, RY, RLY	**carve**	
carrier for hooligan	ROUGHSHOD	carve accent	GRAVE
carrier, *say*	BARER	carve insect	ETCHANT
carrier's confession	IMPORTER	*carved up* [meat]	MATE, TAME, TEAM
carry		*carving* [lamb]	BALM
carried	BORE	**case**	
• carried corpses, *say*	BOARDED	case of pins and needles	ETUI
• carried drill	BORE	*case of* <u>wh</u>isky	WY

cased in a . . .	incl A
cased in *	incl *
• gold *cased in* iron	FORE
cases	CA
casing in *	incl in *
• iron *casing in* gold	FORE
in any *case*	AN–Y
in case of wine	H–OCK, VI–N
pastry *case*	PY
cash	
cash	BRASS
• cash collapses	BRASSFOUNDERS
• cash that is about . . .	BRASSIERE
cash	BREAD
• cash crop	BREADFRUIT
• cash *given to* journalist	BREADED
cash	L
• cash *in the* bag	SLACK
• paid *in* cash? *The reverse*	PLAID
cash	READY, RHINO
cash	TIN
• cash *in* saint's . . .	STINTS
• cash, for example *returns*	TINGE
cash against documents	CAD
cash on delivery	COD
	MATERNITY GRANT
cash present	COINHERE
cash registers	NOTES
cash with order	CWO
cash*less*	omit L
• cash*less* Lapp	APP
casserole	
casserole of [meat]	MATE, TAME, TEAM
casseroled [lamb]	BALM
cast	
cast [a net]	NEAT
cast about ten< . . .	NET
cast about [ten]	–ENT, ENT–, NET
c(as)t as *not wanted*	CT
cast down	MOULT(ED)
cast off	EXEUNT
[cast] *off*	ACTS, CATS, SCAT
cast off here	GREEN ROOM
cast out here	STAGE DOOR
cast, *say*	THROUGH
cast skin	omit 1st and last letters
• (p)up(a) *casts skin*	UP
[cast] *spell*	ACTS, CATS, SCAT
*cast*a[way]	YAW
casting director	PLASTERER
castle	
castle	R(OOK)
castle in the air	FLYING FORTRESS
	ROOK
casual	
casual [remark]	MARKER
casual trousers, *say*	GENES
casual worker	TEMP
• casual worker *with* one . . .	TEMPI
• casual worker in front	TEMPLED
• casual worker overdue	TEMPLATE
and	
• worker is *French*	TEMPEST
• worker, the *French* . . .	TEMPLE
• worker *with* ring	TEMPO
casually dressed	UNSUITED
casualty [ward]	DRAW
cat	
cat	CAT
• cat family	CATKIN
• cat fur	CATNAP
• cat goes to church	CATCH
cat	FELIX, MOG, REX
cat	OUNCE
• black cat	BOUNCE
• flourished cat	FLOUNCE
• girl *with* cat	ANNOUNCE
cat	TABBY
• cat chewed, *say*	TABITUDE
• cat trap *say*	TAB(B)INET
cat	TOM
• a cat	ATOM
• catbird	TOMTIT
• catfish	TOMCOD
• cats	TOM-TOM
cat-o'-nine-tails	BACKMARKER
cat rouses, *say*	KITTIWAKES
cat will, *say*	CATTLE
catcall	MEW, MIAU, MIAOW
cat's home, *say*	MEWS
cat's paw	PUSSYFOOT
catty utterance	PURR
catty utterance, *say*	PER
catalogue	CAT
catch	
catch	NET
• catch spirit	NETRUM
• catch woman's . . .	NETHER
• good catch	BONNET
catch	TRIP
• catch fish	TRIPLING
• catch insect, *say*	TRIPPANT
catch cold	incl C
catch game	CONTRACT
catch Joy	GLEE
catch model	SITTER
catch *up*(D)^	BAN, TEN
catches fish	TAKE SIDES
catching a . . .	incl A
catching some fi/sh or e/els	SHORE
catching the one-five	incl IV
catching *	incl *
• ma–n *catching* one . . .	MAIN
caught a . . .	incl A

caught *	incl *
• ma–n *caught* one	MAIN
caught by *	incl in *
• one *caught by* ma–n	MAIN
caught in m/an t/rap	ANT
(*see also* caught)	
catechism	CAT
cathedral	ELY
cathode-ray	
cathode-ray oscillograph	CRO
cathode-ray tube	CRT
catholic	RC
cattle	
cattle	KINE, NEAT
cattle complaint	BEEF
cattle dealing	STOCK EXCHANGE
cattle drive	STEER
cattle not watered	NEAT
cattle-truck	STOCK-CAR
caught	
caught	C
• caught a married ...	CAWED
• caught an anthropoid	CANAPE
• caught at church	CATCH
• caught bird	CRAVEN, CROOK
• caught *by* leg	CLIMB
• caught fish	CLING
• caught man	CALF, CHAL, CLEW
• caught *on* branch	CLIMB
• caught *with* nothing on	COON
• caught *with* stolen goods	CLOOT
caught	CT
caught *in*	incl C
caught *out*	omit C
caught spirit	SNARE-DRUM
(*see also* catch)	
cause	
cause [alarm]	MALAR
cause of quarrel	ARROWROOT
cause for complaint	BACILLUS, BACTERIUM
	GERM, VIRUS etc
cause relief	EMBOSS
cause, *say*	CAWS
caused by [germ in a] ...	REAMING
causes pain, *say*	HERTZ
caution	
caution, *say*	FOUR, WEAR, WORN
cautious sign(al)	AMBER
cave	
cave, *say*	KV
caveman	DEN
	POTHOLER, SPELEOLOGIST
cavy, *say*	KV
cavity	
cavity	O
• cavity *in* b–at	BOAT
• p–ut *round* cavity	POUT

cavort	
cavorted [like] ...	KIEL
cavorting [lamb]	BALM
celebrate	
celebrate	SING
celebrated	CEL
celebrated dynasty	SUNG
celebration	DO, GALA
• celebration tea, *perhaps*	DOT, DOTE
• celebration drink	GALATEA
celebrity	LION, STAR, VIP
Celtic	
Celt, *say*	GALE
Celtic tax	SCOT
censor	CATO, EDIT
cent	C, CT
centilitre	CL
centime	C, CT
centimetre	CM
centipede	CLIMBS
central	
Central	
–African Republic	CAR, RCA
–America	CUS
–European Time	CET, MEZ
–Standard Time	CST
central	CEN
Central America	(s)TATE(s)
central character in Tosca	S
central defender	FEND
central heating	CH
central heating	T
central letters	M, N
central letters	T
central nervous system	CNS
central processing unit	CPU
central Wales	ALE, L
centre	
Centre Court	U
centre-forwards, *say*	HOSPITAL
centre-*half*	CEN, TRE
centre-half	AL
centre of gravity	CG
centre of gravity	V
centre of Paris	R
centre of *	incl in *
• the *centre of* scared ...	FEATHERED
*centre*fold	OL
centrepiece	K, KING, Q, QU, QUEEN
centrepiece	E
centrepiece of decorations	RAT
Centre Point	MIDDLE EAST
Centre Point	I
centre, *say*	NAVAL
self-*centred*	EL
shopping-*centre*	PP
soft-*centred*	OF

to̲w̲n-*centre*	OW
	(l)OUT(h), (n)EAT(h) etc
century	C, CEN
ceremony	
ceremony, *say*	RIGHT, WRIGHT, WRITE
cereal	
cereal	BRAN
• cereal bowl	BRANDISH
certain	
certain	SURE
• certain sack	SURE-FIRE
certain amount of beer	PINT
certain amount of be̲e̲r	BEE
certain amount of bee/r I se/nt	RISE
certain m/en rol/ling . . .	ENROL
certain parts of c/ar c/an . . .	ARC
certain person	DOGMATIST
certain, *say*	SHORE
certainly	YES, SURE
certainly *not*	omit SURE
• Pleasure? Certainly *not*	PLEA
certificate	
certificate	A, B, U, X
Certificated Master	CM
chain	
chain-letters	MAIL
chain parts, *say*	LYNX
chair	
chair is hard, *say*	CHERISH
chairman	ADAM, CHIPPENDALE
	HEPPLEWHITE, SHERATON
	PROFESSOR
chairman of	
–British Airways, *say*	BAKING
–RAC, *say*	RACKING
–TUC, *say*	TUCKING
chaldron	CH
champion	
champion	ACE
• champion	
water-sportsman	SURFACE
• fine champion	FACE
• formidable champion	GRIMACE
champion	CH
• champion members	CHARMS
• champion *with* style	CHAIR
• supreme champion	STARCH
champion boxer	SPARKING, TOP-DOG
chance	EARTHLY, HAP
change¹	
indicating anagram:	
• *change* [bowler]	BLOWER
• *change* [coins]	ICONS, SONIC
• *change* [into]	–TION
• *change* [into a]	–ATION
• *change of* [heart]	EARTH, HATER, RATHE
• *change of* [scene]	CENSE, –SENCE

• *change*-[over]	ROVE
• *change-over of* [duties]	SUITED
• *changeable* [weather]	WREATHE
• *changing* [gear]	RAGE
• [gear]-*change*	RAGE
• [ship] *changes course*	HIPS, PISH
change²	
indicating substitution:	
change ends of *	
• *change ends* of \l\eve\r\	REVEL
change leader	change 1st letter
• *change* \F\rench	
leader	DRENCH, TRENCH, WRENCH
• \p\arty *changes leader*	TARTY, WARTY
change of hear\t\	HEARS
change of heart	change middle letter(s)
• *change of heart* for T\or\y	TROY
• le\p\er has *change of heart*	LEVER
change of sc\e\ne	SCONE
change partners	change E for W, W for E
	change N for S, S for N
change polarity	change N for S
	change S for N
change sides	change L to R, R to L
• *change* side of \r\oad	LOAD
• *changing* side of \l\oom	ROOM
• gent\l\y *changing sides*	GENTRY
• pee\r\ *changes side*	PEEL
changing character	
of \w\eather	HEATHER, LEATHER
\O\ *for* \a\ *change in* vogue	VAGUE
change³	
other uses:	
change bowler	MONEY-SPINNER
change direction of road<	DR, EVA, IA, IM, TS
change directors	SWITCHBOARD
change gear	RECLOTHE, REDRESS
change girls, *say*	ALTERCATES
change in	
–America	CENT
–France	CENTIME
–Germany	PFENNIG
–Italy	CENTESIMO
–Spain	PESETA
–UK	PENNY
change into suit	BECOME
change its colour, *say*	DIET
change of heart	TRANSPLANT
change, *say*	ALTAR
change sides	RAT
changes	PEAL
changes clothes	SHIFTS
changes colour	TURNSTONE
changes, *say*	PEEL
changing gear	TRANSVESTISM
changing place	CREWE etc
	JUNCTION

Letter replaced \c\at; Omit (a); Pointers *out*; Retain a̲; Split B_ED; Down (D); Backwards <or ^

changing-room	BANK	charge per session, *say*	CITRATE
channel		charge *up*(D)^	NOI–
Channel Islands	CI	charge, *say*	INDITE, LODE
channelled into [thin] . . .	HINT	charged	LIVE
chaos		charged particle	ION
chaos [in the] . . .	THINE	charged *up*(D)^	EVIL
chaotic [mess on] . . .	MESONS	*charged with* a . . .	incl A
[it was] *chaotic*	WAIST	*charged with* *	incl *
chap		• iron *charged with* current	FACE
chap in charge	MANIC	**Charles**	
chaps	(*see* men, two²)	Charles (king)	CR
chapel		• Charles I	CRONE
chapel, *presumably*	NOTCH	Charles *I*	C
chaplain CF, CHAP, HCF, OCF, REV(D)		Charles *II*	H
chaps	(*see* men, two²)	Charlie's better	FOOLSCAP
chapter C, CAP, CH, CHAP		**charm**	
Chapter I	CHI	charm Scot	MAGICIAN
chapters	CC	charmer	MUSIC
Chapters *I & III*	CA	[charming] *disposition*	MARCHING
char		charming islander	CIRCE
char	DAILY	charming man	WARLOCK
• char paper	DAILY	charming woman	WITCH
• chars wages	DAILY BREAD	**chart**	
char	TEA	chart showing errors, *say*	SYNGRAPH
• char got up	TEA-ROSE	**chase**	
• char *has* money	TEAL	chased police	RANCID
character		chasing prostitutes, *say*	OARING
[all the] *characters*	LETHAL	chased, *say*	CHASTE
character	CARD	**chaste**	
• character-actor	CARD PLAYER	chaste	PURE
• character in Greek . . .	CARDING	• chaste saint	PUREST
• port authority *has* character	PLACARD	chaste, *say*	CHASED
character	LETTER	**chat**	
character-forming	PRINTING, TYPING,	*chatting* aloud	ALLOWED
	WRITING	not *chatting*	KNOT
character impression	STAMP	chatterbox	TELEPHONE KIOSK
character, *say*	ROLL	**cheap**	
characters in [play]	PALY	cheap	ID, IP
character's size	POINT	cheap drink	FARTHINGALE
Greek characters	ALPHA, BETA etc	cheap floor	KNOCKDOWN
Hebrew characters	ALEPH etc	cheap ring	LOCAL CALL
charge		cheap, *say*	CHEEP
charge	BILL	cheap shelter, *say*	PENITENT
• angry charge	CROSSBILL	cheap transport	PENNY-FARTHING
• charge alien	BILLET	**cheat**	
• charge directors	BILLBOARD	cheat	BEACON
charge	FEE	cheat	CON
• charge a man, *say*	FEMALE	• cheat two boys	CONVICTED
• charge circuit	FEERING	cheat	DO
• charge circuit, *say*	FEARING	• cheat people	DONATION
• charge family, *say*	FELINE	• cheat soldiers	DOOR
• charge nothing, *say*	PHOENIX	• cheat twice	DODO
• charge *on* the bus, *say*	PHOEBUS	• cheats family	DOESKIN
• charge *to* fish	FEELING	cheating player	FIDDLER
• charges, *say*	FEEZE	**check**	
charge girl	COSTMARY	check	REIN
charge moderate	RUSHLIGHT	• check certain . . .	REINSURE

• check condition	REINSTATE	• chief Cornish saint	ARCHIVES
• check garment	REINVEST	• chief financial backer	ARCHANGEL
• check, *say*	RAIN, REIGN	• chief journalist	ARCHED
	(*see also* control)	chief	CH, CID
check mate	TEST MATCH, TRIAL MARRIAGE	chief	KING
check performance	STUNT	• chief architect	PLANKING
check, *say*	CHEQUE, CZECH	• chief boxer	SPARKING
checked *out*	SE–EN	• chief censor	BANKING
• 5 checked *out*	SEVEN	• chief debt collector	DUNKING
checked, *say*	RAINED, REIGNED	• chief herring-packer	CRANKING
checking again	REVETTING	• chief invoice-clerk *say*	BILKING
checks sound, *say*	KERBSTONE	• chief pastry-cook	BUNKING
cheek		• chief lavatory attendant	LOOKING
cheek	LIP	• chief leather-dresser	TANKING
• cheeky	LIPOID	• chief of tribe	CLANKING
• loud cheek	FLIP	• chief sun-god	RAKING
cheek	NECK	chief accountant	MAJORCA
• cheek allowed	NECKLET	chief manufacturer	KINGMAKER
cheeks men	CHAPS	chief mason	MASTER BUILDER
cheeky	MALAR	**child**	
cheeky drop	TEAR	child	BOY
cheeky novel	FRESH	• child *after* cat	TOMBOY
cheer		• child put to bed	BOYCOTTED
cheer up(D)^	HAR	• childhood, *say*	BUOYAGE
cheering up	STANDING OVATION	child	BRAT
cheerleader	HIP	child	CH
cheerleader	C	• child with guns	CHARMED
cheers	TOAST	• child *in* horses' . . .	MARCHES
cheese		• strike child	HITCH
cheese container	ROLL	child	IMP
cheese insect	BRIEFLY	• child displays	IMPAIRS
cheesemaker	RENNET	child	KID
hard cheese	BAD LUCK	• child *on* knee, *say*	KIDNEY
indifferent cheese	MOUSETRAP	• one *local* child	UNKID
say cheese	SMILE	• child slept	KIDNAPPED
chef's whiskers	BLENDERS, EGG BEATERS	• child *with* joint, *say*	KIDNEY
chemical		• child's family	KIDSKIN
chemical	NITRE	child	TOT
Chemical Society	CS	• child *has* energy	TOTE
chemist	MPS	• child *with* friend	TOTALLY
chemists	CS	• child *with* letter	TOTEM
chess		Child Guidance Officer	JUNIOR COUNSEL
chess player	BLACK, WHITE	childish habits	LAYETTE, ROMPER SUITS
chessman, *say*	NIGHT	childish relation	BEDTIME STORY
chest			FAIRY STORY
chest, *say*	COUGHER	childless	SP
chest expander	MEDAL	childless	omit SON
chevron	V	• child*less* cleric	PAR(son)
chew		• child*less* individual	PER(son)
chew fly, *say*	GNAWING	• child*less* worker	MA(son)
chew lips, *say*	TULIPS	children	ISSUE, SEED
chewed [meat]	MATE, TAME, TEAM	children, *say*	BREWED
chewing up [bone]	EBON	child's	
chews, *say*	CHOOSE	–drink	TOT
chi	X	–play	PANTOMIME, PETER PAN etc
chief		–toy, *say*	WHOOP
chief	ARCH	**Chile**	RCH

Letter replaced \c\at; Omit (a); Pointers *out*; Retain a̲; Split B_ED; Down (D); Backwards <or ^

chill

chill at this place, *say*	FREESIA
chill, *say*	FRIEZE

chime

chiming (=rhyming)	
• *chiming* bell	CELL, DELL, FELL, HELL, SELL, TELL, WELL, YELL
• *chiming* sound	BOUND, FOUND, HOUND MOUND, POUND, ROUND
• *chiming* merrily	VERILY

chimney

chimney	LUM
• base of chimney, *say*	BEDLAM
• cowl *on* chimney	HOODLUM
chimney-pot	CAN

chin

[chin]*wag*	INCH

china

china	PORCELAIN, POTTERY SERVICE
china (plate)	MATE, PAL
china tea	MATE

China

China	CATHAY, CH, CHIN MIDDLE KINGDOM
China area (Far East)	FARE
<u>C</u>hinese *capital*	C
<u>C</u>hinese *flower*	YANGTSE
Chinese fruit	MANDARIN
<u>C</u>hinese *leader*	C
Chinese, *say*	CYNIC
Chinese takeaway	SHANGHAI
river in China	PLATE

chip

chip	UPSHOT
chip bag	KNAPSACK
chips	OLD MASTER
chips *without* fish	(carp)ENTER
chipshot	COUNTERSTROKE

chiropodist   CORN MERCHANT, FOOTMAN

chisel

chiselled [bust]	BUTS, STUB
chiselling [marble]	RAMBLE

choice

choice	OR
• choice cut	ORLOP
• choice of directions	NORE, NORSE SORE, SORN WORE, WORN, WORSE
• make choice *with* pin	ORPIN

chomp

chomp [oats]	STOA
chomping [roots]	TORSO
[horse] *chomped*	SHORE

choose

choose	ELECT
• choose artist	ELECTRA
• choose *by* word of mouth	ELECTORALLY
• choose particle	ELECTION
• choose *to* speak	ELECTORATE
• choosy individual	ELECTOR
choose	OPT
• choose one hundred	OPTIC
• choose one mother	OPTIMUM
• choose worker	OPTANT
choose	PICK
• choose a heretic *say*	PICARIAN
• choose an entrance, *say*	PICADOR
• choose bed, *say*	PICOTTE
• choose correctly, *say*	PICRITE
• choose fish	PICKLING
• choose foolish *Australian, say*	PICCADILLY
• choose prison, *say*	PICCAGE
• chose 'your', *say*	PICTURE
choose passage	EXTRACT

chop

chop down pin(e)	PIN
chop off bran(ch)	BRAN
chopstick	CLEAVE
chopped spice	CLOVE
chopped [spice]	EPICS
chopped (s)pice	PICE
chopper *up*(D)^	EXA–
chopping [logs]	SLOG

Chopin lover   SAND

choreograph

choreograph [dance]	CANED
choreography of [Act IV]	VATIC

chorus girl   SHOWPIECE

chow-chow   DOG'S DINNER

Christ   CHR, X, XT

Christian   CHR, XN

Christian endeavour	CE
Christian era	AD
Christian men	MUTINEERS
Christian service	CS

Christmas

Christmas	PRESENT DAY, XM(AS)
Christmas girl	CAROL
Christmas hangover	MISTLETOE
Christmas period	DEC
Christmas present	FRANKINCENSE, GOLD MYRRH PARTRIDGE etc
Christmas present drawer	REINDEER
Christmas spirit	MARLEY'S GHOST

chromosome   X, Y

chronic patient   LONG-SUFFERING

chuck

chuck out a . . .	omit a
chuck out *	omit *
• ma(s)ter *chucked out* son	MATER
I chucked out. . .	omit I

Anag [cat]; Any *; Begin IGN–; Endings –ING; eg •; Hidden /cat/; Implied add (on); Implied in (in);

church

church	CE
• a church	ACE
• a church ruler	ACER
• a church gallery	ACETATE
and	
• American church	AMERCE
• city church	ESSENCE
• Italian church	ROMANCE
• many in church	MINCE
• mother church	MACE
• when at church . . .	WHENCE
and	
• hurried *in* church	CRANE
• man *in* church	CHIME
• rodent *in* church	CRATE
and	
• church keys	CEDE
• church scriptures	CENT
• Church Street	CEST
church	CH
• church examination	CHORAL
• church like St Paul's	WRENCH
• church militant	CHARMED, CHARMING
• church music (writer)	CHAIR(MAN)
• church painter	CHARTIST
• church songs	CHAIRS
• church vessel	CHURN
• church-woman	CHALICE
• church work	CHOP
• church-worker	CHANT
and	
• church *on* the hill	TORCH
• Egyptian church	ETCH
• German church	HUNCH
• in church	INCH
• low church	MOOCH
• mother church	MACH
• stone church	PITCH
• which church?	THATCH
church	RC
• a church (house)	ARC(H)
• church *has* enemies *all round*	FORCES
• spies *surround* church	CIRCA
church leader	LANG, HUME etc
church *leader*	C
churchman inside, *say*	DOMINEER
churchwarden's home	PIPE-RACK

Churchill

Churchill	WINNIE
Churchill, *say*	WHINNY

churl

churl	CARL
churlish, *say*	RUED

churn

churning [a pint]	PAINT
churning up [earth]	HATER, HEART, RATHE

CID member — YARDARM

cigar(ette)

[cigar]-*maker*	CRAIG
cigarette-*end*	E
cigarette, *say*	REFER

cinema director — USHERETTE

cipher

cipher	O
ciphered [signal]	ALIGNS

circle

[arty] *circles*	TRAY
broken [circle]	CLERIC
circle	DISC
• circle above . . .	DISCOVER
• circle America	DISCUS
• circle drops	DISCLOSES
• circle or ball	DISCORDANCE
circle	O
• Circle line	OL, –ORY
• circle of friends	OPALS
• circle round	OO
• circles the globe	OOSPHERE
• circular letter	OMISSIVE
• dress-circle	GARBO
• lady's circle	HERO
• race *in* circles	OTTO
circle	RING
• a race *in* circle	RATTING
• circle permitted	RINGLET
• circle, *say*	WRING
• lady's circle	HERRING
circle a . . .	incl A
[circle] *around* . . .	CLERIC
Circle Line	CHORD, CIRCUMFERENCE
	DIAMETER, EQUATOR, INNER TUBE
	MERIDIAN, NOOSE, RADIUS
circle of rocks	ETERNITY RING
circle roughly	ROUNDABOUT
circle *	incl *
• rodent *circles* it	CAVITY
* *circled by* . . .	incl in *
• it is *circled by* rodent	CAVITY
circles	DISCO, RING-DIAL
circling [plane]	PANEL
Inner Circle	BULL'S EYE, GOLD, RED

circuit

circuit	O
circuit	RING
• circuit rented	RINGLET
	(*see also* circle)
circuit of [town]	WONT

circular

circular letter	O, OMICRON, OMISSIVE
circular objects	DISCO, RING-DIAL
	(*see also* circle)

circulate

circulate [news or] . . .	OWNERS

circulating [in the] . . .	THINE
circulating note<	ETON
flat *remains in circulation*	LEVEL
[news in] *in circulation*	SEWN, WENS
circumnavigate	
circumnavigate a . . .	incl A
circumnavigate *	incl *
• help *circumnavigate* cape	ACID
circumnavigated by * . . .	incl in *
• cape *circumnavigated with*	
help	ACID
circus character	EROS
circumvent	
circumvent a . . .	incl A
circumvent *	incl *
• writing *circumvents* end . . .	MENDS
circumvented by *	incl in *
• end *circumvented by*	
writing . . .	MENDS
cite	
citation	CIT
cite, *say*	SIGHT, SITE
cites pain, *say*	NAMESAKE
city	
Abrahamville	LINCOLN
Cakesville	ECCLES
citizen	CIT
city	EC
• city house	ECHO
• city retreat	ECLAIR
• res–t *outside* the city	RESECT
city	ELY
• a king *in* city	EARLY
• as I *entered* the city	EASILY
• city diocese	ELYSEE
city	LA
• city representative	LAMP
• city street	LARD, LAST
city	NY
• big *in* New York	NOSY
• tin city	CANNY
city	LA, NY
city church	ESSENCE
city feature	URCHIN
city girl	ADELAIDE, ALICE, CONSTANCE,
	FLORENCE, NANCY, VICTORIA
city judge	TRIER
city (old)	TROY, UR
city press	SHANGHAI
city road	ANCHORAGE
city sailors	BATH SALTS
city, *say*	CITE
city slum	STOKEHOLE
c(it)y *with no centre*	CY
eternal city	ROME
granite city	ABERDEEN
holy city	JERUSALEM, MEDINA

	MECCA, ROME
New York	BIG APPLE, GOTHAM
old city	TROY, UR
Witchville	SALEM
Wyeville	ROSS
civic	
civic *leader*	C
civic leader, *say*	MARE
civil	
civil defence	ARP, CD
civil engineer	CE
civil servant	(in) C–S
civil service	CS
civilian	CIV
civilian dress	MUFTI
clad	
clad in ragg/ed gar/ments	EDGAR
clad with *	incl in *
• gold *clad with* i–vy	IVORY
cladding a . . .	incl A
cladding *	incl *
• I–vy *cladding* for gold . . .	IVORY
claim	
claim	AM
• claiming *French* father	AMPERE
• claiming lamb	AMELIA
• claiming our . . .	AMOUR
• claiming to be essayist	AMELIA
claim	IAM
• claiming *to have* vehicle	IAMBUS
• two claiming . . .	PRIAM
claim	IM–
• claiming goodness	IMPIETY
	IMPIOUSNESS, IMPURITY
• claiming some . . .	IMPART
• claiming to be Bill	IMPOSTER
claim	ME
• claim to be Edward	METED
• claim to be Indian	MEUTE
• claim *to* father	MESON
claim *say*	RITE, WRIGHT, WRITE
	(*see also* admit, confess, declare)
clash	
clashing [sound]	NODUS
[red] *clashes with* [pink]	PRINKED
clasp	
clasp, *say*	BUCCAL
clasped in /her b/reast	HERB
class	
class	CL
• Class 1	CLONE
• class always . . .	CLEVER
• class has...	CLOWNS
classic	
Classic races	DERBY, GUINEAS
	OAKS, ST LEGER
classic trees	OAKS

Anag [cat]; Any *; Begin IGN–; Endings –ING; eg •; Hidden /cat/; Implied add (on); Implied in (in);

Classics (examination)	GREATS	clear	PLAIN
classical		• clear air	PLAINSONG
classical (=Greek or Roman)		clear	RID
• classical art	ES	• clear note	RIDE
• classical god	DEUS	clear bargain	NEGOTIATE
• classical labourer	HERACLES, HERCULES	[clear] *out*	CLARE
• classical man	VIR	*clear out* [drawers]	REWARDS
• classical musician	ORPHEUS	clear photograph	TRANSPARENCY
• classical place	LOCUS	clear the table	DELAY
• classical power	VIS	*clearance* [granted]	DRAGNET
• classical skill	ARS	clearer run	BALDERDASH
• classical supporter	ATLAS	*clearing* [snow]	OWNS
classical character (=Greek letter)		**Cleopatra**	NEEDLEWOMAN
• classical character	ALPHA etc	**clergy**	
• classical character following a . . .	BETA	clergyman's address	SERMON
• first classical character	ALPHA		FATHER, RECTOR, VICAR
classify			MANSE, RECTORY, VICARAGE
classified	AD, ADVERT(ISEMENT)	clergyman *and* I celebrate	REVISING
classified item	ROAD	**cleric**	
classified [item]	EMIT, MITE, TIME	cleric	BD, DD
classified [papers]	SAPPER	clerical error	SPOONERISM
classification of *cabs, say*	TAXIS	clerical gangster	PRIESTHOOD
classmate	FORMALLY	*disguised* [cleric]	CIRCLE
classy	U	**clerk**	
clause		Clerk of the Peace	CP
clause	CL	Clerk to the Signet	CS
clause, *say*	CLAWS	**clever**	
clay		clever Dick	KNOW-ALL, SMART ALEC
clay	ALI	clever person	BA, MA
clay-pigeon	FLYING SAUCER	clever way	STREETWISE
clean		*cleverly* [made]	DAME, EDAM, MEAD
clean her, *say*	GUTTER	**climb**	
clean if I, *say*	PURIFY	climber	AMPELOPSIS, IVY
clean it up, *say*	MOPPET	climber's aid	TRELLIS
[clean] *out*	LANCE	*climbing* party(D)^	OD
cleaner	CHAR	*climbing* rose(D)^	DER
• cleaner fuel	CHARCOAL	*climbing* tor(D)^	ROT
• cleaner hair	CHARLOCK	**clinch**	
• cleaner *in* clear . . .	RICHARD	*clinch* a . . .	incl A
• cleaner porcelain	CHARMING	*clinch* *	incl *
cleaner entertainment	SOAP	• *clinch* deal *in fog*	MISDEALT
cleaner flag	DUSTER	*clinched by* *	incl in *
cleaner paper	DAILY	• deal *clinched in* fog	MISDEALT
clear		**cling**	
clear	JUMP	*cling to* a . . .	incl A
• clear case	JUMP SUIT	*cling to* money	incl L
• clear crypt	VAULT	*cling to* *	incl *
clear	MANIFEST	• bo–y *clings to* ship	BOSSY
• clear round	MANIFESTO	**clip**	
clear	NET	*clip from* fil/m or n/egative	MORN
• clear round	NETBALL	clip wool, *say*	SHEER
• clear spirit	NETRUM	*clip* win(g)	WIN
• clear *up*(D)^	TEN	*clip wings of* (s)nip(e)	NIP
clear	OVERT	clipper	TOPIARIST
• clear cut	OVERTRUMP	**cloak**	
• clear lubricant	OVERTOIL	cloak, *say*	MANTEL, VALE
• clear water	OVERTRAIN	*cloaked in* secre/cy, St/ella . . .	CYST

Letter replaced \c\at; Omit (a); Pointers *out*; Retain <u>a</u>; Split B_ED; Down (D); Backwards <or ^

cloaked in *	incl in *
• hollow *cloaked in* m–ist	MOIST
cloaking a . . .	incl A
cloaking *	incl *
• m–ist *cloaking* hollow	MOIST
clobber	
clobber [one] . . .	NEO–
[get] *clobbered*	TEG
clock	
clock	DIAL
• clock *on* city square	DIALECT
clock	TIMER
• clock *up*(D)^	REMIT
clock cover	VEIL, YASHMAK
clock cover, *say*	VALE
clock repair	FACE LIFT
clock repairer	COSMETIC SURGEON
clockwise	HOROLOGIST
close	
close	NIGH
• close connections	NIGHTIES
• close junction	NIGHT
• close relation	NIGHTIE
close average	MEAN
close book	K
close call	HANG UP, RING OFF
	TALLY-HO
close early	omit last letter
• ban(k) *closes early*	BAN
• *early closing of* gallery	TAT(e)
close friend	NEIGHBOUR
close of play	Y
close, *say*	MIEN
close to Cain's brother, *say*	BUYABLE
close watch	SHUT-EYE
closed	TO
closing of mill	L
closing remark	K
closure of mine	E
cloth	
cloth	CLERGY
• cloth-worker	CLERGYMAN
cloth	SERGE
• cloth-worker	SERGEANT
cloth	TWEED
• cloth in front	TWEEDLED
• cloth runner	TWEED
cloth cap	BIRETTA, MITRE
cloth-worker	VICAR etc
clothed	(in) GE–AR, IN GEAR
clothed by H/art/nell	ART
clothed by *	incl in *
• man *clothed in* re–d	REMAND
clothed in blu/e den/im	EDEN
clothes expert	HABITABLE
clothes fit . . .	SUIT
clothing a . . .	incl A
clothing strike	CLOBBER
clothing workers	SHIFT
clothing *	incl *
• re–d *clothing* man	REMAND
sh/e we/ars *clothing*	EWE
cloud	
cloud nine	EUPHORIA
[cloud]*burst*	COULD
cloudless plain	CLEAR
club	
club	C
club	IRON
• club functions	IRONWORKS
• club team	IRONSIDE
club	MACE
• club charges	MACERATES
• club servant	MACE-BEARER
club	RAC
club	SUIT
club	WOOD
• club talk	WOOD CHAT
• flower club	ROSEWOOD
club-house	VILLA
club magazine	ARSENAL
club sandwich	WEDGE
clubman	CADDY, GOLFER
	HERACLES, HERCULES
	PICKWICK
clubwoman	BATHER
clucking female	HEN, LAYER
clumsy	
clumsily [treads]	TRADES
clumsy [oafs]	SOFA
clutch	
clutch control	GRASP
clutch housing	BIRD'S NEST
clutching a . . .	incl A
clutching *	incl *
• Ra–y *clutching* £50	RALLY
clutched by *	incl in *
• £50 *clutched by* Ra–y	RALLY
CO₂	SECOND-IN-COMMAND
coach	
coach	TRAIN
• coach party	TRAINBAND
• second coach	STRAIN
coach bearing	CARRIAGE
coach building	SCHOOL
coach industry	DILIGENCE
coach look-out	TRAINSPOTTER
coach operator	BUSKING
coach shoe	TRAINER
coach worker	STAGEHAND
coaches	TRAIN
• coaches *aboard* ship	STRAINS
• coaches clayworker	TRAINSPOTTER
coal-hole	MINE, PIT

Anag [cat]; Any *; Begin IGN–; Endings –ING; eg •; Hidden /cat/; Implied add (on); Implied in (in);

coalesce
coalescence of a mass	AMASS
fluorine *coalesces with* it	FLIT

coarse
coarse actors	BROADCAST
coarse aggregate	GROSS
coarse grade	RANK
coarse saint	CRUDEST
coarse, *say*	COURSE, RUFF

coast
coast erosion	BEACHWEAR
[coast] *erosion*	ATOCS, COATS
coastal billet	DRIFTWOOD

coat
coat of paint	PT
coat, *say*	JERKING
coating a . . .	incl A
coating *	incl *
• frost *coating* tree	RIMFIRE
coated by *	incl in *
• tree *coated by* frost	RIMFIRE

cobbler
cobbler, *say*	SUITOR
cobbler's *last*	R
cobbling together [yarn]	NARY

cocaine
	CRACK, SNOW

cock
cock an ear(D)^	GUL, RAE
cocked a [snook]	NOOKS
cocked up [great] . . .	GRATE
cocked up an . . .(D)^	NA
cockerels, *say*	COX

Cockney
Cockney	omit H
• *Cockney* dwelling	(h)OUSE
• *Cockney* fence	(h)EDGE
• *Cockney* girl	(h)ER
• *Cockney* woodman	(h)EWER
• *East Ender's* (h)aunt	AUNT
• *East London* school	(h)ARROW
• *Eliza* getting better	(h)EALING
• fireplace *in Bow*	(h)EARTH
• hirsute *Bowman*	(h)AIRY
• *Londoner's* fish	(h)ERRING
• thin *Cockney*	(h)AIRLINE

Cockney
indicating pronunciation:
• *Cockney* abrasive	SANDPIPER
• *Cockney* behaves	BEE-HIVES
• *Cockney* daily	PIPER
• *Cockney* luggage tag	LIBEL
• *Cockney* rogues	KNIVES

Cockney
indicating rhyming slang:
• apples (and pears)	STAIRS
• china (plate)	MATE
• trouble (and strife)	WIFE

Cockney artist	RAINBOW
	(*see also* bow)

cocktail
coc*k*tail	K
cocktail of [gin]	–ING

code
[code]-*breaking*	CO-ED, DECO
code-name	LAWN
code [words]	SWORD
coded [remark]	MARKER
[German] *code*	MANGER

codex
	COD

codicil
	PS

coffee time
	ELEVEN(TH HOUR)

coffer
coffer, *say*	COUGHER, KISSED

coffin
coffin carrier, *say*	BEER
coffin, *say*	COUGHING

cohabitants
	ITEM

coil
coil here, *say*	WINDIER
coiled [rope]	PORE
coiling [adder]	DREAD

coin
coin a [phrase]	SHAPER, SHERPA
coin factory working	MINTON
coin remains . . .	SOUREST
coin, *say*	GILDER, MILL-RACE
	S(C)ENT, SUE
coin-trick, *say*	DIMETRIC
counterfeit coin	SLIP, STUMER

cold
catch cold	incl C
• Pa–t *catches* cold	PACT
cold	C
• cold earth	CLOAM
• cold meat	CHAM
• cold on . . .	CON–
cold bird, *say*	CHILDREN
cold buffet	ICE-BOX
cold environment	(in) I–CE
cold *front*	C
cold greeting	HAIL
cold look	DEAD-EYE
cold, *say*	CHILE, CHILLI, PARQUET
	KOFF
Cold War missile	SNOWBALL
cold-blooded poisoner	ADDER, ASP, SNAKE
cold-*hearted*	incl C
cold-*hearted*	OL

collage
collage made of [silver]	LIVERS, SLIVER
collage of [flowers]	REFLOWS

collapse
collapse of [dais]	AIDS, SAID
collapsed [arch]	CHAR

collapsible [seat]	EATS, SATE, TEAS	• colour stained, *say*	RED-EYED
collar		colour	FLAG
collar	TORC	• colour bar	FLAG-POLE, FLAG-STAFF
• collar, *say*	TALK, TORQUE	• colours fade	FLAG
• collar turning force, *say*	TORQUE	• without colour	OFLAG
collar fastener, *say*	TYPE-IN	colour	TAN
colleague	COLL	• colour goes, *say*	TANGOS
collect		• coloured man	TANGENT
collect	REAP	• coloured them, *say*	TANDEM
• collect directions	REAPPOINTS	colour	TONE
• collect fruit	REAPPEAR(S)	• colour of fruit	LIMESTONE
collect many	incl D, C, L, M	• fish colour	TROUTSTONE
collect money	incl D, L, P	• sun colour	STONE
• ti–ler *collects* money	TIDDLER	colour bar	LIPSTICK
	TILLER. TIPPLER	colour blind	SHADE
collect *	incl *	colour-sergeant	FLAMENCO
• ma–n *collects* one . . .	MAIN	colour signal	MAROON
collected animals	FAUNA	colour television	CHOCOLATE BOX
collected plants	FLORA	colour *up*(D)^	DER
collected [poems]	MOPES	coloured	(in) R–ED
collection	ANA	coloured	
collection of stories	SKYSCRAPER	–cheese	BRIERED
	TOWER BLOCK	–defender	GREENBACK
collector	COLL	–fish, *say*	BLUE-EYED
	GRASS-BOX, RAKE,	–gown, *say*	REDRESS
	TAXMAN	–people	ORANGEMEN
collectors	IR, TAXMEN	–sailor	BLACKJACK
college		–study	REDDEN
college	COLL, ETON, POLY	colourful article	REDAN
• college that is . . .	COLLIE	colour*less*	omit RED
• railway college	BRETON	• cove(red) *colourless* . . .	COVE
• college training	POLYPE	colourless prairie	PLAIN
college girl	CLARE, MAGDALEN(E)	colourless, *say*	PAIL, PLANE
college president	LINCOLN	**column**	
college window	ORIEL	column	COL
colliery area	MINEFIELD	columnist	NELSON
collision		columns, *say*	PEERS, PIERCE
collision [made] . . .	DAME, EDAM, MEAD	**combat jacket**	WARDRESS
collision of [heads]	HADES, SHADE	**combine**	
[slight] *collision*	LIGHTS	*combination of* [pills]	SPILL
colloquial		Combined Forces	RARE
colloquial	COLL	*combined* [ops]	SOP
colloquially cannot	CANT	Combined Universities	OXBRIDGE
is not *colloquial*	AINT	combines ponds	POOLS
Colombia	CO	*combining* [pairs]	PARIS
colonel	COL	**come**	
colony	C	*come a cropper* [in the] . . .	THINE
colonial building	ANTHILL	come down	(*see* comedown *below*)
Colonial Office	CO	come down in this fashion	SOLAND
colonial worker	ANT	come to halt(D)^	WARD
colonist	ANT	*come to a conclusion*	end with A
colony chief	GO-AHEAD	• he *comes to a conclusion*	MANA
colour		come up	
colour	DYE	• animal *comes up*(D)^	REED
• colour a scarf, *say*	DIASTOLE	• *come up* on . . .(D)^	NO
• colour-meter, *say*	DIMETER	come-uppance	
• colour rope, *say*	DICHORD	• *come-uppance of* prima-donna(D)^	AVID

Anag [cat]; Any *; Begin IGN–; Endings –ING; eg •; Hidden /cat/; Implied add (on); Implied in (in);

- fool's *come-uppance* (D)^   LOOF
comes from N/ew E/ngland   EWE
comes from [Spain]   PAINS
* *comes off* . . .   omit *
  - motor *comes off* (car)ousel   OUSEL
comes out of [court on] . . .   CROUTON
comes out of [past]   PATS, TAPS
comes out of th/e ra/in   ERA
comes to grief in [race]   ACER, ACRE
  CARE
comes to light in s/ear/ch   EAR
comes to surface
  - sub *comes to surface*(D)^   BUS
comes to [terms in] . . .   MINSTER
comes through *   incl in *
  - heat *comes through*
  opening of shed . . .   SHEATH
comedown   HAIL, RAIN, SLEET, SNOW
comeback   ECHO
comeback dance   GIG
comeback made< . . .   EDAM
comes to grief [on court]   CROUTON
coming from Jamai/ca t/o London   CAT
coming into Lon/don ate/evening   DONATE
coming out of thea/tre at/night   TREAT
coming to river   ADVENTURE
  (*see also* came)
comedy   COM
comic
comic [acts]   CATS, SCAT
comic   FUN
- comic fellow   FUNGUS
- comic figure   FUND
- comic soldier   FUNGI
comic   WIT
- comic head   WITNESS
- comic success   WITH-IT
- lavatory humour, *say*   PEEWIT
comic Rugby player   HARLEQUIN
command
command sequence   ORDER
commander   AGA, CINC, CO, COM, OC
- commander *batting*   AGAIN
- commander *has* hard . . .   CINCH
- Commander, Royal Navy   CORN
- commander *has*
  French father   COMPERE
- commander *with* dog   OCCUR
commander   CBE, CDR
commanding officer   CO, OC
commemorative meal   REPAST
commence
commence to . . .   T
commencement of her . . .   H
commencing work   W
commerce
commerce   COM

commercial   AD
- commercial address   ADORATION
- commercial break   ADRIFT
- commercial leader   ADDUCE
commercial traveller   CARGO SHIP
  FREIGHT PLANE, GOODS TRAIN,
  REP
commit
commit (=put into)
- *commit* little girl *to* car–e   CARMINE
committed me to war-d   WARMED
- I am *committed to* prison   CAIN, PEIN
committee   COM
commissioner   COM
common
common   COM
common
indicating colloquialism:
- *common* (h)aunt   AUNT
- *commonly* (h)as . . .   AS
- will not *commonly* . . .   WONT
common haunt   FREQUENT
common man   BLOKE, BO(D), CHAP
  GEEZER, PROLE
common metre   CM
common pleas   CP
common salt   AB, RATING, SAILOR, TAR
commons   FARE, HC, HOUSE
Commonwealth (Relations)
Office   C(R)O
commotion
commotion   ADO, TODO
commotion [in street]   INTEREST
commune   COM
communication system   GRAPEVINE
communion   HC
communist
communist   COM
- communist *apparently*
  intended   COMMENT
- communist *has* strong *French* . . . COMFORT
- communist ruler   COMER
communist   RED
- anarchist deed   REDACT
- communist-*backed* . . .<   DER
- Communist club   REDWOOD
- Communist ring   REDO
- Communist study   REDDEN
- Communist's arrived, *say*   RED-SEAR
- Communist's family   REDSKIN
- Russian food   REDDISH
- tender Communist   KINDRED
communist   TROT
- communist *has* hard . . .   TROTH
- one *in* communist . . .   TAROT
- turn *in* communist . . .   TROUT
Communist Party   CP

community

community	EC
• community home	ECLAIR
• community house	ECHO
• community standing	ECSTATIC
community centre	ABBEY
community *centre*	U
community *leader*	C
community payment	SETTLEMENT
Community Service Order	CSO
Community Service Volunteer	CSV

commute

commute [to an] . . .	NOTA
commuting (= going back and forth)	
• *commuting* to flat	LEVEL
commuting [daily]	LYDIA

compact

compact disc	CD
compact disc	O
compact house	H(O), HSE

companion

companion	CBE
companion	CH
• companion has weapons	CHARMED
• companion in a . . .	CHINA
• see companion	LOCH
companion for	
–Bacon	EGGS
–Bill	COO
–Daisy	BUTTERCUP
–Gilbert	SULLIVAN

company

company	CO
• company doctor	COMB
• company uniform	COHABIT
• company work	COOP
company	FIRM
• company cost	FIRM PRICE
• company employed . . .	FIRM HAND
• company position	FIRM STANCE
company	TWO
• company car	TWO-SEATER
• company *has* a few . . .	TWOSOME
• company work	TWO-PLY
company board	GANGPLANK
company director	IMPRESARIO
company *dismissed*	omit CO
• (co)aching company *dismissed* . . .	ACHING

compare

compare	CF, CP
comparatively cold	COLDER
comparatively cold	
(=cold as)	CHARITY, ICE
compared with Edward	LIKENED

compel

compelled a bird, *say*	MAIDEN
compelled terrorists . . .	MADEIRA

compile

compilation of [news]	SEWN, WENS
compiled [list]	SLIT

complain

complain	CARP
• complain *to* editor	CARPED
• complain *to* queen	CARPER
complain *at* meal	BEEF-TEA
complain, *say*	WINE

complete

complete meal	THOROUGHFARE
completed twice	OVERDONE
completely avian, *say*	AWL-BIRD
c(ompletel)y *gutted*	CY
completion of work	K
half-*completed*	F

complex

complex [design]	SIGNED
complex man	OEDIPUS
complex number	C
complex woman	ELECTRA
complexity of [ideas]	AIDES, SADIE

complicate

complicate [matters]	SMATTER
complicated [affair]	RAFFIA

component

components in mo/tors o/r . . .	TORSO
components of [cars]	ARCS, SCAR

compose

compose poetry	SING
compose some popul/ar son/gs	ARSON
composed by [Elgar]	GLARE, LAGER
	LARGE, REGAL
composed [of nuts]	FOUNTS
composed of [nuts]	STUN
composer	ARNE et al
	SCORER
composer's girl, *say*	MISHANDLE
composer's material	NOTEPAPER
composing music	CRADLE-SONG, LULLABY
composite [alloy]	LOYAL
[later] *composition*	ALTER, RATEL

compost

compost [heaps]	PHASE, SHAPE
compost of [dead] . . .	EDDA

compound

compound of [tin he] . . .	THINE
compound, *say*	OX-EYED, OX-HIDE
compounded [lots] . . .	SLOT

comprehend

comprehend (=take in)	
comprehend a . . .	incl A
comprehend *	incl *
• m–an *comprehends* always	MAYAN
comprehended by *	incl in *
• always *comprehended by* m–an	MAYAN
comprehensive case	SCHOOL-BAG

Anag [cat]; Any *; Begin IGN–; Endings –ING; eg •; Hidden /cat/; Implied add (on); Implied in (in);

compress

compressed	PENT
• compressed fish	PENTANGLE
• compressed toes, *say*	PENTOSE
• second compressed . . .	SPENT
	(see also confine)

comprise

comprised in *	incl in *
• the *French comprised in* s–et	SLEET
comprises [all the] . . .	LETHAL
comprising a . . .	incl A
comprising *	incl *
• s–et *comprising* the *French* . . .	SLEET

computer

computer aided	
–design	CAD
–typesetting	CAT
computer assisted	
–instruction	CAI
–learning	CAL
computer club	BCS
computer firm	BIG BLUE
computer integrated	
–business	CIB
–manufacturing	CIM
computer language	
–recorder	CLR
–translator	CLT
computer managed instruction	CMI
computer oriented language	COL
computer output microfilm	COM
computerised scanner	CAT, CT
computers	IT

conceal

conceal	HIDE
• conceal boy, *say*	HYDRON
• conceal spring	HIDEBOUND
• conceal warden, *say*	HYDRANGEA
conceal head	omit 1st letter
• (n)ail *has concealed head*	AIL
conceal a . . .	incl A
conceal money	incl D, L, P
conceal one can	PALMITIN
concealed by camoufla/ge ne/t	GENE
concealed by *	incl in *
• it is *concealed by* m–e	MITE
concealed in [Dorset]	STORED
concealed in h/er go/wn	ERGO
concealed lair	HIDDEN
concealing a . . .	incl A
concealing, *say*	HAYDN
concealing *	incl *
• m–e *concealing* it	MITE

concern

concern	CO, FIRM
	(see company)
concerning	ON, RE

conclude

concluding remark	K
conclusion	CON
conclusion he *came to*	E
conclusion of play	Y
conclusions the panel	
had made after . . .	ELDER
conclusive proof	F
final *conclusion*	L

concoct

concoct it, *say*	HATCHET
concoction of [report]	PORTER
concocted [recipe]	PIERCE

concubine SULTANA

condemn

condemnation of [those] . . .	ETHOS
condemned [to die in] . . .	EDITION
[liar] *condemned*	ARIL, LIRA, RAIL

condition

condition	IF, STATE
conditioned [to heat]	HOT TEA

conductor BUSBAR, CABLE, WIRE

confection

[a new] *confection*	WANE, WEAN
confection of [meats]	MATES, STEAM
	TEAMS

conference

conference	PEAR
conference *centre*	ER

confess

confess	AM–
• confess aims	AMENDS
• confess to being	
right wing	AMATORY
• confessing I can	AMIABLE
confess	IAM
• *begin to* learn confession	LIAM
• Bob confessing	SIAM
• confess *to* bishop in charge	IAMBIC
confess	IM–
• confess age	IMAGE
• confessing weight	IMPOUND
• confessing *before* jury	IMPANEL
confession of timidity	MESHY
confessor	COUGHER, EDWARD
confessor, *say*	COFFER
	(see also admit, claim, declare)

confide

confidante	GATE POST, YOU
confidential hint	INTIMATE

confine

confine	PEN
• confine drug-dealer	PEN-PUSHER
• confine sheep	PENT-UP
• confines charged	
particles	PENSIONS

(see about[2])

Letter replaced \c\at; Omit (a); Pointers *out*; Retain a̲; Split B_ED; Down (D); Backwards <or ^

confined	PENT
• confined notice	PENTAD
• confined one *Scottish* . . .	PENTANE
• confined verse	PENTODE
	(*see also* compress)
confined by ste/el ba/rs	ELBA
confined by *	incl in A
• winner *confined* by two . . .	PACER
confined, *say*	DAMNED
confined to bed	(in) B–ED, (in) CO–T
• confined to bed	BILLED
confined to bed(=laid up)(D)^	DIAL
confined to hospital	INWARD
confining a . . .	incl A
confining *	incl *
• two *confining* winner	PACER
w/e we/re *confined*	EWE
conflict	
conflict of [wills]	SWILL
conflict, *say*	WORE
conflicted [with her] . . .	WRITHE
conflicting [ways]	SWAY, YAWS
conflicting ways	EW, NS, SN, WE
conforming	INSTEP
confound	
confound [devil]	LIVED
confounding [evil] . . .	LIVE, VILE
confront	
confront	C
confront man	FACETED
confronting	start with CON
• *confronting* dog	CONCUR
confuse	
confuse, *say*	JUMBAL
confused [ideas]	AIDES, SADIE
confusing [item]	EMIT, MITE, TIME
[no greater] *confusion*...	GENERATOR
confute	
confute [all the] . . .	LETHAL
confutation of [rules]	LURES
conglomerate	
conglomerate of [large] . . .	ELGAR, GLARE
	LAGER, REGAL
conglomeration of [things]	NIGHTS
Congo	RCB
congregation	INCE, (in) C–E
	INCH, (in) C–H
conjure	
conjure up [devil]	LIVED
conjuring up [evil] . . .	LIVE, VILE
connect	
indicating addition:	
• father is *connected*	
with church	PACE
• member *connected to* hard . . .	HARM
conquered	
conquered *by Caesar*	VICI

conqueror	WILLIAM
conscientious objector	CO
conservationist	
conservationist	GREEN
• conservationist	
support	GREENBACK
• conservationist wing	GREENFLY
conservationists	GREENS, NT
conservative	
Conservative	BLUE, C, CON, TORY
• conservative dress	BLUEGOWN
• Conservative majority	COVERAGE
• Conservative whip	CLASH
• Conservative state	CONGA
• six hundred	
Conservative . . .	VICTORY
conservative	U
conserve	
conserve *	incl *
• m–an *conserves* energy	MEAN
consider	
consider it, *say*	MULLET
consider summary	DIGEST
considerable	TIDY
conspirator	CADE, CASCA, FAWKES, OATES
Constable's house	ART GALLERY
constant	
constant	C
constant	PI
• constant speed	PIRATE
constant concern	FIRM
constant interference	STATIC
constant suffering	ABIDING
constipated	MOTIONLESS
constitute	
constituent of *	incl in *
• new *constituent of* ba–d . . .	BAND
constituent part of sal/address/ing	ADDRESS
constitute [my bases] . . .	EMBASSY
constitutional support	WALKING-STICK
[his] *constituents*	–ISH
[those] *constituents*	ETHOS
construct	
construct [a redoubt]	OBDURATE
constructed from [clay]	LACY
constructing [a new] . . .	WANE, WEAN
construction of [town]	WONT
constructors of [cars]	ARCS, SCAR
construe	
construe [a line]	ALIEN, ANILE
construing [odes]	DOES
consult	
consult lively *Scots*, *say*	SECANT
consulting room	INSPECTION CHAMBER
consume	
consumed by *	incl in *
• six *consumed* by o–ne	OVINE

Anag [cat]; Any *; Begin IGN–; Endings –ING; eg •; Hidden /cat/; Implied add (on); Implied in (in);

consumed [peas]	APES, APSE
consumer protection	NAPKIN, OVERALL
	SERVIETTE
consuming a . . .	incl A
consuming interest	EATING
consuming *	incl *
• o–ne *consuming* six	OVINE
contact	
contact blue	TOUCH DOWN
contagious disease	CD
contain	
contain, *say*	HOLED
contained in [soup]	OPUS
contained in st/ewe/d lamb	EWE
contained in *	incl in *
• number *contained in* tin	CANON
container for pistols, *say*	JEWEL-BOX
container missing, *say*	JARGON
container ship	BIN LINER
containing a . . .	incl A
containing *	incl *
• tin *containing* number	CANON
containing some th/in k/ind	INK
contents of new/spa/per	SPA
contents of crate	RAT
contents of [crate]	REACT
contents of lar/ge ne/w . . .	GENE
contents of text with . . .	EXIT
contents of the bad egg	HAG
contaminate	
contaminate [pure soil]	PERILOUS
contaminated [meat]	MATE, TAME, TEAM
contamination of [wines]	SINEW, SWINE
contemporary	
contemporary	AD
• contemporary churchman	ADMINISTER
• contemporary poetry	ADVERSE
• contemporary with *German* . . .	ADMIT
contemptible fellow	CAD, TWERP
contentious	
contentious [idea]	AIDE
[speak] *contentiously*	PEAKS, SPAKE
contents	(*see* contain)
continent	ASIA, EUR
Continental	M
continental (=French etc)	
• *continental* art	ES
• *continental* articles	UNDER
• *continental* shelf	ANAQUEL
continental head	FRENCH BEAN
continental *head*	C
continental head	TETE
(*see also* abroad, cross[4], foreign)	
continue	
continue	GOON
continue	
–attacking, *say*	RADON
–beaming	RAYON
–burning	TORCHON
–carrying	CARTON
–chatting	CHATON, YAPON
–decaying	ROTON
–digging	PITON
–drawing	DRAGON
–drilling, *say*	BORON
–drooping	WILTON
–for a long time	DRAGON
–greeting, *say*	HALON
–heaping, *say*	PYLON
–informing, *say*	TALON
–innings	BATON
–interfering, *say*	PRION
–ironing	PRESS ON
–irritating	GALLON
–miaouing	MUON
–mixing, *say*	MELON
–moving	GOON
–nursing	TENDON
–playing	ACTON, BAT(T)ON
–pulling	DRAGON
–pushing	SURGEON
–rasping, *say*	PHYLON
–rushing	SURGEON
–shaking	WAGON
–signalling	FLAGON
–talking	CHATON, YAPON
–the war, *say*	PHYTON
–walking	GOON
–waving	WAGON
–wearing hat	CAPON
–working	ACTON
continue reading	PTO
continue summary	RESUME
continued to indulge, *say*	SINDON
continuing story, *say*	CEREAL
contort	
contorted [face]	CAFE
contortions of [animal]	LAMINA
[weird] *contortions*	WIDER, WIRED
contract	
contract	
indicating abbreviation:	
• always *contracted*	EER
• boys *contracted*	TIMED
• *contract* bridge	BR
• *contract* cannot . . .	CANT
• *contract* illness	FLU
• *contract* written . . .	WRIT
• *contractor's word for* finished	OER
	(*see also* short[1])
contract debts	INCURIOUS
contract manager	BRIDGEMASTER
contracted le(g)	LE
contracted out	CAUGHT

Letter replaced \c\at; Omit (a); Pointers *out*; Retain <u>a</u>; Split B_ED; Down (D); Backwards <or ^

contradict

contradiction of all . . .	SOME
contradiction of young . . .	OLD
contradictions	E–W, N–S, S–N, W–E
contradictory answer	NOYES

contrary

contrariwise, May . . .	YAM
contrary girl	MARY
contrary speech	CONVERSE
contrary way<	YAW

contribute

contribution from te/nor, Man/rico	NORMAN
contributing to t/he ed/itor's . . .	HEED
contribution t/o a f/und	OAF

contrive

[a new] *contrivance*	WANE, WEAN
contrived [a plot]	PLATO
contriving to [get a] . . .	GATE

control

control	REIN
• control animals	REINDEER
• control certain . . .	REINSURE
• control country	REINSTATE
• control violence	REINFORCE
• control what is said	REINSTATEMENT
	(*see also* check)
control animal	STEER
control clutch	GRASP
control knob	BOSS
control of corporation	DIETING
control, *say*	GUYED, RAIN, REIGN
controller of locks	ALICE BAND
	HAIR NET, KIRBIGRIP
	KIRBY-GRIP, SLIDE

controversy

controversial [remark]	MARKER
controversy in [Dail]	DIAL, LAID

convenient

convenience	CON
convenient headgear, *say*	HANDICAP

converse

adults *converse*	CHILDREN
conversation	CON
converse of all . . .	SOME
converse of old . . .	NEW, YOUNG
converse quietly	LOUDLY
conversing aloud	ALLOWED
heard *in conversation*	HERD
heard *in conversation* by . . .	BUY

convert

conversion of [sinner]	INNERS
convert [into] . . .	–TION
convert [into a] . . .	–ATION
convert [lire]	LIER, RILE
convert money	CHANGE
converted [infidel]	INFIELD
convertible [coins]	ICONS, SONIC

convey

convey delight	TRANSPORT
conveyed beforehand	PRESENT
conveyed herd	DROVE
conveying wa/ter ne/ar . . .	TERNE

convict

convict	CON
convict	LAG
• convict *with* nothing on	LAGOON
• fellow-convict	FLAG
• old convict	GREYLAY
	(*see also* criminal)

convulse

convulsed [with anger]	WREATHING
convulsion of [face]	CAFE
convulsive [leap]	PALE, PEAL, PLEA

convolute

convoluted [ideas]	AIDES, SADIE
convolutions of [dance]	CANED

cook

cook [meal]	LAME, MALE
cook, *say*	GRILLE
cook young fish	FRY
cooked [sausage]	ASSUAGE
cooker	POACHER
cooking [pots]	OPTS, SPOT, STOP, TOPS
Cook's craft	ENDEAVOUR
Cook's vessel	ENDEAVOUR
cook's weapon	MACE
cook's whiskers	EGG-BEATERS, BLENDERS
cooks fruit	STEAMSHIP
cooks insects	FIDDLESTICKS
cooks joint	STEAMSHIP
[over]*cooked*	ROVE
undercooked	RARE
[under]*cooked*	RUNED

cool

cool	FAN
• cool cat, *say*	PHANTOM
• cool city	FANNY
• cool food	FANFARE

co-ordinate

co-ordinate	X, Y
co-ordinated [with his] . . .	WHITISH
co-ordination of [arms]	MARS, RAMS

copper

copper	CU
• copper can	CUT IN
• copper (coin)	CUD, CUP
• copper colour	CURED
• copper embargo	CUBAN
• copper ring	CURING
• copper's helmet	CUSHAT
copper	D
• copper *and* unknown . . .	DANDY
• copper I dropped	DISHED
• copper I threw	DICAST

Anag [cat]; Any *; Begin IGN–; Endings –ING; eg •; Hidden /cat/; Implied add (on); Implied in (in);

copper	P
• copper and a . . .	PANDA
• copper fields	PLEAS
• copper I valued	PIRATED
copper	PC
copper disc	POLICE RECORD
copper-skinner	PEELER
coppers	PENNY-FARTHING

copy

copy soldier	GIGI
	(see also double²)
copy some . . .	SUM
copy strip	TAKE OFF
copy Turner	REVOLVE, ROTATE
copying speed	CRIBRATE
copyright	RITE, WRIGHT
copyright	APER, C
cor	BLIMEY, FRENCH HORN

core

apple core	P
core	omit centre
• core a(ppl)e	AE
• f(rui)t cored	FT
core of reactor	C

corn

corn	EARS, FOOTPAD
corn cracker	(WIND)MILL
corn-Indian	CORNUTE
corn plaster	FOOTPAD
corned beef can, say	BULLETIN

corner

corner	L
corner fish	ANGLE
corner man	CASTLE, ROOK
Cornwall	SW
coroner	COR
corporal	CPL, NYM, TRIM

corporate

corporate state	FATNESS, OBESITY
corporation	BEEB, CO, INC, TUM

correct

correct	OK
correct	TICK
• correct marks	TICKS
• correct sovereign	TICKER
• shilling is correct	STICK
correct [fare]	FEAR
correct pronunciation	RITE, WRIGHT
	WRITE
correct, say	RITE, WRIGHT
	WRITE
corrected [angle]	GLEAN
correction of [skid]	KIDS

correspond

correspond completely	FITFULLY
correspond with king	WRITER
correspondence of [lovers]	SOLVER

correspondent, say	PENALLY
corresponding liquid	INK
corresponding member	CM
corresponding sheet	NOTEPAPER
corresponding to [German] . . .	MANGER

corrupt

corrupt [dealer]	LEADER
corrupted [all the] . . .	LETHAL
corruption of [leader]	DEALER

corset

corseted in cali/co st/uff	COST
corseted in *	incl in *
* in corsets	incl *
• a king in iron corsets	FAKE, FARE

cost

cost, insurance, freight	CIF
cost of	
–leather, say	HYDRATE
–ride, say	FAIR, PHARE
–trimming	LACERATE
costs nothing	omit O

Costa Rica

Costa Rica	CR
capital of Costa Rica	C
leaders of Costa Rica	CR
co-tangent	COT

could

could be [Easter]	SEATER
could be Easter	FEAST
could be found in sup/erst/ore	ERST
could be feast	EASTER
could be said aloud	ALLOWED
could be said to . . .	TOO, TWO, TU–
could be said to be . . .	TUBE
could be [worse]	SWORE
could become [easy]	AYES, YEAS
could go into [Leith]	LITHE
could, say	MITE
coulomb	C

council

Council of	
–Engineering Institutions	CEI
–Europe	CE
–Industrial Design	CID
council leader	C
councillor	CR

count

count	TOT
• count gangster	TOTAL
• count them, say	TOTEM
• good count	BIENTOT
counts coins	NOBLES

counter

counter	GEIGER, GM
[counter]-move	RECOUNT, TROUNCE
[counter]-productive	RECOUNT, TROUNCE
[counter]-revolutionary	RECOUNT, TROUNCE

Letter replaced \c\at; Omit (a); Pointers out; Retain a̱; Split B_ED; Down (D); Backwards <or ^

counter strike	BUFFET
counter stroke	BUFFET, CHIP-SHOT
countermarcher	SHOPWALKER
counterfeit	
counterfeit	SHAM
• counterfeit article	SHAMAN
• counterfeit bear, *say*	SHAMPOO
counterfeit [coin]	ICON
counterfeit [note]	ETON, TONE
counterfeit note	DUDE
country	
country	CHINA
• country dishes	CHINA
• country friend	CHINA
• country town	CHINAWARE
country	LAND
• country accent	LANDGRAVE
• country bar	LANDRAIL
• country folk	LANDRACE
country (=dialect)	
• country girl	GAL
• country-lover	SWAIN
• country worker	EMMET
country air	NATIONAL ANTHEM
country food	FIELDFARE
country girl	PERUSAL
country man	JOHN BULL, UNCLE SAM
country music	NATIONAL ANTHEM
country seat	SHOOTING STICK
country style (=dialect)	(*see above*)
country ways	LANES
country woman	BRITANNIA
county	
county	AVON, SOM etc
county	CO
• county exercises	COPE
• county side	COL, COR
• county woman	COW
county	DOWN
• county coach	DOWN STAGE
• county players	DOWNCAST
• county side	DOWNRIGHT
county alderman	CA
county borders	BEDS
county *borders*	CY
county coach	SURREY
county council	CC
county seat	SHOOTING STICK
county's team	CORKSCREW
couple	PAIR, PR, TWAIN
couple of	
–boys	REGAL, ROYAL
–days	WE
–fellows	CHAPMAN
–people	EVADES, SALTED
–times	TT
	(*see also* two)

couples starting <u>lo</u>ve <u>a</u>ffairs	LOAF
first couple	ADAM, EVE
last couples ma<u>ke</u> rott<u>en</u> . . .	KEEN
couplet	TT
course	
course	N, S, E, W
• all courses	NEWS, WENS
• course books	SENT, WENT
	SNOT, SWOT
• three courses	EWE, NEW, SEE, WEN etc
course	RIVER
• course *in* Ne/w Ye/ar	WYE
• course on border	TWEED
• course *of* for/ty ne/w . . .	TYNE
course (=golf, etc)	
• colour of course	GREEN
• course inspected, *say*	LYNX-EYED
• cry of course	FORE, OFF
• end of course	EIGHTEENTH, LINE, TAPE
• side of course	RAILS
• start of course	TEE
course (=part of meal)	PIECEMEAL
• course for beginners	STARTERS
• dampcourse	SOUP
• introduction to course	ENTREE
• main course	SEA-FOOD
course controller	HELM, RUDDER
course fee	REFRESHER
course official	MARSHAL, STARTER
course record	LOG BOOK, SCORECARD30
court	
court	CT
court	WOO
• court beginner	WOOL
• court daughter	WOOD
• court Satan	WOOD-EVIL
court actions	SUITCASE
court activity	BADMINTON, TENNIS etc
court martial	CM
court meeting	DATE
court *say*	SITTING-ROOM
court sessions	CS
courtly animal	KANGAROO
courtly lord	LUD
courtesan	SULTANA
cover	
cover	CAP
• cover cereal	CAPRICE
• cover girl	CAPELLA
• useful cover, *say*	HANDICAP
cover	HOOD
• clergyman *takes* cover	PRIESTHOOD
• cover chimney	HOODLUM
• cover journalist	HOODED
cover charge	PREMIUM
cover-stone	SKINFLINT
coverage in Daily Mirr/or fe/ature	ORFE

covered by *	incl in *	crackpot [idea]	AIDE
• one covered by British . . .	BONER	crackshot	ANNIE (OAKLEY), TELL
covered in sn/ow, Ed/ward . . .	OWED		SURE-FIRE
covering a . . .	incl A	crack[shot]	HOST, HOTS
covering brood	HATCH	**cradle song**	LULLABY, ROCK MUSIC
covering fire	SHELL	**craft**	
covering mu/ch op/era	CHOP	craft	ART
covering of cloth	CH	• crafty deed, say	ARTEFACT, ARTIFACT
covering *	incl *	• crafty girl, say	ARTEMIS
• British covering one . . .	BONER	• hard craft	HART
cover-up(D)^	DIL, POT	craft	SS
covers lar/ge ar/ea	GEAR	craft of wickerwork	CORACLE
covers of magazine	ME	craft [she saw] . . .	WASHES
cow		craftily [sneaks] . . .	SNAKES
cow	LOWER	crafty director	CAPTAIN, NAVIGATOR,
• cowhide	LOWER CASE		HELM, RUDDER
• cowshed	LOWER HOUSE	crafty fellow	ARTISAN, TRADESMAN
• fine cow	FLOWER	crafty group	FLEET, NAVY, SQUADRON
cow pasture	OXLAND	crafty operator	BOATMAN, PUNTER
cowboy	STEERSMAN	crafty [seer]	ERSE, SERE
cowgirl	IO	**cram**	
cowman, say	COWARD, COWERED	cram cloth	STUFF
cowshed	STOCK ROOM, STOCKHOLDER	cram food	TUCK
coward		**cramp**	
coward, say	COWERED, COWHERD	cramped by a c/rowd y/ou . . .	ROWDY
cowardly defender	YELLOWBACK	cramped by *	incl in *
cowardly show	CAVALCADE	• individual cramped by man . . .	MAIN
cowl		cramping a . . .	incl A
cowl	HOOD	cramping *	incl *
• cowl on chimney	HOODLUM	• ma–n cramping individual . . .	MAIN
• stealing cowl, say	ROBIN HOOD	**crank**	
cox		crank case	ASYLUM, BROADMOOR
coxed pair	THREE MEN IN A BOAT	crank [case]	ACES, AESC
coxswain, say	COCKS	cranky [tutor]	TROUT
crack		**crash**	
[Animal] Crackers	LAMINA	crashed [car]	ARC
crack	ACE	crashing [bore]	EBOR, ROBE
• crack king	ACER	**crave**	
• crack note	ACETONE	crave, say	PREY
crack	DAB	craving drink	LUSTRUM
• crack rear, almost	DABSTER	**craze**	
• crack-up(D)^	BAD	crazed [china]	CHAIN
crack	PRO	crazy	MAD
• crack discovered...	PROFOUND	• crazier plant	MADDER
• crack dossier	PROFILE	• crazy about the girl, say	MADONNA
crack n–ut with a . . .	NAUT–	• crazy ruler, say	MADDER
crack [nuts]	STUN, TUNS	crazy fellow	HATTER
crack of dawn	DAYBREAK	Crazy [Horse]	SHORE
crack journalist	REPORTED	crazy proposal	LOCOMOTION
crack picture	SNAP	**crease**	
crack up	EXTOL	crease dresses	RUCKSACKS
crack up [when I] . . .	WHINE	crease us, say	CROESUS
cracked heads	NUTS	creased [sheet]	THESE
cracked [heads]	SHADE	**create**	
crackers [in the] . . .	THINE	create [anew]	WANE, WEAN
cracking [code in] . . .	COINED	create interest	INVEST
crack[pot]	OPT, TOP	creation	HAT

Letter replaced \c\at; Omit (a); Pointers out; Retain a̲; Split B_ED; Down (D); Backwards <or ^

creation of [life]	FILE, LIEF	• criticise teacher, *say*	PANZER
credit		• criticise test	PANTRY
credit	CR	criticise cook	ROAST
• credit cut	CREDITED	criticise fish	CARP
• credit due	CROWED, CROWING	criticise, *say*	REVUE
• credit State	CRAVER	**crock**	
credit notes	–IOUS	*crock* [player]	REPLAY
creditor	CR	*crocked* [a winger]	WEARING
creed	–ISM	**crook**	
creeper	IVY, SNAKE	crook	CRIMINAL
crematorium			CROSIER, CROZIER
crematorium	CREM	*crook* [is not an] . . .	NATIONS
crematorium refuse, *say*	BEAU NASH	*crooked* [leg]	GEL
crew		[detains] *crook*	INSTEAD
crew	BOASTED	**crooner**	
	FOUR, EIGHT	crooner	BING
crew weight, *say*	CROUTON	*in* crooner's . . .	B–INGS
crewed	HANDS-ON	• energy *in* crooner's . . .	BEINGS
crewed, *say*	COARSE, CRUDE	**crop**	
crewed her, *say*	COARSER, CRUDER	*come a cropper* [in the] . . .	THINE
cricket		crop *up*(D)^	NOTE, PINS, POL–
cricket boycott	TEST BAN	sort of crop	ETON
cricket club	BAT, CC	**cross¹**	
cricket ground	HEARTH	cross	IO
cricket ground, *say*	LAUDS	• cross *in* right . . .	RIOT
cricket side	LEG, OFF, ON, XI	• dog crosses . . .	CURIOS
cricket spectator	OVERSEER	• five cross fifty . . .	VIOL
cricket stroke	BATSWING	cross	ROOD
cricketer	BATMAN	• cross *inside* b–y . . .	BROODY
cricketer's hat	BOWLER	• cross-*over*<	DOOR
home of cricket	HEARTH	cross	TAU
criminal		• cross a number	TAUTEN
criminal	CON	• cross to grand . . .	TAUTOG
• criminal evidence	CONSIGNS	• cross *with* cross	TAUTEN
• criminal punished	CONFINED	cross	TEN
• criminal type	CONSORT	• cross a town	TENACITY
criminal	CROOK	• cross-bones	TENTS
criminal	HOOD	• cross legs	TEN-PINS
• criminal circles	HOODOO	• cross over	TENON
• criminal journalist	HOODED	• cross the river	TENURE
• sister *with* criminal	NUNHOOD	cross	X
criminal error	CLUE	• cross-beam	X-RAY
criminal procrastinator	THIEF	• cross one . . .	ELEVEN, XI
criminal pursuit	MANHUNT	• monkey-cross	APEX
Criminal (Records) Office	C(R)O	cross islander	MALTESE
criminal [stole so] . . .	LOOSEST	cross *over the Channel*	CROIX, KREUZ
	(*see also* convict)	*French* Cross	CROIX
crimson		*German* Cross	KREUZ
crimson-*clad*	(in) R–ED	**cross²**	
• crimson-*clad* article	READ	cross	ANGRY
cripple		cross *over the Atlantic*	ORNERY
cripple [master]	REMAST, STREAM	cross *over the Channel*	FURIEUSE
crippled [man is] . . .	MAINS		FURIEUX
crippling [trade]	RATED	**cross³**	
criticise		indicating inclusion:	
criticise	PAN	*cross* a	incl A
• criticise girl	PANADA	*cross* river	incl R

Anag [cat]; Any *; Begin IGN–; Endings –ING; eg •; Hidden /cat/; Implied add (on); Implied in (in);

cross street	incl RD or ST
cross *	incl *
• saint *crosses* friend	SPALT
crossed by *	incl*
• friend *crossed by* saint	SPALT
cross⁴	
other uses:	
cross-channel (=French etc)	
• *cross-channel* bridge	PONT
(*see also* abroad, continent, foreign)	
cross-country runner	RIVER
• cross-country runner *changes* [line]	NILE
• former English cross-country runner	EXE
• French cross-country runner	LOIRE
• German cross-country runner	RHINE
cross-examiner	SCRUTINEER
cross-maker	ELECTOR, VOTER
crossing	PANDA, PELICAN
cross[road]	DORA
cross[words]	SWORD
crowd	
crowd	THREE
crowd crowed	CREW
crowded street, *say*	RUEFUL
crown	
crown	CR
crown commission	MAJORITY, ROYALTY
crown jewels	TIARA
crown of head(D)	H
crowned	
indicating one word written below another word or letter:	
• man *crowned with* gold(D)	ORAL
crowned officer	MAJOR
crude	
crude container	OIL DRUM
crude form of [words]	SWORD
crude [ore]	ROE
crude signature	X
crudely [made] . . .	DAME, EDAM, MEAD
crudely made [table]	BLEAT
cruder *say*	COURSER, RUFFER
cruel	
cruel cut	FELL
cruelly [used]	DUES, DUSE, SUED
crumble	
crumbling [ruins Ed] . . .	INSURED
crumbly [bread]	BARED
crumple	
crumpled	INCREASES
crumpled [papers]	SAPPER
crunch	
crunched [under a] . . .	UNREAD
crunching [nuts]	STUN
crush	
crush newspapers	PRESS
crush pen	POUND
crush spirit	SCOTCH
crushed fabric	WORSTED
crushed [orange]	ONAGER
crushing [ores]	EROS, ROES, ROSE, SORE
crust	
bread *crusts*	BD
crust on port	PT
crustless (p)or(t)	OR
cry	
[cried] *off*	DICER
[cries] *out*	SERIC
cry aloud	ALLOWED
cry 'Foul!'	FOWL
cry of delight	OLE
cry of triumph	IO
cry out	YELLOW
cry *over*<	BULB
cry, *say*	W(H)ALE
crying 'Fore!'	FOR, FOUR
crying, say	W(HA)LING
cryptic	
cryptic [clue]	LUCE
cryptically [signal]	ALIGNS
crystal box	SPAR
Cuba	
Cuba	C
Cuban capital	C
Cuban leader	C
Cuban steps	RUMBA
cube	
cube root	SUGAR BEET
cubic	CU, CUB
cubic feet per	
−minute	CUMIN
−second	CUSEC
cubic metre, *say*	STEER
cuckold	ACTAEON
cuckoo	
cuckoo [in nest]	TENNIS
[man is] *cuckoo*	MAINS
cue	
cue, *say*	Q, QUEUE
cull	
[deer] *cull*	REDE, REED
culling [seal]	ALES, LEAS, SALE
cult	
cult	SECT
• cult worker	SECTANT
• member of a cult	INSECT
• two cults	BISECTS
cultivate	
cultivate stars	PLOUGH
cultivate [stars]	TRASS
cultivated dwarf	BONSAI
cultivated products	BACTERIA, PEARLS
cultivating [soil]	OILS, SILO

Letter replaced \c\at; Omit (a); Pointers *out*; Retain a̲; Split B_ED; Down (D); Backwards <or ^

culture
culture of [animal] ...	LAMINA, MANILA
cultured [pearl]	PALER

cunning
cunning man, *say*	ARCHBISHOP
cunning [ruse]	RUES, SURE
cunningly [plied]	PILED

cup
cup-bearer	GANYMEDE, HEBE
	SAUCER
Cup *Final*	P
Cup game	TIDDLY-WINKS
Cup round	TASSO
cupholder	GANYMEDE, HEBE

cure
cure [my pet]	EMPTY
cure, *say*	HEEL, HE'LL
cure your, *say*	HEALTHY
cured [bacon]	BANCO
cured, *say*	HEALD, HEELED

curie CI

curious
curious book	ODDJOB
curious, *say*	KNICKNACKS
curious [thing]	NIGHT
curiously [shaped]	PHASED
curiously shaped [roots]	TORSO

curl
curl it up, *say*	PERMIT
curling [iron]	NOIR, ROIN
curly [beard]	BARED, BREAD, DEBAR
curly *head*	C

current[1]
current	AC
• current price	ACCOST
• current tax	ACCESS
• current usage	ACCUSTOM
current	AMPS
• 150 current ...	CLAMPS
• c–current	CAMPS
• junction *with* current	TAMPS
current	DC
current	I
• current state	–ICAL
• current representative	IMP
• highest current	MAXI
current account	ELECTRICITY BILL
current-carrying	incl AC
• current-*carrying* lines	RACY
current unit	A, AMP, COULOMB
	KWH(R), VOLT

current[2]
current	TIDE
• current *recession*<	EDIT
• current recession	EBB-TIDE
• current usage	TIDEWAY
current drop	EBB(-TIDE)

current management
structure	BREAKWATER, GROYNE
current, *say*	TIED

(see also current[3]*)*

current[3]
current	RIVER
• current in London	THAMES
• current team	RIVERSIDE
• Indian current	GANGES
current control	WEIR
current drop	CATARACT, FORCE
	WATERFALL
current management	
structure	DAM, EMBANKMENT
current stoppage	DAM

(see also current[2]*)*

current[4]
current cost accounting	CCA
current purchasing power	CPP
current success	WINNOW
current (this month)	CUR(T)

curse
curse	DAMN
• curse China, *say*	DAMMING
• curse people, *say*	DAMNATION
• English curse, *say*	EDAM
curse gentleman, *say*	BLAST-OFF
curse people	CONDEMNATION

curt greeting SHORTWAVE

curtail
curtailed tri(p)	TRI–
curtailing journey	TRI(p)

curtain
curtain material	BAMBOO, IRON
curtains	DEATH

custom
customer	(in) SHO–P
customs	HMC
customs assigned number	CAN

cut[1]
cut	AX(E)
• cut *back*<	EXA–
• cut leg	AXON
• cut *up*(D)^	EXA–
• *cutback*<	EXA–
cut	CUT
• cut *back*<	TUC
• cut note	CUTE
• cut *up*(D)^	TUC
• *cutback*<	TUC
cut	DOCK
• cut it off, *say*	DOCKET
• cut off three feet	DOCKYARD
• cut short	DOCK BRIEF
cut	HACK
• cut joint, *say*	HACKNEY
• cut objections	HACKBUTS

Anag [cat]; Any *; Begin IGN–; Endings –ING; eg •; Hidden /cat/; Implied add (on); Implied in (in);

• second cut	SHACK		DAIS(y), PANS(y), PEON(y)
cut	LOP	cut law(n)	LAW
• 100 cuts	CLOPS	cut off part . . .	ART, PAR
• cut up(D)^	POL	cut-price	COS(t)
• cutback<	POL	cut say	MOAN, MODE
cut	MOW		PAIR, PEAR
• cut name	MOWN	cu(t) short	CU
• cut journalist	MOWED	cut sh(ort)	SH
• cut, say	MOAN, MODE	cut short journey	TOU(r), TRI(p)
cut	NIP	cut skin	FELL
• cut at this point, say	NIPPIER	cut twice, say	MAU-MAU
• cut her, say	NIPPER, NIPTER	cut out a . . .	omit A
• cut support	NIPPIER	cut out *	omit *
cut	PRUNE	• le(ad)er cuts out notice	LEER
• cut fruit	PRUNE	cut out odd bits of (t)w(e)e(d)	WE
• cut monarch	PRUNER	cut *	omit *
• cut you and me, say	PRUNUS	cutting (h)edge	EDGE
cut	SAW	cutting *	omit *
• cut at angle	SAWFISH	I cut	omit I
• cut new . . .	SAWN	• ma(i)ze I cut	MAZE
• cut up(D)^	WAS	**cut⁴**	
• cutback<	WAS	other uses:	
cut	SEVER	cut a dash	HYPHENATE
• cut Edward	SEVERED	cut down afternoon . . .	PM
• cut friend	SEVERALLY	cut down drink	RATIONALE
• cut gangster	SEVERAL	cut-down ship	RAZEE
cut	SNIP	cut down tree	FELL
• cut animal	SNIPPET	cut [finger]	FRINGE
• cut favourite . . .	SNIPPET	cut grass	SPLIT
• cutback<	PINS	cut greeting	SHORTWAVE
cut²		cut later...	GASHOLDER
indicating inclusion:		cut production	CROP
cut *	incl in *	cut senior . . .	GASHOLDER
• king cuts corners	ANGLERS	cut staff	CLEFT STICK
cut by a . . .	incl A	cut the aged . . .	GASHOLDER
cut by *	incl *	cut up [steak]	SKATE, STAKE, TAKES
• corners cut by king	ANGLERS	cut whip	CROP
cut from woo/den se/at	DENSE	cut woman	SLITHER
cut into juic/y ap/ple	YAP	cuts face	CHOPS
cut t/he len/gth . . .	HELEN	**cute**	
cutting the grass	RE–ED	cutie	DISH
cut³		cutie, say	QT
indicating omission:		**cycles per second**	CPS, CS, HERTZ
a cut	omit A	**cyclists**	CTC
• a cut in me(a)t	MET	**cyclopaedia**	CYC(LO)
• he(a)l a cut	HEL	**Cymric**	CYM
cut cloth	CLOT, LOTH	**Cyprus**	CY
cut down ratio(n)	RATIO	**Czech**	
cut down (s)hip	HIP	Czech, say	CHECK, CHEQUE
cut down tree	TRE–, REE	Czechoslovakia	CS
cut fibre	SLIVER	capital of Czechoslovakia	C
cut flower	(b)LOOM, (f)LOWER	Czech (oslovak) leader	C

D

damn, *date*, *daughter*, day, dead, deci, *Dee*, degree, dele, delete, delta, Democrat, denarius, density, department, departs, depth, deserted, deus, deuterium, Deutsch(land), diameter, diamond, died, differential operator, dimension, dinar, director, discantus, doctor, dominant, dominus, duke, Dutch, electrical flux, five hundred, four, four thousand, Germany, had, key, *lot*, many, mark, note, notice, *number*, old penny, penny, ring, Schubert's works, string, vitamin, would

Dad		**damn**	
Dad's Army	HG, PASTA	damn, *say*	DAM
Dad's double	PAPA	damned lucky	BLESSED
daft		**damp**	
daft [idea]	AIDE	damp course	SOUP
[I am] *daft*	AIM	damp environment	(in) MO–IST, (in) WE–T
daggers drawn	OBELI	damp-proof course	DPC
Dahomey	DY	damp-proof membrane	DPM
in Dahomey	D–Y	damp, *say*	WHET
Dai		**damsel**	
Dai's (=Welsh)		[damsel] *in distress*	MEDALS
• *Dai's* violin	CRWTH	**dance**	
home *for Dai*	CARTREF	dance	BALL
daily		• dance poster	BALLAD
daily	PAPER	• dance *on* tiptoe	BALLPOINTS
• daily job	PAPERWORK	• dance *with* alien	BALLET
• daily wager	PAPERBACK	• dance *with* nothing on	BALLOON
daily	CHAR	dance composer	HAYMAKER
• daily paper	CHARMS	dance dress	BOLERO
• one *in* daily . . .	CHAIR	dance in front	TRIPLED
• *put* shirt *on* daily . . .	CHART	(d)ance *not started*	–ANCE
daily	NEWSPAPER	Dance of The Tins	CANCAN
	SUN, TIMES	dance, *say*	HEY, REAL
daily job	REPORTER	dance tour	TRIP
dairy		*dancing* [bear]	BARE, BRAE
dairy girl	MARY	dancing girl	ALMA, ALME(H), GEISHA,
[dairy] *produce*	DIARY		NAUTCH, PAVLOVA, SALOME,
Daisy's transport	BICYCLE		SPINNING JENNY
dam			(WALTZING) MATILDA
dam, *say*	DAMN, WERE	*dancing* [shoe]	HOES, HOSE
dam river, *say*	SEA-LOUSE	[sun] *dance*	NUS, UNS–
damage		[tap]-*dancing*	APT, PAT
damage	MAR	**dandy**	ADONIS, BEAU, MACARONI
• damage container	MARTIN	**Dane**	HAMLET
• damage *in* a way	SMART	**danger**	
• damage key, *say*	MARQUEE, MARQUIS	danger at this point, *say*	RISKIER
damage *limitation*	COS(t), HAR(m)	dangerous driver	ROAD-HOG, TOAD
damage [vase]	SAVE	dangerous man	DAN
damaged [pear]	PARE, RAPE, REAP	dangerous, *say*	RISQUE
damaging footwear, *say*	SOUL DESTROYING	**Danish**	
damaging [remark]	MARKER	Danish	DAN

Anag [cat]; Any *; Begin IGN–; Endings –ING; eg •; Hidden /cat/; Implied add (on); Implied in (in);

Danish capital	KRONE
Danish *capital*	D
Danish *leader*	D
	(see also Denmark)
dark	
Dark [Ages]	SAGE
dark dress	NIGHTGOWN
dark blue	OXONIAN
dark horse	BLACK BEAUTY, NIGHTMARE,
	BLACK BESS
Dark Lady	NEGRESS
dark bird, *say*	BLACKEN
dark sportsman	NIGHTCAP
dark suit	CLUBS, NIGHT CLUB, SPADES
darkness, *say*	KNIGHT
darling girl	GRACE
dart	
dart *back<*	PIN, TRAD
[dart] *playing*	DRAT, TRAD
darts man	CUPID, EROS
dash	
dash about	DARTRE
dashing [about]	U-BOAT
dashing about [town]	WONT
data	
data processing	ADP, DP, EDP
data transfer	DT
date	D
date of birth	DOB
dative	DAT
daughter	
daughter	D
• daughter is hard . . .	DISH
• daughters-*in*-law	RUDDLE
• grand-daughter	GD
• twin daughters	DD
daughter born, *say*	MISBEGOTTEN
David's work	PSALMS
dawn	
dawn (=sun-up)(D)^	NUS
dawn of civilisation	C
dawns on people entering new . . .	OPEN
day¹	DAY
[day] *off*	–ADY
[day] *out*	–ADY
[day] *trip*	–ADY
[day]*break*	–ADY
day²	
day	D
• day *after*	end with D
day after day	DD
day *before*	start with D
day *centre*	A
day *off*	omit D
• ban(d) *took* day *off*	BAN
day *out*	omit D
• la(d)y *had* day *out*	LAY

daybreak	D
days	DD, DS
days after	
–date	DD
–sight	DS
day's date	DD
day³	
day in	incl D
• day in Wye, *say*	WIDE
day in	
–Berlin	TAG
–Paris	JOUR
–Rome	GIORNO
day *return<*	DEW
daybreak	DAWN, SHORT LEAVE
days, *say*	DAZE
daze	
daze, *say*	DAYS
dazed [reaction]	CREATION
in a daze [he was] . . .	HAWSE
d-duster	DRAG
dead	
dead	D
• dead bird, *say*	DOWEL
• dead keen	DAVID
• dead reckoning	DR
• dead right	DR–
dead	LATE
• dead bird	EMULATE
• dead saint	LATEST
• dead space	LATEEN
• deadhead	LATENESS
dead	OBIT
[dead] *beat*	–ADED, EDDA
dead-centre	CEMETERY, CHURCH YARD
	CREMATORIUM
	FUNERAL PARLOUR
dead *centre*	EA
[dead] *drunk*	–ADED, EDDA
dead end	CEMETERY, CHURCHYARD.
	GRAVE, TOMB
dead *end*	D
dead on arrival	DOA
dead policeman	BUSYBODY
dead language	OBIT(UARY)
dead*head*	D
deadheaded (f)lower	(f)LOWER
deadheaded flower	(f)LAG, (v)ETCH etc
deal	
deal with [all the] . . .	LETHAL
dealt with [evil] . . .	LIVE, VILE
dean	
dean	INGE
Dean of Faculty	DF
dean's house, *say*	DENARY
dear	
[dear] . . .	READ-OUT

Letter replaced \c\at; Omit (a); Pointers *out*; Retain a; Split B_ED; Down (D); Backwards <or ^

dear *French* . . .	CHER(E)	• deceive leader	CONDUCE
dear money	SWEETBREAD	• deceive top player, *say*	CONCEDE
death		deceive	GULL
death certificate	END PAPER	• deceive alien	GULLET
death lines	EPITAPH, OBIT(UARY), RIP	• deceive bird	GULL
death of deity	GODSEND	• deceive unknown . . .	GULLY
Death Row, *say*	DICLINIC, DYELINE	deceive	FOX
[death] *throes*	HATED	• deceive Communist	FOX-TROT
death-wish	RIP	• deceive cricketer	FOX-BAT
deathly words	EPITAPH, OBIT(UARY), RIP	• deceive follower	FOXTAIL
debase		deceiver of policeman	SUPER-DUPER
debased [idea]	AIDE	*deceiving* [master]	REMAST, STREAM
[quite] *debased*	QUIET	**December**	DEC
debar		**decentralise**	
debar dog, *say*	BANKER, BARKER	decentralise	CORE
debar Scot	BANIAN	*decentralise* m(inistr)y	MY
debris		**deci-**	
debris of the . . .	ETH, HET	decigramme	DG
debris [piled] . . .	PLIED	decilitre	DL
[much] *debris*	CHUM	decimetre	DM
debt		**decider**	ARBITRATOR, JUDGE, REFEREE
debt	IOU		UMPIRE, JUMP-OFF
debt collector	DUNKING		PLAY-OFF, TIE-BREAK
debtor	DR–	**decimal**	
debtor's documents	–IOUS	decimal	OFTEN
debts	–IOUS	decimal point	(IN)TENSE
debut		decimal, *say*	INTENSE
debut of socialite	S	[decimal] *system*	CLAIMED, DECLAIM,
debut performance	P		MEDICAL
decapitate		decimally	INTENS–
decapitate	omit 1st letter	**decimate**	
• *decapitated* (k)ing	–ING	*decimate* [army]	MARY, MYRA
• *decapitated* (w)oman	OMAN	*decimated* [by a] . . .	BAY
decay		**decipher**	
decay	ROT	*decipher* [signal]	ALIGNS
• decay a number	ROTTEN	*deciphering* [letters]	SETTLER
• decay of jetty	PIERROT	**declare**	
• decay of woman, *say*	ROTTER	declaration	DEC
decay	RUST	declaration of friendship	IMAMATE
• decay at this point, *say*	RUSTIER	*declaration of*	
• decay in article	THRUSTING	–some . . .	SUM
• decay in front	RUSTLED	–spirits	RHUMB
decayed [leaf]	FLEA	–war	WORE
decayed, *say*	DECADE	declare	AM–
decaying bodywork	CÁRROT	• declaring our . . .	AMOUR
decaying [tree is] . . .	RESITE	• declaring rightist views	AMATORY
deceased		• declaring the result	AMEND
deceased	D, DEC	declare	IAM
deceased's title	DEAD MAN'S HANDLE	• declaring vehicle . . .	IAMBUS
deceive		• pair declaring . . .	PRIAM
deceitful [tinker]	REKNIT	• son declaring directions	SIAMESE
deceive	COD	declare	IM–
• deceive fish	COD, CODLING	• declaring agreement	IMPACT
• deceive in river	DECODE	• declaring some . . .	IMPART
• deceive journalist	CODED	• declaring wine	IMPORT
deceive	CON	(*see also* admit, claim, confess)	
• deceive company	CONFIRM	declare perfect	UTTER

Anag [cat]; Any *; Begin IGN–; Endings –ING; eg •; Hidden /cat/; Implied add (on); Implied in (in);

declaring wine — WHINE

decline
decline *old* gamebird — QUAIL
declension — DEC

decode
decode [signal] — ALIGNS
decoded [German] . . . — MANGER

decompose
decomposed [meat] — MATE, TAME, TEAM
decomposing [flesh] — SHELF
decomposition of [fibres] — BRIEFS

deconstruct
deconstruct [verse] — SEVER
[later] *deconstruction* — ALTER

decorate[1]
decorate — DECK
• decorate cards — DECKHAND
• decorate journalist — DECKED
• decorate part of ship — DECK
decorated [plate] — PLEAT
decoration of [room] — MOOR
decoration, *say* — MEDDLE
decorative border, *say* — FREEZE
indicating use of
abbreviation such as OBE:
• company *has* decoration — COMBE
• decorated queen — OMER
• King *with* no decoration — ROOM
• decorated unknown . . . — OBEY
• King decorated . . . — ROBE

decrease
decrease — GODOWN
decreasing (ret)urns — URNS

decrepit
decrepit [cars] — ARCS, SCAR
decrepit girl, *say* — RUSTICATE
decrepit vehicle, *say* — RUSTICA
decrepit, *say* — TATTIE

deduct
deduct from bill — (ac)COUNT, (b)ILL
deduct one point — omit N, S, E or W
deduction from salary — (s)ALARY, (w)AGES
deduction from r/igor/ous . . . — IGOR
deduct two points — omit NE, SE etc
• *deduct* two points *from* (s)cor(e) — COR
• *deduct* two points *from* gam(es) — GAM

Dee
Dee — D
Dee passed away, *say* — DEEDED
Dee's predecessor — C
Deeside, *say* — DECIDE
Deeside tartan — DEEP-LAID

deed
deed of separation — CUT(TING), PARTING
PARTITION, SEVERANCE
SEVERING
(*see also* indeed)

deep
deep — MAIN
• continental *has* deep . . . — SPANISH MAIN
• deep surround — MAIN-FRAME
• make deep . . . — DOMAIN
deep — SEA
• deep breath — SEA BREEZE
• deep pink — SEA-ROSE
• deep tone — SEARING
deep blue — LOW
deep fish — BASS
deep freezer — ICEBERG
deep consideration — OCEANOGRAPHY
Deep South — ANTARCTIC OCEAN

deer
deer — BUCK
• deer have a few, *say* — BUXOM
• deer in front — BUCKLED
• deer's relatives — BUCKSKIN
deer — DOE
• deer-king — DOER
• deer's relatives — DOESKIN
• *invest* money *in* deer — DOLE
deer — ROE
• deer-dog, *say* — ROAD-HOG
• deer, *say* — ROW(DIER)
deer — HIND
• deer *has* the greatest . . . — HINDMOST
• deer spots . . . — HINDSIGHTS
deer, *say* — DEAR, EXPENSIVE

deface
deface — MAR
• deface lines — MARRY
• deface ruler — MARKING
• deface script — MARTEXT

defeat
defeat — PIP
• defeat boy — PIPERIC
• defeat family — PIPKIN
• defeat girl — PIP-EMMA
defeat Brown — TAN
defeat champion — BEST
defeat party — THRASH

defect
defect [of nut] — FOUNT
defective hearing — MISTRIAL
defective [tap] — APT, PAT
[mental] *defective* — LAMENT

defend
defend Scot — GUARDIAN
defendant — DEF, DFT
defender — BACK
Defender of the Faith — DF
defenders drinking — BACKSLAPPING

deficient
deficient of a . . . — omit A
deficient of, *say* — LAX

deficient of *	omit *
• Left *deficient of* part . . .	DE(part)ED
extremely deficient	omit end(s)
• crow(d) is *extremely deficient*	CROW
• (c)row(d) is *extremely deficient*	ROW
very deficient	omit V
• hal(v)e very *deficient* . . .	HALE
defile	
defile [art]	RAT, TAR
defiling [chapel]	PLEACH
defilement of [virgin]	RIVING
define	
defining [words]	SWORD
definitely [was] . . .	SAW
definition	DEF
deflect	
deflect [blade]	BALED
deflection of [sword]	WORDS
deform	
deformed [feet]	FETE
deformity of [arms]	MARS, RAMS
defrost	TAKE OFFICE
degrade	
degradable [type A] . . .	PEATY
degradation of [art]	RAT, TAR
degrade [oils]	LOIS, SILO
degree	
degree	BA
• degree students	BALL
• degree *with* honour	BACH
• mother *has* degree	MAMBA
degree	D, DEG
degree	MA
• degree students	MALL
• degree *with* honour	MACH
• school *with* degree . . .	GAMMA
degree of f/reed/om	REED
degree of hop(e)	HOP
deity	
deity	GOD
• deity appears	GODSON
• deity has urinated	GODSPEED
• deity knew . . .	GODWIT
delay	
delay charge	STALLION
delay exhibit	HOLD UP
delay permit	LET
delay, *say*	PAWS
delay-switch, *say*	LIGHTWEIGHT
delayed	LATE
• delayed ceremony	LATERITE
• delayed recovery	LATERALLY
• son delayed	SLATE
delegate	DEL
delete	
delete	D
delete a . . .	omit A

delete a line	omit AL
• *delete* a line *from* p(al)er . . .	PER
delete line	omit L
• Wa(l)ter *deletes* line	WATER
delete part of (p)age	AGE
delete score	SCRATCH
delete *	omit *
delicate	
delicate	FINE
• delicate lines	FINERY
• soldier has delicate . . .	REFINE
delightful drawing	FETCHING
Delilah's (handi)work	(D)EPILATION
	HAIR-CUTTING
delinquent	
delinquency of [boys]	YOBS
delinquent [kids]	SKID
delirium	
delirious [chatter]	RATCHET
delirium tremens	DT(S)
deliver	
deliver children, *say*	BARE
deliver *up*(D)^	REVILED
delivered from hand/s of	
a/ vandal	SOFA
deliveries	OVER
• 150 deliveries	CLOVER
• deliveries *by* spinner	OVERTOP
• deliveries expected	OVERDUE
delivers fish	HANDSHAKE
delivery	BALL
delivery date	DOB
deliveryman	BOWLER, GYNAECOLOGIST
	LIBERATOR, SPEAKER
delta	D
delusions	DT(S)
demand style	CALL
demented	
demented [Greek in] . . .	REEKING
[made] *demented*	DAME, EDAM, MEAD
demi	
demi-cannon	CAN, NON
*demi*john	JO
Democrat	D, DEM
demolish	
demolish, *say*	RAISE, RAYS, RECK
demolished [barn]	BRAN
demolition of [shed in] . . .	SHINED
demonstrate	
demonstrate	SHOW
• demonstrate a bit	SHOWPIECE
• demonstrate concern	SHOW BUSINESS
demonstrated (fabric)	SATIN
Denmark	
Denmark	DK
• a name *in* Denmark	DANK
• smuggle *into* Denmark	DRUNK

Anag [cat]; Any *; Begin IGN–; Endings –ING; eg •; Hidden /cat/; Implied add (on); Implied in (in);

• we *in* Denmark	DUSK	**depose**	
	(*see also* Danish)	*depose leader*	omit 1st letter
dentist		• *depose leader* of (S)cots	COTS
dentist	BDS, DDS, LDS, MDS	depose monarch	SPURNER
	DRILLER, FILLER, STOPPER	depose monarch, *say*	SACKING
dentist's chair	DRILLING SITE	deposed	DEP
dentist's friend	EXTRACTOR FAN	**deposit**	
dentist's surgery	DRAWING ROOM	*deposit in* *	incl in *
	FILLING STATION	• *deposit* money *in* b–ank	BLANK
dentists	BDA	deposit, *say*	LOAD
deny		deposited, *say*	LADE
denial of her . . .	HIS	* *deposited in* . . .	incl *
denying right . . .	LEFT	• money *deposited in* b–ank	BLANK
depart		**depress**	
depart to . . .	GOAT	depressed fence	HAHA
departed saint	LATEST	depressing outcome	KEYSTROKE
departs quietly	omit P	depression	COL
• (p)arson *departs quietly*	ARSON	**deprive**	
departure	DEP	*deprive of* a . . .	omit A
departure of *	omit *	*deprive of* leader	omit 1st letter
• *departure of* king *from* par(k)	PAR	• (p)arty *deprived of leader*	ARTY
departure platform	BIER	*deprive of* love	omit O
* *departing*	omit *	*deprive of* money	omit L
• King *departing from* No(r)way	NO WAY	*deprived of* *	omit *
department		• (tot)ally *deprived of* drink	ALLY
department	DEPT, DPT	• (p)irate *deprived of* power	IRATE
Department of		**deputy**	
–Economic Affairs	DEA	deputy	DEP, LOCUM
–Education and Science	DES	deputy	STAND-IN
–Employment (and Productivity)	DE, DEP	• deputy stableman	STANDING-ROOM
–the Environment	DOE	*deputy head*	D
–Trade (and Industry)	DOT, DTI	deputy-lieutenant	DL
depend		**derail**	
depend	RELY	*derail* [Engine D]	NEEDING
• depend *on woman, say*	RELIEVE	*derailment of* [trucks]	STRUCK
• depend *on* worker, *say*	RELIANT	**derange**	
indicating one word written		*derange* [mental] . . .	LAMENT
below another word or letter:		*deranged* [or insane]	IN REASON
• Conservative *depends*		**deregulate**	
on his . . .(D)	HISTORY	*deregulating* [more] . . .	OMER, ROME
• expert *depends on* money(D)	LACE	*deregulation of* [Norse] . . .	SNORE
depict		**derelict**	
depicted in larg/e pic/ture	EPIC	*derelict* [chapel]	PLEACH
depicted in [orange]	ONAGER	*dereliction of* [duties]	SUITED
depicting [a last] . . .	ATLAS	[made] *derelict*	DAME, EDAM, MEAD
deplete		**derive**	
depleted (s)tor(e)	TOR	derivation	DER
depletion of (s)oil	OIL	*derivative of* Israe/li ve/rb	LIVE
deplorable		*derivative of* [German] . . .	MANGER
deplorable [lapse]	PALES, PEALS	derived	DER
deplorably [late]	LEAT, TALE, TEAL	*derived from* [one Red's] . . .	ENDORSE
deploy		*derived from* o/ur ge/nes	URGE
deploy [tanks]	STANK	**descend**	GODOWN
deployed in *	incl in *	**desert**	
• soldiers *deployed in*		desert	RAT
exercises	PORE, PORT	• desert animal	RAT
deployment of [guns]	GNUS, SNUG	• desert fighter	RAT

Letter replaced \c\at; Omit (a); Pointers *out*; Retain <u>a</u>; Split B_ED; Down (D); Backwards <or ^

• desert in the East	RATINE
• desert man	RATHE
• desert tribe	RAT RACE
desert animal	RAT
desert band	QUITO
desert fault	DEFECT
desert holiday	LEAVE
desert ship	CAMEL
[Desert] *Storm*	RESTED
deserted	D
deserted by a . . .	omit A
deserted by *	omit *
• pa(la)ce *deserted by* the *French* . . .	PACE
deserted sailor	LEFT-HAND
deserter	RAT
• deserter in front, *say*	RATTLED
• deserter will, *say*	RATTLE
• deserter X	RATTEN
* *deserting*	omit *
• princess *deserting* (di)vine . . .	VINE
design	
design	PLAN
• design alien	PLANET
• design church	PLANCH
• design furniture	PLANTABLE
Design [Centre]	RECENT
Design Council	CID
designed [table]	BLATE, BLEAT
desire	
desire	LUST
• desire at this point	LUSTIER
• desire spirits	LUSTRUM
desire merely . . .	WANTONLY
despatch	
despatch a . . .	omit A
despatch money	omit L
• p(l)an to *despatch* money	PAN
despatched, *say*	SCENT
desperate	
Desperate [Dan]	AND
desperate man	DAN
desperate [shriek]	HIKERS, SHRIKE
desperately [tired]	TRIED
despoil	
despoiled, *say*	PRAYED
despoiler *say*	PRAYER
dessert	
dessert	AFTERS
• dessert wine	AFTERSHOCK
• desserts have . . .	AFTERSHAVE
• king *takes* desserts	RAFTERS
dessert	FOOL, PUD etc
destabilise	
destabilise [regime]	EMIGRE
destabilising [Roman] . . .	MANOR
destroy	
destroyed [castle]	CLEATS

destroy listeners	ENDEARS
destruction of [Troy]	TORY
destructive beauty	SMASHER
destructive [blow Seb] . . .	WOBBLES
desultory	
desultorily [read] . . .	DARE, DEAR
desultory [try at] . . .	RATTY
detach	
detach a . . .	omit A
detach *	omit *
• Set(h) has *detached* house	SET
detached [retina]	RETAIN
detached territory	ISLAND
detail	
detail	DOCK
detail of Picas/so p/ainting	SOP
detailed ca(t)	CA
detailed drawin(g)	DRAW-IN
detain	
detain a . . .	incl A
detain *	incl *
• las–s *detains* her . . .	LASHERS
detain suspect	APPREHEND
detained by detecti/ve al/though . . .	VEAL
detained by *	incl in *
• see her *detained by* las–s	LASHERS
detect	
detect	SPY
• detect Communist, *say*	SPIRED
• detect hooligan, *say*	SPITED
• detect the *German*, *say*	SPIDER
detective	BLOODHOUND, DET, EYE, TEC
detectives	BUSIES, CID, YARD
detectives give information, *say*	EYE-STALK
detective's joke, *say*	HOMESPUN
deteriorate	
deteriorate [in water]	TINWARE
deteriorated, *say*	DECADE
deteriorating [state]	TASTE, TEATS
deterioration of [life]	FILE, LIEF
determine	
determine, *say*	DEESIDE
determined attack	SET ON
detour	
detour [made in] . . .	MAIDEN
[wider] *detour*	WEIRD, WIRED
Deutsch	D
devastate	
devastate [region D]	ERODING
devastated [realm]	LAMER
devastation of [forest]	FOSTER
develop	
developed [a new] . . .	WANE, WEAN
development of [site]	TIES
device	
device [may be] . . .	BEAMY

Anag [cat]; Any *; Begin IGN–; Endings –ING; eg •; Hidden /cat/; Implied add (on); Implied in (in);

[simple] *device*	IMPELS	**diameter**	D
devil		**diarist**	EVELYN, NOBODY, PEPYS
devil	ABADDON, APOLLYON, BELIAL,	**Dickens**	
	CLOOT(IE), DAVY-JONES	[Dickens] *novel*	SNICKED
	NICKNAME, (OLD) SCRATCH	Dickensian dance	TWIST
	RAGMAN	**dicky**	ILL
devil	IMP	*Dicky*, [Sue] *and* [Sam]	ASSUME
• 50 devils	LIMPS	**dictate**	
• devil consumed us, *say*	IMPETUS	*dictate* tail	TALE
• devil performed	IMPACTED	*dictator's* reign	RAIN, REIN
• *give* the devil credit	CRIMP	**dictionary**	OED
• *wandering* devil	IMPROVING	**did**	
devil, *say*	JUICE	Did expert . . . ?	ACCOMPLISHED
devilish control	POSSESSION	did it	FEC(IT), FF
devilish skill	IMPART	*Did you say 'No'?*	KNOW
devilish [skill]	KILLS	**die**	
devilled [lamb]	BALM	die *from* . . .	omit D
devious		• die *from* col(d)	COL
devious *ends*	DS	die *in* Germany	DEFINITE ARTICLE
deviously [went] . . .	NEWT	die of cold	ICE-CUBE
[men are] *devious*	MEANER	[die] *off*	IDE, –IED
devise		[die] *out*	IDE, –IED
devised [name]	MANE, MEAN	die, *say*	GOADED, PASSOVER
devising [means]	MANES, NAMES	died	D
Devon	SW	• died later	DAFTER
devote		• died young	DEARLY
devoted [to her] . . .	THROE	• woman died	SHED
[it was] *devoted* . . .	WAIST, WAITS	died	OB(IT)
devour		died *out*	omit D
devour animals	WOLF-CUBS	died without children	OSP
devoured by *	incl in *	**dieting**	FAST WORK
• one *devoured by* men	MEAN, MIEN	**differ**	
devouring a . . .	incl A	*differ* [from anil]	FORMALIN
devouring, *say*	GOBELIN, GOBLIN	*differ from* [others]	THROES
devouring *	incl *	*difference* [in the] . . .	THINE
• men devouring one . . .	MEAN, MIEN	different *conclusion*	T
devours, *say*	TOCSIN	*different* head	change 1st letter
devout	PI	• \f\ lower has *different*	
diabolic		head	GLOWER
diabolic [idea]	AIDE	*different* [one]	NEO–
diabolically [evil]	LIVE	*different position*	
[it was] *diabolic*	WAIST	*of* [letters]	SETTLER
dial		*different role* for [actress]	RECASTS
dial	O	*different spell of* witch	WHICH
dial(D)^	LAID UP	*different way to* draw<	WARD
dial girl, *say*	DILEMMA	*different way* [to fry]	FORTY
dialling system	STD	different way(s)	N, S, E, W
diamond		• *in* different ways, girl . . .	ENSUES
diamond(s)	ICE	• \N\ orse have *a different way* . . .	WORSE
• diamond case	ICEBOX	*different* [ways]	SWAY, YAWS
• diamond factory	ICE-PLANT	*differential* [gear]	RAGE
• diamonds only . . .	JUSTICE	*differently constructed*	
diamond	ROCK	[steel] . . .	LEETS, STELE
• 100 diamonds	CROCKS	*differing* [points]	PINTOS
• diamond ring	ROCK BAND	**difficult**	
• *give* diamond to alien	ROCKET	difficult at this point, *say*	HARDIER
diamond ring	ENGAGED SIGNAL	*difficult* [time]	EMIT, MITE

difficult manoeuvre	HARD TACK
difficulty	ADO, ER, NET
difficulty [in art]	TRAIN
difficulty, *say*	NOT
diffuse	
diffuse [gases]	SAGES
diffused [glow in] . . .	LOWING
diffusion of [air]	RIA
dig	
dig it	UNDERSTAND
dig *up*(D)^	GID
dig up food	GRUB
dig up [trees]	RESET, TERSE
digging up [soil]	OILS, SILO
digs with hands	GRUB-SCREW
	(*see also* dug)
digest	
digest *	incl *
• h–e *digested* the Bible	HAVE
digest, *say*	SUMMERY
digested [meal]	LAME, MALE
digestion of [oats]	STOA
digit	
digit expires, *say*	TOADIES
digit, *say*	UNDERSTAND
digital recording	BRAILLE
	DAT
	FINGERPRINT
digits, *say*	TOSE, TOZE
dilute	
dilute liquid	WATER
[diluted] *mixture*	LUDDITE
diluted sp(i)rit	SPRIT
dim	
[dimmer] *switch*	RIMMED
dim[wit]	TWI–
[saw it] *dimly*	WAIST, WAITS
dime	IOC
diminish	
diminish th(e) . . .	TH
diminish the girt(h)	GIRT
diminish t/he len/gth	HELEN
diminishing asset	ASS, SET
diminution of	
–height	H
–interest	INT
–power	P
diminutive	
–footballer	HALF
–general	(TOM) THUMB
–man	CHAPLET
–mother	MINIMUM
diminutive	
–father	DAD, FR, PA, POP
–girl	DI, G
–mother	MA(M), MUM
–Senator	SEN

–sister	SIS
(*see also* small²)	
dip cloth	DUCK
dinar	D
dine	
[dine] *out*	ENID, NIDE
dine *with* china	MESSMATE
dined *after* match	TESTATE
dined *out*	F–ED
diploma	
diploma	DIP
Diploma of Art	DA
–of the Imperial College	DIC
–in Industrial Health	DIP
–in Public Health	DPH
–in Ophthalmic Medicine and Surgery	DOMS
–in Psychological Medicine	DPM
diplomat	
diplomatic retreat	CONSULATE, EMBASSY
diplomatic sign	CD
diplomats	CD, FO, UN
Dirac's constant	H
dire	
dire [need]	DENE, EDEN
dire straits	(in) NE–ED
direly [felt, not] . . .	FLETTON
direct	
direct current	DC
direct speech	ADDRESS
directed [fire]	RIFE
direction	
direction-finder	COMPASS, GUIDE
	(ROAD-)MAP
directions	E, N, S, W
• directions *to* the gallery	ESTATE
• in all directions	NEWS, SEWN, WENS
	(*see also* ways)
directions from the staff (=musical directions)	
• *directions from the staff* to all . . .	TUTTI
• *directions from the*	
staff quickly . . .	ALLEGRO, PRESTO
• loud *directions from the staff*	FORTE
director	
change directors	SWITCHBOARD
director	ARROW, DIR, POINTER
Director of Public Prosecutions	DPP
directors	BOARDBOARD
directors *are after* money	BREAD
director's dog	POINTER
directors embark	BOARD
directors of astronomy	STARBOARD
directors, *say*	BORED
dirty	
dirty [dogs]	GODS
dirty film	DUST, SCUM
dirty gorge	DEFILE
dirty old man	DOM

Anag [cat]; Any *; Begin IGN–; Endings –ING; eg •; Hidden /cat/; Implied add (on); Implied in (in);

dirty opening, *say*	MESSIDOR	• prohibit discharge, *say*	BARSAC
dirty, *say*	FOWL	**discharge²**	
dis-		*discharge* a . . .	omit A
many words beginning with		*discharge* *	omit *
dis-, some of which follow,		• fat(her) *discharges* her	FAT
are used to indicate anagrams		discharge debts	ENDOWING
disabled		discharge sailor	TURNABOUT
disabled (income group)	DIG	discharge soldiers	FOOT
disabled [poor Ted] . . .	TORPEDO	discharge *to* river	VENTURE
disadvantage		*finally discharged*	omit last letter
disadvantage (=draw*back*<)	WARD	• deb(t) *finally discharged*	DEB
disagree		*(see also* dismiss)	
disagree with all . . .	PART, SOME	**disclose**	
disagree with many	FEW	*disclose* [secret]	RESECT
disappear		*disclosed in* no/vel vet/ted by . . .	VELVET
disappearance of a . . .	omit A	*disclosed in* [novels] . . .	SLOVEN
disappearance of *	omit *	*disclosure of* [news]	SEWN, WENS
• *disappearance of* shilling from pur(s)e	PURE	**discoloured figures**	LIVID
disappearing drink	EBB-TIDE, SEA-GOING	**discomfit**	
start to <u>d</u>isappear	D	*discomfitted* [king is] . . .	SKIING
start *to disappear*	omit 1st letter	*discomfiture of* [king at]...	TAKING
• flowers start *to disappear*	(f)LAGS	**discompose**	
	(f)LOWERS, (v)ETCHES etc	*discompose* [all the] . . .	LETHAL
disapprove	BOO	*discomposed* [by no] . . .	BONY
disarmers	CND	**disconnect**	
disarray		*disconnect* [lamp]	PALM
army *in disarray*	MARY, MYRA	*disconnected by* a . . .	incl A
disarray in [team]	MATE, MEAT, TAME	*disconnected by* *	incl *
disarray [in team]	INMATE	• r–ing *disconnected by* former	
disaster		pupil	ROBING
[American] *disaster*	CINERAMA	* *disconnects*	incl *
disaster [in the] . . .	THINE	• former pupil *disconnects*	
disastrous [fire]	RIFE	r–ing	ROBING
disastrous court	DIRECT	*disconnection of* [wires]	SWIRE
disastrously [I sailed] . . .	LIAISED	**disconcert**	
disband		*disconcert* [her fat] . . .	FATHER
disband [side]	DIES, IDES	*disconcerted* [by a] . . .	BAY
disbandment of [squad]	QUADS	[it was] *disconcerting*	WAIST
disc		**discontented**	
disc	O	*discontented*	omit centre
disc-jockey	DJ	• *discontented* m(al)e	ME
disc-jockey, *say*	COMPARE	• d(aughte)r *is discontented*	DR
discard		**discontinue**	
discard a . . .	omit A	*discontinuance of* man(y) . . .	MAN
discard hat	omit 1st letter	discontinue diet	PROROGUE
• parent *discards* hat	(m)OTHER	discontinued	DIS
discard reserves	SCRAP-BOOKS	*discontinued* mode(l)	MODE
discard *	omit *	**discord**	
• Wh(it)e, N, *discards* it	WHEN	*discord* [results] . . .	LUSTRES
discharge¹		*discordant* [notes]	ONSET, SETON
discharge	FIRE		STONE, TONES
• certain discharge	SURE-FIRE		
• discharge soldier	FIREMAN	**discount**	
• discharges fish	FIRESIDE	20% *discount on* (c)lock	LOCK
discharge	SACK	50% *discount on* tic(ket)	TIC
• discharge journalist	SACKED	**discourage**	
• discharge girl, *say*	SACELLA	discourage	DETER
		• discourage digging	DETERMINE

Letter replaced \c\at; Omit (a); Pointers *out*; Retain <u>a</u>; Split B_ED; Down (D); Backwards <or ^

• discourage man	DETERGENT
discover	
discover gnomes	SEE-SAWS
discovered by *	incl DIS
• *discovered by* an Old English . . .	ANODISE
discovered in Sou/th Eir/e	THEIR
discovered in *	incl in *
• one *discovered in* m–y . . .	MONEY
discovered journalist	FOUNDED
discovering . . .	incl in DI–S
• *discovering* me . . .	DIMES
discovering [lost] . . .	LOTS
discuss	
discuss ways	WEIGHS
discussion group	GAS-RING
great *discussion*	GRATE
disease	
disease in [China]	CHAIN
diseased [trees]	RESET, STEER, TERSE
disembody	
disembodied [souls]	SOLUS
disembodiment of [flesh]	SHELF
disentangle	
disentangle [threads]	HARDEST
disentangled [nets]	STEN
disfigure	
disfiguration of [Roman] . . .	MANOR
	NORMA, RAMON
disfigure	MAR
• disfigure girl	MARINA
• disfigure leader	MARCID
• disfigure Scot	MARIAN
disfigure [a large] . . .	LAAGER
disfiguring [icon]	COIN
disgraceful	
disgraceful [scene, a] . . .	SENECA
disgracefully [used]	DUES, DUSE, SUED
disguise	
disguised [as priest]	PIASTRES
disguised by *	incl in *
• a king *disguised by* man	LEARN
disguising a . . .	incl A
disguising *	incl *
• man *disguising* a king	LEARN
disguising m/any how/itzers	ANYHOW
dish	
dish covered with yolks	BOW-LEGGED
dish out [gruel]	LUGER
dish-*up*(D)^	TOP
dishing out [wages]	SWAGE
dishearten	
dishearten	omit centre
• *disheartened* b(o)y	BY
disheartened	CORED
	(see also core)
dishevelled	
dishevelled [robes]	BORES, SOBER
[I am] *dishevelled*	AIM
dishonest	
dishonest [ruse]	RUES, SURE, USER
dishonest tendency	BENT
disinclined	HELL-BENT
disintegrate	
disintegrating [meteor]	REMOTE
disintegrations per minute	DPM
disinter	
disinterment of [bone]	EBON
disinterred [remains]	MARINES
dislike	
dislike	THING
dislike	OFF
• dislike gangster	OFFAL
• dislike her ring, *say*	OFFERING
• disliking queen	OFFER
disjointed	
disjointed [speech]	CHEEPS
[elbow] *disjointed*	BELOW
dislocate	
dislocate [knee]	KEEN
dislocated [elbow]	BELOW, BOWEL
dislocation of [arm]	MAR, RAM
dislodge	
dislodge [bails]	BASIL
dislodging [grit in] . . .	TIRING
dismal	
dismal prisoner	GREYLAG
dismally [failed]	AFIELD
dismantle	
dismantle	UNDRESS
dismantle [crane]	CANER, NACRE
dismantling [ship]	HIPS, PISH
dismember	
dismembered [cats]	SCAT
dismemberment of [deer]	REED
dismiss	
dismiss clergy	SACKCLOTH
dismiss, *say*	SAGO
dismiss team	FIRESIDE
dismissed	OFF, OUT
dismissed, *say*	BOLD
dismissing a	omit A
dismissing *	omit *
• co(lone)l *dismissed* single . . .	COL
finally dismissed	omit last letter
• soldier *finally dismissed*	PAR(a)
one's *dismissed*	omit I
	(see also discharge)
disorder	
disorder [I cannot] . . .	CONTAIN
disorder of [bowels]	ELBOWS
disorderly guerrillas	IRREGULARS
disorderly [trainer]	RETRAIN, TERRAIN
disorganise	
disorganise [seminar]	REMAINS

Anag [cat]; Any *; Begin IGN–; Endings –ING; eg •; Hidden /cat/; Implied add (on); Implied in (in);

disorganised [army]	MARY, MYRA
disorient	
disorientation of [brain]	BAIRN
disoriented [by all] . . .	BALLY
dispatch	(*see* despatch)
dispel	
dispel [fears]	FARES
dispelling [gloom in] . . .	LOOMING
dispense	
[all remedies] *dispensed*	EMERALD ISLE
dispensation [granted]	DRAGNET
dispense with a . . .	omit A
dispense with *	omit *
• pa(ye)r *dispenses with*	
the *old* . . .	PAR
dispensed [pills]	SPILL
disperse	
dispersed [much] . . .	CHUM
dispersing [a mob]	BOMA, MOAB
dispersion of [gas]	SAG
dispirited	DISPOSSESSED, EXORCISED
displace	
displace a . . .	omit A
displace *	omit *
• (k)night *displaces* king	NIGHT
displace [silent] . . .	ENLIST, LISTEN
displaced [by a] . . .	BAY
displaced person	DP
displacement of ship	TONNAGE
displacement of [ship]	HIPS, PISH
display	
display	AIR
• display slyness	AIRCRAFT
• display tolerated	AIRBORNE
• displayed beer	AIREDALE
• displays ship's company	AIRSCREW
• displays speed	AIRSPACE
display	SHOW
• display feathers	SHOWDOWN
• display pullovers	SHOW-JUMPERS
• displays headgear	SHOW-STOPPER
and	
• display a pasture, *say*	SHOALY
• display a shirt, *say*	SHOAT
• display weapon, *say*	SHOGUN
display of [art]	RAT, TAR
displayed in Ta/te g/allery	TEG
displaying [wares]	SWEAR, WEARS
displaying wa/res in/side . . .	RESIN
display wound	SPORTS CAR
dispose	
dispose of a . . .	omit A
dispose of bodies, *say*	BARIUM
dispose of leader	omit 1st letter
dispose of money	omit D, L, P
dispose of *	omit *
• moth(er) *disposed of* queen	MOTH
disposed [to rent]	ROTTEN
disposition [of latest],	FALSETTO
disposition, *say*	MOOED
[waste] *disposal*	SWEAT, TAWSE
[ill]-*disposed*	LIL
dispossess	DISPIRIT, EXORCISE
dispute	
disputatious mathematician	WRANGLER
dispute [over] . . .	ROVE
disputed [point]	PINTO
disquiet	
disquiet	omit P or SH
• *disquiet* (P)otter	OTTER
• *disquieted* tram(p)	TRAM
• *disquieting* mar(sh)y . . .	MARY
disrupt	
disrupted [lives]	EVILS
disrupting [life]	FILE, LIEF
disruption [entails] . . .	SALIENT
dissect	
dissect [bird]	DRIB
dissection of [rats]	ARTS, STAR, TARS
disseminate	
disseminate [news]	WENS
disseminated sclerosis	DS
dissipate	
dissipate [boredom]	BEDROOM
dissipated [Poles]	LOPES, SLOPE
dissipating [asset]	SEATS
dissipation of [gas]	SAG
dissolve	
dissolution of [later] . . .	ALTER, RATEL
dissolve into [tears]	RATES, RESAT
	STARE, TARES
dissolving [a gel]	GALE, GAEL
[it was] *dissolved*	WAIST
distant	
distant	FAR
• distant China	FARMING
• distant church	FARCE
• distant object	FARTHING
• distant grass-cutter, *say*	FARCICAL
• distant sea	FARMED, FARMER
distil	
distillation of [oils]	SILO, SOIL
distilled [scent]	CENTS
distiller, *say*	JINKING
distillers	DCL
distilling [gin]	–ING
distinguished	
Distinguished Conduct Medal	DCM
Distinguished Flying	
–Cross	DFC
–Medal	DFM
distinguished member	MBE
Distinguished Service	
–Cross	DSC

Letter replaced \c\at; Omit (a); Pointers *out*; Retain a; Split B_ED; Down (D); Backwards <or ^

–Medal	DSM
–Order	DSO
distort	
distorted [faces]	CAFES
distorted fish, *say*	RILING
distortedly, *say*	RILEY
distorting [views]	WIVES
distortion of [arch]	CHAR
distract	
distracted [all the] . . .	LETHAL
distractedly [paces]	CAPES, SPACE
distraction [of a] . . .	OAF
distraught	
distraught [as one is] . . .	ANOESIS
distraught [parent I] . . .	PAINTER
distress	
distress [signal]	ALIGNS
distressed	BALD, SHORN, UNLOCKED
distressed [wives]	VIEWS
distressing	HAIRCUT(TING)
distressing [news I] . . .	SINEW
distribute	
distribute [alms]	SLAM
distribute children	ISSUE
distributed [alms on] . . .	SALMON
distribution of [rice]	ERIC
distributor, *say*	PO(O)RER
district	
District Attorney	DA
District Commissioner	DC
District of Columbia	DC
District Officer Commanding	DOC
district prize	SEAWARD
disturb	
disturb, *say*	SHEIK
disturbed [sleep]	PEELS
disturbing [reports]	PORTERS
[recent] *disturbance*	CENTRE
disunite	
disunited [team]	MATE, MEAT, TAME
disunity of [friends]	FINDERS
ditch	
ditch	HAHA
ditch digger	OFFA
ditch, *say*	MOTE
ditch worker	TRENCHANT
dither	
dithered [when I] . . .	WHINE
dithering [over] . . .	ROVE
divers	
divers	SOME, SUNDRY
divers [races]	ACERS, ACRES, CARES, SCARE
diverse	
diverse [ways]	SWAY, YAWS
diversely [sent]	NETS, STEN
divert	
[a new] *diversion*	WANE, WEAN

diversion into Turin]	NUTRITION
divert	TURN
• divert canon	TURN ROUND
• divert fish	TURNPIKE, TURNSOLE
• diverts relatives	TURNSKIN
diverted [stream]	MASTER, REMAST
divide	
a *divided* . . .	incl A
• a *divided* group	SEAT
divide	DIV
divide country	SUNDERLAND
divide workers	QUARTERSTAFF
divided by a . . .	incl A
• group *divided by* a . . .	SEAT
divided by *	incl *
• Hull, *say*, *divided by* ten	PORTENT
divided skirt	TU–
divides accommodation	QUARTERS
dividing place	DIVORCE COURT, RENO
dividing *	incl in *
• ten *dividing* Hull, *say*	PORTENT
one *divided by* five	SOLVE
divine	
divine	DD
• divine *intervention* in Cole's . . .	CODDLES
divine substance	SENSE
divorce	
divorced	DIV
divorced husband	omit H
divorced spouse	EX, TIE-BREAKER
divorced wife	omit W
divorcee	EX, TIE-BREAKER
dizzy	
dizzy city	SWIMMING BATH
dizzy [turn]	RUNT
do	
do	DO
• do a *turn*<	OD
• do nothing	DOO–
• do shake her, *say*	DOWAGER
• do *wrong*	OD
• d–o *without*	incl in D–O
do badly	SWINDLE
do entertain us, *say*	PLEASING
do *fully*	DITTO
do gooder	S, ST
do in	HOUSE PARTY
do relief work	EMBOSS
do some drawing	ATTRACT
do without a . . .	omit A
do without money	omit L
do without *	omit *
do you, *say*	JU–
• Do you haver?, *say*	JUDICA
• Do you know?	JUNO
• Do you rave?, *say*	JURANT

Anag [cat]; Any *; Begin IGN–; Endings –ING; eg •; Hidden /cat/; Implied add (on); Implied in (in);

• Do you see?, *say*	JUICY
Do you say so?	SEW, SOUGH
doing a roll, dog< . . .	GOD
doing a roll, [plane] . . .	PANEL
doing aerobatics, *say*	LUPIN
doing the rounds [near the] . . .	EARTHEN
dock	
dock brief	CUT SHORT
dock closing	PORTENDING
dock management	CLIPBOARD
docked animal	DO(g)
docked wages	PA(y)
docker's work	DETAILING
ship *docked*	LINE(r)
doctor	
doctor	BM
doctor	DR
• doctor copying	DRAPING
• doctor not well	DRILL
• doctor *with* one . . .	DRONE
• doctor works . . .	DROPS
doctor	GP, LEECH
doctor	MB
• 51 doctors	LIMBS
• 151 *have* doctor	CLIMB
• a doctor *to* the queen	AMBER
doctor	MO
• Doctor Hill	MOTOR
• doctor on unknown . . .	MOONY
• doctor with your *old* . . .	MOTHY
doctor	MD
doctor	NO, WHO
Doctor [Cameron]	CREMONA, ROMANCE
Doctor of	
–Canon and Civil Law	JUD, UJD
–Civil Law	DCL, JCD
–Dental Surgery	DDS
–Divinity	DD
–Education	DED
–Engineering	DENG, DING
–Law	LLD
–Letters	DLIT, LHD, LITD
–Literature	DLIT, LITD
–Medicine	MD
–Music	DMUS
–Philosophy	DPH, PHD
–Science	DSC, SCD
–Theology	DTH, THD
doctored [wines]	SINEW, SWINE
doctors	BMA
doctor's bag	SAC
doctors' dance	MEDICINE BALL
doctor's paper-knife	LANCET
unpopular doctor	FELL
doctrine	–ISM
document	
document	MS

document *about* . . .	DE–ED, M–S
document case, *say*	PHIAL
in document	DE–ED, M–S
written in document	DE–ED, M–S
doddering	
doddering [old men]	DOLMEN
doddering [into a] . . .	–ATION
dodge	
dodge [past]	PATS, STAP, TAPS
dodged [issues]	SUISSE
dodging [rain]	IRAN, RANI
dodgy [sort]	ORTS, ROTS, TORS
doe	
doe, *say*	BUCKSHEE
	DOH, DOUGH
doesn't	
doesn't close	omit last letter
• *doesn't close* gat(e)	GAT
• doo(r) *doesn't close*	DOO–
doesn't go	REMAINS, STAYS, STOPS
doesn't get a . . .	omit A
doesn't get on	omit ON
doesn't get *	omit *
• B(ill)y *doesn't get ill*	BY
doesn't include a . . .	omit A
doesn't include *	omit *
• fa(the)r *doesn't include* the . . .	FAR
doesn't make amen(ds)	AMEN
doesn't start (p)lay	LAY
dog¹	
Darwin's dog	BEAGLE
director's dog	POINTER
dog	BARKER
dog	CUR
• dog at home	INCUR
• dog-basket	CURBED
• dog devoured	CURATE
• dog-end	CURTAIL
• dog-fish	CURLING
• dog on hill	CURATOR
• dog trial	CURTEST
• dogged, *say*	CURD, KURD
• levy on dogs, *say*	CURT-AXE
• rear of dog	CURTAIL
• dog-bowl, *say*	KIRPAN
• dog droppings, *say*	KERMESS
dog	MUTT
• dog performing	MUTTON
dog	PUG
• dog-bird	PUGREE
• dog understands, *say*	PUG NOSE
dog blanket	AFGHAN
dog devoured . . .	PUPATE
dog does	ENDING
dog-food	CHOW
dog gnawed, *say*	LASSITUDE
dog-lead	D

Letter replaced \c\at; Omit (a); Pointers *out*; Retain a; Split B_ED; Down (D); Backwards <or ^

Dog star	POINTER, SIRIUS
dog tracks	COLLIERY
dog unit	TALBOT
dogfight	BLENHEIM
dogged policeman	HANDLER
dogma	BITCH
dogs' dinner	CHOW-CHOW
dogs notice them, *say*	COLISEUM
guide dog	POINTER
dog²	
dog	FOLLOW
• dog in <u>G</u>ates*head*	FOLLOWING
• dog *with* queen	FOLLOWER
dog	TAIL
• dog food	TAIL-BOARD
• dog breed	TAIL-RACE
• dog killer	TAILENDER
• dog parts	TAILPIECES
• Dog Star	TAIL-LIGHT
dog	TRAIL
• dogfish, *say*	TRAILING
• dog jacket	TRAIL-BLAZER
dole money	UB
dolichocephalic	HEADLONG
doll	
dolled up [tart is] . . .	ARTIST
[she was] *all dolled up*	WASHES
dollar	
a dollar (100 cents)	ACCENTS
dollar	BUCK
• dollar *and* a quarter	BUCKS
• dollar sign	BUCKRAM
• noticed dollar	SAWBUCK
dollar	DOL, S
dollar pieces	CENTS, DIMES, NICKELS
domestic	
domestic boiler	(TEA-)KETTLE
domestic rows	INDOOR FIREWORKS
domesticated saint	TAMEST
dominate	
dominate	
indicating one word written	
above another word or letter:	
• tree *dominates*	
loch(D)	SPRUCENESS
dominant bird	TOPKNOT
dominant general	PREVAILING
don	
don *	incl in *
• king *dons* ha–t	HART
donned by *	incl *
• ha–t *donned by* king	HART
Donald Duck	MANDRAKE
done	
done	OVER
• done twice	OVERDONE
done [in fat]	FAINT

[he's] *done a runner*	SHE
donkey	
donkey	ASS
• donkey always	
ate . . .	ASSEVERATE
• donkey-hire, *say*	ASSUAGE
• donkey is ill	ASSAILS
• donkey's optics, *say*	ASSIZE
donkey	NEDDY
don't	
don't begin (t)o . . .	O
don't change it	STET
don't declare	BATON
don't finish son(g)	SON
don't give up	GOON
don't open (t)he . . .	HE
don't stand	SIT
don't start (t)o . . .	O
don't stop	GOON
don't take a . . .	omit A
don't take *	omit *
• so(me) *don't take* me . . .	SO
don't tear off . . .	RIPON
doodlebug	VI
door	
back door<	ROOD
door catch	WICKET
doo<u>r</u> *closer*	R
door-handle	NAMEPLATE
door-keeper	LATCH, LOCK, TILER
door-knocker	BATTERING RAM
<u>d</u>oor *opening*	D
dope	ASS
Dora	
[Dora]	CROSSROAD
Doric	DOR
dormitory	
dormitory feast	BEDSPREAD
dormitory suburb	LAND OF NOD
dotty character	I, J
double¹	
double	BI–
• double carriageway	BIRD
• double *the* French	BILE
• Doubleday	BID
double	DI–
• Doubleday	DID
• double double	DIKA, KADI
• double poem	DIODE
double	DUAL
• double eyes, *say*	DUALISE
• double, *say*	JEWEL
• double tables, *say*	DUELLISTS
double	KA
• double double	DIKA, KADI
• double-talk	KAYAK
• double *the French* . . .	KALE

Anag [cat]; Any *; Begin IGN–; Endings –ING; eg •; Hidden /cat/; Implied add (on); Implied in (in);

double²			SHOWER, SNOW
double act	DODO	*downfall of* [kings I] . . .	SKIING
double chant	SING–SING	Downtown	NEWRY
double carriageway	MIMI	**drachma**	DR
double dose of sulphur	SS	**Draconian measure**	STERNWAY
double feature	CHIN-CHIN	**draft**	
double grave	STERN-CHASE	draft	DFT
double impact	SMASH-HIT	*drafted* [into]	–TION
double life	ISIS	**drag**	
double meat ration	CHOP-CHOP	drag	DRAW
double negative	NEVER-NEVER	• drag *back*<	WARD
double note	MIMI	• drag lake	DRAWL
double parking	PP	• drag *up*(D)^	WARD
double rations	CHOW-CHOW	drag	LUG
double share of profits	DIVI-DIVI	• drag *back*<	GUL
double stitch, *say*	SO-SO	• drag *up*<(D)^	GUL
double stomach	CRAW-CRAW	• second drag	SLUG
double your money	LL	*drag*-[race]	ACRE, ACER, CARE
(see also two²)		drag-race	TRANSVESTITES
double³		drag swag	HAUL
double bend	Z	*dragging* [a log]	GAOL, GOAL
double cross	TWENTY, TWO TIMES	**drain**	
double eyes, *say*	DUALISE	drain rod, *say*	LOOP-HOLE
double-*header*	D	drainpipe	EXHAUST
double, *say*	WRINGER	**dram**	DR
double table, *say*	DUELLIST	**drama writer**	PLAYPEN
double tea, *say*	DOUBLET	**drank**	
double vision	DOPPELGANGER, LOOK-SEE	drank	TOPED
doublet	TT	drank heartily, *say*	COIFFED
doubly		drank *up*(D)^	DEPOT
doubly deep	SEA-BASS	(*see also* drink, drunk)	
doubly depressed	LOW-DOWN	**drastic**	
doubly finished	OVERDONE	drastic method	STERNWAY
doubly good	BON-BON	*drastic* [step]	PEST, PETS
doubly hard	HH	*drastically* [alter]	LATER
doubly healthy, *say*	WELL-HOLE	**draught**	
doubly loud	FF	draught beer	OUT OF THE WOOD
doubly low	DOWN UNDER	draughty passage	FLUE
doubly mute, *say*	DUM-DUM	**draw**	
doubly quiet	HUSH-HUSH, PP	draw	TIE
doubt		• draw game	TIEPOLO
doubt	ER, UM	• draw*back*<	EIT
doubter	THOMAS	draw	X
doubtful [result]	LUSTRE	draw at this point, *say*	HAULIER
doughboy	GI, GRUNT	draw fee	TOWAGE
down		*draw from* t/he r/anks	HER
down container	BLUEBOTTLE	draw hooligan, *say*	PULL-OUT
down-hearted	incl LOW	*draw in* a . . .	incl A
• s–ing down*heartedly*	SLOWING	*draw in* *	incl *
down-*hearted*	OW	• sh–ow *draws in* everybody	SHALLOW
Down here	IRELAND	draw knight, *say*	TOWSER
down-market bird	EIDER(DUCK)	draw male . . .	PULLMAN
down the pit, *say*	INDAMINE	*drawn in by* *	incl in *
downcast	MOULT(ED)	• everybody *drawn in*	
downfall	AVALANCHE	by sh–ow	SHALLOW
CATARACT, RAPIDS, WATERFALL		*drawn into**	incl in *
HAIL, RAIN, SLEET,		• woman *drawn into*	

wicked . . .	BASHED	• drill for coal, *say*	BORECOLE
[draw] *out*	WARD	drill	PE, PT
draw *up*(D)^	EIT, WARD	drill, *say*	AUGUR, BOAR
draw*back*<	EIT, WARD	*drill* [sergeant]	ESTRANGE
drawback part . . .<	TRAP	drilled, *say*	AUGURED, BOARD
drawer	ARTIST, DR	drilling rig	BRACE
	MAGNET	drilling site	DENTIST'S CHAIR
drawer *overturned*<	RD, REWARD		PARADE GROUND
drawing material	TOBACCO	**drink**	
drawing-room	STUDIO	drink	HOCK
drawn from fa/r an/d wide	RAN	• 100 drinks	CHOCKS
dreadful		• drink joint	HOCK
dreudful [rage]	GEAR	• second drink	SHOCK
dreadful service	BADMINTON	drink	LAP
dreadfully [made]	DAME, EDAM, MEAD	• drink *to* favourite	LAPPET
dreamer	JOSEPH	• drink when flying (=on wing)	LAPWING
dress		• fine drink	FLAP
dress	DON	drink	PORTER
dress	GARB	• claim drink	IMPORTER
• dress circle	GARBO	• drink *before* time	PORTERAGE
• dress in front . . .	GARBLED	• drink stout	SUPPORTER
• dress lubricant	GARBOIL	drink	SHORT
dress	GEAR	• drink before time	SHORTAGE
• dress adjustment	GEAR SHIFT	• drink *with* food	SHORTBREAD
• dress journalist	GEARED	• round of drinks	SHORT CIRCUIT
• dressed	IN GEAR	drink	SUP
dress	HABIT	• drink beer	SUPPORTER
• dress custom	HABIT	• drink *to* model	SUPPOSE
• dress-making	HABIT-FORMING	• drink wine	SUPPORT
• dressed	INHABIT	drink	TEA
dress business	SHIFTWORK	• drink alone	TEASINGLY
dress [circle]	CLERIC	• drink feature	TEACH-IN
dress-maker	CLOTH, FABRIC	• drink increased	TEA-ROSE
	NEEDLE, SATIN, WOOL etc	drink dispenser	GANYMEDE, HEBE
dress [sense]	ESSEN	drink manufacturer	STILL
dress *up*(D)^	EBOR	drink pop	HOCK
dressed by *	incl in *	drink problem	DT(S)
• fish *dressed by* ma–n	MAIDEN	drink round	LAP
dressed hair, *say*	QUAFFED	drink *round*<	EMIL, PAL, PIN, PUS
dressed [hare]	HEAR, RHEA	drink, *say*	(D)JINN, WHINE
dressed up [in gown]	OWNING		TAKES UP
dressed up in *	incl in *	drink too much	OVERLAP
• king *dressed up in* robe	GROWN	drink *up*	STIRRUP-CUP
dresses Arab	CLOTHES HORSE	drink *up*(D)^	EMIL, PAL, PIN, PUS
dressing a . . .	incl A	drink wallop	PUNCH
dressing-table	PLASTERBOARD	*drink* *	incl *
dressing-[table]	BLATE, BLEAT	• wa–g *drinks* gin	WAGING
dressing *	incl *	drinking, *say*	WHINING
• ma–n *dressing* a fish	MAIDEN		(*see also* drank, drunk)
drift		**drive**	
drift into [port so] . . .	TROOPS	drive	DR
drifter	TRAMP STEAMER	drive sheep	RAM
drifting [ship]	HIPS, PISH	*drive up* motorway(D)^	IM–
drill		drivers	AA, RAC
drill	BORE	driver's place	TEE
• drill at a spot, *say*	BORACITE	driving	(in) CA–R
• drill deeper, *say*	BORON	• award *driving* . . .	CAMBER

driving force	HIGHWAY PATROL	drove	(see drive)
	POLICE CAR(S)	**drown**	
	TRAFFIC POLICE	*drowned in* *	incl in *
driving instructor	COACHMAN	• learner *drowned in* river	CLAM
driving [rain]	IRAN, RANI	*drowning* a . . .	incl A
drove one mad	SENTIMENTAL	*drowning* *	incl *
drop¹		• river *drowning* learner	CLAM
indicating inclusion:		**drug**	
dropping in a...	incl A	drug-taking	incl E
dropping in *	incl *	• drug-*taking* m–an	MEAN
• *dropping* students *in* river	TALLY	drug	ACID
drop²		• drug I see, *say*	ACIDIC
indicating omission:		• drug trial	ACID TEST
drop a . . .	omit A	• p(a)l *without* a drug	PLACID
drop a line	omit AL, ARY	drug	SPEED
drop a note	omit A, B, C, D, E, F, G	• drug dealer	SPEED MERCHANT
drop a point	omit N, S, E, W	• drug in college	SPEED UP
drop dead	omit D	• drug rate	SPEED
drop end of plan(k)	PLAN	• drug source	SPEEDWELL
drop money	omit L	drug	UPPER
drop off a . . .	omit A	• drug container	UPPER CASE
drop off *	omit *	• drug worker	UPPER HAND
drop out *	omit *	• second drug	SUPPER
drop quietly *off*	omit P, SH	drug dispenser	CHEMIST
drop *	omit *	drug excess	OD
• ski(p) and *drop* coin	SKI	drug, *say*	COCKAIGNE
*drop*head	omit 1st letter	drug supplier	POPPY, PUSHER
• *drop*head (c)ar *with* my . . .	ARMY	**drum**	
dropped letter		drum music	REEL
• Pat *has dropped* letter	AT, PA	drummer	DR
dropped letter	H	**drunk**	
dropping a . . .	omit A	[dead] *drunk*	–ADED, EDDA
dropping in	omit IN	drunk	(in) AL–E
• pa(in)ter *dropping* in	PATER	• drunk at . . .	ALATE
dropping out	omit OUT	• drunk on . . .	ALONE
• nearly *dropping* out	AB(out)	• four drunken . . .	ALIVE
dropping *	omit *	drunk	HIGH
• (p)arty *dropping* leader	ARTY	• drunken Communist, *say*	HIRED
drop³		• drunken friend, *say*	HIEMATE
other uses:		• drunken people, *say*	HYMEN
drop a little . . .	TASTE	• drunken sailor, *say*	HIGHJACK, HIJACK
drop building	SHED	• drunken woman, *say*	HY(A)ENA, HYGIENE
drop discrimination	TASTE	drunk	LIT
drop in current	CASCADE, WATERFALL	• drunk about . . .	LITRE
drop in the ocean	EBB(-TIDE), LOW TIDE	• drunken man	LITHE
drop litter	FARROW, WHELP	• saint *in* drunken . . .	LIST
drop note	MINIM	drunk	OILED
drop of water	W	• 100 drunken . . .	COILED
drop of water	EBB(-TIDE), WATERFALL	• drunken counsel	OILED SILK
drop off	SLEEP	• second drunk	SOILED
[drop]-*off*	DORP, PROD	drunk	TIGHT
[drop]-*out*	DORP, PROD	• drunk on H₂O	WATERTIGHT
drop rent	TEAR	• drunk on hemp	TIGHTROPE
dropped letter	H	• drunken head	TIGHTNESS
dropping stones	HAIL	*drunk and disorderly* [men at] . . .	MEANT
dropping zone	PARASITE	*drunk by* *	incl in *
drops of water	FALLS, RAIN, RAPIDS	• gin *drunk by* wa–g	WAGING

Letter replaced \c\at; Omit (a); Pointers *out*; Retain a; Split B_ED; Down (D); Backwards <or ∧

drunk on [gin]	–ING
drunken characters from	
[Leeds are] . . .	RELEASED
drunken nap	TIDDLYWINKS
drunken [sots]	TOSS
drunken [speech]	CHEEPS
drunken speech	
substitute SH for S	
• *drunkard's* sort . . .	SHORT
• *drunken* sort	SHORT
• selfish *in the pub*	SHELLFISH
(*see also* drank, drink)	
dry	
dried grape, *say*	RAISING
dry	AIR
• dry *up*(D)^	RIA
• dry wine	AIRPORT
dry	SEC
• dry *up*(D)^	CES
• dry worker	SECANT
dry	TT
dry in the open air	SUNDRY
dual carriageway	MIMI
dubious	
dubious [dealing]	LEADING
dubious dealing in [lira]	ARIL, LAIR
	LIAR, RAIL
dubious [fate]	FEAT
[stare] *dubiously*	ASTER, RATES
	TARES, TEARS
ducal footwear	WELLINGTONS
duck	
Donald Duck	MANDRAKE
duck	O
• duck feathers	OPINIONS
• duck-house	OCELLAR, OPEN
• duck liver	OLIVER
• duck's eggs	OO
• portion of duck	ORATION
and	
• duck *in* the mud	MOIRE
• duck *in* the road	SOT
• eat meal *including* duck	SOUP
and	
• duck *on* her . . .	HERO
• father-duck	DADO
• leg of duck	LIMBO
• shoot at duck	POTATO
duck á l'orange	MANDARIN
duck *eaten* . . .	incl O
duck-farm, *say*	QUACKERY
duck shooter, *say*	FOULER
ducked	UNDERWENT
duck-*keeping*	incl O
due	
[due] *for conversion*	EDU, –UDE
due, *say*	DUE

duly performed	DP
duff	
duff [part]	RAPT, TRAP
[lamp] *is duff*	PALM
[treacle] *duff*	ELECTRA
dug	
dug	MINED
dug out of ear/th in G/ermany	THING
dug, *say*	MIND
dug *up*(D)^	DEMIN
[dug]*out*	–UDG–
(*see also* dig)	
duke	FIST
duke's handwriting	FIST
duke's protector	KNUCKLE-DUSTER
dull	
dull	DIM
• dull eater, *say*	DIMETER
• dull porcelain	DIMMING
dull	FLAT
• dull accommodation	FLAT
• dull man	FLATTED
• dull trial	FLATTEST
dull *and* fat, *say*	DULLARD
dull film	TARNISH
dull hooter	GREY-OWL
dumb man	MALEMUTE
dunderhead	
dunderhead	D
dunderheaded boy	DREG
dunderheaded [male]	LAME, MEAL
duplicate	
duplicate essays	GOGO
duplicate *French* word	MOT-MOT
duplicate keys	AA, BB, CC
	DD, EE, FF, GG
duplicate sounds	HUM-HUM
duplicate tests	MOT-MOT
duplicating your . . .	YORE
(*see also* double, two)	
Durham area	NE
during	
during he/r ear/ly . . .	REAR
during March	INFRINGE
during Prohibition	(in) DO–NT
during race	(in) T–T
during, *say*	WILE
during school	(in) TER–M
during *	incl in *
• fiddle *during* pla–y	PLAGUEY
	(*see also* in²)
Dutch	
Dutch	DU
Dutch capital	GUILDER, GULDEN
Dutch *capital*	D
Dutch *leader*	D
Dutch ship, *say*	COUGH

Anag [cat]; Any *; Begin IGN–; Endings –ING; eg •; Hidden /ca*t*/; Implied add (on); Implied in (in);

dwarf
  dwarf   DOC, MINUTEMAN
  dwarf fish   TROLL
  dwarf's sayings   GNOMES

dwindle
  dwindling hop(e)   HOP
  (s)tore(s) *dwindled*   TORE

dynamic
  dynamic [action]   CATION
  dynamically [leads]   DALES, DEALS
                          LADES, SLADE

dynamo(meter)   DYN
dyne   DYN

E

Asian, Balearic Islands, boat, bridge player, Canary Islands, Earth, east, Easter, eastern, Ecstasy, Edward, eight, eight thousand, electromotive force, electron charge, electronic, Elizabeth, energy, England, English, epsilon, eta, European, exa-, five, five thousand, food additive, key, layer, logarithm base, *low-grade*, *mail*, natural base, note, *Orient*, *Oriental*, region, Spain, Spanish Guinea, Spanish Sahara, string, two hundred and fifty (thousand), universal set, vitamin.

each	
each	AHEAD, EA
each	PER
• each change	PERMUTATION
• each letterhead	PERMISSIVENESS
• each employer	PERUSER
each side of . . .	
indicating inclusion:	
• *put* on *each side of* one	ONION
• ways *on each side of* pond	SPONDEE
each way	
indicating a palindrome:	
• blow *each way*	TOOT
• look *each way*	PEEP
• looks *each way*	SEES
• time *each way*	NOON
each year	PA
ear	
ear, nose and throat	ENT
ear ornament, *say*	HEARING
ear, *say*	ORACLE
ears burning	EARSHOT
earl	COUNT
earl's daughter, *say*	MISCOUNT
early	
earlier, *say*	PRIER, PRYER
early bath	BAPTISM
early bird ARCHAEOPTERYX, PTERODACTYL	
	EVE
	SATELLITE
early birds	BI
early examples of Roman art	
form to . . .	RAFT
early flier ARCHAEOPTERYX, PTERODACTYL	
	ICARUS, WRIGHT
early landfall	ARARAT
early letters	ATOC
early morning	IAM
early picture	FRONTISPIECE
early riser	SUN

early risers	FIRST STEPS
early sign	S
early sign *of* spring	S
early stage	BUD
early stage	S
early stages of his life	HL
early transport	PERAMBULATOR, PRAM
	PUSH-CHAIR
early warning system	DEW
earn	NET
earth	
[earth]-*moving*	HATER, HEART, RATHE
[earth]-*shattering*	HATER, HEART, RATHE
earthling	GLOBE-FISH
[earth]*quake*	HATER, HEART, RATHE
[earth]*work*	HATER, HEART, RATHE
ease	
ease burden	CONTENT
ease, *say*	EE, ES
easily [won]	NOW, OWN
Easy	MIDSHIPMAN
easy remedy	SIMPLE
east	
east	E
• East River	–ER
• h–ard *out* East	HEARD
• in the East	–INE
East Africa	EA
East Central	EC
East *End*	T
east end of town	N
East Ender	(*see* Cockney)
East *Ender*	T
East *French*	EST
East *German*	OST
east-north-east	ENE
east *of* Berlin	OST
east *of* Paris	EST
East River	GANGES
east-south-east	ESE

Anag [cat]; Any *; Begin IGN–; Endings –ING; eg •; Hidden /cat/; Implied add (on); Implied in (in);

out East	omit E
out [East]	SATE, SEAT
eastwards	TOE
from East	TOW
eastern	
eastern	E
• Eastern agent	ESPY
• Eastern country	ESTATE
• Eastern property	EQUALITY
• Eastern ruler	EKING
• Eastern traveller	EMIGRANT
and	
• in Eastern . . .	–INE
eastern dish	HOURI
eastern garment, *say*	JIBBER
Eastern Standard Time	EST
easy	
easy, *say*	EEC
(*see* ease)	
eat	
eat	WOLF
• eat animals	WOLF-CUBS
• eat fish, *say*	WOLFISH
• eat sheep	WOLFRAM
• eat *with* family	WOLFKIN
cat a . . .	incl A
eat, *say*	BIGHT, BYTE
	IN JEST
eat turkey	GOBBLE
eat vegetables	SUPPLANTS
eat *	incl *
• man *eats* roll	TROLLED
eaten by *	incl in A
• roll *eaten by* man	TROLLED
eaten by mo/st Ar/menians	STAR
eating away part of (c)oast	OAST
eating fish	FINISHING SCHOOL
eating into *	incl in *
• the *French eat into* foo–d	FOOLED
eau de Cologne	RHINE
eavesdrop	
eavesdropper	ICICLE
eavesdropping on one	
who interferes	MEDLAR
two *eavesdropping*	PEAR, TU–, TOO
ebb	
ebb-tide	WATERFALL
ebbing sea<	DEM–, REM–
ebbing tide<	EDIT
eccentric	
eccentric	CAM
• eccentric age	CAMERA
• eccentric fool	CAMASS
• eccentric man	CAMBRIAN
eccentric	CARD
• eccentric's instrument	CARDSHARP

eccentric	CRANK
• eccentric suit	CRANKCASE
• eccentric will, *say*	CRANKLE
• eccentric's handle . . .	CRANKSHAFT
eccentric	NUT
• eccentric *and* mad	NUT-CRACKERS
• eccentric breed	NUTHATCH
• eccentric woman	NUTMEG
eccentric	RUM
• eccentric in workers' . . .	RUMINANTS
• eccentric, *say*	RHUMB
• eccentrics' dance	RUM-SHOP
eccentric [teacher]	CHEATER
ecclesiastical member	CHARM
echo	
echo of guns<	SNUG
echoing a noise	ANNOYS
echoing sound	RHYME
echoist	PARROT
economy	
economical bowl	MAIDEN
economise	USELESS
economist	MILL, SMITH, *et al*
ecstatic	
Ecstasy (drug)	E
ecstatic	SENT
ecstatic [state]	TEATS
Ecuador	
Ecuador	EC
capital of Ecuador	E
leader of Ecuador	E
eddy	NELSON
edge	
edge cut	RIMSAW
edge of cliff	LANDSLIP
edge of cliff	C
edge of court	ADVANTAGE
edge of court	C
edge of pine	SIDELONG
edge of pine	P
edged by *	incl in *
• feature *edged by* silver	ACHING
edging a . . .	incl A
edging *	incl *
• silver *edging to* feature	ACHING
edges of table	TE
edit	
edit<	TIDE OVER
edited	ED, EDIT
edited [indent]	INTEND, TINNED
editing instruction	STET
editing [text or] . . .	EXTORT
edition	ED, EDIT
edition of [a last] . . .	ATLAS
editor	ED
[editor] *edited*	RIOTED
editor of 'Playboy'	FUNKING

Letter replaced \c\at; Omit (a); Pointers *out*; Retain a̱; Split B_ED; Down (D); Backwards <or ^

editor, *say*	CENSER, SENSOR
editor [wrote]	TOWER
educate	
educated man	MA
• educated Scot	MASCOT
educational centre	MIDDLE SCHOOL
educational *centre*	T
educational journal	TES
educational establishment	ETON, U
educational skill	R
educational supplement	TES
educationalist	BED
educationally subnormal	ESN
educationist	BED
educationists	DES
English education	RRR
Edward	
Edward II	SECONDER
Edward II	D
Edward expired	EDDIED
Edward Knight	SIRED
Edward made, *say*	EDDIED
Edward struck her, *say*	EDITOR
EEC	
EEC	TWELVE
EEC, *say*	EASY
e–emperor	EKING
effort	
effortless	omit TRY
• effort*less* indus(try)	INDUS
effortless flight	ESCALATOR
egg	
egg	O, OVAL, SPUR
egg container	NEST, SHELL
egg-making, *say*	OVATION
egg supplier	HEN, OVARY
egg-*topping*(D)	E
egg white, *say*	GLARE
egg yellow, *say*	LUTINE
*egg*head	E
scrambled [eggs]	SEGG
ego	
[ego]-*trip*	GEO–
egoism, *perhaps*	EYE TROUBLE
Egypt	
Egypt	ET
• Egypt *almost* alon(e)	ETALON
• Egypt *and* her ...	ETHER
• Egypt *joins with* North America	ETNA
and	
• archdeacon *in* Egypt	EVENT
• father *in* Egypt	EPOPT
• I study *in* Egypt	EIDENT
• the record is *in* Egypt	ELOGIST
and	
• draw Egypt ...	PULLET

• charge Egypt ...	BILLET
• odds in Egypt	SPINET
Egyptian capital	PIASTRES
Egyptian *capital*	E
Egyptian *flower*	NILE
Egyptian *leader*	E
Egyptian king, *say*	FARO
Egyptian kings, *say*	FAROES
eight	
eight Christmas presents	MILKMAIDS
eight hundred	O, OMEGA
eight hundred thousand	O, OMEGA
eight-nil	EIGHTY
eight-nil, *say*	ATE TEA
eight notes	OCTAVE
eight rowers	CREW
eight, *say*	AIT, ATE, EYOT
one over the eight	DRUNK, NINE
eighteen	
eighteen	MAJORITY, MANAGE
eighteen holes	ALL ROUND
	GOLF COURSE
eighteen in team	AUSTRALIAN RULES
eighteen leaves	
per sheet	EIGHTEENMO
	OCTODECIMO
eighteen letters	–ATOR
eighth	
eighth note	QUAVER
eighth part of circle	OCTANT
eighty	
eighty	P, PI, R
eighty-eight	PIANO
eighty, *say*	ATE TEA
eighty thousand	P, PI, R
either	
either end of <u>house</u>	HE
either way	
indicating a palindrome:	
• blow *either way*	TOOT
• *either way*, it's flat	LEVEL
• look *either way*	PEEP
	(*see also* each)
eject	
eject a ...	omit A
eject Turner	SPIT
eject *	omit *
• escort *ejects* hard ...	US(h)ER
• man *ejected by* small(les)t ...	SMALT
ejected from mee/tin/g	TIN
El Salvador	ES
elaborate	
elaborate [robes]	BOERS, BORES, SOBER
elaboration of [ideas]	AIDES, SADIE
el	
el	L
els	LL, LS

Anag [cat]; Any *; Begin IGN–; Endings –ING; eg •; Hidden /cat/; Implied add (on); Implied in (in);

elastic	
elastic [rope]	PORE
elasticated [edges]	SEDGE
elbow bender	BICEPS
elderly convict	GREYLAG
elect	
elected	IN
• *elected* friend	INMATE
• *elected* officer	IN GENERAL
• steal from *elected* . . .	ROBIN
election day, *say*	TUESDAY
election fever, *say*	BALLETOMANIA
electoral system	PR
electric	
electrical charge	Q
electric current	AC, DC, I
electric fence	RADIO RECEIVER
electric *lead*	E
electric unit	AH, AMP, VOLT
electrical capacity	C
electrical unit, *say*	WHAT, WOT
electricity	AC
• electricity *in* iron	FACE
• electricity money	ACCENTS
• price of electricity	ACCOSTS
electricity bill	CURRENT ACCOUNT
	(*see also* current)
electro-	
electro-cardiogram	ECG
electro-convulsive therapy	ECT
electro-encephalogram	ECG
electro-magnetic unit	EMU
electromotive force	EMF
electro-plated	EP
electrostatic unit	ESU
electron	
electron-volt	EV
electronic data processing	EDP
elegant	
elegant beasts	NEAT
elegant cape	NEATNESS
elegant, *say*	SHEIK(H)
element[1]	
ancient	AIR, EARTH, FIRE, WATER
modern	
commonly used names:	
argon	A
barium	BA
calcium	CA
carbon	C
chlorine	CL
chromium	CR
cobalt	CO
copper	CU
fluorine	F
gold	AU, OR
helium	HE

hydrogen	H
iodine	I
iridium	IR
iron	FE
krypton	KR
lead	PB
magnesium	MG
manganese	MN
mercury	AZOTH, HG
neon	NE
nickel	NI
nitrogen	AZOTE, N
oxygen	O
phosphorus	P
platinum	PT
plutonium	PU
potassium	K
radium	RA
radon	RN
silicon	SI
silver	AG, ARGENTUM
sodium	NA
strontium	SR
sulphur	S
tin	SN
titanium	TI
tungsten	W
uranium	U
zinc	ZN
elements	–IC, –CK, SC etc
element[2]	
element in mo/st ar/ticles	STAR
element of trage/dy in g/reat . . .	DYING
elevated	
elevated land	UP COUNTRY
elevated railway	EL
elevated road	EL
elevated road(D)^	DR, EVA, IM, TS
eleven	
eleven	LEGS, O, TEAM, XI
eleven	SIDE
• eleven children	SIDE ISSUE
eleven Christmas presents	PIPERS
eleven hundred	MC
eleven thousand	O
elevens(es)	SNACK
eleventh	
eleventh hour	COFFEE TIME
eleventh hour revival	LATERALLY
eliminate	
eliminate a . . .	omit A
eliminate about . . .	omit C, CA, RE
eliminate *	omit *
• pur(g)e *eliminates* 1000	PURE
• (p)urge *eliminates* leader	URGE
Eliza	
Eliza (=Cockney)	

• *Eliza's* (h)at	AT	*embracing* *	incl*
• (h)old *for Eliza*	OLD	• b–oy *embracing* you, *say*	BUOY
	(see also Cockney)	**embroider**	
Elizabeth		[altar] *embroidery*	TALAR
Elizabeth II	SECONDER	*embroider* [T-shirt]	THIRST
El̲izabeth II	L	embroidered yarn	TALL STORY
ell	L	**embroil**	
ells	LL, LS	*embroiled in* *	incl in *
elocution		• a king *embroiled in* row	TARIFF
elocution heard	HERD	*embroiling* a . . .	incl A
maid *in elocution*	MADE	*embroiling* *	incl *
elsewhere		• row *embroiling* a king	TARIFF
elsewhere, say	KNOTTIER	**emend**	
elusive		*emendation of* [line]	LIEN, NEIL, NILE
elusive [bird]	DRIB	*emended* [phrase]	SHAPER
[act] *elusively*	CAT, TAC–	*emending* [verses]	SERVES
em		**emerge**	
em	M	*emerging from* mi/st at e/nd . . .	STATE
ems	MM, MS	**eminent pupil**	BIG APPLE
emaciated ruler	THINKING	**emit**	
emancipated worker	FREE HAND	emit fire	SHOOT
embargo		emit, *say*	POOR, PORE
embargo	BAN	**emperor**	
• embargo expired	BANDIED	emperor	EMP, NERO, OTTO
• embargo *on* 500 . . .	BAND	emperor, *say*	SEIZE HER, SEIZER, SEIZOR
• embargo *on* one building	BANISHED	**empire**	
embark		empire state	NY
embark on journey	J	empire woman	DBE
embarkation of t̲roops	T	**employ**	
embarrass		*employ* a . . .	incl A
be embarrassed	GORED	*employ* *	incl *
embarrassed	RED	• student *employed in* b–and	BLAND
• embarrassed player	REDACTOR	employ painter	MOOR, TIE-UP
embarrassed [all the] . . .	LETHAL	employ, *say*	EWES, YEWS
embarrassing [remark]	MARKER	employed	INFIRM, INWORK
embed		*employed by* manu/fact/urer	FACT
embedded in so/lid o/nyx	LIDO	*employed in* m/unit/ions	UNIT
embedded in *	incl in *	Employment Exchange	TRADE
• queen *embedded in* stones	ROCKERS	**empty**	
embedding a . . .	incl A	empty	O
embedding *	incl *	• *empty*, empty space	OVOID
• stones *embedding* queen..	ROCKERS	• *empty* space	OZONE
embody		• *empty* wood	OPINE
embodied in *	incl in *	empty	incl O
• old *embodied in* attempt . . .	TRAGEDY	• *empty* bed	COOT
embodied in o/ne st/atute	NEST	• *empty* container	–TION
embody a . . .	incl A	• *empty* ship	SOS
embodying *	incl *	empty drain	EXHAUST
• attempt *embodying*		empty-*headed*	start with O
old . . .	TRAGEDY	• *empty-headed* boy	ODES
embrace		• e̲mpty-*headed* girl	OKAY
all-*embracing*	incl ALL	• e̲mpty-*headed* teacher is . . .	OSIRIS
• m–et all-*embracing* . . .	MALLET	e̲mpty-*headed*	E
embraced by *	incl in *	• empty-*headed* agent	ESPY
• you, *say, embraced by* b–oy	BUOY	• empty-*headed* boy	EVICTOR
embraced in stron/g ar/ms	GAR	• empty-*headed* girl	EROSE
embracing a . . .	incl A	empty net	CLEAR

Anag [cat]; Any *; Begin IGN–; Endings –ING; eg •; Hidden /cat/; Implied add (on); Implied in (in);

empty, *say*	VANE, VEIN
empty vault	CLEAR
indicating omission	
of middle:	
• *emptied* m(agazin)e	ME
• *empty* h(ous)e	HE
• *empty* b(a)r	BR
• r(apidl)y *emptied*	RY
en	
en	N
en route	(in) CA–R, (in) R–D, (in) S–T
en voyage	(in)S–S
ens	NN, NS
encage	
encaged	(in) C–AGE
encaged by *	incl in *
• owl *encaged by* B–ing	BOWLING
encaged in ste/el m/esh	ELM
encaging a . . .	incl A
encaging *	incl *
• B–ing *encaging* owl	BOWLING
encapsulate	
encapsulated in word/s	
of a/ sage	SOFA
hi/s word/s *encapsulated*	SWORD
encase	
encased in concre/te ar/ound . . .	TEAR
encased in *	incl in *
• gold *encased in* iron	FORE
encasing a . . .	incl A
encasing *	incl *
• iron *encasing* gold	FORE
enchanting insect	SPELLING BEE
encipher	
encipher [signal]	ALIGNS
encipherment of [all the] . . .	LETHAL
encircle	
encircle a . . .	incl A
encircle *	incl *
• water *encircles* rat	DERATE
encircled by *	incl in *
• rat *encircled by* water	DERATE
enclose	
enclose nerve	BOTTLENECK
enclosed in a b/ig loo/p	IGLOO
enclosed in *	incl in *
• auditor *enclosed in* sh–ed	SHEARED
enclosed, *say* BLOCK-TIN, WAULED, WAWLED	
enclosing a . . .	incl A
enclosing *	incl *
• sh–ed *enclosing* auditor	SHEARED
enclosure in wi/de cor/ral	DECOR
large *enclosure*	BI–G
• family *in* large *enclosure*	BIKING
encompass	
encompass a . . .	incl A
encompass *	incl *

• pla–n *encompassing* one . . .	PLAIN
encompassed by *	incl in *
• one *encompassed by* pla–n	PLAIN
encompassed in Engli/sh ed/ition	SHED
encounter	
encounter (=run into)	
• run *into* BT . . .	BRUNT
encounter, *say*	MEAT, METE
	POULTRY-KEEPER
encountered	MET
• encountered a number,	
say	METAPHOR
• encountered a road	
marker, *say*	METACONE
• encountered engineer	METRE
• encountered	
previously, *say*	METAPHOR
encountered in mo/st	
art/ists . . .	START
encrypt	
encrypted [verses]	SEVERS
encryption of [German] . . .	MANGER
end	
end of/*end of*	
–cake	ROLLOVER
–cak<u>e</u>	E
–crossing	PASSOVER
–crossin<u>g</u>	G
–go	TURNOVER
–g<u>o</u>	O
–draw	PULLOVER
–dra<u>w</u>	W
–filming	TAKEOVER
–filmin<u>g</u>	G
–June	THIRTIETH
–Jun<u>e</u>	E
–line	BUFFERS
–lin<u>e</u>	E
–music	CODA
–musi<u>c</u>	C
–prayer	AMEN
–praye<u>r</u>	R
–quarrel	ARROWHEAD
–quarre<u>l</u>	L
–race	TAPE
–rac<u>e</u>	E
–season	(sum)MER, (win)TER
–seaso<u>n</u>	N
–the . . .	E
–the roa<u>d</u>	D
–the war	VE, VJ
–the wa<u>r</u>	R
–the world	ARMAGEDDON, RAGNAROK
–the worl<u>d</u>	D
–training	TERMINUS
–trainin<u>g</u>	G
end paper	DEATH CERTIFICATE

Letter replaced \c\at; Omit (a); Pointers *out*; Retain <u>a</u>; Split B_ED; Down (D); Backwards <or ^

end protest	OBJECT	• English clergyman	ERECTOR
end-to-end lever	REVEL	• English country	ELAND, ESTATE
end *up*(D)^	MIA, PIT, POT, POTS	• English flower	EASTER
endless bel(t)	BEL	• English landowner	ESQUIRE
endless (f)light	LIGHT	• English team	EXI–
endlessly talk	DISCUS(s)	• English trees	EYEWASH
ends of <u>May</u> and <u>April</u>	MYAL	• English woman	EPAULETTE
ends *off* th(e) ree(d)	THREE	• Englishmen	EVICTED
ends *up*(D)^	SPIT, SPOT, SPOTS	English	ENG
loose [ends]	DENS, SEND	• English nation	ENGRACE
<u>loose</u> *ends*	LE	• English period	ENGAGE
endear	LOBE	• English waterfall	ENGRAIN
enemy		• English lunatic	ENGRAVING
enemy	TIME	English banker	THAMES etc
• enemy *retreating<*	EMIT	English capital	STERLING
<u>enemy</u> *front*	E	<u>English</u> *capital*	E
energy		English country music	NATIONAL ANTHEM
energy	E	English *flower*	THAMES etc
energy figures	VIM	<u>English</u> *leader*	E
engage		English linesman	KEATS et al
engaged in [war]	RAW	[English] *resort*	SHINGLE
engaged in w/ar t/o . . .	ART	English vale	FAREWELL, GOODBYE
engaged in *	incl in *	**English²**	
• chief *engaged in* de–ed	DECIDED	English as a	
engagement ring	ARENA, WARRING	–foreign language	EFL
	(*see also* battle)	–second language	ESL
engaging a . . .	incl A	English Chamber Orchestra	ECO
engaging *	incl *	English Church Union	ECU
• de–ed *engaging* the		English Dialect Society	EDS
chief . . .	DECIDED	English Golf Union	EGU
engender		English language teaching	ELT
engender [fear]	FARE	English Speaking Union	ESU
engendered by [lots] . . .	SLOT	**engrave**	
engendering [hate]	HEAT	engrave	BURY, INTER
engine		engrave worker	ETCHANT
engine driver	STEAM	engraved line, *say*	HATCHER
engine noise	CARPING	engraver	ENG
engineman	STEPHENSON, WATT		FUNERAL DIRECTOR
engineer			UNDERTAKER
engineer(s)	CE	engravers	RE
• engineers *almost* well off	CERIC (h)	engraving	ENG
• engineer *gets* wage increase	CERISE	**engulf**	
• engineer learners *have* nothing	CELLO	*engulfed by* *	incl in *
engineer	ENG	• one *engulfed by* wa–ve	WAIVE
engineer(s)	RE	*engulfed in* re/bell/ion	BELL
• engineer designs	REDRAWS	*engulfing* a . . .	incl A
• engineer *with a* vehicle	REBUS	*engulfing* *	incl *
• engineer's gallery	RESTATE	• wa–ve *engulfing* one . . .	WAIVE
• engineers teach . . .	RESTRAIN	**enigma**	
engineer(s)	REME	*enigma* [of Al] . . .	FOAL, LOAF
• engineer's graduated scale	REMEDIAL	[Enigma] *Variation*	GAMINE
• engineer's unknown quantity	REMEX	[real] *enigma*	LEAR
• test engineers, *say*	TRIREME	**enjoying hot weather**	(in) SU–N
engineer [has to] . . .	OATHS, SHOAT	**enlist**	
English¹		*enlist* a . . .	incl A
<u>England</u>'s *opening pair*	EN	*enlist* *	incl *
English	E	• navy *enlists* first-class . . .	RAIN

enlisted by *	incl in *		*(see also* entrance)
• I've *been enlisted by*		**entertain**	
the navy	RIVEN	*entertain* a . . .	incl A
enliven		*entertain* *	incl *
enliven [dance]	CANED	• drink *to entertain* judge	ALLUDE
enlivened [by a] . . .	BAY	• ho–st *entertains* beginner	HOLST
enlarge paper	REAM	• I am *entertained by* par–ty	PARITY
enough		entertainment finished	SHOW-OFF
enough for [all the] . . .	LETHAL	**enthrall**	
enough to make [many] . . .	MYNA	*enthralled by* *	incl in *
enrol		• see me *enthralled by* state	CAMEL
enrol a . . .	incl A	*enthralled by* cine/ma st/ars	MAST
enrol student(s)	incl L(L)	*enthralls* a . . .	incl A
enrol *	incl *	*enthralls* *	incl *
• I *enrol in* par–ty	PARITY	• state *enthralled* me	CAMEL
ensconce		**enthusiast**	
ensconced in ch/ape/l	APE	enthusiast	FAN
ensconced in *	incl in *	• enthusiast follows	FANTAILS
• Premier *has* queen		• enthusiast *grabs* money	FLAN
ensconced in..	PERM	• enthusiast's food	FANFARE
ensemble		enthusiastic	HOT
ensemble [she saw] . . .	WASHES	• enthusiastic soldiers	HOTFOOT
[German] *ensemble*	MANGER	• enthusiastic trial	HOTTEST
enshrine		• enthusiastic, urges . . .	HOTSPURS
enshrine a . . .	incl A	enthusiastic *about*< . . .	DAM
enshrine *	incl *	enthusiastic girl	NANKEEN
• church *enshrines* a saint	CASTE	**entire**	
enshrined by *	incl in *	entire	STALLION
• a saint *enshrined by* church	CASTE	entire, *say*	HOLE
enshrined by wor/ship/pers	SHIP	**entomology**	ENT
ensign	ENS	**entrance¹**	
enslave	DELIBERATE	entrance money	INCOME
ensnare		*entrance to* building	B
ensnare a . . .	incl A	entrance, *say*	WEIGH-IN, WEIGHING
ensnare *	incl *	*entry* form	F
• rustic *ensnares* learner	PLEASANT	*Entry of the* Gladiators	G
ensnared by *	incl in *	entry to profession	ADMISSION
• learner *ensnared by* rustic	PLEASANT	entry to profession	P
ensnared in pl/ot her s/on . . .	OTHERS	No *Entry*	N
entangle			*(see also* enter)
entangle a . . .	incl A	**entrance²**	
entangle *	incl *	entranced, *say*	WRAPPED
• re–ed-*entangled* fin	REFINED	entrancing flier	WITCH
entangled in *	incl in *	entrancing flier, *say*	WHICH
• fin *entangled in* re–ed	REFINED	**entreat**	
entangled [nets]	STEN	entreat	BEG
enter		• entreat a single . . .	BEGONE
enter in/to a st/and	TOAST	• entreat Barnaby	BEGRUDGE
enter plant	(in) RE–ED	• entreat Clark	BEGGABLE
entered	INGOT	entreat	PRAY
entered by *	incl *	• entreated, *say*	PREYED
• animals had *entered*	SHADOWS	• entreats, *say*	PRAISE
• the river *entered by* stream	THRILLER	• entreaty, *say*	PREYER
entered in da/ta b/ank	TAB	entreaty	PLEA
I *enter*	incl I	• entreaty finished, *say*	PLEADED
* *enters*	incl *	• entreaty *to* daughter	PLEAD
• stream *enters* th–e river	THRILLER	• entreaty *to* Edward	PLEATED

Letter replaced \c\at; Omit (a); Pointers *out*; Retain <u>a</u>; Split B_ED; Down (D); Backwards <or ^

entry	(see enter)
entwine	
entwine [arms]	MARS, RAMS
entwined by *	incl in *
• a king *entwined by*	
st–ring	STARRING
entwined in fi/bre d/rawn . . .	BRED
entwining a . . .	incl A
entwining *	incl *
• st–ring *entwining* a king	STARRING
entwining [roots]	TORSO
enunciate	
enunciated clause	CLAWS
enunciation of phrase	FRAYS
envelop	
envelop a . . .	incl A
envelop *	incl *
• f–og *envelops* king	FROG
enveloped by *	incl in *
• king *enveloped by* f–og	FROG
environment	
environment of Lond/on	
set/tlement	ONSET
* *environment*	incl in *
• a king *in* city *environment*	EARLY
environmentalists	GREENS
envy	
envious	GREEN
envy, say	NV
epistle	EP
epsilon	E
equal	
equal	PAR
• equal bargain	PARSNIP
• equal monarch	PARKING
• equal shares	PARTAKES
equal contest	MATCH
equal manufacturer	MATCHMAKER
Equal Opportunities Commission	EOC
equal *returns*	LEVEL
equal to or more than, *say*	KNOTLESS
equalise scales	BALANCE
equality, say	PARROTTY
equally	AS
• equally determined	ASSET
• equally hot	ASWARM
• equally sharp	ASTART
equals, say	PIERCE, PIERS
equestrian	
equestrian appendage	RIDER
equestrian humour	HORSE LAUGH
equestrienne	GODIVA
equitation, say	MANAGE
eradicate	
eradicate a . . .	omit a
eradicate *	omit *
• fat(her) *eradicates* her . . .	FAT

is *eradicated*	omit IS
• r(is)e is *eradicated*	RE
Erato	
Erato, *say*	AMUSE, MUSE
erect	
are *erected*(D)^	ERA
erect bat(D)^	TAB
erect cooker	REARRANGE
erected dam(D)^	MAD
erection of part(D)^	TRAP
was *erected*(D)^	SAW
ergo	SO
erode	
erode, *say*	WARE
eroded [coastline]	SECTIONAL
eroded, *say*	WARN
eroding [slope]	LOPES, POLES
erosion of coast	BEACHWEAR
erosion of [coast]	ATOCS, COATS
erosion, *say*	LANDWEHR
errant	
errant character	MISPRINT, TYPO
errant [Poles]	LOPES, SLOPE
erratic	
erratic [drive]	DIVER
[spoke] *erratically*	POKES
error	
erred in Italy, *say*	SYNDROME
erroneous [step]	PEST, PETS
error	SIN
• error by family	SINK IN
• error-trap	SINNET
• error unusual, *say*	SYNOD
error [in the] . . .	THINE
errors excepted	EE
errors and omissions excepted	EOE
[human] *error*	NAHUM
[on a quite] *erroneous* . . .	EQUATION
erupt	
erupt [in a] . . .	AIN, –IAN, INA
erupting [like] . . .	KIEL
eruption of [Etna]	NATE, NEAT
escape	
escape route	FLIGHT PATH
escaped a . . .	omit A
escaped [deer]	REED, REDE
escaped from Ber/lin g/aol	LING
escaped king	omit R
escaped queen	omit ER
I *escaped*	omit I
one *escaped*	omit A, I
* *escaped*	omit *
• she *escaped* ma(she)r	MAR
escudo	ESC
Eskimo	
Eskimo	HUSKY, IN(N)UIT
Eskimo *leader*	E

Anag [cat]; Any *; Begin IGN–; Endings –ING; eg •; Hidden /cat/; Implied add (on); Implied in (in);

especially	ESP
esquire	ESQ
essay	
essay, *say*	SA
essayist	ELIA, LAMB
essayist's claim	AMELIA
Essen	
[Essen] *demolished*	SENSE
Essen, *say*	SN
essence	
essence of roses	S
vanilla *essence*	I
essential	
essential in bre/ad mix/ture	ADMIX
essential part of en/gin/e	GIN
essentially sound	U
Essex	
Essex, *perhaps*	COUNTY
Essex, *say*	SX
establish	
established	EST, PROVEN
• established at eastern . . .	ESTATE
• established state	PROVENCAL
established church	EC, CE
established company	FIRM
* established	incl *
• one *established in* pos–t	POSIT
estate agent	
Estate	VIRGINIA etc
estate agent	STEWARD
estate agent's brochure	SEMI-CIRCULAR
estimated	
estimated time of	
–arrival	ETA
–departure	ETD
eta	E
etchers	RE
Ethiopia	ETH
etymology	ETY
European[1]	
European	E, EUR
European Broadcasting Union	EBU
European Council	CE, EC
European Defence Community	EDC
European Development Fund	EDF
European (Economic) Commission	E(E)C
European (Economic) Community	E(E)C
European Monetary Agreement	EMA
European Payments Union	EPU
European Productivity Agreement	EPA
European[2]	
European agreement	JA, OUI, OUIJA, SI
European articles	ELLA, LATHE, UNDER
European *capital*	E
European country, *say*	OSTREA
European fashion, *say*	UROSTYLE
European friend, *say*	CHECKMATE
European journalist	POLISHED
European *leader*	E
European measure	POLE
European on strike, *say*	CHECK-OUT
European property	SLAVE STATE
European, *say*	CHECK, CHEQUE, DEIGN
Evangelical Union	EU
even	
even characters abandon p(l)a(y)	PA
even characters in play	LY
eve(n) *less*	EVE
even match	FLATTEST
even number	FLATTEN, PLAINSONG
fairly *even*	–ARY
evening	
evening air	NOCTURNE, SERENADE
evening dress, *say*	TALES
evening journey, *say*	NITRIDE
evening out	IRONING, PLANING, PRESSING
evening sun	RED SETTER
evening work	IRONING, PLANING, PRESSING
eventually	
eventually	(in) EN–D
• certain *eventually*	ENSURED
ever	
ever	AY, AYE, ER, EER
[ever]-*changing*	REVE
evermore	EVERT, LEVER, NEVER
evermore	NEVERTHELESS
every	
every evening, *say*	KNIGHTLY
every other day	EOD
every other part of Spain	PI, SAN
every player	TUTTI
every year	PA
everyone	ALL, EACH
everyone *up*^ North(D)	LLAN–
everything does	ENDING
everything due	ALLOWING
evict	
evict a	omit A
evict people	omit MEN
evict *	omit *
• *evict* girl *from* sor(di)d . . .	SORD
evident	
evident *in* hi/s ap/proach	SAP
evil	
evil boy	VICEROY
evil ruler	SINKING
evolve	
evolution of [man is] . . .	MAINS
evolve [a new] . . .	WANE, WEAN
evolving from [past] . . .	PATS, TAPS
ewe	
ewe, *say*	U, YEW, YOU

Letter replaced \c\at; Omit (a); Pointers *out*; Retain a; Split B_ED; Down (D); Backwards <or ^

ewes, *say*	US, UU, YEWS, YOUSE
ex-	
ex-	X
ex-captain	MAJOR
ex-pupil	GRADUATE, OB
ex-works	incl OP
• *ex*-works sl–ed	SLOPED
exact	
exact money	BLACKMAIL
exactly (=to a T)	
• ten *exactly*	TENT
• meet *exactly*	JOINT
• *exactly to* his . . .	HIST, THIS
exact time	DEAD MARCH
exalt	
exaltation of new . . .(D)^	WEN
exalted cleric *has* order(D)^	MOVER
examine	
examination	ORAL, TEST, VIVA
• spring exam	MAYORAL
• try examination	TEST
• examination town	VIVACITY
examination	A-LEVEL, CSE, GCE
	O-LEVEL
examination level	A, O
examination paper	SEARCH WARRANT
examine	CON
• examine bivouacs	CONTENTS
• examine evidence	CONSIGN(S)
• examine punishments	CONFINES
examine	TEST
• examine *after* warm . . .	HOTTEST
• examine river	TEST
• examine vessel, *say*	TESTERN
examine	PRY
• examine friend, *say*	PRIMATE
• examine lad	PRISON
• examine porcelain, *say*	PRIMING
examine	TRY
• examine cereal, *say*	TRICORN
• examine cult, *say*	TRISECT
examined	EX
examines, *say*	CHEQUES, CZECHS
example	EX
excavate	
excavate(=dig up)(D)^	GID
excavated boat	DUGOUT
excavated from de/ep ic/e	EPIC
excavated, *say*	HOLLOAED, MIND
excel	
excel, *say*	XL
excellency	HE
excellency, *say*	XLNC
excellent	AI
• excellent wine	AIRED
• excellent ball	AIDANCE
• excellent fish	AILING
excellent	SUPER
• excellent book	SUPERB
• excellent disguise	SUPERVISOR
• excellent eyesight	SUPERVISION
excellent	VG
excellent brandy	FINE
excellent character	CAPITAL
excellent drug	CRACKPOT
excellent guess	DIVINE
excellent ruler	SOVEREIGN
except	
except a . . .	omit A
except Edward	BUTTED
except *	omit *
• *except* the fa(the)r	FAR
exception	EX(C)
exceptional [talent]	LATENT
exemplary	EG
excess	
excess weight	GLUTTON
excessive love	MANIA
excessive *rise*(D)^	OOT, REVO
excessively	OTT
exchange	
exchange currency	TRADEMARKS
exchange of letters	ANAGRAM
exchange of [letters]	SETTLER
exchange [rate]	TARE, TEAR
exchanging punches	HORSE-TRADING
[heat] *exchange*	HATE, THEA
in exchange for [lira]	ARIL, LIAR, RAIL
stock exchange	CATTLE MARKET
excise	
excise a	omit A
excise one . . .	omit A, I
excise some t(um)ours	TOURS
excise *	omit *
• fa(the)r *excised* the . . .	FAR
excite	
excite dogs	FANTAILS
excited [dogs]	GODS
excitement of [atoms]	MOATS, STOMA
exciting [times]	EMITS, SMITE
[great] *excitement*	GRATE
exclude	
exclude outsiders	omit 1st and last
• (b)oar(d) *excludes outsiders*	OAR
excluding a . . .	omit A
excluding nothing	incl ALL
• wicked *excluding* nothing	BALLAD
excluding nothing	omit O
• l(o)ad *excluding nothing*	LAD
excluding *	omit *
• Char(le)s *excluding*	
the *French*	CHARS
excruciate	
excruciating [pains]	SPAIN

Anag [cat]; Any *; Begin IGN–; Endings –ING; eg •; Hidden /cat/; Implied add (on); Implied in (in);

excruciatingly [sharp]	HARPS
excursion	
excursion [by bus]	BUSBY
excursion route	TRIPLANE
excursus	EX
Exe	X
execute	
execute agent	IMPLEMENT
execute player	HANG BACK
executed (k)ing	–ING
executioner	KETCH, TOPPER
executive	EX
executive officer	HANGMAN
executor	EXR, EXOR
exemplified	EG
exempt	
exempt at the end	omit last letter
• mat(e) *exempt at the end*	MAT
exempt at the start	omit 1st letter
• (m)ate *exempt at the start*	ATE
exercise	
exercise	PE
• artillery exercise	RAPE
• company exercise	COPE
• exercise books	PENT
exercise	PT
• artillery exercise	RAPT
• company exercise	COPT
• field exercise	LEAPT
exercise [dogs]	GODS
exercise sequence	TRAIN
exercising [men at] . . .	MEANT
exhaust pipe	DRAIN
exhibit	
exhibit	HANG
• exhibit in Greece	HANGING
• exhibit pet	HANGDOG
• exhibit sack	HANG FIRE
exhibit	SHOW
• exhibit county . . .	SHOWDOWN
• exhibit garments	SHOWJUMPERS
• exhibit *before* queen	SHOWER
exhibited by *	incl in *
• spectacles *exhibited by* musician	BOOM
exhibiting a . . .	incl A
exhibiting ar/t at T/ate	TATT
exhibiting *	incl *
• musician *exhibiting* spectacles	BOOM
exhibition of wa/res t/ of . . .	REST
exhibitor	ARTIST, RA
exist	
exist in this way	SOLIVE
existing	LIVE
• an existing . . .	ALIVE
• existing king	LIVER

• existing lines	LIVERY
existing place	HOME, RESIDENCE
existing present	TENSE, TENURE
existing rate	COST OF LIVING
existing, *say*	REEL
existing state	ASIS
exists *on* earth	ISLAND
exit	
exit permit	OUTLET
exit, *say*	WEIGH-OUT
exits	OUTDOORS
Exodus	EX
exonerate	
exonerate	CLEAR
• exonerate journalist	CLEARED
• exonerate king	CLEARCOLE, CLEARER
exorcise	
exorcise	DISPOSSESS
exorcise a . . .	omit A
exorcise alien . . .	omit ET
exorcise one . . .	omit A, I
exorcise, *say*	EXERCISE, PE, PT
exorcise *	omit *
• p(ri)est *exorcises* king-emperor	PEST
exotic	
exotic (=foreign language)	
• *exotic* flower	FLEUR
• *exotic* friend	KAMERAD
• *exotic* girl	SENORITA
• *exotic* garden	GIARDINO
exotic	ALIEN, ET
exotic character (=letter from a foreign language)	
• first *exotic character*	ALEPH, ALPHA
• *exotic character is after* a . . .	BETA, BETH
exotic [trees]	STEER, STERE
expand	
indicating an abbreviation to be written in full:	
• *expanded* her . . .	HERALDRY
• it *expanded*	ITALIAN
• no *expansion*	NOBELIUM
expect	
expectant mother	LADY-IN-WAITING
expected, *say*	JEW
expel	
expel a . . .	omit A
expel those present	TURNOUT
expel *	omit *
• *expel* head of (c)lass	LASS
• Henry *expelled from* school	(h)ARROW
• (l)over *expels* student . . .	OVER
experiment	
experiment [in the] . . .	THINE
experimental [plane]	PANEL

Letter replaced \c\at; Omit (a); Pointers *out*; Retain <u>a</u>; Split B_ED; Down (D); Backwards <or ^

[painter] *experimented*	REPAINT

expert

expert	ABLE
• expert *has* square . . .	ABLET
• good man *has* expert . . .	STABLE
• run expert . . .	MANAGEABLE
expert	ACE
• expert *with* twitch	ACETIC
• expert sound	ACETONE
and	
• British expert	BRACE
• friend and expert	PALACE
• quiet expert	PACE
• stern expert	GRIMACE
and	
• fifty experts	LACES
• many experts	MACES
expert	DAB
• expert *goes round* the bend	DAUB
• expert lost blood	DABBLED
• expert worker	DAB HAND
expert	PRO
• expert examination	PROTEST
• expert in good shape	PROFIT
• expert remedy	PROCURE
expert did . . .	ACCOMPLISHED
expert oarsman	MASTERSTROKE
expert's knowledge	ONIONS
	(*see also* ace, profess)

expire

expire	DIE
• expire, *say*	DAI, DYE
expire	PASSOVER
expired persons, *say*	WEEDED
expiration of leas<u>e</u>	E

explode

explode	GOBANG
exploding [mine]	MIEN
explosion of [rage]	GEAR
explosive	HE, TNT
• explosive mixture	HEBREW
• I *put in* explosive	TINT
explosive finale	KO
explosiv<u>e</u> *finale*	E
explosive [rate]	TARE, TEAR
explosive, *say*	TONIGHT

exploit

exploit [forests]	FOSTERS
exploit, *say*	FEET
exploitation of [slaves]	SALVES
exploits fish	MILKSHAKE

exponential — EXP

export — EX(P)

expose

expose some l/aye/rs	AYE
exposing hid/den t/alent	DENT
exposition of cle/ver ge/neral	VERGE

express

express condition	STATE
express fare	FAST FOOD
expressions of regret, *say*	SIZE

expurgate

expurgated t/ext end/ing . . .	EXTEND
expurgation b/y obs/erving . . .	YOBS

extend

extend plan	PROJECT
extend time	STRETCH
extended her . . .	HERALDRY
extended play	EP
extended speech	DRAWL
extension	EXT
extent, *say*	SIGHS
it *extended* . . .	ITALIAN

exterior

exterior of <u>cabin</u>	CAN
* *exterior*	incl in *
• animal has re–d *exterior*	REAPED

external

external measurements‵	OUTSIZE
external *	incl in *
• university's *external* entrance	AUDIT
externally	EXT

extinct — EXT

extinguish

extinguish a . . .	omit A
extinguish *	omit *
• fa(the)r *extinguished* the . . .	FAR
• fir(e) *finally extinguished*	FIR

extol

extol queen	PUFFER
extol summer	PUFF-ADDER

extort

[crude] *extortion*	CURED
extort [ransom]	MANORS
extort, *say*	RING

extra

extra	BYE
• extra reading	BY-ELECTION
• extra rules	BYE-LAWS
• extras	BYE-BYE
extra	EXT
• extra bit	EXTORT
• extra boorish	EXTRUDE
• extra worker	EXTANT
extra	MORE
• cut extra, *say*	HUMOR
• extra cut, *say*	MORLOP
• extra flower, *say*	MOROSE
extra	NO-BALL
extra	WIDE
• extra child	WIDE-BOY
• extra food	WIDESPREAD
• extra run	WIDER
extra damage	SURCHARGE

Anag [cat]; Any *; Begin IGN–; Endings –ING; eg •; Hidden /cat/; Implied add (on); Implied in (in);

extra delivery	NO-BALL, WIDE	*extremely* light	LT
extra large	EXCEL, XL, OS	extremes	N–S
extra-sensory perception	ESP	*extremes of* paranoia	PA, PANDA
extra-terrestrial	ALIEN	*extremists abandoned* (W)ale(s)	ALE
• extra-terrestrial scoffed	ALIENATE	*extremists in* Paris	PS
extra-terrestrial	ET	extremities	N, S
	(*see also* alien)	*extremities of* endurance	EE
extra thought	PS	extremity	TOE
extract		pedal *extremities*	PL
extract a . . .	omit A	**extricate**	
extract a/n oun/ce	NOUN	*extricate from* [a mesh]	HAMES, SHAME
extract from fun/gus t/ype	GUST	*extricate from* ditc/h aft/er . . .	HAFT
extract of [roe]	ORE	**exuberant**	
extract *	omit *	[act] *exuberantly*	CAT
• *extract* lubricant *from* b(oil)ed...	BED	*exuberant* [dancer]	CRANED
extracted from par/t of fee/t	TOFFEE	**eye**	
extracted from [skin]	INKS, SINK	*eye of* needle	E
extraction of bit/ter m/elon	TERM	eye, *say*	AYE, I
extraordinary		eye-dropper	TEAR
extraordinarily [like] . . .	KIEL	eye-liner	RETINA
extraordinary [caper]	PACER	eye-opener	ALARM (CLOCK), COCKEREL
extravagant			LID
extravagant [claim]	MALIC	eye-*opener*	E
extravagantly [used]	DUES, DUSE, SUED	eye-*opener*	start with I
[Irish] *extravaganza*	RISHI	• member has eye-*opener*	IMP
extreme		eye trouble, *say*	EGOMANIA, EGO(T)ISM
extreme characters	AZ	eyeball	ORB
extreme characters in play	PY	eyeblack, *say*	COAL
extreme left	E	eyeless	omit I
extreme left	L, T	eyelid	SHUTTER
extreme *right*	E	eyepiece	CORNEA, IRIS, LENS
extreme right	R, T		RETINA
extreme state	UTTER	eyes at the back, *say*	REARISE
extremely handy	FINGERTIP	eyes, *say*	II, IS, –ISE, –IZE
extremely handy	HY	eyesore	STYE
extremely light	VERY	**Ezra**	EZ

F

clef, Fahrenheit, farad, Faraday's constant, farthing, fathom, fellow, female, feminine, femto-, fighter plane, filial generation, filly, *fine*, fluorine, folio, following, foot, force, forte, forty (thousand), franc, France, e, frequency, Friday, Helmholtz free energy, hole, key, layer, loud, *noisy*, note, number, stop, vitamin, word

fabricate		*(see also* indeed)	
fabricate	LIE	**factory**	
• fabricate opening, *say*	LIGATE	factory dance	WORKSHOP
• fabrication speed, *say*	LYRATE	factory output	RUN OF THE MILL
• fabricator, *say*	LYRE	factory owner, *say*	MILKING
fabricate [cruel] . . .	LUCRE	**Faculty of Actuaries**	FA
fabricated song	LIED	**fade**	
fabrication of [steel]	LEETS, STELE	[fade] *out*	DEAF
fabulous		fade, *say*	WAIN
fabulous bird	ROC	*fadeout of final* ac(t)	AC
fabulous country, *say*	COCAINE	**Faeroe Islands**	FR
fabulous loser	HARE	**fag-end**	
fabulous place	COCKAIGNE, ELDORADO	*fag-end*	G
fabulous supporter	UNICORN	*fag-end of* join<u>t</u>	T
fabulous winner	TORTOISE	**Fahrenheit**	F
facade		**fail**	
facade of <u>r</u>espectability	R	fail, *say*	WAIN
<u>i</u>mposing *facade*	I	fail to declare	BATON
face		fail to finish	omit last letter
face	DIAL	• a girl *fails to finish*	ALAS(s)
• engineer's face	REMEDIAL	• *fail to finish* bee(r)	BEE
• face shock treatment	DIALECT	• sh(e) *fails to finish*	SH
• face with eyes, *say*	DIALISE	*fail to get a* . . .	omit A
• face *up*(D)^	MUG, LAID	*fail to get* money	omit L
face job	CLOCKWORK	*fail to get* *	omit *
face lift(D)^	GUM	• *fail to get son out of* vessel	(s)HIP
face pain	PANACHE	• the(y) *fail to get* unknown . . .	THE
face saver	MASK, VISOR	*fail to open*	omit 1st letter
face up	BACK DOWN	• *fail to open* (g)ate	ATE
face wall	PLASTER, RENDER	failed	CAMEO
• *faces of* <u>t</u>he <u>o</u>ld <u>w</u>omen	TOW	*failed* [in the] . . .	THINE
facing		failed, *say*	MIST
–east	TOE	*failing a* . . .	omit A
–north	TON	*failing* *	omit *
–west	TOW	• *failing* her fat(her)	FAT
facing the other way, tip		*failing* [test]	SETT, STET
was< . . .	SAW PIT	*fails to start*	omit first letter
rats *faced the other way*<	STAR	• (b)us *fails to start*	US
fact		• *fails to start* (r)ace	ACE
facts	DATA, GEN	*failure of* [arch]	CHAR
facts, *say*	FAX	failure to decide, *say*	ETHERISM

Anag [cat]; Any *; Begin IGN–; Endings –ING; eg •; Hidden /cat/; Implied add (on); Implied in (in);

[heart] *failure*	EARTH, HATER, RATHE	*falling over* [step]	PEST, PETS
one *failing*	omit I	*falling* [star]	ARTS, RATS, TARS
[renal] *failure*	LEARN	* *falls off*	omit *
faint		• nose *falls off* (p)lane	LANE
faint boundary	PALE	falls over carrier	SLIPSHOD
fa*i*nt *heart*	I	**false**	
faint letter	WEAKEN	*false* [or true]	ROUTER, TOURER
faint point	WANE	*false* [start]	TARTS
faint *sound*	FEINT	f*alse start*	F
fair		*falsely* [said] . . .	AIDS, DAIS
fair	F	falsifies marks	FIDDLESTICKS
• fair, always	FEVER	*falsify* [report]	PORTER
• Fair Isle	FIONA	**Falstaff's tipple**	SACK
• mark *on* fair . . .	SCARF	**falter**	
fair account	EXPOSITION	*falter* [over]	ROVE
fair *and* square	EVENT	*faltering* [steps]	PESTS, PETS
fair game	AUNT SALLY, HOOPLA,	**familiar**	
	SKITTLES, etc	familiar	FAM
fair location	PLEASURE GROUND	indicating: colloquial	
fair punishment	FINE	diminutive	
fair *shares*	FA, IR	slang	
fair treatment	BLEACH(ING), PEROXIDE	*familiar* face	MUG
fairy		*familiarity with* Philip	PIP
fairy	HOB, IMP, PERI, PUCK	*familiarly* eccentric	LOOPY
• fairy ring	HOBO	**family**	
• fairy tales	IMPLORE	family	BLOOD
• fairy fish	PERICARP	• athlete's family	BLUE BLOOD
• fairy queen	PUCKER	• family *with* unknown . . .	BLOODY
fairy dance	MOTH BALL	• family row	BLOOD BANK
fairy king	OBERON	family	FAM
fairy queen	MAB	• bovine family	OXFAM
falcon		• family in the East	FAMINE
falcon, *say*	JERKING	• family *takes* drug	FAME
falconer's pastime	HOBBY	family	KIN
fake		• feline family	CATKIN
fake	SHAM	• interrogate family	PUMPKIN
• fake article	SHAMAN	• odd family	RUMKIN
• fake diamonds	SHAMROCK	family	LINE
• fake drug	SHAME	• incorporated family . . .	INCLINE
fake ache, *say*	CHAMPAGNE	• family friend	LINEALLY
fall		• family *has* king's . . .	LINERS
fall	HAIL, RAIN, SLEET, SNOW	Family Income Supplement	FIS
	SLIPOVER	family mess	LITTER
fall *for a Frenchman*	AUTOMNE	Family Planning Association	FPA
fall *for American* . . .	AUTUMN	family story	RELATION
fall from *	omit from *	family works	HOUSE PLANT
• he *falls from* t(he) . . .	T	**famous**	
• he *falls from* (he)avens	AVENS	famous day	VE
fall in *	incl in *	famous fish	STARLING
• rat *falling in* river	DERATE	famous saw	NOTED
fall short of targe(t)	TARGE	**fancy**	
fall short of th(e) . . .	TH	*fanciful* [ideas]	AIDES, SADIE
fallen [angel]	ANGLE, GLEAN	fancy catalogue	IDEALIST
falling about [in the] . . .	THINE	fancy food shop	DELI
falling apart [when I] . . .	WHINE	fancy heel	IDEALIST
falling house	USHER	*fancy* [I can] . . .	CAIN
falling out [over] . . .	ROVE	fancy man/woman	SUSPECT

fancy table	IDEALIST
fancy [table]	BLATE, BLEAT
fanlight	BLOW-TORCH
fantasy	
fantastic aircraft	BROOMSTICK
fantastic relation	FABLE, FAIRY STORY
fantastic [scene I] . . .	NIECES
fantasy [in B]	BIN, NIB
far	
[far] *away*	FRA, RAF
far-fetched [idea]	AIDE
[far]-*flung*	FRA, RAF
far-flung [clime]	MELIC
[far] *off*	FRA, RAF
far side of road	D
farad	F
fare	
fare-carrier	LUNCH-BOX
	PICNIC HAMPER
fare from China	CHOW-MEIN
fare from Italy	PASTA
fare from Spain	PAELLA
farewell	
farewell	BV, SUCCEED
farewell speech	A BIENTOT, ARRIVEDERCI,
	ADIEU, ADIOS, ALOHA, AU REVOIR,
	AUF WIEDERSEHEN, CIAO, CHEERIO,
	GOODBYE, HASTA LA VISTA,
	SAYONARA, SO LONG, TATA, VALE
farm	
farm boss	STUD
farm butter	GOAT, RAM
farm victims	MIC(e)
farmer	GILES, YEOMAN
farmer's punch	HAYMAKER
farmhouse victims	MIC(e)
farming	(on) LAND
• fish*farming*	GARLAND
farming policy	CAP
farthing	F, Q
fashion	
fashion	ALA
• fashion *in* South Dakota	SALAD
• fashion lines	ALARY
• note fashion	BALA, GALA
fashion	RAGE
• current *in* fashion	RAMPAGE
• note fashion	MIRAGE
• see company bend *to* fashion	COURAGE
fashion	TON
• fashion *in* Home Counties	STONE
• fashion notes	TONDO, TONGA
• South American fashion	SAT ON
fashion	
indicating use of foreign	
language:	
• a *Greek fashion*	ALPHA
• leader *in Italian fashion*	DUCE
• new *French fashion*	NOUVEAU
• older *Spanish fashion*	MAYOR
• *Paris fashion* is . . .	EST
• sweet *American fashion*	CANDY
• the *German fashion*	DAS, DER, DIE
fashion bench	FORM
fashion city	BRISTOL
fashion class	FORM
fashion models	FORMS, MAKES, SHAPES
fashion [models]	SELDOM
fashion, *say*	MOWED
fashion shop	BOUTIQUE
fashion [shop]	HOPS, POSH
fashion that is . . .	CUTIE
fashion you and me, *say*	STYLUS
fashioned, *say*	MAID
[old]-*fashioned*	DOL, LOD
fashionable	
fashionable	CHIC
• fashionable fellow	CHICKEN
• fashionable girl	CHICHESTER
• fashionable in the past	CHICAGO
fashionable	HIP
• fashionable curves	HIPS
• kin(g)s *almost* fashionable...	KINSHIP
• woman *with* fashionable . . .	WHIP
fashionable	IN
• fashionable dress	INHABIT
• fashionable group	INSECT, INSET
• fashionable sound	INTONE, INVOICE
fashionable	U
• fashionable *and* quiet	UP
• fashionable evening, *say*	UNITE
• fashionable fur	USABLE
fashionable [gear]	RAGE
[not] *fashionable*	ONT, TON
fast	
fast	LENT
• fast one	LENTI
• in so fast . . .	INSOLENT
fast buck	DEER, HARE, RABBIT
fast car	GT, ROD
fast company	FIRM
fast delivery	CHATTER
fast finish	EASTER
fas*t finish*	T
fast freeze	STARVE
fast mover	CLAPPER
fast ships	FLEET
fast start	F
fast work	DIETING, STARVATION
fasten	
fasten	PIN
• fasten a number, *say*	PINNATE
• fasten to	PINTO
• fasten *to* land	TERRAPIN

Anag [cat]; Any *; Begin IGN–; Endings –ING; eg •; Hidden /cat/; Implied add (on); Implied in (in);

fasten	TIE
• fasten correctly, *say*	TYRITE
• fasten joint, *say*	TINY
• fasten, *say*	THAI
fasten	LOCK
• 100 fasten . . .	CLOCK
• fasten hair	LOCK
• fasten it, *say*	LOCKET
fasten folder	NAIL FILE
fasten in this way	SOLACE
fasten marine animal	SEAL
fasten opening	BOLT-HOLE
fastened a weight	PENTAGRAM
fastened [gates]	STAGE
fastened in *	incl in *
• four *fastened in* str–ing	STRIVING
fastened thus	SOLACED
fastening in a . . .	incl A
fastening in *	incl *
• str–ing *fastening in* four . . .	STRIVING
fastener	LOCK
• fastener for flat	PADLOCK
• fine fastener	FLOCK
• fastener *with* eccentric . . .	LOCKNUT
fastener, *say*	BUCCAL
fat	
fat	LARD
• cut *back<* fat . . .	POLLARD
• fat boy	LARDED
• fat monarch	LARDER
fat	
• fat goat	BUTTER
• fat prize	BUTTERCUP
fat	GREASE
• a fat, *say*	AGREES
• fat, *say*	GREECE, GREES
• fat Scot, *say*	GRECIAN
fat people	ROUND FIGURES
fat porter	STOUT
fat ruler	STOUTER, UNTHINKING
fat, *say*	OBIES, PICNIC
fathead	BROAD BEAN, BUTTERNUT
fathead	F
fattening food	BLOATER
fatted calf	STOCKING FILLER
fatter, *say*	GROCER
father	
father	ABBA
father	DAD
• father *has* cut . . .	DADDOCK
• father *with* a . . .	DADA
• father *with* nothing	DADO
father	FR
• father at church	FRATCH
• father should . . .	FRAUGHT
• father *with* East *German*	FROST
father	PA
• father-figure	PAD, PAL, PAM
• father married	PAWED
• Father Thomas and	PATHOS
• father's amusement	PASSPORT
• father's beer-mug, *say*	PASTE-IN
• father's wise	PASSAGE
father	POP
• father *after* money, *say*	LOLLIPOP
• father examined . . .	POP-EYED
• father is hot	POPISH
father	THAMES, TIME
father of pride	HELION
father, *say*	SIGHER
father*less*	omit PA
• father*less* (Pa)than	THAN
fatherless gangster	ORPHANHOOD
father's letters	PA, PANDA
fathom	F, FTH, FTHM
fatuous	
fatuous	
• *fatuous* [grin is] . . .	RISING
• [smile] *fatuously*	LIMES, MILES
fault	
fault*less* ser(vice)	SER
faulty hearing	MISTRIAL
faulty head	BADNESS
faulty [sign]	GINS, SING
[his] *fault*	–ISH
favour	
favour sage	LIKEWISE
favoured	IN
favourite	PET
• favourite man	PETAL, PETTED
• favourite ruler	PETER
• transport favourite . . .	CARPET
fear	
fear of Germans, *say*	HUNDRED
fearful [rage]	GEAR
fearfully [tried]	TIRED
feature	
feature	CHIN
• feature article	CHINA
• feature monarch	CHINK
• firm feature	COCHIN
feature a . . .	incl A
feature directors	STARBOARD
feature editor	COSMETIC SURGEON
feature of t/he be/st	HEBE
feature *	incl *
• *feature* article *in* story	LIANE
featured in [all the] . . .	LETHAL
featured in cine/ma ne/ar . . .	MANE
features in n/ew e/xperiment	EWE
featuring *	incl in *
• story *featuring* article	LIANE
featuring remarka/ble st/unt	BLEST

Letter replaced \c\at; Omit (a); Pointers *out*; Retain <u>a</u>; Split B_ED; Down (D); Backwards <or ^

February	FEB
feed	
fed *up*(D)^	DEF
feed*back*<	DEEF
feeding, *say*	FAIRING
feel	
feel sad	BELOW, TOUCHDOWN
feel the weight	TOUCHSTONE
feeling fit	INFORM
[feeling] *poorly*	FLEEING
felt, *say*	CENSED
feet	
feet	FT
feet *up*(D)^	DRAY
FEG	EFFIGY
fell	
fell	DOWN, MOOR, HILL
• fell *back*<	ROOM
• fell down	MOOR, HILL
• fell *over*<	ROOM
• fell *up*(D)^	ROOM
• fell twice	DOWNHILL
fell *back*<	DENNIS
fell over	HIDE-OUT
fell sergeant	DEATH
fellow[1]	
fellow	CO–
• fellow-archdeacon	COVEN
• fellow-European	COBALT
• fellow fellow	CODON
• fellow-friend	COPAL
fellow	COVE
• a *French* fellow *with* king	UNCOVER
• fellow Russian	COVERED
• gangster fellow	ALCOVE
fellow	DON
• fellow *at* tea, *say*	DONT
• fellow dined	DONATE
• fellow fellow	CODON
• fellow soldiers	DONOR
• fellow *with* a Conservative	DONATORY
fellow	F
• fellow *has* a cow	FLOWER
• fellow is not . . .	FAINT
• fellow *with* spectacular fish	FOOLING
fellow	GENT
• brown fellow	TANGENT
• fellow the *French* . . .	GENTLE
• fellow *with* Scots boy	GENTIAN
fellow	MAN
• fellow is *back* < on	MANSION
• fellow-man	MANAL, MANED
• the *French* fellow	LEMAN
fellows, *say*	FELLOES, GUISE
Fellow[2]	
Fellow of the	
–Antiquarian Society	FAS

–British Academy	FBA
–Chartered Accountants	FCA
–Historical Society	FHS
–Institute of Journalists	FJI
–Royal Society	FRS
–Society of Antiquaries	FAS
–Society of Arts	FAS
female	
female	DI
• female journalist	DIED
• female poet	DISPENSER
• female sign	DIARIES
female	F
• female duck	FO
• female *has* no spirit	FORUM
• female is ill	FAILS
female	GAL
• engineer *with* female . . .	REGAL
• female insects	GALLICE
• female *with* money	GALL
female	HEN
• female *at* church	HENCE, HENCH
• female line	HENRY
• female part	HENBIT
female	HER
• female *and* male	HERM
• female with *German* . . .	HERMIT
• female working	HERON
female	MISS
• engineer *with* female . . .	REMISS
• female gangster	MISSAL
• female journalist	MISSED
and	
• female bank clerk, *say*	MISCALCULATING
• female flatfish, *say*	MISPLACE
• female magistrate, *say*	MISJUDGE
female	SHE
• female and *French* . . .	SHEET
• female antelope, *say*	BUCKSHEE
• female Berber	SHERIFF
• female flies	SHEWINGS
• female monarch	SHEER
female adviser	EGERIA
female bookmaker	AUTHORESS, RUTH
female cat	ANNOUNCE
female donkey, *say*	ASSESS
female figurehead, *say*	PROWESS
female friend, *say*	PALETTE
female gangster	ANNEAL, MISSAL, SHEAL
female graduates	MALADIES
female horse, *say*	MAYOR
female lawyer	BARMAID
female mouse, *say*	MINI
female *lead*	F
female relative, *say*	ANTI
female supporter	BRA(SSIERE)
	(*see also* girl)

Anag [cat]; Any *; Begin IGN–; Endings –ING; eg •; Hidden /cat/; Implied add (on); Implied in (in);

feminine		*made of* [fibre]	BRIEF
feminine	F	**fickle**	
• feminine appearance	FLOOK	*fickle* [friend]	FINDER
• feminine limbs	FARMS	[man is] *fickle*	MAINS
• feminine usefulness	FUTILIY	**fiction**	
feminine	FEM	*fictional* [giant he] . . .	HEATING
femme fatale	MURDERESS	*fictionalised* [life] . . .	FILE, LIEF
fence		**fiddle**	AMATI, CREMONA
fenced in by *	incl in *		STRAD(IVARIUS)
• animal *fenced by* saints	SCOWS	*fiddled* [a lot]	TOLA
fencing in a . . .	incl A	fiddler	NERO
fencing in *	incl *	fiddlesticks	BOWS
• saints *fencing in* animal	SCOWS	*fiddling* [takings]	SKATING, STAKING
ferment		**field**	
fermentation of [wines]	SINEW, SWINE	field division	FENCE, HEDGE
fermented [in a glass]	ASSAILING	field-dressing	FERTILISER
fermenting [cask]	SACK		NITRE, POTASH
ferryman	CHARON	[field]-*dressing*	FILED
fertile		field-effect transistor	FET
fertile crescent	GROWING	field frog	PADDOCK
fertiliser	NITRE, STAMEN	Field-marshal	FM
fester		field of beans	RUNNERS
festered [like] . . .	KIEL	Field Officer	FO
festering [sore]	EROS, ORES, ROES, ROSE	field sport	MEADOW LARK
[it was] *festering*	WAIST	[field] *sport*	FILED
festival		field study	LEADEN, LEYDEN
festival	GALA	fieldfare	GRASS, GRAZING
• festival drink	GALATEA		PICNIC
• festival had . . .	GALAHAD	fielding side	ONSET
• festival writings	GALANT	**fiery**	
fetch		fiery mount	ETNA, VOLCANO
fetch companion	CARRY	fiery revolutionary	IXION
fetch, *say*	GOPHER	**fifteen**	RU TEAM
fête		**fifth**	
fête say	FATE	*fifth* of circle	L
fête tea	GALATEA	November *Fifth*	M
fetter		**fifty**	
fetters donkey	CHAIN–SMOKE	50% of people	PEO, PLE
fever		fifty	A
fever [I ran] . . .	RAIN, RANI	fifty	L
feverish [turn]	RUNT	• 50-50	LL
[hay]-*fever*	YAH	• fifties	LL, LS
few		• fifty copies	LIMITATIONS
few fish	SCANTLING	• fifty experts	LACES
few, *say*	FU–	• fifty I know	LIKEN
• few lay floors, *say*	FUTILE	• fifty I know, *say*	LINO
• few vocalise, *say*	FUSING	• fifty in cage, *say*	LINKAGE
• few *will have* me, *say*	FUME	• fifty in store	LINSTOCK
fewer clothes	LESSON	• fifty or five hundred	LORD
fewer directions	LESSEE(S),	• fifty points	–LES(S), –LESSNESS
	LESSEN(S)	• fifty-first	LIST
fewer fowl, *say*	LESSENS	• fifty refuse	LASH
fewer net serves	MOREOVER	fifty	N, NU, V
f–fish	FEEL, FIDE, FLING	fifty cents	DOL, LAR
fibre		• fifty-cent note	DOLE
fibre diet	BRANDISH	• fifty cents a thousand	LARK
fibre*tip*	F or E	fifty-fifty	EVENS

Letter replaced \c\at; Omit (a); Pointers *out*; Retain <u>a</u>; Split B_ED; Down (D); Backwards <or ^

fifty one	LI, LONE	• (c)an figure *out*	AN
• fifty-one can . . .	LIABLE	• figure *out* c(l)ues	CUES
• fifty-one directions	LINES	figure *out*	CON–E, F–IVE, N–INE
• fifty-one doctors	LIMBS		ON–E, TE–N
• fifty-one extremely . . .	LIVERY	figures (in Rome)	C, D, L, M
• fifty-one iron ships	LIFEBOATS		CI, CL, DI, LI, MI, MM
• fifty-one on	LION	• cut a figure	SLICED
• fifty-one pounds	LIQUIDS	• figure eight, *say*	CATE, DATE
• fifty-one ran	LISPED		LATE, MATE
• fifty-one support . . .	LIBRA	• figure on	CON, DON, LION, MON
• fifty-one swindle . . .	LISTING	• figure out	CLOUT, LOUT
fifty-nine	LIX	figures *out*	incl in numbers
Fifties	LL, LS	• girl figures *out*	MADAM
fifty States	US, USA	• man figures *out*	CALL
fifty thousand	L, N, NU, V	figurehead	BUST
fight		figure*head*	F
fight	BOX	**file**	
• fight churchman	BOX-ELDER	[file]	WILDLIFE
• fight *with* mother	BOX-DAM	file one class, *say*	FILIFORM
• ready *to* fight	MONEY-BOX	file poem, *say*	PHYLLODE
fight	SPAR	file them, *say*	PHYLUM
• fight *and* beat	SPARTAN	filing assistant	MANICURIST
• fight Brown	SPARTAN	**filial claim**	MESON
• fight Communist	SPARRED	**fill**	
• fight with Territorials	SPARTA	fill coach	CRAMBUS
fight*back*<	RAW	*fill the gap in* *	incl in *
fighter	MIG	• always *fill the gap in* r–ed . . .	REVERED
• fighter raves	MIGRANTS	*fill the gap with* *	incl *
• fighter speed	MIGRATE	• *fill gap in* bo–rder *with* a . . .	BOARDER
fighter	GI, MAN, SOLDIER	fill the sea	CRAMMED, CRAMMER
fighter in the ring	PICADOR, TOREADOR	filled bread roll, *say*	BURGHER
	TORERO	*filled with* a . . .	incl A
fighter register	TERRIER	*filled with* *	incl *
fighting	(in) AC–TION, INACTION	• a *French* bed *filled with*	
fighting	WAR	men	ALIMENT
• fighting China	WARMING	*filling* *	incl in *
• fighting Communist	WARRED	• men *filling* a *French* bed	ALIMENT
• fighting *in* Communist . . .	REWARD		(*see also* full)
fighting		**film**	
–American	DOUGHBOY, GI, GRUNT	dull film	DUST, TARNISH
–Frenchman	SOLDAT	film	A, ET, U, X
–German	SOLDAT	film distributor	AEROSOL, SPRAY(-GUN)
–Italian	SOLDATO	film girl	GIGI
–Spaniard	SOLDADO	film sponsor	GODFATHER
fighting figure	MARS	filmed	(*see* picture)
fighting situation	BATTLEFIELD	filming	(on) SET
	(BOXING) RING	*filming* high ground	SET-DOWN
fighting weight	WARRINGTON	• scholars *filming*	BASSET
fighting woman	AMAZON, ATS	old film	PATINA
fighting worker	COMBATANT	**filter**	
figure		filter tip	SMOKESCREEN
figuratively	FIG	*filter tip*	F
figure	FIG	*filter* [wines]	SINEW, SWINE
figure-*hugging*	incl number	**final**	
• figure-*hugging* p–ants	PLANTS	final blow	KO
figure of eight	OCTAGON	*final* blo<u>w</u>	W
figure *out*	omit number	final drink	LAST LAP

final drin*k*	K
final examination	ENDPAPER
final examinatio*n*	N
final home	GRAVE, TOMB
final hom*e*	E
final judgement	EPITAPH, OBIT(UARY)
final judgemen*t*	T
final letter	OMEGA, Z
final lette*r*	R
final mark	FULL STOP
final mar*k*	K
final message	OBIT(UARY), RIP
final messag*e*	E
final piece of evidenc*e*	E
final point	LANDS END
final poin*t*	T
final odds	SP
final odd*s*	S
final venue	ARMAGEDDON, RAGNAROK
	TWICKENHAM, WEMBLEY
final venu*e*	E
final word	AMEN, GOODBYE
final wor*d*	D
final words	EPITAPH, OBIT(UARY), RIP
finalists at Wimbled*on*	ON
finally	(in) EN–D
• *finally* certain	ENSURED
finally arrive*d*	D
finally failing	omit last letter
• hear(t) *finally failing*	HEAR
finally left	end with L
• Al *finally* left	ALL
finally left	omit last letter
• the(y) *finally* *left*	THE
finally lost	omit last letter
• Franc(e) *finally* *lost*	FRANC
finally, *say*	ATTEND
losing *finalist*	G
	(*see also* last)
finale	
finale of concert	T
gran*d finale*	D
finance	
finance company	BRASS BAND
finance record	BACKLOG
financial liabilities	–IOUS
Financial Times	FT
find	
find a [log, ruin] . . .	LOURING
find [a log], *ruin* . . .	GAOL, GOAL
find another way to [drive] . . .	DIVER
find another way to say so	SEW, SOW
finding a synonym	LOCATING
finds it in ver/y ear/ly . . .	YEAR
	(*see also* found)
fine	
fine	AI

fine	F
• fine book	FACTS
• fine wine	FASTI
fine boy	ERIC
fine breed	GOODS TRAIN
fine	NOBLE
• *directions to* fine . . .	ENNOBLE
• fine coin	NOBLE
• fine fellows	NOBLEMEN
• fine queen	NOBLER
fine	OK, SCOT
fine fellow	JUDGE, MAGISTRATE
[fine] *form*	FEIN
fine leisure, *say*	GRANDEES
fine man	JUDGE, MAGISTRATE
fine manservant	GOOD FRIDAY
fine note	SHARP
fine scholar	GRANDMA
fine spring	WELL
finer, *say*	MORPHINE
finest *accommodation for* . . .	(in) B–EST
finest agent, *say*	SPIKING
finest mount	BESTRIDE
finest trip	BESTRIDE
finesse	
finesse [by Dan]	BANDY
finessing [in game]	GAMINE
finger	
fingerbowl	TOUCHWOOD
fingered fabric	FELT
fingerprint expert	DAB
finial	
finial of spire(D)	S
tall *finial*(D)	T
finish	
all *finished*	L
finish at Epsom	(THE) LINE
finish at Epso*m*	M
finish	END
• finish club	ENDIRON
• finish cross	ENDANGERED
finish game	MATE
finish gam*e*	E
finish needlework	CLOSEKNIT
finish off	omit last letter
• finish off boo(k)	BOO
finish of*f*	F
finish off pudding	G
finish shed	OVERSPILL
finished she*d*	D
finish work	RETIRE
finish wor*k*	K
finished exam	PASTORAL
finished gardening	HOEDOWN
finished gardening	G
finished skating	OFFICE
finishes letter	DIESEL

finishing touc**h**	H
matt *finish*	T
Finland	SF
Finnish	
Finnish author	TWAIN
Finnish *capital*	F
Finish *leader*	F
fir	
[fir-cone] *producer*	CONIFER
fir rod, *say*	FIRST HALF
fi**r**, *say*	FUR
firs, *say*	FURS, FURZE
fire	
fire	SACK
• fire clergy	SACKCLOTH
• fire people	SACKRACE
• fire rifle	SACK
[fire]-*fighting*	RIFE
fire hydrant	FH
fire plug	FP
fire-ship	LIGHTER
fired	LIT
• fired engineer	LITRE
• fired man	LITHE
• son fired . . .	SLIT
firelighter	ARSONIST
fireman	GUNNER
firemen	GUNNERS, RA
firm	
firm	CO
• firm agreement	COOK
• firm friend	COPAL
• firm support(er)	COBRA, COPIER
• firm's a . . .	COCOA
firm agreement	COMPACT
firm building	STABLE
firm control	HOUSEHOLD, STRONGHOLD
firm grasp	STRONGHOLD
firm hand	IRON DUKE
fi**rm**-*hearted*	IR
firm-*hearted*	incl CO
• a firm-*hearted* saint	ASCOT
• firm-*hearted* i–n . . .	ICON
firm ruler	HARDER, (MANAGING) DIRECTOR
firm undertaking	FUNERAL CONTRACTORS
first[1]	
first	A
• first man	AGENT
• first team	ASIDE
• girl first	GALA
first	–IST
• fat man first	FATALIST
• first *after* many . . .	LIST, MIST
• first the *French*	ISTLE
first	NOI
• first *back*<	ION
• first directions	NOISE

• first *to return*<	ION
first[2]	
First XI	E
First-**a**id	A
first-born	start with NE, NEE
• *first*-born intend . . .	NEMEAN
• *first*-born died	NEED
first **b**atsman	B
first-**b**orn	B
first character in **H**amlet	H
first character *to*	
leave	omit 1st letter
• first character *to leave* (p)lay	LAY
first-**c**lass	C
first couple on **st**age **en**tered	STEN
first **h**alf	H
first half of **ga**me	GA
first-**h**and	H
first item in **s**ale	S
First **L**ady	L
first **l**etter	L
first **l**ight	L
first **m**an	M
first man	start with MAN
• man *has* appointment	MANDATE
first **m**ate	M
first of **a**ll	A
first of **A**pril	A
first of **t**he . . .	T
first of the **m**onth	M
first **o**ffender	O
first **p**erson	P
first **p**ost	P
first **p**rize	P
first **q**uality	Q
first **r**ate	R
first **r**ound	R
first **s**ervice	S
first showings of **p**lay **i**n **N**eath	PIN
first sightings of **W**est **I**ndies	WI
first sign of **S**pring	S
first **s**lice	S
first slice of **c**ake	C
first **s**tage	S
first stage of **r**ocket	R
first to **w**in	W
first **t**o win	TWIN
first[3]	
first act of play	BREAK, FACE-OFF
	KICK-OFF, SERV(IC)E
first-aid station	DRESSING-ROOM
first *American*	FOIST
first and foremost	A
first batsman	OPENER
first cardinal	ONE
first chance	OPENING
first character	A, ADAM, ALPHA

Anag [cat]; Any *; Begin IGN–; Endings –ING; eg •; Hidden /cat/; Implied add (on); Implied in (in);

first character *to leave*	omit A
• first character *to leave* pl(a)y	PLY
first-class	(*see* first-class)
first clue	–IAC
first-day cover	AMNION, AMNIOTIC SAC
	BIRTHDAY SUIT, CAUL
	FIG-LEAF, SKIN
first drink	ADAM'S ALE, ADAM'S WINE
first gear	FIG-LEAF, LAYETTE
first generation	FRONTAGE
first in, first out	FIFO
first item in sale	LOTI
First Lady	EVE
first letter	A, ALPHA
first light	ONE ACROSS
first man	ADAM
first mate	ADAM, EVE
first mother	EVE
first mover	WHITE
first murderer	CAIN
first nine characters *returned*<	IOTA
first novel	ORIGINAL
first object	LEADING ARTICLE
first of April	MARCH PAST
first offender	ADAM, EVE
first opportunity	OPENING
first person	ADAM, I, ME
first place	EDEN
first prize	GOLD, PALM
first quality	A, AI
first question	QI
first reading book	ABC, ABCEE, ABSEY
	PRIMER
first sign	INITIAL
first slip	(ORIGINAL) SIN
first string	A, HEADLINE
first to be struck	PENNY BLACK
first victim	ABEL
first water	ADAM'S ALE, ADAM'S WINE
first wife	EVE

first-class

first-class	A
• father *has* first-class . . .	DADA
• first-class degrees	ADD
• fish *with* first-class . . .	CODA
first-class	AI
• first-class ball	AIDANCE
• first-class fish	AILING
• first-class *return*<	–IA
first-class	ACE
• first-class flower	ACEROSE
• first-class gallery	ACETATE
• fist-class sound	ACETONE
first-class	PRO
• first-class colliery	PROMINE
• first-class degree	PROD
• first-class match	PROTEST

first-class	CRACK, SMASHING
first class	KINDERGARTEN, NURSERY
	PLAYSCHOOL
first class attender	KINDERGARTENER
	INFANT

fish¹

fish	ANGLE
• black fish	BANGLE
• fish-club	ANGLE-IRON
• many fish	MANGLE
fish	BASS
• fish caught, *say*	BASSINET
• fish devoured, *say*	BASSETTE
• fish-kettle	BASS-DRUM
fish	CARP
• criticise fish	CARP
• fish arrives	CARPENTERS
• fish-container	CAR PARK
fish	CHAR
• cleaner fish	CHAR
• fish cleaner	CHAR(LADY), CHARLOTTE
• fish tea	CHAR
fish	COD
• fish-stream	CO-DRIVER
• fish strike	CODSWALLOP
• fish freezes	CODICES
fish	DAB
• fish expert	DAB
• fish *rising*(D)^	BAD
• fish-worker	DAB HAND
fish	EEL
• female fish	FEEL
• fish *rising*(D)^	LEE
• k–ing *without* fish	KEELING
fish	GAR
• *bring* fish *to* shore	GARLAND
• fish lost blood	GARBLED
• fish trap	GARNET
fish	ID(E)
• flaccid fish	LIMPID
• kingfish	KID
• square fish	SQUID
and	
• hot fish	HID(E)
• kingfish	RID(E)
• sunfish	SID(E)
fish	RUDD
• fish at this spot, *say*	RUDDIER
• fish in front	RUDDLED
• fish unknown	RUDDY
fish	LING
• few fish	SCANTLING
• fine fish	FLING
• sunfish	SLING
fish	SHAD
• fish here, *say*	SHADIER
• fish unknown	SHADY

Letter replaced \c\at; Omit (a); Pointers *out*; Retain a̲; Split B_ED; Down (D); Backwards <or ^

• fish *with* journalist	SHADED
fish	SKATE
• Fish Authority	SKATEBOARD
• inexpensive fish	CHEAPSKATE
• fish died	SKATED
fish	PIKE
• divert fish	TURNPIKE
• fishes Welsh river	PIKESTAFF
• sunfish	SPIKE
fish²	
fish	SWIMMER
fish	
–*at* sea	CLAMMED
–*at* the seaside	PORTRAY
–*at* this point, *say*	RUDDIER, SHADIER
fish-boat	DORY
fish-boy	SCHOOLMASTER
fish cake	POMFRET
fish eggs, *say*	RHO, ROSE, ROW(S)
fish-house	BLEAK
fish-like	OFFISH
fish roost	PERCH
fish, *say*	ERRING, POLLEN, SOUL
fish-spear	PIKE
fish-spear, *say*	GAFFE
fish stank	SMELT
fish struggles	FLOUNDERS
fish vessel	CAR PARK
fish-woman	SALMONELLA
fish worker	CLAMANT
fisherman	PEDRO, PETER
fisherman's problem	NONET
fisherman's tale	BANK ACCOUNT
fishing (industry)	NETWORK
fishmonger	SOLE AGENT
fishplate	SCALE
fishing rod	PIKESTAFF
two fish	CODLING, IDLING
	TROUTLING
two fish, *say*	EALING
fit	
fit clothing	SUIT
fit condition	AGUE, EPILEPSY
fitness competition	NATURAL SELECTION
five	
five	CINQUE
five	V
• 5 x 50	VIOL
• five drinks	VALES
• five I lease	VIRENT
• five in debt	VOWING
• five *in* low island	CAVY
• five *to* nine	VIX
• five *with* no instrument	VOLUTE
• five *with* one German . . .	VEIN
five Christmas presents	GOLD RINGS
five hundred	A
five hundred	D
• 501	DI
• five hundred in time	DINT
• five hundred is, ,	DIS–
• five hundred pounds	DL
five in Magnet (comic)	FAMOUS
five iron	MASHIE
five lines	STAVE
five nil	FIFTY
five-star	FIRST CLASS
five thousand	A, V
five-year olds	FIRST CLASS
five year prison sentence	HANDFUL
fix	
fix	PIN
• fix flower	PINASTER
• fix in front, *say*	PINAFORE
• fix puncture	PIN-PRICK
fix	SET
• fix *up*(D)^	TES
• fixed pay	SET SCREW
• scholars fixed . . .	BASSET
fixed course	RUT
fixed stud	STABLE
fixed up [a new] . . .	WANE, WEAN
fixed wages	SETSCREW
fixing [tiles]	STILE
fizzy	
fizzy wines	CHAMPAGNE, PERRY
fizzy [wines]	SWINE, SWINE
flabbergast	
flabbergast [all the] . . .	LETHAL
flabbergasted [when I] . . .	WHINE
flag	
flag	IRIS, LIS
flag *on* fleet	COLOUR-FAST
flag in front	SETTLED
flag officer	ENSIGN
flags *to* rent	WILTSHIRE
flail	
flail [oats]	STOA
flailing [arms]	MARS, RAMS
flak	AA
flaky	
flaky [skin]	SINK
flaky stuff	SNOW
flame	
flaming desire	ARSON, PYROMANIA
flaming [desire]	RESIDE
flaming redhead	MATCH, VESTA
flank	
flankers of platoon	PN
flanking army	AY
flap	
[emerge in a] *flap*	MENAGERIE
flapper	BIRD
flapping [about]	U-BOAT

Anag [cat]; Any *; Begin IGN–; Endings –ING; eg •; Hidden /cat/; Implied add (on); Implied in (in);

in a flap [over] . . .	ROVE
[sails] *flapping*	SILAS
flare	
flared trousers	HOTPANTS
flaring [gas]	SAG
flash	
flashing character	ROBOT
flashy boat	LIGHTSHIP
flashy building	LIGHTHOUSE
flat	
flat	UNNATURAL
Flat 10	FLATTEN
flat-*bottomed*(D)	T
flat dweller	PLAINSMAN
flat *opposite*	HILLY, SHARP, UNEVEN
flat-finding agency	SPIRIT LEVEL
flat fish, *say*	PLACE, SOUL
flattens note	IRONSTONE, SANDSTONE
flatter	
–animal	FAWN
–fabric	FLANNEL
flaunt	
flaunting [a new] . . .	WANE, WEAN
[was it] *flaunting* . . .	WAIST
flaw	
flaw in [glass]	SLAGS
flawed [sense]	ESSEN
flay	
flay pirate	SKINFLINT
flay [steer]	REEST, RESET, TREES
flea	
flea *in the ear*	FLEE
fleas jump	TICK-SHOP
jumping [flea]	LEAF
fleet	RN
flesh	
flesh, *say*	MEET, METE
flesh wound	SCRATCH
	SHOT IN THE ARM
flexible	
flexible [friend]	FINDER
flexing [arms]	MARS, RAM
flick	
flick [over]	ROVE
flicker of [life]	FILE, LIEF
flickering [lamps]	PALMS
flier	
flier, *say*	BURRED
fliers	RAF
	(*see also* fly)
flies	(*see* fly)
flight	
flight	HEGIRA, HEJ(I)RA, HIJRA(H)
flight cover	STAIR CARPET
flight demonstrator	SHOWER
flight of [swan I] . . .	SWAIN, WAINS
flight member	RISER, STAIR, TREAD

flight of locks	ALOPECIA, BALDNESS
flight path	STAIRCASE
flight unit	STAIR
flight, *say*	STARES
flighted delivery	AIRLIFT, AIRMAIL
flightless	OWING
flighty poet	HOMER
flighty [sort]	ROTS, TORS
fling	
[dance] *fling*	CANED
fling frill	FLOUNCE
fling [stone]	NOTES, ONSET, TONES
flint	
flint breaking, *say*	NAPPING
flint breaker, *say*	NAPPER
flip	
flipside	RECORD TURNOVER
flip over LP<	PL
flipping lid<	DIL
flit	
[bats] *flitting*	STAB, TABS
flitted [about]	U-BOAT
float	
flotation of [ship]	HIPS, PISH
floating	(in)S–S
floating about [lake]	KALE
floating [voter]	TROVE
flog	
flog queen, *say*	WHIPPER
flog twice	WHIPLASH
flood	
flood of [tears]	RATES, STARE, TARES
flood survivor	HAM, JAPHET, NOAH
florin	FN, SS, TWOS
flounder	
flounder [in sea in] . . .	ASININE
floundering [in sea]	ANISE
flourish	
flourished [when I] . . .	WHINE
flourished	FL
flourishing [guns]	GNUS, SNUG
flow	
[flow]	WILDFOWL
flow *over*<	NUR
flow, *say*	PEARL
flow through *	incl in *
• river *flows through* Sp–ain	SPRAIN
flowing [ale]	LEA
flowing through wa/ter m/eadow	TERM
flower[1]	
flower	ARUM, ROSE etc
flower arrangement	BOUQUET, GARLAND
	WREATH
[flower] *arrangement*	FOWLER, REFLOW
flower-bird	POPPYCOCK
flower-cutters	CLEAVERS
flower girl	DAISY, ROSE, etc

Letter replaced \c\at; Omit (a); Pointers *out*; Retain a̲; Split B_ED; Down (D); Backwards <or ^

flower, *say*	FLOCKS, LOOPING, ROWS
flower seed, *say*	POLLAN
flower spray	ROSE, WATERING-CAN
flower stores	STOCKS
flowers	LEI
flower's colour	FLAGSTONE
flowery item	PETAL, SEPAL
flowering shrub, *say*	FUTURE

flower²

flower	RIVER
• blue and white flower	NILE
• blue flower	DANUBE
• border flower	TWEED
• flower experiment	INDUSTRY
• flower for each . . .	CAMPER
• flower of France	RHONE, SEINE
• flower of Hades	STYX
• flower of oblivion	LETHE
• flower seen in Ireland	SHANNON
• German flower	RHINE
• that *French* flower	CELADON
flower-cutter, *say*	DREDGER
flower-power	HYDRO-ELECTRICITY
	(*see also* river)

fluctuate

fluctuating [beat is not] . . .	OBSTINATE
fluctuation of [tide]	EDIT, TIED

fluff

fluff [lines 'e] . . .	SENILE
fluffed [it when] . . .	WHITEN

fluid

fluid	FL
• fluid *has* unknown . . .	FLY
• fluid measure	FLINCH
• fluid style	FLAIR
fluid extract, *say*	DEUCE
fluid loss	SEEPAGE, SPILLAGE
fluid [made to] . . .	MOATED
fluidity of [style 'e] . . .	SLEETY

flurry

flurry of [snow]	OWNS, SOWN
flurried [man or] . . .	ROMAN

flush

flush	GORED
flush toilet	WATERLOO
flushed	RED
• flushed *out*	R–ED

fluster

flustered [and red]	DANDER
[never] *flustered*	NERVE

flutter

flutter of [wings]	SWING
fluttering [lids]	SLID
[heart] *aflutter*	EARTH, HATER, RATHE

fly

flies *up*(D)^	STANG, STOB
fly *about*	F–LY, W–ING

fly *about*<	TANG
fly bird	CRANE, DRAKE
fly *buzzing around*<	TANG
fly-by-night	BAT, MOTH
fly high, *say*	SORE
fly in this fashion	SOWING
fly saint	WIDEST
fly spider	SPINNER
fly *to*	
–France	MOUCHE, VOLER
–Germany	FLIEGE(N)
–Italy	MOSCA, PILOTARE
–Spain	MOSCA, VOLAR
fly *up*^(D)	TANG, TOB
flying	(in) SK–Y
• a king *flying*	SARKY
• sick, *flying*	SKILLY
flying	(on) PLANE
• test *flying, say*	TRIPLANE
• *flying* time	PLANET
flying	(on) WING
• about *flying*	CAWING
• father *flying*	PAWING
flying animal	BULLDOG, CAMEL
flying [animal]	LAMINA, MANILA
flying [ants]	STAN, TANS
flying around a . . .	incl A
• b–ird *flying around* a . . .	BAIRD
flying around [China]	CHAIN
flying around E, isle<	ELSIE
flying around *	incl *
• ti–t *flying around* pole	TINT
flying [bluetits]	SUB-TITLE
flying broomstick	WITCHCRAFT
flying club	BAT
flying fish	PILOT
flying fortress	CASTLE-IN-THE-AIR
flying machine, *say*	PLAIN
flying officer	ENSIGN, FO
flying out [airman]	MARINA
flying saucer	CLAY PIGEON
flying *start*	F
flying up on an(D)^ . . .	NANO–
flyover	HIGH ROAD

focus

focus of attention	N
focus of *	incl in *
• learner *is focus of* mu–ch . . .	MULCH

fog

fog, *say*	MISSED
foggy [day]	–ADY

fogey

fogey	SQUARE

foil

['e soon] *foiled*	NOOSE
foiled [a gun raid]	GUARDIAN

fold

fold [diaper]	REPAID

Anag [cat]; Any *; Begin IGN–; Endings –ING; eg •; Hidden /cat/; Implied add (on); Implied in (in);

fold knife	CREASE	food crusher	MOLAR, TOOTH
fold linen	CRASH	food for supporter	FANFARE
fold net	TUCK	food of the gods	PANCAKES, RADISHES
fold over [ends]	DENS, SEND	food processor	STOMACH, TUM(MY)
fold over top<	POT	food purveyor	GULLET, OESOPHAGUS
fold you and me, *say*	CROESUS	food raiser	CHOPSTICK, FORK, SPOON
folded [sheet]	THESE	food, *say*	FAIR
folding [arms]	MARS, RAMS	• food pulverised, *say*	FAIRGROUND

folio

folio	F, FO, FOL	• food unknown	FAIRY
• First Folio *in front*	FIBT	food, *say*	PHARE
folios	FF	food store, *say*	DELHI

follow

a *follower*	B	food tokens	CHIPS

fool

follow	DOG	fool about	NITRE
• follow *up*(D)^	GOD	fool *around*	AS-S
• follow hunter	DOG-WATCH	fool will, *say*	PRATTLE
• follows sailor	DOG-STAR	*fooling around* [in the] ...	THINE
follow	TAIL	*foolish* [boy]	YOB
• follow *after* bird	COCKTAIL	foolish creature	FONDANT
• follow dog	TAIL	foolish girl, *say*	SILICATE
• follow soldiers	TAILOR	*foolishly* [I went] ...	TWINE
follow	TRACK	[general] *foolishness*	ENLARGE

foot

• followed a Conservative, *say*	TRACTATORY	foot	DANCE
• followed a number, *say*	TRACTATE	foot	F
• followed girl, *say*	TRACTOR	• nothing *on* foot	OF
follow <u>my</u> *leader*	1st letter M	• one *on* foot	IF
I'll *follow* <u>my</u> *leader*	MILL	• pertaining to foot	OFF
follow win	SUCCEED	foot	FT
followed, *say*	CHASTE	• man *on* foot	HEFT
followers		• see US state *on* foot	RIFT
–*of* ABC	DE	• the *French* foot	LEFT
–*of* CND	DOE	foot fault	BUNION, CORN, HAMMER TOE
of star	TUBS	foot joint, *say*	PAWNEE
following	AFTER	foot lever, *say*	PEDDLE
• following mathematics	AFTER MATHS	foot-pound-second	FPS
• following smack	AFTERTASTE	footpad	CORN PLASTER
• king *has* following	RAFTER	footman	CHIROPODIST, PEDESTRIAN
following	F	footnote	PS
• following behind	FRUMP	footwear, *say*	SHOO
• following deed	FACT	footwear *with* spikes	BOOTLACES
• mark following ...	SCARF		SHOELACES
following	SQ, SEQ, SEQUENS		

football

following <u>his</u> *leader*	1st letter H	football	FA
• little Arthur *following* <u>his</u> *leader*	HART	• football in square	FAINT
how *to follow* teams	SIDESHOW	• football near church	FACE
	(*see also* dog²)	• football on street	FAST

		Football Association	FA
		football club	AFA, FA

foment

foment [riots]	TRIOS	football club-house	VILLA
fomenting [revolt]	TROVER	football club incentives	SPURS

food

		football	RU
Food and Agriculture Organisation	FAO	• football *in* these islands	GRUB
food container	EGGSHELL, NUTSHELL	• football match	RUB OUT
	STOMACH, TUM(MY)	• football revival	RURALLY
		footballers	FA, RU
		footballers' magazine	ARSENAL

footwear   (*see* foot)
for¹
  for example, for instance, maybe,
  perhaps, possibly and say are largely
  interchangeable and are used to
  indicate anagrams, homophones and
  one of a class
for²
  for   FOR
  • for a friend   FORMATE
  • for me   FOREGO
  • for teacher, *say*   FORCER
  for   PRO
  • for and against   PROV–
  • for good measure   PROTON
  • for one   PROA
  for and against   NOYES
  for and on behalf of   PP
  for each   PER
  • for each boy   PERSON
  • for each king   PERK
  • meat for each . . .   HAMPER
  for example   EG, VG
                                              (*see also* for³)
  for starters have egg
    mayonnaise   HEM
  for the ear, I . . .   AY(E), EYE
  for the family   OVERSTRAIN
for³
  indicating a foreign language:
  • boy *for Benito*   RAGAZZO
  • dog *for Hans*   HUND
  • house *for René*   MAISON
  • sing *for Emilio*   CANTAR
  indicating a homophone:
  • *for example*, a weight   AWAIT
  • *for instance*, hire   HIGHER
  • *for the ear*-wax   WHACKS
  indicating one of
  a class:
  • *for example*, it . . .   PRONOUN
  • *for example*, Jeeves   SERVANT
  • *for example*, she'll   ELISION
  • *for instance*, servant   JEEVES
  • *for one*, Constable   PAINTER
  indicating substitution:
  • \p\enny *for* \s\on sent . . .   PENT
  • \t\ime *for* \c\old chicken   TOWARD
forbid
  forbidden in future, *say*   TABULATOR
  forbidden *to speak*   BAND, BARD
force
  force   F
  • force cow   FLOWER
  • one force   IF
  • story *about* force   LIFE
  force   G

  • force oar   GROWER
  • force out   GOUT
  • out in force   OUTING
  force of gravity   GRATE
  force of law   POSSE
  forced   FZ
  forced [into] . . .   –TION
  forced [into a]   –ATION
  forced into [action]   CATION
  forced, *say*   RESTED
  forceful reportage   TELLING
  forcibly break into   ENTERPRISING
  forcibly remove   TEARAWAY
fore
  fore and aft   1st and last letters
  • *fore and aft of* the . . .   TE
  • *fore and aft of* ship   SP
  fore part of ship   S
forefront
  forefront   F
  forefront of the army group   TAG
  soldiers in battledress *at*
    *the forefron*t   SIB
  the *forefront*   T
forego
  forego a   omit A
  forego money   omit L
  forego, *say*   WAVE
  forego *   omit *
  • mot(her) *foregoes* her . . .   MOT
forehead
  forehead   F
  forehead   H
  foreheads, *say*   BROWSE
foreshorten
  foreshorten girl   (m)ARIA
  for(e)shortened   FOR
  foreshortened, *say*   THREE
foreign¹
  indicating use of other
  languages:
  • *foreign* castle   SCHLOSS
  • *foreign* character   ALPHA
  • *foreign* field   CHAMP
  • *foreign* man   HOMBRE
  • *Foreign* Office   BUREAU
  • *foreign* town   VILLE
  • *foreign* wine   VIN(O)
                          (*see also* abroad, cross⁴, continent)
foreign²
  foreign (= not English)   NOTE
  Foreign (and Commonwealth)
    Office   F(C)O
  foreign *capital*   F
  foreign company   AG
  foreign exchange   AU PAIR
  foreign goddess   ALIENATE

Anag [cat]; Any *; Begin IGN–; Endings –ING; eg •; Hidden /cat/; Implied add (on); Implied in (in);

foreign [to me]	MOTE	**format**	
foreign warship	USS	*format* [disk]	KIDS, SKID
foreign wife	DUTCH	*formation of* [planes]	PANELS
foremost		[page] *format*	GAPE, PEAG
foremost <u>a</u>uthority	A	[place in] *formation*	PELICAN
*foremost character in p*arty	P	**former**	
foremost in <u>a</u>ny good <u>E</u>nglish . . .	AGE	former	
foresters	AOF	indicating old words:	
forfeit		• *former* housewife	HUSSY
forfeit a . . .	omit A	• *former* queen	PRINCE
forfeit (a) hundred	omit (A)C	• sailor *formerly*	SHIPMAN
forfeit a pound	omit AL	former	EX
forfeit money	omit D, L, P	• *former* coins, *say*	EXPENSE
forfeit *	omit *	• *former* nurse	EXTEND
• mate(lot) *forfeits* much . . .	MATE	• *former* model	EXPOSE(R)
forge		• *former* player	EXACTOR
forge money	MAKE READY	• *former* position, *say*	EXCITE
forged [coin]	ICON	• *formerly* a miner	EXAMINER
forger's art	METALWORK	• *formerly* healthy	EXHALE
forger's shop	SMITHY	• *formerly* plenty	EXAMPLE
forging [note]	ETON, TONE	former	LATE
forget		• engineer's former . . .	RELATE
forget a . . .	omit A	• *former* ceremony	LATERITE
forget money	omit D, L, P	• *former* meeting	LATERALLY
forget name	omit N	former copper	D
forget nothing	omit O	former monk	OUT OF ORDER
forget *	omit *		PRIOR
• (To)by *forgets* to . . .	BY	former painter	OLD ROPE
half-*forgotten* parent	PAR, ENT	former pupil	FP, GRADUATE
fork		former pupil	OB
fork out *	omit*	• 100 former pupils	COBS
• cut(l)er *forks out* pound	CUTER	• *former* pupil *takes* exam	OBTEST
• m(al)e *forks out* a pound	ME	• *former* pupils' meeting	OBSESSION
forlorn		former, *say*	YOUR
[Ted is] *forlorn*	SITED	formerly	NE, NEE
forlorn [but not] . . .	BUTTON		(*see also* old)
form		**formidable champion**	GRIMACE
Form [One]	EON, NEO–	**formulate**	
form [a line]	ANILE	*formula for* [Cartesian] . . .	ASCERTAIN
form of [stapler]	PLASTER	*formulate* [his new] . . .	WHINES
form of worship	PEW	*formulation of* [idea]	AIDE
form queue	BRAID, PLAIT	**tort**	FT
form round a . . .	incl a	**forte**	
form round *	incl *	forte	F
• r–ing *forms round* a king	RAKING	forte-piano	FP
form union	WED	forte, *say*	FOR TEA, FORTY
forming [words]	SWORD	fortissimo	FF
formal		**forty**	
formal	PRIM	Forties	ROARING, SEA AREA
• formal park	PRIMP	forty	F, M, MU, XL
• formal period	PRIMAGE	forty, *say*	EXCEL, FOR TEA, FORTE
• formal states	PRIMUS	forty days	LENT
formal body	STIFF	forty-five	DISC, EP, RECORD
formal garden, *say*	NOT	forty-five minutes	(h)OUR, HOU(r)
formal *introduction*	F	forty-nine	IL
formally attired	(in) TA–ILS	forty-niner	GOLD-SEEKER, PROSPECTOR
formally dressed	INVESTMENT	forty, *say*	FOR TEA, FORTE

forty thousand	F, M, MU
forty winks	NAP
forward	
forward-<u>l</u>ooking	L
forward part of ship	BOW, FOCSLE
	FORECASTLE, PROW
forward part of <u>s</u>hip	S
forwards of <u>A</u>rsenal play	
<u>t</u>ogether	APT
forzando/forzato	FZ
foul	
<u>f</u>oul-*mouthed*	F
foul punch	LOWLANDER
foul, *say*	FOWL
fouled [nest]	NETS, SENT, STEN
found	
found	CAST
• found gold	CASTOR
• found out	CASTAWAY
• found the *French* . . .	CASTLE
found abroad	
indicating use of	
foreign word:	
• coin *found in Spain*	PESETA
• flower *found in France*	FLEUR
• girl *found in Italy*	RAGAZZA
• I *found in Germany* . . .	ICH
• man *found abroad*	HOMME, HOMBRE
	UOMO, MANN
found at last	COBBLER, SHOEMAKER
found in S/anti/ago	ANTI–
found in *	incl in *
• we are *found in* building	SHEWED
found out [why it] . . .	WITHY
found vessel	LAUNCH
	(*see also* find)
founder	
foundering [yacht]	CATHY
[ship] *founders*	HIPS, PISH
foundation	
foundation of hous<u>e</u> (D)	E
strong *foundation*(D)	G
four	
four	IV, TWO-BY-TWO
four Christmas presents	CALLING BIRDS
four-in-hand	COACH, FINGERS, NECKTIE
four-letter word	TETRAGRAM
four-nil	FORTY
four of <u>hear</u>ts	HEAR
four of the best	ACES
four points	NEWS, SEWN, WENS
	TRY
four, *say*	FOR
• four airs, *say*	FORTUNES
• four feet, *say*	FORFEIT
• four old people, *say*	FORAGED
four, *say*	FORE

• four have left, *say*	FOREGONE
• four seas, *say*	FORESEES
• four toys, *say*	FORETOPS
fourth	
fourth	D, QUARTER, UNPLACED
fourth dimension	TIME
fourth man	SETH
fourth of December	DE, CE, MB, ER
fourth of Dec<u>e</u>mber	E
fourth of Jul<u>y</u>	Y
fourth part of play	ACTIV–
fourth part of pla<u>y</u>	Y
fowl	
fowl	HEN
• fowl part	HENBIT
• fowlpest	HENBANE
• woman *with* fowl	WHEN
fowl, *say*	FOUL
fox	
fox	TOD
• fox devoured	TO-DATE
fox, *say*	RUSTLE
fracas	
fracas in the	THINE
[she saw] *fracas*	WASHES
start of <u>f</u>racas	F
fraction	
fraction of the	T, HE
fraction of t/he len/gth	HELEN
fractionate [oils]	LOIS, SILO
<u>prop</u>er *fraction*	PROP
fractious	
fractious [babe]	ABBE
[spoke] *fractiously*	POKES
fracture	
badly fractured	BALDLY
fracture [hip]	PHI
fracturing [arm]	MAR, RAM
fragile	
fragile [plate]	PETAL, PLEAT
fragile, *say*	WEEK
fragile vessel	TENDER
[quite] *fragile*	QUIET
fragment	
fragment	FR
fragmented [bone]	EBON
fragments of <u>petal</u>s	PEAL
fragments of [petals]	PLEATS, STAPLE
frail	
frail [prince]	PINCER
frail, *say*	WEEK
frailty of [old Ed] . . .	DOLED
frame	
framed by ug/ly re/mains	LYRE
framed by *	incl in *
• aim *framed by* manuscript	MENDS
framed in fi/ne st/eel	NEST

Anag [cat]; Any *; Begin IGN–; Endings –ING; eg •; Hidden /cat/; Implied add (on); Implied in (in);

framing a . . .	incl A	free³	
framing *	incl *	other uses:	
• manuscript framing aim	MENDS	free a . . .	omit A
franc	FR	free alongside ship	FAS
France		free of charge	GRATIS, NEUTRAL
France	FR, RF		UNLOADED, VINDICATE
France, say	GALL	free of charge	FOC
Franco-British articles	LATHE, LETHE	free on board	FOB
Franco-German agreement	OUIJA	free on rail	FOR
Franco-German articles	UNDER	Free Presbyterian	FP
	(see also French)	free publication	RELEASE
Frank		free-range eggs	LAID OUT
frank character	STAMP	free supply	DELIVER
Frank scoffed	CANDIDATE	free TV	AUNTIE, BEEB
Frank's deception	BLUFF	free *	omit *
frantic		• free her from fat(her)'s . . .	FATS
frantic [leap]	PALE, PEAL	insect-free	omit FLY
[stare] frantically	RATES, TARES, TEARS	• (f)air(ly) insect-free	AIR
fraudulent		freeze	
[act] fraudulently	CAT	freezing	ATOC, TEMPO
fraudulent [deal]	DALE, LADE, LEAD	freezing-point	FP, OC
fraudulently [alter]	LATER	freezing-point	F
[he's] fraudulent	SHE	freezing waterfall	HAIL(STORM)
fray		frozen bird, say	CHILDREN
frayed [nerves]	SEVERN	frozen vegetable	CORNICE
fraying [rope]	PORE	French	
freak		French	FR
freak [show]	HOWS	• a French help	AFRAID
freakish [result]	LUSTRE	• French caper	FRANTIC
free¹		• French crew	FREIGHT
free	RID	French and English money	SOUL,
• exist without free . . .	BRIDE		SOUP
• free ball	RIDDANCE	French art gallery	ESTATE
• free return, for example<	RIDGE	French banker	LOIRE, SEINE etc
• free-standing(D)^	DIR	French brother	JACQUES
• free study	RIDDEN	French capital	EURO, FRANC
free admission	incl RID	French capital	F
• free admission to		French capitalist	PARISIEN(NE)
Geological Society	GRIDS	French fort	STRONG
free²		French friend	AMI(E)
indicating anagram:		• French friend can . . .	AMIABLE
[Born] Free	BRNO	• French friend in the	
[dust]-free	STUD	Louvre initially	TAMIL
free-[for-all]	FLORAL	• French friend with 500 . . .	AMID
[free] movement	REEF	French horn	COR
free movement of [cars]	ARCS, SCAR	French leader	F
[free]-range . . .	REEF	French manger	EAT
free-[range I] . . .	GAINER, REGAIN	French private	ENTRE NOUS
free [slaves]	SALVES, VALSES	French-speaking girl	FILLE(TTE)
free-style [event seen] . . .	SEVENTEEN	French underground	MAQUIS, METRO
free [trade]	RATED, TREAD	Frenchman	M, RENE
free transfer for [player]	REPLAY	• Frenchman married	RENEWED
free [vote]	VETO	Frenchmen	MM
free[dom]	MOD		(see also France)
free[lance]	CLEAN	frenetic	
freely [as her] . . .	HARES, HEARS, SHARE	frenetic [pace]	CAPE
freely occurring [in the] . . .	THINE	[it was] frenetic	WAIST, WAITS

Letter replaced \c\at; Omit (a); Pointers out; Retain a; Split B_ED; Down (D); Backwards <or ^

frenzy

frenzied [dash]	SHAD
frenzy of [swine]	SINEW, WINES

frequent

frequency	F
frequency modulation	FM
frequently	FR

fresh

fresh	NEW
• fresh deposit	NEW-LAID EGG
• fresh people	NEWGATE
• fresh weight and	NEWTON
• fresh choler, *say*	NUBILE
• fresh song, *say*	NUDITY
• fresh work, *say* and	NUT-OIL
• fresh mother, *say*	PNEUMA
• freshly cut here, *say*	PNEUMONIA
fresh [bread]	BARED, BEARD, DEBAR
fresh edition	GREENED
fresh impression	REISSUE
fresh oar	CLEAN SWEEP
fresh spell of rain	REIGN, REIN
fresh start for boy	COY, GOY, HOY ROY, SOY, TOY
fresh support	GREENBACK
freshly cut [flowers]	FOWLERS
freshly gathered [grapes]	PAGERS, SPARGE
freshly [made]	DAME, EDAM, MEAD
freshly made [bread]	BARED, BEARD, DEBAR
freshness of [dawn]	WAND
	(*see also* new)

friar

friar	TUCK
• friar fights . . .	TUCK-BOXES
• friar's dance	TUCKSHOP
• son *with* friar	STUCK

Friday

Friday	F, FR, FRI
• Friday's child	FRISSON
Friday	MAN

friend

friend	ALLY
• alternative friend	ORALLY
• boy-friend	REGALLY, ROYALLY
• little boy friend	TOTALLY
• stout friend	FATALLY
• support friend	LEGALLY
friend	CHINA
• friend *on* island, *say*	CHINAMAN
• friend wears, *say*	CHINAWARES
friend	OPPO
• friend's height, *say*	OPPOSITE
• friend's ways	OPPOSES
friend	MATE
• deceives friend	FOOL'S MATE

• European friend, *say*	CHECKMATE
• friend *with* much . . .	MATELOT
friend	PAL
• friend *and* expert	PALACE
• friend *at* sea	PALMED, PALMER
• friend ate nothing, *say*	PALMETTO
• friendless	OPALS
• girl-friend	PALMARY, PALMYRA
• good friend	PIPAL
• no friend	OPAL
friend*less*	omit ALLY
• truly friend*less*	RE(ally)
friend*less*	omit PAL
• (pal)try, friend*less* . . .	TRY
friendly	PALLY
• friendly animal, *say*	PALLIASSE
• friendly father	PAPALLY
• friendly language, *say*	PALI
friendly cat	FAMILIAR
friendly *converse*	HOSTILE
friendly Russian	KINDRED
Friendly Society	OUTGOINGS
Friends of Europe	FOE
Friends of the Earth	FOE

fright

frighten	AWE
• frighten a few	AWESOME
• frighten completely, *say*	AWFULLY
• frightening, *say*	AURIFIC
• learner frightens, *say*	LAWS
frighten	COW
• frighten fish	COWLING
• frighten writer	COWPEN
• son frightens . . .	SCOWS
frightful [time]	EMIT, MITE
frightfully [ugly, Nott] . . .	GLUTTONY

fringe

fringe report	BANG
fringed by *	incl in *
• motorway *fringed by* tre–es	TREMIES
fringes a . . .	incl A
fringes *	incl *
• tre–es *fringe* motorway	TREMIES
fringes of society	SY

frisk

frisky [horse]	SHORE
[lamb] *frisking* . . .	BALM

fritter

fritter [asset]	TESSA
fritter, *say*	WAIST

Fritz

Fritz (=German)	
• *Fritz's* house	HAUS
• with *Fritz's* . . .	MIT

frog

frog	FRENCHMAN
frog clearer	AHEM

Anag [cat]; Any *; Begin IGN–; Endings –ING; eg •; Hidden /cat/; Implied add (on); Implied in (in);

frog march	MARCHE MILITAIRE	from London	DOWN
	MARSEILLAISE	*from* [Mali]	MAIL
frolic		from North-west	TOSE
frolic [in sea in] . . .	ASININE	from point to point (= between N, S, E, W)	
frolic about [in nude]	UNDINE	• Bill King *goes from*	
frolicking [lionesses]	NOISELESS	point to point	NACRE
from¹		• goddess *goes from*	
from	EX	point to point	EATEN
• from a pit	EXAMINE	• Hal *goes from point to point*	WHALE
• from shelter	EXTENT	from South	TON
• from the first	EXIST	from South-west	TONE
from	OFF	*from* Sou/th-ea/st	THEA
• from the freezer	OFFICE	from the air (=song)	
• from worker	OFFHAND	• *from the air*, London	
• shirt from . . .	TOFF	river	OLD FATHER THAMES
from *French*	DE	• *from the air*, Surrey feature	FRINGE
• from *French* girl	DECLARE	*from the back of* beyon<u>d</u>	
• from *French* islands	DECAYS	they cam<u>e</u>	DYE
• from *French* records	DEFILES	from the beginning	AB INIT(IO)
from *Latin*	AB	*from the beginning of* <u>t</u>ime	
• from *Latin* customs	ABUSES	<u>o</u>n <u>E</u>arth	TOE
• from *Latin* scholar	ABBA	*from the end of* <u>t</u>he Big	
• from *Latin* spoken . . .	ABORAL	Bang	EGG
from the *French*	DELA, DES, DU	*from the finish of* pla<u>y</u>	
• from the *French*		he went	YET
bird, note	DELAMINATE	*from the front* <u>h</u>e <u>i</u>s <u>s</u>ure . . .	HIS
• from the *French* in the East	DELAINE	*from the heart of* t/he be/ast	HEBE
• from the *French* youth	DELATED	*from the mouth of*	
and		• heard *from the mouth of* . . .	HERD
• from the *French* city	DESTROY	from the queen	OFFER
• from the *French* couple	DESPAIR	*from the rear of* <u>t</u>he parad<u>e</u> A<u>l</u>	EEL
• from the *French* I call	DESIRING	*from the rear* rank<	KNAR
and		*from the start of* <u>t</u>he <u>o</u>ld <u>y</u>ear	TOY
• from the *French* church	DUCE	from West	TOE
• from the *French* scholar	DUMA	*from what we hear*, he'll . . .	HEAL, HEEL
• from the *French* members	DUMPS	*from what's said*, I'd . . .	EYED, IDE
from²		**front**	
indicating omission:		<u>B</u>righton *front*	B
• alternative *from* the(or)y	THEY	<u>c</u>old *front*	C
• doctor *from* Bor(d)e(r)s	BORES	<u>e</u>nemy *front*	E
• letter *from* (m)other	OTHER	front	BOW
from³		• artist in front	RAINBOW
indicating origins:		• front learner	BOWL
• agreement *from Moscow*	DA	• front letter	BOWESS
• boy *from Milan*	RAGAZZO	front cover	APRON
• *Cairngorm*-stone	STANE	*front* <u>c</u>over	C
• children *from Germany*	KINDER	*front* <u>d</u>oor	D
• dog *from Lyons*	CHIEN	front line	POLE POSITION
• girl *from Perth*	SHEILA	*front* <u>l</u>ine	L
• man *from Ayr*	MON	front of house	FACADE
• uncle *from Pretoria*	OOM	*front of* <u>h</u>ouse	H
• woman *from Malaga*	SENORA	front of vehicle	CARNOSE
from⁴		*front of* <u>v</u>ehicle	V
other uses:		front page	PI, RECTO
from A-K and M-Z	NOEL	*front* <u>p</u>age	P
from Bir/ming/ham	MING	front runner	ADAM
from East	TOW	*front* <u>r</u>unner	R

Letter replaced \c\at; Omit (a); Pointers *out*; Retain <u>a</u>; Split B_ED; Down (D); Backwards <or ^

front-runner in Derby	D	• *full-length* cot	COTTAGE
sea-*front*	S	full meal	THOROUGHFARE
warm *front*	W	full moon	O
frontier		*full of* *	incl *
frontier of Russia	R	• bo–x *full of* gunners' . . .	BORAX
frontier restriction	LIMIT	Full Organ	FO
Russian *frontiers*	RN	full rank	ABUNDANT
frost		full version of	
frost	DAVID	indicating abbreviation to be expanded:	
	HOAR, JACK, RIME	• *full version of* sect	SECTION
frost, *say*	RHYME, WHORE	• *full version of* Mass	MASSACHUSETTS
froth		fully	
frothing [over]	ROVE	indicating abbreviation to be expanded:	
frothy [surf]	FURS	• do *fully*	DITTO
frozen	(*see* freeze)	• *fully* met	METEOROLOGICAL
fruit		**fumble**	
fruit	LIME	*fumble* [about]	U-BOAT
• fruit flavour	LIMESTONE	*fumbling* [in the] . . .	THINE
• fruit underweight, *say*	LIMELIGHT	**function**	
• second fruit	SLIME	function	PI
• under fruit . . .	SUBLIME	• function *in* city	EPIC
fruit	PEAR	• function noted, *say*	PICENE
• a soft fruit	APPEAR	• second function, *say*	SPY
• fruit *and* fish	PEARLING	function	SIN(E)
• fruit *carried in* ship	SPEARS	• firm function	COSINE
• fruit, *say*	PARE, PAIR	• function, *say*	SIGN
• harvest fruit	REAPPEAR(S)	• function-like, *say*	CYNICAL
fruit	PLUM	**funeral**	
• *fruit-fly*	PLUMPEST	funeral contractors	FIRM UNDERTAKING
• fruit garden	PLUMBED	funeral party	GRAVEDO
• fruit, *say*	PLUMB	**funky**	
• fruit season	PLUMAGE	*funky* [notes]	SETON, STONE, TONES
fruit and veg, *say*	MELANCHOLY	[quite] *funky*	QUIET
fruit-bats	BANANAS	**funny**	
fruit dish	FOOL	funny-bone	
fruit only	LEMON SOLE	operation, *say*	HYSTERECTOMY
fruit pulp	SQUASH	funny cry	SCREAM
fruitful area	ORCHARD, ORANGE GROVE	*funny*-[face]	CAFE
	VINEYARD	*funny* [idea]	AIDE
fruitful, *say*	TEAMING	*funny* [thing]	NIGHT
frustrate		*funny* [turn]	RUNT
frustrate [action]	CATION	[How] *funny*!	WHO
[it was] *frustrated*	WAIST, WAITS	[it was] *funny*	WAIST, WAITS
fuddled		**fur**	
fuddled [in bar]	BAIRN, BRAIN	fur, *say*	FIR
fuddling [ales]	LEAS, SALE	furs, *say*	FIR, FURZE, MINX
fudge		*local* fur	FAR
fudged [issue]	SUSIE	**furious**	
[lemon] *fudge*	MELON	*furious* [rage]	GEAR
full		furious woman	ALECTO, MEGAERA
full	DRUNK, FED, STONED, TIGHT		TISIPHONE
full-*back*<	DEF	furious women	ERINYES, EUMENIDES
full board	THOROUGHFARE	*furiously* [blame] . . .	MABEL
full length		**furl**	
indicating abbreviation		*furled* [sails]	SILAS
to be expanded:		*furling* [tops'l]	PLOTS
• Al, *full-length* . . .	ALUMINIUM	**furlong**	FUR

Anag [cat]; Any *; Begin IGN–; Endings –ING; eg •; Hidden /cat/; Implied add (on); Implied in (in);

furniture	
furniture maker	ADAM, CHIPPENDALE
	SHERATON el al
	MAHOGANY, OAK etc
furniture remover	CASTOR
furniture remover's garment	SHIFT
furrowed brow	HEADLINES
further	
further	MORE
• further money	MOREL
• further *round* the bend	MORSE
• no further	NEVERMORE
furthest part of China	A
furtive	
furtive [leer]	REEL
[I creep] *furtively*	PIERCE
fury	
furious [when I] . . .	WHINE
[I am] *furious*	AIM, AMI
in a fury [over] . . .	ROVE
[in a] *fury*	AIN, –IAN
furze	
furze	GORSE, WHIN
furze, *say*	FIRS, FURS, WIN
fuse	
fused [lights]	SLIGHT
fusion of [alloy]	LOYAL
[nuclear] *fusion*	UNCLEAR
fuss	
fuss	ADO
• fuss about	ADORE
• fuss *about* one . . .	ADIO
• fuss *in* the Navy	RADON
fuss [about] . . .	U-BOAT
fussy [gown in] . . .	OWNING
fussy individual	PARTICULAR
[get] *fussed*	TEG
futile	(in) VA–IN
future	FUT

G

acceleration, agent, clef, conductance, four hundred (thousand), gallon, gamma, gamut, gauss, gee, gelding, general intelligence, George, German, Germany, Gibb's function, giga-, girl, good, gram, gram(me), grand, gravity, group, guinea, gulf, key, man, note, shear modulus, spot, string, suit

G-man's son	GLAD	game	
gabble		game	BRIDGE
gabbled [words]	SWORD	• attract game	DRAWBRIDGE
[stop] *gabbling*	POTS, SPOT, TOPS	• game *follows* animal . . .	OXBRIDGE
gad		• game *on* river	CAMBRIDGE
gad*about*	GA–D	game	LOO
gad*about*<	DAG	• game *with* king's . . .	LOOKS
gadding about [in the] . . .	THINE	• give directions *after* game	LOOSE
gain		• I *have* grand game	IGLOO
gain admission to *	incl in *	game	POLO
• I *gain admission to* club	BAIT	• draw game	TIEPOLO
• we *gain admission to* s–et	SWEET	• game *near* city	POLONY
gain honour	APPRECIATE	game	RU, RUGBY
gain points	WINTRY	• game at home	RUIN
gain, *say*	PROPHET	• game fish	RULING
gained weight	WONTON	• game, second-class	RUB
gained weight, *say*	WANTON	game bird	HOBBY
Galatians	GAL	game birds	DUCKS AND DRAKES
gale	WINDLASS	game couple	TWOSOME
gallery		game leader	BRIDGEHEAD
gallery	TATE	game *leader*	G
• second gallery	STATE	game *over*<	UR
• gallery-owner's daughter	MISSTATE	game redhead	MATCH
gallery idols	GODS	game reserve	SUBSTITUTE, TWELFTH MAN
galley	PROOF	game reserves	POOL
Gallic king	ROI, SM	**gamma**	G
gallon	GAL(L)	gang	
gallop		gang-girl	BANDANNA
gallop [off in Reg's] . . .	OFFERINGS	gang leader	FOREMAN
gallop, *say*	CHOREA	gang leader	G
galloping [horse]	SHORE	gangster	AL
Gallup poll	GP	• gangster fellow	ALCOVE
Gambia	WAG	• gangster *with* President	ALIKE
gamble		• gangster *with* weapon	ALARMED
gamble	BET	gangster	HOOD
• gamble a small amount	BETA PARTICLE	• gangster bats an eye	HOODWINKS
• gamble on unknown . . .	BETONY	• gangster's moll	GIRLHOOD
• gamble *with* a monarch	BETAKING	• second gangster, *say*	SHOULD
gamblers	BETTER AND BETTER	gaol	
gambling theorist	SPECULATOR	[gaol]-*break(ing)*	GOAL, OLGA
gambol		gaol disturbance	STIR
gambol [in the] . . .	THINE	[gaol] *disturbance*	GOAL, OLGA
gambol, *say*	BET, SPECULATE	gaoled	(in) C–AGE, (in) PE–N
gambolling [lambs]	BALMS	*riot in* [gaol]	GOAL, OLGA

gap
gap-filler	ER, UM
gap, *say*	WHOLE

garage
garage for vintage car, *say*	CARPORT
garage, *say*	CARCASE

garbage in, garbage out — GIGO

garble
garbled [speech]	CHEEPS
garbling [words]	SWORD

Garbo — DRESS CIRCLE

garden
garden	BED
• garden refuse	BEDASH
• gardener	BEDMAKER
• tool *used in* garden	BAWLED
garden	EDEN
garden	PLOT
• garden plan	PLOT
ga*rd*en *centre*	RD
garden maker	ADAM
[garden] *maker*	DANGER
garden-party	OUTDO
garden tool, *say*	SEA-DRAKE
gardener	ADAM, BEDFELLOW
gardener's share	ALLOTMENT

garrison dance — BASEBALL

gas
gas consumed	NEONATE
gas-cooled reactor	AGR
gas main	NORTH SEA
gas ring	DISCUSSION GROUP, SEMINAR

gate
gate-crasher	BATTERING-RAM
[gate]-*crashing*	–TAGE
gateman	WICKET-KEEPER

Gateshead
*G*ateshead	G
• *G*ateshead owns . . .	GOWNS
• in *G*ateshead	–ING

gather
gather a . . .	incl A
gather food	TUCK
gather fruit	REAPPEAR(S)
gather round	incl O
gather [nuts]	STUN, TUNS
gather *	incl *
• bo–y *gathers* weight	BOOZY
gathered by *	incl in *
• weight *gathered* by bo–y	BOOZY
gathering	DO
gathering of [men at] . . .	MEANT
gathering of shea/ves t/aken . . .	VEST

gaunt
gaunt bird	HAGGARD
gaunt writer	HAGGARD

gauss — G

gazette(er) — GAZ

gear — FIRST, SECOND, THIRD, FOURTH, NEUTRAL, REVERSE
gear change	NEW SUIT
[gear] *change*	GARE, RAGE
gear changing	TRANSVESTISM
gearbox	SUITCASE

gee — G

gelignite — JELLY

gem
gem merchant, *say*	DUELLIST
gem, *say*	PURL
gem study, *say*	RUBICON
gem weight	STONE
gem weight, *say*	CARROT

gender — GEN

general[1]
general	BOOTH
• general stall	BOOTH
• general *swaps* book for shirt	TOOTH
general	GRANT
• general assistance	GRANT-AID
• my general, *say*	MIGRANT
general	LEE
• general's introduction	MELEE
• *in* general	LE–E
general	GEN(L)
• general *has* square . . .	GENT
• general *in* boat	PUNGENT
• general name	GENEVA
general	GORDON
[General] *Assembly*	ENLARGE
[general's] *order*	ENLARGES
order from [general]	ENLARGE

general[2]
General Assembly	GA
[General] *Assembly*	ENLARGE
general certificate	U
General Certificate of Education	GCE
General Court Martial	GCM
General Electric Company	GEC
general issue	GI
General Medical Council	GMC
General Motors	GM
General Officer Commanding	GOC
general paralysis of the insane	GPI
General Post Office	GPO
general practitioner	GP
general-service	GS
General staff	GS
General staff officer	GSO
[general] *surgery*	ENLARGE
General Teaching Certificate	GTC

generate
generate [steam]	MATES, MEATS, TAMES
generation	ERA

Letter replaced \c\at; Omit (a); Pointers *out*; Retain a̲; Split B_ED; Down (D); Backwards <or ^

generation of [heat]	HATE, THEA	• fear of Germans, *say*	HUNDRED
genesis		• German church	HUNCH
Genesis	GEN	• German dogs, *say*	HUNKERS
Genesis *I and II*	GE	• German youth	HUNTED
genesis of life	L	German	JERRY
genitive	GEN	• German is able, *say*	JERRICAN
genius	ID, KA	German	KRAUT, TEUTON
gentle		German *banker*	ODER, RHINE etc
gentle death	EASY GOING	German capital	(DEUTSCH)MARK, EURO
gentle game	LIGHTHOUSE	German *capital*	G
gentle type	KIND, MAGGOT	German capitalist	BERLINER
gently	P	[German] *dancing*	MANGER
very gently	PP	German fellow	OTTOMAN
	(*see also* quiet, soft)	German flower	ODER, RHINE etc
gentleman		German *leader*	G
gentleman Scot	GENTIAN	German linesman	GOETHE
gentleman's home	VERONA	German shell (WWI)	PIPSQUEAK
genuine		*German-speaking* woman	FRAU
genuine	REAL	German trooper, *say*	WRITER
• genuine fish	REALGAR	German way	AUTOBAHN
• genuine document	REALMS	two Germans	HUNGER
• genuine table, *say*	REALIST	**Germany**	D, GER
• over genuine . . .	SURREAL	**gerund**	GER
genuine, *say*	REEL	**get¹**	GET
• 100 genuine, *say*	CREEL	[Get] *lost!*	TEG
• genuine fish, *say*	REELING	[get] *organised*	TEG
genus	GEN	get *out*	GE–T
geology		[Get] *out!*	TEG
Geological Society	GS	get-*up*(D)^	TEG
geologist's work	FAULT-FINDING	**get²**	
Geordie		indicating implied inclusion:	
Geordie	NE	getting a tan	(in) SU–N
Geordie-land	NE	getting wet	(in) RA–IN
George		**get³**	
George I	GRACE	indicating inclusion:	
George *I*	G	*get into* t/he ar/my	HEAR
George Bernard Shaw	GBS	*get into* *	incl in *
George Cross	GC	• we *get into* sea	MEWED
George Medal	GM	*get left in* . . .	incl L or LT
germ		*get on*	incl ON
germ	BUG	• I *get* on both sides	ONION
• germ carries . . .	BUGBEARS	*get out for* a duck	incl O
• germ deficiency	BUGLOSS	• h–e *gets out for a* duck	HOE
• germ *with* the *French* . . .	BUGLE	*get out of* a . . .	incl A
• sound germ	HUMBUG	*get out of* brea/th an/d . . .	THAN
germ, *say*	CEDE	*get out of* line	incl I or L
German¹		• he–m *gets out of* line	HELM
German	BOCHE, FRITZ	• ma–n *gets out of* line	MAIN
German	G	*get out of* *	incl *
• German landlord	GHOST	• German soldier *gets*	
• German rage	GANGER	*out of* car	SCARS
• German state	GUTTER	*get right in* . . .	incl R or RT
German	GER	*get round* a . . .	incl A
• German and *German*	GERUND	*get round* *	incl *
• German *follows* male . . .	MANGER	• soldier *gets round* it	RITE
• German transport system	GERRY	**get⁴**	
German	HUN	indicating omission:	

Anag [cat]; Any *; Begin IGN–; Endings –ING; eg •; Hidden /cat/; Implied add (on); Implied in (in);

get out of a	omit A
get out of *	omit *
• (Ch)arles gets out of church	ARLES
get rid of a . . .	omit A
get rid of money	omit L
get rid of *	omit *
• the(y) get rid of unknown . . .	THE
• get rid of odd members of (p)a(r)t(i)e(s) . . .	ATE

get[5]
other uses:

get a big haul, say	CACHALOT
get a good result	PASSABLY
get a rise(D)^	
• before getting a rise	ETNA
get aboard, say	COMMON
get awkward [and not] . . .	DANTON
get cracking	DECIPHER, DECODE
get down	DUCK
get drunk	BESOTTED
get drunk [on ale]	ALONE
get from e/vide/nce	VIDE
get in a mess [over] . . .	ROVE
get [into] shape	–TION
get involved in [war]	RAW
get lost in [forest]	FOSTER
get married, say	TAKE AMISS
get moving [when I] . . .	WHINE
get out of bed	DIG UP
get out of [breath]	BATHER
get over it<	TI
get ready	(EN)CASH, REALISE
get ready [to pin] . . .	PINTO, POINT
get shot	SNAP, TAKE PICTURE
get to work [in car]	CAIRN
get to work on [time]	EMIT, MITE
get up mad(D)^	DAM
get very 'ot	OVEREAT
gets help	GAINSAID
getting better sport	RALLYING
getting firsts in Science, English and Maths	SEAM
getting on train	BOARDING SCHOOL
getting warm	NOTICED

ghastly

ghastly [green end]	ENGENDER
[paints] ghastly . . .	PINTAS

ghost

ghost, say	GOAL
ghost-writer	IBSEN
ghostly remains, say	GOULASH
in ghost, say	INSPECTOR

giant

giant	ATLAS
giant	TITAN
• giant in charge	TITANIC
• giant, say	TIGHTEN
giant-killer	DAVID, JACK

Gibraltar — GIB, GBZ

giddy

giddy [goat]	TOGA
[spin] giddily	NIPS, SNIP

gift

gift	GAB
gift coin	TALENT
gift of money	TALENT
gift-wrapped	(in) PRES–ENT
• I'd gift-wrapped . . .	PRESIDENT
gifted father	SANTA CLAUS

giga-electron-volt — GEV

Gilbert and Sullivan — GS, GANDS

gilded — (in) O–R

gilt

gilt	OR
gilt-edged	O–R

gimmick

gimmick [used]	DUES, DUSE, SUED
gimmicky [means]	MANES, NAMES

gin

[gin] cocktail	IGN–, –ING, NIG
gin mixer	ATONIC
[gin] sling	IGN–, –ING, NIG
gin user	TRAPPER

girdle

girdles a . . .	incl A
girdles *	incl *
• staple girdling the . . .	BREATHED

girl[1]
commonly used names:

girl	ADA
• girl in millions	MADAM
• girl takes exercise	ADAPT
girl	ALMA
• girl has a joke, say	ALMAGEST
• quiet girl	PALMA
girl	ANN
• black girl, say	BAN(N)
• girl in sea in France	MANNER
• girl overweight(D)	ANNOUNCE
girl	ANNA
• 100 girls	CANNAS
• girl in telecommunications	BANNAT
• girl puts on pounds	ANNALS
girl	ANNE
• girl in transport	BANNER
• girl with hat on	ANNELID
• quiet girl	PANNE
girl	ANNIE
• girl lost, say	ANIMIST
• girl married, say	ANIMATED
• Greek girl, say	GRANNIE
girl	AVA
• girl takes cereal	AVARICE

Letter replaced \c\at; Omit (a); Pointers out; Retain a̲; Split B_ED; Down (D); Backwards <or ^

- learner *takes* girl ...   LAVA
- quiet girl *has* name ...   PAVAN

girl   DI
- girl employees   DISTAFF
- rotter *with* girl's ...   CADDIS
- spoil girl   MARDI

girl   DINAH
- girl might, *say*   DYNAMITE
- girl, *say*   DINER

girl   ENA
- girl *goes to* court   ENACT
- girl *in* Lebanon   RENAL

girl   EVE
- girl *after* transport   BREVE
- girl *has square*   EVET
- girl *in* sides   LEVER

girl   IDA
- *girl has* a call   IDAHO
- girl *without* energy   IDEA

girl   JOY
- girl *almost* complete   JOYFUL
- girl *has* name, *say*   JOIN
- girl's credit   JOYSTICK

girl   KATE
- girl out of practice, *say*   RUSTICATE
- girl performed, *say*   KATYDID
- second girl   SKATE

girl   MAY
- girl *has* spoken   MAYORAL
- girl *on* river, *say*   MAYFLOWER
- this girl, *say*   DISMAY

girl   MEG
- girl *and* a boy   MEGARON
- girl *on* the edge   MEGRIM
- girl *with* a ...   MEGA–

girl   MONA
- girl died   MONAD
- girl's twitch   MONASTIC
- off-white girl, *say*   CREMONA

girl   PAT
- former girl   EXPAT
- girl fastens ...   PATTIES
- second girl   SPAT

girl   PEG
- girl like you and me   PEGASUS
- girl on ...   PEGLEG
- girl spinner   PEGTOP

girl   ROSE
- girl devoured ...   ROSEATE
- girl is prepared, *say*   ROSEWOOD
- quiet girl   PROSE

girl   * RUBY
- girl devoured *say*   RUBIATE
- girl *with* criminal, *say*   RUBICON
- girl is prepared, *say*   RUBYWOOD

girl   SAL
- girl from South America   PERUSAL

- girl *with* dog   SALCHOW
- girl working   SALON

girl   SUE
- girl died   SUED
- girl *without* right ...   SURE
- is the girl?   ISSUE

girl   TESS
- girl *takes* time   TESSERA
- girl *with* boy, *say*   TESTED
- shouts *to* girl   HOSTESS

girl   UNA
- girl *in* sides   LUNAR
- girl-struck   UNABASHED
- square girl   TUNA

girl   VERA
- girl *in* time ...   AVERAGE
- girl *reaches* big town   VERACITY
- girl with a ... , *say*   VERANDA

girl   VI
- a girl died   AVID
- girl has arrived, *say*   VISCUM
   VISIER, VIZIER
- girl poses   VISITS

girl²

girl   DEB
- a royal girl   ARDEB
- girl broadcasting   DEBONAIR
- girl *goes to* America   DEBUS

girl   G
- girl *in* ...   GIN
- girl *in* the money   COIGN
- in girl   –ING

girl   GAL
- girl runner   GALLOPER
- girl *with* nothing on   GALOON
- girl *with* one lion   GALILEO

girl   LASS
- 100 girls   CLASSES
- ginger-*headed* girl   GLASS
- girl took action, *say*   LASSOED

girl   MAID(EN)
- girl gangster   MAIDENHOOD
- girl *has* a point   MAIDENHEAD
- worker *with* girl   HANDMAID

girl   MISS
- composer's girl, *say*   MISHANDLE
- girl and French ...   MIS-SET
- girl locked up   MISSPENT

girl³

girl *and* boy   ANNEAL, BETHANK, DIJON, DIARCHY, DINED, GALLEON, MISSAL, PATRON, PATTED, SALIAN, SALTED

girl *and* man   SALMON
girl *and* two boys   BETRAYAL
   (*see also* boy and girl)
girl can handle gun   PEARL

girl carrying camera	DOLLY	give voice *about*	S–ING
girl cyclist	DAISY	*given* a . . .	incl A
girl-friend	MANDATE, PALMARY	*given* <u>h</u>is *head*	incl H
	PALMYRA, SALAMI	*given shelter by* *	incl in *
girl from		• English queen *given*	
−America	BROAD	*shelter by* sh–ed	SHEERED
−Australia	ADELAIDE, ALICE, SHEILA	*given* *	incl *
−France	FILLE(TTE), NANCY	• she *is given* £50	SHELL
−Germany	FRAULEIN	**give²**	
−Ireland	COLLEEN	indicating omission:	
−Italy	RAGAZZA, SIGNORINA	*give away* a . . .	omit A
−Picardy	ROSE	*give away* money	omit D, L, P
−Scotland	CUMMER	*give away* *	omit *
−Spain	MUCHACHA, NINA, SENORITA	• (p)layer *gives away* pawn	LAYER
−Tralee	ROSE	*give* nothing *away*	omit O
−Troy	HELEN	*give out* a . . .	omit a
−Wales	MEGAN	*give out* *	omit *
−Wessex	TESS	• fat(her) *gives out* her . . .	FAT
Girl Guide	USHERETTE	*give up* a . . .	omit A
girl in		*give up* leader	omit 1st letter
−[gaol]	OLGA	*give up* *	omit *
−opera	AIDA, CARMEN, MIMI	• mot(her) *gives up* her . . .	MOT
	NORMA, TOSCA	**give³**	
−[silo]	LOIS	other uses:	
−the [army]	MARY, MYRA	give	HAND
−the drink	OLIVE	• give at this point, *say*	HANDIER
−the garden	MAUD	• give the sack	HANDBAG
−the shrubbery	MYRTLE, VERONICA etc	• support *and* give . . .	BACKHAND
−Wonderland	ALICE		SECONDHAND
girl *making* [coral]	CAROL	*give a lift to* diva(D)^	AVID
girl of the soft left	MILDRED	give attention to	EAR
girl, *say*	GENE, MAIDAN	give birth	
girl who		−at one,, *say*	LITERATI
−did	KATIE	−to eight, *say*	LITERATE
−gets gun	ANNIE	give girl a weapon	ARMADA
−sparkles	BERYL, RUBY	give no indication	SHAKE ONE'S HEAD
−takes issue	SUE	*give* nothing *for* a . . .	
−*took the* [blame]	MABEL, MELBA	• Chin\a\ *gives* nothing *for* a . . .	CHINO
girl with cold hands	MIMI	*give rise to* [leer]	REEL
girl *working the* [oracle]	CAROLE	*give rise to* leer(D)^	REEL
girlish *denial*	BOYISH	give up, *say*	SEED
girl's	HER	give worker a break	RESTANT
• girl's love	HERO	*given* a *hearing*, Paul . . .	PALL, PAWL
• girl's ring in . . .	HEROIN	*given* a *lift*, boy(D)^	YOB
girl's claim	AMRITA	*given in* hi/s pare/nts' . . .	SPARE
girl's best friend	DIAMOND	*gives* [praise]	ASPIRE
growing girl	DAISY, ERICA, ROSE etc	giving away purchases	SHOPPING
	(*see also* female)	giving consultation	CONFERRING
give¹		giving [her a] . . .	HARE, HEAR
indicating inclusion:		giving up drink	(on) WAGON
give key *to* . . .	incl A, B, C, D, E, F, G	**Gladstone**	
give money *to*	incl D, L, P	Gladstone	BAGMAN, GOM
give oxygen *to*	incl O	Gladstone's admission	ALIBI
give shelter *to* a . . .	incl A	**glamour**	
give shelter *to* *	incl *	glamour	IT
• sh–ed *gives shelter to*		• glamour-queen dined	ITERATE
English queen	SHEERED	glamour	SA

Letter replaced \c\at; Omit (a); Pointers *out*; Retain <u>a</u>; Split B_ED; Down (D); Backwards <or ^

• glamour-girl	SAGENE, SAUNA
glass	
acrobat's glass	TUMBLER
glass-maker	QUARTZ
glass of beer, *say*	PINTAIL
glass-paper	MIRROR
glass vessel	SCHOONER
stranger glass	RUMMER
gleaner	RUTH
glider	SNAKE
gloat	
gloat *over<*	LEVER
globe	
globe	O
globe-fish	EARTHLING
gloomy crypt	GRAVE
gloria	HEADLIGHT, O
glovemaker	BUCKSKIN, DOESKIN
	KID, LEATHER
gnarled	
gnarled [oaks]	SOAK
gnarly [trees]	REEST, RESET, STEER
go¹	GO
go *a bit* si<u>ll</u>y	GOLLY
go *abroad*	ALLER
go *and* cut	GOSNICK
go *and* throw	GOSLING
go *back<*	OG
[go] *out*	OG
go *over<*	OG
go *round<*	OG
[go] *round*	OG
[go] *wrong*	OG
[goes] *funny*	EGOS
[gone] *bad*	–GEON
go²	
go	PEP
• go *and* do wrong	PEPSIN
• go both ways	PEP
• go *with* the tide	PEPTIDE
go	TRY
• directions *to go* . . .	ENTRY
• go *by* road	TRYST
• succeed with go	WINTRY
go	TURN
• go *on* board	TURNTABLE
• go *to* fish	TURNPIKE
• go *to* university	U-TURN
go³	
indicating anagram:	
go astray [in the] . . .	THINE
go bad [in keg]	EKING
go into [slide]	IDLES, SIDLE
go off [meat]	MATE, TAME, TEAM
go off with [a tenor]	ORNATE
go to the dogs [or be] . . .	BORE, ROBE
go wild [over]	ROVE

go wrong [over an] . . .	VERONA
go⁴	
indicating inclusion:	
go round the bend	incl S, U
going about a . . .	incl A
going about *	incl *
• fish *going about* the . . .	GATHER
going around a . . .	incl A
going around *	incl *
• i–s *going around* a square	ITS
going inside *	incl in *
• he, *going inside*, swat–s . . .	SWATHES
going outside a . . .	incl A
going outside *	incl *
• w–ere *going outside* house	WHERE
go–ing *outside*-right	GORING
going round a . . .	incl A
going round *	incl *
• c–at *going round* circle	COAT
going through *	incl in *
• Scot *going through* Per–th	PERIANTH
going without a . . .	incl A
going without *	incl *
• w–e are *going without* her	WHERE
go⁵	
indicating omission:	
go away from	omit N, S, E, W
go East from	omit E
go North from	omit N
go off a . . .	omit A
go off *	omit *
• brother *goes off* the edge	(br)INK
* *goes*	omit *
• win(k) when king *goes*	WIN
go South from	omit S
go West from	omit W
going without a . . .	omit A
going without *	omit *
• fat(her) *going without* her	FAT
go⁶	
other uses:	
go	GREEN
go against it, *say*	BUCKET
Go back, fool!*<*	PAS
go before	PREDECEASE
go by sea, *say*	CREWS, SALE
go crazy	DEPARTMENTAL
go fishing	CASTANET
go into action	PROSECUTE, SUE
go mad	DEPARTMENTAL
go metric	SCRAPYARD
go north	QUITS
go on	RIDE
go on a bender	KNEEL
go over	(see over)
go over plot	CROSSPATCH
go to pot [when I] . . .	WHINE

Anag [cat]; Any *; Begin IGN–; Endings –ING; eg •; Hidden /cat/; Implied add (on); Implied in (in);

go upstairs	TAKE FLIGHT
go west	QUITE
goes in front, *say*	LEEDS
going around <u>s</u>lowly	SLY
going around [there]	ETHER
* *going about*	
• saw *going about*<	WAS
* *going around*	
• gnat *going around*<	TANG
going astray, *say*	HERRING
going by air (=in a song)	
• cyclist, *going by air*	DAISY
• *going by air*, sailorman . . .	POPEYE
going north, walker . . . (D)^	RECAP
* *going round*	
• bus *going round* . . . <	SUB
going rate	MPH, SPEED, VELOCITY
going *to* a dance	WORKSHOP
going up step(D)^	PETS
goad her	NEEDLEWOMAN
goal	
[goal]	GAOLBREAK
goal-less draw	O–O
goat	
• goat	BUTTER
• female goat	BUTTRESS
• goat's milk	BUTTERMILK
• goat-fat	BUTTER
goat	KID
• goat expires	KIDDIES
• goat family	KIDSKIN
• goat in ship	SKIDS
goat tender	NANNY
god	
god	LAR
• god is dead, *say*	LARDED
• god-like	LAROID
• river-god	POLAR
god	PAN
• god does his best	PANTRIES
• god fastens . . .	PANTIES
• god knows, *say*	PANNOSE
god	RA
• god *has* many . . .	RAM
• god *in* th–e . . .	THRAE
• horse-god	COBRA
god	RE
• god exists	REIS
• god *in* th–e . . .	THREE
• son to god	STORE
goddess	DEVI
• goddess devoured . . .	DEVIATE
• goddess in front	DEVILED
• goddess said, *say*	DEVISED
goddess, *say*	HEARER, MEWS, SERIES
godfather	CAPO, DON
godsend	GOTTERDAMMERUNG, RAGNAROK

going	(*see* go)
gold	
gold	AU
• gold *and* potassium	AUK
• gold cross in . . .	AUXIN
• gold rocks, *say*	AUROCHS
• gold the *French* . . .	AULA
gold	OR
• gold *and* iron	ORFE
• gold key	ORE
• gold coin	ORBIT
• gold letters	ORLANDO
• gold trade	ORDEAL
and	
• gold *in* church	CORE
• gold *in* iron	FORE
• gold sh–e *took in*	SHORE
and	
• measure gold	METEOR
• old gold	PASTOR
• win gold	SUCCESSOR
gold-*bearing*	incl AU, OR
• gold-*bearing* race	TAUT
• gold-*bearing* river	TORRENT
gold-bearing, *say*	HORRIFIC
gold coloured, *say*	GUILT
gold-*covered*	(in) O–R
gold-*edged*	(in) O–R
gold mint	BULL'S-EYE
gold-*mounted*	(in) O–R
gold-*mounted*(D)^	RO, UA
gold painter, *say*	GUILDER
gold-*plated*	(in) O–R
gold sovereign	MIDAS
gold-*wrapped*	(in) O–R
• the *old* gold-*wrapped* . . .	OYER
gold *wrapped in* . . .	incl AU, OR
• gold *wrapped in* pound note	LAUD, LORD
golden colour, *say*	GUILT
golden handshake	MIDAS TOUCH
golden retriever	ARGONAUT, JASON
golf	
golf course, *say*	LYNX
golf suit	CLUBS
golfer's curse	ROUND OATH
golfers	PGA
poor golfer	RABBIT
gone	(*see* go)
good¹	
good	A
• good journey	ATRIP
• good relations	AKIN
• good team	ASIDE
good	AI
• good colour	AIRED
• good contest	AIR-ACE
• good fish	AILING

Letter replaced \c\at; Omit (a); Pointers *out*; Retain <u>a</u>; Split B_ED; Down (D); Backwards <or ^

good	BON
• good figure	BOND
• good note	BONA, BOND, BONE, BONG
• good *to* us	BONUS
good	FAIR
• good distance	FAIRWAY
• good head	FAIRNESS
• *put* animal *to* good . . .	HORSE-FAIR
good	G
• embarge *has* good . . .	BANG
• good lad	GLAD
• good-*hearted* roué	ROGUE
good	OK
• good always	OKAY
• good-*hearted* man	BLOKE
• behold good . . .	LOOK
good	PI
• good friend	PIPAL
• good laugh, *say*	PILAFF
• good value	PIRATE
good *French*	BON
• good *French* beef	RIBBON
• good *French* journalist	BONED
• good *French* vehicle	CARBON
good²	
good book	BIBLE, NT, OT
good butter	GOAT
good-bye	TATA, VALE
good chap	JAKE, S, ST
good flan, *say*	OKAPI
Good Food Guide	DIETICIAN
good friend(D)^	LAP UP
good friends(D)^	SLAP-UP
good golfer	BOGEY MAN
go*od-hearted*	OO
good looker	DISH, PEACH
	SEARCHER, SPOTTER
good looking, *say*	HANSOM
good man	DEAN
good man	S, ST
• good man is not well	STILL
• good man *in* first class . . .	ASTI
• see a good man	LOST
good number	ANAESTHETIC, ANTHEM,
	HYMN
good people	SS
good reading	BIBLE, NT, OT
good rhyme	COULD, WOOD etc
good score	PAR
Good Service Pension	GSP
good sort	KIND
good speller	MAGICIAN, WARLOCK
	WITCH
good writing	BIBLE, NT, OT
goodness	MY, WELL-HEAD
goodnight, *say*	GALAHAD
goods, *say*	WEAR, WEIGHER, WHERE

goose	
gooselike	ANSERINE
gooselike, *say*	ANSWERING
Gort's men	BEF
Gospels	NT
got	(*see* get)
Gotham	NY
Gotterdammerung	GODSEND
gouge	
gouged out e(ye)s	ES
m(iddl)e *gouged out*	ME
w(it)h *middle gouged out*	WH
w(rass)e *with middle gouged out*	WE
govern	
governed by policy	UNDERLINE
governess	ANNA
government	GOV(T)
government controlled	UNDERSTATE
government house, *say*	STATOHM
government issue	GI
government	
representatives, *say*	CONSOL(E)S
government	
securities, *say*	CONSOLES,
	CONSULS
governor	GOV, HE
governor of Paris	PRIAM
governor's position	OVERSTATE
grab	
grab a . . .	incl A
grab *	incl *
• do–g *grabs* a tin	DOTING
grabbed by *	incl *
• tin *grabbed by* do–g	DOTING
gradually	ERIC
graduate	
graduate	BA
• graduate circle	BARING
• graduate fool, *say*	BASILIAN
• graduates are late	BASTARDY
• graduates *have a* hair-cut	BASS-HORN
• wicked graduate	BASINFUL
and	
• mother *and* graduate	MAMBA
• peculiar graduate	RUMBA
• Uncle *with* graduate	SAMBA
graduate	MA
• graduate queuing	MAINLINE
• graduate's quarrel	MASTIFF
• graduates are wise	MASSAGE
• graduates celebrate	MASSING
	(*see also* scholar)
grain	
grain	GR
grain, *say*	SERIAL
grain vessel	BRANDISH
gram(me)	G, GM, GR

Anag [cat]; Any *; Begin IGN–; Endings –ING; eg •; Hidden /cat/; Implied add (on); Implied in (in);

grammar	GR
gran turismo	GT
grand	
grand	G
• grand circle	GO
• grand entrance	GENTRY
• grand total	GADDING
• grand tour	GRANGE
grand *deficiency*	omit G
grand	IMPOUNDS
gran<u>d</u> *finale*	D
Grand Old Man	GOM
grand *opening*	G
Grand Union	MARRIAGE, WEDDING,
	WEDLOCK
grandfather clock	OLD TIMER
graphite	KISH
grasp	
grasp, *say*	HOLED
grasped by *	incl in *
• king *grasped by* duke	FIRST
grasp twig	REALISE, UNDERSTAND
grasp woman, *say*	CAESAR
grasping a . . .	incl A
grasping compact	TIGHT
grasping hi/s hand, y/oung . . .	SHANDY
grasping , *say*	CEASING
grasping *	incl *
• duke *grasping* a king	FIRST
grass	
grass	FIELDFARE
	MARIJUANA, POT(-PLANT)
grass	BETRAY, INFORM
	SQUEAL, TELL
grass	SING
• grass and ecstasy	SINGE
• grass twice	SINGLETON
• tea-grass	TEASING
grass brush	FOXTAIL
grass-covered	(in) RE–ED
grasser	BETRAYER, INFORMER
	SQUEALER, TELLER
grate	
grate [on her] . . .	HONER, RHONE
grating [noises]	ESSOIN
grating *sound*	GRILL
gratings in pighouse, *say*	STYRAX
gratings, *say*	GRILSE
gratitude	TA
grave	
grave description	DEAD END, TOMB
grave-digger, *say*	CRYPTOLOGIST
grave, *say*	CEREOUS
grave situation	CEMETERY, CHURCHYARD
	CREMATORIUM
gravestone	CARVE, SCULPT
grave testimonial	HEADSTONE
gravity	
gravity	G
gravity-*free*	omit G
• gravity-*free* (g)lobe	LOBE
graze	
graze, *say*	BROWS
grazing	FIELDFARE
great	
great	GT, MEGA–, OS
great artist	TOP DRAWER
Great Britain	GB
great city	WEN
great composer	TOP SCORER
great conductor	COPPER, CU
great craft	LARGESS
Great Dane	HAMLET
great deal	BAGS, LOTS
great deceiver	SUPER-DUPER
great dog	DANE
great fiddle	CELLO
great flier	AUK, TIT
great flow(er) (=large river)	
• great flow of German . . .	RHINE
• great flower in South America	AMAZON
• Indian's great flower	GANGES
great fool	BF
great healer	TIME
great lady	BIGAMY
great letter	CAPITAL, LARGESS(E)
great names	ALEXANDER, ALFRED
	CATHERINE
great physician	TIME
great sea	MEDITERRANEAN
great swimmer	WHALE
great town	YARMOUTH
Great Universal Stores	GUS
Great Western Railway	GWR
greater alarm, *say*	MORPHIA
Greater London Council	GLC
greater, *say*	GRATER, MOOR
greatness	BIGHEAD
Greece	GR
Greek	
Greek	GK
Greek	GR
• Greek in debt	GROWER, GROWING
• Greek river	GROUSE
• Greek state	GRAVER
Greek bedroom	ATTIC
Greek capital	DRACHMA
Greek *capital*	G
Greek capitalist	ATHENIAN
Greek character (=Greek letter)	
• 3rd character in Greek . . .	GAMMA
• Greek character *has* no large . . .	OMEGA
Greek garret	ATTIC
Greek judge, *say*	DIE-CAST

Letter replaced \c\at; Omit (a); Pointers *out*; Retain <u>a</u>; Split B_ED; Down (D); Backwards <or ^

Greek labourer	HERACLES, HERCULES	grip, *say*	BIGHT, BYTE
Greek *leader*	G	*grip* *	incl *
Greek story	ATTIC	• a v–ice *grips* a king	AVARICE
green		*gripped by* wa/ter m/onster	TERM
green	GO, NAIVE, RAW	*gripped by* *	incl in *
[green] *bananas*	GENRE, NEGRE	• a king *gripped by* a v–ice	AVARICE
green city	LINCOLN	gripper	CLAM(P), VICE, VISE
green cotton	LAWN	gripping article	CLAM(P), VICE, VISE
green-eyed monster	ENVY	lo/ve st/ory *is gripping*	VEST
green light	PERMISSION	**gritty fellow**	SANDY
[Green] *Movement*	GENRE, NEGRE	**groggy**	
[green] *salad*	GENRE, NEGRE	*groggily* [rise]	SIRE
greenkeeper	CONSERVATIONIST	*groggy* [males]	LAMES, MEALS
	EVERGREEN, LAUREL etc	**gross national product**	GNP
greenstuff	LAWN	**grotesque**	
Greenwich Mean Time	GMT	*grotesque* [icon]	COIN
greet		*grotesquely* [fat]	AFT
greet icily	HAIL	**ground**	
greeting	AVE	ground control approach	GCA
• greeting king	AVER	ground plan	PLOT
• greeting *with* anger	AVERAGE	ground rent	CREVASSE, FISSURE
• woman greeting . . .	WAVE	ground rent deposit	LAVA
greeting	HI	*ground* [rice]	CIRE, ERIC
• greeting Asian	HIMALAYAN	**group**	
• greeting child, *say*	HYSON	group	BAND
• greeting sailor	HIJACK	• group noticed	BAND-SAW
greet	HAIL	• group rented	BANDLET
• greet, *say*	HALE	• group, *say*	BANNED
• greets Franchot	HAILSTONE	group	CLASS
• second greeting, *say*	SHALE	• group directions	CLASSES
Grenada	WG	• group in charge	CLASSIC
Grenadines	WV	• group *with* fewer . . .	CLASSLESS
grey		group	GANG
grey suit	SLATE CLUBS	• function *in* group	GAPING
greyish carpet	SLATE	• group considers, *say*	GANGWAYS
greylag	GAOLBIRD	group	SECT
grievous		• belonging to group	INSECT
grievous bodily harm	GBH	• group insects	SECTANTS
grievous [hurt]	RUTH	• two groups	BISECTS
grievously [stinted]	DENTIST	group	SET
grill		• group of fliers	POSSET
grill for breakfast, *say*	FRIARLY	• group of graduates	BASSET
grill [lamb]	BALM	• group of officers	COSSET
grilled [sole]	LOSE	group of workers	BEE
grilling [steak]	SKATE, STAKE, TAKES	groups of sheep, *say*	PHLOX
grim		**grouse**	
grim	GRIZZLY	grouse	GR
grim situation	STERNPOST	grouse-meat	BEEF
grimace	MOUE, MOW	**grow**	
grind		grow back	REAR
grind coin	POUND	growing attractive	BECOMING
grind [into]	–TION	growing division	HEDGE
grind [into a] . . .	–ATION	growing girl	MYRTLE, ROSE, VIOLA et al
grind it, *say*	MILLET	growing incentive	CARROT
grinding [oats]	STOA	growing wrinkled	INCREASES
grip		growth industry	FARMING, FORESTRY
grip a . . .	incl A		MARKET GARDENING

Anag [cat]; Any *; Begin IGN–; Endings –ING; eg •; Hidden /cat/; Implied add (on); Implied in (in);

guard

guard	SCREW
• follow guard	DOG-WATCH
• guard alien	WATCHET
• guard timepiece	WATCH
guarding a . . .	incl A
guarding *	incl *
• do–g *guarding* a tin	DOTING
guarded by *	incl in *
• tin *guarded by* a do–g	DOTING
Guatemala	GCA
Guernsey	GBG
guide	
guide animal	STEER
guide animal, *say*	STEAR, STERE
guide dog	POINTER
guide, *say*	GUYED
	LIEDER, PILATE
	STEAR(E), STERE
guide to cinema	USHERETTE
guilder	GLD
guile	
guile of [devil]	LIVED
guileful [ways]	SWAY, YAWS
[slid] *guilefully*	LIDS, SILD
guillotine	
guillotine	omit 1st letter
• *guillotine* cleric	(p)ARSON
• Marie's *guillotined* . . .	ARIES
guinea	G, GU
gules	GU
gulf	G
gullible fool	CHARLEY, CHARLIE
gulp	
gulp (=knock back)	
• *gulp* brandy<	CRAM

• *gulping* bun<	NUB
gum	
gum(D)^	MUG-UP
gum-*up*(D)^	MUG
gun	
gun	ARM
	BREN, GAT, LEWIS
	MAXIM, ROD, STEN
gun carrier	HOLSTER
gun-dogs	POMPOM
gun-running	PASSAGE OF ARMS
[gun]-*running*	GNU
[gun]-*whip*	GNU
[gun]*maker*	GNU
gunman	COLT, WEBLEY et al
gunmen	GRS, RA
gunner	FIREMAN, GR
gunners	FIREMEN, GRS, RA
guns	GRS, RA
gut	
c(ompletel)y *gutted*	CY
gut fish	STRIPLING
gutted h(ak)e	HE
gutless m(al)e	ME
Guy	
Guy	FAWKES, PLOTTER
Guy's companions	DOLLS
Guy's part	WARD
Guy's partner	DOLL
Guy's revolver	CATHERINE WHEEL
Guyana	GUY
gyrate	
gyrate [orb]	ROB
gyrating [top]	OPT, POT
gyration of [centre]	RECENT

H

beam, bomb, complex cube root, Dirac's constant, enthalpy, Hamiltonian, hand, hard, heart, heat content, hearts, hecto-, height, Helmholtz free energy, henry, heroin, *horse*, hospital, hot, hotel, hour, house, Hungary, husband, hydrant, hydrogen, magnetic field strength, Planck's constant, tap, total energy, two hundred (thousand), vitamin

Habakkuk	HAB
habit	
annoying habit	HAIR SHIRT
habit-forming	DRESSMAKING, TAILORING
habitat	
habitat for *	incl *
• garden *habitat for* steer	BOXED
• organ *found in* dr–y *habitat*	DREARY
had confessed	OWNED
Haggai	HAG
Haggard girl	SHE
hail	
hail	AVE
• hail *after* sun	SAVE
• hail king	AVER
• hailstorms	AVERAGES
hail Mary	AM
hailing from Rome	ROAM
hair	
hair	FUR
• hair in front	FURLED
• hairline	FURROW
• made of hair, *say*	OFFER
Hair	MUSICAL
hair-*covered*	(in) MAN–E
hair fasteners	LOCKS
h<u>air</u>-*piece*	AIR
hair-remover	BARBER, HAIRDRESSER, RAZOR, SCISSORS
hair shirt	ANNOYING HABIT
hair-style	
–for the beach	SHINGLE
–report	BANG
–report, *say*	BHANG
hair*cut*	(h)AIR
hairdresser	COMB(ER)
hairdressers' dance	BARBERSHOP
hairy	DANGEROUS, LOCKED
hairy	(in) FU–R
hairy, *say*	INFER
Haiti	RH
half[1]	

half	DEMI–
• half egg	DEMIURGE
• half square	DEMIT
• half-way	DEMIST
half	HF
half	SEMI–
• half-*back*<	–IMES
• half-cold	SEMIC
• half-note	SEMITE
• half *with* no . . .	SEMINARY
half a score	TEN, X
half alphabet	ATOM
half-century	L
half-*cut*	ALF, HAL
half-day	AM, PM
half-dozen	VI
half-*hearted*	AL
half-inch	PINCH, STEAL
half-minute	MO
half moon	FORTNIGHT
half *of France*	DEMI
half open	AJAR
half time	AM, PM
half[2]	
comm<u>only</u> *halved*	ONLY
half a jiffy	OND, SEC
half afraid	AID, AFR
*half*back	BA, CK
half-baked	COO, KED
half day	FRI, MON, SUN
• *half*-day closing	FRIEND
• *half*-day early	MONSOON
• *half*-day *and* night, *say*	SUNNITE
half days	DA, YS
half dead	AD, DE
half dry	T
half-*forgotten* parent	ENT, PAR
	FAT, HER
	HER, MOT
half full	FU, LL
half-hearted bel(l)ow	BELOW
half <u>len</u>gth	LEN

Anag [cat]; Any *; Begin IGN–; Endings –ING; eg •; Hidden /cat/; Implied add (on); Implied in (in);

half length of tunnel	TUN, NEL
half-mast	MA, ST
half mile	MI, LE
half minute	MIN, UTE
half-moon	MO, ON
half Nelson	NEL, SON
half of bitter	BIT, TER
half of ditch	HA
half of th/e ar/c	EAR
half open	EN, OP
half-sister	SIS, TER
half-sovereign	ARD, EDW
	KI, NG
half the capital	DON, LON
half-time	TI, ME
half volume	OK, BO
*half*way	PA, TH
	AD, RO
	EET, STR
half-witted	TED, WIT
halo	AUREOLE, GLORIA
	HEADLIGHT, NIMBUS, O
ham	
ham	OVERACT
ham [actor]	CROAT, –OCRAT
Hamlet	
Hamlet, *say*	DEIGN
Hamlet's agreement	SETTLEMENT
Hamlet's rest	SILENCE
hammer	
hammered [with] . . .	WHIT
<u>hammer</u>*head*	H
hammering [nails]	SLAIN
Hampton	
[Hampton] *maze*	PHANTOM
hand[1]	
hand	AB
• hand-loom	ABLOOM
• hand-out	ABOUT
• hands pamphlet . . .	ABSTRACT
hand	FLUSH, FULL HOUSE
	STRAIGHT
hand	H
• hand fish . . .	HEEL, HID, HIDE
• hand permits . . .	HALLOWS
• hand-work	HOP
hand	L, R
• bird *in* hands	LEMUR
• copper hands	CURL
• hands *round* girl	LANNER
	LEVER, REVEL
hand	MAN
• colour *round* hand	HUMANE
• hand *has* army . . .	MANTA
• warning *to* hand	FOREMAN
hand	PAW
• hand-*out*	PA–W

• hands	PAWPAW
• hands *back*<	SWAP
• hands *over*<	SWAP
• hands *to* ears	PAUSE
• hands *up*(D)^	SWAP
hand	PALM
• hand ate, *say*	PALMETTE
• hand ate nothing, *say*	PALMETTO
• name a hand	NAPALM
hand in . . .	incl L, R
• had hand *in* ma–king	MARKING
• hand *in* f–ew . . .	FLEW
hand-*out*	omit L, R
• (l)a(r)ge hand-*out*	AGE
hand[2]	
hand over [reins]	RESIN
hand, *say*	SIGHED
handbook, *say*	MANUEL
handed out [dole]	LODE
handover of loot<	TOOL
hands down	SIX-THIRTY
hands up	MIDNIGHT, NOON, TWELVE
handy	
–cleaner	NAILBRUSH
–cover	GLOVE
–fitter	GLOVE
–fruit	BANANAS
–joke, *say*	REDIGEST
–pair	THUMBS
–sketch	THUMBNAIL
–way	CLOCKWISE
handicap	
handicap	EBOR
handicapped [male]	MEAL, LAME
handle	
handle	EAR
• 150m handles	CLEARS
• handle money	EARMARK(S)
• long handle	LEAR
handle eyes, *say*	TREATISE
handle, *say*	EWES, YEWS
	HANDEL
handle stores	STOCK
handled [adroitly]	IDOLATRY
handled fabric	FELT
handling [dogs]	GODS
hang	
hang alien	LYNCHET
hang over a lot(D)^	TOLA
hang-up	CLOSE CALL, MOBILE
hanger-on	BARNACLE,
	CLAM, ICICLE,
	STALAGMITE
hangman	(JACK) KETCH
haphazard	
haphazard [sort]	ORTS, ROTS, TORS
[picks] *haphazardly*	SPICK

Letter replaced \c\at; Omit (a); Pointers *out*; Retain <u>a</u>; Split B_ED; Down (D); Backwards <or ^

happy		Hardy companion	LAUREL
happier, *say*	MORGAY	Hardy's superior	NELSON
happy few	GLADSOME	**harm**	
happy fish, *say*	MERICARP	*harm* [a fly]	FLAY
happy ignorance	BLISS	harmless female, *say*	VENUS
happy members	CONTENT	harmless glider	GRASS SNAKE
happy people, *say*	MERIONES	[not] *harmed*	TON
harass		**harness**	
harassed [teacher]	CHEATER	harness	TACK
harassment of [all the] . . .	LETHAL	• can harness . . .	TINTACK
[it was] *harassing*	WAIST	• harness in front	TACKLED
harbour		• harness *in* ship	STACKS
harbour a . . .	incl A	**harry**	
harbour	PORT	*harried* [master]	REMAST, STREAM
• harbour charges	PORTIONS	*Harry* [lived] . . .	DEVIL
• harbour fruit	MULBERRY	*harry* [deer]	REDE, REED
• harbour lights	PORTRAYS	**harsh name**	BITTERN
harbour *	incl *	**harvest**	
• ship *harbouring* convict	SLAGS	harvest	REAP
harboured by *		• harvest conference, *say*	REAPPEAR
• convict *harboured by* ship	SLAGS	• harvest fruit	REAPPEARS
hard[1]		• *use* a hundred *in* harvest	RECAP
hard	H	harvested, *say*	MOAN, MODE
• hard and fast	HANDFAST	**has[1]**	
• hard ground	HEARTH	has	HAS
• hard *to* say	HAVER	[has] *difficulty*	ASH
• hard work	HOP	h–as gone out	HA–S
• hardwood	HASH, HELM	has leased	HASLET
hard black	HB	has *to be made smaller*	HA, AS
hard *for outsiders* . . .	H–H	[has] *trouble*	ASH
• as hard *for outsiders* . . .	HASH	**has[2]**	
• hard *going*	omit H	*has a role in* T/he M/ousetrap	HEM
h̲ard-*headed*	H	*has a way with*	incl N, S, E, W
hard-*hearted*	incl H	• he *has a way with* . . .	HEN, HEW
• hard-*hearted* c–ad	CHAD	*has a way with*	incl RD, ST
hard *to avoid*	omit H	• she *has a way with* . . .	SHERD
• *hard to avoid* t(h)e . . .	TE	has arrived	NOWHERE
h̲ard*top*(D)	H	[has made] *mistakes*	ASHAMED
very hard	HH	*has no* . . .	incl NO
hard[2]		*has no* money	omit L
hard bed	STRATUM	*has no* time	omit T
hard case	SAFE, SHELL	*has no* *	omit *
hard drop	HAILSTONE	• I(r)an *has no* king	IAN
ha̲r̲d-*hearted*	AR	*has nothing*	incl O
hard job	STERNPOST	*has nothing on*	end in O
hard, *say*	TUFF	*has nothing on*	incl OON
hard tack	WARFARE	*has on*	incl ON
hard time	ROUGHAGE	* *has gone off*	omit *
hard times, *say*	CORSAGE	• clot(he)s he *has gone off*	CLOTS
hard water	GLACIER, ICE, ICICLE	*hasn't* a . . .	omit A
hardback	STERN	*hasn't* left	omit L
harden tablet	CAKE	• p(l)ane *hasn't* left	PANE
hardly credible	TALL	*hasn't* married	omit M
hardly [human]	NAHUM	• (m)an *hasn't* married	AN
hardtop	CARAPACE, HELMET, SKULL	*hasn't* *	omit *
hardy		**hash**	
Hardy girl	TESS	*hash* of [meal]	MALE, LAME

hashy [mess a] . . .	SEAMS
made a hash of [it when] . . .	WHITEN
hassle	
[badly] *hassled*	BALDY
hassle [players]	REPLAYS
hasty	
hasty [words]	SWORD
hastily [hide]	HIED
[speak] *in haste*	PEAKS, SPAKE
hat	
hat maker	FELT, STRAW
hat measurement	CAPSIZE
hatless black woman(D)	(n)EGRESS
hatch	
[eggs] *hatching*	SEGG
hatch [new] . . .	WEN
hatching [plot]	POLT
haughty clique	UPSET
haul	
haul it, *say*	PULLET
haul on	PULLOVER
haul sail	LUG
haul, *say*	HALL, VESTIBULE
have	
(h)ave *an hour off*	AVE
have an hour *off*	omit H
• Cat(h) has an hour *off*	CAT
have it *at heart*	incl IT
having	WITH
• having base . . .	WITHSTAND
• having bear	WITHSTAND
• having drug	WITHE
• having *nearly* al(l)	WITHAL
• they are having, *say*	THEREWITH
having a . . .	incl A
having a run	LADDERED
having a row	OARING, SCULLING
having *a synonym*	OWNING
having an edge, *say*	RIMMON
having an overdraft	(in)R–ED
having changed [a note]	ATONE
having eyes, *say*	CITED, SITED
having keys, *say*	QUAYED
having large eyes, *say*	OX(H)IDE
having money	incl D, L, P
having mosquitoes, *say*	NATTY
having small fruit, *say*	BURIED
having wharves, *say*	KEYED
having wheels, *say*	WEALD, WIELD
having *	incl *
• s–py *having* cut . . .	SLOPPY
hawk	
hawk, *say*	TARSAL
hawker, *say*	PEDALLER
Haworth residence	PARSONAGE
hay	
[hay] *fever*	YAH

[hay]*maker*	YAH
made [hay]	YAH
[went] *haywire*	NEWT
hazard	
hazard [I ran]	RAIN, RANI
hazardous [task]	SKAT
hazel	
Hazel's descendant	AMENT, CATKIN
Hazel's protector	NUTSHELL
hazy	
hazily [recall]	CALLER
hazy [idea]	AIDE
he¹	
he	HE
• he copied	HEAPED
• he exploded, *say*	EPOPT
• he got up, *say*	EROSE
• he *has* a telephone	HEARING
• he is *local*	HEBE
• he licks, *say*	HELIX
• he licks her, *say*	ELIXIR
• he lifted, *say*	ERASED
• he makes tea	HEBREWS
• he spoke to, *say*	HEADREST
• he went on horseback, *say*	ERODE
• he will dance, *say*	HEEL-BALL
• he will ring, *say*	HELLO
he *abandons* . . .	omit HE
• he *abandons* (he)r	R
• he *abandons* t(he) . . .	T
he *escapes from* . . .	omit HE
• he *escapes from* (h)ol(e)	OL
• he *escapes from* t(he) . . .	T
he *leaves* . . .	omit HE
• he *leaves* (he)r . . .	R
• he *leaves* (h)om(e)	OM
• he *leaves* t(he) . . .	T
(h)e *lost his head*	E
he-man	HEART, HELEN
	HEROD, HERON
he *objectively* . . .	HIM
he *quits* . . .	omit HE
• he *quits* (he)ad . . .	AD
• he *quits* t(he) . . .	T
he *turned over*<	EH
he will, *say*	HEEL, HELL
he would, *say*	HED, HEED
he's *put out*	omit HE
he²	
he	MALE
• Effie *and* he, *say*	FEMALE
• he, *say*	MAIL
he	MAN
• he beat it	MANGETOUT
• he gets older	MANAGES
• he is aware, *say*	MANNOSE
• he leaves	MANGOES

• he names . . .	MANHANDLES	deputy *head*	D
• the *French* he . . .	LEMAN	*head* boy	B
he makes one cross	ELECTOR	*head* first	F
he painted (it)	PINXIT, PXT	*head* of beer	B
he sculpted (it)	SC, SCULP(SIT), SCULPT	*Head* of Department	D
head¹		*head* of Intelligence	I
head covering	HAT, SCALP	head *first*	H
head garment	CAPE	head *first*	F
head measurement	CAPSIZE	head office	O
head specialist	HAIRDRESSER	head *start*	H
	TRICHOLOGIST	head *start*	S
headlight	AUREOLE, GLORIA	head *teacher*	T
	HALO, NIMBUS	headman	M
headlines	CROWS'-FEET, WRINKLES	*heading* ball	B
headlining	BRAIN(S)	headgear	G
headlong	DOLICHOCEPHALIC	headland	L
headpiece	EAR, NOSE	headlong *into*	incl L
headroom, *say*	SCULLERY	headmaster	M
head's side	OBVERSE	heads I win	IW
Head's trophy	SCALP	heads of State are gathered . . .	SAG
head²		heads off towards any large	
head	LOAF	emporium	TALE
• head *has* gin *cocktail*	LOAFING	heads you lose	YL
• head monarch	LOAFER	headship	S
head	NESS	King's *Head*	K
• hard head	TOUGHNESS	**head⁵**	
• head of beer	BITTERNESS	indicating omission:	
• wide head	THICKNESS	head *away*	omit 1st letter
head	NUT	• head *away* from (S)lough	LOUGH
• girl *with* head . . .	HAZELNUT	head *leaves*	omit 1st letter
• head girl	NUTMEG	• head *leaves* study	(d)EN, (c)ON
head	PATE	head *missing*	omit 1st letter
• head *aboard* . . .	SPATES	• head *missing from* (f)lower	LOWER
• head king	PATER	head *not seen*	omit 1st letter
head	RAS	• head *not seen* in (c)lass	LASS
• English head *has* English . . .	ERASE	head *not shown*	omit 1st letter
• head *in* church	CRASH	• *head not shown* on (s)nap	NAP
head	TOP	*head off* (b)ear	EAR
• head in charge	TOPIC	*heading from* (W)are	ARE
• head missing	TOPLESS	heading *off*	omit 1st letter
head *covering*	(in) N–ESS, (in) NU–T	• heading off (t)he . . .	HE
	(in) P–ATE, (in) RA–S	headless (f)lower	LOWER
head³		headless woman (m)ARIA, (j)ILL, (w)OMAN etc	
head East		**head⁶**	
• agent *headed* East	ESPY	other uses:	
• man *heading* East	MANE	head harness, *say*	BRIDAL
head North		head of Intelligence	MISCHIEF
• apes *headed* North	NAPES	*head-over-heels*, Eros . . . <	SORE
• girl *heading* North	MAIN	head pastry-cook, *say*	BUNKING, FLANKING
head South		head race	CROWN DERBY
• sailor *headed* South	STAR	shook *head to* foot(D)	HOOKS
• sailor *heading* South	TARS	*head-to-tail* pins<	SNIP
head West		headlong rush, *say*	CHOREA
• everyone *headed* West	WALL	**headmaster**	ARNOLD, HM
• woman *heading* West	SHEW	**headquarters**	
head⁴		headquarters of sect	SE
indicating 1st letter(s):		Police headquarters	PEE, PEN, PEW

Anag [cat]; Any *; Begin IGN–; Endings –ING; eg •; Hidden /cat/; Implied add (on); Implied in (in);

<u>S</u>cout *head*quarters	SEE, SEN, SEW
<u>Y</u>outh *head*quarters	YEN, YES, YEW
heal	
heal priest	CURE
healer	DR, GP, MB, MD, MO
	(*see* doctor)
health	
good health	TOAST
health authority	WHO
hea<u>l</u>th-*centre*	AL
health expert	TOASTMASTER
health food	TOAST
health official	MO
health resort	CLINIC
healthy	omit ILL
• *healthy* PM	CHURCH(ill)
• *healthy* hatmaker	M(ill)INER
• *healthy* tree	W(ill)OW
healthy	WELL
• healthy family, *say*	WELKIN
• healthy man, *say*	WELTED
• partner healthy	BRIDEWELL
healthy, *say*	HAIL
healthy stock	GOODS TRAIN
heap	
heap of fruit	LIMERICK
heaps of [soil]	OILS, SILO
[slag]-*heap*	GALS, LAGS
hear[1]	
hear	TRY
• fathers hear . . .	PASTRY
• hear *about*	TR–Y
• hear holy man	TRYST
hear[2]	
indicating a homophone:	
• *do we hear* rain	REIGN, REIN
• hear a loud . . .	ALLOWED
• *hear* forty . . .	EXCEL, FORTE, XL
• hear *in conversation*	HERE
• hear, *say*	HERE
• *hear* wails	WALES, WHALES
• hear why . . .	WYE, Y
• *heard* a noise	ANNOYS
• Heard? *Heard!*	HERD
• *heard* in conversation	HERD
• *hearing* a girl	ALAS
• *hearing* aid	–ADE, AIDE
• *hear*say	HERE
• *hearsay* cited	SIGHTED, SITED
• intended *to hear*	–MENT
• more *hearsay*	MOOR
• Paul *given a hearing*	PALL, PAWL
• rumour *that is hearsay*	ROOMER
hear[3]	
(he)ar he *left*	AR
heard more than ever	CLEVER, TREVOR
hearing aid	EAR
hearing test	TRIAL
heart	
at heart s/he w/as . . .	HEW
gr<u>eet</u> *heartily*	REE
heart	H
heart-*breaking*	(in) CO–RE
[heart]-*breaking*	EARTH, HATER, RATHE
[heart]-*broken*	EARTH, HATER, RATHE
• [heart]-*broken* American	ARETHUSA
[heart]-*failure*	EARTH, HATER, RATHE
heart of Fren/ch Arm/y	CHARM
heart of go<u>ld</u>	OL
Heart of Midl<u>oth</u>ian	OT
heart of <u>t</u>he . . .	H
heart of the ma<u>tt</u>er	TT
heart recording	TICKER TAPE
[heart] *surgery*	EARTH, HATER, RATHE
[heart] *transplant*	EARTH, HATER, RATHE
heart transplant for Be\g\in	BEING
heartless f(emal)e	FE
heart-throb	PULSE
heart-th<u>r</u>ob	R
hearty	AB, SAILOR, TAR
hearty drink	CORDIAL
Li<u>on</u>heart	IO
m/aide/n's *heart*	AIDE
* *to heart*	incl *
• captures *with* blow *to heart*	TRAPS
• see m–e *take* it *to heart*	MITE
heat	
[heat] *exchange*	HATE, THEA
[heat] *treatment*	HATE, THEA
heated issue	LAVA, STEAM
heath	
heath	TED
heath, *say*	MORE
heavens	COO, COR, MY, SKY
heavy	
heaviness, *say*	WAIT
heavy accent	GRAVE
Heavy Artillery	HA
heavy artillery, *say*	CANONRY
heavy blow	CYCLONE, GALE, HURRICANE
	ONER
heavy breather	GRAMPUS
heavy going	(in) MU–D
Heavy Goods Vehicle	HGV
heavy round	DOORSTEP
heavyweight	ANTON, BOXER, STONE, TON
Hebrew	
Hebrew	HEB(R)
Hebrew character (=Hebrew letter)	
• first character in	
Hebrew . . .	ALEPH
• Hebrew character looks	
crippled	LAMED
Hebrew	JEW

Letter replaced \c\at; Omit (a); Pointers *out*; Retain <u>a</u>; Split B_ED; Down (D); Backwards <or ^

• Hebrew baby, *say*	JUNIPER	*hemmed in by* *	incl in *
• Hebrew beauty will, *say*	JUDICIAL	• us *hemmed in by* sea	MUSED
• Hebrew is acute	JEW'S-HARP	**hemi-**	
• Hebrew, *say*	DEW, DUE	*hemi*hedron	HED, RON
Hebrew diet	KNESSET	*hemi*olic	OL, IC
Hebrew leader	MOSES	**hen**	
Hebrew *leader*	II	hen	LADYBIRD, LAYER
hectare	HA	hen, *say*	FOUL, LAIR
hectic		hen's head, *say*	FOULNESS
hectic [time]	EMIT	**henna**	TONE CONTROL
[rushes] *hectically*	USHERS	**henry**	
hectolitre	HL	Henry	H
hedge		• Henry I	HI
hedge	HAW	• Henry VIII	HEIGHT
hedge shrub , *say*	PRIVATE	Henry	HAL
heed		• Henry Bird, *say*	HALBERD
heed, *say*	MINED, WRECK	• Henry *on* the stairs	HALF-LIGHT
heeds, *say*	REX, WRECKS	Henry	HANK
height		• Henry went in front	HANKLED
height	H	• Second Henry	SHANK
height of _f_ashion(D)	F	Henry I	H
held		Henry II	E
held back by man/y		**her¹**	
reve/rent . . . <	EVERY	her fish, *say*	HURLING
held by lar/ge ne/w . . .	GENE	her man, *say*	URGENT
held in banks (indicating a river):		her *counterpart*	HIS
• *held in English banks*	THAMES etc	her other case	SHE
• *held in French banks*	SEINE etc	her view, *say*	URSINE
• *held in German banks*	RHINE etc	**her²**	
held in *	incl in *	Her (Britannic) Majesty	H(B)M
• nitrogen *held in* ba–g	BANG	Her Exalted Highness	HEH
• nothing *held back in* ba–g	BALING	Her Grace	HG
held Italian capital	HADROME	Her Imperial Majesty	HIM
	(*see also* hold)	Her Majesty's Customs	HMC
Hell		Her Majesty's Government	HMG
hell	ABADDON, AVERNUS	Her Majesty's Inspectorate	HMI
hell	DIS	Her Majesty's Service	HMS
• gangster *in* hell	DIALS	Her Majesty's Ship	HMS
• hell-bent	DISINCLINED	Her (Royal) Highness	H(R)H
hell	EREBUS, PIT, HADES, TARTARUS	Her Serene Highness	HSH
hellhound	CERBERUS, PLUTO	**herald**	
hellish boss	DEVIL, DIS	[Herald] *Extraordinary*	HARELD, HARLED
help			–HEDRAL
Help!	SOS	heraldry	HER
help get o/ver y/our . . .	VERY	Heralds' College	HC
help mot/her d/ust . . .	HERD	**herb**	SIMPLE
help out	AI–D	**herd**	
• five help *out*	AVID	herd of cows	OXGANG
help to make aero/plan/es	PLAN	herd, *say*	HEARD
help to make [notes]	ONSET, STONE, TONES	**here**	
helpful officer	ADC, AIDE	here *in France*	ICI
helping of beer	RATIONALE	here *in Rome*	HIC
hem		h_ere_ *in the middle* . . .	ER
hem of skir_t_	T	here is (laid)	HS
hemmed in a . . .	incl A	**hereafter**	
hemmed in *	incl *	hereafter	HEAVEN
• sea *hemmed* us *in*	MUSED	here*after*	

• guard here*after*	HEREWARD
• firm here*after*	COHERE
heretic	ARIAN
hero	
hero	LADYLOVE
Hero worshipper	LEANDER
Hertz	CS, CPS, HZ
hesitate	
hesitation	–ER, UM, UR
• *hesitant* claim	ERMINE
• hesitation *in* time . . .	HUMOUR
• *hesitating in* church	CURE
without hesitation	omit ER, UM, UR
h-hem	HEDGE
hide	
hidden in h/er go/wn	ERGO
hidden in [forest]	FOSTER
hidden in *	incl in *
• fruit *hidden by* divine	DAPPLED
hidden piece of wo/od in/side . . .	ODIN
hide pepper	PELT
hide shield	SCREEN
hiding a . . .	incl A
hiding in cupboar/d un/der . . .	DUN
hiding in [field]	FILED
hiding *	incl *
• divine *hiding* fruit	DAPPLED
hideous	
hideous [face]	CAFE
[Medusa's] *hideous* . . .	ASSUMED
hi-fi	
hi-fi buff	STEREOTYPE
hi-fi *sound*	HYPHAE
Higgins's girl	ELIZA
high	
high	TOP
• high bend	TOPARCH
• high note	TOPE
• high notes	TOPE(E)S
• high speed	TOPKNOTS
high-alumina cement	HAC
high-class	A, AI, U
high-class band	CORONET, TIARA
high diver	OFFENDER
high explosive	HE
high flier	AEROPLANE, AIRSHIP BIRD, CONDOR etc COMET, ICARUS TRAPEZE(-ARTIST) WHIZZ-KID
high flier's home	EYRIE, NEST
high flier's home, *say*	EERIE
high frequency	HF
high honour	KING
high jump	OFFSPRING
high-king, *say*	HIKING, TALKING
High Noon	HANDS UP
high place	UP
high point, *say*	PEEK, PIQUE
high-powered firm	STRONG
high priest	AARON, ELI, LAMA etc
high revs	(ARCH)BISHOPS
high-rise building	ANTHILL
high road	FLYOVER
high score	TON
high-*sounding*	HI(E)
• high-*sounding* girl	HYENA
high summer	ADDER, (SENIOR) WRANGLER
High Table	PLATEAU
high tars	SMELLING-SALTS
high tension	HT
high time	NOON
high tower	UPKEEP
high wager	TREBLE
high water	TARN
high water mark	HWM
high wind	JETSTREAM
higher, *say*	HIRE, LEASE, RENT
• higher row, *say*	HYALINE
• higher lamp, *say*	HYALITE
Higher National Certificate	HNC
Higher National Diploma	HND
higher number	NUMERATOR
highest chief	TOPARCH
highest common factor	HCF
highest honour	ACE
highest point, *say*	PEEK, PIQUE
highest speed	C
highlight	MOON, STAR, SUN
highly charged	DEAR, EXPENSIVE
highway, *say*	LAIN, RODE
highball	
highball	LOB
• highball money	LOBLOLLY
• highball specialist	LOBSTER
• second highball	SLOB
Highland	
Highland Light Infantry	HLI
Highland(er) (=Scottish)	
• *Highland* shoemaker	SOUTAR, SOUTER SOWTER
• *Highlander's* salutation	BECK
highlight	MOON, STAR, SUN
hill	MT, TOR
Hill 11	TORII
hill-billy	MOUNTAIN GOAT
hill-*climbing*(D)^	ROT
hill-dweller	ANT, TERMITE
hill-guide	TORMENTOR
<u>hill</u>*side*	H
<u>hill</u>*top*(D)	H
Himalayan	SHERPA
hinder	
hinder man	DETERGENT

hindrance	LET
• hindrance *to ruler, say*	LETTER
hip	
[hip] *replacement*	PHI
[hip]-*shaking*	PHI
hippy	SCIATIC
replacement of [hips]	PISH, SHIP
his¹	
his	GREETINGS
his	HIS
• his attempt, *say*	HISTRION
• [his] *characters*	–ISH
• [his] *cocktail*	–ISH
• [his] *fault*	–ISH
• his knight, *say*	HISSER
• his teacher, *say*	HISSER
his *counterpart*	HER
his eyes, *say*	MAN-SIZE
his *head*(D)	H
his²	
His (Britannic) Majesty	H(B)M
His Catholic Majesty	HCM
His Eminence	HE
His Exalted Highness	HEH
His Excellency	HE
His Grace	HG
His Imperial Highness	HIH
His Imperial Majesty	HIM
His Majesty's Customs	HMC
His Majesty's Government	HMG
His Majesty's Inspectorate	HMI
His Majesty's Service	HMS
His Majesty's Ship	HMS
His (Royal) Highness	H(R)H
His Serene Highness	HSH
hiss	
hiss *at*	incl S
• hiss *at* play	SPLAY
hissing sound	S
history	
historian	ACTON
history teacher	PASTMASTER
hit	
hit	PAT
• hit bird	PATTERN
• hit girl	PATELLA, PATINA
• hit man	PATRON, PATTED
hit	PUNCH
• hit horse	PUNCH
• hit *with* wood	PUNCH-BOWL
• hit woman, *say*	PUNCHER
hit	RAP
• hit double	RAPID
• hit *in* church	CRAPE
• hit the drink	RAPPORT
hit	SOCK
• hit girl, *say*	SOCCER

• hit him, *say*	SOCMAN
• hit it, *say*	SOCKET
hit	SLOG
• hit one . . .	SLOGAN
• hit woman, *say*	SLOGGER
hit	SMACK
• hit boat	SMACK
• hit queen	SMACKER
• hit woman, *say*	SMACKER
hit American, *say*	WAMMUS
hit and run	BLOWFLY, SLAPDASH
hit for six [by real] . . .	BARLEY
hit it, *say*	WAPPET
hit number	SCORE
[hit] *out*	–ITH
hit a Pole, *say*	LAMP-HOLE
hit timekeeper	CLOCK
hit vehicle, *say*	LASHKAR
hitman	PATRON, PATTED
hitch	
hitch in [part] . . .	RAPT, TRAP
hitching-post	GRETNA GREEN
	REGISTRY OFFICE
Hitler's bodyguard	SS
hive	
hive, *say*	BEHOLDER
hoard	
hoard, *say*	CASH, HORDE, WHORED
hoarded by *	incl in *
• it is *hoarded by* saints	SITS
hoarding a . . .	incl A
hoarding *	incl *
• saints *hoarding* it	SITS
hoarse	
hoarse, *say*	CROQUET, RUPEE
hoarse sound	CROAK
hoarse *sound*	HORSE, MAYOR
sounding hoarse	CROQUET, RUPEE
	HORSE, MAYOR
hogshead	
hogshead	HHD
hogs*head*	H
hoist	
hoist bird	CRANE
hoist headgear, *say*	WHIN-CHAT
hoist it . . . (D)^	TI
hoist up(D)^	PU
hoist sail(D)^	LIAS
hold	
hold	KEEP
• hold *back*<	PEEK
• hold girl, *say*	KEEPER
• hold liquor	KEEPSAKE
• hold up(D)^	PEEK
hold firm	incl CO
hold on	incl ON
hold stock	STEM

Anag [cat]; Any *; Begin IGN–; Endings –ING; eg •; Hidden /cat/; Implied add (on); Implied in (in);

hold-up	DAM
hold up	incl UP
• firms *hold* up . . .	COUPS
hold-up man	ATLAS, JACK, TURPIN
hold up paws(D)^	SWAP
holding a . . .	incl A
holding agency	CLAMP, VICE
	FIXATIVE, GLUE, GUM, PASTE
holding company	CANOODLING, CUDDLING
	SNOGGING, SMOOCHING
holding back	
• girl *holding back* about . . . <	LASERS
holding hose	HASSOCKS
holding on	incl LEG, ON
• drink *holding* on . . .	ALONE
• Sally *holding* on	SORTILEGE
holding together t/wo k/inds . . .	WOK
holding up(D)	
• doctor *held up by* girls	MOLASSES
• girl *holding up* a . . .	AMISS
and	
• Mo–ses *holding*	
up girl(D)	MOLASSES
holding *	
• pai/r are st/ill *holding*	RAREST
holding *	incl *
• ba–g *holding* nitrogen	BANG
holds	
• holds hose	HASSOCKS
• holds *in* church	CHASE
• holds a row	HASTIER
holds bonds	STOCKS
holds colour	CLINGSTONE
	(*see also* held)
hole	
hole	O
hole, *say*	WHOLE
hole in one	CELLINI
holed	incl O
holed, *say*	HOLD
holiday bay	RECESS
hollow	
hollow (=nothing inside)	
• *hollow* s(oun)d	SD
• *hollow* t(ub)e	TE
• *hollow* v(ictor)y	VY
hollow	O
• cover *hollow* . . .	LIDO
• *hollow* sound	ODIN
• *hollow* tree	OPINE
hollow(ed)	incl O
• d–ry *hollow*	DORY
• *hollow* ro–d	ROOD
• sh–e *hollowed* . . .	SHOE
hollow	PAN
• hollow feature	PANNOSE
• hollow pain	PANACHE

• second hollow	SPAN
Hollywood	
Hollywood area	CAL, LA
in Hollywood area	C–AL, L–A
holy	
holy	PI
• holy child	PITOT
• Holy City	PILA
• holy man	PINED
Holy City	JERUSALEM, MEDINA, MECCA,
	ROME ETC
Holy Communion	HC
holy day, *say*	SUNDAE
holy man	S, ST
Holy Mother Mary	SMM
holy orders	TEN COMMANDMENTS
holy river	GANGES
Holy Roman Empire	SRI
Holy Virgin	HV
Holy Writ	NT, OT
home¹	
home	FLAT
• home club	FLAT-IRON
• home *in* the river	DEFLATE
• home trial	FLATTEST
home	IN
• home bird	INTERN
• Home Rule	INLAW
• home stretch	INTENSE
• home team	INSIDE
home²	
home club	VILLA
Home Counties	SE, THESE
home following	CARAVAN
home *front*	H
Home Guard	HG, WATCHDOG
home-made soup	BIRDS'-NEST
home	
–of gentlemen	VERONA
–of natives	OYSTER BED
–of the brave	HOGAN, TE(E)PEE
	TIPI, WIGWAM
home team	VILLA
Homer	
Homeric	
indicating use of Greek word or character:	
• *Homeric* character	
wagered . . .	ALPHABET
• *Homeric* character recently . . .	PHILATELY
Homer's place	DOVECOT(E)
	(PIGEON-)LOFT
honest	
honest footballer	STRAIGHTFORWARD
honest member	SQUARE LEG
honeymoon express	BRIDAL TRAIN
Hong Kong	HK
• a river *in* Hong Kong	HARK

Letter replaced \c\at; Omit (a); Pointers *out*; Retain <u>a</u>; Split B_ED; Down (D); Backwards <or ^

honour	
honorary	HON
honour	A, ACE, J, JACK
	K, KING, Q, QUEEN
honour	CH
• graduate with honour	MACH
• honour a member	CHAMP
• honour *among* mayors, *say*	MARCHES
honour	OBE
• 50 honour . . .	LOBE
• honour revolutionary	OBECHE
• honourable name	OBERON
• honours, *say*	OBESE, OBIS
honour	OM
• act *with* honour	DOOM
• honour *in* about . . .	COMA
• honour it	OMIT
(*see also* award, order)	
Honourable	HON
Honourable Artillery Company	HAC
honoured companion	CH
hooded bird	CROW, ROBIN
hook	
hook	PIRATE
• hooklike	ASPIRATE
hoop	
hoop	O
hoop for crinoline	DRESS CIRCLE
	DRESS-RING
hooter	
hooter	NOSE
second feature	SHOOTER
hop	
hopping about [room]	MOOR
hopping [mad]	ADM–, DAM
hope	
Hope's territory	RURITANIA
hopelessly [lost]	LOTS, SLOT
hopin'	ASPIRIN
Horace's work	ODES
horizontal	
horizontal	HOR
horizontal angle	FLATFISH
horizontal equivalent	HE
hormone	
hormone	AUTOCOID
[hormone] *treatment*	MOORHEN
horology	
horology	HOR
horologist	CLOCKWISE
horrible	
horrible [fate]	FEAT
horrible, *say*	VIAL
horribly [made]	DAME, EDAM, MEAD
horrific	
horrific [tale]	LATE, LEAT, TEAL
[it was] *horrifically* . . .	WAIST

horse¹	
[horse]-*breaking*	SHORE
[horse]-*racing*	SHORE
[horse]*play*	SHORE
horse²	
horse	ARAB
• horse *in* the desert	SARABAND
• horsewoman	ARABELLA
• namely, a horse	SCARAB
horse	ASS
• black horse	BASS
• horse drawing . . .	ASSART
• horse *in* the *French* . . .	LASSES
horse	BARB
• horse one can . . .	BARBICAN
• horse devoured . . .	BARBATE
• horse measures, *say*	BAR-BELLS
horse	BAY
• horseman	BAYED
• mountain horse	TORBAY
• horse, very odd	BAY-RUM
horse	COB
• Horse Artillery	COBRA
• horse-food	COBLOAF, COBNUT
• horse painter	COBRA
horse	G, GEE
• ban horse	BARGEE
• horse-road	GEEST
• horse *without* new . . .	GENE
horse	GG, GEE-GEE
• horse *in* a rage	BAGGIT
• horse *without* an . . .	GANG
• Oriental horse	EGG
horse	H
• horseman	HALF, HANDY
• horse in river	HINDEE
• horse *with* no bit	HOBIT
horse	HACK
• horse joint, *say*	HACKNEY
• horse list	HACKLOG
• second horse	SHACK
horse	NAG
• horse collection	NAGANA
• horse *in* ship	SNAGS
• horse or . . .	NAGOR
• horse*back<*	GAN
horse³	
dark horse	NIGHTMARE
horse-drawn carriage	HACKNEY
• horse-drawn carriage, *say*	ACNE
horse disease, *say*	MAL-DE-MER
horse drug	HEROIN
horse-laugh, *say*	NAY
horse pistol	COLT
horse race	HOUYHNHNM
horse-race	DERBY, NATIONAL, OAKS etc
	PLATE

Anag [cat]; Any *; Begin IGN–; Endings –ING; eg •; Hidden /cat/; Implied add (on); Implied in (in);

horse-riding	(in) S–ADDLE, UP
horse-riding, *say*	MANAGE
horse, *say*	BEY, HOARSE, RHONE
horse sound	NEIGH, WHINNY
horse *sound*	HOARSE, MAYOR
horse's foot	TROTTER
horse's head	H
horse trading	STOCK EXCHANGE
horse*back<*	BOC, GAN
horse*less*	omit G
horseman	CENTAUR
horseplay	EQUUS, RICHARD THE
	THIRD, POLO
horse's refusal, *say*	NEIGH
horseshoe	MULE
sound horse	HOARSE, MAYOR
steady horses	STABLE
unhealthy horse	SICK-BAY
white horse	BREAKER, WAVE
Hosea	HOS
hospital	
hospital	H
• hospital *has* changed	HALTERED
• hospital *has* no use . . .	HOUSE
• hospital-planes	HAIRLINE
hospital department	ENT
hospital sign	H
hospital wing, *say*	WARDROOM, WARRED
hospitalised	INWARD, (in) W–ARD
hot	
hot	H
• hot *and nearly* ful(l)	HANDFUL
• hot *at* church	HATCH
• hot fish	HEEL, HID(E)
• hot oven	HOAST
hot *and* bothered	RED CROSS
hot-rod driver	RIVETER
hot tip	FIRE ALARM
h̲ot *tip*	H
hothead	VOLCANO
h̲ot*head*	H
hotline	EQUATOR, TROPIC
hotplate, *say*	FRIARY
hour	H, HR
house¹	
house	CO, COT
• a royal house	ARCO
• house *in* the street	SCOT
• houses collections	COSSETS
house	H, HO
• house *and* home	HONEST
• house in good order	HOOK
• housework	HOOP
house	SEMI
• house colours	SEMITONES
• house insect, *say*	SEMITIC
• house shakes	SEMIQUAVERS

house²	
house	BINGO
house-boat	HOMECRAFT
house builder	JACK
house buzzer	FLY
house-coat	PLASTER, STUCCO
house deposit	LODGE
house for	
–scientist	LODGE
–team	VILLA
House of Keys	HK
House of Lords	MANOR
house-party, *say*	SEA-TROUT
house-room	AUDITORIUM
housed in de/relic/t . . .	RELIC
housed in *	incl in *
• scholar *housed in* for–t	FORMAT
housemaid	WENDY
housemaid's knee	BURSITIS
houseman	INTERNE, RESIDENT
	MEMBER OF PARLIAMENT, MP
housemaster	PM, PRIME MINISTER
	SPEAKER
housework	COTTAGE INDUSTRY
	LEGISLATION
housing a . . .	incl A
(ho)*using shortage*	USING
housing ol/d art/efacts	DART
housing *	incl *
• for–t *housing* scholar	FORMAT
White House	IGLOO
house³	
house	HANOVER, STUART
	WINDSOR etc
• house in Holland	ORANGE
• house plant	TUDOR ROSE
• houses sound	YORK STONE
houseman	LANCASTRIAN, TUDOR etc
how	
how	QM
how [far is a] . . .	SAFARI
how fast	MPH
[How] *funny*	WHO
how *to follow* teams	SIDESHOW
Howard	
Howard's End	D
Howard's rhyme	COWARDS
hug	
hug a . . .	incl A
hug *	incl *
• Pa–t *hugs* son	PAST
hugged by *	incl in *
• son *hugged by* Pa–t	PAST
huge	
huge	OS
huge quarry	OSPREY
huge cost	EARTH

Letter replaced \c\at; Omit (a); Pointers *out*; Retain a̲; Split B_ED; Down (D); Backwards <or ^

huge *majority*	HUG	• 150 in s–ly . . .	SILLY
	(*see also* large)	• 150 plus 50	ILL
Hugh		• fast 150	LENTIL
Hugh *said* . . .	HEW, HUE	hundred and sixty	T
Hull transport	BOTTOMRY	hundred and fifty thousand	Y
hum		hundred and sixty thousand	T
hum, *say*	DEMISING	hundred thousand	LAC, LAKH, P, R, RHO
humming-*top*(D)	H	hundred thousand pounds	SEYMOUR
human		hundredth	CENTI–
human	MAN	hundredweight	CWT
• human *meets* alien	MANET	Old Hundred	PSALM
human error	MORTAL SIN	**hung**	(*see* hang)
[human] *error*	NAHUM	**Hungary**	
Humberside	NE	Hungarian capital	FORINT
hundred		Hungarian *capital*	H
hundred	C	Hungarian *leader*	H
• 100 I examine	CIVET	Hungarian steps	CZARDAS
• 100 in church	CINCH	Hungary	H
• 100 girls	CLASSES	**hungry**	
• 100 to one	CAN, CI	hungry (=nothing inside)	incl O
	CLONE, CONE	• *hungry* c–at	COAT
• 100 with nothing on	COON	hungry boy	OLIVER
• a hundred	AC	**hunt**	
• centipede	CLIMBS	hunter	ACTAEON, ESAU, ORION
• hundred pound note	CLA–, CLE	hunters lay about	GUNSLINGER
• hundred pounds	CL	hunting area	SHIRE(S)
• hundreds	CC, CS	hunting leopard, *say*	CHEATER
• one hundred	IC	hunting whales, *say*	WA(I)LING
hundred	CENTUM, CENTURY	huntress	ARTEMIS, DIANA
	P, R, RHO	huntsman's drink	CHASER
hundred	TON	**hurl**	
• hundred directions	TONES	*hurled* [spear]	PARES, RAPES, SPARE
• hundred *in* the Home Counties	STONE	*hurling* [stone]	NOTES, ONSET
• one hundred	SINGLETON		SETON, TONES
hundred (county division)	CANTRED	**hurry**	
	CANTREF	hurried	RAN
–hundreds	CHILTERN	• hurried *back*<	NAR
hundred and one	CI	• hurried firing	RANSACKING
• 101 fish	CIGARS	• hurried *up*(D)^	NAR
• 101 grave . . .	CISTERN	• *hurried to* the square	RANT
• 101 surgeons	CIVETS	hurry	DART
hundred and four	CIV	• hurry *back*<	TRAD
• 104 I record	CIVILIST	• hurry *up*(D)^	TRAD
• 104 in charge	CIVIC	• hurry *to* the South	DARTS
• 104 with one learner	CIVIL	hurry	NIP
hundred and twenty	GREAT HUNDRED	• hurry back<	PIN
	LONG HUNDRED	• hurry *up*(D)^	PIN
hundred and forty nine	CIL	• hurry *to* the East	PINE
hundred and fifty	CL, Y	hurry	RUN
• 150 deliveries	CLOVER	• hurry back<	NUR
• 150 listeners	CLEARS	• hurry *up*(D)^	NUR
• 150 to one	CLAN, CLONE	• hurry *to* the East	RUNE
and		**hurt**	
• a girl *in* 150	CAVIL	*hurt* [pride]	PRIED
• a graduate *in* 150	CABAL	*hurting* [arm]	MAR, RAM
• or one *in* 150	CORAL	**husband**	
hundred and fifty (one-fifty)	IL	husband	H, MAN

husband and wife	MATES	**hydrant**	
husband of May Queen, *say*	MAKING	hydrant	H
husbandman	CARL	hydro-electricity	FLOWER POWER
hush	SH, ST	**hymns**	AM
husky food	BRAN	**hypocrite**	PECKSNIFF
hybrid		**hypothesis**	IF
hybrid [animal]	LAMINA, MANILA	**hypoteneuse**	ALONGSIDE
hybrid bacteria, *say*	GERMULE	**hysteria**	
hybrid [tea rose]	ROSEATE	*hysteria* [in the] . . .	THINE
hybridised [roses]	SORES	[spoke] *hysterically*	POKES
hybridising birds, *say*	CROSS-HATCHING		

Letter replaced \c\at; Omit (a); Pointers *out*; Retain a̲; Split B_ED; Down (D); Backwards <or ^

I

a, an, ane, ay, aye, beam, che, dotted, electric current, ego, eye, in, independence, independent, individual, institute, iodine, *iota*, island, isle, Italy, *line, lunchtime*, moment of inertia, one, single, *straight line*, square root of -1, ten, ten thousand, *un, upright, yours truly*

I¹	
I	A, AN, ANE
	EGO
	SPEAKER, VOWEL
I *abandon* . . .	omit I
I am	IAM, IM
I am *in* . . .	incl IAM, IM
I *am in*	incl I
I am *standing*(D)^	MAI, MI
I caught	–IC
I collapse, *say*	ICE-LUMP
I come ashore again	IRELAND
I come ashore, *say*	ISLAND
I deceive	ICON
I defame	ISLANDER
I demonstrated	ISATIN(E)
I disembark, *say*	ISLAND
I *don't appear in*	omit I
I don't know mother, *say*	ADENOMA
I *escape from* . . .	omit I
I *get* about	–IC
I *get* on	–ION
I *get out of* . . .	omit I
I get smaller, *say*	ICE-RINK
I *go out*	omit I
I had	–IATE
I had	ID(E)
• I had been ahead	IDLED
• time I had, *say*	TIDE
I have	IVE
I have *at heart*	incl IVE
I have left	omit I
I *have* left	IL
I inform Scot, *say*	ITALIAN
I *intervene*	incl I
I *leave*	omit I
I *left*	omit I
I look ahead, *say*	PHARISEE
I *lost*	omit I
I married . . .	IM–
I note	–IA, –IC, ID, IE, IF
	IRE, –ITE
I notice	–IAD

I object	ME
I offered	IBID
I *omitted* . . .	omit I
I owe you	IOU
I perform afterwards	IDOLATER
I possess	–IVE
I postpone	IDOLATER
I prepare a rota	IDOLIST
I *quit*	omit I
I rented, *say*	ISLET
I ride a bike, *say*	ICICLE
I see	–IC, IV
I see, *say*	ICY
I shall	ILL, ISLE
I shout, *say*	ICE-CREAM
I spotted, *say*	ICE-SAW
I state	–ICAL
I *take* on . . .	–ION
I trust	INT–
I will, *say*	ILL, ISLE
I *won't be there*	omit I
I²	
I am	
–a Conservative	AMATORY
–a fish	AMID, AMIDE
–an essayist	AMELIA
–a fool	AMASS
–complete	AMUTTER
–dead	AMENDED
–dying	AMENDING
–employing	AMUSING
–Lamb	AMELIA
–present, *say*	AMEER, AMERE, AMIR
–working late, *say*	AMMONITES
I am	
–a bird	MEAL-ARK
–a building	MESHED
–a child	MESON
–a detective, *say*	MEDICK
–a fish	METOPE
–a mediaeval noble	METHANE
–a peg, *say*	MEAT-TEA
–a reviver	METONIC

Anag [cat]; Any *; Begin IGN–; Endings –ING; eg •; Hidden /cat/; Implied add (on); Implied in (in);

–a Welsh girl	MESIAN	**idol**	
–an Indian	MEUTE	idol	MAMMET, MAUMET
–Edward	METED		MAWMET, MOMMET
–fly	MEWING	idol, *say*	IDLE, LAZY
–Kenneth, *say*	MEEKEN	idolatry	MAMMETRY
–Sally	MESAL(LLY)	**if**	
–stern	MEGRIM	if it	ANT
–timid	MESHY	if *old*	AN
I am	IM	**igloo**	BLOCKHOUSE
–a maiden	IMAM	**ignite**	
–a nuisance	IMPEST	ignite	FIRE
–an animal	IMBRUTE	• girl ignited, *say*	MISFIRED
–an attendant	IMPAGE	• ignites joint	FIRESHIP
–chaste	IMPURE	• sack	FIRE
–debarred, *say*	IMBAND	ignites offal	LIGHTS
–old-fashioned	IMPASSE	**ignore**	
–two	IMPAIR	*ignore* a . . .	omit A
–wan	IMPALE	ignore command	SHUN
I^3		ignore feast	PASSOVER
I am told your . . .	YORE	*ignore* the odds	omit alternate letters
I *declared*	AY(E), EYE	• (t)r(i)e(d) t(o) *ignore*	
I (dialect)	CHE	*the odds*	RET
I hear news	GNUS	*ignore* the odds	omit SP
I *heard*	AY(E), EYE	• *ignoring* the odds in (sp)ort	ORT
I *say*	AY(E)	• jumped *ignoring* the odds	(sp)RANG
I *say*	EYE	*ignore* *	omit *
• I am clean, *say*	EYE-BATH, EYEWASH	• (ac)tress *ignores* bill	TRESS
• I quote, *say*	EYESIGHT	ignorant alien	THICKET
• I rented, *say*	EYELET	**i-issue**	IDEAL
• I witnessed, *say*	EYESORE	**ill**	
I *say*	OPTIC, VOWEL	*ill-advised* [remark]	MARKER
I say nothing	EGO	ill bird, *say*	ILLEGAL
I say you . . .	EWE, U, YEW	*ill-disposed* [sort]	ORTS, ROTS, TORS
I'd *say*	EYED, IDE	*ill-fated* [ship]	HIPS, PISH
I'll burn them, *say*	ALBURNUM	ill feeling, *say*	ACRIMONY
ice		*ill-fitting* [shoe]	HOES, HOSE
ice	HARD WATER	*ill-organised* [trips]	SPIRT, SPRIT
[ice]-*breaking*	CIE	ill *in* b–ed	BILLED
ice-cream, *say*	SUNDAY	ill temper, *say*	BHYLE
icy greeting	HAIL	[ill]-*treated*	LIL
icy rain, *say*	HALE	*ill-treated* [animal]	LAMINA, MANILA
icy, *say*	–IC	*ill-treatment of* [salt-mine]	AILMENTS
icthyology	ICT(H)	[ill]-*used*	LIL
ideal partner	SOUL MATE	*ill*-[used]	DUES, DUSE, SUED
identify		ill-used vehicle	AMBULANCE
identification	ID		INVALID CHAIR, WHEEL-CHAIR
identified in Fren/ch arm/y	CHARM	*ill-written* [verse]	SERVE, SEVER
identify spirit	NAMESAKE	illness	FLU
idiot		• illness better, *say*	FLUE-CURED
idiot breeds	NUTHATCHES	[it goes] *ill*	EGOIST
idiot's headgear	FOOLSCAP	**illegal**	
idle		illegal army	ETA, IRA, PLO
idle head	LOAF	*illegal* [army]	MARY, MYRA
idle, *say*	IDOL, LAYS	**illegitimate**	
idler	DRONE	*illegitimacy of* [male] . . .	LAME, MEAL
idly [stroll]	TROLLS	*illegitimate* [son can] . . .	CANONS

Letter replaced \c\at; Omit (a); Pointers *out*; Retain a̱; Split B_ED; Down (D); Backwards <or ^

illiberal

illiberal	omit L
• *illiberal* (l)out	OUT
• *illiberal* regime	RU(l)E

illicit

act *illicitly*	CAT
illicit [affair]	RAFFIA
illicit diamond buying	IDB

illiterate signature	X
illuminated note	LITRE

illusion

illusion of [speed train] . . .	PEDESTRIAN
[optical] *illusion*	TOPICAL

illustrated

illustrated	ILL
• saint illustrated	STILL
illustration	ILL

image

[formed] *image*	DEFORM
image building	PR
image converter	RETINA
image of [Mary]	ARMY, MYRA
imaginary	INFANCY

imbecile

imbecile [can see] . . .	SEANCE
imbecility of [all the] . . .	LETHAL

imbibing

imbibing a . . .	incl A
imbibing *	incl *
• he–r *imbibing* drink	HEALER
imbibed by *	incl in *
• drink *imbibed by* he–r . . .	HEALER

imitate

imitate tenor	TENNER
imitation of male . . .	MAIL
poor *imitation*	PORE

immediate success	WINNOW

immersed

immerse a . . .	incl A
immerse *	incl *
• king *immersed in* study	DERN
immersed	(in) WA–TER
• one *immersed*	WAITER
immersed in wa/ter, m/y . . .	TERM
*immersing	incl in *
• study *immersing* king	DERN

impair

impaired [speech]	CHEEPS
impairment of [taste]	STATE, TEATS

impecunious American	NOCENT
imperative	IMP

imperfect

imperfect	IMP
imperfect speech	
• fully	FURRY
• kith	KISS

• tree	TWEE
imperfect [tense]	TEENS

imperial

imperial	IMP
imperial measure	THEFT
Imperial Service Order	ISO

impersonal	IMP

impersonate

impersonate insect	AUNT, BE, NAT
impersonating peer	PIER

impetuous rascal	TEARAWAY

implicate

implicate a . . .	incl A
implicate *	incl *
• Ro–n *implicates* master	ROMAN
implicated by *	incl in *
• master *implicated by* Ro–n	ROMAN
implicated in scanda/lous y/arn	LOUSY

import

import a . . .	incl A
import *	incl *
• ship *imports* drug	SPOTS
imported	FAR-FETCHED
imported by *	incl in *
• drug *imported by* ship	SPOTS
imported, *say*	–MENT
Swe/dish ed/itor's *import*	DISHED

important

important	LARGE
• important letter	LARGESS(E)
• important saint	LARGEST
• measure important . . .	ENLARGE
important	MAJOR
• important officer	MAJOR
• important party method	MAJOR-DOMO
• important prison	MAJORCAN
important connection	EARTH

impose

impose on	
indicating one word written	
above another word or letter:	
• cat *imposed on by* a . . . (D)	ATOM
• he *imposes on* the king(D)	HETHER
imposition, *say*	TACKS
impositions, *say*	TAXIS

imposter

imposter	SHAM
• imposter lost blood	SHAMBLED
• imposter *with* drug	SHAME
imposter's [real] . . .	LEAR
[smart] *imposter*	MARTS, TRAMS

impound

impound a . . .	incl A
impound *	incl *
• German soldiers *impound* cow	SCOWS
impounded by sherif/f in	

d/efault   FIND
impounded by *   incl in *
• cow *impounded by* German
  soldiers   SCOWS
impoverished
impoverished   (in) NE–ED
• a king *impoverished*   NEARED
• *impoverished* journalist   NEEDED
impressive
impress city   SHANGHAI
impressive marks   EMBOSSING, ETCHING
imprison
A/rab bi/d *to imprison* . . .   RABBI
imprison gangster   INTERNAL
imprisoned   (in) C–AGE, (in) PE–N
imprisoned by Fren/ch Arm/y   CHARM
imprisoned by *   incl in *
• American *imprisoned*
  by German soldiers   SUSS
imprisoned in Al/cat/raz   CAT
imprisoning a . . .   incl A
imprisoning *   incl *
• German soldiers
  imprisoning American   SUSS
impromptu
impromptu [remark]   MARKER
[quite] *impromptu*   QUIET
improper
improper [remark]   MARKER
improperly [made]   DAME, EDAM, MEAD
improperly dealt with [much] . . .   CHUM
improve
improved [lamp]   PALM
improvement in [pay]   YAP
improvise
improvise [tale]   LATE, LEAT, TEAL, TELA
improvising [ploy]   POLY–
improvisation [on a set] . . .   ATONES
in¹
                                            IN
in a class   INFORM
in a new way   INANE
[in a] *flap*   AIN, –IAN
[in a] *fury*   AIN, –IAN
[in a] *new way*   AIN, –IAN
[in a] *panic*   AIN, –IAN
[in a] *spin*   AIN, –IAN
[in a] *novel*   AIN, –IAN
in a way   –INE, INN, INS
in about . . .   INCA
in another key   INA, IND, –INE, –ING
in apple juice, *say*   INSIDER
in autumn   INFALL
in *capturing*   I–N
• i–n *capturing* firm . . .   ICON
in church   INCE, INCH
in company   INFIRM

in English   –INE
• in English ship   –INESS
in *French*   EN
• in *French* church   –ENCE
in G and S   –INGS
in *Gates*head   –ING
in *German capital*   –ING
in hospital   INWARD(S)
in imagination   INFANCY
in love   INO
in one . . .   INA, INI
in one quarter   –INE, INN, INS–
[in or] *out*   IRON
in order, *say*   INTERN(E)
in *retirement*<   NI
in *return*<   NI
in rhyme   INVERSE
in, *say*   INN, PUB
in *some* cas(es)   INCAS
in *sound*   INN
in Spain   –INE
in syrup, *say*   INDUCE
in *the beginning*   INT–
in *the beginning*   start with IN
• obtained in *the beginning*   INGOT
in *the centre*   incl IN
• in *the centre of* the
  London area   SINE
in the East   –INE
in *the end*   –INE
in *the end*   end with IN
• firm in *the end*   COIN
in the Orient   –INE
in the papers   INQUIRE
in the pipeline   INDUCT
in time   INT–
in *turn*<   NI
in turn, *say*   INTERN(E)
in wheat, *say*   INKHORN
in*turned*<   NI
in²
implying inclusion:
in can be used to imply
the inclusion of one word
or letter in another word, as in
• retired   (in) B–ED), (in) C–OT
• under canvas   (in) T–ENT
and so on: other examples will be found
throughout the book under the appropriate
headword.
in³
indicating an anagram:
in [ascent]   STANCE
in a bad way [after red] . . .   RAFTERED
in a blur [when I] . . .   WHINE
in a different order

[but not] . . .	BUTTON
in a flap [over] . . .	ROVE
in a form [that] . . .	TATH
in a mess [for us]	FOURS
in a muddle [I went] . . .	TWINE
in a tizzy [about] . . .	U-BOAT
in a way [mad]	DAM
in action [St Michael] . . .	ALCHEMIST
in agony [poisoned] . . .	POSEIDON
in circulation [in the] . . .	THINE
in confusion [I ran]	RAIN, RANI
in disarray [his team]	HAMITES
in disorder [when I] . . .	WHINE
in distress [some lad] . . .	DAMOSEL
in error [sent] . . .	NETS, STEN, TENS
in exchange for [lira]	ARIL, LAIR, LIAR
in form [player]	REPLAY
in motion [it ran] . . .	TRAIN
in need of repair [shoes] . . .	HOSES
in order to [play she] . . .	SHAPELY
in poor shape [I cant] . . .	ANTIC
in ruins of [Rome]	MORE, OMER
in smithereens [when it] . . .	WHITEN
in the guise of [an old] . . .	NODAL
in the lurch [when I] . . .	WHINE
in the manner of [a Serb]	BARES,
	BEARS
	BRAES, SABRE
in turmoil [I ran] . . .	RAIN, RANI

in⁴

indicating inclusion:

in 2000	M–M
in a certain situation	S–URE
in a rush	RE–ED
in a way	A–RD, AS–T, R–D, S–T
in act	AC–T, DE–ED
in action	AC–T, DE–ED
in agony	PA–IN
in agreement	A–Y
in America	U–S
in American money	C–ENT
in an attempt	TRI–AL, TR–Y
in animal	DE–ER
in any *case*	AN–Y
in [bad] *shape*	AB–D
in bed	B–ED, CO–T, PA–D, S–ACK
in bed *in France*	LI–T
in camera	SL–R
in car	R–R, V–W
in Carlisle	N–W
in case	
• a letter *in* m–y *case*	MESSY
• gun *in case of* ne–ed	NEGATED
• it *is in* pastry *case*	PITY
• provided *in* b<u>rief</u>*case*	BIFF
in character	CAR–D

in charge	FE–E
in church	C–E, C–H
in city	E–C, E–LY
in communist . . .	RE–D, TRO–T
in concert	PRO–M
in conclusion	EN–D
in Cornwall	S–W
in credit	C–R
in crib	BE–D, CO–T
in damp environment	D–AMP, WE–T, MO–IST
in death	EN–D
in debt	R–ED
in deep water	MA–IN
in Devon	S–W
in dictionary	O–ED
in different ways	N–S, WE–S, etc
in dismal *environment*	GRA–Y, GRE–Y, SA–D
in document	DE–ED, M–S
in doorway	ENTR–Y
in drink	AL–E
in dry . . .	T–T
in dry grass	T–ED
in expensive coat	FU–R
in exploit	DE–ED
in exposed situation	BAR–E
in face of . . .	DI–AL
in fact	DE–ED
in favour	BO–ON
in fear	AW–E
in feat	DE–ED
in fixed position	SE–T
in flight	W–ING
in general	LE–E
in Gilbert & Sullivan	G–S
in gold	O–R
in grass	S–ING
in harmony	TU–NE
in hat	LI–D
in heaven	SK–Y
in Holy Writ	N–T, O–T
in Home Counties	S–E
in hospital	WAR–D
in icy clutches	COL–D
in Ireland	E–IRE
in Kent	S–E
in large amounts	C–M, M–C, M–M
• unknown *in* large amounts	CYM
• article I *found in* large amounts	MANIC
• first-class, *in* large amounts	MAIM
in large measure	ROO–D
in lead	P–B
in legal document	DE–ED
in Lincoln	AB–E
in London area	S–E
in long grass	RE–ED

Anag [cat]; Any *; Begin IGN–; Endings –ING; eg •; Hidden /cat/; Implied add (on); Implied in (in);

in low *surroundings*	MO–O
in Manhattan area	N–Y
in many ways	SN–ES, N–ESE etc
in mid<u>wee</u>k	E–E
in moist conditions	D–AMP, W–ET, MO–IST
in motorcycle race	T–T
in my *case*	M–Y
in need	NE–ED
in Newcastle	N–E
in newspaper	SU–N
in Norfolk town	DIS–S
in olden days	B–C
in opposition	E–W, N–S, S–N, W–E
in order	C–H, OB–E, O–M
in pain	ST–ING
in pastry *case*	P–Y
in performance	DE–ED
in pipe	RE–ED
in plot	BE–D
in port	DE–AL
in prepaid container	SA–E
in prison	C–AGE, CA–N, GA–OL, P–EN
in pub	BA–R, IN–N, LO–CAL
in question	E–H
in raincoat	MA–C
in residence	N–EST
in retirement	B–ED, C–OT
in retreat	DE–N
in Russian	RE–D
in salt water	SE–A
in Second City	MO–NY
in shape	CON–E
in ship	S–S
in ship's clothing	S–S
in silks	BA–R
in silver	A–G
in Slough	BO–G, FE–N
in some circles	O–O
in some ways	N–ESE, W–E, etc
in tall grass	RE–ED
in temporary home	T–ENT
in the afternoon	P–M
in the air	SK–Y
in the *back* row<	EN–IL
in the Bible	N–T, O–T
in the City	E–C, E–LY
in the clutches of *	incl in *
• I'm *in the clutches of* the *French* . . .	LIME
in the cold	I–CE, I–CY
in the desert	SAN–D
in the drink	AL–E, BE–ER, TO–T
in the end	EN–D
in the face	DI–AL
in the fall	R–AIN
in the Fifties	L–L
in the front	FOR–E
in the garden	B–ED
in the grass	RE–ED
in the grip of *	incl in *
• one *in the grip of* a ca–d	CAID
in the heavens	SK–Y
in the King's name	LEA–R
in the last month	DE–C, UL–T
in the lead	P–B
in the long grass	RE–ED
in the main	DE–EP, SE–A
in the market	E–C
in the match	T–EST
in the middle	COR–E
in the money	CO–IN, C–ENT
in the nude	BAR–E
in the open	OVER–T
in the race	T–T, N–ATION
in the rain	WE–T
in the red	R–ED
in the right	LI–EN, THE–R
in the sea	DE–EP, MA–IN
in the ship	S–S
in the snuggery	N–EST
in the street	AV–E, R–D, S–T
in the vessel	S–S
in the way	AV–E, R–D, S–T N–E, N–W, S–E, S–W etc
in this era	A–D
in this *case*	THI–S
in time	AG–E, D–ATE, DA–Y, H–R, MI–N
in traffic	DE–AL
in twenty–four hours	DA–Y
in two hundred . . .	C–C
in two thousand	M–M
in two ways	L–L, L–R, R–L, R–R N–S, W–E, etc ST–ST
in warm clothing	HO–T
in wet conditions	DA–MP, MO–IST
in wintry conditions	COL–D, IC–Y
in writing	M–S
in * *environment*	incl in *
• king *in* t–ough *environment*	TROUGH

in⁵

meaning:
accepted
- • father *accepted*   PAIN
at home
- • mother *at home*   MAIN
at the wicket
- • *batting* after tea, *say*   TIN
batting
- • champion *batting*   CHIN
belonging to

• *belonging to* party consisting of	INSECT, INSET
• *consisting of* alloy	INTERNE
during	
• *during* autumn	INFALL
elected	
• *elected* to seat	INSTALL
esoteric	
• *esoteric* class	INFORM, INSECT, INSET
fashionable, etc	
• *trendy* view	INSIGHT
favoured	
• *favoured* friend	INMATE
governing	
• staff *governing*	RODIN
member of	
• *member of* group	INSECT, INSET
planted	
• *planted* meadow	INFIELD
popular	
• good man and *popular*	STAND-IN
smart	
• *smart* group	INSECT, INSET
wearing	
• *wearing* undergarments	INVESTS
well-favoured	
• *well-favoured* position	INSTANCE

in[6]

other uses:

in a jam, *say*	BLOCK-TIN
in a manner of speaking, bare	BEAR
in accordance with	SEC
in agreement	ATONE
in all directions	NEWS
in audition (=homophone)	
• *in audition*, I . . .	AY(E), EYE
• *in audition*, tenor . . .	TENNER
• Perry *in audition* . . .	PERI
in banks (=river)	
• *in English banks*	THAMES
• *in French banks*	SEINE
• *in German banks*	RHINE
in bed (=flower, plant, shrub)	
• girl *in bed*	MYRTLE, VIOLA et al
in capacity of	QUA
• *in the capacity of* a daughter	QUAD
• *in the capacity of* a ruler	QUAKING
in-car music, *say*	CARTOONS
in case	IF
in charge	IC
• Duke in charge	FISTIC
• graduates in charge	BASIC
• scholar *and* saint in charge	MASTIC
in connection with	ON, RE
	(*see* about[2])
in conversation (=homophone)	

• *in conversation*, mayor . . .	MARE
• Marie *in conversation* . . .	MARRY
in country style (=dialect)	
• grimace *in country style*	MUMP
• *in country style* lunch . . .	TIFT
in court	UP
in debt	BILLOWED, BILLOWING
in every detail (=to a T)	
• past *in every detail*	OVERT
in extremis take . . .	TE
in favour of	FOR
• *in favour of* charity	FORGIVING
• *in favour of the* majority, *say*	FOREMOST
in favour of	PRO
• *in favour of* leader	PRODUCE
• *in favour of* timber, *say*	PROLOGUE
in foreign parts (=foreign language)	
• arrive *in foreign parts*	ANKOMMEN
• live *in foreign parts*	VIVRE
• travel *in foreign parts*	VIAJE
• work *in foreign parts*	LAVORO
in full (=expanded abbreviation)	
• do *in full*	DITTO
• do *fully*	DITTO
• *in full* fig	FIGURE
in Gateshead	–ING
in gear	CLOTHED, DRESSED
in German	–ING
in good condition	ASSENT
in hell	DISPLACED
in-house publication	HANSARD
in imagination	INFANCY
in London (=Cockney)	omit H
• (h)ouse *in London*	OUSE
in my direction	TOME
in opposition	V
in other words	SC
in part di/vide/d	VIDE
in place of (=substitution)	
• l\an\e with one *in place of* an . . .	LIE
in place of	VICE
• *in place of* boy	VICEROY
• *in place of* sin	VICE
• refusal in place of . . .	NOVICE
in report, he'd . . .	HEED
in retirement<	NI
in retirement, star . . . <	RATS
in retreat, the *German* . . . <	RED
in return<	NI
in short, cannot	CANT
in some parts (=dialect)	
• go astray *in some parts*	MISGO
• *in some parts* favourable . . .	TOWARD
in speech, told . . .	TOLLED

Anag [cat]; Any *; Begin IGN–; Endings –ING; eg •; Hidden /cat/; Implied add (on); Implied in (in);

in splendour	POMPON
in su/ch ef/fort	CHEF
in support of	(*see* support[3])
in talkies, Hugh . . .	HEW, HUE
in talking, I'd . . .	EYED, IDE
in the Black Watch (=Scottish)	
• man *in the Black Watch*	MON
in the cast	ACTING, ONSET
in the club	ENCEINTE, PREGNANT
in the country (=dialect)	
• *in the country* crowd	MONG
• wander *in the country*	STROAM
in the course of	
goin/g over n/ew . . .	GOVERN
in the first instance, she	
was at pains . . .	SWAP
in the Foreign Legion (=French)	
• man *in the Foreign Legion*	HOMME
in the glens (=Scottish)	
• home *in the glens*	HAME
in the last month	ULT(IMO)
in the meantime	AD INT(ERIM)
in the middle of total/ly re/d . . .	LYRE
in the nude (=with nothing on)	add O
	add OON
• father in the nude	DADO
• dance in the nude	BALLOON
	(*see also* with[?])
in the open	ALFRESCO, OUTDOOR
in the past (=old words)	
• bury *in the past*	INEARTH
• *in the past*, boxer . . .	PUGIL
in the pub	(*see* drunk)
in the role of . . .	AS
• in the role of a bird	ASHEN
• in the role of husband	ASH
• in the role of a Scot	ASIAN
in the saddle	UP
in the same place	IB, IBID
in the sticks (=dialect)	
• farm *in the sticks*	WICK
• *in the sticks*, a spider . . .	ATTERCOP
in the style of	ALA
in the time of	TEMP(ORE)
in the wrong direction a rat . . . <	TARA
in the year of . . .	AN, ANNO
–(human) salvation	A(H)S
–the flight	AH
–the king's reign	ARR
–the queen's reign	ARR
–the reign . . .	AR
–the world	AM
in (town) (=foreign language)	
• bridge *in Paris*	PONT
• house *in Milan*	CASA
• inn *in Madrid*	POSEDA
• street *in Berlin*	STRASSE
in turn, *say*	INTERN(E)
in waterproof clothing	MACON
in what manner	QM
in woman's clothes	DRAGON
inaccurate	
inaccuracy of [shot]	HOTS, TOSH
inaccurate [report]	PORTER
[wrote] *inaccurately*	TOWER
inane	
inane [laugh in] . . .	HAULING
inane	AN–E
inapplicable	NA
inaugurate	
inaugurating bursary	B
inauguration of scheme	S
incessant	
incessant (=without end)	
• grumble *incessantly*	MOA(n)
• sin(g) *incessantly*	SIN
inch	
inch	IN
[inch]	CHINWAG
incipient	
incipient growth	G
incisive treatment	SURGERY
incite	
incite	CIT–E
incite *by speech*	INSIGHT
incitement, *say*	PHILIP
include	
included	INC(L)
included in sho/p lea/se	PLEA
included in *	incl in *
• Herb *included in* group	SHERBET
including a . . .	incl A
including *	incl *
• group *including* Herb	SHERBET
incognito	
incognito [prince]	PINCER
[king is] *incognito*	SKIING
income	
income	COM–E
income tax return	REVENUE
incompetent	NOTABLE
incomplete	
incomplete, *say*	KNOTHOLE
incomplete boo(k)	BOO
incomplete de/liver/ies	LIVER
incomplete volume	BOO(k)
incomprehensible	
incomprehensible [argot]	GROAT
incomprehensible	
language	DOUBLE DUTCH, GREEK
inconclusive	
discus(s) *inconclusively*	DISCUS

Letter replaced \c\at; Omit (a); Pointers *out*; Retain a̲; Split B_ED; Down (D); Backwards <or ^

inconclusive kin(d)	KIN	*indefinite* [time]	EMIT, MITE
inconclusive battle	SALAMI(s)	[remain] *indefinitely*	MARINE
inconsistent		**independent**	IND
inconsistency in [speech]	CHEEPS	Independent Broadcasting Authority	IBA
inconsistent [views]	WIVES	Independent Labour Party	ILP
inconsistently [said] . . .	AIDS, DAIS	Independent Television Authority	ITV
inconstant		independent worker	FREE HAND
inconstant [love]	VOLE	**Indian**	
[man is] *inconstant*	MAINS	Indian	CREE
inconvenience		• Indian food, *say*	CREEPIE(S)
inconvenienced by [much] . . .	CHUM	• Indian friend, *say*	CREMATE
[when I] *inconvenienced* . . .	WHINE	• Indian money	CREED, CREEL, CREEP
incorporate		• Indian name	CROWN
incorporate a . . .	incl A	Indian	CROW
incorporate *	incl *	• Indian pub	CROWBAR
• South Africa *incorporates*		• Indian's home	CROW'S NEST
section	SPARTA	Indian	IND
incorporated	INC	• Indian *and* one man	INDIGENT
incorporated by *	incl in *	• Indian *with* no alternative	INDOOR
• section *incorporated by*		• Indian *with* no fast . . .	INDOLENT
South Africa	SPARTA	Indian	UTE
incorporated in hou/se in E/rith	SEINE	• Cape Indian	CUTE
incorrect		• Indian girl	SALUTE
incorrect	(in) R–T, (in) O–K	• Indian *in* credit	CUTER
incorrect [dates]	SATED, STEAD	Indian city, *say*	BOMB–BAY
incorrectly [laid]	DIAL	Indian coin, *say*	ROUPY
increase		Indian fashion	FILE
increase	GROW	Indian ox, *say*	BILE
• increase head, *say*	GROCER	Indian station	CASTE
• increase *almost all* th(e) . . .	GROWTH	Indian uncle, *say*	PAWNEE
• increase weight, *say*	GROGRAM	(*see also* brave)	
increase labour	WAXWORK	**indicate**	
increased by a . . .	incl A	indicate a number, *say*	SIGNATE
increased by one	incl A or I	indicated horse power	IHP
increased by 100	incl C	*indicates* [where] . . .	HEWER
increased by *	incl *	*indicates* where	WARE, WEAR
• weight *increased by* king	TORN	indicative	IND
incredible		**indirect**	
incredible ascent	INDIAN ROPE TRICK	*indirect* [route]	OUTER, OUTRE
incredible soak	STEEP	*indirect* [speech]	CHEEPS
indebted		[speak] *indirectly*	PEAKS, SPAKE
indebted	(in) R–ED	**indiscriminate**	
• Eli *indebted*	RELIED	*indiscriminate* [sort] . . .	ROTS, TORS
• *indebted* following . . .	RAFTERED	[throw] *indiscriminately* . . .	WORTH
indecent		**indispose**	
indecent picture	BLUEPRINT	[his] *indisposition*	–ISH
indecent, *say*	RISKY	*indisposed* [when I] . . .	WHINE
[pose] *indecently*	PESO	**indistinct**	
indeed		*indistinct* [note]	ETON, TONE
indeed	AC–T, DE–ED	[said] *indistinctly*	AIDS, DAIS
• companies *indeed* . . .	ACCOST	**individual**	
• *indeed* allowed . . .	DELETED	individual	I, ME, ONE, SOLE
indefinite		individuality	KA
indefinite(ly)	SUR–E	**indoor**	
indefinite number	N, NO	*indoor*	DO–OR, ENTR–Y
	X, Y, Z	• caught *in*do–or	DOCTOR

Anag [cat]; Any *; Begin IGN–; Endings –ING; eg •; Hidden /cat/; Implied add (on); Implied in (in);

• eat *indoor*	ENTREATY	• insect *infesting* Paul	PANTRY
induce		**infiltrate**	
induced [trance]	NECTAR	*infiltrate* *	incl A
inductance	L	*infiltrated by* a . . .	incl A
indulge		*infiltrated by* *	incl *
indulge in *	incl in *	• c–amp *infiltrated by* fifty . . .	CLAMP
• lieutenant *indulged in* drink	BELTER	**infinite**	
industrialist	BEE	infinite (=unending)	
inefficient		• *infinite* tim(e)	TIM
*in*efficient	A–BLE	• *infinitely* wealthy	–RIC(h)
• *in*efficient artist	ARABLE	infinitive	INF
inefficient	NOTABLE	**inflate**	
inefficient Hoover, *say*	SLOVAK	inflated (=containing air)	
inefficient person	CHARLEY, CHARLIE	• company *after inflation*	CAIRO
inefficiently	NOTABLY	• *inflated* afterthought	PAIRS
inept		**inflow**	
inept [player]	REPLAY	*inflow*	F–LOW
ineptly [sung]	GNUS, GUNS, SNUG	**inform**	
[spoke] *ineptly*	POKES	inform	GRASS, SQUEAL
inexperienced		inform, *say*	TALON
inexperienced driver	CARL	information	GEN
inexperienced footballers	GREENBACKS	• information about . . .	GENRE
infantry		• information *found in* old	
infantry	FOOT	city square	URGENT
• infantry dance	FOOTBALL	information office	COI
• infantry march	FOOTSTEP	information technology	IT
• powerful infantry	HOTFOOT	information unit, *say*	BIGHT, BITE
infantry	INF, PBI	informer	GRASS, NOSE, SQUEALER
infantry instructions	MARCHING ORDERS	informs, *say*	TELSON
infectious disease	ID	**informal shirt**	T
inferior		**infuriate**	
inferior	B	*infuriated* [master]	REMAST, STREAM
inferior	BAD	*infuriating* [leer he] . . .	REHEEL
• inferior china	BADMINTON	*infuriatingly* [smug]	GUMS, MUGS
• inferior drug	BADE	**ingest**	
• son in inferior . . .	SINBAD	*ingest* a . . .	incl A
inferior	POOR	*ingest* *	incl *
• inferior journalist, *say*	PO(U)RED	• m–an *ingested* drug	MEAN
• inferior key, *say*	PORKY	**ingenious**	
• inferior ring, *say*	PO(U)RING	[act] *ingeniously*	CAT
inferior	SUB	*ingenious* [idea]	AIDE
• inferior position	SUBSTANCE	**ingredient**	
• inferior sailor	SUBMARINE	*ingredient of* s/orb/et	ORB
• inferior writer	SUBSCRIBE	*ingredients of* [pie]	EPI–, –IPE
inferior	UNDER	**inhabit**	
• inferior *in* ship	SUNDERS	*inhabitant of* wo/od in/Norway	ODIN
• inferior novelist	UNDERWRITER	*inhabits* fla/t in Ge/rmany	TINGE
• like inferior . . .	ASUNDER	**inhale**	
inferior cow	LOWER	*inhale* a . . .	incl A
inferior horse	ROSINANTE, TIT	*inhale* *	incl *
infest		• h–e *inhaled* oxygen	HOE
infested by a . . .	incl A	**inharmonious**	
infested by *	incl *	*inharmonious* [airs]	SAIR, SARI
• Paul *infested by* insect	PANTRY	[sung] *inharmoniously*	GUNS, SNUG
* *infesting*	incl *	**inherent**	
• infested with insects, *say*	MIGHTY	*inherent in* mo/st Et/hiopians	STET

Letter replaced \c\at; Omit (a); Pointers *out*; Retain a; Split B_ED; Down (D); Backwards <or ^

inhibit
inhibit a . . .	incl A
inhibit *	incl *
• woman *inhibits* fine . . .	EVOKE
inhibited by t/he r/ules	HER
inhibited by *	incl in *
• chant *inhibited by* h–er	HOMER

inhuman
inhuman	ANIMAL, BEASTLY
in[human]	NAHUM

initial
initial combination	ACRONYM
initial letters	SIGNPOST
Initial Teaching Alphabet	ITA
initially deficient	omit 1st letter
initially they . . .	T
initially they were only . . .	TWO

initiate
commercial *initiate*	C
initiate scheme	S
initiating doctrine	D
initiative to start	S

inject
inject a . . .	incl A
inject *	incl *
• *inject* nitrogen *into* bo–y	BONY
inject drug	incl E
* *injected with*	incl in *
• bo–y *injected with* nitrogen	BONY
injection	JAB, TAB

injure
injured [parties]	PIASTRE
injuring [arm]	MAR, RAM
injury to [horse]	SHORE

ink slinger   OCTOPUS

inland
inland	OFFSHORE
*in*land	LAN–D
Inland Revenue	IR, TAXMAN

inmate
*in*mate	M–ATE
in[mate]	MEAT, TAME, TEAM
inmate of c/ell en/gaged in . . .	ELLEN

innate
innate in so/me Et/thiopians	MEET
innate part of Am/erica/n . . .	ERICA

innards
a/nim/al's *innards*	NIM
innards of com/put/er	PUT

inner
inner chamber, *say*	CELLAR, SELLA, SELLER
Inner Circle	BULL('S-EYE), GOLD, RED
inner circle	incl O
• line *with inner* circle	ROY
• test *inner* circle	MOOT
inner elements of	

reac/tor que/nched	TORQUE
inner part of city	IT
inner parts	ART
inner roof, *say*	SEALING
inner tube	CIRCLE LINE
	ENTERON, INTESTINE

innkeeper   BONIFACE

innovate
[act] *innovatively*	CAT
innovation [made] . . .	DAME, EDAM, MEAD
innovative [idea]	AIDE

inoffensive figures   MILD

inordinate
inordinate [praise]	PERSIA
inordinately [weak]	WAKE

insane
insane [despot]	POSTED
insanely [rages]	GEARS
insanity [plea]	LEAP, PALE, PEAL

inscribe
inscribe a . . .	incl A
inscribe *	incl *
• *inscribe* name *in* 100 ha–ts	CHANTS

insect
insect	ANT
• insect biting	ANTACID
• insect *impersonator*	AUNT
• insect persecution	ANTABUSE
insect	BEE
• insect bites	BEESTINGS
• insect *given* name	BEEN
• insect *impersonator*	B, BE
insect	BUG
• insect damage	BUGLOSS
• insect drinks . . .	BUGGINS
• noise of insect	HUMBUG
insect	GNAT
• insect *impersonator*	NAT
• insect *returns<*	TANG
insect	TICK
• at insect's . . . , *say*	ATTICS
• insect in front	TICKLED
• second insect	STICK
insect breeding establishments, *say*	MOTHERY, NATTERY
insect dances	MOTH-BALLS
insect egg, *say*	KNIT
insect-*free*	omit FLY
• (f)air(ly) insect-*free*	AIR
insect hangover	BEETLE
insect, *say*	AUNT, BE, MIGHT, NAT
insecticide	DDT
insect's mouth parts, *say*	TROPHY

insecure
insecure [door]	ROOD
insecurity of [tenure]	RETUNE

[tied] *insecurely*	DIET, EDIT, TIDE	• inspect stomach, *say*	CERUMEN
insert		inspect closely, *say*	STAIRWELL
insert in document, *say*	TIE-PIN	inspected dossier	SAWFILE
inserted in docum/ent Eric/ . . .	ENTERIC	inspection chamber	CONSULTING ROOM
inset		inspector	HMI
*in*set	SE–T	inspects	SEES
in[set]	–EST, TES	• boy inspects	LESSEES
inside		and	
*in*side	LE–G, L–T, O–N	• inspects drink, *say*	SEA-SWINE
	S–IDE, R–T	• inspects fingertips	SEA-SNAILS
• *in*side left	SLIDE	• inspects fish, *say*	SEASIDE
in[side]	DIES, IDES	**inspiring**	
inside left	L–T, POR–T	inspiring group	MUSES, NINE
• very large *inside*-left	LOST	inspiring passage	BRONCHIOLE, BRONCHUS
• ten *inside* left . . .	PORTENT	**install**	
inside left	incl L	*install* a . . .	incl A
• footballer, *inside*-left	BLACK	*install* *	incl *
inside man	PRISONER	• *installed* king *in* state	CARL
inside out	incl in OU–T	*installed in* re/gal a/partment	GALA
• bend *inside* ou–t	OUST	instalment system	HP
inside out	incl OUT	**instant**	
• about *inside* out	ROUTE	instant	INST
inside right	R–T	instant	MO
• holes *inside* right . . .	ROOT	• instant assault	MOONSET
inside right	incl R	• instant tea	MOCHA
• child *inside* right . . .	TROT	instant	SEC
inside t/he Ar/ctic	HEAR	• *after* an instant, worker . . .	SECANT
inside *	incl in *	• equal instant	PARSEC
• measure *inside* crate	CREMATE	instant	TICK
is *inside*	incl IS	• instant credit	TICK
• old fiddle is *inside*	GUISE	• second instant	STICK
insolvent	(in) R–ED	instant assessment	SECOND RATE
inspect		**instead**	
inspect	EYE	instead	STEA–D
• inspect ship	EYE-LINER	• me instea–d	STEAMED
• inspect molar	EYE-TOOTH	*in*[stead]	DATES, SATED
• inspects mineral	EYESORE	**instinct**	ID
inspect	SCAN	**institute**	
• inspect bonds	SCANTIES	Institute/Institution of	
• inspect junction	SCANT	–Actuaries	IA
• union inspects . . .	TUSCANS	–Advanced Motorists	IAM
inspect	SEE	–Bankers	IB
• inspect corpses, *say*	SEEDED	–Building	IOB
• inspect cut	SEE-SAW	–Civil Engineers	ICE
• inspect porcelain	SEEMING	–Contemporary Artists	ICA
and		–Journalists	IOJ
• inspect coins, *say*	SERIALS	–Linguists	IL
• inspect island, *say*	SECRETE	–Mining and Metallurgy	IMM
• inspect vegetable, *say*	SECALE	–Municipal Engineers	IMUNE
and		–Physics	IP
• inspect drink, *say*	SEAPORT	–Practitioners in Advertising	IPA
• inspect porcelain, *say*	SEAMING	**instruct**	
• inspect telephone, *say*	SEARING	instructed	TAUGHT
and		• instructed a number, *say*	TAUTEN
• inspect corpses, *say*	CEDED	• instructed a woman, *say*	TAUTER
• inspect fish, *say*	CEILING	• instructed, *say*	TAUT

instructing team	COACHWORK	interchangeable	
instructs snooker player	TRAINSPOTTER	indicating substitution:	
insufficient		• *interchangeable* ends	
insufficient money	SHORTBREAD	of \l\eve\r\	REVEL
insufficiently appreciated	UNDERFELT	• \m\ate\s\ *with*	
insure		*interchangeable* ends	SATEM
insurance premium, *say*	PROLIFERATE	**interest**	INT
*in*sure	SUR–E	interest	INT
insure	TAKE COVER	• interest *in* writing	MINTS
*in*sured	SUR–ED	• interest *on* pound	LINT
• horse *in*sured	SURMOUNTED	**interfere**	
intake		interfere, *say*	MEDAL
in[take]	KATE, TEAK	*interfere with* [car]	ARC
intake a . . .	incl A	*interference with* [signal I] . . .	SAILING
intake *	incl *	**interior**	
• he–r beer *intake*	HEALER	interior	INT
• w–e *have* an *intake*	WANE	*interior of* Am/eric/a	ERIC
integer		*interior* o/f Ame/rica	FAME
integers	Z	*interior of* *	incl in *
integral	INT	• horse *in interior of* be-ar	BEGGAR
integral part of mo/tor c/ar	TORC	interior views	X-RAYS
integrated circuit	IC	**interject**	
intellectual games	MARBLES	*interject* a . . .	incl A
intelligence		*interject* *	incl *
intelligence	MI, NI	• "Pla–n", I *interjected*	PLAIN
intelligence department	ID, MI, NI	**interminable**	
intelligence factor	NEWSAGENT	*interminable* journey	TRI(p)
intelligence group	CID	rod(e) *interminably*	ROD
intelligence operation	COGITATION	**intermittent**	
	THINKING	*intermittent signs of* me<u>asle</u>s	MALE
intelligence quotient	IQ	p<u>ainted</u> *intermittently*	ANE
intelligence, *say*	WHIT	**intern**	
intend		*intern* a . . .	incl A
*in*tend	TEN–D	*intern* *	incl *
in[tend]	DENT	• Hu–ns *intern* mother	HUMANS
intended	FIANCE(E), –MENT	*interned by* *	incl in *
*in*tent	T–ENT	• mother *interned by* Hu–ns	HUMANS
in[tent]	NETT	**internal**	
inter		internal combustion engine	ICE
inter	BURY	*internal to* househ/old	
inter	T–ER	est/ablishment	OLDEST
in[ter]	–ERT, RET, TRE	*internally* a . . .	incl A
inter alia	AL–IA	*internally* *	incl *
[inter]-*reaction*	NITRE, TRINE	• carrier *with internal* skin	BASKING
inter, *say*	BERRY	**international**	
inter-*state*	BERRY	International	
inter-state	AVE–R, C–AL, SA–Y,	–Bank	BIS
inter them, *say*	BARIUM	–Development Association	IDA
interred, *say*	BERRIED	–Electrotechnical Commission	IEC
intercept		–Finance Corporation	IFC
intercept a . . .	incl A	–Labour Organisation	ILO
intercept *	incl *	–Monetary Fund	IMF
• sh–ot *intercepted by*		–Olympic Committee	IOC
everyone	SHALLOT	–Organisation for Standardisation	ISO
interchangeable		–Phonetic Alphabet	IPA
[inter]*changeable*	INERT, NITRE, TRINE	–Publishers' Association	IPA

Anag [cat]; Any *; Begin IGN–; Endings –ING; eg •; Hidden /cat/; Implied add (on); Implied in (in);

–Publishing Corporation	IPC	• *interview* reserves	SETAE
–Rail Transport	TIF	**interweave**	
–Road Transport	TIR	*interweave* [cane]	–ANCE
–Social Services	ISS	[inter]*woven*	NITRE, TRINE
–Subscriber Dialling	ISD	*interwoven* [mesh]	HEMS, SHEM
–Telecommunications Union	ITU	**into**	
–Trade Organisation	ITO	*into a mess* [I ran]	RAIN, RANI
–Vehicle Registration	IVR	*into* [town]	WONT
international	CAP	into hospital	TOWARD(S)
• deceives international . . .	FOOLSCAP	pop *into*	incl PA
• international award	CAP	• pop *into* Pole's . . .	SPAN
• international drug	CAPE	run *into*	incl R
international	INT	• run *into* f–og	FROG
international banker	GNOME	see *into*	incl C
international organisation	UN	• see *into*, s–oon	SCOON
international unit	IU	turn *into*	incl GO
interpolate		• turn *into* a–ny . . .	AGONY
interpolate a . . .	incl A	**intoxicated**	
interpolate *	incl *	*intoxicated* [by all] . . .	BALLY
• doctor *interpolating*		*intoxication of* [men at] . . .	MANET
figure is . . .	LIMBS		MEANT
interpose		**intricate**	
interpose a . . .	incl A	*intricacy of* [plot I] . . .	PILOT
interpose *	incl *	*intricate* [design]	SIGNED
• *interpose* it *in* directions	SITE(S)	**intrigue**	
interpret		*intriguing* [idea]	AIDE
interpret [Norse] . . .	NOSER, SNORE	[nasty] *intrigue*	TANSY
interpretation of [Pali]	PAIL	**intrinsic**	
interpreter	INT	*intrinsically* honc/st	
interrupt		and s/sane	STANDS
interrupted by a . . .	incl A	s/he w/as *intrinsically* . . .	HEW
interrupted by *	incl *	**introduce**	
• hundreds *interrupted by* shout	CHIC	introduce force	ENTERPRISE
interrupting *	incl in *	*introduced to* *	incl in *
• shout *interrupting* hundreds	CHIC	• man *introduced to* woman	SUEDE
intersect		*introducing* a . . .	incl A
intersect *	incl in *	*introducing* *	incl *
• many *intersect* pat–h	PATCH	• girl *introducing* man	SUEDE
[inter]*section*	INERT, NITRE, TRINE	*introductions to* new owner	NO
intertwined		introductory letters	INITIALS
intertwined [coil]	–OLIC	**intruding**	
intertwining [arms]	MARS, RAMS	*intruding into* *	incl in *
intervene		• one *intruding into* party	COIN
intervention of a . . .	incl A	**invade**	
intervention of *	incl *	*invaded by* a . . .	incl A
• *intervention of* men		*invaded by* *	incl *
in this *French* . . .	CEMENT	• ship *invaded by* lice	SLICES
• student *intervenes in* b–est . . .	BLEST	*invaded by* fier/ce de/mons	CEDE
interview		*invading* Ameri/can ter/ritory	CANTER
interview	SEE	*invading* *	incl in *
• interview royalty	SEEKING	• lice *invading* ship	SLICES
• interview servant	SEEPAGE	**invalid**	
• interview thousands	SEEMS	*invalid* [claim]	MALIC
interview	(in) SE–E	*invalidly* [claimed]	DECIMAL, DECLAIM
• in *interview*	SEINE		MEDICAL
• *interview* king	SERE	**invariably**	EER

Letter replaced \c\at; Omit (a); Pointers *out*; Retain a; Split B_ED; Down (D); Backwards <or ^

invent		Irish sailors	CORKSCREW
invent plant	MINT	Irish team	DOWNSIDE
invented	INV	Irish warder	CORKSCREW
invented [a thing] . . .	HATING	Irishman, *say*	WRYLY
invention of part(D)^	PANEL	**iron**	
inventor	EDISON	iron	DECREASE
invert		iron	CLUB
inversion of part(D)^	TRAP	iron bed	CLUBBED
inversion of [sense]	ESSEN	• ironworker	CLUBMAN
invert parts(D)^	STRAP	iron	FE
inverted cheese(D)^	MADE	• gold *and* iron	ORFE
invest		• iron *in* loa–d	LOAFED
invest a . . .	incl A	• iron lady	FEDORA
invest *	incl *	• iron man	FETED, FEMALE
• mother's *investing* £50	MALLS	iron bird	GOOSE
invested in sha/res t/oday	REST	iron*bound*	(in) F–E
invested in *	incl in *	• iron*bound* curve	FARCE
• £50 *invested in* mother's . . .	MALLS	iron*clad*	(in) F–E
invests at this place, *say*	BANKSIA	• American iron*clad*	FUSE
invisible		iron	PRESS
* *invisible*	omit *	• engineers have iron	REPRESS
• biscuit that is *invisible*	COOK(ie)	• ironworkers	PRESSMEN
• val(is)e is *invisible*	VALE	iron hand	LAUNDRY WORKER
invite		Iron Lady	MAGGIE
invite round	COURT CIRCULAR	iron rations	HARD TACK, STAPLE DIET
invitation	CARD	ironmonger	SCRAP MERCHANT
invitation, *say*	OAKUM	Ironside	EDMUND
invitation to entertain	DOSING	ironside	HARDLINER, HARDSHIP
invoice	INV	ironwork	DECREASING, EVENING, PRESSING
involve		**irregular**	
involved in sc/hem/e	HEM	*irregular* [army]	MARY, MYRA
involved in *	incl in *	*irregular* [verb], English	BREVE
• me *involved in* state	CAMEL	*irregularity of* [line]	LIEN, NEIL, NILE
involved [me in] . . .	MIEN, MINE	*irregularly* [formed]	DEFORM
involving a . . .	incl A	**irreversible letter of credit**	ILC
involving [much] . . .	CHUM	**irritate**	
involving *	incl *	irritability, *say*	BHYLE
• state *involving* me	CAMEL	irritate	PIQUE
inward		• irritate insect, *say*	PIQUANT
inward	HOSPITALISED	• irritate ruler, *say*	PEAKING, PEEKING
in[wards]	DRAWS, SWARD	• irritated, *say*	PEAKED, PEEKED
Iran		irritate(D)^	BUR
[Iran]	RAINMAKER, RAINSTORM	irritate animal	BUGBEAR
Ireland	EIRE, ERIN, EMERALD ISLE	*irritated* [these] . . .	SHEET
	GREEN ISLE, IR, IR(E)L	irritates nose	TROUBLESHOOTER
Irish		*irritation of* [horse's] . . .	SHORES
Irish	IR	**is**	IS
Irish banker	SHANNON	is *about*<	SI
Irish capital	PUNT	is *about*	I–S
Irish *capital*	I	is *absent*	omit IS
Irish capitalist	DUBLINER	is *ahead of* time	–IST
Irish clergyman, *say*	REVERSE	is English	–ISE
Irish *flower*	SHANNON	is *forgotten*	omit IS
Irish house	DAIL	• lift is *forgotten*	HO(is)T
Irish *leader*	I	is *found in* . . .	incl IS
Irish police-chief	RUCKING	• is *found in* poem	EPISODE

Anag [cat]; Any *; Begin IGN–; Endings –ING; eg •; Hidden /cat/; Implied add (on); Implied in (in);

is *French*	EST	Isle of Man	GBM, IOM
is *German*	IST	Isle of Wight	IOW, IW
is *given* Eastern . . .	–ISE	isle, *say*	AISLE, I'LL
is hard	–ISH	islet	LEASED, TENANTED
is hot	–ISH	our islands	GB
is *in France*	EST	this island	UK
is *in Germany*	IST	**isle**	(*see* island)
is *in Spain*	ES	**issue**	
is *in* time	DAISY	issue	CHILD(REN), LITTER, SON
is leased	ISLET	*issue* [shares]	SHEARS
is married	–ISM	**it**	
is no . . .	ISO–	it	SA, T
is nothing	ISO–	*it appears* plain	PLANE
is prosecuted	ISSUED	it is	–ITIS, TIS
is *removed*	omit IS	(i)t is *short*	T
• hagg(is) is *removed* . . .	HAGG	*it might be* great	GRATE
is rented	ISLET	*it might be* [great]	GRATE, TARGE
is *Spanish*	ES	*it sounds like* rain	REIGN, REIN
is square	–IST	*it turns out* [fine]	NIFE
is *taking* time	–IST	[it's] *broken*	–IST, SIT, TIS
is *the first*	–IST	[it's] *free*	–IST, SIT, TIS
is²		[it's] *Greek*	–IST, SIT, TIS
Is he able? *say*	CANNY	it's hot, *say*	SWARM
Is he obliged? *say*	MUSTEE, MUSTY	it's not a bird	SNOWBIRD
is not	AINT, ANT	it's not footwear	SNOWSHOE(S)
is not *commonly* . . .	AINT, ANT	it's not, *say*	SNOT, TAINT
is not [considerate]	DESECRATION	It's [Not] *Unusual*	TON
Is the girl able?	CANADA	it's not your, *say* . . .	TAINTURE
Isaiah	IS(A)	it's nothing, *say*	SNOUT
island		[it's] *rough*	–IST, SIT, TIS
island	AIT, EYOT, I, INCH	*it's said* you . . .	EWE, YEW
	IONA, MONA	[it's] *unusual*	–IST, SIT, TIS
island	CAPRI	[it's] *wrong*	–IST, SIT, TIS
• island crop	CAPRICORN	**Italy**	I
island	COS	**Italian**	
• island group	COSSET	Italian	AUSONIAN, EYETI(E), EYTIE
• island unknown	COSY	Italian	IT
island	CRETE	• Italian *and* English share	ITERATION
• princess's island	DISCRETE	• Italian church	ITCH
• study island	CONCRETE	• Italian letters	ITEMS
island	ELBA	Italian	ROMAN
• island *retreat<*	ABLE	• Italian *and* Scot	ROMANIAN
island	HERM	• Italian church	ROMANCE
• island goddess	HERMAPHRODITE	• Italian capitalist	ROMAN
• island with *German, say*	HERMIT	• Italian insect, *say*	ROMANTIC
island	IS	Italian banker	TIBER etc
• island occupied	ISLET	Italian *capital*	I
• islands	ISIS	Italian capital	EURO, LIRA
island	MAN	Italian *flower*	TIBER etc
• first island	FOREMAN	Italian *leader*	I
• island bird	MANDRAKE	Italian linesman	DANTE
• island *with* unknown . . .	MANY	*Italian-speaking* boy	RAGAZZO
island edge	INCH	Italian way	AUTOSTRADA
island king	SOLOMON	**item**	
islands, *say*	PHARAOHS	item of make-up	CHROMOSOME, GENE
Isle of Dogs	NEWFOUNDLAND	*item in* news/pap/er	PAP

Letter replaced \c\at; Omit (a); Pointers *out*; Retain <u>a</u>; Split B_ED; Down (D); Backwards <or ^

itemise [all the] . . .	LETHAL	**Ivory Coast**	CI
Ivan		**ivy**	
[Ivan] *the Terrible*	VAIN	ivy *maybe* . . .	CREEPER
makes [Ivan] . . .	VAIN	ivy, *say*	IV

J

curve, heat, Jack, Japan, *jay*, *joint*, joule, journal, judge, justice, *knave*, one, pen, spin quantum number, square root of -1

Jack

Jack	J, KITTY, KNAVE
Jack's wedding	UNION
	(*see also* sailor)

jacket

jacket	REEFER
jacket, *say*	REFER

jade YU

jagged

jagged [scar]	ARCS, CARS
[made] *jagged*	DAME, EDAM, MEAD

jailed (in) C–AGE, (in) CA–N, (in) PE–N

Jamaica JA

James

James	JAS
James	JIM
• James is working	JIMSON
• Jim, can I? *say*	GYMKHANA

jammed cylinder SWISS ROLL

January JAN

Japan J, NIPPON, VARNISH

Japanese

Japanese	JAP
Japanese capital	YEN
Japanese *capital*	J
Japanese *leader*	J
Japanese palace, *say*	DAIRY
Japanese purchaser	YEN

jaunt

jaunt [in Wye]	WINEY
[stride] *jauntily*	DIREST, DRIEST

jay J

jazz

jazz	TRAD
• jazz queen	TRADER
• jazzman	TRADED
jazz fan	CAT
jazz figure	RIFF
jazzy [coat]	ATOC, TACO

jeer

jeer leader	BOOKING
jeer *leader*	J
jeers, *say*	BOOZE

jelly

jellied	SET
jellied [eel]	LEE
jelly	GELIGNITE, SHAPE

jenny

Jennifer, *say*	DONKEY-SKIN
Jenny Hill, *say*	GENITOR
jenny, *say*	ASSESS

jerk

jerking [rein]	RINE
jerking, *say*	JACKET
jerky [stride]	DIREST, DRIEST
[speak] *jerkily*	PEAKS, SPAKE
[tear]-*jerking*	RATE, TARE

Jerry

Jerry's (=German)	
• for *Jerry's* . . .	FUR
• *Jerry's* house	HAUS
• with *Jerry's* . . .	MIT

Jersey

Jersey	GBJ
Jersey, *say*	COW
	PULLOVER

Jesus IHC, IHS, JC, JHC

(*see also* Christ)

jet

jet	BLACK
• jet flier	BLACKBIRD
• jet pilot	BLACK FLY
• jetstream	BLACKBURN
• *see* jet land	BLACK COUNTRY
jet flier	CROW, RAVEN, ROOK
jet set	AIR CREW
jetstream	HIGH WIND

jewelry

jewelry	PASTE
• jewelry catalogue	PASTELIST
• jewelry lines, *say*	PASTRY

Jewish (*see* Hebrew)

jilt

jilted [Delia]	AILED
[she was] *jilted*	WASHES

jittery

jittery [leader]	DEALER

Letter replaced \c\at; Omit (a); Pointers *out*; Retain a̲; Split B_ED; Down (D); Backwards <or ^

jittery *leader*	J	**jolly**	
[she was] *jittery*	WASHES	jolly	MARINE, RM
j-jaguar	JOUNCE	• a jolly old fellow	ARMAGEDDON
Joan's friend	DARBY	• in jolly style	ALARM
job		• laugh *and have* jolly . . .	HARM
job description	PATIENT	jolly fellow	ROGER
job-finder	DEVIL, SATAN	**jolt**	
job in the theatre	OPERATING, SURGERY	*jolted* [arm]	MAR, RAM
jockey		*jolting* [blow 'e] . . .	ELBOW, BELOW
jockey's lawyers	SILKS	**Jonathan's bearer**	APPLE-TREE
Joe's double	GIGI	**Jordan**	HKJ
jogging		**jostle**	
jogger	PROMPT(ER)	jostle boat	BARGE
jogging [arm]	MAR, RAM	*jostle* [master]	REMAST, STREAM
[the pony is] *jogging*	HYPNOTISE	*jostling* [elbow]	BELOW
John		**joule**	J
John	JNO	**journalist**	ED
John's place	GAUNT	**journey**	
join		journey after dark, *say*	NITRIDE
join a chief	ACID	journey *by* road	TRIPLANE
join	SEAM	journey shared	GO-BETWEEN
• join an . . .	SEAMAN	journey's end	DESTINATION
• join forces	SEAMSTRESSES	Journey's End	Y
join an orchestra	ALSO	journeyman	GULLIVER, ODYSSEUS
joined forces	INTERPOL	**joy**	
joined in son/g at E/aster	GATE	joyful cry	IO
joined, *say*	TIDE	joyous hoot, *say*	HOOP
joined sect	INCULT	**judge•**	
joiner	AND, HYPHEN	judge	HEAR
	DOWEL, STAPLE	• judge aboard ship	SHEARS
	SNUG	• judge man	HEARKEN
joining in cele/brat/ion	BRAT	• second judge	SHEAR
joining together, *say*	TEEMING	judge	J
joining train	BOARDING SCHOOL	judge	REF
joint	CO–	• judge Indians	REFUTES
–at this point	COHERE	• judge not well	REFILL
–friend	COMATE, COPAL	• judge took advantage	REFUSED
–ruler	COKING	judge instrument	RECORDER
–support	COBRA, COPIER	judge, *say*	GAGE
joint	DIVE, ELBOW	judge's chauffeur	MASTER OF THE ROLLS
joint	KNEE	judge's condition	SOBER, SOBRIETY
• joint fish	KNEELING	Judges	JUD(G)
joint	REEFER	**judo expert**	DAN
joint, *say*	REFER	**juggle**	
joint	SEAM	*juggle* [plates]	PALEST, PETALS, PLEATS,
• joint help	SEA-MAID		STAPLE
• joint, *say*	SEEM	*juggling* [rings, I]	RISING
joint cleaners	KNUCKLEDUSTERS	**July**	JUL
joint guardian	PATELLA	**jumble**	
Joint Matriculation Board	JMB	*jumble* [sale]	ALES, LEAS, SEAL
joke		*jumbled* [letters]	SETTLER
joke mildly	PUNGENTLY	**jumbo pilot**	MAHOUT
joke, *say*	JESSED	**jump**	
joker	RAGMAN	jump aboard, *say*	NIPPON
jokingly ingest . . .	(in) J–EST	*jump* [over]	ROVE
jokingly, *say*	INGEST	*jump over* *	incl *

Anag [cat]; Any *; Begin IGN–; Endings –ING; eg •; Hidden /cat/; Implied add (on); Implied in (in);

• h–e *jumps over* a street	HASTE	junior common room	JCR
jump t<u>o</u> *conclusions*	PO	junior minister	CURATE
jump through	HOPPER	**junk food**	TRIPE
jump up		**just**	
• dog *jumps up*(D)^	GOD	*just a bit of* bro/ken t/ableware	KENT
jump well	SPRING	just a piano	UPRIGHT
jumped aboard, *say*	LEPTON	just blond	FAIR
jumper CRICKET, FLEA, KANGAROO,		just characters	FOUR MEN
JERSEY, PULLOVER,		• just characters, *say*	FOREMEN
PARACHUTIST, PARATROOPER		just fine	FAIR
• jumper store	FLEA MARKET	• just line, *say*	PHARAOH
jumper fastener	FROG	• just *the reverse*	UNFAIR
jumping [bean]	BANE	just water	MERE
jumping deer<	REED	just words	SENTENCE, VERDICT
jumpy soldier	PARA(TROOPER)	**justice**	
jumpy [soldier]	SOLIDER	justice	FREEZING
junction			J
junction	T		SHALLOW
junction of a line	ALINE	Justice's clerk	JC
square junction	TT	Justice of the Peace	JP
June	JUN	**Jutes**	SACK RACE
jungle queen	FORESTER	**juvenile**	
junior		juvenile game	KIDNAP
junior	JUN(R), JR	juvenile *lead*	J

K

Boltzmann's constant, carat, conductivity, constant, dissociation constant, kacha, kalium, Kampuchea, kangha, kaon, kappa, kara, karat, kay, *Kay*, kelvin, kesh, Khmer Republic, kilo, kina, king, Kirkpatrick, kirpan, knight, Köchel, krona, krone, kwacha, *monarch*, Mozart's works, potassium, radius of gyration, Scarlatti's works, thousand, twenty (thousand), two-hundred and fifty, velocity constant, vitamin

K9	CANINE	Keeper of the Privy Seal	KPS
kale	KL	Keeper of the Royal Swans	SWANKING
kaleidoscope		*keeping* a . . .	incl A
kaleidoscope of [scenes 'e] . . .	ESSENCE	*keeping* *	incl *
kaleidoscopic [lights]	SLIGHT	• m–an *keeping* girl	MAIDAN
kangaroo		keeps mum	SAY-SO
kangaroo	JOEY	*kept (in) by* t/each/er	EACH
kangaroo	ROO	*kept (in) by* *	incl in *
• kangaroo boss, *say*	ROOKING	• girl *kept in by* m–an	MAIDAN
• kangaroo burrow	ROOPIT	• girl *kept by* parents	PANORAMA
kappa	K	kept quiet	RESERVED
Kay	K	kept waiting (=on ice)	
Kayo	LADY-LOVE	• *kept waiting with* daughter	ICED
keel		• king *kept waiting*	RICE
keeling over, Ben . . .<	NEB	• many *kept waiting*	DICE, LICE, MICE
sloop *keels over*<	POOLS	**keel**	
keen		*keeling over*, Ben . . . <	NEB
keen cricket side	CRY OFF	sloop *keels over*<	POOLS
keen on	INTO	**Kelly's eye**	I, ONE
keen on something, *say*	MADONNA	**kelvin**	K
keen, *say*	EAGRE	**kennel**	
keener	NIOBE	kennel fee	CURRENT
keep		kennel club	KC
keep burning, *say*	BLAZON	**Kensington district**	WEIGHT
keep commission	RETAIN	**Kent**	SE
keep flying	NEVER-NEVER-LAND	**Kenya**	EAK
keep healthy	BEFIT	**kept**	(see keep)
keep in	GATE	**kernel**	
• keep in job	GATEPOST	br<u>ok</u>en *kernel*	OK
keep playing	ACTON, BATON	b/roke/n *kernel*	ROKE
keep going	DRAGON	*kernel of* p/roble/m	ROBLE
keep notice	OBSERVE	**kewpie (doll)**	QP
keep quiet	incl P, SH	**key**	
• Ro–y *keeps* quiet	ROPY	key	A, B, C, D, E, F, G
• Mar–y *keeps* quiet	MARSHY	• key hole	BO, DO, GO
keep quiet, *say*	WIST	• key note	ATE
keep signalling	FLAGON	• key points	AS, ASS, BE, BEE, EWE etc
keep sovereign	KING OF THE	• key ring	DO, GO
	CASTLE	• key-stone	COPAL
keep tractor	TOWER	• key *to* room	EDEN
keep waving	WAGON	• key *to* the door	GENTRY

Anag [cat]; Any *; Begin IGN–; Endings –ING; eg •; Hidden /cat/; Implied add (on); Implied in (in);

• two keys *with* lock	ACTRESS
key	CAY
• key, key, key	DECAY
• key-worker	CAYMAN
key batsman	OPENER
key feature	WARD
key figures	EX, EMIL, CIVIC etc
key	
–for legumes, *say*	PEAKY
–for vehicle, *say*	KHAKI
–for relations, *say*	KINKY
key personnel	SKELETON STAFF
key-worker	PIANO TUNER, TYPIST
keyboard, *say*	MANUEL
kick	
kick	BOOT
• kick sailor	BOOT-JACK
• kick son	BOOTS
• kick the drink, *say*	BOOTLICKER
kick	HACK
• kick horse	HACK
• kick *on* the knee, *say*	HACKNEY
• son *takes* kick	SHACK
kick-off	KO
kick *out*	HA–CK
kick-out [cat]	ACT
kicked about [field]	FILED
kickstart	K
[unit alive and] *kicking*	ANTEDILUVIAN
kid	
kid brother	BILLY
kid sister	NANNY
kids curse	CHILDRENSWEAR
kid's father	BILLY, GOAT
kid's mother	GOAT, NANNY
kidnap	
kidnap children	TAKE ISSUE
kidnapped schoolgirl, *say*	MISTAKEN
kidnapper	LEATHERHEAD, PARIS
kill	
kill	END
• kill debtor	ENDOWER
• kill nettles	ENDANGERS
• second kill	SEND
kill	SLAY
• kill ruler, *say*	SLAKING
• kill Scot, *say*	SLATE-AXE
• kill dog, *say*	SLAP-UP
• killed, *say*	SLADE
kill mother	DOMAIN
kill you and me, *say*	CROCUS
killed slug	SHOT
killer	CAIN
kilo	K
kind	
kind	MODE

• kind helping	MODERATION
kind	TYPE
• kind appearance	TYPEFACE
• kind author	TYPEWRITER
kind	NATURE
• kind husband	NATURE RESERVE
• kind mother	NATURE
• kind note	NATURED
kind of [animal]	LAMINA, MANILA
king¹	
king	HM
king	K
• king-fish	KEEL
• king in fear, *say*	KINDRED
• The King and I	KI
king	KING
• graduate king	BAKING
• island king, *say*	CAKING
• king-like	ASKING
• river-king	POKING
• royal architect	PLANKING
• royal yacht	KINGSHIP
• slim ruler	THINKING
king	R
• king is dead	LATER
• king-bird	REGRET
• The King and I	RI
king	REX
• king lives, *say*	RHEXIS
• king, *say*	(W)RECKS
• model king, *say*	TREKS
king (Charles)	CR
• king *at* work	CROP
• King Charles I	CRONE
• king has . . .	CROWNS
• king I see	CRISPY
king (Edward)	ER
• king at home, OK	ERINYES
• King-rat with a . . .	ERRATA
• King's English	ERSE
king (George)	GR
• king and heir	GRANDSON
• King George I	GRIST
• king *with* one son	GRISON
kings	
• two kings dine at home	KREATIN
	(*see also* royal¹)
king²	
Cockney king	PEARLIE, PEARLY
King Cole	NAT
King Edward	LEAR, LEARNED
king-emperor	RI
king, *maybe*	CARD, CHESSMAN, PIECE
king of France	ROI, SM
king of sin	VICEROY
king watcher	CAT

kingly men	REGAL, ROYAL	*knead* [knead]	NAKED
king's associate	ANNA	knead, *say*	WANT
King's Bench	KB	*kneaded* [clay]	LACY
King's College	KC	*kneading to* [paste]	PATES, PEATS, SPATE
king's constitution	COLESLAW	**knew**	
King's Counsel	KC	knew (old)	WIST
king's downfall	CHECKMATE	knew, *say*	GNU, NEW
King's *Head*	K		WHIST
king's highway	ROYAL ROAD	**knight**	
king's mistress	NELL	knight	K, KT, N
king's rule	COLESLAW	knight	SIR
king's weapon	EXCALIBUR	• knight copies, *say*	SERAPES
mad king	LEAR	• knight devoured, *say*	SERRATE
merry king	COLE	• knight *with* Scot, *say*	SERMON
old king	COLE, OG	and	
Sun king	LOUIS	• knight employed . . .	CERUSED
king³		• knight is English	CERISE
*Cha*rles *I*	C	• knight was familiar	
*Cha*rles *II*	H	with us, *say*	CERNUOUS
*Ed*ward *II*	D	and	
Edward II	SECONDER	• knight *and* a man, *say*	SURGENT
*Ed*ward *III*	W	• knight bachelor, *I'm told*	SURCINGLE
George *IV*	R	• knight *has* a title, *say*	SURNAME
Henry *V*	Y	• knight overtakes, *say*	SURPASSES
*Edwar*d *VI*	D	and	
kinky		• knight got up, *say*	CIRROSE
kinky [male]	LAME, MEAL	Knight	
[quite] *kinky*	QUIET	–of Labour	KL
Kipling		–of Malta	KM
Kipling's character	KIM	–of the Bath	KB
Kipling's work	IF	–of the Legion of Honour	KLH
kipper		–of the Order of the Garter	KG
kipper	NAPPER	–of the Thistle	KT
kipper's head	NAPPER	Knight Bachelor	KB
kipper's *head*	K	knight bachelor, *I'm told*	SURCINGLE
kippe*r's tail*	R	Knight Commander	
Kirkpatrick	K	–of the Bath	KCB
kiss		–of the British Empire	KBE
kiss	BUSS	Knight Grand Cross	
kiss	PECK	–of the Bath	GCB
• Kiss me, Hardy	PECKING ORDER	–of the British Empire	GBE
• kiss toes, *say*	PECTOSE	–of Hanover	GCH
• kissed a number, *say*	PECTATE	knight, *say*	NIGHT
• knock-out kiss	KOPECK	• Knight E, *say*	NIGHTIE
kiss	X	• Knight Lee, *say*	NIGHTLY
• a kiss (English)	AXE	**knit**	
• kiss boy	X-RAY	*knit* [coat]	ATOC, TACO
• the *French* kiss	LAX, LEX	knit, *say*	NIT, PEARL, WE'VE
kiss striker	SMACKER	*knitted* [a scarf]	FRACAS
kite	BUS, PLANE	knitting expert, *say*	PINKING, PINNACE
kitten		*knitting* [pins]	SNIP, SPIN
kitten's father, *say*	CAT'S-PAW	**knock**	
kitty, *say*	KITE	knock *back*<	KNOB, PAR, PAT
k-kip	KNAP	*knock back* drink<	REGAL
KN	CAYENNE	knock door	CARPENTRY
knead		*knock down* house	H(O)

Anag [cat]; Any *; Begin IGN–; Endings –ING; eg •; Hidden /cat/; Implied add (on); Implied in (in);

knock down, *say*	RAISE, RAYS	knot in ham, *say*	NOTTINGHAM
knock it *back*<	TI	*knotted* [ties]	SITE
knock-[knee]	KEEN	*knotty* [timber]	BETRIM, TIMBRE
knock out a . . .	omit A	**know**	
knock out *	*omit* *	know Edward, *say*	KENNED
• *knock out* one of he(i)r's . . .	HERS	*know no bounds*	omit ends
knock over pins<	SNIP	• (g)loo(m) *that knows*	
knock, *say*	WRAP	*no bounds*	LOO
knockabout	PA–T, RA–P, TA–, –P	know, *say*	NO, WATT, WHAT
knockabout<	PAR, PAT, TAP	know-all	CLEVER DICK, SMART ALEC
knockabout [farce]	FACER	knowing	FLY
knockdown [prices]	PRECIS	• knowing baseball player	FLYCATCHER
knocked, *say*	RAPT, WRAPPED	• knowing history	FLY-PAST
• knocked America, *say*	RAPTUS	• knowing sportsman	FLY-FISHER
knocked [into] . . .	–TION	knowledge	–OLOGY
knocked into [shape]	HEAPS, PHASE	knowledge of elves	IMPLORE
knockout	KO	**Köchel**	K
knocks down fish	FELLSIDE	**Korea**	ROK
knee		**kreutzer**	KR
knee-*cap*	K	**krone**	KR
knock-[knee]	KEEN	**Kuala Lumpur**	KL
knot		**Kuwait**	KWT, Q8
knot	KN	**KV**	CAVY

L

angle, angular momentum, apprentice, Avogadro's number, corner, driver, el, elevated railway, ell, fifty (thousand), half century, hand, inductance, Labour, lady, la(e)vo-, l(a)evorotatory, lake, lambda, lambert, latent heat, Latin, latitude, league, learner, learning, lecturer, left, length, Liberal, licentiate, line, libra, library, lira, lire, litre, live, loch, long, longo, lough, lumen, luminance, Luxembourg, many, molar latent heat, new driver, novice, number plate, overhead railway, port, pound, pupil, quantum number, right angle, side, specific latent heat, student, tyro, vitamin

£1	LI	*lacking* *	omit *
£1.51	CLIP	• mot(her)'s *lacking* her . . .	MOTS
£s	LL	**lack**	
label		lack	NEED
label	TAB	• lack at this point, *say*	NEEDIER
• label plot	TABBED	• lack fish	NEEDLING
• label 'Rented'	TABLET	• lack, *say*	KNEAD, KNEED
• label the *French* . . .	TABLE	lacking	NO
label	TAG	• *lacking* direction	NOSE
laboratory	LAB	• *lacking* medicine	NODOSE
labour	LAB	• *lacking* money	NOCENT
labour extremists	WORKAHOLICS	lacking	O
labour *extremists*	LR	• *lacking* people	OMEN
labour leader	FOREMAN	• *lacking* stretch	OGIVE
Labour leader	ATTLEE	• *lacking* trees	OPINES
Labour *leader*	L	lacking, *say*	IN-KNEED
labour movement	CONTRACTION	**ladder**	
labour pains	EFFORT	ladder	RUN
Labour Party	LP	ladderman	JACOB
Labour supporter	MATERNITY BED	**lady**	
Labour [ward]	DRAW	Ladies' Gold Union	LGU
laboured [speech]	CHEEPS	ladies' magazine	POWDER ROOM
Labour's record	BOOK OF JOB	Ladies Only	NOMEN, OMEN
labourer	HAND	lady	DAME, EVE, LUCK
	HERACLES, HERCULES	lady	MISS
lace		• lady gangster	MISSAL
laced [into a] . . .	–ATION	• lady is . . .	MISSIS
[strait]-*laced*	TRAITS	• lady *with* a . . .	MISSA
lack		and	
lack foresight	LOOK AFTER	• Lady Bountiful, *say*	MISGIVING
lacking a . . .	omit A	• lady fly-fisher, *say*	MISCASTING
lacking an alternative	omit OR	• lady magistrate, *say*	MISJUDGE
lacking dash	MINUS	lady	SHE, TRAMP
lacking finish	omit last letter	lady bookmaker	AUTHORESS, RUTH
lacking nothing	omit O	Lady Day	LD
lacking one	omit A, I	lady-in-waiting	EXPECTANT
lacking sex appeal	omit IT, SA		MOTHER
lacking the right . . .	omit R, RT	lady-killer	BLUEBEARD

lady-love	HERO, KAYO, LASSO, MAYO
Lady of the Lake	CONSTANCE, WINDERMERE
lady *of the* [manor]	NORMA
lady's	HER
• lady's a . . .	HERA
• lady's on trains	HERONRY
• lady's ring	HERO
and	
• lady's clothes, *say*	HIRSUTE
• lady's fish, *say*	HURLING
lady's maid	ABIGAIL
Lady with the lamp	USHERETTE
ladybird	HEN, PEN, SALTERN

laid

laid *back<*	DIAL
laid new grass, *say*	RECEDED
[laid] *out*	DIAL
laid to rest	(in) B–ED, (in) CO–T
• English deserter *laid to rest*	BERATED
• son *laid to rest*	COST
laid up	(in) B–ED, (in) CO–T
laid *up*(D)^	DIAL
laid out [wares] . . .	SWEAR, WEARS
	(*see also* lay)

lake

lake	ERIE
• lake*side* dwelling	COTERIE
lake	L, LOCH
	WATER COLOUR

Lamb

lamb	ELIA
• lamb lover	ELIAN
lamb	RAMSON

lambast

lambast [players]	REPLAYS
[master] *lambasting*	REMAST, STREAM

lambda L

lambert L

lament

lament, *say*	GREEVE, MOWN
lamented, *say*	SIDE
laments, *say*	SIZE

land

Land Army	TILLER GIRLS
land girls	WLA
land in the water	AIT, EYOT
	ISLAND, ISLE(T)
Land of Hope	RURITANIA
land of rest	BEULAH
land of the wizard	OZ
landed explosive	LITHE
Land's End	WEST POINT
Lan*d's End*	D
landholder, *say*	FEWER
landing on	
indicating one word written	

above another word or letter:	
• flier *landing on*	
prison(D)	BIRDCAGE
• insect *lands on* ring(D)	MOTHBALL
landline	BR, RLY, RY
landlocked	(in) L–AND
	(in) EST–ATE
landlord's job	INNKEEPING
landlord's job, *say*	IN KEEPING
landlords of multi-storey flats	BLOCK LETTERS
landmark	RUT

lampholder ALADDIN

language

language buff	POLISH
language of love	ROMANCE
language refinement	POLISH
languish	LYDIA

lap

lap a . . .	incl A
[lap]-*dancing*	ALP, PAL
lap speed	LICK
lap *	incl *
• wa–ter *lapping round* one . . .	WAITER
lap *up*(D)^	PAL
lapdog	GREYHOUND
lapped by *	incl in *
• one *being lapped by* wa–ter	WAITER
la*ptop*(D)	L

large

large	BIG
• can *in* large *enclosure*	BITING
• large girl	BIGAMY
• large head	BIGNESS
• king *in* large . . .	BRIG
large	GRAND
• large degree	GRANDMA
• large letters	GRANDEE
• large poster, *say*	GRANDDAD
large	MAJOR
• large container	MAJORCAN
• large officer	MAJOR
large	OS
• large duck	OSTEAL
• large flag	OSIRIS
• large tin	OSCAN
• large vehicle	OSCAR
large amount of timber	WOO(d)
large cat, *say*	LINKS
• can *in* large *enclosure*	BITING
large-eyed, *say*	OX–HIDE, OXIDE
large jumper	KANGAROO
large letters	OS
[large] *letters*	ELGAR, LAGER, REGAL
large mouthful, *say*	MEGABYTE
large needle-case	HAYSTACK
large number	ARMY, D, M, NATION
large part of c/once/rt	ONCE

large part of many . . .	MAN, ANY
large pieces	ARTILLERY
large scale	EPIC, OS
large stand	GREAT BEAR
large step	GRANDPAS
large sum	IMPOUNDS
large tent, *say*	MARQUIS
large tree, *say*	RED-WUD
largely wast(ed)	WAST
larger offer, *say*	MORBID
larger, *say*	HIRE
lariat	STOCKHOLDER
lark	
larking about [in the] . . .	THINE
[it was] *larking about*	WAIST, WAITS
lasso	LADY-LOVE, STOCKHOLDER
last	
last	END
• last debtor	ENDOWER
• last man	ENDED
• way *to* last . . .	SEND, WEND
last bit of foo<u>d</u>	D
last carrier	BIER, HEARSE
• last carrier, *say*	BEER, HERS
last chanc<u>e</u>	E
last characters in A<u>ida</u>	DA
last couple danc<u>ed</u> lamb<u>ada</u>	EDDA
last drink	HEMLOCK
last horse in Derby, *say*	ENDORSE
last in, first out	LIFO
last in, last out	LILO
last interminably	DRAGON
last laug<u>h</u>	H
last letter	OMEGA, Z
last man	COBBLER, SHOEMAKER
last ma<u>n</u>	N
last minut<u>e</u>	E
last minute improvement	LATERALLY
last month	DEC
• last month I married	DECIMATED
last month	ULT(IMO)
last mont<u>h</u>	H
last object	END
last of th<u>e</u> . . .	E
last of the	
−beef	OXTAIL
−series	OMEGA, Z
−wine	GRAVESEND
Last of the Mohican<u>s</u>	S
last offer	HOLD OUT
last resort	HOSPICE
[last] *resort*	ALTS, SALT
last stop	STAY
last stra<u>w</u>	W
last things	BOOTS, SHOES
last train	CORTEGE
	FUNERAL PROCESSION
last vehicle	BIER, HEARSE
• last vehicle, *say*	BEER, HERS
last war	ARMAGEDDON, RAGNAROK
last word	AMEN, CUE, GOODBYE
last words	PS
• last words *about*	P–S
• last words *about*<	SP
last words	EPITAPH, OBIT(UARY)
last words	RIP
last worker	COBBLER, SHOEMAKER
[the last] *resort*	STEALTH
	(*see also* final)
late	
late	
• late *getting up*(D)^	−ETAL
• late *rising*(D)^	−ETAL
late	EX
• late *getting up*(D)^	−XE
• late *rising*(D)^	−XE
late ball	ATTENDANCE
late fruit	SLOE
late opening	POST MORTEM
late pressing	EVENING
<u>l</u>ate *starter*	L
late shift	NIGHTDRESS, NIGHTGOWN
	NIGHTIE, NIGHTSHIRT
[late] *shift*	LEAT, TAEL, TALE, TEAL
late worker	BEHINDHAND
latecomer	JOHNNY
later message	PS
[later] *model*	ALTER, RATEL
later postscript	PPS
latest mode<u>l</u>	L
latest information	SP
latest informatio<u>n</u>	N
latest of thos<u>e</u> . . .	E
	(*see also* old)
latent	
latent [heat]	HATE, THEA
latent in yo/ung love/r	UNGLOVE
Latin	
Latin	L
• Latin in church	LINCH
• Latin is part . . .	LISSOME
• Latin poem	LODE
Latin	LAT
• Latin queen	LATER
• Latin *in* the Home Counties	SLATE
• strong Latin . . .	FLAT
Latin	ROMAN
• Latin affliction	ROMANTIC
• Latin church	ROMANCE
• Latin unknown	ROMANY
latitude	L, LAT
laugh	
laugh	HA, HAHA, HAWHAW
	HEHE, HOHO

laughter, *say*	GESTATION
launch	
launch of ship	S
*launch*pad	P
launching yacht	Y
laundry	
laundering [sheet]	THESE
laundry helper	DETERGENT, SOAP, SODA
	DOLLY, IRON
law	
law	COPS, FUZZ
law agent	LA
[law]-*breaking*	AWL
law lord	LUD
lawman	BL, DA, EARP
lawmen	COPS, POLICE, POSSE
	VIGILANTES
lawgiver	MOSES, SOLON
lawmaker	DRACO, MEDE, MP
lawyer	BL, DA
lawyers	BAR
• international lawyers	UNBAR
• lawyers see . . .	BARELY
• lawyers' stooge	BARSTOOL
lawyers	
indicating use of legal term:	
• bar *for lawyers*	ESTOP
• *lawyer's* house	MESSUAGE
• *lawyers'* right	LIEN
lax |laws|	AWLS, SLAW
Lawn Tennis Association	LTA
lax	
lax [rule]	LURE
[law is] *lax*	WAILS
lay	
lay	AIR
• lay *behind* saint	STAIR
• lay drunk	AIRTIGHT
• quiet lay	PAIR
lay*out*	LA–Y, SE–T
[lay]*out*	–ALY
lay up nuts(D)^	STUN
lay*about*	LA–Y, SE–T
lay*about*<	TES, YAL
layer	E
	BIRD, HEN, WYANDOTTE etc
laying out [cash, Tom] . . .	STOMACH
layout man	PLANGENT
layout of [town]	WONT
[nice] *layout*	CINE
	(*see also* laid)
lazy monk	ABBEY-LUBBER
LC	ELSIE
lead¹	
lead (=1st letter)	
• juvenile *lead*	J
• *lead* off	O

• *lead off* roof	R
• *leads to* better things	BT
lead *off*	omit 1st letter
• *lead off* (t)he . . .	HE
• lead *off* the (c)limb	LIMB
leader (=1st letter)	
• leader *dropped from* (p)arty	ARTY
• Oriental *leader has gone*	(e)ASTERN
• *leader of* flock	F
• *leader of* Marathon	M, MU
• *leaderless* (w)omen	OMEN
• *leaders of* Cyprus	CANDY
• *leaders of* Patagonia	PANDA
• *leaders of* Syria	SANDY
• squadron *leader*	S
• wartime *leader*	W
leading (=1st letter)	
• *leading* article	A
• *leading* character	C
• *leading character in* play	P
• *leading edges of* technological advance	TA
• *leading* lady	L
• *leading* light	L
• *leading* man	M
• *leading* seaman	S
led by a . . .	start with A
led by *	start with *
• heir *led by* me	MESON
lead²	
lead	GUIDE
• lead on, *say*	GUIDON
• lead, *say*	GUYED
lead	STAR
• leading directors	STARBOARD
• leading light	STARLIGHT, STARSHINE
• leading performer landed	STARLIT
lead in(to) *	incl in *
• *lead* a king *into* r–ing	RAKING, RARING
lead soldiers	SCOUTS, VANGUARD
leader	A, NOI–
leader	AGA
• leader in the street	AGAINST
• leader lashes, *say*	AGATISE
• leader missed, *say*	AGAMIST
leader	CID
• a leader	ACID
• managed leader	RANCID
• PLA leader	PLACID
leader of	
–flock	BELLWETHER
–queue	HEAD WAITER
leader, *say*	GUYED
leader's address	DOWNING STREET
leading	FRONT
• leading gangster	FRONTAL
• leading journalist	FRONTED

• store leading . . .	SHOP-FRONT
leading	NOI–
• leading a few . . .	NOISOME
• leading student	NOIL
leading	(in) VA–N
• I am *leading*	VAIN
• *leading*, for example . . .	VEGAN
leading artist	PRA
leading character	A, NOI–
leading characters	INITIALS
leading feature	CHIN
leading figure	A, NOI–
leading firm	UPTIGHT
leading lady	EVE
	USHERETTE
leading light	POLE STAR
	STAR OF BETHLEHEM
leading man	ADAM
	GUIDE, USHER
	KING, STAR
leading model	MAINFRAME
leading monk	PRIOR
• leading monk, *say*	PRIER, PRYER
leading player	FIRST VIOLIN
	PIED PIPER
leading seaman	FIRST HAND
[led] *astray*	–DLE, ELD
lead³	
lead	PB
• lead-*covered*	P–B
lead-coloured figures	LIVID
lead soldiers	SCOUTS, VANGUARD
leaf	
leaf-eater	BOOKWORM
leaf-insect	PAGEANT
[leaf]-*mould*	FLEA
	(*see also* leaves)
league	
league	L
league match	UNION
league members	REDHEADS
lean	
lean diet	SLIM
lean nurse	TEND
leak	
leak at this point, *say*	SEPIA
leak, *say*	LEEK
leaking, *say*	HOLED, HOLY, WHOLLY
leap	
leap over net	CLEAR
leap over tomb	VAULT
leap shrub	CAPER
leap-year	SPRINGTIME
leaping [over] . . .	ROVE
learn	
learn	CON
• I learn . . .	ICON

• learn only . . .	CONSOLE
• learn *to* dance	CONTANGO
learn *about*	CO–N, REA–D
learn to swim	MASTERSTROKE
[learned] *characters*	LEANDER
learned man	DR, MAGUS, SAGE
learner	L
• learner finished	LOVER
• learner in study	LINDEN
• learner *with* spectacles	LOO
learner's figure	FIFTY, L
learning	LORE
young learner	BABEL
lease	
lease it, *say*	WREN-TIT
lease more properties	OUTLET
lease*back*<	TEL
leased	ISLET
least common multiple	LCM
leather	
leather	KID
• leather joint, *say*	KIDNEY
• leather *with* woolly surface	KIDNAP
• Leatherhead	KIDNAPPER
leather	LOWER CASE
leather	BUFF
• concerning leather	REBUFF
• leather polish	BUFF
• *place* leather *before* queen	BUFFER
leather dresser, *say*	COURIER
leather, *say*	HIED, OXIDE
Leather*head*	L
leave¹	
indicating omission:	
he *leaves* t(he) . . .	T
I *leave* . . .	omit I
head *leaves*	omit 1st letter
king *left* . . .	omit K or R
leave home	omit in
leave a . . .	omit A
leave it *out*	omit IT
leave me *out*	omit ME
leave out a . . .	omit A
leave out *	omit *
• p(l)ayers *leave out*	
beginner	PAYERS
leave quietly	omit P
leave *	omit *
time *to leave*,	omit T
leave²	
leave	GO
• leave drink	GOSLING
• leave *in* interior . . .	INGOT
• leave in two directions	GOES, GONE
	GOWN
• leave quickly, *say*	GOSSOON
• man *has* leave	MANGO

Anag [cat]; Any *; Begin IGN–; Endings –ING; eg •; Hidden /cat/; Implied add (on); Implied in (in);

leave	PART
• I am *on* leave	IMPART
• leave hilltop	PARTRIDGE
• leave *in* river	SPARTEINE
leave	QUIT
• leave bird *without* . . .	REQUITE
• leave the ring	QUITO
• leaves level	QUITS
leave	RAT
• leave church	RATCH
• leave baseball player	RAT-CATCHER
• leave *in* church	CRATE
leave *by* No.1 bus	PARTIBUS
leave harbour	CROSSBAR
leave work	HOLIDAY JOB
leave room for a . . .	incl A
leave room for *	incl *
• *leave room for* it *in*	
south-east	SITE
leave the North	LEAVEN
leave the South	LEAVES
leaving word	ADIEU, ADIOS, GOODBYE
	(*see also* left[1])

leaves

leaves	TEA
• leaves directions	TEASE
• leaves *in* tin . . .	STEAN
• leaves space	TEA-ROOM
leaves his dinner	HERBIVORE
leaves producer	TREE
leaves supporter	STEM
Lebanon	RL
led	
led, *say*	METAL
	(*see also* lead)

left[1]

left	L
• 100 left	CL
• excessively left	TOOL
• fruit left	PEARL
• left home	LIN–
• left in church	LINCH
• left in debt	LOWING
• left *on* road	LAVE
• left *on* time	LAD, LEON
• left port	LADEN
• left to burn	LIGNITE
• left turn	LU
• left *with* no ship	LOSS
left *behind*	last letter L
• friend left *behind*	PALL
• gangster left *behind*	ALL
• girl left *behind*	NORMAL
left *inside*	incl L
• left *inside* c–ove	CLOVE
• left *ins*–ide	SLIDE
left *out*	omit L

left *right out*	omit L
left-over(D)	
indicating L written	
over another word:	
• left-*over* fluid	LINK
left[2]	
left	LEFT
left *centre*	EF
Left? *Left*	L
Left, *Right* . . .	T
left[3]	
left	LT
• is *in* left . . .	LIST
• left *back<*	TL
• left *out* last word	LAMENT
• left *without* spectacles	LOOT
• left *turns<*	TL
left *out*	omit LT
left *right out*	omit LT
left *outside*	(in) L–T
left[4]	
left	OFF
• 100 left	COFF
• left side	OFFHAND
• left team	OFFSIDE
left[5]	
left	PORT
• I am left	IMPORT
• left one company	PORTICO
• left *in* the act	DEPORTED
left *outside*	(in) POR–T
left-over(D)	
indicating 'left' written	
over another word:	
• left-*over* fish	PORTRAY
left[6]	
left	RED
• father left	PARED
• left-handed club	REDWOOD
• left, I see	REDIVIDE
• left *in* company	CREDO
• left leg	REDSHANK
left wing	RED
leftist	RED
left[7]	
Bolton *left-half*	BOL
left centre	C
left hand	H
left hand of God	G
left of target	T
left[8]	
left again	OVER
left at sea	PORT
left boot	SIDEKICK
left centre	LC
left for dead	GONE
left-hand	LH, VERSO, VO

Letter replaced \c\at; Omit (a); Pointers *out*; Retain a; Split B_ED; Down (D); Backwards <or ^

left-hand man	COMMUNIST, SOCIALIST
left hands	LABOUR
left *on road*	NEAR(SIDE)
left *on ship*	PORT
left right *out*	omit R, RT
nothing *left<*	LIN
peek *to left<*	KEEP
	(*see also* leave)

leg

left leg	REDSHANK
leg	LEFT, ON
leg armour, *say*	GRIEVES
leg before (wicket)	LB(W)
[leg]-*break*	GEL, –GLE
leg in front	GAMBLED
leg of lamb/mutton	SHEEPSHANK
leg of mutton, *say*	RAMPART
leg-*over<*	GEL, NO
leg-ring	LIMBO
leg, *say*	ELEGY
leg *up*(D)^	GEL, NO
leg*less*	omit ON
• leg*less* bird	CAP(on)
• R(on) *is* leg*less*	R
legs	ELEVEN

legal

legal	LEG
legal argument	BARROW
legal division	DIVORCE
legal document	DEED
legal exercise	CONSTITUTIONAL
legally	IN-LAW

legate

legate	HE
legatees cried, *say*	AIRSWEPT

legend   FOOT, TOE

legislate

legislating	HOUSEWORK
legislator	DRACO, MEDE, MP
legislature	LEG

legit   RUN

length

fine length	FINCH
length	L
length that is . . .	YARDIE
length in ship	SMILES
length of	
–fish	PERCH
–links	CHAIN
–stick	POLE, ROD
length untied	FOOTLOOSE
lengthy stay	LONGSTOP

Lent

Lent	FAST
• lent a dollar	FAST BUCK
• Lent fare	FAST FOOD
• lent [gin] *cocktail*	FASTING

leopard's weight	OUNCE
Lesotho	LS

less

doe(s) *less*	DOE
less correct, *say*	RONGEUR
less costly, *say*	CHEEPER
less dash	MINUS
less hairy god	BALDER
less important	B
less labour, *say*	MORATORY
less, *say*	FUAR
less smooth, *say*	RUFFER
less than a second	–ATIC(k)
less than al(l) . . .	AL
less than tw/o-pen/ce	OPEN
less than four	THREE
less than (f)our	OUR
less than (t)he *whole* . . .	HE
less than *the whole* (t)own	OWN
less than their . . .	THE, HEIR
less than twenty	UNDERSCORE
less than (t)went(y)	WENT
lessen	GODOWN

let

let	(in) R–ENT
let down	ABSEIL
[let] *free*	TEL, –TLE
let in a . . .	incl A
let in *	incl *
• sh–e *lets in* a student	SHALE
let loose [all the] . . .	LETHAL
[let] *loose*	TEL, –TLE
[let] *off*	TEL, –TLE
let out a . . .	omit A
let out *	omit *
• t(he)ory he *let out* . . .	TORY
[let] *out*	TEL, –TLE
let us, *say*	LETTUCE
let wine breathe	AIRPORT

letter[1]

letter	CHI
• burnt letter	LITCHI
• letter slopes	CHILEANS
• letter only . . .	CHIMERE
letter	DEE
• letter *in* Indian . . .	INDEED
• letter writer	DEEPEN
• odds on letter . . .	SPONDEE
letter	EFF
• letter employed	EFFUSED
• letter service	EFFACE
• letter *with* a bit . . .	EFFORT
letter	EM
• hard letter	HEM
• letter finished	EMENDED
• letter *in* th–e . . .	THEME
letter	EN

• hard letter	HEN
• letter binder	ENTWINE
• letter *written in* afterthought	PENS
letter	ESS
• letter from Holland, *say*	DUCHESS
• letter *in* m–y . . .	MESSY
• letter *with* directions	ESSENE
letter	MU
• English letter	EMU
• letter *found in* the road	SMUT
• letter-list	MUTABLE
• letter, *say*	MEW
• letter *to* MP	MUMP
letter	O
• lady's letter	HERO
• letter, *say*	OH, OWE
• letter writer	OPEN
letter	PHI
• delete letter	DELPHI
• letter *in* the present day	APHID
• letter recently . . .	PHILATELY
• letter, *say*	FIE
letter	PI
• approve a letter	OKAPI
• letter *found in* the road	SPIT
• letter overdue	PILATE
• letter, *say*	PIE
letter	RHO
• letter, *say*	ROE, ROW
• letter *to* boy	RHODES
• letter *to* girl	RHODORA
letter²	
letter-card	CHARACTER
letter from	
–America	REALTOR
–Holland, *say*	DUCHESS
letter *from* [Stell(a)], *maybe*	TELLS
letter *from* Sp(a)in	SPIN
letter *of* condolence	C
letter of inquiry, *say*	WYE, Y
letter of thanks	COLLINS
letter opener	ADDRESSEE, DEAR
	PAPER KNIFE
letter *opener*	L
letter *opening* . . .	L
letter or two	BORED, DORIC, HORSE
	KORAN, LORIS, PORCH
	SORRY, TORUS, WORTH
letter *out of* li(n)e	LIE
letter *to* a policeman	COPE, COPS
	COPT, COPY
letter *to* hotel	FRITZ
letters *enclosing* money	MY
letters *from* (Am)erica	ERICA
letters *in* [Times]	ITEMS, MITES, SMITE
letters *for* father	PANDA
letters *from* Spa(in)	SPA
letters *from* (S)tell(a)	TELL
letters of credit	LC, CR
letters of introduction	INITIALS
letters of [love]	VOLE
letters of thanks	TA
letters *said*	AS(E), BEES, SEAS, EASE,
	GEES, EYES, JAYS, ELLS, EMS, ENS,
	OHS, PEAS(E), CUES, QUEUES,
	ARS, TEAS(E), TEES, USE, WISE
letters, *say*	MALE
letters sent	OUTPOST
letters *to*	
–editor	MAILED
–friends	PALSHIP, PALSIED
–queen	MAILER
letters written in [haste]	HATES, HEATS
letter*head*	L
letterheads	CAPITALS
letterpress	EMPRESS, MUSQUASH
[love] *letters*	VOLE
[send] *letters*	DENS, ENDS
lettuce	
lettuce	COS
• lettuce bag	COSSACK
• lettuce grower, *say*	COSMOLOGIST
• lettuce plants	COSSETS
level head	EVENNESS
levitate	
levitating boy(D)^	YOB
levitation of new . . . (D)^	WEN
Leviticus	LEV
levy	
levy on the obese	CORPORATION TAX
levy, *say*	LEVEE
lexicon	LEX
liable	
liable to tax	DIFFICULT
liability is ours	ONUS
liar	ANANIAS, MATILDA
Liberal	
liberal	BROAD
• liberal clergy	BROADCLOTH
• liberal king	BROADER
• Liberal Party	BROADSIDE
liberal	L
• liberal Emperor	LOTTO
• Liberal loses seat	LOUT
• liberal President	LIKE
Liberal	LIB
• good liberal . . .	GLIB
• Liberal devoured . . .	LIBATE
• liberal share	LIBRATION
liberal	WIDE
• liberal feast	WIDESPREAD
• liberal head	WIDENESS
• liberal king	WIDER
[liberal] *characters*	BRAILLE

Letter replaced \c\at; Omit (a); Pointers *out*; Retain a̲; Split B_ED; Down (D); Backwards <or ^

liberal [regime]	EMIGRE	lifeboatman	NOAH
liberally [I grant]	GRATIN, RATING	**lift**	
Liberals	LL	ban *lifted*(D)^	NAB
liberate		lift beams, *say*	RASE, RAYS, RAZE
liberate [slaves]	VALSES	lift cup	JACKPOT
liberation of [Paris]	PAIRS	lift, *say*	RASE, RAYS, RAZE
Liberia	LB	lifted flower	ROSE
library		*lifting* leg(D)^	GEL
librarian	BOOK-KEEPER	**light**	
Library Association	LA	light	MATCH
Libya		• light entertainment	MATCHPLAY
Libya	LAR	• light meals	MATCHBOARD
• Libya *and* America	LARUS	• light staff	MATCHSTICK
• Libya *has* many . . .	LARD	light	MOON
• Libya *has* railway	LARRY	• light drink	MOONSHINE
and		• light *round* king	MORON
• Libya *without* iron	FLARE	light	STAR, SUN, VERY
• live *outside* Libya	BLARE	light a cigarette	FIREWEED
• talk *about* Libya	SALARY	light appearance	DAWN, DAYBREAK
and			SUNRISE
• directions *in* Libya	LASER	light clothing	WINDOW DRESSING
• grow old *in* Libya	LAAGER	light covering	RAYON
• woman *in* Libya	LASHER	light-emitting diode	LED
and		light heart	DAY CENTRE
• doctor *goes to* Libya	MOLAR	light *heart*	G
• Libya *follows* a . . .	ALAR	Light Infantry	LI
• thus Libya . . .	SOLAR	light machine-gun	LMG
Libyan capital	DINAR	light material	CANDLEWICK, TINDER
Libyan *capital*	L	light music	TORCH-SONG
Libyan *leader*	L	light of danger	RED
licence		light pastry, *say*	PISOLITE
[dog] *licence*	GOD	light sauce	WINDOW DRESSING
licence [may be] . . .	BEAMY	light soil	LAND
licentiate	L	light spasm	ARCTIC
Licentiate		light symbol	FLOODMARK
–of Apothecaries' Company	LAC	light worker	DAY LABOURER
–of College of Preceptors	LCP	lighter	ARSONIST, FIRESHIP
–of Society of Apothecaries	LSA	lighter propeller	BARGE-POLE, SCREW
–in Dental Surgery	LDS	lighter push	BARGE
–in Surgery	LCH	lighter stone	FLINT
–in Theology	LTH, THL	lighthouse, *say*	FAIR, FARE
lick		lighting offence	ARSON
lick [airmen] *into shape*	REMAIN	lightweight	CARAT, CT
[man is] *licked into shape*	MAINS		FEATHER G, GRAIN, GRAM(ME)
lie			OUNCE, OZ
lie-abed	OYSTER	lightweight animal	OUNCE
lie about	FIBRE	lightweight monarch	THINKING
[lie] *about*	ELI	**like¹**	
lie in warmth, *say*	BASQUE	like	ALA
Liechtenstein	FL	• black like . . .	BALA
lief		• like a marine	ALARM
[lief]	WILDLIFE	• like *in* m–y . . .	MALAY
lieutenant	LOOT, LT	• like scholars	ALABAMA
life		like	AS
[life]-*style*	FILE, LIEF	• like a bird	ASHEN, ASTERN
life symbol	ANKH	• like a buccaneer	ASPIRATE
lifeboat	ARK	• like a carrier	ASTRAY

• like a coin	ASCENT	• like an embargo	BANISH
• like a coin, *say*	ASSENT	• like an equal	PARISH
• like a container, *say*	ASSAPAN	• like anger, *say*	IRISH
• like a drunkard	ASSOT	• like cereal	CORNISH
• like a fish	ASHAKE, ASIDE	• like dough	FLOURISH
• like a flan	ASTART	• like fruit, *say*	PERISH
• like a loch	ASLAKE	• like German writer	MANNISH
• like a lubricant, *say*	ASSOIL	• like head, *say*	POLISH
• like a mariner, *say*	ASSAILER	• like motor fuel	DERVISH
• like a nun	ASSISTER, ASSAULT	• like Norse gods	VANISH
• like a philosopher	ASKANT	• like part of Yorkshire	MOORISH
• like a relative	ASSISTER	• like preserved meat	HAMISH
• like a ruler	ASKING	• like the Air Force, *say*	RAFFISH
• like a Scot	ASIAN		(*see also* rather)
• like a swan	ASPEN	**like²**	
• like a tar, *say*	ASSAILER, ASSAULT	like	
• like a tree	ASOAK	–a blender, *say*	WHISKEY
• like a writer	ASPEN	–a Communist	LOVERED
• like acid	ASCETIC	–a corsair, *say*	PYRITOUS
• like dirt	ASSOIL	–a detective, *say*	DICKY
• like foreign articles	ASUNDER	–a hamster, *say*	PETTISH, PETTY
• like Henry	ASH	–a nun	INHABIT
• like the CIA, *say*	ASPIRING	–a parrot, *say*	PARITY
• like a smell, *say*	ASCENT, ASSENT	–a policeman, *say*	COPPERY
• like Thomas, *say*	ASTOMOUS	–a sandwich-filling, *say*	INBRED
• like wine	ASPORT	–a soldier	UNCIVIL
and		–a vegetable, *say*	PELIKE
• as *in* church	CASE	–a young dog	PUPOID
• beetle-like	DORAS	–an aristocrat	U
and		–Cain's brother	LIKABLE
• like a detective, *say*	AZTEC	–Edward	LIKENED
• like a part, *say*	AZAROLE	–fruit	PEARLY
• like a waste product, *say*	AZURINE	–kippers	ASLEEP
	(*see also* as)	–rain	RIGHT
like	–ISH	–Venus	ARMLESS
• like a European, *say*	FINISH	**like³**	
• like a bounder, *say*	KADDISH	indicating a homophone:	
• like a bridge	SPANISH	• *like* meat	MEET
• like a cleaner	MOPISH	• *like* one . . .	WON
• like a comb, *say*	RAKISH	• *like* rain	REIGN, REIN
• like a couple, *say*	PERISH	• *like* some . . .	SUM
• like a cryptogam, *say*	FURNISH	• *like* thyme	TIME
• like a father	POPISH	• *like* wood	WOULD
• like a fish	GARISH	• *like* you	EWE, U, YEW
• like a French woman, *say*	FAMISH	**like⁴**	
• like a friend	PALISH	*likely to appear*	(in) OFF–ING
• like a gala, *say*	FETISH	• object *likely to appear*	OFFENDING
• like a joke	PUNISH	• queen *likely to appear*	OFFERING
• like a judo expert	DANISH	liken, *say*	COMPERE
• like a lake	TARNISH	likes *to* dine	LOVE-SEAT
• like a rod	POLISH	**lime**	
• like a Russian	SLAVISH	lime *peel*	LE
• like a slipper	MULISH	[lime] *squash*	EMIL, MILE
• like a stamp	FRANKISH	*peeled* (l)im(e)	IM
• like a stew	HASHISH	**limit**	
• like a vehicle	VANISH	limit drink	RATIONALE
• like a WC, *say*	LAVISH	*limitation of* damage	COS(t), HAR(m)

limited amount of ca/sh I p/ut	SHIP	*lining* *	incl in *
limited amount	LO(t)	• copper *lining* city . . .	BASCULE
limited are(a)	ARE	**link**	
limited a/rea m/ay . . .	REAM	link-*up*(D)^	EIT
limited by an . . .	incl in A–N	link up *with* Edward	JOIN(T)ED
• state *limited by* an . . .	AMEN	linked characters	SIAMESE TWINS
limited edition	ED	**Linnean Society**	LS
limited liability	LTD, PLC	**lino**	
limited number	N(O)	lino*cut*	LIN(o)
limited subscription	INITIALS	[lino]*cut*	LION
limiting a . . .	incl A	**lion**	
limiting *	incl *	lion family	CATKIN, LEO
• s–un *limiting* power	SPUN		PRIDE
limited by *	incl in *	• lion family, *say*	PRIED
• power *limited by* s–un	SPUN	lion-tamer	ANDROCLES, DANIEL
limits of patience	PE	lioness	ELSA
limousine	OSCAR	Li*on*heart	IO
Lincoln		**lip dressing**	SAUCE
Lincoln	ABE	**liquid**	
• Lincoln Square	ABET	liquid courage	INK BOTTLE, SPIRIT
• Lincoln *with* the *French* . . .	ABELE	*liquidate* [a mob]	BOMA, MOAB
• the morning *after* Lincoln . . .	ABEAM	*liquidation* [by a] . . .	BAY
Lincoln, *say*	BISCUIT	liquefied natural gas	LNG
line		liquefied petroleum gas	LPG
line	I, L	**lira(e)**	L, LR
line across curve, *say*	CORD, CORED	**lisp**	
line manager	SIGNALMAN	lisp	substitute th for s
line of music	CONGA	• *lisp* in song	THONG
line-*out*	omit I	• *lisping* sigh	THIGH
[line]-*out*	LIEN, NEIL, NILE	• sing *lispingly*	THING
line, *say*	RHO, ROE	**list**	
line worker	GENEALOGIST	list at this point, *say*	TABLIER
lined by *	incl *	list of vehicles	CARLIST
• city *lined by* copper	BASCULE	listed building	TOWER OF PISA
lined characters	OG(H)AM	**listen**	
liner	SS	for *listening to*	FORE, FOUR
lines	BR, RLY, RY	I see why *listeners* . . .	ICY
• lines have . . .	BROWN	*listen* to . . .	TOO, TWO
• doctor the lines	MOTHERLY	*listen* to peace . . .	TWO-PIECE
• street *with* no lines	STORY	*listen to* piece	PEACE
lines	ODE	listen to, *say*	HERE
• lines *up*(D)^	EDO	listened to, *say*	HERD
• many lines	LODE, MODE	listener	AUDITOR
• right lines	RODE	listener	EAR
• straight lines	STRODE	• dry *without* listener	DREARY
lines	VERSE	• good listener	GEAR
• fashionable lines	INVERSE	• listener panics	EARFLAPS
• lines *written to* daughter	VERSED	listener	LUG
• study lines	CONVERSE	**lit**	
lines, *say*	ROES, ROSE	lit	DRUNK, LANDED
lines up	DRESSES	lit-*up*(D)^	–TIL
lines *up*(D)^	RB, YR	**literal(ly)**	LIT
linesman	PLIMSOLL	**literature**	
linesman	POET	literacy examiner, *say*	SPELEOLOGIST
• English linesman	KEATS et al	literary giant	DESPAIR
• German linesman	GOETHE	literary hack	ROSINANTE
• Italian linesman	DANTE	literary prop	BOOK-END

literary set	ALPHABET
literature	LIT
litre	L
litter	
litter container	STY, UTERUS, WOMB
[papers] *littered about*	SAPPER
little[1]	
little	WEE
• little boy	WEENED
• little for each . . .	WEEPER
• little king	WEEK
• little Mark	WEEM
• little tart	WEEPIE
• shirt *has* little . . .	TWEE
and	
• little boy, *say*	WEAKEN, WEANED
• little king, *say*	WEAK, WEAR, WEIR
	(*see also* small[1])
little	SHORT
• little food	SHORTBREAD
• little letter	SHORTEN
• little petticoat	SHORT SLIP
• little ring	SHORT CIRCUIT
• little time	SHORTAGE
• little workman	SHORTHAND
little[2]	
indicating abbreviation:	
• little Bill	AC
• little bounder	ROO
• little Boy Blue	VICTORY
• little brother	BRER
• little brothers	BROS
• little change	D, –ID, P, –IP
• little chap	GENT
• little coin	D, –ID, P, –IP
• little couple	PR
• little horse	GEE, GG
• little John	JNO
• little money	D, –ID, IP, P
• little mother	MA
• little notice	AD
• little response	ANS
• little river	R
• Little Rock	GIB
• little theatre	REP
• little time	D, H, HR, M, MIN,
	MO, S, SEC, T
• little way	RD, RY, ST
	(*see also* reduce, small[2])
little[3]	
other uses:	
a little of t/he be/ef	HEBE
little bird, *say*	ROBINET
Little Boy Blue	PUT TO SEA
little bounder	JOEY
little bread	CRUMB, PETTY CASH
little butter	KID, PAT

little by little	ERIC
little change	D, P, PENNY
little change in sha\p\e	SHADE
little change in [shape]	HEAPS, PHASE
little charge	ION
little class	TOUCHTYPE
little crone, *say*	HAGLET
little cut, *say*	SNIPPET
little difference in board . . .	BEARD
little donkey, *say*	ASSET
little fellow, *say*	COVELET
little fight	SCRAP
little fish, *say*	BASSET, PIKELET
little growth	BUD, LEAFLET
little help	MINUTE HAND
little horse, *say*	HACKLET
little idiot	ASSET
little Indian	PAPOOSE
little lighter	FIREFLY
little lower	CALF
little man	MINUTE HAND
little Mark	SCARLET
little marmalade	KITTEN
little Mary	STOMACH, TUM
little money	D, P, PENNY
little mother	MINIMUM
little music	NOTE
little mus<u>ic</u>	–IC
little of <u>his</u> . . .	H
little of h/is le/ave	ISLE
little ox, *say*	BULLET
Little Rock	BOULDER, PEBBLE
little runner	BROOK, RILL, RIVULET
	STREAM(LET)
little support	TEE
little taxi, *say*	CABLET
little Tommy	SON OF A GUN
	(*see also* small[3])
live	
live	BE
• live animal	BEHIND
• live more violently	BEWILDER
• live *on* fertile land	BEARABLE
• live *on* the street	BEST
live teams	BESIDES
[live] *broadcast*	EVIL, VILE
live long, *say*	DILATE
live round	BEO–
live *round*<	EVIL
live teams	BESIDES
lived so long	AV
lively [dance]	CANED
lively figures	VIVID
<u>l</u>ively *start*	L
lively voice	ACTIVE
lives	IS
• lives *in* about . . .	RISE

• lives in a vessel	ISINGLASS	*located in* t/he w/oods	HEW
• lives round city	ISOBATH	Location of Offices Bureau	LOB
• Scot lives . . .	TAXIS	location for pub, *say*	INCITE, INSIGHT
living person	INCUMBENT	location, *say*	CITE, SIGHT
living	QUICK	**loch**	NESS
• living space	QUICKSTEP	**lock**	
• living tree	QUICKLIME	lock	TRESS
one *lives in* . . .	incl A, I	• a lock-*up*(D)^	ASSERT
* *lives in* . . .	incl *	• girl's locks	DISTRESSES
• we *live in* he–r . . .	HEWER	• the *Camptown* lock-*up*(D)^	DESSERT
lizard		lock keeper	HAIR NET, HAIR PIN
<u>lizard</u> *skin*	LD		KIRBIGRIP, KIRBY-GRIP
lizard's place	CORNWALL	lock, stock and barrel	RIFLE
l-letter	LEN, LESS	lock up	INTERN
load		• lock up drug	INTERNE
load-bearing female, *say*	ASSESS	• lock up gangster	INTERNAL
load, *say*	LAID, LODE	• lock up journalist	INTERNED
loaded	BULLETIN, DRUNK, RICH	locked	HAIRY
loan		locker	KEY
loan records	–IOUS	locker, *say*	QUAY
loan, *say*	LONE, SINGLE	locks out	ALOPECIA
lob	HIGHBALL, UPSHOT	locksmith	WIGMAKER
lobby correspondent	DIETED	**lodge**	
local		*lodged in* *	incl in *
local	BAR	• convict *lodged in* vil–e . . .	VILLAGE
• local employee	BARMAID, BARMAN	lodger	GUEST
	BARTENDER	• lodger, *say*	GUESSED
• local paper	BARMS	lodger	PG
• local profit	BARGAIN	lodgings	PAD
local	INN	**logarithm**	LOG
• local worker	INNKEEPER	**logic**	
• location for pub, *say*	INCITE, INSIGHT	logical *extremes*	LL
• pub *in* service	LINNET	**London**	
local	PH	London	SMOKE, WEN
• local *has* no style	PHOTON	–and North-Eastern Railway	LNER
• local one	PHONE	–County Council	LCC
• local one *has almost* al(l) . . .	PHIAL	–Midland and Scottish	LMS
local	PUB	–Missionary Society	LMS
• local is . . .	PUBIS	–Philharmonic Orchestra	LPO
• local student in charge	PUBLIC	–School of Economics	LSE
local		–Symphony Orchestra	LSO
indicating colloquialism:		London area	SE
• is not *local*	AINT	• *in* London area, it . . .	SITE
• *local* (h)aunt	AUNT	• London area squares	SETS, SETT
• *locally* (h)otter	OTTER	• the London area	THESE
local		London banker	THAMES
indicating dialect:		London-bound	UP
• *local* branch	GRAIN, SHROUD	London landlord	CAPITAL LETTER
• *locally* caught	CATCHED	London magazine	ARSENAL
• *locally* worse	WUSS	London police	MP
Local Defence Volunteers	HG, LDV	London town	DERRY
local deliveryman	BREWER, DRAYMAN	*London* train	TRINE
Local Education Authority	LEA	to London	UP
local target	DARTBOARD	**long**	
locate		long	DIE
located in *	incl in *	• long dead	DIED
• I am *located in* Avon	AVION	• long for Edward	DIETED

Anag [cat]; Any *; Begin IGN–; Endings –ING; eg •; Hidden /cat/; Implied add (on); Implied in (in);

• long time	DIET
long	L
• long • one foot	LIFT
• long round cask	LOVAT
• longboat	LARK
long	PINE
• circle *has* long . . .	OPINE
• long fruit	PINE-APPLE
• long line	PINERY
• long mallet	PINE BEETLE
• long nettle	PINE NEEDLE
• long stomach	PINETUM
• long tree	PINE
• street *without* long . . .	SPINET
• second long . . .	SPINE
long-awaited man	GODOT
long dispute	FARROW
long distance runner	AMAZON, NILE etc
long metre	LM
long-playing record	LP
long range	ALPS, ANDES etc
long ruler, *say*	HIKING
long runner	THE MOUSETRAP
long service	OUT OF COURT
long-standing friend	CHRONICALLY
Longfellow	SILVER
longing *after* god	PANACHE
longing for food	LUSTRATION
longitude	LON(G)
look¹	
look	AIR
• look left	AIRPORT
• Look, mister!	AIRMAN
• look unprepossessing, *say*	AIRPLANE
• look *up*(D)^	–RIA
look	EYE
• look *both ways*	EYE
• look lively	EYEBRIGHT
• look *up and down*(D)	EYE
• looks warm	EYESHOT
look	LA
• look *almost* de(a)d	LADED
• look *at* the . . .	LATHE
• look in	LAIN
• look-*in*	incl LA
• look-*out*	omit LA
• look *round*<	AL
• look *round*	L–A
• look under	LAUNDER
• look *up*(D)^	AL
look	LO
• look in	LOIN
• look-*in*	incl LO
• look *on*	LOON
• look-*out*	omit LO
• look *round*<	OL

• look *round*	L–O
• look round	LOO
• look *up*(D)^	OL
and	
• a look of . . .	ALOOF
• look *in* two directions	SLOW
• look one way	LOWEST
look	PEEK
• look *back*<	KEEP
• look *up*(D)^	KEEP
• look, *say*	PEAK, PIQUE
look	SEE
• look *at* five hundred . . .	SEED
• look *out*	SE–E
• look *over*<	–EES
• look *round*<	–EES
• look *round*	SE–E
• look *up*(D)^	–EES
• looks *both ways*	SEES
look	V
• look *at* fever	VAGUE
• look-*in*	incl V
• look in about . . .	VINCA
• look in square	VINT
• look-*out*	omit V
look	VID(E)
• look *about* an . . .	VIAND
• look *round*<	DIV
• look *round*	VI–D
• look *round* a soft	VAPID
• look no . . .	VIDEO
• look *up*(D)^	DIV
look²	
look ahead, *say*	FARCY, FARSI
look *around*	PE–ER
look *around*<	KEEP
look at	
–American	GAZEBO
–fish, *say*	PEOPLING
–letter	PEERESS
–speech	WATCHWORDS
look *both ways*	EYE, PEEP
look equal	PEER
look for	SEEK
• look for ruler	SEEKER
• look for ruler, *say*	SEEKING
and	
• look for Alf, *say*	SEA-CALF
• look for argument, *say*	SEA-CROW
• look for beer, *say*	SEA-KALE
• look for wine, *say*	SEA-COCK
and	
• look for, *say*	SIKH
and	
• look for them, *say*	CAECUM
look out	CAVE, FORE
look *out*	SE–E

lookalike caller	RINGER
looked *around*	SE–EN
looked *back<*	WAS
looked *up*(D)^	WAS
looking about	REGARDING
looking *at* cat	PEEPING TOM
looking into ne/w ide/as	WIDE
lookout	SE-E
• look*out* dog	SECURE
• Lookout, Sam!	SESAME
lookout man	EXTRAVERT, EXTROVERT
looks both ways	SEES
tots *looking up*(D)^	STOT
loony	
loony-[bin]	NIB
loony *left*	L
loony *[left]*	FELT
loop	
loop	O
loophole, *say*	ISLET
loops in chain, *say*	LYNX
loose	
loose *ends*	LE
loose *[ends]*	DENS, SEND
loose painter	CAST OFF
loosely fastened, *say*	HALF-TIDE
loosely *[tied ends]*	DESTINED
loosen *[ties]*	SITE
loosen up *[a bit]*	BAIT
loosens part of roof, *say*	FREESTYLE
loosens trousers	SLACKS
[screw] *loose*	CREWS
lop	
lop *of*(f)	OF
lopping (b)ranch	RANCH
lord	LD
Lord	
–Chief Justice	LCJ
–Justice	LJ
–Provost	LP
lord in court	LUD
Lord North	SIREN
Lord's ground	EARLDOM
Lordship	LDP, LP
Los Angeles	LA
lose¹	
indicating an anagram:	
lose [heart]	EARTH, HATER, RATHE
[lose] *out*	SLOE, SOLE
lose sequence of [letters]	SETTLER
lose series of [sets in] . . .	STEINS
lost [a set]	SATE, SEAT, TEAS
lose²	
indicating omission:	
lose all . . .	omit ALL
• b(all)oon *loses* all . . .	BOON
lose bishop	omit B

lose energy	omit E
lose half that	TH, AT
lose head	omit 1st letter
• (s)he *loses* her head	HE
lose heart	omit middle
• pat(i)ent *loses* heart	PATENT
• sc(hol)ar *loses* heart	SCAR
• t(he)y *lose* heart	–TY
lose his shirt	omit T
lose key	omit A–G
lose king	omit K, R
lose knight	omit N
lose lead	omit 1st letter
lose money	omit D, L, P
lose nothing	omit O
lose odds and ends	omit OD
lose one	omit A, I
lose one's shirt	omit T
lose one's shirt	omit IST
lose opener	omit 1st letter
• (M)CC *lose* opener	CC, HUNDREDS
lose pawn	omit P
lose power	omit P
lose prisoner	omit CON
lose rook	omit R
lose queen	omit ER, Q
lose silver . . .	omit AG
lose tail	omit last letter
• do(g) *loses* tail	DO
lose the right	omit R
lose the round	omit O
lose the way	omit N, S, E, W
	omit AVE, RD, ST
lose time	omit AGE, MO, SEC, T
losing a . . .	omit A
losing *	omit *
• fa(the)r *losing* the . . .	FAR
loss of first . . .	omit 1st letter
• *loss of first* (p)awn	AWN
loss of ship	omit SS
loss of wicket	omit W
lost in . . .	omit IN
• *lost* in Spa(in)	SPA
lose³	
lose bottle	COWER, PANIC
lose colour	GOWAN
lose girl	MISS
lose *heart*	
• diplomats lose *heart*	CLOSED
lose most	WINSOME
loses colour, *say*	GRAZE
lost colour, *say*	GRADE
lost editor	UNFOUNDED
loss	(*see* lose)
lost	(*see* lose)
lot	
a lot of wo/men, tall,	

Anag [cat]; Any *; Begin IGN–; Endings –ING; eg •; Hidden /cat/; Implied add (on); Implied in (in);

y/oung . . .	MENTALLY
lot	C, D, L, M
lot of fruit	ORANG(e), PEA(r)
lot of lines	BR, RY
	ODE, POEM, VERSE
lot of money	IMPOUNDS
lot of <u>sea</u>ts	SEA
lots of beer	NINEPINS
lots of ships	FLEET, NAVY, RN
	(*see also* many[1])

loud

loud	F
• a loud anger	AFIRE
• a loud blonde	AFFAIR
• a loud listener	AFEAR
and	
• loud instrument	FLUTE
• loud music	FROCK
• loud yob	FLOUT
loud, *say*	FORTY
loudspeaker	BOANERGES, STENTOR
	PA
very loud	FF
• a very loud blow	AFFRIGHT
• a very loud attack	AFFRAID
• a very loud song	AFFAIR

lousy

lousy [at reading]	TRAGEDIAN
[it was] *lousy*	WAIST, WAITS

love

love	O
• love a little	OBIT
• love china	OPAL
• love divine	ODD
• love letter	O
• love letter	OF, OH, ON, OR, OS
	OMISSIVE
• love letters	OAR, OBE etc
• love offal	OLIVER
• no love	OO
and	
• dog I love	CURIO
• lady's love	HERO
• time for love	MAYO
and	
• accountants in love	CASINO
• love-*in*-a-m–ist	MOIST
• love*less*	omit O
• love*lorn*	omit O
and	
• fifty loves	LOO
• loves old coin	OORIAL
• loves speed	OOMPH
love	ZERO
• earth-love	GROUND-ZERO
• love in a cold climate	ZERO
love	POINTLESS

love-letter	LIKEN
love-sickness	AFFECTION
love *to* search	HONEYCOMB
lovebird	DUCK
lovelight	FLAME
lover	LOTHARIO
lover-boy	CUPID, EROS
lover *of the country*	SWAIN
loving son	TENDERS

low

low	BASE
• low pedestal	BASE
• Low Street	BASEST
• low trap	BASENET
low	MOO
• low church	MOOCH
• low Latin	MOOL
• low point	MOON
• low quarters	MOONS, MOOSE
• low-*rise*(D)^	–OOM
• low river	MOOR
• low stream	MOOR-ILL
• low table	MOOTABLE
• low trap	MOONET
• lowed, *say*	MOOD
Low character	BLIMP
[low] *characters*	OWL
low class, *say*	DEGRADE, FORESEE
[low] *cunning*	OWL
low dance	BASEBALL, LIMBO
low-down	GEN
low fellow	HEAL, HE'LL
low frequency	LF
Low German	LG
low grade	E
• low-grade German . . .	EG
• low grade, *say*	EATEN
• low grades, *say*	EASE
low grade, *say*	DEGRADE, FORESEE
low interest	BOREDOM, ENNUI
Low Latin	LL
low note, *say*	DEEP SEA
low pot	BLUEGRASS
low pressure	LP
low priced	PEACH
low ranker	PAWN, PRIVATE
low *sound*	LO
low swinger	CHARIOT
low tar	SUBMARINER
low tension	LT
lower	COW
• lower class	BOVINE, CATTLE, COWS
• lower fare	CATTLE CAKE, GRASS
• lower fellow	COWMAN
• Lower House	BYRE, COWSHED
• lower in front	COWLED
• lower jumper	JERSEY

Letter replaced \c\at; Omit (a); Pointers *out*; Retain <u>a</u>; Split B_ED; Down (D); Backwards <or ^

- lower sound — MOO
- lower tender — COWHERD, COWMAN
- lower writer — COW-PEN

lower case — LC
lower classes — DE–
lower number — DENOMINATOR
lower percentage — CUT
lowered, *say* — GLAIRED
lowest note — FIVER
loyal friend — ACHATES
lubricate
  lubricate eyes, *say* — GRECISE
  lubricate surface, *say* — OILSKIN
  lubricates family — OILSKIN
Lucifer's home — MATCHBOX
lucky man — JIM
lumen — L
luminance — L
lump
  lump of bee/f is h/ard — FISH
  lump of earth — EAR
  lumps of rock are . . . — ROAR
lunatic
  [it was] *lunatic* — WAIST, WAITS
  lunatic [king is] . . . — SKIING

lunchtime — ONE, I
lurk
  lurking in hi/din/g — DIN
  lurking in [trees] — REEST, RESET, STEER
  lurking in * — incl in *
  - she is *lurking in* a–n . . . — ASHEN
lux — LX
Luxembourg — L
luxury
  luxurious drinker — LUSH
  luxury car — LIMO, RR
lying
  lying around a . . . — incl A
  lying around * — incl *
  - the–y were *lying around* or . . . — THEORY
  lying cleric — INCUMBENT
  lying in s/un if y/ou . . . — UNIFY
lyrics — AIRLINES
lysergic acid — LSD

M

Bond's boss, em, emma, *Frenchman, lot*, Mach number, magnetisation, maiden, male, Malta, *man, many, mare*, mark, married, masculine, mass, master, medium, medius, member, meridian, meso-, meta-, metre, middle voice, mile, mille, milli-, million, modulus, Monday, monsieur, month, moon, motorway, mu, noon, number, quantum number, roof, *small square, spymaster*, thousand, vitamin

£1,000,000	IMPOUNDS
M1	MOTORWAY, RIFLE
Mac	ASCOT
Mac (=Scottish)	
• look warily *for Mac*	GLEDGE
• Mac *on* the wagon	WAINSCOT
• *Mac's* cottage	BOTHIE, BOTHY
• *Mac's* laugh	LAUCH
Maccabees	MAC
machination	
[cruel] *machination*	LUCRE, ULCER
machination [that Ed] . . .	HATTED
machine-gun	MG
light machine-gun	LMG
mad	
mad character	HATTER
[mad] *characters*	ADM–, DAM
mad	BATS
• I am *in* mad	BAITS
• mad creatures	BATS
• mad individual	BATSMAN
• mad strikers	BATS
mad [dog]	GOD
mad *French* . . .	FOLLE, FOU
mad *German*	VERRUCKT
Mad [Hatter]	THREAT
mad *Italian*	MATTO
mad king	LEAR
• mad king, *say*	LEER
mad Leigh, *say*	CRAZILY
mad Roman	NON COMPOS MENTIS
mad Scot, *say*	REDWOOD
mad *Spanish* . . .	LOCO
mad strikers	BATS
maddened [beast]	BASTE, BATES, BEATS
madly [keen]	KNEE
madman	HATTER
madmen curse . . .	NUTSHELL
Madagascar	RM
madam	MDE, MDM

made	
freshly [made]	DAME, EDAM, MEAD
made better, *say*	HEALD, HEELED
made by hand, *say*	HANDMAID
made *comeback<*	EDAM
made *for the ear*	MAID
made it	FEC(IT), FF
made it up [so we] . . .	OWES, WOES
made late	KILLED, SLEW
made [late]	LEAT, TALE, TEAL
made man	ROBOT
made notes	COMPOSED, EARNED
	PLAYED, SANG
made of [gin]	–ING
made of [steel]	LEETS, STELE
made out [case]	ACES, AESC
made out of p/latin/um	LATIN
made *over<*	EDAM
made *speech*	MAID
made tea, *say*	BROOD
made terrorists, *say*	MADEIRA
made [to run race]	RACONTEUR
made *up*(D)^	EDAM
made up of [parts]	PRATS, SPRAT, STRAP
made up [tales]	LEATS, SLATE, STALE, TEALS
made [worse]	SWORE
[made] *worse*	DAME, EDAM, MEAD
made worse [wines]	SINEW, SWINE
made you, *say*	MAY-DEW
	(*see also* make)
magazine	
magazine	GLOSSY, MAG
	POWDER-ROOM
magazine	PUNCH
• magazine editor	PUNCHED
• magazine policy	PUNCH-LINE
• poor golfer's magazine	RABBIT
	PUNCH
magazine	TIME
• display magazine	AIRTIME
• magazine article	TIMEPIECE

Letter replaced \c\at; Omit (a); Pointers *out*; Retain <u>a</u>; Split B_ED; Down (D); Backwards <or ^

• magazine list	TIMETABLE
magazine article	BOMB, BULLET
	DYNAMITE, EXPLOSIVE
	GUNPOWDER, SHELL

maggot

maggot	GRUB
• maggot-cutter	GRUB-AXE
• maggot food	GRUB
• maggot near	GRUBBY

magic

Magic [Circle]	CLERIC
magical flier	FILER
magical flier	CARPET
magical [trips]	SPIRT, SPRIT
magician, *say*	TRICKING
magician's bird	MERLIN

magistrate

magistrate	BEAK
• magistrate *takes in* money	BLEAK
• magistrate *with* queen	BEAKER
• magistrate's bill	BEAK
magistrates note . . .	BENCHMARK

magnetic MAG

maiden

Maid of the Mountains	OREAD
maiden	M
• maiden in shirt	MINT
• maiden over	MENDED, MOVER
• Yes, *German* maiden . . .	JAM
maiden	GAL
• maiden, *after* about . . .	REGAL
• maiden cut . . .	GALLOP
• maiden *over*<	LAG
maiden(D)	IO
maiden production	PARTHENOGENESIS
	VIRGIN BIRTH
two maidens	MALICE, MANNA, MM

mail

[mail]-*order*	LIAM, MALI
mail sent out	OUTPOST
[mail]-shot	LIAM
mailboat	RMS

main¹

main	DEEP
• cover main . . .	SKINDEEP
• main ruler	DEEPER
• main note, *say*	DEEP SEA
main	SEA
• main course	SEA-FOOD
• main issue	SEASON
• main meal	SEAFOOD
• main picture	SEASCAPE
• main road	SEA-LANE
• main square	SEAT
• main support	SEASHORE
• main weapon	SEASHELL

main battle	TRAFALGAR etc
main course	HARD TACK, SHIP'S BISCUIT
main event	REGATTA
main force	NAVY
main robber	PIRATE
main scene	SEASCAPE
main supervisor	NEPTUNE, POSEIDON
	SEA-GOD
main support	MAST, YARD(-ARM)
main tower	TUGBOAT

main²

main	COCK
• main battle	COCKFIGHT
• main scene	COCKPIT
• prevent main	STOPCOCK
main aisle, *say*	KNAVE
main distributor	AORTA
main mass of her(d)	HER
main part of arm(y)	ARM
main partner	MIGHT
main road	AI, BROADWAY, MI
mainly woo(d)	WOO
mainstream	RIVER

maintain

maintain a . . .	incl A
maintain tower	KEEP
• maintain issue	KEEPS ON
maintain worker	AVOWANT
maintain *	incl *
• pi–es *maintain* king	PIKES
maintained by m/	
an ent/irely . . .	ANENT
maintained by *	incl in *
• king *maintained by* pi–es	PIKES

Majesty

His/Her Majesty	HM
Majesties	MM
Majesty	M

major

major	BARBARA
• major film	BARBARA
major	GROWN UP, MAJ
major sin, *say*	PRIM(A)EVAL
majority of th(e) . . .	TH

make

make	CREATE
• make charged particle, *say*	CREATION
• make journalist, *say*	CREATED
• make mineral, *say*	CREATOR
• making *say*	CREATIN(E), KREATIN
make	DO
• make a bet	DOWAGER
• make fast	DOLENT
• make money	DOCENT, DOYEN
• make note	DOB, DOC, DOE, DOG
	DODO, DOME, DOTE

• make notes	DOFF, DOGE	making waves	CRIMPING, CURLING
make-*up*(D)^	OD		HAIRDRESSING
make	FORM	[she had] *makeover*	HASHED
• make gangster . . .	FORMAL	[shoe]-*making*	HOES, HOSE
• make queen	FORMER		(*see also* made)
• tablet I make, *say*	PILIFORM	**Malachi**	MAL
make a dash	HYPHENATE	**maladjusted**	
make a hash of [it when] . . .	WHITEN	*maladjusted* [boy]	YOB
make a joke of it, *say*	PUNNET	[she was] *maladjusted*	WASHES
make a mess of [things]	NIGHTS	**Malawi**	MW
make a song *about*	S–ING	**Malaysia**	MAL
make an offer	BIDON	**male**	
make changes in [Cremona]	ROMANCE	male	BUCK
make comfortable bed	WELLSPRING	• male artist	BUCKRA
make damp, *say*	WHET	• male sheep	BUCKRAM
ma<u>k</u>e *ends* . . .	ME	• noticed male . . .	SAWBUCK
make headlines	FROWN	male	GENT
make her quiet, *say*	USHER	• male fish	GENTEEL
make holes in, *say*	PEERS, PIERS	• male *in* early, *say*	URGENTLY
make it go	WINTRY	• male partner	COGENT
make it safe, *say*	LOCKET	• male Scot	GENTIAN
make it wobble, *say*	ROCKET	• old city male	URGENT
make light of	IGNITE	male	HE
make little difference		• male bird	HEMINA
to design	RESIGN	• male birds	HEAVES
make mention of witch	WHICH	• male cat	HELION
make notes	SING	• male departed, *say*	HEEDED
ma<u>k</u>e notes *about*	S–ING	• male flower	HEAVENS
make of [gin]	–ING	• male group	HELOT
make one	MARRY, UNITE, WED	• male *in* group	SHEET
make people laugh	BEDROLL	• male journalist	HEED
make play	BRAND	• male representative	HEMP
make room	CAUSEWAY	• male sheep	HET-UP
make [tea]	ATE, EAT, ETA	• male students	HELL
make up [a bed]	BADE, BEAD	• male *with* a fellow . . .	HEAD-ON
make-up of [stars]	TSARS	male	HIM
make-up unit	CHROMOSOME, GENE	• male *aboard*	SHIMS
make us		• male *in* church	CHIME
–redundant, *say*	SACCOS, SACCUS	• woman *has* male . . .	WHIM
–sad, *say*	GRIEVOUS	male	M
–stand up, *say*	COCCUS	• male as first-class . . .	MASAI
make wager	BETON	• male in a shirt	MINT
make waves	CRIMP, CURL, PERM	• male tree	MACER, MASH
ma<u>k</u>e way	FASHION	• male *with* nothing on	MOON
*make * heard*		male	MAN
• horse *makes itself heard*	HOARSE	• English male dined . . .	EMANATE
• *make itself heard* by . . .	BUY	• male animal	MANTIGER
*make * redundant*	omit *	• male composer, *say*	MANHANDLE
• fat(her) *makes* her *redundant*	FAT	• male *with* English . . .	MANE
makes [cars]	ARCS, SCAR	male birds, *say*	COX
makes progress	STEPSON	male chauvinist pig	MCP
makes some of t/he Be/lgians . . .	HEBE	male deer, *say*	HEART
making a contribution		male dog	BOBTAIL
to jo/int o/peration	INTO	ma<u>l</u>e *lead*	M
making [tarts]	START	male principle	YANG
making of [Mary]	ARMY, MYRA	male reeve, *say*	ROUGH

Letter replaced \c\at; Omit (a); Pointers *out*; Retain <u>a</u>; Split B_ED; Down (D); Backwards <or ^

male *said* . . .	MAIL
male twins, *say*	BISONS
males	MEN
• male champions	MENACES
• male pickpockets	MENDIPS
• males curse	MENSWEAR
• without male . . .	OMEN, NOMEN
	(*see also* man)

malform

malformation of [part]	RAPT, TRAP
malformed [arm]	MAR, RAM

malfunction

malfunction of [part]	RAPT, TRAP
malfunctioning [timer]	REMIT

Mali   RMM

malicious

malicious light	ARSON
malicious publisher	LIBELLER

malleable

malleable [as putty]	STAY PUT
[quite] *malleable*	QUIET

Malta   M

maltreat

maltreated [horses]	HOSERS, SHORES
maltreatment of [animal]	LAMINA, MANILA

man¹

commonly used names:

man	AL
• man *carrying* weapon	ALARMED
• man *in* the Home Counties	SALE
• quiet man	PAL
man	BEN
• man *goes to* church	BENCH
• man *on* the square	BENT
• man *with* one child	BENISON
man	DES
• lou–t *set about* man	LOUDEST
• man slays . . .	DESKILLS
• the *French*man	LADES
man	DON
• a number *take* man . . .	TENDON
• man devoured . . .	DONATE
• man *in* shape	CONDONE
man	ED
• he *is with* a man	HEED
• man *has* it or . . .	EDITOR
• man lacking . . .	NEEDED
man	HERB
• man *in* group	SHERBET
• man rented . . .	HERBLET
• shoot man	POT HERB
man	REG
• man *flanked by* daughter and son	DREGS
• man *takes* beer	REGALE
• man without feeling, *say*	REGNUM

man	SID
• a man *takes* drug	ASIDE
• man in front	SIDLED
• *put* hat *on* man	CAPSID
man	TED
• iron man	FETED
• man promises to pay	TEDIOUS
• mother *takes* man	MATED

man²

man	CHAP
• man killed in action	CHAP-FALLEN
• man rented . . .	CHAPLET
• man *without* energy	CHEAP
• man's trousers	CHAPS
• mantrap	CHAPNET
man	CREW
• man aboard	SCREWS
• manned *say*	CRUDE
• second man	SCREW
man	FELLOW
• man, *say*	FELLOE
• man's at home, *say*	FELLAHIN
• plot *with* man	BEDFELLOW
man	IOM, ISLE
man	HE
• man behind	HEARSE
• man speaks to . . .	HEADDRESSES
• man *with* gun	HEROD
• man *with* more than one wife	HEBRIDES
man	M
man *and* boy	GENTLES, JACKSON
	ROBINSON, WILLIAMSON
man *and* woman	EVADES, MANGAL
	REGINA, SALTED, VIAL
man doing housework	BETTY
man from	
–Adelaide	DIGGER
–America	BO
–Am/eric/a	ERIC
–[Ayr]	RAY
–Berlin	MANN
–Glasgow	IAN, MAC, MON
–Madrid	HOMBRE
–New Ze/alan/d	ALAN
–O/reg/on	REG
–Paris	HOMME
–[Roma]	OMAR
–Rome	
ancient	VIR
modern	UOMO
–the river	DON
man *has* one over the eight	LEONINE
man in	
–a tub	DIOGENES
–<u>the</u> . . .	HE
man of	

−determination	WILL	**mangle**	
−force	NEWTON	mangle, *say*	MANGEL, RINGER
−India	CLIVE	*mangled* [arm]	MAR, RAM
−letters	PAUL, POSTMAN	*mangling* [English]	SHINGLE
−magnetism	GAUSS	**manifold divers**	MANY
−might	SMITH	**manipulate**	
−power	WATT	[cruel] *manipulation*	LUCRE, ULCER
−pride	LEO	*manipulate* [men as] . . .	MEANS, NAMES
−Savoy	GILBERT, SULLIVAN	*manipulating* [pawns]	SPAWN
−the match	BRIDEGROOM	*manipulation of* [bone]	EBON
	LUCIFER	**manoeuvre**	
−Verona	GENTLEMAN,PROTEUS,	*manoeuvrable* [plane]	PANEL
	VALENTINE	*manoeuvred* [his car]	CHAIRS
−war	BOER	*manoeuvring* [ship]	HIPS, PISH
man on		**manor**	
−board	DRAUGHT	manor	HOUSE OF LORDS
	BISHOP, KING, KNIGHT, PAWN	manor, *say*	GUISE, MANNER
−watch	ALBERT	**manual**	
man, *say*	FELLOE, MAIL	manual work	BOOKMAKING
man the ring	THEO	manual worker	BOOKMAKER, ORGANIST
man who makes hay	TED	**manufacture**	
man *with* suit	JUST IN CASE	manufactured	MFD
man's at home, *say*	FELLAHIN	manufacturer(s)	MFR(S)
man's drink	PORTER	*manufacturer of* [china]	CHAIN
man's man	VALET	*manufactures* [tables]	BLEATS, STABLE
Man's man	DOUGLAS	**manuscript**	
manservant	FRIDAY, JEEVES	manuscript	MS
	VALET	• cleaner manuscript	CHARMS
manservant, *say*	VALLEY	• military manuscript	WARMS
	(*see also* male)	• the lady's manuscript	HERMS
manage		manuscripts	MSS
manage	COPE	**Manx**	
• fairies manage . . .	PERISCOPE	Manx cat	CA(t), PUS(s)
• manage daughter	COPED	Manx *leader*	M
• managing jewellery	COPING STONES	Manx man	DOUGLAS, KELLY, MA(n)
manage	EIGHTEEN	**many**	
manage	RUN	many	HOST
• manage English . . .	RUNE	• good many	GHOST
• manage *in* exercise	PRUNE	• many *in* Gilbert &	
• managing directors	RUNNING-BOARD	Sullivan . . .	GHOSTS
manage doctor	TREAT	• many times	HOSTAGES
manage [horse]	HOSER, SHORE	many	LOT
managed	RAN	• afterthought *about* many . . .	PLOTS
• 100 managed	CRAN	• many aboard	SLOTS
• managed a few *say*	RANSOM	• many charged particles	LOTIONS
• managed *without* one . . .	RAIN	• many not working	LOTUS
management	ADMIN, BOARD	many	
management blunder	OVERSIGHT	indicating Roman	
management group, *say*	BORED	numerals:	C, CL, D, K, L, M
management [team]	MATE, MEAT, TAME	• many long . . .	CACHE
managing director	MD	• many have . . .	CLOWN
managing [director]	CREDITOR	• a lot *have* a right . . .	DART
mandarin		• many sick	KILL
mandarin	DUCK A L'ORANGE	• many articles	LATHE
mandarin's coat	ORANGE PEEL	• fight *with* many . . .	WARM
mandarin's *coat*	MN	(*see also* number)	

Letter replaced \c\at; Omit (a); Pointers *out*; Retain a̲; Split B_ED; Down (D); Backwards <or ^

many ate, *say*	FORTITUDE
many larks	EXALTATION
many mad, *say*	FUSAIN
ma(n)y *nameless* . . .	MAY
many old, *say*	FU YUNG
[many] *parts*	MYNA
many sane, *say*	FUSILLI
many welcome, *say*	FUSION
m(an)y *won't have an* . . .	MY
mapmakers	OS
marathon runner	(THE) MOUSETRAP
marble	
[marble] *bust*	RAMBLE
marbles champion	ELGIN
march	
March	MAR
• army *on the* march	TAMAR
• March 10	MARIO
• March *with* 1000 . . .	MARK
march	TRAMP
• fish *after* March	TRAMPLING
• march in front	TRAMPLED
march	YOMP
March Militaire	FROG MARCH
	MARSEILLAISE
marching order	L–R
	BEAT IT, SCRAM
marching together	INSTEP
mare	
mare	DAM
• a mare	ADAM
• English mare	EDAM
• mare got old	DAMAGED
mare, *say*	MAYOR
marginal advantage	EDGE
marijuana	
marijuana	POT
• marijuana *found in* vessel	SPOTS
• marijuana refuse	POTASH
• son *has* marijuana	SPOT
marine	
Marine	JOLLY
marine animal, *say*	SELION, WAIL, WALE
Marine band	CREW
marine biologist, *say*	SEA-LACE
marine detachment	ISLAND, ISLE(T)
marine, *say*	NAVEL
Marines	RM
• a jolly girl	ARMADA
• company of Marines	CORM
• he *joined* the Marines	HERM
[Marines] *at sea*	REMAINS, SEMINAR
mark¹	
mark	DM
mark	M
• Mark I	MI

• Mark is tired	MISSPENT
• Mark *wearing* a tie	TIME
• *see* Mark *after* tea	TEAM
mark	MK
mark *out*	omit M
• mark *omitted by* (m)ale . . .	ALE
• (m)aster *omits* Mark	ASTER
mark²	
mark	ANTONY
mark	BRAND
• Mark will, *say*	BRANDLE
• the revolutionary *in* Mark	BRANCHED
mark	SCAR
• mark church	SCARCE
• mark sailor	SCARAB
• the *French* mark . . .	LASCAR
Mark I	MI
Mark II	(MARK) TWAIN
mark butterfly	COMMA
Mark of the Beast	MB
mark, *say*	MINED
mark time	DOTAGE, LINEAGE
marksman, *say*	CHICO, GROUCHO
	HARPO, KARL
market	
market	CM, E(E)C
market square	FAIR
maroon thread	STRAND
marriage	(*see* marry)
marry	
marriage-bowl	MATCHWOOD
marriage	UNION
• marriage declines	UNION FLAGS
• second-rate marriage	BUNION
• marriages	UNITED STATES
married	M
• a married woman	AMERICA
• married man	MART
• married quarters	MESE, MESS, MEW(S)
• married woman	MALICE, MANNA,
	MINA
married	WED
• American married . . .	BOWED
• father married . . .	PAWED
• married girl	UNAWED
• name *in* married . . .	WEND
married couple	H–W
married people	THEWED
marry again	REPAIR
marry many	MATELOT
marry, *say*	TAKE AMISS
marrying man	PRIEST, REGISTRAR,
	VICAR
Mars	
[Mars]	ORDER ARMS
order [mars] . . .	ARMS, RAMS

Anag [cat]; Any *; Begin IGN–; Endings –ING; eg •; Hidden /cat/; Implied add (on); Implied in (in);

Marshal

marshal	FOCH, NEY
Marshal [Ney]	YEN
[race] *marshal*	ACER, ACRE, CARE

martyr

martyr	M
martyrs	MM

marvellous

marvellous	FAB
• page about marvellous . . .	PREFAB
• marvellous girl	FABELLA
• marvellous man	FABIAN

Marxist drug — OPIUM

Mary's follower — LAMB

masculine — M, MAS(C)

mash

[bran]-*mash*	BARN
mashed [peas]	APSE
mashing [tea]	ATE, EAT, ETA

Masonic chief — MASTER BUILDER

masquerade

masquerade as [Oriental]	RELATION
masquerading [in gown]	OWNING

mass

mass	M
mass producer	LITURGIST, PRIEST
mass production	EUCHARIST

Massachusetts Institute of Technology — MIT

massacre

[Herod's] *massacre*	HORDES
massacre of [babes]	ABBES

massage

massage	RUB
• daughters massages	DRUBS
• massage donkey, *say*	RUBASSE
• massage girl	RUBELLA
massage [arm]	MAR, RAM
massaging [leg]	GEL

master

master	AM
• 150 masters	CLAMS
• master *has* afterthought	AMPS
• master *in the French* . . .	LAMA, LAME(S)
master	DAN
• directions *to* master	SEDAN
• master is hard	DANISH
• master *at* church	DANCE
master	M
• master *and* emperor	MOTTO
• master in America	MINUS
• master *with* a girl	MALICE
master	MA
• master *has* one study	MAIDEN
• master-key	MAB, MAC, MAD, MAE, MAG

• masterly figure	MAC, MAD, MAL, MAM, MAX
master	SIR
• master approves, *say*	SURPASSES
• master *has* awful . . . *say*	SERVILE
• raise master, *say*	GROCER
[master]-*builder*	REMAST, STREAM
master key for . . .	HEADLOCK

Master of

−Arts	MA
−Dental Surgery	MDS
−Foxhounds	MOF
−Laws	LLM
−Science	MSC
−Surgery	MCH, MS, CHM, CM
−the Rolls	MR, CHAUFFEUR
−Theology	MTH

Master of Ceremonies	MC
Master of Ceremonies, *say*	COMPARE
[master] *switch*	REMAST, STREAM
master*piece*	MAS, TER
master*stroke*	COUP, HOLE IN ONE
maths master	EUCLID

mat

mat *finish*	T
matted [fibre]	BRIEF

match

match	LIGHT, VESTA
match	TEST
• match-box	TEST CASE
match goddess	VESTA
match colour	TIERED
match level	SET ASIDE
match points	COMPARE
matches [none]	NEON
matchmaker	WOOD
matchmaker, *say*	PARER, WOULD

mate

mate	CHINA, PAL, WIFE
mating of bears	BARES
mating of pairs	PEARS

material

material	REP
• material consumer	REPEATER
• material *in* church	CREPE
• sit *on* material	SITREP
material	SERGE
• material on, *say*	SURGEON
• Russian material	SERGE
material [part]	PRAT, TRAP
material for [book]	BOKO
material used in [a cheap] . . .	APACHE

maths

maths function	COS, LOG, SINE, TAN
• function put . . .	COSSET
• function in charge	LOGIC

• function makes better . . .	SINECURES
• function with grand . . .	TANG
maths master	EUCLID
Mauretania	RIM
Mauritius	MS
maximum	
maxim*um*	MAX
maximum speed	C
may	
May 8th	V-DAY
may appear [later]	ALTER
may be [sent]	NETS, STEN, TENS
may become [weak]	WAKE
may he/she rest well	BQ
May's follower	JUNE
maybe	
indicating anagram:	
• *maybe* [Manet]	MEANT
• [I can] *maybe* . . .	CAIN
indicating homophone:	
• *maybe* right	WRITE
• nose, *maybe*	KNOWS
indicating one of a class:	
• *maybe* setter	DOG
• dog, *maybe*	SETTER
Mayday	SOS
Mayfair	WI
mayhem	
mayhem [in the] . . .	THINE
[or cause] *mayhem*	CAROUSE
Mayo	LADY-LOVE, TREE RING
mayor	
mayor, *say*	MARE
mayor's allowance, *say*	MACERATE
maze	
[Hampton] *maze*	PHANTOM
maze in [garden]	DANGER, RANGED
me	
me and the girl, *say*	MEANDER
me *following* the *French* . . .	LAME
me *in France*	MOI
me *in Germany*	MICH
me *in Italy*	MI
me *in Spain*	MI
meadow	
meadow	LEA
• exercise *around* meadow	PLEAT
• fine meadow	FLEA
• meadow grass	LEASING
meal	
meal	TEA
• meal *in* tin	STEAN
• meal *with* king	TEAK, TEAR
• meals will, *say*	TEASEL, TEASLE, TEAZEL
meal, *say*	FLOWER
meal ticket	LV

meal times	LUNCHEONS
meals on wheels	MOVEABLE FEASTS
mean	
mean	POOR
• mean, *say*	PORE, POUR
• mean city, *say*	PAUCITY
• mean old city, *say*	POROSITY
mean business	USURY
mean monarch	NEARER
mean person	AVERAGE MAN
mean, *say*	MIEN
mean sea-level	MSL
mean time	MT
means of	
–identification	PIN
–travel	BR
meant, *say*	–MENT
meantime	PARAGE
meander	
meander [about]	U-BOAT
meandering [stream]	MASTER, REMAST
measure	
measure	EL(L)
• good measure	GEL
• measure *in* king's . . .	HELMS
• measure part of fish	ELFIN
and	
• fine measure	FELL
• measure *in* grass	SELLING
• measure edges, *say*	ELLIPSE
measure	EM
• hard measures	HEMS
• measure corpse	EMBODY
• measure vehicle	EMBUS
measure	EN
• hard measures	HENS
• measure coin	ENNOBLE
• measure *in* doctor's . . .	MENDS
measure	FT
• a measure	AFT
• measure *about* a . . .	FAT
• the *French* measure	LEFT
measure	Y(D)
• measure *about* the *Spanish* . . .	YELD
• measure a street	YARD
• reasonable measure	FAIRY
measure	M
measure	PINT
• measure *about* a . . .	PAINT
• measure can . . .	PIN-TABLE
• measure nothing	PINTO
measure depth, *say*	PLUM
measure of a/le d/runk	LED
measure ribbon	TAPE
measure, *say*	GAGE, MEAT, MEET, WAY
measure stick	ROD

measure union	LEAGUE
measured, *say*	GAGED, WADE
meat	
meat sandwich	(in) MEA–T
meat *to* scoff	HAMMOCK
meat was bleeding	HAMBLED
meat *with* pickle, *say*	LAMPLIGHT
mechanical	
mechanical engineer	ME
mechanical transport	MT
medal	
medal	GONG
• king *wearing* medal	GORING
• one *wearing* medal	GOING
medal	MC, MM, TD
medal, *say*	MEDDLE
mediaeval	MED
medical	
[medical] *disorder*	CLAIMED, DECIMAL
	DECLAIM
medical graduate	MB
medical man	DR, GP, MB, MO
Medical Officer (of Health)	MO(H)
Medical Research Council	MRC
medical social worker	MSW
medical speciality	ENT
[medical] *treatment*	CLAIMED, DECIMAL,
	DECLAIM
medicine	
medicine	MED
medicinal group	WHO
medicine ball	PILL
medicine-man	DR, GP, MB, MO
medicine-men	DRAUGHT
Mediterranean	MED
medium	
medium	MED
medium-sized jumper	CRICKET, KANGAROO
medium standard frequency	MSF
medium wave	MW
medley	
medley [in A Flat]	FANTAIL
medley [race]	ACER, CARE
medley of [tunes]	UNSET
meet	
meet	SEE
• meet daughter	SEED
• meet finest girl, *say*	SEBESTAN
• meet girl-friend, *say*	SEDATE
and	
• meet Arab, *say*	SEA-HORSE
• meet prostitutes, *say*	SEA-HORSE
• meets prostitute, *say*	SEA-SHORE
meet people	HUNTSMEN
meeting	AGM
meeting-house	AUDIENCE

meeting place for merry men	ROUND ROBIN
meeting-points	AGENDA
	(*see also* met)
mega-	(*see* million)
mélange	
mélange of [cream]	CRAME, MACER
[taste] *mélange*	TEATS, STATE
mêlée	
mêlée [in street]	INTEREST
[recent] *melée*	CENTRE
melt	
melt [fat]	AFT
melt, *say*	THOR
melting point	MP
melting [snow]	OWNS, SOWN
molten [steel]	LEETS, STELE
member	
member	ARM, LEG, M, MP, TOE
• church member	CHARM
• member makes a mistake	LEG-SLIPS
• member *takes* cereal	MOATS
• member of Dail	EMPIRE
• member *takes in* new . . .	TONE
member	MEM
Member of	
• Congress	MC
• Council	MC
• County Council	MCC
• House of Representatives	MHR
• Institute of Journalists	MJI
• Legislative Assembly	MLA
• Council	MLC
• Order of the British Empire	MBE
• Parliament	MP
• Pharmaceutical Society	MPS
• Philological Society	MPS
• Royal Victorian Order	MVO
member of fir/m an/d . . .	MAN
member's movement	STEP
members of [SAS]	ASS
memorial service	OBIT
men	
men jump	PAWNSHOP
men of intelligence	AGENTS, CIA, SPIES
men, *say*	GUISE
men with guns	RA
	(*see also* man)
mend	
mend [plate]	PETAL
mending [china]	CHAIN
mental	
mental case	CRANIUM, SKULL
[mental] *case*	LAMENT
[mental] *defective*	LAMENT
mention	
make mention of a juice	ADDUCE

mention their . . .	THERE	metal oxide silicon	MOS
mentioned new . . .	GNU, KNEW	metal, *say*	METTLE, LED, STEAL
mentioning some . . .	SUM	metal van	LEAD
merchant		metal washer	COPPER
Merchant Navy	MN	**metamorphosis**	
Merchant of Venice	ANTONIO, POLO	*metamorphose* [into a] . . .	–ATION
merchant vessel	MV	*metamorphosis*	
mercy		of [an insect's] . . .	INCESSSANT
mercy	QUARTER	**metaphorical**	MET
• mercy returned	QUARTERBACK	**metaphysics**	MET
mere		**meteorology**	MET
mere colour	LAKE	**mete**	
mere existence	POND-LIFE	[mete] *out*	MEET, TEEM
mere reserve	JUSTICE	**meter**	(*see* metre)
merry		**Methodist Episcopal**	ME
[a small] *merry-go-round*	LLAMAS	**metre**	
Merry Christmas (=[Noel])	LONE	metre	M
merry fellow	ANDREW	metre*less*	omit M
merry-go-round	GA-Y	metrically rendered	INVERSE
merry minute	TIDDLY	**metrical**	INVERSE
Merry [Wives]	VIEWS	**Metropolitan Police**	MET, MP
Merseyside	NW	**Mexico**	MEX
mess		Mexican capital	M
in a mess [it ran] . . .	TRAIN	Mexican *flower*	RIO GRANDE
make a mess of [things]	NIGHTS	Mexican *leader*	M
mess *about*	M–ESS	**mezzo**	
mess-box	CANTEEN	mezza-voce	MV
messed up [a paper] . . .	APPEAR	mezzo-forte	MF
messing about in [boats]	BOAST	mezzo-piano	MP
messy [eaters]	RESEAT, TEASER	**Micah**	MIC
met		**mickey-taker**	CAT, MOUSER
met her again, *say*	REJOINDER	**mid-**	
Met line	ISOBAR	*mid*-air	I
Met office	(NEW) SCOTLAND YARD	mid-morning	ATTEN–
met *on the way back*<	TEM	*mid*-morning	N
met *up*(D)^	TEM	*mid*-stream	RE
	(*see also* meet)	*mid*-summer	MM, THOUSANDS
metal		*mid*-West	ES
metal	IRON	*mid*-Western	T
• iron man	IRONED	midday	N, NOON
• metal club	IRON	midday	A
• "Metal", I state	IRONICAL	midday *break*	NO–ON
• metal unknown	IRONY	*Mid*lands	N
metal	LEAD	*mid*night	G
• metal guide	LEAD	*mid*off	F
• metal ruler	LEADER	*mid*riff	IF
• soft metal	PLEAD	midriff, *say*	WASTE
metal	TIN	midshipman	EASY, SNOTTY
• metal cover	TIN-HAT	*mid*shipman	P
• metal *found in* the road	STINT	*mid*week	EE
• metal key	TINE, TING	midweek, *say*	EASE
• metal ruler	TINKING	*mid*wife	IF
• metal trophy	TINPOT	midwife's fee	CASH ON DELIVERY
metal container	ORE, TIN	**middle**	
metal *in* s/cu/lpture	COPPER, CU	*middle* age	G
metal money	BRASS	Middle America	CENTER

Anag [cat]; Any *; Begin IGN–; Endings –ING; eg •; Hidden /cat/; Implied add (on); Implied in (in);

Middle America	R
middle class	BOURGEOIS
middle class	A
Middle East	CENTRE POINT
Middle East	AS
Middle English	ME
Middle English	L
middle gear	LOINCLOTH
middle of the . . .	H
middle of the road	OA
middle, *say*	CENTAUR, COLONEL
Middle School	HO
middle way	MIDST
middleman	MEDAL
middleman	A
midst	
in the midst of lif/e we/ are . . .	EWE
we a/re in/ *the midst*	REIN
might	
might appear [that Ed] . . .	HATTED
might be [a pet]	PATE, PEAT, TAPE
might he, *say*	MIGHTY
mighty king	STRONGER
mighty man	SMITH
mighty queen	STRONGER
mild	
mild case	PATIENT
mild man	CLEMENT
mild temper	MODERATE
mile	M
miles *away*	omit M
• miles *away from* ho(m)e	HOE
• Pa(m) *was miles away*	PA
miles per gallon	MPG
miles per hour	MPH
milestone	MS
military	
military	MIL
military agent	TEAR GAS
military band	GUERRILLAS
	PLATOON, TROOP
military bands	CHEVRONS, SASHES
	STRIPES
military briefing	PRIVATE LESSONS
Military Cross	MC
military exercise	OP
Military Intelligence	MI
Military Medal	MM
military (personnel)	RA
• horse *with* military . . .	COBRA
• military exercises	RAPE, RAPT
• military victory is hard	RAVISH
military (personnel)	RE
• military district	REWARD
• military intelligence	RENEWS
• military vehicle	REHEARSE

military (personnel)	REME
• former square *with*	
military . . .	EXTREME
• military clock	REMEDIAL
• three military . . .	TRIREME
Military Police	(R)MP
military rations	WARFARE
military study	WARDEN
military uniform	WARDRESS
military unit, *say*	TROUP(E)
milk	
milk of magnesia	WINDCHEATER
milky eyes, *say*	OPALISE
mill	
[grist] *to the mill*	GRITS, STRIG, TRIGS
miller	DUSTY
miller's corn	GRIST
milling [oats]	STOA
milli-	
millibar	MB
milligram(me)	MG
millilitre	ML
millimetre	MM
millisecond	MS
million	
million	M, MEGA
million cycles per second	MPS
million electron-volts	MEV
million joules	MJ
million pounds	IMPOUNDS
mimic	
mimic nun	NONE
mimicry of male . . .	MAIL
mince	
minced [lamb]	BALM
mince[meat]	MATE, TAME, TEAM
mine	
mine	PIT
• mine collapses	PITFALLS
• mine *in* the Home Counties	SPITE
• mine working	PITON
mine entrance	ADIT
mine *entrance*	M
mine expired, *say*	MINDED
mine had, *say*	MAENAD
mine, *say*	WEAL, WE'LL, WHEEL
miner, *say*	MINOR
miners	NUM
mining engineer	ME
mineral	
mineral water	EVIAN, PERRIER
	SERPENTINE
mineralogy	MIN
minimal	
minimal amount	D, P, ID, IP
minimal amount of drug	D

Letter replaced \c\at; Omit (a); Pointers *out*; Retain a; Split B_ED; Down (D); Backwards <or ^

minimal change	D, P, ID, IP
minimal ta(x)	TA
minimum lending rate	MLR
minister	
minister	DD
minister's assistant	CURATE, PPS
ministerial box	CABINET
ministry	D(O)E, FO, MIN
Ministry of Defence	MOD
Ministry of Transport	MOT
minor	
minor	WARD
• concerning minor . . .	REWARD
• minor aboard	SWARDS
• minor opportunity	WARDROOM
• minor, *say*	WARRED
minor	WEE
• minor coin	WEED, WEEP
• minor note	WEED
• shirt *has* minor . . .	TWEE
minor burn	BROOK(LET), RILL
	STREAM(LET)
minor county	OXON, YORKS etc
minor cut	SLIGHT
minor *disagreement*	MAJOR
minor highway	BROAD
minor key	AIT, AYOT, INCH, ISLET
minor points	LESSEE(S)
minor railway	INFANTRY
minor road	B
minor road	RD
minor work	COTTAGE INDUSTRY
minor work	OP
Minority Rights Group	MRG
minor, *say*	MINER
minor street	ST
mint	
mint centre	BULL'S-EYE
mi<u>nt</u> *centre*	IN
mint money	NEW GUINEA
minted [coins]	ICONS, SONIC
minus	
minus a . . .	omit A
minus five	omit V
• se(v)en minus five	SEEN
minus *	omit *
• song *minus* all . . .	B(all)AD
minute	
minute	M, MIN
minute	MO
• a pair of minute . . .	DUOMO
• minute flower	MOROSE
• minute boy	MODES, MORON
minute	SMALL
mis-	
many words beginning with	

mis-, some of which follow,	
are used to indicate anagrams	
misadventure	
misadventure [in great] . . .	TEARING
[recent] *misadventure*	CENTRE
misaligned	
[gears] *misaligned*	RAGES
misalign [stream]	MASTER, REMAST
misalliance	
[German] *misalliance*	MANGER
misalliance of [Norse] . . .	SNORE
misanthrope	TIMON
misbehave	
misbehaving [with] . . .	WHIT
misbehaviour of [boys]	YOBS
miscast	
mis[cast]	CATS, SCAT
[mis]*cast*	–ISM
miscast [role]	LORE
miscellaneous	
miscellaneous [items]	METIS, MITES
	SMITE, TIMES
miscellany of [tunes]	UNSET
mischief	
mischief [done]	NODE
mischievious [kids]	SKID
misconceive	
misconceived [idea]	AIDE
misconception [that Ed] . . .	HATTED
misconstrue	
misconstrue [words]	SWORD
misconstrued [what] . . .	THAW
miscreant	
mis[creant]	RECANT
miscreant [gave ear]	AVERAGE
miscreant, *say*	RETCH
[vile] *miscreant*	EVIL, LIVE
miscue	
miscue on [break]	BRAKE
mis[cued]	DUCE
miscued [on red]	DRONE
misdirect	
mis[directed]	CREDITED
misdirected [players]	PARSLEY
misdirection of [throw]	WORTH
miser	HARPAGON, SCROOGE
miserable	
[made] *miserable*	DAME, EDAM, MEAD
miserable	BLUE
• miserable china, *say*	BLOOMING
• miserable daughter	BLUED
• miserable scum	BLUE FILM
miserable	DOWN
• display miserable . . .	SHOWDOWN
• miserable *about* king	DROWN
• miserable team	DOWNSIDE

miserable	SAD	misprinted [page]	GAPE
• miserable *about* the *French* . . .	SALAD	[name] *misprinted*	MANE, MEAN
• miserable girl	SADINA	**misquote**	
• miserable lair	SADDEN	*misquotation* from [bard]	BRAD, DRAB
miserable outlook, *say*	PORCINE	*misquote* [poem]	MOPE
miserable [sinner]	INNERS	*misquoting* [verse]	SERVE
miserably [cried]	DICER	**misread**	
misfire		*mis*[read]	DARE, DEAR
mis[fire]	RIFE	*misread* [words]	SWORD
mis[fired]	FRIED	*misreading of* [text or] . . .	EXTORT
misfired, *say*	BLUE-BACK	**misrepresent**	
misfiring [car]	ARC	*misrepresent* [case]	ACES, AESC
misfortune		*misrepresented* [a lot in] . . .	TALION
[great] *misfortune*	GRATE	**misrule**	
misfortune to [meet] . . .	TEEM	*mis*[rule]	LURE
misguide		*mis*[ruling]	LURING
misguided [souls]	SOLUS	[Tsar's] *misrule*	STARS
misguidedly [said] . . .	AIDS, DAIS	**miss**	
[more] *misguided*	OMER, ROME	miss	GAL, GIRL
mishandle		Miss America	MISSUS
mis[handle]	HANDEL	*miss* [bus]	SUB
mishandled [case]	AESC	miss girl, *say*	LACUNA
mishap		miss lady	SPINSTER
[large] *mishap* ELGAR, GLARE, LAGER, REGAL		*miss* nothing	omit O
mishap [in game]	GAMINE	Miss Sybil, *say*	MISCIBLE
mishmash		missed a number, *say*	LACTATE
[mish]*mash*	SHIM	missed, *say*	MIST
mishmash of [all the] . . .	LETHAL	missed *speech*	MIST
misinform		missing	AWOL
misinform *in speech*	SCHOOLGIRL	*missing* a . . .	omit A
misinformed [editor]	RIOTED	missing journalist	UNFOUNDED
misinterpret		*missing* journalist	omit ED
misinterpret [false] . . .	FLEAS	missing husband	omit H
misinterpretation of [words]	SWORD	missing mark	CARET
mislay		*missing* mark	omit M
mis[laid]	DAIL, DALI, DIAL	*missing* money	omit L
mislaid [ring]	GRIN	*missing* motorway	omit M, MI
mislay a . . .	omit A	*missing* out	omit OUT
mislay card	LOSE HEART	*missing out part of* st(or)y	STY
mislay [coin]	ICON	missing person	BUTTER FINGERS
mislay head	omit 1st letter	*missing start of* (r)ace	ACE
mislay one	omit I	*missing* student	omit L
mislay *	omit *	*missing* *	omit *
• *mislay* her rat(her) . . .	RAT	• th(row) *missing* tier	TH
mislead		[near] *miss*	EARN
mislead [solver]	LOVERS	misstate, *say*	MISSISSIPPI
misleading [clue]	LUCE	**misshape**	
mis[led a] . . . DALE, DEAL, LADE, LEAD		*misshape* [form]	FROM
mismanage		*misshapen* [arm]	MAR, RAM
mismanaged [much] . . .	CHUM	**missile**	
mismanagement of [team] MATE, MEAT, TAME		missile	ARROW
misplace		• many missiles	MARROWS
misplaced [letters]	SETTLER	• missile base	ARROWROOT
misplacing [words]	SWORD	missile	BULLET
misprint		• missile enters . . .	BULLETIN
misprint	LITERAL, TYPO	• snap missile	BITE THE BULLET

Letter replaced \c\at; Omit (a); Pointers *out*; Retain <u>a</u>; Split B_ED; Down (D); Backwards <or ^

missile	IBM, SAM, VI
missile plant	ROCKET
missiles	AMMO, DARTS
missionaries	CMS
misspell	
misspelled [words]	SWORD
misspelt [a notice]	ACONITE
mist	
mist, *say*	HAYS, MISSED
misty [start]	TARTS
mistake	
mistake in [line ten]	LENIENT
mistake problem	SLIP-KNOT
mistaken [for the] . . .	FOTHER
mistakenly [said] . . .	AIDS, DAIS
mistakes underwear	BLOOMERS
mister	MR
mistreat	
mistreat [horse]	HOSER, SHORE
mistreating [cat]	ACT
misuse	
misuse [mails]	ISLAM
misused [cutlery]	CRUELTY
mix	
mix, *say*	(K)NEED
mix-up of [dates]	SATED
mix up, *say*	JUMBAL
mixed drinks	SHANDY
mixed [blessing]	GLIBNESS
mixed-[up Mel] . . .	PLUME
mixed-up type	PI
mixed-up [type I] . . .	PIETY
mixture [of beer]	BEFORE
Mk II	(MARK) TWAIN
mm!	EMS
m-mokes	MASSES
mob	
mob's sponsor	GODFATHER
mobster	OCHLOCRAT
mobile	
mobile [crane]	CANER, NACRE
mobile home	CARAPACE, SHELL, TENT
Mobile state	ALABAMA
mobile workers	SHIFT
[the] *mobile*	ETH, HET
mock	
[man I] *mocked*	MAIN
mock battle	COD WAR
mock [duel Ed] . . .	ELUDED
mock food	SCOFF
mock-*up*(D)^	DOC
mocked, *say*	GUIDE
mocking sheep, *say*	WRITE-UP
model	
model	POSE(R)
• girl's model	DISPOSE(R)

• model city	POSEUR
• model question	POSER
model	STANDARD
• model colours	STANDARD
• model servant	STANDARD-BEARER
Model Army	PLANTA
Model [Army]	MARY, MYRA
model car	T
model [cars]	ARCS, SCAR
model [models]	SELDOM
model support	CATWALK
moderate	
moderate	MOD
moderate means	MEDIUM
moderate mood	TEMPER
moderate [views]	WIVES
moderate weight, *say*	KERBSTONE
moderations	MODS
modern	
Modern Language Associaton	MLA
modern miss	MS
modern power	US(A)
modern *sound*	GNU, KNEW
modern-*sounding* race	NUMEN
modern times	AD, ADAGE
	NEWT
modern ways	NEW(S)
modify	
modification of [rules]	LURES
modified [brakes]	BAKERS, BASKER
	BREAKS
modulate	
modulate [note]	ETON, TONE
modulation of [tone]	ETON, NOTE
modulus	M
moist	
moist, *say*	WHET
moisten her, *say*	W(H)ETHER
mole	
mole	ADRIAN, MOL
mole	PIER
• mole, *say*	PEER
• power *in* mole	PIPER
mole	SPY
molten	(*see* melt)
mon	ASCOT
Monaco	MC
monarch	
monarch	ER, K, R
Monarch of the Glen	CLANKING
monarch's chair, *say*	THROWN
	(*see also* king)
monastic custom	HABIT
Monday	
Monday	M, MON
[Monday] *off*	DYNAMO

Anag [cat]; Any *; Begin IGN–; Endings –ING; eg •; Hidden /cat/; Implied add (on); Implied in (in);

money

money	BRASS
• money-belt	BRASS BAND
• money collapses	BRASSFOUNDERS
money	BREAD
• little money	SHORTBREAD
• money policy	BREADLINE
• money to directors	BREADBOARD
money	CASH
• king in the money	CRASH
• only after money	CASHMERE
money	CENT
• about money	RECENT
• make money	DOCENT
money	COIN
• money present	COINHERE
• money safe	CO-INSURE
money	DOUGH
• bad money	SOURDOUGH
• son after money	DOUGHBOY
• money, say	DOE, DOH
money	L
• money I have	LIVE
• p–ot with money in	PLOT
money	OOF(TISH)
• hard money	HOOF
• woman has money	WOOF
money	P
• money has much . . .	PLOT
• money to every . . .	PEACH
money	READY
• money earned	READY-MADE
money	SHEKELS
money	SUM
• money raised	SUM UP
• money with German . . .	SUMMIT
money	TIN
• money-box	TINPOT
• money less restricted	TIN-OPENER
money belt	POUND
money maker	MINT, FORGER
money, say	CACHE, COIGN, CAPITOL, DOE, DOH, QUOIN

monk

monk in possession	FROWNING
monk with unknown . . .	PRIORY

monkey

monkey, say	LANGOUR
monkey's brother	CAPUCHIN

monkshood COWL
monseigneur MGR
monsieur M
monstrous regiment WOMEN
month

month	JAN, FEB etc M, MO, MOON, MTH

month after sight	MS

Moon River RILL(E)
moor

Moor	SARACEN
moor about . . . <	ROOM
moor, say	GREATER, HIGHER, MORE
moor space	HEATHEN
moored (=alongside)	
• vessel moored by firm beach	HARDSHIP
Moorish cover	HEATH(ER), MOROCCO

mop

mop up(D)^	POM
mop up a . . .	incl A
mop up [ink]	KIN
mop up *	incl *
• ra–g mops up French wine	RAVING
mopped up by *	incl in *
• French wine mopped up by r–ag	RAVING

Moral Rearmament MRA
more

more	MORE
• more cereal, say	MORRICE
• more cleaners, say	MORMOPS
• more fiddles, say	MORGUES
• more fools, say	MORASSES
• more or less, say	MORPHEW
[more] complicated	OMER, ROME
more cross	PLUS
more daughters, say	LESSONS
more discomfort, say	LESSEES
more equitable method, say	WAYFARER
more free	RIDDER
more frivolous period	LIGHTERAGE
more frozen	EVEN NUMBER
more hearsay	MOOR
More ideal	UTOPIA
more ill, say	SICCAR
more impressive, say	GRATER
more incorrect, say	RONGEUR
more offensive soldier	RANKER
more perforated, say	HOLIER
more polluted, say	FOWLER
more than 500	DI–
more than enough for mo/st ar/mies	STAR
more than one	BONE, CONE, DONE, GONE, HONE, LONE, NONE, ONER, PONE, TONE
more than one, say	PLEURAL
more tinny, say	CANNIER
[more] stirring	OMER, ROME
More work	UTOPIA
o/ne pal/ace is more than enough	NEPAL

Letter replaced \c\at; Omit (a); Pointers out; Retain a; Split B_ED; Down (D); Backwards <or ^

morning	
mid-mor<u>ni</u>ng	N
morning	AM
• many mornings	CAMS, DAMS, LAMS,
	MAMS
• morning in the East	AMINE
• morning *in the French* . . .	LAME
• morning service	AMUSE
morning air	AUBADE
morning off	omit AM
• entertain with *morning* off	(am)USE
• S(am) *has* morning *off*	S
Morocco	MA, MOR
Morris garage	MG
mosaic	
[marble] *mosaic*	RAMBLE
mosaic of [pieces]	SPECIE
most	
most *disagreeable*	LEAST
Most Excellent	ME
most of	
–all	AL, LL
–<u>the</u> . . .	TH
–the <u>time</u>	TIM
most parts	PAR, ARTS
most perforated, *say*	HOLIEST
most severe person	GRAVESTONE
most stupid	LEASTWISE
most tinny, *say*	CANNIEST
most w/omen s/*ay*	OMENS
mostly fashionable	ALAMO, CHICK
mostly tall	ALL, THIGH
mother	
mother	DAM
• mother *and* son	DAMSON
• mother country	DAMNATION
• mother swan	DAMPEN
mother	MA
• mother *and* child	MASON
• mother at home	MAIN
• Mother Earth	MAGE
• mother in court	MAINYARD
• mother's double	MAMA
• mother's picture	MAINFRAME
• mother-ship	MASS
• mother wearing blouse	MAINTOP
• mother *with* robe	MAKIMONO
• motherlessness	NOMA
mother	MAM
• mother *and* friend	MAMMATE
• mother encountered . . .	MAMMET
• mother *with* Scotsman	MAMMON
mother	MUM
• little mother	MINIMUM
• mother *has* directions on . . .	MU-MESON
• mother *has* power	MUMP
motherless	omit MA
• mother*less* wo(ma)n	WON
Mothers' Union	MADAM, MAMA, MAMMA
two mothers	MADAM, MAMA, MAMMA
motion	
motion of [moon]	MONO–
[tram] *in motion*	MART
[tram in] *motion*	MARTIN
motley	
motley [garb]	BRAG, GRAB
[robed] *in motley* . . .	BORED
motor	
motor	CAR
• bird *follows* motor	CARGOOSE, CAROUSEL
• motor race	CARNATION
• motor travels . . .	CARGOES
motor fleet vessel	MFV
motor sport improving	RALLYING
motor torpedo boat	MTB
motor vessel	MV
motoring	(in) CA–R
motoring friend	CARPAL
motoring organisation	AA, RAC
motoring people	CARNATION
motorists	AA, RAC
motorist's club	DRIVER
motorway	M, MI
• motorway building	MISTY
• motorway in Germany	MING
• motorway madness	MIRAGE
• motorway restaurant	MIDINETTE
• motorway *turn*<	IM–
• motorways merge	MIMI
• posts *on* the motorway	MISTAKES
mould	
moulded [clay]	LACY
moulded, *say*	DICAST, DIKAST
moulding [vase]	AVES, SAVE
mouldy, *say*	MUSTEE
moult	
moult(ed)	CAST DOWN
	DOWNCAST, DOWNFALL
mount	
mount	MT
mount drama	HORSEPLAY
mounted	UP
• mounted coach	UPSTAGE
• mounted players	UPCAST
• mounted team	UPSIDE
mounted artillery(D)^	SNUG
mounted huntsman's . . . (D)^	SLEEP
mounted police	MP, RCMP
mounted police(D)^	PM
mounted soldiers(D)^	AR, AT, ER, SIG–
mounting disorder	RIOT, UPRISING
mounting step(D)^	PETS

mounts stairs	TAKES FLIGHT

mountain

a Scandinavian *mountaineer*(D)^	APPAL
mountain	ALP
• eastern mountain	ALPINE
• mountain-*climbing*(D)^	PLA
• mountain *retreat*<	PLA
mountain	ETNA
• mountain-*climbing*(D)^	ANTE
• mountain *retreat*<	ANTE
mountain	TOR
• mountain-*climbing*(D)^	ROT
• mountain guide	TORMENTOR
• mountain *retreat*<	ROT
• mountain split	TORRENT
mountain goat	HILL-BILLY
mountain in	
–France	MONTAGNE
–Germany	BERG
–Italy	MONTAGNA, MONTE
–Scotland	BEN, MUNRO
–Spain	MONTANA
Mountain Standard Time	MST
mountaineer	SHERPA
mountaineer, *say*	CLIMATOLOGIST

mourn

mourn, *say*	GREAVE, MORN, W(H)ALE
mourned, *say*	SIDE
mourner, *say*	SIRE, W(H)ALER
mourns, *say*	GREAVES, SIZE, W(H)ALES

mouse

mouse	MICKEY
mousey female	MINNIE

mousse

[orange] *mousse*	ONAGER
mousse [made] . . .	DAME, EDAM, MEAD

mouth

big-*mouth*	B
foul-*mouthed*	F
mouth of *r*iver	R
mouth ointment	BALMORAL
mouthpiece	GUM, LIP, MOLAR
	TONGUE, TOOTH
mouth*piece*	M

move¹

indicating an anagram:

• [counter]-*move*	RECOUNT, TROUNCE
• [epic] *movie*	PICE
• *move* out of [range]	ANGER
• *move* [castle]	CLEATS
• *moved* [it to] . . .	TITO
• *movement* of [tide]	DIET, EDIT, TIED
• *movie* [actor]	CROAT
• *moving* [parts]	PRATS, SPRAT, STRAP
• *movingly* [depict an] . . .	PEDANTIC
• [slow] *movement*	LOWS, OWLS

move²

indicating changed position
of some letter(s):

move *

• c\l\am *moves* left	CALM
• fou\r\ thousand *move* right	FORUM
• *move* East of L\e\ith	LITHE
• *move* south *in* \s\cow	COWS

move³

indicating omission:

move in	omit IN
move on	omit ON
move out	omit OUT
• *move* out, p(out)ing	PING
move * *from*	omit *
• *move* North *from* Bar(n)es	BARES
• *move* South *from* (S)lough	LOUGH
• *move* pawn *from* s(p)ot	SOT
moving a . . .	omit A
moving *	omit *
• *moving* animal from c(rat)e	CE

move⁴

move	GO
• move *after* god . . .	LARGO
• move away from the south-west	GONE
• move *into* the interior	INGOT
• move sheep	GOT-UP
• move *to* the back, *say*	GORIER
move *round*<	OG

move⁴

other uses:

move quickly	HARE
• move quickly, *say*	HAIR
move right *round*<	TR
move round on< . . .	NO
move something, *say*	BUDGET
move to North	LEAVES
move to South	LEAVEN
moveable feasts	MEALS ON WHEELS
moved camp	AFFECTED
moved into *	incl in *
• animal *moved into* church	CRATE
moving about	TOUCHING
moving ceremony	FLY-PAST, MARCH-PAST
moving picture	DRAWING
moving proposal	MOTION
moving spirit	PETROL

Mozart's works   K

MP   HOUSEMAN

Mr

Mr, *say*	MISSED HER
Mr *Turner*<	RM

mu   M

much

much	BAGS, LOTS
much-liked	IN

Letter replaced \c\at; Omit (a); Pointers *out*; Retain <u>a</u>; Split B_ED; Down (D); Backwards <or ^

mud   212   my

much money	IMPOUNDS
much of Sept<u>ember</u>	EMBER
much <u>time</u>	TIM
much-used	(see Old)
much-v/aunt/ed	AUNT
mud	
muddied [pool]	LOOP, POLO
muddy [waters 'e] . . .	SWEATER
muddle	
muddle [things]	NIGHTS
muddled [men eat a] . . .	EMANATE
muff	
muffed [shot]	HOST, HOTS
muffing [every]	VEERY
mug	
mug(D)^	GUM UP
[mug]-*shot*	GUM
mug up	SWOT
mug *up*(D)^	GUM, TOWS
mulch	
mulch	BEDSPREAD
mulch of [dead] . . .	EDDA
mulched [petals]	PLATES, PLEATS
	STAPLE
mull	
mulled [ales]	LEAS, SALE, SEAL
mulling [over] . . .	ROVE
multiple sclerosis	MS
multiplication stable	STUD
mum	
mum	MA
	(*see* mother)
mum	SH
• mum *at* work	SHOP
• turn mum	GOSH
mum	ST
• father *has* Mum . . .	PAST
• mum always . . .	STAY
munch	
munched [grain in] . . .	RAINING
munch grass, *say*	BROWS, GRAYS, GREYS
munching [oats]	STOA
Municipal Police	MP
murder	
murder mother	DOMAIN
murder *on the rebound*<	RED RUM
murder [sister]	RESIST
murder victim	ABEL
murderer	CAIN
museum	BM, MUS, VA, VANDA
mush	
mushed up [snow]	OWNS, SOWN
mushy [peas]	APES, APSE
music	
music	MUS
mu<u>s</u>ic *centre*	S

music directors	SCOREBOARD
Music of the Muses	NONET
music school	RAM
musical	CATS
• musical animals	CATS
• musical mounted	CATSUP
• tolerate musical . . .	BEARCAT
musical	HAIR
• fewer *following* musical . . .	HAIRLESS
• musical party	HAIR-DO
• musical season	HAIRSPRING
musical cleric	CANON
musical girl	ANNIE, BOHEMIAN
musical number	SCORE
musical prince	IGOR
musical show, *say*	REVIEW
musical tempo	AIRSPACE
musical whim	CAPRICE, CROTCHET
musicians	RAM, MCM
musician's character	FLAT, NATURAL
	NOTE, SHARP
musicians cried	WINDSWEPT
musician's house	FLAT
muster	
muster [army]	MARY, MYRA
mustering [regiment]	METERING
mutate	
mutant [ape]	PEA
mutated [trees]	RESET, STEER, STERE
mutation of [flies]	FILES
mutiny	
mutinous [sepoy]	POESY
mutiny in [army]	MARY, MYRA
[regiment] *mutinied*	METERING
mutton	RAMPART
mutual friend	COPAL
muzzle velocity	MV
my	
my	MY
• my lamp is, *say*	MYELITIS
• my scythe, *say*	MYTHICAL
• my stick will, *say*	MYSTICAL
and	
• my anger, *say*	MIRAGE
• my bet, *say*	MISTAKE
• my porcelain,say	MIMING
• my tea, *say*	MIGHTY
• my wife, *say*	MIMESIS
My!	COO
• my fish	COOLING
• my money	COOL
• my shirt	COOT
My!	COR
• my boy	CORDON, CORED
• my name	CORN
• my soldier	CORGI

Anag [cat]; Any *; Begin IGN–; Endings –ING; eg •; Hidden /cat/; Implied add (on); Implied in (in);

My!	GEE	my name is	
• my daughter	GEED	–Kenneth, *say*	MEEKEN
• My, my!	GEE-GEE	–Sally	MESAL(LY)
• my son	GEES	–Sian	MESIAN
My!	O, OH	My, *no!*	omit MY
• my fast . . .	OLENT	• Fa(m)il(y)? My, *no!*	FAIL
• My, my!	OGEE	**mystery**	
• my tree	OPINE	*mystery of* [death]	HATED
my bet, *say*	MISTAKE	*mysterious* [tribe]	BITER
My measurements	GO SHARES		

N

Avogadro's number, born, bridge player, en, half an em, indefinite number, knight, name, nano-, natural numbers, natus, neper, neuter, neutral, neutron number, new, newton, ninety, ninety thousand, nitrogen, no, noon, normal, north, northern, Norway, note, noun, nu, number, quantum number, unknown number, unlimited number, viscosity

1984	YEAR BOOK	**name³**	
1986 car	DREG	name	
Nahum	NAH	indicating origins:	
nail		• *Emilio's* city	CIUDAD
nail in front	TACKLED	• *Fritz's* farm	BAUERNHOF
nail policeman	PINCOP	• *Pierre's* town	VILLE
nail, *say*	TINGAL	• *Dante's* house	CASA
naked		(*see also* from⁴)	
naked	OUT OF GEAR	**name⁴**	
naked (=with nothing on)		named	DIT
• dance naked	BALLOON	named, *say*	HEIGHT, SIGHTED, SITED
• naked girl	SALOON	name*less* (di)ve	VE
• naked light	LAMPOON	namely	SC, SCIL, SCIZ, VIZ
(*see also* bare, nothing)		**nanny goat**	BUTTRESS
naked	BARE	**nanosecond**	NS
• naked musical, *say*	BEARCATS	**Napoleon**	
• naked saint	BAREST	Napoleon's child	PIGLET
naked, *say*	WORN-OUT	Napoleon's foot	TROTTER
name¹		Napoleon's supporters	TROTTERS
name	CALL	**narrow**	
• concerning names	RECALLS	narrow road	BROAD
• name in Germany	CALLING	narrow ruler	THINK(ING)
• naming vocation	CALLING	**nasal**	(*see* nose)
and		**nasty**	
• name her, *say*	COLLAR	nasty attack	OFFENSIVE
• name it, *say*	COLLET	na*sty* end	STY
and		*nasty* [end]	DEN, NED
• name, *say*	CAUL	**nation**	
name	CITE	nation	RACE
• former name	EXCITE	• black nation	BRACE
• name, *say*	SIGHT, SITE	• hand *in* nation's . . .	RACHES
• popular name	INCITE	• nation state	RACEME
name	TERM	**national¹**	
• abbreviated name	SHORT TERM	national	NAT
• name I note	TERMITE	national composer	GERMAN
• name ruler	TERMER	national extremists	ETA, IRA, PLO
name²		n̲ational *extremists*	NL
name	N	N̲ational *Front*	N
• name unknown	NU, NY	national *flower*	THAMES
• new name	NN	National Hunt jockey	OVER-RIDER
• write name *in* re–d . . .	REND	national issue	SUBJECT
name-*dropping*	omit N	national register	SWISS ROLL
name*less*	omit N	national roll	SWISS

Anag [cat]; Any *; Begin IGN–; Endings –ING; eg •; Hidden /cat/; Implied add (on); Implied in (in);

National runner	RED RUM	• naughty girl	BLUEBIRD
national *runner*	THAMES etc	• Naughty Nineties	BLUE PERIOD
national tax	SCOT	• naughty pictures	BLUEPRINTS
national writer	FRANCE	naughty age	NINETIES
nationalists	SDP	*naughty* [boys]	YOBS
national²		naughty girl	BAD FAITH, BLUEBIRD
National			(*see also* naught)
–Board for Prices and Incomes	PIB	**naval**	(*see* Navy)
–Book League	NBL	**navigate**	
–Broadcasting Company	NBC	navigation	NAV
–Bureau of Standards	NBS	navigator	HENRY
–Cash Register Company	NCR	**Navy**	
–Coal Board	NCB	naval	NAV
–Enterprise Board	NEB	naval architect	WREN
–Exhibition Centre	NEC	naval assistance, *say*	MARINADE
–Farmers' Union	NFU	naval commander	CORN
–Fire Service	NFS	naval directors	HELMS, RUDDERS, SEABOARD
–Front	NF	naval port	LARBOARD, LEFT
–Graphical Association	NGA	Naval Reserve Decoration	NRD
–Health		naval, *say*	NAVEL
Insurance	NHI	navy	BLUE
Service	NHS	• Navy flier	BLUEBIRD
–Incomes Commission	NIC, NICKY	• Navy officer	BLUE ENSIGN
–Insurance	NI	Navy	RN
–Opinion Poll	NOP	**NE**	
–Physical Laboratory	NPL	NE	NORTH-EAST
–Portrait Gallery	NPG	NE, *say*	ANY
–Rifle Association	NRA	**near**	
–Trust (for Scotland)	NT(S)	factory *nearly complete*	PLAN(t)
–Union of		near average	MEAN
Journalists	NUJ	near (old)	NIE
Mineworkers	NUM	[near] *disaster*	ARNE, ANER, EARN
Railwaymen	NUR	*Near* East	EAS, AST
Seamen	NUS	near London	(THE)SE
Students	NUS	near mealtime, *say*	NIGHTIE
Teachers	NUT	near miss	OUTER
–University of Ireland	NUI	*near* redundant	NEEDLES(s)
–Youth Orchestra	NYO	[near]-*riot*	ARNE, ANER, EARN
native		*nearside of road*	R
native	ABO(RIGINAL)	near the drier, *say*	NIGHT-OWL
native chief	BLACKHEAD	nearest figure	MISER
native's home	OYSTER BED	*nearly* al(l)	AL
Nativity of the Virgin Mary	NVM	*nearly all* gon(e)	GON
natural		*nearly all* skin	KIN, SKEIN
natural base	E		SKINK, SKINT
natural *base*(D)	L	*nearly all* th(e) . . .	TH
natural cover	FIG LEAF	*nearly complete* volume	BOO(k)
natural drawing	MAGNETISM	*nearly* finished	DON(e), MAD(e)
natural order	NO	*nearly finished* drink	BEE(r), BRAND(y)
natural topic	SUBJECT		WIN(e), WHISK(y)
naught		nearly naked	INVEST
naught	O	*nearly* (n)ew	EW
• came to naught	CAMEO	*nearly* read(y)	READ
• naughty, *say*	OE	*nearly* there	HERE, THER
naughty		ver(y) *nearly*	VER
naughtily [trips] . . .	SPIRT, SPRIT	**neat¹**	
naughty	BLUE	[neat]	ALTERNATE

Letter replaced \c\at; Omit (a); Pointers *out*; Retain a̲; Split B_ED; Down (D); Backwards <or ^

neat *ending*	T	needlewoman	CLEOPATRA
n̲e̲a̲t̲ *start*	N		GOAD HER
neat²		needle worker	ACUPUNCTURIST
neat	CATTLE		TATTOOIST
• neat building	CATTLE SHED	**negative**	
• neat diagram	CATTLE GRID	negative	NEG, NONPLUS
• neat writer	CATTLE PEN	negative principle	YIN
neat	COW	negative, *say*	KNOT
• neat accommodation	BYRE	negatives, *say*	NAZE, NEIGHS, NOSE
	COWHOUSE, COWSHED	**neglect**	
• neat mistake	COWSLIP	*neglect* a . . .	omit A
• neat underwear	COWSLIP	*neglect* *	omit *
• son *has* neat . . .	SCOW	• per(son) *neglected* child	PER
neat	KINE	**negotiate**	
neat	OX	*negotiable* [terms at] . . .	MATTERS
• 100 neat . . .	COX	negotiate *with* monarch	TREATER
• neat ending	OXTAIL	*negotiation of* [lease]	EASEL
• neat look(er)	OX-EYE	*negotiated* [truce]	CUTER, RECUT
• neat mistake, *say*	OXLIP	**Nehemiah**	NEH
• neat ornament	OX-BOW	**neither**	
neat control	STEER	neither	NOR
neat couple	YOKE	• mother *has* neither . . .	MANOR
neat description	BEEFY	• neither *found in* the road	SNORT
neat drive	ROUND-UP	• neither person	NORMAN, NORROY
neat leg	CALF	**Nelson**	
neat little animals	CALVES	Nelson's employer	WRESTLER
neat pullover	GUERNSEY, JERSEY	Nelson's ship	VICTORY
neat *Scotch*	KY(E), SNOD	Nelson's woman	EMMA
neat sound	LOWING, MOO	**neper**	N
neat theft	RUSTLING	**Neptune**	NEP
neat³		**nerve**	
neat	TRIM	nerve, *say*	STEAL
• a neat . . .	ANTRIM	[nerve]-*shattering*	NEVER
• neat compound	TRIMESTER	*nervous* [friend]	FINDER
• neat eater, *say*	TRIMETER	nervous twitch, *say*	CAREER
Neath river	UNDERWEAR	**nest**	
necessary		a nest of agents, *say*	ASPIRING
necessary [part]	PRAT, TRAP	bird *nesting in* ship	SPIES
necessary part of		*nesting in* li/me tre/e	METRE
ste/am en/gine	AMEN	**net**	
necessary to ass/emble		net	CLEAR, GAIN
m/any . . .	EMBLEM	[net] result	ENT, TEN
[no tips] *necessary*	POINTS	*netting* a . . .	incl a
neck		*netting* *	incl *
neck hair, *say*	MAIN	• prisoner *netting* fish	CRAYON
neckband, *say*	CALLER, CHOLER	**Netherlands**	NL
neckline	LANYARD, NOOSE	Netherlands Antilles	NT
	TIDEMARK, V	**network**	
need		network	BR, RY, RLY
needed for mo/st aff/airs	STAFF	[net]*work*	ENT–, TEN
needed in man/y ear/ly . . .	YEAR	**neuralgia**	TIC
needing kicks, [take] . . .	KATE, TEAK	**neuter**	N
needing repair, [shoe]	HOES, HOSE	**neutral**	
needs [a set] . . .	SATE, SEAT, TEAS	neutral	(in) L–R
		• woman *is neutral*	LEVER
needle		neutral	N
needle*point*	N	• neutral area	NACRE

Anag [cat]; Any *; Begin IGN–; Endings –ING; eg •; Hidden /cat/; Implied add (on); Implied in (in);

never

[never]-*changing*	NERVE
never-*ending*	WHENEVER
neve*r*-*ending*	R
never-ending	omit last letter
• *never-ending* night	NIGH
• *never-ending* journey	TRI(p)
never leaves off	EVERGREEN
nevertheless	EVER MORE
never*theless*	omit O

new¹

new	FRESH
• concerning new . . .	REFRESH
• new layer, *say*	FRESHEN
• new novel	FRESH
• new ruler	FRESHER
	(*see also* fresh)
new	N
• New Age	NEON
• new member	NEAR
• new safety-measure	NEAR-THING

new²

indicating anagram:

new-born [lamb]	BALM
new course of [action]	CATION
new development in [Neath]	THANE
new edition of [Wells]	SWELL
[new]-*fangled*	WEN
new-fangled [tools]	LOOTS, STOOL
new form [master]	STREAM
new form of [words]	SWORD
New [Forest]	FOSTER
new formula [oils]	SILO
new layout of [E Street]	TEETERS
new order for [shoes]	HOES, HOSE
New [Orleans]	SALERNO
new position of [table]	BLEAT
new production of [Tosca]	ATOCS, COATS
new regulation [made in] . . .	MAIDEN
new role for [director]	CREDITOR
new setting for [garnets]	STRANGE
new [shoes]	HOSES
new sort of [medical]	CLAIMED, DECIMAL, DECLAIM
new style of [shoe]	HOES, HOSE
New [Testament]	STATEMENT
new use for [tool]	LOOT
new version of [stage] . . .	GATES
new way to [run] . . .	NUR, URN
New [Year]	YARE
newly-built [town]	WONT
newly-coined [words]	SWORD
newly-gathered [flower]	FOWLER, REFLOW
newly-planted [forest]	FOSTER
newly-[wed]	DEW
New[town]	WONT
New[castle]	CLEATS

new²

indicating homophone:

new capital, *say*	NEUROMA
new flower, *say*	NEUROSE
new *rhyme*	GNU, KNEW
new river, *say*	NEURONE
new, *say*	GNU, KNEW
new *sound*	GNU, KNEW
new sound of waves	WAIVES
new spell of weather	W(H)ETHER

new³

New Church	NC
New England	NE
New English	
–Bible	NEB
–Dictionary	NED
New Jersey	CALF, NJ
New Orleans	NO
New Providence	NP
New South Wales	NSW
New Testament	NT
New York	BIG APPLE, GOTHAM, NY
–City	NYC
–district	BOWERY, BRONX
	HARLEM, MANHATTAN, QUEENS
–opera	MET
–Times	NYX
New Version	NV
New Zealand	(*see separate entry*)

new⁴

other uses:

new coat	WET PAINT
new driver	L
New Forest	GREENWOOD
new girl	DEB(UTANTE)
• a right new girl	ARDEB
• new girl scoffed	DEBATE
New Left	UNUSED
new lines	AD LIBS
new look	NOVELLO
new partner	BRIDE(GROOM)
new start for felon	MELON
new suit	GEAR CHANGE
new tip on \p\ike	BIKE, LIKE, MIKE
New World (=American)	
• criticise New World . . .	PAN-AMERICAN
• New World clergy	AMERICAN CLOTH
new writing	NOVEL
New Year's Day(=Jan 1st)	J
newly arrived	JUSTIN

New Zealand

New Zealand	NZ
New Zealand *flower*	CLUTHA
New Zealand *leaders*	NZ

newcomer

newcomer	DEB
new[comer]	CROME

Letter replaced \c\at; Omit (a); Pointers *out*; Retain a; Split B_ED; Down (D); Backwards <or ^

Newry	DOWNTOWN	nil	O
news		nil-nil	OO
news	GEN		*(see also no)*
• News at Eleven	GENII	**nine**	
• news that is . . .	GENIE	nine	IX, THETA
• newsboy	GENERIC	nine Christmas presents	LADIES
news, *say*	GNUS, WHIRRED	nine dancers	MORRIS MEN
newspaper		nine days' . . .	WONDER
newspaper	RAG	nine days of devotion	NOVENA
• 100 newspapers	CRAGS	nine eyes	LAMPREY
• newspaper *in* the river	DRAGEE, DRAGON	nine hundred	CM, SAMPI
• newspaper magazine	RAGTIME	[nine] *letters*	NEIN
• newspaper published	RAGOUT	nine letters *returned<*	IOTA
newspaper	FT, SUN, TIMES	nine lives of . . .	CAT
newspaper column	STANDARD	nine nil	NINETY
newspaper boss	ED, EXPRESSED	nine points of . . .	LAW
	PRESS STUD, PRESSED	**nineteen**	
newspaper leader	ED, EXPRESSED, PRESSED	1984	YEARBOOK
newspaper *leader*	N	1986 cars	DREGS
newton		nineteenth (hole)	BAR, CLUBHOUSE
newton	N	**ninety**	
new[ton]	NOT	Nineties	NAUGHTY
next		ninety	N, Q, XC
next county	CLOSE DOWN	ninety-nine	IC
next month	PROX(IMO)	ninety thousand	N, Q
next to nothing	add O	**nip**	
• room <u>next to nothing</u>	CELLO	nip(D)^	PIN-UP
	(see also nothing³)	nipped *round*	BI–T
Nicaragua	NIC	**NME**	
nice		NME, *say*	ENEMY
Nice chap	FRENCHMAN	**no¹**	
nice man	KINDLES	no	LOVE
Nice people	FRENCH	• 100 love	CLOVE
Nice policeman	GENDARME	• no fruit	LOVE-APPLE
Nice surroundings	RIVIERA	• no home	LOVE-NEST
nickname	DARTMOOR, PARKHURST, etc		*(see also love)*
	PRISON	no	NIL
	DEVIL	• greeting *in* no . . .	NIHIL
Nigel		• no point	NILE
[Nigel] *Twist*	ELGIN		*(see also nil)*
Nigella (=Love-in-a-mist)	MOIST	**no²**	
Niger	RN	no	NO
Nigeria	WAN	• no directions	NOSE
niggard	CARL	• no good	NOOK
night		• no medicine	NODOSE
night air	NOCTURNE, SERENADE	• no-one	NOI–
night-light	MOON, STAR	• no right	NOR(T)
[night]-*out*	THING	• no spare key	NOTHING
night, *say*	ENNOBLE	<u>no</u> *beginning*	N
[night]-*shift*	THING	no *end*	O
night-time, *say*	DAGON	no *entry*	incl NO
night watchman	CHARLEY, CHARLIE	• there is no *entry in* a–n . . .	ANON
	STARGAZER	no French . . .	NON
nigh(t) *without end*	NIGH	no *going back<*	LIN, ON
nightmare	BLACK BEAUTY, DARK HORSE	no *head*	start with NO
nil		<u>no</u> *head*	N
nil	LOVE	no *heart*	incl NO

Anag [cat]; Any *; Begin IGN–; Endings –ING; eg •; Hidden /cat/; Implied add (on); Implied in (in);

• knight *has* no *heart*	KNOT
No, no!	omit NO
• Learner? *No,* no!	(no)VICE
no *return<*	LIN, ON
no Scot, *say*	GNOMON
no *Scotch*	NA, NAE
no *turning back<*	LIN, ON
no way	NOE, NON, NOS, NOW

no³

no	O
• no co-ordinates	OXY–
• no cover	OLID
• no employment	OUSE
• no food	ORATIONS
• no friends	OPALS
• no love	OO
• no noise	OBANG, ODIN
• no people	OMEN
• no part	OBIT, OE, ON, OS, OW
• no right	OR(T)
• no share	ORATION
• no space	OVOID
• no theologian	ODD
• no trees	OPINES
• no VAT	ORATED
• no-way	OE, ON, OS, OW
	ORD, OST

and

• company *has* no . . .	COO
• cover *with* no . . .	LIDO
• girl *with* no . . .	MAYO
• father *has* no . . .	DADO
• no credit	LENTO
• no *support for* leg(D)	LIMBO
no *entry*	incl O
no *love*	omit O
no score	incl O
no score draw	O–O

no⁴

indicating omission:

no account	omit AC
• no *account performer*	(ac)TRESS
no alternative	omit OR
• st(or)y *with* no alternative	STY
no aspiration	omit H
• (h)as *no* aspiration	AS
• (h)e *has* no aspiration	E
• *no* aspiration to (h)arm . . .	ARM
no bounds	omit ends
• (c)it(y) *has no bounds*	IT
no claim	omit AM, IAM, IM
no conclusion	omit last letter
• ha(s) *no conclusion*	HA
no end	omit END
no *end* of th(e) . . .	TH
no *entrance* to (p)ort	ORT
no go	omit GO

no good	omit G
no head	omit 1st letter
no heart	omit H
no heart	omit centre
• M(ar)y *has no heart*	MY
no initial . . .	omit 1st letter
no limits to (w)eight(s)	EIGHT
no love	omit O
no money	omit L
no *need for* a . . .	omit A
no *need for* *	omit *
• do(l)t *has no need for* money	DOT
no novice	omit L
no-one	omit I
no opening	omit 1st letter
no parking	omit P
no point *in* . . .	omit N, S, E, W
no power	omit P
no publicity	omit AD
no resistance	omit R
no right	omit R, RT
no ring	omit O
no *roof on*(D)	omit 1st letter
no saint	omit S, ST
no *sign of* a . . .	omit A
no sign of *	omit *
• moth(er) *shows no sign*	
of hesitation	MOTH
no *start for* . . .	omit 1st letter
no *stomach for* ba(tt)le	BALE
no thanks	omit TA
no time	omit AGE, T
• men(age) *has no* time . . .	MEN
• (t)hey *have no* time	HEY
no way	omit N, S, E, W
• *no* way pa(s)t	PAT
no way	omit RD, ST
• *no* way ha(rd)y . . .	HAY
• *no* way pa(st)	PA

no⁵

indicating opposite:

no admission	DENIAL
no expert	L, LEARNER
no handicap	SCRATCH
no high-flier	LOWLANDER
no inclination	FLAT, LEVEL
no mistake	CORRECT, R, RT, RIGHT

no⁶

other uses:

no bloody good	NBG
no charges	FREE FOR ALL
no commercial value	NCV
no date	ND
no drink	TT
no film	NEGATIVE
no good	NG, US
no-good [liar]	ARIL, LIRA, RAIL

no longer	LATE	*noisy* band	BANNED
no longer (=old word)		noisy preacher	BOANERGES
• song *no longer*	FIT(T), FITTE, FYTTE	noisy unit	(DECI)BEL
no *meaning*	REFUSAL	• noiseless	NOBEL
no (place of publication)	NP	rumour *noised abroad*	ROOMER
no proper [cures]	CURSE	**nomadic**	
no rain *about*	(in) DR–Y	[Is Arab] *nomadic?*	ARABIS
no trumps	NT	*nomadic* [tribe]	BITER
no value declared	NVD	**nominal**	
Noah		nominal subscription	SIGNATURE
Noah ANCIENT MARINER, ARKWRIGHT		nominal winner	VICTOR
Noah's lamp, *say* ARCLIGHT, FLOODLIGHT		**nominative**	NOM
Noah's wife, *say* JOAN OF ARC		**non-¹**	NON–
nob	JACK, KNAVE	non-*extreme members*	NN
noble		non-*finisher*	N
noble churchman	DUKEDOM, EARLDOM	[non]-*runner*	ONN
noble friend, *say*	DUCALLY	non-*starter*	N
noble journalist	COUNTED	**non-²**	
noble queen	COUNTER	indicating omission:	
noble, *say*	MARQUEE, PIER	*non*-British	omit B
noble vessel	LORDSHIP	*non*-English	omit E
noble's joint	COUNTSHIP, DUKESHIP	*non*-European	omit E
nobles, *say*	MARQUEES, PIERCE, PIERS	*non*-extreme (m)ember(s)	EMBER
nobility, *say*	PIERAGE	*non*-U	omit U
nobody		• *non*-U ho(u)se	HOSE
nobody	ALL SOULS, POOTER	*non*-union	omit TU, U
nobody called	ORANG	• *non*-union (tu)tor	TOR
nod		• *non*-union to(u)r	TOR
nod *back<*	DON	*non*-university . . .	omit U
[nod] *off*	DON, –OND	**non-³**	
noise		other uses:	
noise	DIN	non-commissioned officer	CPL, CQMS, CSM
• noise abates	DINGOES		NCO, RQMS, RSM,
• noiseless	ODIN		SGT, SM
noise	RACKET	*non-conformist* [priest]	RIPEST, STRIPE
• noise in court	RACKET		TRIPES
• noise of showjumping BADMINTO RACKET		non-drinker	TT
• noise, *say*	RACQUET	non-medal-winner	FOURTH
• noisy dance, *say*	RACQUET BALL	non-military numbers	CIVIL
noise and number index	NNI	non-professional	LAY
noise of rain	REIGN, REIN	non-specific urethritis	NSU
noiseless	NOBEL, OBANG, ODIN	non-striker	SCAB
	QUIETER	non-U	NAFF
noiseless ty(ping)	TY	**none**	
noisily opening	DOR, GAIT	none	NOTARY
noisy (very noisy)	F(FF)	none left	ALL RIGHT
• a noisy attack	AFRAID	none oversleep	ON A PLATE
• a noisy carnival	AFFAIR	none*theless*	omit O
• a noisy company	AFFIRM	• *nonetheless* s(o)lid	SLID
and		• s(o)ap *nonetheless* . . .	SAP
• noisy cow	FLOWER	**nonsense**	
• noisy way	FEAST	*nonsense* [verses]	SERVES
• noisy work	FOP	nonsensical fellow	LEAR
and		**noon** AMENDS, HANDS UP, M, N	
• a very noisy listener	AFFEAR	**Norfolk town**	
• a very noisy tune	AFFAIR	Norfolk town	DISS
(*see* also loud, strong)		*in* Norfolk town	DIS–S

Anag [cat]; Any *; Begin IGN–; Endings –ING; eg •; Hidden /cat/; Implied add (on); Implied in (in);

• wine *in* Norfolk town	DISPORTS	• not any *local* . . .	NOTARY
normal		• not church	NOTCH
normal	PAR	• not decorated	NOTICED
• I am *in* normal . . .	PAIR	• not English	NOTE
• normal family	PARKIN	• not frozen	NOTICE
• ship *outside* normal . . .	SPARS	• not if I, *say*	NOTIFY
normal colour	STANDARD	• not in key	NOTING
normal soldier	REGULAR	• not well	NOTABLY
normal temperature and pressure	NTP	[not](D)^	TON-UP
Norman		not a sign	NOTARIES
Norman (=French)		not *as before*	NE
• *Norman's* residence	CHATEAU, MAISON	not *back*<	TON
• present *for Norman*	CADEAU	[not] *bad*	TON
Norman French	NF	not *backward-looking*<	TON
north		not *beginning*	start with NOT
north	N	• not *beginning* sweet . . .	NOTICE
North Africa	NA	not *beginning*	N
• North African girl	NASAL	not *central*	O
• North African perfume	NASCENT	not *closing*	T
• North African tree	NAPALM	not *coming back*<	TON
North America	NA, US, USA	[not] *converted*	TON
North American (=Red Indian)		n(o)t *disheartened*	NT
• North American wife	SQUAW	n(o)t *emptied*	NT
(*see also* brave, Indian)		not *ending*	T
North British	NB	not *extremely* . . .	–NT
North Circular (Line)	NO	not *finally* . . .	T
North-east	NE, PREMIERE	not *French*	NON
north-facing door(D)^	ROOD	not *head* . . .	N
north-north-east	NNE	not *heard*	KNOT
north-north-west	NNW	not *hurried*	NT
north of the Border (=Scottish)		not *known before*	NE
• go *north of the Border*	GANG	not *lacking*	omit NOT
• man *north of the Border*	MON	• (not)ably not *lacking*	ABLY
• town *north of the Border*	TOON, TOUN	not *listened to*	KNOT
North Pole	NP	not *long ago*	NE
north-west	NW	not *missing*	omit NOT
northern	N	• not *missing* s(not)ty . . .	STY
Northern French	NF	[not] *moving*	TON
Northern Ireland	NI	not *old*	NE
• Northern Ireland apprentice	NIL	not *once*	NE
• Northern Ireland church	NICE	not *one*, twice	NENE
• Northern Ireland tre(e) *cut*	NITRE	not *opening*	N
Northern Territory	NT	not *opening*	start with NOT
northwards	TON	• not *opening* sweets	NOTICES
Norway	N	[not] *out*	TON
nose		n(o)t *out* nought	NT
nasal drip	DEWDROP	[not] *out of place*	TON
nose	HOOTER	not *raised*(D)^	TON
nose of rocket	R	not *reduced*	NO, NT
nose *off* (f)ace	ACE	not *round*	NO–T
[nose] *put out*	EONS, NOES	not, *say*	KNOT
nosey client	PARSON	• not all, *say*	KNOT-HOLE
Nosey Parker, *say*	PRIOR	• not that man, *say*	KNOTTY
noseless, *say*	NONOSE	not *Scottish* . . .	NA, NAE
not¹		not *seen on the Continent*	NON
not	NOT	not *starting*	start with NOT
• not a child	NOTCH	• not *starting* directions	NOTES

Letter replaced \c\at; Omit (a); Pointers *out*; Retain a; Split B_ED; Down (D); Backwards <or ^

not *starting*	N
not *up*(D)^ . . .	TON
not *using* a . . .	NOTA
not *very old*	NE
not *without*	NO–T
n(o)t *without* love	NT
not²	
not	O
• not at all	–OWAY
• not empty	OVOID
• not marked	OSCAR
• not married	OWED
• not pleasant	ON ICE
• not taxed	ORATED
not³	
indicating anagram:	
[it was] not *true*	WAIST
not *normally* [made]	DAME, EDAM, MEAD
not *really* [new]	WEN
not *right* [in the] . . .	THINE
not *true* [by her] . . .	HERBY
not *usual* [in an] . . .	NAIN
not *usually* [said]	AIDS, DAIS
not⁴	
indicating hidden word:	
not *all* tha/t in t/he . . .	TINT
not *all* of t/he ar/tist's . . .	HEAR
not *altogether* c/lear n/ow . . .	LEARN
not *complete* in/stall/ation	STALL
not *entirely* c/lea/r	LEA
not *full* s/tom/ach	TOM
not *fully* a/war/e	WAR
not *much* of t/he m/oney	HEM
not *the whole* tru/th in/side	THIN
not *wholly* finish/ed, it/ was . . .	EDIT
not⁵	
indicating omission:	
not a co(a)t	CAT
not about	omit C, CA, RE
not accepted	omit U
not al(l)	–AL
not *all* that . . .	THA, HAT
not *altogether* (c)lear	LEAR
not America	omit US
• A(us)tria not America	ATRIA
not approved	omit OK
not available	(see unavailable)
not *beginning*	omit 1st letter
• not *beginning* (r)ace	ACE
not *big enough for* (m)any	ANY
not *charged*	omit ION
• rat(ion) not *charged*	RAT
not *complete*	FUL(l)
not *completely* done	DON, ONE
not *completely* finished	DON(e), MAD(e)
not *constant*	omit C
• (c)over not *constant*	OVER
• grip not *constant*	(c)LAMP
not dead	omit D
not *entirely* (c)lear	LEAR
not *entirely* cle(ar)	–CLE
not *equal to* teacher	(m)ASTER
not *exactly* (w)hat . . .	HAT
not fifty	omit L
not *finally* sen(t)	SEN
not *finishing*	omit last letter
not *finished* wit(h)	WIT
• not *finishing* of(f) . . .	OF
not *following*	omit F
• (F)red not *following*	RED
not *full* co(mpany)	CO
not *full* stoma(ch)	STOMA
not *fully* (o)pen	PEN
not good	omit G
• sharp pain not good	TWIN(g)E
not *got* *	omit *
• mot(her)'s not *got* her . . .	MOT
not *half*!	omit half of word
• Hun(gry)? Not *half*!	HUN
• (Sca)red? Not *half*!	RED
not hard	omit H
not *having* it	omit IT
not *having* money	omit L
not *head* of (p)arty	ARTY
not in	omit IN
not *keeping* a . . .	omit A
not *keeping* quiet	omit P
not *keeping* time	omit T
not *keeping* *	omit *
• r(up)ee not *keeping* up	REE
not *long*	omit L
not *long enough for* the(m)	THE
not male	omit M
not married	omit M
not me	omit ME
not *much* t(ime)	T
not new	omit N
not noisy	omit F
not OK	omit OK
not old	omit O
• c(o)at not old	CAT
not on	omit ON
not one	omit I
not *opening*	omit 1st letter
• (p)lay not *opening*	LAY
• pub not *opening*	(i)NN
not popular	omit IN
not posh	omit U
not quiet	omit P
not quit(e)	QUIT
not *quite* 50%	HAL(f)
not *quite* al(l)	–AL
not *quite* certain	SUR(e)
not *quite* the finest	THEBES(t)

not right	omit R, RT
not round	omit O
not so	omit SO
• *not* so (so)on	ON
not soft	omit P
not square	omit T
not starting	omit first letter
• (t)rain *not* starting	RAIN
not the capital	omit 1st letter
• *not the capital of* (C)had	HAD
not the doctor . . .	omit DR or MO
not the first	omit T
not the first one	omit first I
• *not the first* one wa(i)ling	WALING
not th(e) *whole* . . .	TH
not the whole thin(g)	THIN
not there *	omit *
• *not there*, we (we)ren't . . .	RENT
not trendy	omit IN
not unknown	omit X, Y, Z
• point *not* unknown	APE(x)
• pixie *not* unknown	FAIR(y)
• Jerusalem *not* unknown	(z)ION
not upper class	omit U
not using head	omit 1st letter
not using motorway	omit M(I)
not using *	omit *
not very	omit V
not wearing tails	omit last letters
• ne(w) on(c) *not wearing tails*	NEON
not wholly manufactured . . .	MAD(e)
* *not seen*	omit *
• king *not seen in* Dove(r)	DOVE

not⁶

indicating opposite:

not a man	FEMALE, WOMAN
not acting	OFFSET
not all	APART, SOME
not all black, *say*	JETSAM, JETSOM
not at home	OUT
not automatic	MANUAL
not bad	FAIR, GOOD
not batting	FIELDING, OUTSIDE
not big-*hearted*	SWEET, TWEED
not bound	FREE
not bulls	INNERS
not exactly	ROUGHLY
not even	ODD
not fair	DARK
not far	NEAR
not fast	ADRIFT, SLOW
not favouring	ANTI, CON–
not fielding	BATTING, INSIDE
not first class	B
not for	ANTI, CON–
not full	STILLROOM
not fully dressed, *say*	BEARER, LESSON

not good	BAD, OFF
not grand	UPRIGHT
not here	THERE
not I	CONSONANT, YOU
not in employment	OUTWORK
not in form	OUTCLASS
not left	R, RT, RIGHT
not long	SHORT
not natural	FLAT, SHARP
not one, *say*	MOOR, NUN, TOO
not ordained	LAY
not out	IN
not partial	TOTAL
not positive	NAY, NEGATIVE, NO
not qualified	ABSOLUTE, AMATEUR, LAY
not reacting	INERT, NEUTRAL, NOBLE
not recorded	LIVE
not right	L, LEFT, LT, WRONG
not singular, *say*	PLEURAL
not so good, *say*	PORER, POURER
not spliced	SINGLE
not tart, *say*	SUITE
not the main . . .	LÀND
not that	THIS
not those	THESE
not tired	BARE, NAKED, NUDE, UNDRESSED
not top quality	B
not upright	GRAND
not 'urtful	ARMLESS
not vacant	ISLET
not watered	NEAT
not worn out	UNDERWEAR
not written	ORAL

not⁷

other uses:

not at all	NO–WAY
not clear	NL
not crazy	NOMAD
not dated	ND
not decimal	UNTENABLE
not exactly weak	TEAK, WEAN, WEEK
not fine enough	UNDERGROUND
not full stomach	TUM(MY)
not identified	X, Y
not just hot	SHOT, HOTEL
not many vocalise, *say*	FUSING
not often if I, *say*	RAREFY
not on purpose	OFFEND
not otherwise provided	NOP
not out	NO
not paid	AMATEUR, HON
not permitted	NL
not quite beautiful	DUTIFUL
not so much chicken, *say*	LESSEN
not so much comfort, *say*	LESSEES
not so bright	MATTER
not specific	NS

not suited	BARE, NAKED, NUDE
	UNDRESSED
not *to get* left in . . .	incl R, RT
• f–ight *not to get* left *in*	FRIGHT
• ma–y *not get* left *in*	MARTY
not *to get* right into	incl L, LT
• f–ight *not to get* right in	FLIGHT
• ma–y *not get* right *in*	MALTY
not upper class	NON-U
not 'urt	UNARMED
not willing	INTESTATE
not working	DOWN
• not working properly	DOWNRIGHT
notable	
notable	CANNOT, CANT
notably (=in music)	
• *notably* fast	ALLEGRO
• *notably* slow	LENTO
	(*see also* note)
Notary Public	NP
notch	V
note¹	
group of notes	ABE(D), ACE
	BAD(E), BAG, BEAD, BEE, BEG
	CAB, CAD, CAFE
	DAB, DEB, DEAD, DEAF
	EBB
	FAD(E), FEE(D)
	GAD, GAFF, GEE
note	A, B, C, D, E, F, G, N
• cover note	CACHED
• love-notes	ODD, OFF
• notebooks	ENT–
• pound notes	LADE, LEE, LEG
note	DO, DOH, UT, RE
	ME, MI, FA, FAH
	SO, SOH, SOL, LA
	LAH, SI, TE, TI
• note most . . .	UTMOST
• note, *say*	DOE, DOUGH
• notebook	SOB
• two notes	FARE, FATE
note	FLAT, NATURAL, SHARP
• note *to* Times	FLATTEN
• note *to* first . . .	NATURALIST
• notes owl	SHARPSHOOTER
note	BREVE, MINIM etc
• note shirt	BREVET
• note viewers, *say*	MINIMISE
note *from* . . .	omit A, B, C etc
	omit DO(H) etc
noted	incl A,B, etc
	incl DO(H) etc
noted	COMPOSED
noted (=in music)	
• *noted* boy	DANNY
• *noted* man from Seville	BARBER
• *noted* waltzer	MATILDA
noted group	CHORD
	OCTET, QUARTET etc
	(*see also* notable)
note²	
note well	NB
note landlord	LETTER
notebook	MARK noted,
	say SCENE
notes	–IOUS
printed notes	FIVER, TENNER
written notes	PS, PPS
nothing¹	
nothing	LOVE
• fifty *to* nothing	CLOVE
• nothing right	LOVER
• nothing's right	LOVE-STORY
	(*see also* love, no)
nothing²	
nothing	NIL
• nothing *back* in s.a.e	SALINE
• nothing English	NILE
• nothing *in* bishop's office	SENILE
	(*see also* love, no)
nothing³	
nothing	O
• nothing American	–OUS
• nothing changes	OVARIES
• nothing left	OL
• nothing pleasant	ON ICE
• nothing right	OR, ORT
• nothing the matter	OPUS
• nothing *to* America	–OUS
• nothing to eat	OATMEAL, ORATIONS
and	
• advanced nothing	LENTO
• came *to* nothing	CAMEO
• cover *with* nothing . . .	LIDO
• order nothing	COMMANDO
• surgeon *has* nothing . . .	VETO
nothing *forgotten*	omit O
nothing *in* it	incl O
nothing *is lacking*	omit O
nothing *less*	omit O
nothing *lost*	omit O
nothing *missing*	omit O
nothing *more*	add O
• father *has nothing more*	DADO
• girl *has nothing more*	MAYO
• record *with nothing more* . . .	DISCO
nothing *on*	–O
• father *with* nothing *on*	DADO
• man *with* nothing *on*	HALO
• sailor *with* nothing *on*	TARO
nothing on	–OON
• dance *with* nothing on	BALLOON
• girl *with* nothing on	SALOON

Anag [cat]; Any *; Begin IGN–; Endings –ING; eg •; Hidden /cat/; Implied add (on); Implied in (in);

• many *with* nothing on	MOON
	(*see also* with)
nothing *short*	omit O
nothing *to lose*	omit O
• b(o)y has nothing *to lose*	BY
nothing⁴	
nothing but	PURE
nothing on the clock	BAREFACED
nothing, *say*	KNOUT
nothing to declare	DUMB, MUTE
notice	
notice	AD
• distant notice	FARAD
• notice *in* m–e . . .	MADE
• notice the mud	ADMIRE
notice	D
• notice dog	DROVER
• notice *to* paper	DREAM
• notice perused	DREAD
notice	SEE
• notice article	SEETHE
• notice Frenchman, *say*	SERENE
• notice many . . .	SEED, SEEL, SEEM
and	
• notice child, *say*	SEASON
• notice him, *say*	SEAMAN
• on notice, *say*	OVERSEA
notice	SPY
• notice feature, *say*	SPINOSE
• notice joint, *say*	SPINODE, SPINY
• notice woman, *say*	SPIRE
notice keep	OBSERVE
noticed	SAW
• dance noticed	JIGSAW
• noticed magistrates	SAW BENCH
• noticed poster	SAWBILL
and	
• noticed a wise man, *say*	SAUSAGE
• noticed you and me, *say*	SAURUS
noticed *in* Dai/ly Re/cord	LYRE
notices	SEES
• notices, *say*	SEAS, SEIZE
• notices boy, *say*	SEISMAL, SEISTAN
noticing, *say*	CITING, SITING
short notice	AD(VERT)
notorious kisser	JUDAS
notwithstanding	LOW CLASS
nought	LOVE, NIL, NO, O
	(*see also* naught, nothing)
noun	N
novel	
novel	NEW
• concerning novel . . .	RENEW
• novel race	NEWSPRINT
• novel shirt	NEWT
• novel style	NEWTON
and	

• novel, *say*	GNU, KNEW
novel	SHE
• novel articles	SHEATHE
• novel many . . .	SHED
• novel record	SHEEP
• novel report	SHEBANG
novel headgear	TRILBY
novel place	UTOPIA, WESTWARD HO etc
novel [present]	SERPENT
novelist	MANN, STERNE et al
novel[ist]	SIT
[Proust] *novel*	SPROUT, STUPOR
[wrote] *novel*	TOWER
November	NOV
novice	
novice	L
• novice *has* current . . .	LAMP
• novice priest	LLAMA
• *place* horn *before* a novice	CORAL
	(*see also* learner)
now	
now	AD, ANON
nowadays	AD(AGE)
noxious	
[it was] *noxious*	WAIST, WAITS
noxious [weeds]	SEWED, SWEDE
n-number	NONE
NTT	
NTT, *say*	ENTITY
nu	N
nucleus	
nuclear	(in) COR–E
• five nuclear . . .	CORVE
• nuclear rod	CORRODE
• nuclear sheep	CORTEGE
[nuclear] *fallout*	UNCLEAR
[nuclear] *fusion*	UNCLEAR
nucleus of a<u>to</u>m	TO
nude	OUT OF GEAR
	(*see also* bare, naked)
number¹	
number	C, CL, D, L, M, N, V
• a number of coins	ACCENTS
• number one	CLONE
• number in Queen's . . .	DINERS
• number *in* c–are	CLARE
• number in America	MINUS
• number at church	NATCH
• number one *German*	VEIN
number	EIGHT
• number unknown	EIGHTY
• French number	FREIGHT
• women number . . .	WEIGHT
number	NINE
• firm number	CONINE
• number of matches	NINETIES
• write nine . . .	PENNINE

Letter replaced \c\at; Omit (a); Pointers *out*; Retain <u>a</u>; Split B_ED; Down (D); Backwards <or ^

number	NO	number of French . . .	MARSEILLAISE
• live *with* a number	BEANO	number of Germans	LIED
• number play badly	NOSTRUM	number of Hungarians	CSARDAS
• round number	ONO	number of Spaniards	PASA DOBLE
and		**number one**	
• *back* number<	ON	number one	ADAM, I, ME, NOI
number	ONE	number one craze	EGOMANIA
• number *following* saint	STONE	*number one from* London	L
• number *in* trains	BONER	number one *French*	UN, UNE
• square number	TONE	number one *German*	EIN
number	TEN	number one *Italian*	UNA, UNO
• number expert	TENACE	number one man	ADAM
• number he intended, *say*	TENEMENT	number one mother	EVE
• number of workers	TENANTS	number one on ship	MATE
• numbered apartment	FLATTEN	number one *on* ship	S
• round a number	OATEN	number one *returning*<	–ION
number her feet, *say*	COUNTERFEIT	number one wife	EVE
number of Romans	C, CL, D, L, M, V	number one woman	EVE
number chooser	ERNIE	**numerical control**	NC
number cruncher	COMPUTER	**nurse**	
number eight, *say*	FORTITUDE	nurse	EDITH (CAVELL)
number, *say*	WON		FLORENCE (NIGHTINGALE)
	TO, TOO		SCN, SEN, SRN, VAD
	FOR, FORE	nurse	SHARK
	AIT, ATE, EYOT	nurse	TEND
	FOR TEA, FORTE	• nurse working	TENDON
numbers	NOS	• popular nurse	INTEND
Numbers	NUM(B)	nurse goat	NANNY
		nurse, *say*	MISTREATING
number²		nursemaid	ALICE
number	ANAESTHETIC, LOCAL	nursery gardener	MARY
	OPIATE	nursery *rhyme*	BURSARY, CURSORY
back number	EPIDURAL, SPINAL	*nursing* a . . .	incl A
number [three], *say*	ETHER	*nursing* *	incl *
number³		• a *French* female *nursing* boy	UNDONE
number	SONG, TUNE	**nut**	
number of Argentinians	TANGO	[I am] *nuts*	AIM, MAI
number of Brazilians	SAMBA	[nut]*cracker*	TUN, UNT–
number of Cubans	R(H)UMBA	nuts	BANANAS, MAD

O

all-rounder, **anthem**, *around*, **aught**, *bald patch*, *ball*, *band*, *blob*, **blood group**, *cavity*, **cipher**, *circle*, *circuit*, *circular letter*, *descendant of*, *dial*, *disc*, *duck*, *egg*, **eleven (thousand)**, *empty*, **examination**, *full moon*, **globe**, **grade**, *gulf*, *hole*, *hollow*, *hoop*, *level*, *loop*, **love**, **meditation**, **naught**, **nil**, **nothing**, **ought**, **Ohio**, **old**, **omega**, **omicron**, **on**, *opening*, **ordinary**, *ortho-*, **ought**, *oval*, **oxygen**, *pellet*, *pill*, *rotund*, *round*, *ring*, *spangle*, *vacancy*

O	
O	CIRCLE, CIRCULAR LETTER
	LOVE LETTER
O	RING
• garbo	DRESS RING
• Mayo	TREE-RING
• Soho	KEY-RING
O	ROUND
• good round	GROUND
• fine round, *say*	FROWNED
• OUP	ROUND-UP
O, *certainly*	OXYGEN
oatmeal	BRANDISH
Obadiah	OB(AD)
obese	
obese	FAT
• obese friend	FATALLY
• obese man	FATAL, FATED
• obese woman	FATHER
• test for obesity	FATTEST
object	
object	IT, OBJ
objection	BUT
• objection *following* looting	SACKBUT
• objection *to* hair	BUTTRESS
• objection *to* weight	BUTTON
objection to [prices]	SPICER
objective	OBJ
objective, *say*	GHOUL
objector	CO
oblige	
obligation, *say*	DHOOTIE
obliged to jump	BOUND
oblique	
oblique	OBL
oblique [angle]	GLEAN
[laid] *obliquely*	DIAL
obliterate	
obliterate a . . .	omit A
obliterate *	omit *

• uproar *eliminates* us	RUCK(us), RUMP(us)
oblong	OBL
obscure	
obscure book	BLURB
obscure note	DIME
obscure [views]	WIVES
obscured by mu/ch ar/gument	CHAR
obscuring [a scene]	SENECA
obsequious man	FUNERAL DIRECTOR
	UNDERTAKER
observe	
observation	OBS
observe	SEE
• observe mortals, *say*	SEMEN
• observe ruler	SEEK, SEER
• observe square, *say*	SEAT
• observe vehicle, *say*	CEBUS
observe branch	TWIG
observed	SAW
• observed deer	SAWBUCK
• observed skeleton	SAWBONES
• worker observed . . .	HANDSAW
observed in [Leith]	LITHE
observed in Lei/th en/tirely . . .	THEN
observed, *say*	SCENE
Observer Magazine	SPECTATOR
observes retinue	EYE STRAIN
	(*see also* notice, see)
obsolete	(*see* old[3])
obstacle	
obstacle *on* journey	TRIPLET
obstacle race	HANDICAP
obstacle, *say*	ITCH
obstreperous	
[he acted] *obstreperously*	CHEATED
obstreperous [men are] . . .	RENAME
obtain	
obtainable from [large] . . .	LAGER, REGAL
obtainable from lar/ge an/imals	GEAN
obtainable in b/ig, loos/e packets	IGLOOS

Letter replaced \c\at; Omit (a); Pointers *out*; Retain <u>a</u>; Split B_ED; Down (D); Backwards <or ^

obtained from [lime]	EMIL, MILE
obtained from li/me tre/es	METRE
obtains support	GAINSAID
obvious disagreement	PLAINTIFF
occupy	
occupational therapy	OT
occupied by a	incl A
occupied by *	incl *
• sh–ed *occupied by* a king	SHARED
occupied this place, *say*	STADIA
occupying position	INSTANCE
occupying Russi/an vil/lages	ANVIL
occupying *	incl in A
• a king *occupying* sh–ed	SHARED
ocean	
ocean	MAIN
• about the ocean	REMAIN
• ocean-drilling rig	MAINBRACE
• ocean race	MAIN COURSE
• ocean, *say*	MANE
ocean-going junk	FLOTSAM
	(*see also* sea)
ochlocrat	MOBSTER
octavo	OCT
October	OCT
odd	
odd	RUM
• many odd . . .	DRUM
• odd coin	RUMP
• odd family	RUMKIN
• odd matter	RUMPUS
• Oddfellow	RUMAL
odd bits of fo_o_d	FO
odd character	CARD, ECCENTRIC
odd characters in p_l_ay	PA
odd [shape]	HEAPS, PHASE
oddball [actor]	CROAT
oddfellow	OF
_oddfell_ow	FLO
oddity of [Norse] . . .	SNORE
oddly deficient (s)t(o)r(e) (w)e (s)e(t) . . .	TREE
oddly neglected (o)p(e)r(a) (b)y . . .	PRY
oddly [shaped]	PHASED
odds	SP
sho_rt_ *odds*	SOT
of¹	
of *French*	DE
• of *French* fathers	DESIRES
• of *French* money	DECENT
• of *French* wine	DEPORT
of *German*	VON
of *French* and *German*	DEVON
of the *French*	DELA, DES, DU
• of the *French* hill	DELATOR
• of the *French* note	DELATE
• of *the French* unknown	DELAY
and	

• of the *French* city	DESTROY
• of the *French* couple	DESPAIR
• of the *French* hypocrisy	DESCANT
and	
• of the *French* affliction	DUG-OUT
• of the *French* share	DURATION
• of the *French* sportsman	DUSKIER
of the *Italian*	DEL
• of the *Italian* measurement	DELFT
• of the *Italian* river	DELOUSE
• of the *Italian* sweet	DELICE
of the *Spanish*	DEL
• doctor of the *Spanish*	MODEL
• of the *Spanish* army	DELTA
• of the *Spanish* victory	DELVE
of²	
indicating origins:	
• half *of France*	DEMI
• lady *of Madrid*	SENORA
• leader *of Italy*	DUCE
• soldiers *of Germany*	SOLDATEN
of³	
other uses:	
of course	(*see* course)
of some c/once/rn	ONCE
of ten, *say*	DEANERY
of the lungs, *say*	PLURAL
of them, *say*	THERE
of th/in mate/rial	INMATE
of use [in the] . . .	THINE
of use in [the war]	WREATH
* of	
–a boy	BROTH
–a gun	SON
–cake	PIECE
–my eye	APPLE
–the month	FLAVOUR
–the walk	COCK
–the world	MAN
off¹	
off	BAD
• *put* off *after* error	SINBAD
• off English . . .	BADE
off	OUT
• 150 off	CLOUT
• off the team	OUTSIDE
• road off . . .	STOUT
off	R, RT, RIGHT
off²	
indicating an anagram:	
[I went] *off the rails*	TWINE
[let] off	–TLE
[Monday] *off*	DYNAMO
off course [in a golf] . . .	FOALING
off-[drive]	DIVER, VERDI
off [hooks]	SHOOK
off the rails [a train]	ANITRA

Anag [cat]; Any *; Begin IGN–; Endings –ING; eg •; Hidden /cat/; Implied add (on); Implied in (in);

off[beat]	BATE
offbeat [march]	CHARM
off[cuts]	SCUT
off-key [note]	ETON, TONE
off[side]	DIES, IDES
[take]-*off*	KΛTE, TEAK
[trade]-*off*	DATED, TREAD
[write]-*off*	TWIER
[wrote]-*off*	TOWER

off³

meaning:

away
- away result — OFFEND

bad
- that is bad — SCOFF

right
- daughter with right . . . — DOFF

stale
- stale buffet — OFFBEAT

off⁴

other uses:

off Cowes	(in) SO–LENT, INSOLENT
off cricket	R, RT, RIGHT
off its food	
(=taking nothing in)	incl O
• c–at *is off its food*	COAT
off-key	omit A, B, C, D, E, F, G
• *off*-key (b)ass	ASS
• *off*-key son(g)	SON
off-peak call	YODEL
off them	ONUS
offhand impression	FINGERPRINT
offensive striker	BATTLE-AXE, CLUB
	COSH, SWORD

offer

offer	BID
• artist *takes* offer	RABID
• four offer study, *say*	FORBIDDEN
• offer English . . .	BIDE
offer sweet, *say*	SERVICE
offer *up*(D)^	DIB
offer up a jar(D)^	RAJA
offer vessel	TENDER
offered in so/me sh/ops	MESH
wom/an des/iring *offers*	ANDES

office

office	MASS
• office provided . . .	MASSIF
• soldiers *in* office	MORASS
• state office	MASS
office girl	TEMP
Office of Fair Trading	OFT

officer

officer	COL
• officer in charge	COLIC
• officer *in* service dress	SCOLD
• officer *with* daughter	COLD

officer	LT
• commander *with* lieutenant	COLT
• lieutenant *outside* the ring	LOT
officer-commanding	CO
• ban officer-commanding	BANCO
• officer-commanding engineers	CORE
• officer-commanding in prison, *say*	COINCIDE
• officer-commanding, married	COWED
officer-commanding	OC
• officer-commanding (Mediterranean)	MEDOC
• officer-commanding sect	OCCULT
officer-in-charge	OIC
officer is able	MAJORCAN
officer of the crown	MAJOR
Officer of the Order of the British Empire	OBE
officer, *say*	KERNEL
Officer Training Corps	OTC

official

official	MARSHAL
• display official . . .	AIR-MARSHAL
• official, *say*	MARTIAL
official	OFF
official	REF
• jerk official	CANTREF
• official purposes	REFUSES
• official *without* English . . .	REEF
Official Chaplain to the Forces	OCF
official language	MANDARIN
official *opening*	O
official receiver	ADDRESSEE
officinal	OFF

offspring

offspring	HEIR
• offspring, *say*	AIR
offspring	LITTER
• fine offspring	FLITTER
• offspring scoffed, *say*	LITERATE

often

often	DECIMAL
often *reduced*	OF, TEN

ogee

ogee	RING-HORSE
ogee, *say*	OG

oh

oh	O
oh, why, *say*	OY
ohs	OO, OS

oil

change [oil]	OLI–
oil container	PICTURE FRAME
[oil] *rig*	OLI–
oil sellers	OPEC
[oil]-*spill*	OLI–
OK	ROGER

old¹

old	OLD
• *late* queen	OLDER
• *much-used* letter	OLDEN
• *retired* head	OLDNESS
[old]-*fashioned*	DOL, LOD
[old]-*fiddler*	DOL, LOD
old *French*	VIEILLE, VIEUX
old *Scottish*	AULD
<u>o</u>ld *leader*	O
older tree	ELDER

old²

old	AGED
• old cards	PACKAGED
• old fellow	MANAGED
• Old English	ENGAGED
• old fish	GARAGED
• old fruit	PLUMAGED
• old hounds	PACKAGED
• old mare	DAMAGED
• old medication	PILLAGED
• old orchestra	BANDAGED
• old players	BANDAGED
• old spirit, *say*	RUMMAGED
• old swindle	RAMPAGED
• old weir	DAMAGED
• old woman	DAMAGED
old	EX
• *former* deed	EXACT
• *late* claim	EXCLAIM
• *no longer* clear	EXPLAIN
• old *and* ugly	EXPLAIN
• old nurse	EXTEND(ER)
• *once* stood	EXPOSED
• *one-time* shelter	EXTENT
• *outdated* tax	EXCESS
• *past* it	EXIT
• *previous* pamphlet	EXTRACT
• *retired* player	EXACTOR
• *stale* wine	EXPORT
• *used to be* the thing	EXIT
old	LATE
• *Old and* New Testament	LATENT
• *old* cross	LATEX
• *old* king	LATER
old	O
• Old Age Pension(er)	OAP
• old boy	OB
• Old English	OE
• Old Etonian	OE
• Old French	OF(R)
• Old Irish	OIR
• Old Measurement	OM
• old newspaper	OFT
• Old Norse	ON
• Old Style	OS
• Old Testament	OT

old	PAST
• *old* gold	PASTOR
• *old, old* use	PASTURE
• *old* one, *German*	PASTE-IN
• old soldiers	PASTOR
old	STALE
• old friend	STALEMATE
• old saint	STALEST

old³

indicating ancient, archaic, obsolete, previously expressed, out of fashion, superannuated: etc:

old bag	RETICULE
old does . . .	DOTH
old enough	ENOW
old measure	HAY, MINUET etc
old writer	STYLE
	(*see also* ancient)

old⁴

other uses:

old banger	MUSKET
old boy	ALUMNUS
old coppers	PENNYFARTHING
old crocks	MING
old digger	ABORIGINE
old Dutch	WIFE
old Englishman	ANGLE
old-fashioned corsets	OUTSTAYS
old-fashioned medium	STEAM RADIO
old fellow	STALEMATE
old fiddler	COLE, NERO
old flame	LOVER, SWEETHEART
old girl	ALUMNA
	(*see also* old woman *below*)
old hat	DATED
old king	COLE, LUD, OG
old lady	(*see* old woman *below*)
old man	DAD, PA, POP
old man of Paris	PRIAM, VIEUX
old master	CHIPS, PAINTER
	TOP DRAWER
old model	T
Old Nick	MARSHALSEA
old player	HARPSICHORD, SPINET
	KEAN, TREE
old port	LARBOARD, SANDWICH
old Prime Minister	EDEN, PEEL, PITT *et al*
old queen	BESS
old scholar	ERASMUS
old ship	ARGO
old sloth	MEGATHERIUM
old stager	KEAN, TREE
old timer	CLEPSYDRA, HOUR-GLASS
	SUNDIAL, WATER-CLOCK
old woman	BETTER HALF, DUTCH
	EVE, GRAN, HAG, MA, WIFE

Anag [cat]; Any *; Begin IGN–; Endings –ING; eg •; Hidden /cat/; Implied add (on); Implied in (in);

Olympic

Olympics *entrants*	OL
Olympic *finalists*	IC
omega	Z
omelette	
[made] *omelette*	DAME, EDAM, MEAD
omelette of [eggs or] . . .	GORGES
omicron	O
omit	
omit captain	SKIP
omit nothing	incl ALL
• sh–ow *omits nothing*	SHALLOW
on¹	
on	ON
on *ending*	end in ON
o<u>n</u> *ending*	N
on *entering*	incl ON
• on *entering* ship	SONS
o<u>n</u> *entering*	O
on *finishing*	end in ON
o<u>n</u> *finishing*	N
on *leaving*	omit ON
on/*off*	omit ON
• on/*off* bat(on)	BAT
• on/*off* butt(on)	BUTT
on *opening*	start with ON
• on *opening* hospital wing	ONWARD
<u>on</u> *opening*	O
on points	ONES
on *reflection<*	NO
<u>on</u> *starting*	O
on *the inside*	incl ON
• painter on *the inside*	LONELY
on time	ONT–
on²	
on	LEG
• four on, *say*	FORELEG
• on a peg	LEGATEE
• on a rota	LEGALIST
• on *about* an error	LEASING
on³	

implying inclusion:
on can be used to imply the addition
of one word to another word,
as in

flying	(on) PLANE, (on) WING
• father *flying*	PAWING
• test *flying, say*	TRIPLANE
sailing	(on) SHIP
• teacher *sailing*	HEADSHIP
walking	(on) LAND
• bird *walking*	CROWFOOT

and so on: other examples will be
found throughout the book under the
appropriate headword
on⁴
indicating addition:

about *on* time	CAGE, CAT, RET–
company *on* the way	CORD, COST
look *on* board	LOSS
put *on* about . . .	CAPUT
on⁵	

indicating origins:
on Clydeside (=Scottish)

• man *on Clydeside*	MON
on Fujiyama (=in Japan)	
• temple gateway *on Fujiyama*	TORII
on Mont Blanc (=French)	
• man *on Mont Blanc*	HOMME
on⁶	

meaning:
aboard

• islander *aboard*	MINOR CANON
above	
• pass *above*	COLON
acceptable	
• *acceptable to* you and me	ONUS
acting	
• *acting* group	ONSET
advanced	
• John's *more advanced*	JACKSON
ahead	
• right *ahead*	RON
appearing	
• Greek letter *appearing*	MUON
attached	
• orb *with* ring *attached*	BALLOON
available	
• cricketer *available*	BATON
bowling	
• bat *before bowling*	BATON
charged to	
• *charged to* group	ONSET
continue	
• *continue to* signal	FLAGON
forward	
• haul *forward*	DRAGON
functioning	
• officer *functioning*	COLON
further	
• weaken *further*	WILTON
further forward	
• bed-time *further forward*	COTTON
in	
• *in* the reeds	ONRUSHES
lit	
• lamp *lit*	TORCHON
operational	
• 100 *operational* types	CONSORTS
over	
• *over*price	ONCOST
performing	
• *performing* one on . . .	ONION
playing	

• *playing* before church	ONCE
re	
• *re* Advent	ONCOMING
running	
• go running	GOON
supported by	
• vehicle *supported by* . . .	CARTON
working	
• Marx *working*	HARPOON
worn by	
• hat *worn by* . . .	CAPON
on⁷	
other uses:	
on a ramble [in the] . . .	THINE
on account of . . .	OA
on active service	OAS
on behalf of	FOR, PP
• exist on behalf of, *say*	BEFORE
• on behalf of	
some . . .	FOUR-PART, FOURSOME
• on behalf of Sybil, *say*	FORCIBLE
• on behalf of the	
majority, *say*	FOREMOST
on board	(in) BOA–T, (in) LIN–ER,
	(in) S–S
• son *on board*	BOAST
• king *on board*	LINKER
• a prince *on board*	SAPS
* *on board*	incl *
• king *on board* galle–y	GALLERY
on either side	
• *on either side of* the . . .	TE
• *on either side of the* road	RD
on head	
• Ron *standing on* his head(D)^	NOR
• pat *on head*(D)^	TAP
on holiday	OFFBREAK
on horseback	UP
on it	ONT
on purpose	–MENT
on set	ACTING
on side	L, LEG, LT, LEFT
on side, *say*	RITE, WRIGHT, WRITE
on target earnings	OTE
on top(D)	
• parking sign *on top*	RAMP
• parking *on top of* sign . . .	PRAM
on tour [in the] . . .	THINE
on the conservative side	RIGHT
on the Continent	(*see* abroad)
on the contrary, parts . . . <	STRAP
on the fire	INGRATE
on the go [nurse] . . .	RUNES
on the loose [in Greek] . . .	REEKING
on the move [when I] . . .	WHINE
on the panel	INJURY
on the prowl, [animal] . . .	LAMINA

on the radio, news . . .	GNUS, NOOSE
on the rampage, [Huns] . . .	SHUN
on the run [in Glos]	LOSING
on the ship	(in) S–S
on the way	incl N, S, E, W
• he's *on* the way	HEN, HEW
• it *is on* the way	NIT, SIT, WIT
• stop *on* the way	BARE, BARN BARS
on the way North, walker . . . (D)^	RECAP
on the wing	UP
on this very spot, *say*	WRIGHTIA
on trial	UP
once	
once	EX
• flourished once	FLEX
• once clear	EXPLAIN
• once working	EXACTING
(*see also* old²)	
once	
indicating old word:	
• host *once*	HARBINGER
• *once* in spite of . . .	MA(U)LGRE
• *once* more	MO(E)
(*see also* old³)	
one¹	
one	A, AN
• one *and* one	AI
• one daughter	AD, AND
• one-fifteen	ASIDE
• one-fifty	–AL
• one gets up	ARISES
• one in Poplar, *perhaps*	AINTREE
• one *in* a tree, *perhaps*	FAIR
• one son	AS
• one-time	ANT, AT–
one *inside*	incl A, AN
one *leaving*	omit A, AN
one *less (than)* . . .	omit A, AN
ones	AA, AI, ANA, AS
one²	
one	I
• one about . . .	–IC
• one account	–IAC
• one *after* another	ELEVEN
• one against	ICON
• one *and* one	–AI, –IAN, II
	ELEVEN
• one answer	IANS–
• one boy	IDES
• one *by* one	–IA, –IAN, II
	ELEVEN
• one cold . . .	–IC
• one cross	IX
• one daughter	ID
• one-fifty	IL
• one-five	IV
• one gets up	IRISES

Anag [cat]; Any *; Begin IGN–; Endings –ING; eg •; Hidden /cat/; Implied add (on); Implied in (in);

• one *has a* point	–INESS	• one twitch	ACETIC
• one head	–INESS	one	AN
• one hundred	–IC	• one *and* one	ANA–, ANI–
• one *in* a hundred	–TION	• one *in the French* . . .	LANE
• one *in* 100,000	LAIC	• one man	ANDES
• one *in* record-book	EPITOME	one	EA
• one kiss	IX	• one church	EACH
• one leg	–ION	• one *in* transport	BEAR
• one man	IRON(SMITH)	• square one	TEA
• one measure	–ICT, –IFT, ILB	one	EACH
• one member	IMP–	• copper one	PEACH
• one member in the cast	IMPACTING	• learner *has* one . . .	LEACH
• one metre stake	IMPALE	• square one	TEACH
• one mile	IM–	one	ONE
• one name	IN, IRON(SMITH)	• 101	CONE
• one name is suitable	INAPT	• [one] *broken* . . .	NEO–
• one-nil	IO	• (o)ne *loses* nothing	NE
• one no-good . . .	–ING	• one *might say*	WON
• one on	–ION	• *one might say* we've . . .	WEAVE
• one *on* the road	–IRD, –IST	• [one] *wrongly* . . .	NEO–
• one *performing*	–ION	one	UN
• one politician	IMP–	• one *local* local	UNBAR
• one quarter	IE, IN, IS	• one *locally* bred	UNBORN
• one race	–INATION	• one *rustic* hat	UNCAP
• one right	IR	one	UNIT
• one saint	IS–, –IST	• one devoured . . .	UNITATE
• one silver ring	IAGO	• one *in* one	UNIAT
• one son	IS	• one particle	UNITION
• one son *has* nothing	ISO–	• one *short*	UNI–
• one state	–ICAL, –IME	**one⁴**	
• one thousand	IM	other uses:	
• one thousand *and* two	IMPAIR	$^1/_{100}$	ONCE
• one thousand pounds	IMPOUNDS	one	EVERYBODY
• one-time	IT		LUNCH-TIME
• one way	–IE, IN, IS	MONAD, SINGULAR, SOLO, UNIT(Y)	
	–IRD, –IST	one after another, *say*	INTERN(E)
• one *with* a . . .	–IA	one *and* two	TWELVE
and		one capable	PERSONABLE
• hard ones	HIS	one Christmas present	PARTRIDGE
• one's	–IA, II, IS		PEAR-TREE
• one's girl	ISSUE	one cross	IX, NINE
• one's *in* the sea	MISER	one desiring, *say*	LUSTRE
• one's ruler	–ISER	one *divided by* 100	ONCE
one-eyed	incl one I	one drawing	TOWER
• *one-eyed* man	MAIN	one Dutch state	MONOGAMY
• *one-eyed* painter	TIT(i)AN	one each	PER
one *inside*	incl I	• about one each	CAPER
one *leaving*	omit I	• one each child	PERCH
one *less (than)*	omit I	• one each *in* support	SPERLING
one *missing*	omit I	one expert	ACE
one *out of* . . .	omit I	one *French*	UN, UNE
ones	ELEVEN, IS	• one *French* prison	UNCAGE
one's *double*	ELEVEN, IS	• North *with* one *French* . . .	NUN
one³		• king *with* one *French* . . .	RUNE
one	ACE	one *German*	EIN
• one flower	ACEROSE	one in	
• one king	ACER	–a quarter	NUMERATOR

–bed	FLOWER, ROSE, SHRUB etc
–bingo	KELLY'S EYE
–cast	FERRET
–colony	ANT, BADGER, PENGUIN
–eight	OAR, STROKE
–exaltation	LARK
–flight	SWALLOW
–mob	KANGAROO
–parliament	MP, OWL
–pod	DOLPHIN, WHALE
–school	FISH, PORPOISE, WHALE
–sounder . . .	BOAR, PIG
–swarm	BEE, LOCUST
–ten	NEXT TO NOTHING
–the pack	ACE etc, CARD
	DOG, WOLF
	SCOUT, WOLF-CUB
one *Italian*	UNA, UNO
one lamenting, *say*	W(H)ALER
one left money	COINHERITOR
one letter	SINGLET
one *local*	UN
one missing, *say*	LACQUER
one nil	TEN
one not identified	X, Y
one (number one)	FIRST MATE
	LIEUTENANT
one of 9	MUSE
one of 27	BOOK
one of 39	BOOK, STEP
one of these	THIS
one of those	THAT
one of us	ME, YOU
	ISLANDER
one *old*	J
one on the staff	BREVE, MINIM
	NOTE, FLAT
	NATURAL, SHARP
one or the other, *say*	ETHER
one out for a duck	(WILD)FOWLER
one over the eight	COX(SWAIN)
	DRUNK
	NINE
one round *short*	omit O
one *Scots*man	SOLOMON
one *Scottish* . . .	AE, ANE
one *short of* team	TEN
one sided	BIAS(S)ED
one-sided	incl L, R
• *one-sided* recess	LAPSE
• *one-sided* tree	LASH, RASH
one spot	ACE
one taking	
–over	BOWLER
–the pledge	PAWNBROKER
one thousand	LAC
–pounds	GRAND

one time	SINGLET
	(*see also* old, one-time)
one under par	BIRDIE
one up	RIDER
one way and another	STANDARD
one way or another	LR, RL
one who	
–can	PERSONABLE
–conceals, *say*	EIDER
–eats pigmeat, *say*	AMMETER
one's performance	SOLO
one's pixie	ONESELF
one's successor	TWO
one-time	
one-time	
indicating old word:	
• *one-time* British soldier	LOBSTER
• *one-time* feat	POINT
• *one-time* lover	PARAMOUR, SWAIN
only	
only	BUT
• loot only . . .	SACKBUT
• only a note	BUTTE
• only hair	BUTTRESS(ES)
only	JUST
• only fish, *say*	JOSTLING
• only sweet	JUSTICE
• only the queen	JUSTER
only	SOLE
• at home only . . .	INSOLE
• only daughter	SOLED
• only fish	SOLE
• only son	SOLES
• only you and me	SOLEUS
only	NO
• only bread	NOCAKE
• only East	NOW
• only NW	NOSE
• only SW	NONE
only a boundary	MERE
only a small lake	MERE
only *half*	ON, LY
only one *	omit the other *
• dul(l)y *with only one* pound	DULY
onset	
gradual *onset*	G
onset	ACTING
onset of <u>w</u>inter	W
onward	
onward	FORTH
• onward, *say*	FOURTH
• onward together	FORTHWITH
o-ort	OBIT
open	
<u>eye</u> *opener*	E
open	FRANK
• open anger	FRANKINCENSE

Anag [cat]; Any *; Begin IGN–; Endings –ING; eg •; Hidden /cat/; Implied add (on); Implied in (in);

• open commitment	FRANKPLEDGE
• open ravine	FRANKLIN
open	OVERT
• open parliament	OVERTRUMP
• open vessel	OVERTURN
• open works	OVERTOPS
open (=start with)	
• ally *opens with* spades	SALLY
• man *to open* road	HERD
open accounts	PUBLIC RELATIONS
open air	CANDOUR
open air	A
open-air actors	OUTCAST
open [arms]	MARS, RAMS
open arms	A
open country, *say*	WIELD
open house	NEST
open house	H
open order	DIRECT, SESAME
open order	O
open plain	TRANSPARENT
open safe	CRACK
open safe	S
open season	FREE FALL
open season	S
Open University	OU
Open University	U
open up [crate]	CATER, TRACE
open vault	CLEAR
opener	KEY
opening	ACTI–
opening	GATE
• an opening	AGATE
• opening fall	GATECRASH
• opening, *say*	GAIT
opening	HOLE
• daughter *has* opening	DHOLE
• opening a few, *say*	WHOLESOME
• opening *in front of* son	HOLES
opening	PORE
• opening *in* vessel	SPORES
• opening, *say*	POOR, POUR
• son *has* opening	SPORE
opening	O
opening batsman	B
opening gambit	PLOY
opening gambit	G
opening loss	UNDOING
opening of Parliament	P
opening out [ends]	DENS, SEND
opening pair	ADAM AND EVE
	HINGES
opening pair	P
opening part	DOOR, WINDOW etc
opening part	P
opening [part]	RAPT, TRAP
opening of play	ACTI–, BREAK, FACE-OFF,

	KICK-OFF, SERV(IC)E
opening of play	P
opening stages of tennis	
tournament	TT
opening time	T
Opening Today!	T
opening *up*(D)^	ROOD
opening word	SESAME
opening word	W
openwork	OVERTOP
tin-*opener*	T
opera	
opera	OP
opera girl	AIDA, CARMEN, LOUISE
	MARTHA, MIMI, NORMA
	TOSCA
opera house	MET
opera wives	SERAGLIO
operatic drivers	CARMEN
operatic game	PATIENCE
operatic part	ACT, SCENA
operatic ruler	THE MIKADO
operate	
operating	ON
operating [on her] . . .	HERON
operating system	(D)OS
operation(s)	OP(S)
operation of [levers]	REVELS
operational research	OR
Operations Officer	OPS
Operations Room	OPS
opiate	NUMBER
oppose	
opponents	(*see* bridge)
opponents of them	US
opponents of us	THEM
oppose(d)	CON, OPP, V
opposing them	US
opposing us	THEM
opposite	
opposite	COUNTER
• opposite direction	COUNTERPOINT
• opposite table	COUNTER
• space opposite	ENCOUNTER
opposite	OP(P)
opposite directions	EW, NS, SN, WE
opposite ends of the . . .	TE
opposite ends of the field	FD
opposite number<	ON
opposite of new	OLD
opposite of new<	WEN
opposite prompt	OP
opposition to tall . . .	SHORT
oppress	
indicating one word written	
above another word or letter(D):	
as *oppressed by* ruler	KINGLIKE

Letter replaced \c\at; Omit (a); Pointers *out*; Retain a̲; Split B_ED; Down (D); Backwards <or ^

man *oppressed by* weight	TONAL	order it, *say*	WILLET
opt		order member	FRIAR, MONK, NUN,
[easy] *option*	AYES, YEAS		PRIOR
[opt] *out*	POT, TOP	order member, *say*	FRYER, NONE
optative	OPT	Order of	
optional [extra]	TAXER	–British Empire	OBE
optional music	VOLUNTARY	–Merit	OM
optional score	VOLUNTARY	order tub	BATH
optic		*ordered* [wines]	SINEW, SWINE
optical character reading	OCR	*orderly*-[room]	MOOR
optical character recognition	OCR	[rest is] *ordered*	RESIST, SISTER
[optical] *illusion*	TOPICAL	**ordinary**	
optical learner	PUPIL	ordinary	ORD
optical solution	EYEWASH	Ordinary National	
optician, *say*	CYTOLOGIST, SEEKING	–Certificate	ONC
optician's fee, *say*	IRATE	–Diploma	OND
option	(*see* opt)	ordinary pedestrian	PROSAIC
opus	OP	ordinary seaman	AB, OS
or		**ordnance**	
or nearest offer	ONO	ordnance	ORD
or ox, *say*	AUROCHS	ordnance datum	OD
or verbal, *say*	AURORAL	Ordnance Survey	OS
	(*see also* alternative, gold)	**organ**	
oral		organ cover	EARWIG
oral examiner	DENTIST	[organ]-*grinding*	GROAN
oral, *say*	AURAL	organists	RCO
oral tale	TAIL	organ stop	COLON, EAR PLUG
orally I'd . . .	EYED, IDE		HEART ATTACK
orange		**organisation**	
[Orange] *Free State*	ONAGER	Organisation of African Unity	OAU
orange peel	OE	Organisation of American States	OAS
orange spot	JAFFA, SEVILLE	*organisation of* [women is] . . .	WINSOME
[orange] *squash*	ONAGER	**organise**	
Orangeman	MANDARIN	organise	RUN
orator	CICERO, LOUDSPEAKER	• organise English . . .	RUNE
orb	O	• organise *in* fast car	GRUNT
orchestra		*organise* [seminar]	REMAINS .
orchestra	BAND	organised	RAN
• orchestra sash	BAND	• 100 organised . . .	CRAN
• orchestra noticed . . .	BANDSAW	• organised detectives	RANCID
• orchestra, *say*	BANNED	• organised *in* church	CRANE
• state orchestra	RIBAND	*organised* [demo]	MODE
orchestra	LSO	**orient**	E, ELAND, FARE
orchestra *leader*	O	**oriental**	
ordained	ORD	oriental	E
order		• man *has* Oriental . . .	MANE
order	CH, OBE, OM	• Oriental network	–ERY
	(*see also* award, honour)	oriental	INE
order	ORD	• Oriental right . . .	INERT
order alteration	ANAGRAM, (MATISE)	• swindle Oriental	CONINE
order cooker	RANGE	oriental	SHAN
order duck	COMMANDO	oriental meal	FARE
order fish	RANKLING		(*see also* eastern)
order form	CLASS	**origami figure**	PAPER BOY
order [form]	FROM	**origin**	
order house	FRIARY, MONASTERY	*Origin of* Species	S
	NUNNERY, PRIORY	origin, *say*	DECENT

Anag [cat]; Any *; Begin IGN–; Endings –ING; eg •; Hidden /cat/; Implied add (on); Implied in (in);

original address	MAIDEN SPEECH
original clothes	FIG-LEAVES
original manuscript	AUTOGRAPH, MS
	SIGNATURE
original odds	SP
original plot	EDEN
original [plot]	POLT
original story	AVERSION
originally [lived] . . .	DEVIL
originally <u>s</u>een <u>i</u>n <u>N</u>ewark	SIN
originally seen in Ne/war/k	WAR
originates from A/sia M/inor	SIAM
originating from [Rome]	MORE
originator of <u>p</u>lan	P
origins of <u>t</u>he <u>U</u>niverse	TU
ornate	
ornate [garb]	BRAG, GRAB
ornately [tooled]	LOOTED
orphan	ANNIE
oscillate	
oscillating [wires]	SWIRE
oscillation of [A string]	STARING
other	
other people	THEM
other people's	OPS
other ranks	OR
other [times]	ITEMS, MITES, SMITE
others *from Rome*	ET CETERA, ETC
others relax	REST
otherwise	
otherwise	OR
otherwise [it was] . . .	WAIST, WAITS
otherwise used [by a] . . .	BAY
otorhinolaryngology	ENT
ought	O
I ought	IO
ought he, *say*	OE
	(*see* no², nothing, zero)
ounce	CAT, SNOW LEOPARD
	OZ
OUP	ROUND-UP
our	
our era	AD
our leader	ER
our leader	
indicating a word written	
in front of our:	OUR
• officer is our *leader*	COLOUR
<u>o</u>ur *leader*	O
our man	HE
our opponents	THEM
our ships	NAVY, RN
our time	AD
ours	ONUS
oust	
ousted leader	omit 1st letter
• (p)arty *ousted* leader	ARTY

ousted [leader]	DEALER, REDEAL
ousts a . . .	omit A
ousts *	omit *
• s(imp)ly *ousts* the little devil	SLY
out¹	
out and many words beginning	
with out, some of which follow,	
are used to indicate anagrams,	
inclusion or omission	
out²	
indicating an anagram:	
[bail] *out*	BALI
[bale] *out*	ABLE
[chickened] *out*	CHECKED IN
[make] *out*	KAME
out [in the] . . .	THINE
out[take]	KATE, TEAK
	(*see also* out of³)
out³	
indicating inclusion:	
call *out*	CITE, CIT-E
day *out*	DA–Y
dry *out*	DR–Y
last *out*	LAS–T
out-date	D–ATE
out East	incl E
• f–ast *out* East	FEAST
out West	incl W
• ha–s *out* West	HAWS
out West	W EST
• is *out* W–est	WISEST
sit *out*	SI–T
time *out*	A–GE
tire *out*	T–IRE
way *out*	WA–Y
wear *out*	WEA–R
out⁴	
indicating omission:	
out East	omit E
• fin(e) *out* East	FIN
out West	omit W
• (w)omen *out* West	OMEN
*out*line	omit I
• ma(i)n *out*line	MAN
• sing(l)e *out*line	SINGE
out⁵	
meaning:	
abroad	
• girl *abroad*	MISS OUT
asleep	
• king *asleep*	ROUT
away	
• start <u>s</u>cratching *away*	SCOUT
beyond bounds	
• 150 *beyond bounds*	CLOUT
blooming	
• *blooming after a* time	TOUT

bowled	
• <u>G</u>uiana *opener bowled*	GOUT
caught	
• learner *caught*	LOUT
considering verdict	
• *considering verdict*	
suitable . . .	OUTFIT
dismissed	
• Black *dismissed*	BOUT
exceeding	
• *exceeding* the call	OUTCRY
excluded	
• *excluded* group	OUTSET
fielding	
• *fielding* players	OUTCAST
fired	
• quietly *fired*	POUT
flowering	
• *flowering* head	OUTNESS
in error	
• *in error* with offer	OUTBID
in the field	
• run *in the field*	ROUT
not acceptable	
• odds *not acceptable*	SPOUT
not allowed	
• Rod *not allowed* . . .	STICK OUT
not in	
• *not in* key	BOUT, GOUT
old hat	
• *old-hat* group	OUTSET
on strike	
• actors *on strike*	OUTCAST
published	
• paper *published*	RAGOUT
square	
• *T-square*	TOUT
strike	
• *strike* actors	OUTCAST
• *striking* clothes	OUTWEAR
unacceptable	
• *unacceptable* timber	OUTBOARD
unconscious	
• 150 *unconscious* . . .	CLOUT
unfashionable	
• *unfashionable* fashion	OUTRAGE
out⁶	
other uses:	
• [he's] *out* and *about* in . . .	SHINE
out and about	OUTRE
out least	INMOST
out West	–INE
outer cover of <u>air</u>ship	AP
outer covers of <u>book</u>	BK
out of¹	
out of	EX–

• out of beer	EXPORTER
• out of breath	(in) WIN–D
• out of money	EXPOUNDS
• out of sight, *say*	EXCITE
out of²	
implying inclusion:	
out of action	(in) B–ED
out of water	(in) DR–Y
out of³	
indicating an anagram:	
[letters] *out of sequence*	SETTLER
out of [breath]	BATHER, BERTHA
out of control [I ran] . . .	RAIN, RANI
out of form [player]	REPLAY
out of kilter [after he'd] . . .	FATHERED
out of line [steps] . . .	PESTS
out of order [today]	TOADY
out of place [in the] . . .	THINE
out of sequence [when I] . . .	WHINE
out of [step]	PEST, PETS
out of the ordinary	
[sort] . . .	ORTS, ROTS, TORS
out of the way [town]	WONT
out of [time]	EMIT, MITE
out of tune [in song]	NOSING
out of turn [he is] . . .	HIES
out of⁴	
indicating inclusion:	
out of line	incl I, L
out of money	incl L
out of the race	incl TT
out of the way	incl N, S, E, W
• ge–t *out of* the way	GENT
• *out-of-*the-way h-at	HEAT
out of the way	incl RD, ST
• *out-of-*the-way river	TARDY, TASTY
out of time	incl T
out of turn	incl U
out of work	incl OP
out of *	incl *
• w–e *are out of* an . . .	WANE
out of⁵	
indicating omission:	
out of date	omit D
• (d)ye is *out of date*	YE
• *out of date* fat	LAR(d)
out of time	omit T
• despatched *out of* time	POS(t)ED
• sen(t) *out of* time	SEN
out of *	omit *
• he *is out of* t(he) . . .	T
• I am *out of* ra(i)n	RAN
• I'm *out of* sl(im)y . . .	SLY
• Jack *out of* (j)ob	OB–
• one *out of* m(one)y	MY
• ran *out of* cur(ran)t . . .	CURT
• (r)an right *out of sight*	AN

Anag [cat]; Any *; Begin IGN–; Endings –ING; eg •; Hidden /cat/; Implied add (on); Implied in (in);

• run *out of* b(r)ead　　　　　　　BEAD
• run *out of* (ru)i(n)ous . . .　　　　–IOUS

out of[6]

other uses:

out of breath, *say*　　　　　　　PUFFIN
out of court　　　　　　　LONG SERVICE
out of date　　　　　　　(*see* old)
out of date medication　　　　　　PILLAGED
out of gear　　　　　BARE, NAKED, NUDE
　　　　　　　　　　　　　　UNDRESSED
out of gear, *say*　　　　　　　BEAR
out of key　　　　　　　NOTING
out of order　　　　FORMER MONK, LAY
out of or/der at E/nglish,　　　　DERATE
out of print　　　　　　　OP
out of sight, *say*　　　　　PASTEURISE
out of the sun here, *say*　　　　SHADIER
out-of-t/he-w/ay　　　　　　　HEW

outbreak

outbreak　　　　　　　BOIL, RASH
[out]*break*　　　　　　　TOU–
out[break]　　　　　BAKER, BRAKE
outbreak of [flu]　　　　　　–FUL
outbreak of herpes　　　　　　H

outburst

[nasty] *outburst*　　　　　　TANSY
[out]*burst*　　　　　　　TOU–
outburst [in night]　　　　　HINTING

outcast

outcast　　　ISHMAEL, LEPER, PARIAH
out[cast]　　　　　　　CATS

outcome

[bad] *outcome*　　　　　ABD–, DAB
outcome of [a new] . . .　　WANE, WEAN
outcome of te/st on e/engine　　　STONE

outcry

outcry　　　　　　　C–RY
out[cry]　　　　　　　–RCY

outdated　　　　　　　(*see* old)

outdo

outdo　　　　BARBECUE, PICNIC
outdo　　　　　　　D–O

outdoor

outdoor　　　　　EGRESS, EXIT
outdoor　　　　　　DO–OR
out[door]　　　　　　ROOD
outdoor meal, *say*　　FIELDFARE, PYKNIC
outdoor seat　　　SHOOTING STICK

outlandish

outlandish (=foreign)
• *outlandish* course　　　PASTA etc
• *outlandish* tongue　　　FRENCH etc
• *outlandish* way　　RUE, STRASSE etc
outlandish [garb]　　　BRAG, GRAB
outlandish place　　ISLAND, ISLE(T)

outlaw

out[law]　　　　　　AWL

outlaw　　　　　　　incl LAW
• f–ed *outlaw*　　　　　FLAWED
outlaw gangster　　　　　BANAL
out[lawed]　　　　WALED, WEALD
outlaws' meeting place　　ROUND ROBIN

outlay

outlay　　　　　　　LA–Y
out[lay]　　　　　　　–ALY

outlie

mineral *outliers*　　　　　　ML
outlie　　　　　　　LI–E
outlying parts of town　　　　TN

outline

outline　　　　　　　LIN–E
out[line]　　　　　LIEN, NILE
outline a . . .　　　　　　incl A
outline *　　　　　　incl *
• r–ed *outlining* ear　　　REARED
outlined in *　　　　　incl in *
• ear *outlined in* r–ed　　　REARED

output

output　　　　　　　PU–T
out[put]　　　　　　　TUP
output of [men she] . . .　　ENMESH
out of sewers　EMBROIDERY, TAPESTRY

outrace

outrace　　　　　　　T–T
outrace　　　　　　　incl TT
out[race]　　　　　ACER, ACRE

outrage

outrage　　　　　　R–AGE
out[rage]　　　　GARE, GEAR
outrage in [Iran]　　　RAIN, RANI
outraged [mother]　　　THERMO–
outrageous　　　　　　OTT
outrageous [plot on a] . . .　　PLATOON

outré

[it was] *outré*　　　WAIST, WAITS
outré [garb]　　　BRAG, GRAB

outright

outright　　　　　　incl R, RT
• *outright* li–e　　　　　LIRE
• pa–y *outright*　　　　PARTY
outright　　　　　　R–T
• I have *outright* . . .　　　RIVET
outright　　　　　omit R, RT
• *outright* fa(r)ce　　　　FACE
• *outright* pa(rt)y . . .　　　PAY

outset

at the *outset* she told youth . . .　　STY
outset　　　　　　　SE–T
out[set]　　　　　　–EST
outset of expedition　　　　E
unpromising *outset*　　　　U

outside

is *outside*　　　　　　I–S
• member i–s *outside*　　　IMPS

outside	PEEL, SKIN
out[side]	DIES, IDES
[outside] *broadcast*	TEDIOUS
outside a . . .	incl A
outside right	incl R, RT
• *outside* right ha–d . . .	HARD
• *outside* right ma–y . . .	MARTY
outside <u>Torbay</u>	TAY
outside *	incl *
• fa–r *outside* the . . .	FATHER
outsides of <u>house</u>	HE
<u>rank</u> *outsiders*	RK
outsize	
outsize	OS
• h–e *goes round* outsize . . .	HOSE
• king *in* outsize . . .	OHMS
• outsize vehicle	OSCAR
• tub *has* outsize . . .	BATHOS
outskirts	
outskirts of	
–<u>Bombay</u>	BANDY, BY
–<u>city</u>	CANDY, CY
–<u>Holloway</u>	HANDY, HY
–<u>Mandalay</u>	MANDY, MY
outspoken	
he'll *outspokenly* . . .	HEAL, HEEL
out*spoken*	FOURTH
outspoken leader	LIEDER
outspoken male	MAIL
outspoken Pete	PEAT
outspread	
out[spread]	RASPED, SPARED
[out]*spread*	TOU–
outspread [arms]	MARS, RAMS
outstanding	
outstanding	OS
outstanding account	BILLOWING, BILLOWED
outstanding characters	BRAILLE
outstanding colour	ACETONE
outstanding item	CHIN, PARTICULAR
outstanding man	SENTRY
outstanding message	SIGNAL
outstanding rota, *say*	DUELLIST
outstanding vocalist	CAROL SINGER
outstanding work	CAMEO, RELIEF
outstanding *	incl in *
• th–e *outstanding* queen	THERE
• som–e *outstanding* British . . .	SOMBRE
outward	
*out*ward	W–ARD
out[ward]	DRAW
outward bound	TI–ED
outwardly <u>nice</u>	NE
outwardly *	incl in *
• hard, *outwardly* nic–e	NICHE
• *outwardly* courageous god	BOLLARD
oval	EGG, O

oven-ready	
oven-ready, *say*	FRIABLE
over[1]	
[over]*cooked*	ROVE
[over] *excited*	ROVE
over *half*	OV, ER
over[2]	
indicating inclusion:	
• c–ry *over* old city	CURRY
• pass *over* ring	COOL
• ru–n *over* one . . .	RUIN
over[3]	
indicating one word written	
above another word or letter(D):	
• engineers *with* one *over*due	RESIDUE
• girl *over*age	TESSERA
• girl *over*worked	KATYDID
• he *is going over* the road	HERD
• he is *over*bearing	HEN, HEW
• in lieu of *over*time	FORAGE, FORT
• large *over*head	BIGNESS
• live *over*night	BENIGHT
• no *over*charge	ORATE
• no *over*dose	NODOSE
• numbers *over*see	TENSELY
• skill is *over*t	ARTIST
over[4]	
indicating reversal:	
• *over* ten<	NET
• *over*laid<	DIAL
• *over*pay<	YAP
• war *over*<	RAW
over[5]	
meaning:	
about, anent, concerning,	
in connection with, on,	
regarding	RE
• about over	CARE
• over the bar	REPUBLIC
• overseas	REMAINS
above	
• above the table	ON BOARD
• animal above . . .	CATSUP
completed, done, ended,	
finished	
• fifty *completed*	LOVER
• *done to a* turn	OVERTURN
• *ended with* highest . . .	OVERTOP
• doctor *finished* . . .	DROVER
over[6]	
other uses:	
over half mad(e)	MAD
over matey	BIGAMOUS, POLYGAMOUS
over ten	ELEVEN, TENT
over [ten]	ENT, NET
overbearing	
indicates a word written	

Anag [cat]; Any *; Begin IGN–; Endings –ING; eg •; Hidden /cat/; Implied add (on); Implied in (in);

above a compass point(D):

- be *over*bearing — BEE, BEN
- found *over*bearing — CASTE, CASTS
- the *over*bearing . . . — THEE, THEN, THEW

overcast

overcast but . . . < — TUB

was *overcast*< — SAW

overcoat — BENJAMIN

overcome

indicating one word written
above another word or letter(D):

- boy *overcomes* the *French* . . . — LADLE
- I *overcome* Bible queen — INTER
- we *overcome* the backs — WESTERNS
- woman *overcomes* 500 . . . — SHED

overcook

overcook< — WETS

[over]*cook* — ROVE

overcooked, *say* — CHARD

overdose — OD

overdrawn

overdrawn — OD

overdrawn — (in) R–ED

- *overdrawn* account — RACED

overdue

overdue — LATE

- overdue books — LATENT
- overdue improvement — LATERALLY
- overdue Times — LATEX

over[due] — UDE

overhaul

overhaul [car] — ARC

overhauled dray< — YARD

overhead

*over*head — O

*over*head< — POT

*over*head — (see over³)

overhead cover — CAUL, HAT, SKY

overhead light — AURORA, GLORIA
HALO, MOON,
STAR, SUN

overhead lines — AIRWAYS

overheads — ANTLERS, HATS, HORNS

over[heads] — HADES, SHADE

overlong

overlong — TOOL

*over*long

indicating a word
written over L(D):

- ditch–digger *has*
  *over*long . . . — OFFAL
- *over*long charge — FEEL

overlook

overlook a . . . — omit A

overlook nothing — omit O

overlook * — omit *

- ba(n)ker *overlooks* new . . . — BAKER

overnight

over[night] — THING

overnight cover — BLANKET, DUVET etc,
NIGHTDRESS, PYJAMAS etc

overnight trip, *say* — NITRIDE

overrun

overrun

indicating one word written
above another word or letter(D):

- one animal *overruns* another — WOLFRAM
- vehicle *overruns* soldiers — CARMEN

overrun

indicating a word written
above run (cricket)(D):

- planet *over*run — WORLDWIDE
- site *over*run — PLACER
- well *over*run — GOODBYE

overrun — EXTRA

*over*run< — NUR

over[run] — NUR, URN

*over*run a . . . — incl A

*over*run * — incl *

- soldiers *over*run Georgia — MEGAN

*over*run by * . . . — incl in *

- Georgia is *over*run by
  soldiers — MEGAN

overseas

overseas

indicating a word written
above seas or main(D):

- not closed *overseas*
  on . . . — OPEN SEASON
- make *overseas* — DOMAIN

overseas

indicating a foreign
language: — (see abroad)

overseas, *say* — SUPERVISES

overshoot

over[shoot] — HOOTS

overshot the airport — PASTORLY

overtake

overtake, *say* — CATCHUP, KETCHUP

overtake worker — PASSANT

*over*take son(D) — STAKE

overthrow

[emir] *overthrown* — MIRE, RIME

overthrow tsar< — RAST

overtime¹

*over*time< — EMIT

*over*time — (see over³)

over[time] — EMIT, MITE

overtime, *say* — NITRATE

overtime²

indicating a word written above
a word or letter for time(D):

- double *over*time — BIT
- hard *over*time — HERE

Letter replaced \c\at; Omit (a); Pointers *out*; Retain a̲; Split B_ED; Down (D); Backwards <or ^

- single *over*time   SAGE
- work *over*time   OPERA
     (*see also* over[3])

overture
overture to Aida   A
William Tell *overtures*   WT
overturn
overturn it   TI–
overturn it, *say*   TIPPET
[over]*turning*   ROVE
overturning dray<   YARD
overturning [dray]   –ARDY, YARD
overweight
overweight   EXTRACT
overweight
indicating a word written
over weight(D):
- Black *is over*weight   BOUNCE
- fruit *is over*weight   LIMESTONE
- vehicle *is over*weight   CARTON
overweight ladies   FATHERS
overwhelm
overwhelm a . . .   incl A
overwhelm *   incl *
- weight *overwhelms* a student   TALON
overwhelmed by *   incl in *
- a student *overwhelmed*
     by weight   TALON
overworked
[over]*worked*   ROVE
overworked *rhymes*   BURKED, IRKED etc
overwrought
overwrought [man is] . . .   MAINS
[she is] *overwrought*   SHIES
owe
owe(s)   O, (OO, OS)
owing knight, *say*   OWENITE
owing money   (in) DEB–T, (in) R–ED
     –IOUS

own
own goal   OG
own jewelry   HAVERINGS
own *Scottish*   AIN
owned   HAD
- doctors owned . . .   MOSHAD
- owned *in* the Home Counties   SHADE
- owned quays   HADDOCKS
owned by *   incl in *
- company *owned by* drunkard   SCOOT
owned by com/pan/y   PAN
owner   CONFESSOR
owner *with* wine   HAVERSACK
owner's claim   LANDMINE
owning a . . .   incl A
owning *   incl *
- drunkard *owning* company   SCOOT
owns   HAS
- owns a number . . .   HASTEN
- owns a vegetable, *say*   HASBEEN
- owns vehicle   HASSLED
Oxford
lower part of Oxford   SOLE, WELT
Oxford accent   BROGUE
Oxford dreamer   SPIRE
Oxford English Dictionary   OED
Oxford manufacturer   SHOEMAKER
Oxford Street   BROAD, HIGH
upper part of Oxford   TONGUE
ox
oxhide   LOWER CASE
slaughter ox, *say*   KILLOCKS
oxygen
oxygen   O
oxygenate   incl O
- *oxygenated* drink   ALOE, POINT
oyster
oyster   BEDMAKER
oysters, *say*   AUSTRIA

P

Angola, Cape Verde Islands, Celt, *copper*, four hundred (thousand), Kelt, momentum, Mozambique, page, parity, park, parking, participle, Pastor, pawn, *pea*, pedal, *pee*, *peg*, penny, peseta, peso, peta-, phosphorus, pi, piano, pico-, poise, Portugal, Portuguese Guinea, Portuguese Timor, positive, power, president, pressure, priest, prince, Principe Islands, pula, quiet, rho, Sao Tome, semi-conductor type, soft, vitamin

Pa	PANDA	[paint] *mixing*	INAPT, PINTA
pace		painted	PXT
pace stage	STEP	painter	ARA, PRA, RA
pacer, *say*	STRIDOR		ETTY, TURNER et al
pacify			(*see also* artist)
pacifist	CO, DOVE	painter	ROPE
• pacifist *goes to* New York	CONY	painterman RADON, RALES, RAMON, RATED	
• pacifist conclusion	DOVETAIL	painter's jacket	SPENCER
paci<u>fist</u> *conclusion*	T	painting and drawing, *say*	ARTERY
pacify journalist	CALMED	painting book	PRIMER
pack		painting, *say*	CANVASS
pack dress	DECK	painting with rollers	SEASCAPE
pack of hounds	CRY	paints family	OILSKIN
pack *up*(D)^	MAR(C)	**pair**	
package of [papers]	SAPPER	pair	OO, PR
packaged [crate]	CATER, TRACE	pair of	
packed with *	incl in *	–braces	FOUR
• ship *packed with* relatives	SKINS	–clubs	CC
packer, *say*	STOA	–diamonds	DD
packing a . . .	incl A	–ducks	OO
packing *	incl *	–hearts	HH
• relatives *packing* ship	SKINS	–slippers	SKIS
packing [extra] . . .	TAXER	–spades	SS
paddy		–students	LL
Paddy (=Irish)		pair, *say*	TO, TOO, TOU, TU
• flattery *for Paddy*	BLARNEY	• fashionable pair, *say*	INTO
• *Paddy's* accent	BROGUE	• pair in front, *say*	TOOLED
	(*see also* Pat)	• pair is able, *say*	TOUCAN
page	P	• pairs, *say*	TUTU
page *in front of* book	PRESERVE		(*see also* two)
pages	PP	**Pakistan**	PAK
page(s) *missing*	omit P(PP)	**pale**	
paid		pale	WAN
paid	PD	• become pale	GOWAN
paid model	PROPOSER	• pale fashion	WANTON
pain		• pale man	WANTED
pain *in France*	BREAD	pale yellow alien	BUFFET
pained expression	OUCH, OW	**Palestine**	
painful, *say*	SOAR	Palestine	PAL
paint		Palestine Liberation	
paint distributor	ARTIST, BRUSH	Organisation	PLO

Letter replaced \c\at; Omit (a); Pointers *out*; Retain <u>a</u>; Split B_ED; Down (D); Backwards <or ^

palm	
palm-house, *say*	DATARY
palm oil	BRIBE(RY)
pamphlet	PAM
Panama	PA(N)
panda	PA
Pan's pipes	SYRINX
panic	
panic [over]	ROVE
panicking [over] ...	ROVE
panicky [fear]	FARE
pant	
panting *say*	PUFFIN
pants advertisements	PUFFS
paper	
paper	COMIC
• paper-boy	COMICAL
paper	MAIL
• links paper ...	CHAIN-MAIL
• paper, *say*	MALE
• paper*back*<	LIAM
paper	MS
• a royal paper	ARMS
• daily paper	CHARMS
• is *in* the paper	MISS
• paper*back*<	SM
• papers	MSS
paper	RAG
• paper published	RAGOUT
• paper seller	RAG MERCHANT
• paper*back*<	GAR
paper	SUN
• American *with* paper	BOSUN
• paper flower	SUNBURN
• paper*back*<	NUS
paper	TIMES
paper*back*<	SEMIT–
paper carrier	BRIEF CASE
paper cupboard	PRESS
paper headgear	FOOLSCAP
paper maker	CELLULOSE, ESPARTO
	PAPYRUS, (WOOD) PULP
	EDITOR
papers, *say*	CHOIR
parachute	
parachutist	JUMPER
parachutist	PARA
• parachutist's headgear, *say*	PARABOLA
• parachutist's height gauge, *say*	PARAMETER
parade	
parade ground	DRILLING SITE
parade ground, *say*	MAIDEN
parade time	EASTER
paradise	EDEN
paragon	S, SAINT, ST
paragraph	
paragraph	PAR(A)
paragraph, *say*	CLAWS
Paraguay	PY
parallel	PAR
paramount cover	OVERALL
paranormal	
[heard] *paranormally* ...	HARED
paranormal [views]	WIVES
parasite	
parasite	(in) HO–ST
• one *parasite*	HOAST, HOIST
• right *parasite*	HORST
parcel	
parcel	LOT
parcel it up, *say*	PACKET
parcel of [food let] ...	FOOTLED
parcel [post]	OPTS, POTS, STOP, TOPS
parcelled, *say*	RAPT
parent	
parent	DAD
• parent expires	DADDIES
• parent *goes round* English ...	DEAD
parent	MA, MUM
• follow parent	DOGMA
• parent *has* an afterthought	MUMPS
parent	PA, POP
• parent *is after* money, *say*	LOLLIPOP
• son *with* parent	SPA
Parent Teachers Association	PTA
Paris	
Paris-style hat	CHAPEAU
	(*see also* foreign)
parish priest	PP
park	
park	P
• park at ten	PATIO, PATTEN
• park in a street	PINARD
• park in New York	PINNY
• vehicle park	TRAMP
parked in s/tree/t	TREE
parking	P
• parking *beyond* the edge	HEMP
• parking *in* South America	SPA
• parking in the square	PINT
• parking space	PLATITUDE, PLOT
parking space	CARLOT
parliament	
parliament	DIET
Parliamentary Labour Party	PLP
parliamentary opponents	CAVALIERS
Parliamentary Private Secretary	PPS
parrot	
parrot	ECHO(IST), POLLY
parrot, *say*	POLI–, POLY

• parrot-fish, *say*	POLIGAR
• parrot *has* fleas, *say*	POLITICS
• parrot *has* the right mark and	POLITIC
• parrot-fish, *say*	POLYCARP
• parrot has escaped *say*	POLYGON
• parrot *with* cat, *say*	POLYPUS

part

[many] *parts*	MYNA
part	PT
Part I	CHARACTER
part company	DIVORCE
part company	PLATOON
part company	CO, PAN, ANY
[part]-*exchange*	PRAT, TRAP
part of . . .	incl in *
• it *is part of* m–e	MITE
part of Ayrshire	UDDER
part of Ayrshire	A
part of Ayrs/hire d/airy	HIRED
part of bird	PARSON'S NOSE
part of bird	BITTERN, HAWKBIT, HENBIT
part of bird	B
part of bir/d I sh/ot	DISH
part of chestnut	FETLOCK
part of chestnut	C
part of collar	S, ESS
part of collar	COL, LAR
part of collar	C
part of col/lar ge/ts . . .	LARGE
part of county	HUNDRED, RIDING
part of foot, *say*	HEAL, HE'LL, TOW
part of leg	L
part of leg	THEFT
part of leg, *say*	THY
part of mercy	QUARTER
part of Oxford	SOLE, UPPER, WELT
part of school	GAMBIT
part of the . . .	T
part of yard	THEFT
part in dra/ma p/layed . . .	MAP
part-pierced	EAR-LOBE
part, *say*	PEACE
part-tim(e)	TIM
part-time doctor	JEKYLL
partial s/hade s/should . . .	HADES
partially demoli/sh a pe/rgola	SHAPE
partly close, *say*	PUSHTU
partly-grown snake	AS(p)
partly Ic/eland/ic	ELAND
partly mad(e)	MAD
partly reveal . . .	SHOWPIECE
partly spirit(ual)	SOMEBODY
parts of coffee table	FEEBLE
parts of cof/fee t/able	FEET
parts of police force	CANDID

parts of [speech]	CHEEPS
Parts 1 & 3 of thesaurus	TE
[remote] *parts*	METEOR

partake

partake of ho/spit/ality	SPIT
partaking of fo/od in/side . . .	ODIN

partial   (*see* part)

participate

participants in the mat/ch I p/layed	CHIP
participate in t/he re/vels	HERE
participate in *	incl in *
• me *participating in* a–n . . .	AMEN

participle   P

participial adjective	PA

particle

[grit] *particles*	GIRT
particle, *say*	MOAT, WIT
particles [or waves]	OVERSAW

particular

particularly nice	PEDANTIC
particularly well(=to a T)	
• live *particularly well*	BET
• ran *particularly well*	RANT

partnership   EW, NS, SN, US, WE

party

party	BAND
• girl *at a party, say*	SARABAND(E)
• party girl	BANDANNA
• party-time	BANDAGE
• party, *say*	BANNED
party	CON
• one party	ICON
• party in charge	CONIC
• party outing	CONTOUR
party	DO
• one party *after* another	DODO, LIBIDO
• party *cancelled*	omit DO
• party member	DOM
• party workers	DOMINIONS
party	LAB
• party *at which* I ate . . .	LABIATE
• party speeches	LABORATORY
• second party	SLAB
• strong party	FLAB
party	LIB
• grand party	GLIB
• party I do . . .	LIBIDO
• party *with* the *Spanish* . . .	LIBEL
party	TORY
• declare party	AMATORY
• not her party	HISTORY
• second party	STORY
party-giver	MAD HATTER
party habit	BALL GOWN, COCKTAIL DRESS
	DINNER JACKET, GLAD RAGS

party *leader*	P	• past wrong	EXTORT
party line	CONGA		(*see also* old)
party *piece*	P	past	OVER
part(y) *piece*	PART	• 150 past . . .	CLOVER
p/art/y *piece*	ART	• past directors	OVERBOARD
par<u>ty</u> *pieces*	PRY	• run past	ROVER
party whip	THRASH	past	PA
pascal	PA	• past *in* error	SPAIN
pass¹		• past tense	PAT
come *to* pass, *say*	COMPASS	past Grandmaster	PGM
[pass] *muster*	ASPS, SAPS, SPAS	past Master	PM
pass *out*	PAS–S	past participle	P(A)P
• Hill's pass-out	PASTORS	past president	PP
[pass] *out*	ASPS, SAPS, SPAS	past, *say*	PASSED
pass time	PASSAGE	pastmaster	HISTORIAN
pass²			HISTORY TEACHER
pass	COL	**paste**	
• pass 500	COLD	paste diamond	SHAMROCK
• pass on	COLON	paste equipment	CLOBBER
• pass our . . .	COLOUR	*paste* [papers]	SAPPER
and		paste table	PLASTERBOARD
• find artist *in* pass	CORAL	[spread] *paste*	SPARED
• find nothing *in* pass	COOL	**pastry**	
and		pas<u>try</u> *case*	PY
• Passover<	LOC	*short* past(ry)	PAST
pass *out*	CO–L	**pat**	
• gunners pass out	CORAL	Pat (=Irish)	
pass³		• judge *Pat's* . . .	BREHON
pass	HAND	• *Pat's* old doctor	OLLA(H)M, OLLAV
• back pass	SECOND HAND		(*see also* Paddy)
• pass a few	HANDSOME	pat *on* the head	PATNESS
• passes the fish	HANDSHAKE	**patch**	
• passing nothing	HAND IN GLOVE	*patch* [over an] . . .	VERONA
pass girl	VERONICA	*patched* [sleeve]	LEVEES
pass out cube	DIE	**paté**	
pass round a . . .	incl A	[meat] *paté*	MATE, TAME, TEAM
pass, *say*	GOBY	*paté of* [game] . . .	MEGA–
• pass rat, *say*	GOBI DESERT	**patent**	
• pass the fish	GOBY	patent agent	CPA
pass time, *say*	WILE	*patent in* nav/al ar/chitecture	ALAR
passed out, *say*	FEINTED	*patent in* [steam] . . .	MATES, MEATS
passed round *	incl *		TAMES, TEAMS
• prince *passed round* beer	PALER	**pathetic**	
passed round by *	incl in *	pathetic meeting	TOUCHING
• beer *passed round by* prince	PALER	*pathetic* [meeting]	TEEMING
passed, *say*	PAST	**patient**	
• passed exam, *say*	PASTORAL	patient	CASE
passed staff college	PSC	patient attention	NURSING, TREATMENT
passenger-carrying flight	ESCALATOR	patient helper	DOCTOR, MATRON
passion			NURSE, SISTER
passion-fruit drink	CRUSH	patient man	JOB
passionate love	FLAMINGO	patient sewer	SURGEON
past		patient woman	GRISELDA
past	EX	**pawn**	
• past alteration	EXCHANGE	pawn	P
• past terrorists *with* it	EXPLOIT	pawn *opening*	P

Anag [cat]; Any *; Begin IGN–; Endings –ING; eg •; Hidden /cat/; Implied add (on); Implied in (in); •

pawnbroker's daughter	NIECE	pees, *say*	PEACE, PIECE
pawnbroker's son	NEPHEW	**peel**	
pawnee	UNCLE	<u>o</u>range *peel*	OE
pawn's complaint	AMUSED	*peeled* (o)rang(e)	RANG
pay		peeler	BOBBY, POLICEMAN, ROBERT
pay *back*<	YAP	peeler, *say*	PAIRER
pay on delivery	POD	peeling, *say*	BARKHAN
pay *out*	PA–Y	**peep**	
[pay]-*out*	YAP	peeped, *say*	PRIDE
pay-phone	WAGERING	peeper	TOM
pay soldiers	FOOTMEN	peephole, *say*	PEOPLE
pay *up*(D)^	YAP	**peg**	P, T, TEE, TOT
paying guest	PG	**pellet**	O
paymaster	PMR	pellets	OO, OS
Paymaster General	PMG	**pen**	
payment order, *say*	CHECK, CZECH	pen	PEN
pea		• pen friend	PENALLY
pea	P	• pen-name	PENAL
pea-jacket	POD	• penman	PENAL
[pea] *soup*	APE	pen	SWAN
peas, *say*	PEACE, PIECE, PP, PS	• I am *in* the pen	SWAIN
peace		• pen-pusher	SWAN-HERD
peace, *say*	PACKS, PIECE, PP, PS	pen	WRITE
peacekeeper	UNMAN	• finished pen	OVERWRITE
peacekeepers	UN	• write *say*	RIGHT, RITE
peacemakers	ACAS	*penned in by* *	incl in *
peak		• woman *penned in by* youngster	LASHED
peak	BEN, TOR	**penal**	
peak of <u>R</u>ockies(D)	R	[penal] *reform*	NEPAL, PANEL, PLANE
peak performance	MOUNTAINEERING	[penal] *settlement*	NEPAL, PANEL, PLANE
	YODELLING	**penetrate**	
Pearl's mother	NACRE	*penetrate* *	incl in *
peculiar		• hard *to penetrate* t–in	THIN
peculiar	ODD	penetrate log	ENTER
• peculiar child	ODDS-ON	**peninsula**	PEN
• peculiar head	ODDNESS	**penny**	
• throw *round* peculiar . . .	SHODDY	penniless	NOCENT
peculiar	RUM	penni*less*	omit D, P
• 500 peculiar . . .	DRUM	penny	D
• footpath *round* peculiar . . .	FRUMP	• penny a go	DAGO
• peculiar stomach	RUM-TUM	• penny fine	DWELL
peculiar [ways]	SWAY, YAWS	• penny paper	DRAG
peculiarly [placed S]	SCALPED	penny	P
pedagogue	BED	• penny and a . . .	PANDA
pedal		• penny each	PEACH
pedal	P	• penny fine	POKE
pedal appendages, *say*	TOWS, TOZE	• pennyweight	POUNCE
pedal, *say*	PEDDLE	penny off	omit D, P
peddle		pennyweight	DWT, PWT
peddle bird	HAWK	**Pentateuch**	T(H)ORAH
peddle, *say*	PEDAL	**penthouse**	LEAN-TO
peddled, *say*	SOLED	**penultimate**	
pedestrian	FOOTMAN, PED	penultimate letter	Y
pee		*penultimate* lett<u>e</u>r	E
pee	P	**people**	
pees	PP, PS	people	MEN

Letter replaced \c\at; Omit (a); Pointers *out*; Retain <u>a</u>; Split B_ED; Down (D); Backwards <or ^

• a people	AMEN	• of cat, *say*	TABESCENT
• people expired, *say*	MENDED	• of *French* perfume	DESCENT
• people *in* high places	TORMENTOR	• perfume, *say*	CENT, SENT
• people *start* talking	–MENT	**perfunctory goodbye**	SHORT WAVE
people	NATION	**perhaps**	
• mother *has* people . . .	DAMNATION	indicating anagram:	
• people *have* a friend	NATIONALLY	• [maybe], *perhaps* . . .	BEAMY
• transport people	CARNATION	• *perhaps* [not]	TON
people	RACE	indicating homophone:	
• black people	BRACE	• might, *perhaps*	MITE
• people *found in* Eliot	TRACES	• *perhaps* not	KNOT
• people *taking* drug	RACEHORSE	indicating one of	
people get older	MASSAGE	a class:	
people inside	MORTAL SIN	• *perhaps* private . . .	SOLDIER
people, *say*	PEEPHOLE	• soldier, *perhaps*	PRIVATE
people say "When!"	WEN	**perilous**	
per		*perilous* [trips]	SPIRT, STRIP
per	PR	[totters] *perilously*	STRETTO
per annum	PA	**period**	
perambulate		period	AD
perambulating [Pole]	LOPE	• hard period	HAD
perambulation of [master]	REMAST, STREAM	• period *in* novel . . .	SHADE
perceive		• period with the *German* . . .	ADMIT
perceived in ti/me to l/end . . .	METOL	• two periods	ADAGE
perceived, *say*	SCENE	period	AGE
perceptible in ol/d art/icles	DART	• period books	AGENT
percentage		• period aboard	SAGES
percentage of t/urn/over	URN	• Second Period	SAGE
small percentage of profit	P	• two periods	ADAGE
perch on		period	BC, EPOCH, ERA
indicating one word written			FULL STOP
above another word or letter(D):			PER
• bird *perching on* an . . .	TITAN	period charm	SPELL
• monkey *perching on* line	APERY	period drama	TIMEPIECE
perfect		period of	
perfect	NOVICES	–play, *say*	CHUCKER
perfect	UTTER	–revolution	DAY, MONTH, YEAR
• perfect fit	UTTERABLE	period *piece*	PER
• perfect son	UTTERS	pe/rio/d *piece*	RIO
• saint *has* perfect . . .	STUTTER	period *piece*	ER(a), TIM(e)
perfect letter	T	periodical	MAG
perfect order	APPLE PIE	periodical row	PUNCH-LINE
perfect state	UTOPIA, UTTER	**peripatetic**	
perfect weapon	SPEARMINT	*peripatetic* [dealer]	LEADER
perfection	NOVICES	*peripatetical* [priest]	STRIPE
perform		**permanent position**	STANDING
performing	(in) A–CT, (in) DE–ED	**permit**	
performing	ON	permission to depart	LEAVE
• cricketer performing	BATON	permissive	
• the lady's performing	HERON	–missive	LETTER
performing [bear]	BARE, BRAE	–occupation	LETTING
perfume		permit Henry . . .	LETHAL
perfume	ESSENCE	**perpetuate**	
• perfume from fuel, *say*	COALESCENCE	perpetuate driving area	COMMITTEE
perfume	SCENT	*perpetuating* [evil]	LIVE, VILE
• inapplicable perfume	NASCENT	*perpetuation of* [line]	LIEN, NILE

perplex
perplexed [by a] . . .   BAY
perplexing [poser]   ROPES, PORES, SPORE
Persian   PERS
person
  person   BOD, BLOKE, CHAP
     MAN, ONE, PER(S)
  person of note   COMPOSER
     VERDI et al
  person speaking   I
  personal ambition   OWN GOAL
  personal assistant   PA
  personal column   BACKBONE, SPINE
  personal computer   BRAIN, PC
  personal cover   SKIN
  personal donation   BLOOD
  personal hint   INTIMATE
  personal letters   INITIALS,
     SIGNATURE
  personal subscription   SIGNATURE
     YOURS SINCERELY
     YOURS TRULY
  personal to Benjamin, *say*   BENZOIN
  personal transport   FEET, LEGS
  personal voucher   GODPARENT, REFEREE,
     SPONSOR
  personnel carrier   (SEDAN-)CHAIR
     STRETCHER
pertain
  pertaining to
  –a number   OFTEN
  –cavity lining, *say*   PLURAL
  –cheek, *say*   BUCKLE
  –Christmas, *say*   OVULE
  –focus, *say*   PHOCAL
  –food, *say*   ELEMENTARY
  –seals *say*   FOCAL
  –the ear, *say*   ORAL
  –the mouth, *say*   AURAL
perturb
perturbation of [N orbit]   BRITON
perturbed [by a] . . .   BAY
Peru
  Peru   PE
  Peruvian parentage   INCANDESCENT
pervade
pervade *   incl *
  • colour *pervading* vessel   STONES
pervaded by *   incl in *
  • lines *pervaded by* one . . .   BONER
perverse
[act] *perversely*   CAT
perverse boy<   YOB
perversion of [desire]   RESIDE
perverted [love]   VOLE
peso   P

pet
  pet   CAT
  • pet boy   CATALAN
  • pet name   CATCALL
  • strike pet   WHIPCAT
  pet   DOG
  • execute pet   HANGDOG
  • pet lost   DOGGONE
  • pet that is . . .   DOGIE
  pet food   LIGHTS
petition
  petition, *say*   PREY
  petition *to* queen   PRAYER
  petitions, *say*   PRAISE, PREYS
petrol engine   ICE
petty
  petty cash   P
  • officer *takes* petty cash   COP
  • petty cash book   PRESERVE
  • petty cash *hidden in* bed   COPT
  Petty Officer   PO
pewter toy   TRIFLE
Pharmaceutical Society   PS
phase
phase of [moon]   MONO–
[phase] *out*   HEAPS, SHAPE
phase, *say*   FAZE
Philological Society   PS
philosopher
  philosopher   BACON, ERASMUS
     HUME, PLATO et al
  philosopher   LOCKE
  • philosopher-king   LOCKER
  • philosopher *has* many . . .   LOCKED
  philosopher   PHB, PHD
  Philosophy, Politics
   and Economics   PPE
phobia   THING
phone
  phone *about*   R–ING
  phone, *say*   FOEN, FO(E)HN, FONE
phoney
phoney tale   TAIL
phoney, *say*   SUED
phoney [tale]   LATE, LEAT, TEAL
photo-electric cell   PEC
phrase   PHR
physical
  physical education   PE
  physical training   PT
physician
  physician   BM, DR, GP, MB, MD, MO
     LUKE
  physicians   RCP
     (*see also* doctor)
physiologists   CSP

Letter replaced \c\at; Omit (a); Pointers *out*; Retain a̲; Split B_ED; Down (D); Backwards <or ^

pi	P
piano	
piano	GRAND
• piano keys	GRANDEE
• piano scholar	GRANDMA
• pianos playing	GRANDSON
piano	P
• girl *at* piano	PALMA
• piano keys	PAD, PEA, PED, PEE
	PEACE, PEG
• piano music	PAIR
piano	UPRIGHT
piano piece	KEY(BOARD), IVORY
	PEDAL, STRING
piano *piece*	P
pianissimo	PP
pianoforte	PF
pick	
pick horse	HACK
pick *over<*	LOOT
pick-up	PU
pick up a . . .	incl A
pick up *	incl *
• ma–n *picks up* one . . .	MAIN
pick-up notes(D)^	SETON
picked up by *	incl in *
• one *picked up by* ma–n	MAIN
pickle	
pickle factory	TANNERY
pickled [cauli]flower *head*	AULIC
[quite] *pickled*	QUIET
pickpocket	
pickpocket	DIP
• pickpocket *takes* each	DIPPER
• pickpockets *get* right mark	DIPSTICK
picnic	
picnic	OUTDO, OUTSPREAD
picnic food	FIELDFARE
picture	
picture	SHOT, SNAP
picture-house, *say*	SYNEMA
picture only	SOUND OFF
picture postcard	PPC
pictured	
indicating character in	
film or painting:	
• *pictured* deer	BAMBI
• *pictured* dog	LADY, LASSIE
	PLUTO, TRAMP
• *pictured* mouse	MICKEY, MINNIE
• *pictured* sad lad	BLUE BOY
• two soldiers *pictured*	GIGI
pie	
pie [is hot]	HOIST
[pie]-*throwing*	EPI–
[steak] *pie*	SKATE, STAKE, TAKES
piece	
party *piece*	P
piece	MAN, PAWN etc
piece of bread	SLICE
piece of bread	B
piece of cake	EASY
piece of cake	C
piece of fencing	EPEE, FOIL, SABRE
	PANEL, POST
piece of music	BAR, NOTE etc
piece of music	MU, SIC
piece of p/arch/ment	ARCH
piece of the cloth	BISHOP
piece of toast	CHEER(s)
pieces of eight	OCTET
pieces of eight	EI, GHT
pieces of [stone]	NOTES, ONSET, TONES
pieces of stone	ST, ONE
*piece*meal	M
*piece*meal [way]	YAW
piecework	MOSAIC
*piece*work	WOR
pierce	
pierce alien	PRICKET
pierce fish	STABLING
pierce flower	PINK
pierce it, *say*	PRICKET
pierce, *say*	PEERS, PIERS
pig	
pig devoured, *say*	BORATE
pig feed	MAST
*pig*headed	P
pighouse rented	STYLET
pig*tail*	G
pile	
pile	NAP
pile-*up*(D)^	PAN
pile up [earth]	HATER, HEART, RATHE
pile up maps(D)^	SPAM
pilfer	
pilfer, *say*	STEEL, STEIL, STELE
pilfered scarf	STOLE
pilgrim's token	ABBEY-COUNTER
	ABBEY-PIECE
pill	MEDICINE-BALL, O
pilot	
pilot	GEORGE
Pilot-Officer	PO
pin	
case of pins and needles	ETUI
pin-*up*(D)^	–LIAN, NIP
pincer	
[pincer] *movement*	PRINCE
pincer operator	CRAB
pinch	
pinch(D)^	PIN-UP

Anag [cat]; Any *; Begin IGN–; Endings –ING; eg •; Hidden /cat/; Implied add (on); Implied in (in);

pinch a . . .	incl A	pixie, *say*	PERRY
pinch *	incl *	**pizzicato**	UNBOWED
• bo–y *pinches* books	BOOTY	**place**	
pinched by *	incl in *	place	PUT
• books *pinched by* bo–y	BOOTY	• fashionable place	INPUT
pine		• place at this spot	PUTTIER
chop down pin(e)	PIN	• place bonds	PUTTIES
pine	LONG	place	SET
• live pine	BELONG	• fashionable place	INSET
• pine building	LONGHOUSE	• he *is in* place . . .	SHEET
• pine marten, *say*	LONGFELLOW	• place peg	SETTEE
[pines] *away*	SNIPE, SPINE	place	SITE
Ping's other half	PONG	• fashionable place, *say*	INCITE, INSIGHT
pink		• place, *say*	CITE, SIGHT
pink haze, *say*	PIN-CASE	• soft *in* places	SPITES
pink jumper	SALMON	place	LIEU
pint		• motorway place	MILIEU
pint	P, PT	• place occupier	LIEUTENANT
pint of beer, *say*	PINTAIL	place for	
pip		–animals	INSTALL
pip	ACE	–blow-out	ETNA, VOLCANO
• many pips	LACES, MACES	–hanging	GALLERY, TATE
• Pip got up	ACEROSE	–napkin	OVERLAP
pipe		–players	ONSET
piped music	PIBROCH	–putting club	GREENWOOD
pipeline, *say*	HOES	–soldiers	TOAST-RACK
piper's child	TOM	place of service	BASELINE, COURT
pirate			CHURCH
pirate	CORSAIR, PRIVATEER	*placed in* s/ome ga/rdens	OMEGA
	MORGAN, SILVER et al	*placed in* *	incl in *
pirate flag	(JOLLY) ROGER	• silver *placed in* r–ing	RAGING
pirate treasure	SILVER	*placed round* *	incl *
pirate's place	PENZANCE	• r–ing *placed round* silver	RAGING
pirouette		placeholder	LIEUTENANT
[neat] *pirouette*	ANTE, ETNA	**plagiarise**	
pirouetting [dancer]	CRANED	*plagiarise* [article]	RECITAL
pit		plagiarise musical	COPYCATS
pit *closure*	T	**plain**	
pit men	NUM	plain bicycle	ORDINARY
pit stratum	MINELAYER	plain chant	EVENSONG
pit workers	NUM	plain colour	PRAIRIE-OYSTER
pithead	BROW	plain creature	PRAIRIE-DOG
pit*head*	P		PRAIRIE-OYSTER
pit-stop	MINEFIELD	plain glass	PRAIRIE SCHOONER
pitch		plain *speaking*	PLANE
pitch	TAR	plain words	PROSE
• pitch container	TARPAN	**plan**	
• pitch sticks	TARGUMS	plan garden	PLOT
• second pitch	STAR	Plan Position Indicator	PPI
pity		plan table	IDEALIST
[cried] *piteously*	DICER	plans of action, *say*	POLLICES
piteous [pleas]	PALES	**Planck's constant**	H
pity girl	RUTH	**plane**	
pity Herb	RUE	*accident to* [plane]	NEPAL, PANEL
pixie		plane	SMOOTHER
pixie is warm	ELF-SHOT	[plane] *crash*	NEPAL, PANEL

[plane] *disaster*	NEPAL, PANEL	play part	ROLE
plane driver, *say*	PILATE	*play part in* t/he m/atch	HEM
plane, *say*	PLAIN	play patience	TOLERANCE
plank		play-school	RADA, RUGBY, SCANDAL
a plank	ABOARD	play-time	TEMPO
plank *say*	BORED	play-*up*(D)^	HON, ON
planking, *say*	WAILING, WHALING	played first in rubber	WHISTLED
plant		player sacked	BACKFIRED
plant	INTER	players	CAST
• plant seed, *say*	INTERCEDE	• 501 players	DICAST
• second plant	SINTER	• players service . . .	CASTLET
• wide plants	WINTERS	• players went ahead	CASTLED
plant	SOW	players	SIDE
• plant in good . . .	SOWING	• players *have* true . . .	SIDEREAL
• plant *in* rows	DISOWNS	• players in pavilion	OFFSIDE
plant banner	FLAG	• reserve players, *say*	BESIDES
plant cut back	DOCK	players	TEAM
plant fertiliser	STAMEN	• players aboard	STEAMS
plant goddess	HEBE, KALI	• players *follow* second . . .	STEAM
planted *	incl *	• players in good . . .	TEAMING
• the *Spanish planted*		players	BRASS, STRINGS
in row–s	ROWELS	• players *have* a way . . .	BRASSARD
planted round a . . .	incl A	• central players	HEARTSTRINGS
planted round *	incl *	player's	
• row–s *planted round*		indicating words relating	
the Spanish . . .	ROWELS	to music:	
planter's dog	SETTER	• *player's* slow . . .	LENTO
planting period	BEDTIME	• *player's* softly . . .	PIANO
plasma injection	BLOODSHOT	• quickly *for the players* . . .	ALLEGRO
plaster			PRESTO
plaster jacket	RENDER(ING),ROUGHCAST	players' style	CAST
plastered [niche]	CHINE	playful chief	ARCH
plastering [over]	ROVE	playground	REC
plastic		playhouse	CAPULET, MONTAGUE
plastic [bag]	GAB	playing	IN, INSIDE, ON
[thermo]*plastic*	MOTHER	*playing about* [with Alf]	HALFWIT
plate		playing-field	REC
plate	L	*playing*-[field]	FILED
plate, *say*	PLAITER	playing-field, *say*	POLOCYTE
play		*playing* [Hamlet]	THELMA
[nine-act] *play*	ANCIENT [parts] *in*	*playing* [role]	LORE
	play PRATS, STRAP, TRAPS	playpen, *say*	DRAMATIST
play	TOY	**plea**	
• play-boy	TOYED	plea	O
play *around*	PLA–Y, TO–Y	• plea for organ	OLIVER
play-boy	BRANDED, WINSLOW	• plea to allow some, *say*	OMASUM
	TOYED	• plea to congregate	ORALLY
play-group	BRASS, STRINGS		*(see also* PLEASE)
	CAST, SIDE, TEAM	plea, *say*	PREYER
	(see also players *below)*	pleas, *say*	PLEASE
play-group, *say*	MINISCULE	**plead**	
play (Japanese)	NO(H)	plead	BEG
play of [T S Eliot]	LITOTES	• continue pleading, *say*	BEGONE
play on	ACTON, BATON	• plead for island, *say*	BEGUILE
	GAME LEG	• plead strongly	BEGHARD
play on [words]	SWORD	• plead *with* alien	BEGET

pleasant

pleasant *at first*	P
pleasant associations	NICETIES
pleasant Sunday afternoon	PSA
pleasant pasture, *say*	FAIRLY, NICELY
pleasant, *say*	GNEISS

please

please	
–be Ronald	OBERON
–be revolutionary	OBECHE
–change	OVARY
–dance, *say*	OGIVE
–don't die	OLIVE
–fly	OWING
–line up	ORANGE
–scrap	OPHITE
–snap her, *say*	OBITER
–stay, *say*	OTARY
	(*see also* plea)
please make notes	DOSING
please, *say*	PLEAS

pledge

pledge, *say*	GAUGE
pledge taker	TT, UNCLE
pledges	–IOUS

plenty

plenty of remedies, *say*	MANICURES
plenty of scope	A–Z

plough

plough [field]	FILED
ploughed up [earth]	HATER, HEART, RATHE
ploughman	SHAREHOLDER
ploughman, *say*	MANTILLA
ploughman's position	ATTRACTOR

plucky

plucky attempt	PIZZICATO
plucky player	HARPIST

plug | AD(VERT)

plumbers' association | SOUNDING BOARD

plump

plump friend	FATALLY
plump man	FATAL

plunder

plunder a . . .	omit a
plunder gold	omit AU, OR
plunder money	omit L
plunder, *say*	LUTE
plunder *	omit *
• *plunder* silver *from* vill(ag)e	VILLE

plural	PLU(R)
Pluto	DIS
Plymouth Brethren	PB
PM's address	TEN, X
pneumatic drill	AEROBICS
poacher	COOKER

pocket

pocket a . . .	incl A
pocket *	incl *
• Ma–e *pockets* a penny	MADE
pocketed by *	incl in *
• penny *pocketed by* Ma–e	MADE

Poe

letter *to* Poe	POEM, POET
[Poe's] *characters*	POSE

poem | IF, ODE, VERSE

poet

poet	AE, DANTE, DUNNE, ELIOT EZRA, HOOD et al BARD, SWAN
poet laureate	PL
poet *with* economist	MILTON KEYNES
poet's flower	CAMPION
poet's inspiration	ERATO
poet's pen	POUND
poet's weight	POUND
poets	PEN

poetic

poetic	INVERSE
poetic	
indicating old words	
used by various poets	
by phrases such as	
• *according to Spenser*, bent	CORBE
• *as the poet said* again	AGEN
• *often used in poetry*	OFT
• *poetic* peasant	SWAIN
• *poetically* gloomy	DARKSOME
• *Shakespeare's* child	COLLOP

point¹

point	PT
• a point	APT
• point *behind* painter	RAPT
• princess *has* point . . .	INAPT
point	HEAD
• girl *has a* point	MAIDENHEAD
• point *to* vessel	HEADSHIP
• *put* point *to* teacher	HEADMASTER
point	NESS
• good point	FAIRNESS
• invalid point	ILLNESS
• tapering point	SHARPNESS

point²

point	N, S, E, W
• game point	NAPE
• point *to* point	EN, WE
• point to point	ETON, STOW
and	
• he points *out*	SHEW
• points out	SNOUT
• points *out* a woman	SEVEN
point behind	EASTERN

Letter replaced \c\at; Omit (a); Pointers *out*; Retain <u>a</u>; Split B_ED; Down (D); Backwards <or ^

point *out*	omit N, S, E, W
point *taken*	incl N, S, E, W
pointed	incl N, S, E, W
• *pointed* ears	NEARS, SEARS
	SWEARS, WEARS
• *pointed* gun	WARMS
• *pointed* heels	SCADS
pointed stake, *say*	PICQUET
pointer *to* worker, *say*	NORTHERNER etc
pointless	LOVE, TIP-OFF
pointless	omit N, S, E, W
• *pointless* li(e)	LI
• *pointless* (s)ort . . .	ORT
points against	ENCOUNTER
points *out*	N, S, E, W at each end
• he points *out* . . .	WHEN
poise	P
poisoner	
poisoner	ASP, SNAKE
poisonous [snake]	SKEAN, SNEAK
Poland	PL
pole	
in polar regions	(in) N–S
• *French* one *in* polar regions	NUNS
polar regions	NS
• he *goes to* polar regions	HENS
pole	N, S
• he *is leading* Poles	HENS
• pointer *between* poles	NARROWS
• Poles *in* characteristic . . .	TRANSIT
pole	NP, PO, SP
	PERCH, ROD, STAFF
pole-axed [beast]	BASTE, BATES, BEATS
pole position	POST
Pole Star	POLARIS
Pole-star gazer	COPERNICUS
poles *apart*	omit N, S
polesquatter's home	PERSONAL COLUMN
police	
police	CID
• managed police	RANCID
• police *with* queen	CIDER
• port authority police	PLACID
police	FORCE
• character *has* police . . .	AIRFORCE
• county police	DOWNFORCE
• police *nearly* complete . . .	FORCEFUL
police	MET
• police have English . . .	METE
• police in charge	METIC
• policeman	METAL, METED
police	RUC
• police *break* [into] . . .	RUCTION
• police *in* live . . .	BRUCE
• police *return*<	CUR
police	YARD

• police truncheon	YARDSTICK
• police weapon	YARDARM
• support the police	BACKYARD
police artist	CONSTABLE
police car	BLACK MARIA, PANDA
	STATION WAGON
Police Constable	BOBBY, PC
Police Corps	RMP
police district	MANOR
police power	FORCE
policeman	BIZZY, BLUEBOTTLE
	BOG(E)Y, BUSY, MP
	MR PLOD, PC, ROZZER
policeman	COP
• policeman *standing in*	
front of queen	COPER
• policemen *with* one lot . . .	CO-PILOT
• policeman *with* unknown	
animal	COPYCAT
policemen, *say*	COPSE
policewoman	FAIR COP
polish[1]	
polish	RUB
• good polish	GRUB
• polish statue	RUBICON
and	
• polish (=rub-up)(D)^	BUR
polish	SHINE
Polish[2]	
Polish capital	ZLOTY
Polish *capital*	P
Polish *flower*	VISTULA
Polish expert	BUFF
Polish *leader*	P
Polish translation	GLOSS
Reverse Polish Notation	RPN
politic	
Political and Economic Planning	PEP
political leader	PM
political *leader*	P
political opponents	CLEFT
politician	CON
• become a politician	BEACON
• politician punished	CONFINED
politician	LAB
• fine politician	FLAB
• politician's speech	LABORATORY
politician	LIB
• good politician	GLIB
• politician *has the Spanish* . . .	LIBEL
politician	MP
• a politician *in* the study	DAMPEN
• lawyer *with* politician	DAMP
politician	TORY
• politician's claim	AMATORY
• *put* list *in front of*	

politician	ROTATORY
politicians do . . .	PARTY
poll	
poll tree	(l)ARCH
poll (t)ree	REE
polling (d)ay	AY
pollute	
[oil] *pollution*	–OLI
polluted [air]	RIA
pollution of [stream]	MASTER, REMAST
polo	MERCHANT OF VENICE
pond	ATLANTIC (OCEAN)
ponder	
ponder it, *say*	MULLET
ponder, *say*	MEWS, WAY (UP)
pondered, *say*	WADE
pontifical	AARONIC
Pooh	
Pooh	BEAR
• on behalf of Pooh	FOR(E)BEAR
• Pooh can . . .	BEARABLE
• Pooh's relatives	BEARSKIN
poor	
poor	BAD
• learner *in* poor . . .	BALD
• poor china	BADMINTON
poor	BROKE
• 100 poor . . .	COFF
• poor finish	OFFEND(ING)
poor, *say*	PORE, POUR
poor	(in) NE–ED
• *poor* race	NETTED
• *poor* saint	NESTED
• poor meal, *say*	POORT
• son *has* poor . . .	SPOOR
and	
• poor *and* thin, *say*	PAULINE
• poor Kate, *say*	PORCATE
• poor solution, *say*	PORKY
poor	STONY
poor	WEAK
• junction *with* poor . . .	TWEAK
• poor fish	WEAKLING
poor builder	JERRY
poor golfer	RABBIT
poor grades	DE–
poor horse	JADE, ROSINANTE, TIT
poor [relation]	ORIENTAL
poor service	FAULT, LET
poorly	ILL, SICK
poorly [made]	DAME, EDAM, MEAD
poorly made [table]	BLEAT, BLATE
poorly qualified, *say*	DEGRADE(D)
pop	
pop	FATHER

pop	PA
• pop *back*<	AP
• pop in	PAIN
• pop *up*(D)^	AP
pop *in*	incl PA
• the others pop *in*	REPAST
pop *into*	incl PA
• pop *into* a–rt . . .	APART
pop	DAD
• pop *back again*	DAD
• pop *up* again(D)^	DAD
pop song	INLAY
pop up again(D)^	ER
rat *pops up* (D)^	TAR
	(*see also* popular)
pope	
pope	ALEXANDER, CLEMENT, PAUL et al
pope	PAPA
• pope *takes* a diocese, *say*	PAPACY
• pope with . . .	PAPAW
• pope's rota	PAPALIST
	SSD
popular	
popular	LAIC, LAY
popular	IN
• popular *and* cosy, *say*	INKOSI
• popular demand	INEXACT
• popular dog	INCUR
• popular food, *say*	INBRED
• popular form of writing	INCURSIVE
• popular group	INSET
• popular leader	INDUCE
• popular monarch	INKING
• popular officer	IN GENERAL, INMATE
• popular nurse	INSISTER
• popular place	INPUT
• popular present	INHERE
• popular team	INSIDE
popular	HOT
• popular song	HOT AIR
• son *has* popular . . .	SHOT
• son *in* popular . . .	HOST
popular	POP
• pop song	INLAY
pork-pie wrapper	HATBAND
pornographic	
pornographic publication	BLUEPRINT
pornographic writer	BLUE PENCIL
porridge	
porridge	PRISON
porridge-maker	OATMEAL
port	
port	ADEN, DOVER, ORAN, RIO etc
• student *has* port	LADEN
• port only	DOVER SOLE
• port *surrounded by* iron . . .	FORANE

Letter replaced \c\at; Omit (a); Pointers *out*; Retain a̱; Split B_ED; Down (D); Backwards <or ^

• port *with* square . . .	RIOT
port	L, LEFT, LT
• port in debt	LOWING
• sea port	SEAL
and	
• port deliveries	LEFT-OVERS
• port that is . . .	LEFTIE
• port worker	LEFT HAND
and	
• exist *before* port . . .	BELT
• space *in* port	LENT
port	WINE
• port authority	OENOPHILE
• second port	SWINE
port authority	PLA
• port authority building	PLASHED
• port authority fiddle	PLAGUE
• port authority leader	PLACID
port wine	BORDEAUX, MALAGA
portable lamp	LIGHT
portion	
portion of cake	CA, KE
portion of h/is sue/t . . .	ISSUE
portion of lobster	CLAW
portion, *say*	PEACE, PEAS, PEES
portly porter	STOUT
portmanteau	GEAR-BOX
portray	
portrayed in Gothi/c art on/ show	CARTON
portrayed in [oils]	SILO, SOIL
Portugal	LUSITANIA, P
posh	
posh	U
• posh fur	USABLE
• posh knight, *say*	USER
• posh party	UDO
posh car	LIMO, RR
position	
position of	
–actor	ONSET
–Americans, *say*	OVERHEAR
–school governor	OVERHEADS
–sleeper	UNDERLINES
position, *say*	CITE, SIGHT
positive	
positive negative	NEVER
positive principle	YANG
possess	
possess *	incl *
• w–e *possess* an . . .	WANE
possessed by mo/st ag/es	STAG
possessed by *	incl in *
• mineral *possessed by* the–m	THEOREM
possible	
indicating an anagram:	
• *possibility of* [rain]	IRAN, RANI

• *possibly* [an erg]	RANGE
indicating a homophone:	
• made *possibly* . . .	MAID
• *possibly* grown	GROAN
indicating one of a class:	
• Rover, *possibly*	SCOUT
• scout, *possibly*	ROVER
post	
post card	PC
post-chaise	MAIL COACH
post-date	APPOINTMENT
post-graduate	BA, MA
post-holder	LETTER BOX
post-impressionism	FRANKING, STAMPING
post office	PO
• post office advanced a,	POLENTA
• post office is over . . .	POISON
• post office work	POOP
post-office order	POO
post, *say*	MALE, STEAK
post town	PT
postal order	PO
postman, *say*	MAIL
postmaster	PM
Postmaster-General	PMG
postscript	PS
poster	
poster	AD
• 50 posters	LADS
• poster at this point	ADHERE
• poster *placed by* Liberal	AD LIB
poster	BILL
pot	
pot-bellied, *say*	TUBIFORM
pot-plant	GRASS
pot-thrower	PITCHER
potman's jacket, *say*	REEFER
potted bird, *say*	SHOTTEN
potter's achievement	BREAK, CLEARANCE
potter's ball	WHITE
potter's craft	GAMESMANSHIP
	ONE-UPMANSHIP
potter's colours	BLACK, BLUE, BROWN,
	GREEN, PINK, YELLOW
potato	
potato	MURPHY, SPUD
	TATER, TAT(T)IE
potato disease, *say*	TUBERCULOSIS
potato king	EDWARD
potat͟o *peel*	PO
potential	
[great] *potential*	GRATE
[it was] *potentially* . . .	WAIST
potential [in postman]	POINTSMAN
potential queen	PAWN
potentially [a choir man]	HARMONICA

Anag [cat]; Any *; Begin IGN–; Endings –ING; eg •; Hidden /cat/; Implied add (on); Implied in (in);

poultry

poultry country	TURKEY
poultry-maid, *say*	ENCOUNTER

pound

£1.05	NEW GUINEA
five hundred pounds	MONKEY
pound	L, LB
• each one pound	PERIL
• fifty pounds	LL
• one pound	AL, ALB, IL, ILB, L, LB
• pound *and* a quarter	LE, LEAST
• pound *and* three quarters	LEES, LENS
• pound note	LA, LB, LC, LD, LE, LF, LG
• pound notes	LAC(E), LAD(E), LAG
	LE(A)D, LEAF, LEE, LEG
pound	QUID
• pound will, *say*	QUIDDLE
• *put a pound on by* morning	QUIDAM
• second pound	SQUID
pound for poet	EZRA
pound notes	STRUM
pound sign	LIBRA
pounded [table]	BLEAT, BLATE
twenty-five pounds	PONY

pour

poured into *	incl in *
• drink *poured into* jug–s	JUGGINS
poured out [gins]	–INGS, SING

powder

powder-room	MAGAZINE
powdered [face]	CAFE
powdered head	GROUNDNUT
powdery [snow]	OWNS, SOWN

power　　　　　　　HP, P, VIS

power bloc	E, W
powerboat	STEAMSHIP
powerful dives	PLUTOCRAT
powerful influence	STRONGHOLD
powerful man	QUEEN
powerful tug	TOWER OF STRENGTH
powerhouse	MOD, PENTAGON
powerless	omit P
• powerless (p)resident	RESIDENT

p-piece	PARTICLE, PENNY-WHISTLE
p-pole	PROD
practice	–ISM
practice costume	HABIT

praise

praise	CLAP
• praise gin	CLAPTRAP
• praise woman, *say*	CLAPPER
• shout praise	THUNDERCLAP
praise	LAUD
• a very quiet praise	APPLAUD
• praise a politician	LAUDATORY
• praise ruler	LAUDER

and	
• praises, *say*	LORDS
praise, *say*	PRAYS, PREYS

prance

prance [about]	U-BOAT
prancing [horse]	SHORE

precede

following precedent	T
precedence of king	K
preceding MP	LO
preceptors	CP

precious

precious fish	TWEELING
precious girl	PEARL, RUBY

precise

precise time	PRIMAGE
precise particle	EXACTION
precisely (=to a T)	
• everything *precisely* . . .	TALL
• Pale? *Precisely*	WANT
• *precisely* because . . .	FORT

preferred girl	BLONDE
pregnant woman	LADY-IN-WAITING
prelate	DD

prelude

prelude to Act I	A
spirited *prelude*	S

premature

premature *end*	E
premature end to tri(p)	TRI–

premiere

film *premiere*	F
premiere of play	P

pre-pack

pre-packed	(in) BA–G
• *pre-packed* tin	BATING
pre-*packed*	(in) PR–E
• *pre-packed* at . . .	PRATE

prepare

preparation of [team and] . . .	MANDATE
prepare(D)^	WARD
prepare for execution	ENGROSS
prepare [meal]	LAME, MALE
prepared	ALA
prepared letter	SAE
prepared [tea]	ATE, EAT
prepared to	
–play about, *say*	WOODLARK
–stand up, *say*	WOODCOCK
–take a job, *say*	WOODWORK
–talk, *say*	WOODCHAT

preposterous

preposterous [idea]	AIDE
preposterously [garbed]	BADGER, BARGED

present

present	AD

Letter replaced \c\at; Omit (a); Pointers *out*; Retain a; Split B_ED; Down (D); Backwards <or ^

• many present	MAD	press	IRON
• present with *German* . . .	ADMIT	• press agent	IRON
present	GIVE	• Press Club	IRON(WOOD)
• no present	OGIVE	• press teams	IRONSIDES
• present name	GIVEN	• pressing	IRONWORK
present	HERE	• press function	IRONWORK
• fashionable present	INHERE	press agent	(STEAM) ROLLER
• present company	COHERE	press ahead	SURGEON
• present for daughter	HEREFORD	Press Association	PA
• present song, *say*	HEREDITY	press cutting	PAPER CLIP
and		press gang	CROWD
• present, *say*	HEAR	press game	SQUASH
• second present, *say*	SHEAR	press notice	NEW-SAD
present	PR	**pretend**	
• I'm present above . . .	IMPROVER	pretend, *say*	FAIN, FANE
• present at . . .	PRAT	pretend to look	SEEM
present at robbery	ATHEIST	*pretending to be* [dead]	EDDA
present day	AD	**pretty**	
• people *in the present day*	AMEND	pretty	DISHY
• present day period	ADAGE	pretty	FAIR
• *present day* clothes	ADDRESSES	• a quiet, pretty . . .	AFFAIR
present day	BIRTHDAY, CHRISTMAS	• pretty road	FAIRWAY
present day animals	REINDEER	and	
present day visitor	FATHER	• pretty line, *say*	PHARAOH
	CHRISTMAS	pretty clever	CUTE
	SANTA CLAUS	pretty *conclusive*	TY
present pupil	PP	pretty girl	BELLE, CUTIE, DISH
present stream	CURRENT		DOLLY, PEACH, STUNNER
present time	AD, BIRTHDAY, CHRISTMAS	**prevent**	
present writer	I, ME	prevent profit	BARGAIN
preserve		prevent *revolutionary<* . . .	POTS
preservationists	NT	**previous**	
preserve	BOTTLE	previous	EX
• athlete preserves . . .	BLUEBOTTLES	• previous wrong	EXTORT
• preserve nerve	BOTTLENECK	• previously first	EXIST
preserve	CAN	• previously played	EXACTED
• German preserves, *say*	JERRICANS		(*see also* old)
• preserve *aboard*	SCANS	previous address	
• preserve city	CANNY	indicating title used	
preserve	TIN	in front of name:	
• preserve city	TINNY	• ambassador's	
• preserve *in very Spanish* . . .	MUTINY	address	EXCELLENCY, HE
• the *French* preserve . . .	LATIN	• king's address	MAJESTY
preserve cat	MARMALADE	• vicar's address	REV
preserve jam	PICKLE		(*see also* address)
preserve tar	SALT	**price**	
preserved	(in) CA–N, (in) TI–N	price	PR
preserved in bri/ne ver/y . . .	NEVER	(p)rice *cut*	RICE
president		price-earnings ratio	PE
president	ABE, IKE et al	price I have . . .	COSTIVE
	CHAIR	price index	CPI, RPI
	P, PR, PRES	price maintenance	RPM
presidential address	WHITE HOUSE	price of beer, *say*	ALECOST
president's position	OVERSTATES	price per page, *say*	PERFORATE
press		Prices and Incomes Board	PIB
press	DECREASE	**pride**	GANGLIONS

priest

French priest	ABBE, CURE
priest	AARON
priest	ELI
• priest dead, *say*	ELIDED
• priest quoted	ELICITED
• priest *takes* note	ELIDE
priest	ENOCH
priest	PR
• priest *and* philosopher	PRAYER
• priest *has* no dossier	PROFILE
• priest *with* order	PROBE
priest	REV(D)
• priest *by* lake	REVERIE
• priest is fine	REVOKE
• priest is Irish	REVERSE
priest *with* friend	PASTORALLY
priestess	HERO, PYTHIA
priesthood	COWL

Priestley

characters in [Priestley]...	PERISTYLE
[Priestley] *novel*	PERISTYLE

primary

primary colour	CARDINAL
primary colour	C
primary school	S
primarily about the ...	AT
primarily seen in very young ...	IVY

prime

prime example of the ...	T
prime example of the style	S
prime item in collection	C
prime material	GUNPOWDER
Prime Minister	CABINET MAKER, PM
Prime Minister	M
prime mover	M
prime mover in revolt	R
prime piece (=first letter)	
• *prime piece of* beef	B
prime requirement in politician	P
prime sheep	START-UP

primitive

primitive	UR
primitive man	URGENT
primitive instinct	ID
primitive, *say*	ALIMENTARY

Primrose League PL

prince

prince	P, PR, RAS
Prince Albert	ELECTORAL
Prince Edward Island	PEI
princess	ANNE, DI, IDA
	INA, REGAN

principal

principal	HEAD
• power in principal ...	PINHEAD
• principal country	HEADLAND
• principal method	HEADWAY
principal	TOP
• bend principal ...	STOP
• principal problem	TOPKNOT
• principal spinner	TOP
principal charge	PRIME
Principal Clerk of Sessions	PCS
principal directors	STARBOARD
Principal Medical Officer	PMO
principal assistant	A
principally made of wood	MOW

print

print supplier	FINGER(TIP)
printed material	BATIK
printer's measure	EL, EM, EN
printers	CUP, OUP
	NGA, SOGAT

prison

prison	BIRD
prison	CAN
• prison area	CANZONE
• prison *has* so ...	CANTHUS
• prison work	CANOPUS
prison	CLINK, COOLER
prison	HOCK
• prison in Greek ...	HOCKING
• second prison	SHOCK
prison	JUG
prison	NICK
• ancient prison	OLD NICK
• prison *with* the Spanish ...	NICKEL
• second prison	SNICK
prison	NICKNAME
prison	PEN
• prison monster	PENDRAGON
• prison *near* New York	PENNY
• second prison exactly	SPENT
prison	QUAD
• prison animal	QUADRAT
• prison square	QUAD
• second prison	SQUAD
prison	STIR
• live *with* prison ...	BESTIR
• prison breakfast	STIR-FRY
• prison circle	STIRRING
prison camp	OFFLAG, STALAG
• prison-camp child, *say*	STALAGMITE
prison food	PORRIDGE
prison labour	CONFINEMENT
prisoner	BIRDMAN
prisoner	CON
• educated prisoner	MACON
• prisoner in Eastern ...	CONINE
• prisoner's rights	CONSTRUES
prisoner	LAG

Letter replaced \c\at; Omit (a); Pointers *out*; Retain a; Split B_ED; Down (D); Backwards <or ^

• escaped prisoner	OFFLAG
• strong prisoner	FLAG
• prisoner *with* nothing on	LAGOON
prisoner of war	POW

private

private	GI
• private member	GIMP
• private road	GIST
• private transport	GIBUS
private	GUNNER
• private article	GUNNERA
private	INNER
• 500 private . . .	DINNER
• private chapel	INNER TEMPLE
• private circle	INNER RING
• private soldier	INNER MAN
private	TOMMY (ATKINS)
• private bunk	TOMMY ROT
• private saloon	TOMMY BAR
• private weapon	TOMMY GUN
private automatic exchange	PAX
private branch exchange	PBX
private carrier	TROOPSHIP
private *entrance*	P
private *French* . . .	ENTRE NOUS
private home	BARRACKS, DUGOUT
	FOXHOLE, TENT,
	TRENCH
private hope	STRIPE(S)
private soldier	PTE
private soldier, *say*	RANCOUR
private soldiers	OR
private transport	TROOPSHIP
Privy Councillor	PC

prize

prize animal	MEDALLION, START-UP
prize-ring	PR
prize, *say*	PRIES, TROPHI
probationary	PRO

probe

probe *	incl in *
• one *probing* scheme	PILOT

problem

[great] *problem*	GRATE
problem	SUM
problem children	ISSUE
problem	RUB
• 500 problems	DRUBS
• namely, a problem	SCRUB
• problem I leave	RUBIGO
problem putter	POSER
problem [solved is] . . .	DISSOLVE
problematical, [the gain] . . .	HEATING

proceed

proceed	GOAT, GOON
proceeds of [sale]	ALES, LEAS, SEAL

process

[nuclear] *process*	UNCLEAR
process of [law]	AWL
processed [peas]	APSE
processing [past] . . .	PATS, TAPS
processor	CPU

proclaim

proclaim birth	BERTH
proclaiming great . . .	GRATE
procrastinator's declaration	IDOLATER

produce

[counter]-*productive*	RECOUNT, TROUNCE
[garden] *produce*	DANGER, RANGED
produce air	COMPOSE, PLAY, SING
produce animal	BEAR
produce notes	PLAY, SING
produced by goats	MOHAIR
produced by [goats]	TOGAS
produced in mo/st are/as	STARE
producer of [fir cone]	CONIFER
producer of turnips	WATCHMAKER
produces eggs, *say*	LAZE
producing [notes]	ONSET, STONE
	TONES
product [I sent]	INSET, TINES
product of [Iran]	RAIN, RANI
product of I/ran, Ge/rmany . . .	RANGE
production of [stage] . . .	GATES

profess

profession, *say*	CHOREA, KOREA
professional	ACE
• many professionals	LACES, MACES
• professional *follows*	
the sun	SOLACE
• quiet professional	PACE
professional	DAB-(HAND)
• acceptable *in* a professional	DAUB
• professional lost some blood	DABBLED
• professional plot	DABBED
professional	PRO
• professional criminal	PROROGUE
• professional *in* service dress	SPROD
• professional model	PROPOSER, PROSIT
Professional Golfers'	
Association	PGA
Professor of Theology	STP
professor's address	LECTURE
	(*see also* expert)

profit

ban profit	BARGAIN
profit continues	PROCEEDS
profit, *say*	PROPHET, SEER
profit *to* the people	DIVINATION

prohibit

prohibit	BAN
• prohibit 500 . . .	BAND

Anag [cat]; Any *; Begin IGN–; Endings –ING; eg •; Hidden /cat/; Implied add (on); Implied in (in);

• prohibit fruit, *say*	BANBURY
• prohibit ruler	BANK(ING)
and	
• bone prohibited, *say*	RIBBAND
• prohibited mineral, *say*	BANDORE
prohibit	BAR
• prohibit cartel	BARRING
• prohibit fruit, *say*	BARBARY
• prohibit profit-making	BARGAIN
and	
• prohibited obstruction, *say*	BARDLET
• reserves prohibited, *say*	TABARD
prohibitionist placard	BANNER

project

project players	CAST
projected, *say*	THRONE, THROUGH
projecting place	CINEMA
projection	EAR
projectionist	MERCATOR

prominent

prominence	TOR
prominently-featured Communist	STARRED

promiscuous

[a bit] *promiscuous*	BAIT
promiscuous [roués]	ROUSE

promise

promise peg	COMMITTEE
promises to pay	–IOUS
promissory note	IOU, PN

promote

promote ruler	RAISER
promote ruler, *say*	RAZOR
promote star(D)^	RATS
promote worker, *say*	RASANT
promoting, *say*	RAISIN
promotion of tiler(D)^	RELIT

prompt service	AUTOCUE
prone to perjury	LYING

pronounce

pronounce complete	UTTER
pronounced gait	GATE
pronouncement is not . . .	KNOT

proof	GALLEY

prop

prop up bar(D)^	REVEL
prop, *say*	SURE

propagate

propagate [roses]	SORES
propagate, *say*	SEW, SO, SOUGH
propagation of [tubers]	BRUTES, BUSTER

proper

proper	MEET
• assist proper . . .	HELPMEET
• proper encounter	MEET
and	
• proper *and* good, *say*	MEAT-PIE

• proper, *say*	MEAT, METE
proper	PRIM
• one *in* proper . . .	PRIAM
• proper ruler	PRIMER
• proper sign	PRIMARIES
proper	REAL
• proper amount	REALLOT
• proper eyes, *say*	REALISE
• proper place	REALLOCATION
properly built [theatre]	THEREAT

property

property	PTY
property charge	ATTRIBUTE
property conveyance	ESTATE CAR
Property Services Agency	PSA

prophet

prophet	AMOS, ELI, ELISHA
	MOSES et al
prophetess	CASSANDRA, DEBORAH
	SIBYL, SYBYL
prophetic article	VATICAN
prophet's grandmother	MOSES

proportion

proportion of e/lector/ate	LECTOR
proportional representation	PR

proprietary	PTY

prosecute

prosecute	SUE
• is prosecuted	ISSUED
• prosecute Edward, *say*	SUITED
• prosecute it, *say*	SUET
• prosecute Scotsman, *say*	SUMACH
and	
• prosecuted a politician, *say*	SUDATORY
• prosecuted, *say*	PSEUD

prosperous

prosperous part	SE
pros/per/ous *part*	PER

prostitute

prostitute	HOOKER
• prostitute, *say*	HOOKA(H)
prostitute	PRO
• prostitute's clientele	PROFILE
• prostitute's weight . . .	PROGRAM(ME)
	PROTON
prostitute	TART
• prostitute *in* ship	STARTS
• prostitute *has* a run . . .	TARTAR
• prostitute's fee	TARTRATE
prostitute	WHORE
• prostitute laments, *say*	HORMONES
• prostitute, *say*	HOAR

protect

protected by *	incl in *
• a king *protected by* c–at	CARAT

Letter replaced \c\at; Omit (a); Pointers *out*; Retain a̱; Split B_ED; Down (D); Backwards <or ^

protecting a . . .	incl A
protecting *	incl *
• c–at *protecting* a king	CARAT
protector	CROMWELL, NOLL
	GLOVE, OVERALL, HELMET
Protestant Episcopal	PE
proton number	Z
Proust	
[Proust] *novel*	SPROUT, STUPOR
prove	
prove of use [in the] . . .	THINE
proves to be [wrong]	GROWN
Provencal	PR
proverb	
proverbially	
–bald	COOT
–black	DEVIL, INK, SOOT, YOUR HAT
–blind	BAT
–bright	BUTTON
–brown	BERRY
–clean	WHISTLE
–clear	BELL
–cold	CHARITY, ICE
–cool	CUCUMBER
–cunning	FOX
–daft	BRUSH
–dead	DODO, DOORNAIL, MUTTON
–deaf	POST
–deep	OCEAN
–drunk	LORD
–dull	DITCHWATER
–fast	LIGHTNING
–fat	PIG
–flat	PANCAKE
–fresh	PAINT
–happy	LARK, SANDBOY
–high	KITE
–hot	HELL
–mad	HATTER, MARCH HARE
–miserable	SIN
–nice	PIE
–old	HILLS
–patient	SAINT
–plain	PIKESTAFF
–poor	CHURCH MOUSE
–pretty	PICTURE
–pure	SNOW
–quick	FLASH, LIGHTNING
–red	BLOOD
–rich	CROESUS
–right	NINEPENCE, RAIN, TRIVET
–rough	BADGER
–sick	DOG, PARROT
–slow	SNAIL, TORTOISE
–sly	FOX
–smooth	SILK

–snug	BUG (IN A RUG)
–soft	BUTTER, PUTTY
–strong	BULL, LION, OX
–sweet	HONEY, SUGAR
–thick	(TWO) PLANK(S), THIEVES
–thin	LATH, RAKE
–tight	DRUM, NEWT
–ugly	DEVIL, SIN
–weak	KITTEN, WATER
–white	GHOST, LILY, SHEET, SNOW
–wide	BARN DOOR
provide	
provide a seat	ELECT
provide material for [a new]	WANE, WEAN
provide refuge for a . . .	incl A
provide refuge for *	incl *
• *provide refuge for*	
sheep *in* time	HEWER
provide shelter for a . . .	incl A
provide shelter for *	incl *
• w–e *provide shelter for* an . . .	WANE
provided	IF, LENT, SO
provided by [friends]	FINDERS
provided in lar/ge ar/eas	GEAR
providing	IF
providing [arms]	MARS, RAMS
provision-merchant, *say*	GROSSER
province	
some Canadian provinces:	
Alberta	ALBA, ALTA
British Columbia	BC
Manitoba	MAN
New Brunswick	NB
Newfoundland	NF(D)
Nova Scotia	NS
Ontario	ONT
Quebec	PQ, Q, QUE
provincial	
provincial (=dialect)	
• *provincial* girl	GAL
• *provincial* man	MUN
• *provincial* partner	BUTTY
• *provincial* worker	EMMET
provision	
provisional accommodation	DEEP FREEZE
	FREEZER, FRIDGE, LARDER
	PANTRY, REFRIGERATOR
provoke	
provoke	NEEDLE
• provoke lady	NEEDLEWOMAN
• provoke saints	NEEDLESS
provoke	STIR (UP)
• provoke *following* live . . .	BESTIR
• provoke king	STIRK
• provoke, *say*	STIRRUP
Provost Marshal	PM

Anag [cat]; Any *; Begin IGN–; Endings –ING; eg •; Hidden /cat/; Implied add (on); Implied in (in);

prowl		[rice] *pudding*	CIRE, ERIC
prowling [lion]	LINO	**Puerto Rico**	PR
[wolf] *on the prowl*	FLOW, FOWL	**puff**	
Prudential	PRU	puff	AD
prune		puff oxygen	GUSTO
prune (h)us(h)	US	puff will, *say*	TOOTLE
prune plan(t)	PLAN	puffy nose	SNOUT
prune spruce	TRIM	**pull**	
psalm		pull	DRAW
psalm	PS(A)	• having pull	WITHDRAW
psalmist	DAVID	• pull in front	DRAWLED
Psalms	PSA(A)	• pull spanner	DRAWBRIDGE
psychokinesis	PK	pull	LUG
psychotic state	DT	• pull *aboard*	SLUGS
public		• pull fruit	LUGGAGE
public	OVERT	• quietly pull	PLUG
• many public . . .	COVERT	pull	TOW
• public ballot-box	OVERTURN	• pull *aboard*	STOWS
• public individual	OVERTONE	• pull knight, *say*	TOWSER
• public works	OVERTOPS	pull	TUG
public address (system)	PA	• pull *in front of* artist	TUGRA
public building	PO	• pull *round* king	TRUG
public good	PB	pull American	YANK
pub(lic house)	BAR	pull *back<*	GARD, GUL, GUT, WARD
• bird *in front of* pub	CROWBAR	*pull out of* dangerou/s	
• pub brawl	BARROW	ent/erprise	SENT
• pub storage	BARRACKS	*pull out* [stops]	SPOTS
pub(lic house)	INN	pull punch	CLOUT
• local queen	INNER	pull sail	LUG
• pub ghost, *say*	INSPECTOR	pull, *say*	HALL, TOE
pub(lic house)	LOCAL	pull *up*(D)^	GARD, GUL, GUT, WARD
• pub *has* English . . .	LOCALE	*pull up* robe(D)^	EBOR
• pub *is* English	LOCALISE	pull *up round* bend(D)^	GUARD
pub(lic house)	PH	*pull * from*	omit *
• ducks *in* local . . .	POOH	• king *pulled from* T(r)ent	TENT
• pub *has* nothing to . . .	PHOTO	• *pull* wife *from* (w)aves	AVES
public lending right	PLR	*pulled out of* t/he p/lace	HEP
public library	PL	pulling punches	CARTHORSES
public record office	PRO	*pulling* [rank]	KNAR
public relations (officer)	PR(O)	pull*over<*	GARD, GUL, GUT, WARD
Public Service Vehicle	PSV	**pulse code modulation**	PCM
Public Services Authority	PSA	**pulverise**	
publicise		[it was] *pulverised*	WAIST, WAITS
publicise	AIR	*pulverisation of* [oats]	STOA
• publicise *after* many . . .	LAIR	*pulverise* [bran]	BARN
• publicise skill	AIRCRAFT	*pulverise* [pulverise]	REPULSIVE
• publicise wine	AIRPORT	*pulverised* [ash]	HAS
publicity	AD, PR, PUFF	pulverised earth	GROUND
• he *gets* publicity	HEAD	*pulverised* [earth]	HATER, HEART, RATHE
• publicity is over . . .	PRISON	**punch**	
• publicity in second . . .	PUFFINS	punch drunk	WALLOP
publishers	CUP, OUP	punch-*up*(D)^	MAL, PAR
pudding		**punish**	
pudding inside	SAGOIN	*punish* [evil]	LIVE, VILE
pudding [made in] . . .	MAIDEN	*punishing* [sinner]	INNERS
pudding, *say*	SUITE	punishment tires . . .	FATIGUES

Letter replaced \c\at; Omit (a); Pointers *out*; Retain a̲; Split B_ED; Down (D); Backwards <or ^

pupil

pupil	APPLE, L
pupil teacher	PT
pupil's cover	EYELID
pupil's environment	EYE, IRIS

purchase

purchase	BUY
• purchase *round* ring	BUOY
• purchase ruler	BUYER
• purchase cable, *say*	BIFLEX
• purchase cereal, *say*	BICORN
• purchase paper, *say*	BIREME
• purchase ruler, *say*	BIKING
purchase tax	PT

pure

pure	NOVICES
[pure] *chaos*	PUER
pure lake	MERE
pure, *say*	CHASED
pure *sound*	CHASED
pure water	MERE
purify insects	DISINFECTANTS

purée

[orange] *purée*	ONAGER
purée of [leeks]	KEELS, SLEEK

purgatory

purgatory for misers	CLAMSHELL
purgatory for the crazy	NUTSHELL

purify (*see* pure)

purloin

purloin painting	ABSTRACT
purloined, *say*	STOLON

pursue

indicating one word after or
below another word or letter:

• award *pursued by* VIP	MEDALLION
• mother *pursues the French* . . . (D)	LAMA

push

push Black	RAMJET
push forward	SURGEON
push in a . . .	incl A
push in *	incl *
• fish *pushed in* the . . .	GATHER
push in *	incl in *
• *push* penny *into* s–lit	SPLIT
push lighter	BARGE
push over [stool]	LOOTS, TOOLS
push over stool<	LOOTS
push up part . . . (D)^	TRAP
pushover [for a] . . .	FARO
pushover was<	SAW

pussyfoot (CAT'S) PAW

put¹

put *down*(D)^	TUP
put *back*<	TUP
[put] *out*	TUP, UPT–
put *over*<	TUP

put²

indicating inclusion:

put in a . . .	incl A
put in *	incl *
• Greek *put in* cha–ins	CHAGRINS
put round a . . .	incl A
put round *	incl *
• cha–ins *put round* Greek . . .	CHAGRINS
put through *	incl in *
• tyro *put through* p–aces	PLACES

put³

indicating omission:

put aside a . . .	omit A
put aside money	omit D, L, P
put aside *	omit *
• c(are)s are *put aside*	CS
put away a . . .	omit A
put away *	omit *
• ha(sten) *to put away* gun	HA
put out a . . .	omit A
put out *	omit *
• s(cat)ty *to put out* cat	STY

put⁴

other uses:

[nose] *put out*	EONS, NOES
put across	VOTE, X
put an end to	
• Con/stable/ *puts an end to* . . .	STABLE
• *put an end to* man	MANY
• time *puts an end to* man	MANAGE
put an end to Edward	CLOSETED
put away	EAT
put back part<	TRAP
put clock back<	REMIT
put down	BURY, INTER
put down again, *say*	RELAYED
put down ramps	SQUASH RACKETS
put 'em *up*(D)^	ME
put heads together	
• m̲akers o̲f pens s̲hould put heads together	MOPS
put out [cat]	ACT

Q

boat, Celt, cue, electric charge, factor, farthing, fever, five hundred (thousand), heat energy unit, Kelt, koppa, ninety, ninety thousand, Qatar, quadrans, quality, quark, quart, quarter, *quarto*, quartz, Quebec, queen, Queensland, query, question, quetzal, *queue*, quintal, quintus, rational number, ship, sort, train, trichosanthin

Q8	KUWAIT
QE	ER
QEII	SECONDER
quail	COLIN
quake	
[aspen] *quaking*	NAPES, PANES, PEANS
[earth]*quake*	HATER, HEART, RATHE
quaking [in the] . . .	THINE
Quaker City	PHILADELPHIA
qualified	
qualified	BA, MA
qualification of [terms as] . . .	MASTER
	REMAST, STREAM
qualified mother	MAMBA
qualified teacher	BED
qualified [teacher]	CHEATER, RETEACH
quality	
quality	Q
quality improved	STANDARD ROSE
quantity	
quantity of gold	GO
quantity of g/old en/closed	OLDEN
quantity, *say*	WAIT
quarry	
quarry manager	GAME WARDEN
quarry, *say*	PRAY
quart	QT, QU(AR)
quarter	
quarter	N, S, E, W, NE, NW, SE, SW
• quarter horse	SHACK, WHACK
• quarter *to* one	EA, NA, SA, WA
	EI, NI, SI, WI
	NAN, SAN, SWAN, WAN
	NONE
• quarter *to* five	EV, VE
• quarter *to* six	EVI–, VIE, VIN, VIS
• quarter to nine	SIX
• quarter *to* ten	EX–
• quarterly	ELY, SLY
quarter	FRACTION, MERCY, QR, QU(AR)
quarter-deck	D, E, C, K
quarter-deck	C, CLUBS, D, DIAMONDS
	H, HEARTS, S, SPADES
	SUIT
quarter of loaf	L, O, A, F
quarter of Paris	LATIN
quarter of tongue	LATIN
quarter-sessions	QS
quartermaster(-general)	QM(G)
quartermaster(-sergeant	QM(S)
quartet	
quartet	IV
quartet *from* Beethoven	BEET, HOVE, OVEN
quarto	QTO
quash	
quash [riots]	TIROS, TRIOS
['e soon] *quashed* . . .	NOOSE
quasi-stellar object	QSO, QUASAR
quay	
quay, *say*	KEY
quay(side)	PORTEND
queasy	
queasy [when I] . . .	WHINE
[quite] *queasy*	QUIET, –TIQUE
Quebec	Q
queen[1]	
queen	BESS
queen	ER
• queen's circle	ERRING
• queen in charge	ERIC
• Queen Street	ERST
and	
• composer *to* Queen	HOLSTER
• kneel *to* Queen	BENDER
• me and the Queen	MEANDER
• Queen Elizabeth II	SECONDER
• Queen's hotel	INNER
queen	HM, Q, QU, R
Queen Anne	AR
Queen Elizabeth	ER

Queen Mary	MR	question of place	WHERE
Queen Victoria	VIR, VR(I)	question of time	WHEN
queen's letters	ER	question, *say*	GRILLE
queen²		*questionable* [deal]	DALE, LADE
Queen of			LEAD, LEDA
–Carthage	DIDO	questionnaire	FORM
–Cockneys	PEARLIE, PEARLY	**queue**	
–Douglas	MANX CAT	queue	CUE, Q, TAIL
–France	REINE	queue, *say*	CUE, KEW, TALE
–Germany	KONIGIN	**quick**	
–heaven	ASHTORETH	quick	ALIVE
–Italy	REGINA	quick century	C
–Navarre	MARGUERITE	quick cleaner	NAIL FILE
–Sheba	AAZIZ, BALKIS	quick diet	FAST
–spades	BASTA	quick digest	SUMMARY
–Spain	REINA	quick dip	PICKPOCKET, SNEAK THIEF
–the dead	HEL	quick hundred	C
–the fairies	MAB, TITANIA, UNA	quick trim	SMART
–the Nile	CLEO(PATRA)	quick way	FLEET STREET
queen³		quick writer	SWIFT
queen	CAT	quickly (=careless speech)	
• queen of Douglas	MANX CAT	• *quickly* I would . . .	ID(E)
• queen's admirer	TOM(-CAT)	• we will *quickly* . . .	WEAL, WE'LL, WHEEL
• queen's children	KITTENS	quickest way	BEELINE
• queen's mate	TOM(-CAT)	**quid**	
queen city	CINCINATTI	quids *in*	incl LL, LS
queen, *maybe*	CARD, PIECE	• 'e's quids *in*	ELSE
Queen Anne's Bounty	QAB	• she's quids *in*	SHELLS
Queen Elizabeth Hall	QEH	**quiet¹**	
Queen's Bench	QB	fairly quiet	MP
Queen's College	QC	• one fairly quiet . . .	AMP, IMP
Queen's Counsel	QC	• one *in* fairly quiet *surroundings*	MAP
queen's carriage	VICTORIA	• soldier *has* fairly quiet . . .	GIMP
Queen's pudding	CHARLOTTE	quiet	EASE
Queensland	Q	• many quiet . . .	LEASE, MEASE
queer		• quiet, quiet . . .	PEASE
queer	RUM(MY)	• quiet sovereign	EASEL
• queer animal, *say*	RUMBLE	quiet	ODIN
• queer game	RUMMY	quiet	P
• queer graduate	RUMBA	• a quiet bit, ,	APORT
• queer period, *say*	RUMMAGE	• a quiet friend	APPAL
queer practices	CAMPUSES	• a quiet man	APRON
Queer [Street]	RETEST, TESTER	• a quiet square	APT
queerly [spelt]	PELTS	and	P
query	EH	• quiet drink	PALE
question		• quiet road	PLANE
question	EH	• quiet woman	PROSE
• pictures *in* question	EARTH	• quiet worker	PARTISAN
question	PUMP	and	
• energy question	FORCE-PUMP	• insect *has* quiet . . .	BEEP
• question family	PUMPKIN	• little quiet . . .	WEEP
• question MPs	PUMPHOUSE	• motor quietly	CARP
question	Q	quietly *drop off*	omit P
question cook	GRILL	• (p)lumber quietly *drops off*	LUMBER
question of identity	WHO	quietly *left*	omit P
question of motive	WHY	• aircraft quietly *left*	(p)LANE

Anag [cat]; Any *; Begin IGN–; Endings –ING; eg •; Hidden /cat/; Implied add (on); Implied in (in);

very quiet	PP	quintet *from* St/ravin/sky	RAVIN
• a very quiet dog	APPROVER	**quirk**	
• a very quiet fish	APPROACH	*quirk of* [fate]	FEAT
• a very quiet man	APPAL, APPLES	*quirky* [sort]	ROTS, TORS
and		**quip**	
• very quiet *in* the valley	DAPPLE	quip	SALLY
• very quiet *round* a . . .	PAP	quip, *say*	SALLIE
	(*see also* gentle, soft)	**quit**	
quiet²		quit	LEFT
quiet	QT	• 100 quit	CLEFT
• you and I, *say, in* quiet . . .	QUIT	• quit hospital	LEFTWARD
quiet	SH	quit twice	DESERT RAT
• quiet listener	SHEAR	**quite**	
• quiet person	SHONE	quite fair	JUST
• quiet stream	SHRILL	quite heavy, *say*	TONISH
and		quite high	SOUP
• I *am in* quiet *surroundings*	SHIP	quite likely	ON
quiet³		quite sane	NOMAD
quiet dinner, *say*	PIECEMEAL	[quite] *wrong*	QUIET, –TIQUE
quiet in here, *say*	MUTINEER	*quite wrongly* [wrote] . . .	TOWER
quiet thief	RUSTLER	**quiver**	
quiet words	ASIDE, WHISPER	*quivering* [lump]	PLUM
quietener	KO, SH	*quiveringly* [take]	KATE, TEAK
quieter road	TAMERLANE	**quote**	
quietly *converse*	LOUDLY	I *quote*	AYE, EYE
quintal	Q	not *quoted*	KNOT
quintet		*quote* news	GNUS
quintet	V	*quote* [Shaw]	HAWS, WASH

Letter replaced \c\at; Omit (a); Pointers *out*; Retain <u>a</u>; Split B_ED; Down (D); Backwards <or ^

R

are, arithmetic, canine letter, castle, eighty, eighty thousand, gas constant, hand, *king, monarch, month, queen,* radius, *rain,* rand, *ray, reading,* real numbers, Réaumur, received, recipe, rector, regina, registered trademark, Republican, resistance, respond, rex, rho, right, river, *road, Roger,* Romania, röntgen unit, rook, *rotund character, r(o)uble, royal,* run, rupee, Russia, Ryberg's constant, side, *writing*

rabbit		**radiation protection adviser**	RPA
rabbit	BRER, POOR GOLFER	**radio**	
tailless rabbi(t)	RABBI	radio frequency	RF
rabid		radio receiver	ELECTRIC FENCE
[acts] *rabidly*	CATS, SCAT	radio technique	AIRCRAFT
rabid [animal]	LAMINA	radio telephone	RT
race¹		**radiological safety officer**	RSO
race	NATION	**radius**	R, RAD
• change race	ALTERNATION	**ragged**	
• motor race	CARNATION	*ragged* [edges]	SEDGE
• race *with* friend	NATIONALLY	[robes] *ragged . . .*	BORES, SOBER
race	TT	**Ragnarok**	GODSEND
• race *in* circles	OTTO	**Raffles port**	SINGAPORE
• race *round* circuits	TOOT	**rage**	
• race *round* Westminster	TWIT	[depart] *in a rage*	PARTED, PRATED
• road race	MITT	*raging* [gale]	GAEL
race	DERBY, (GRAND) NATIONAL	**railway**	
	OAKS	rail connection	FISH-PLATE
• racehorse	DERBYSHIRE	[rail] *trip*	LIAR, LIRA, RIAL
• gamble *on* race	NATIONAL	railway	BR
	LOTTERY	• railway in Greece	BRING
• southern race	SOAKS	• railway not working	BRIDLE
race²		• railway points	BREW
[horse]*racing*	SHORE	railway	MET
race broadcast	RELAY	• company railway	COMET
race commentator	ETHNOGRAPHER	• put railway *round* a . . .	MEAT
race description	BLOOD RELATION	• railwayman	METAL, METED
race leader	ADAM	railway	RLY
r̲ace *leader*	R	• lay railway *round* east . . .	RELY
race starter	ADAM	• mother *on* the railway	MARLY
r̲ace *starter*	R	• railway *without* record . . .	REPLY
racehorse, *say*	COARSER	railway	RY
races	HEATS	• and *in* railway . . .	RANDY
Racing Club	FLAT IRON	• put railway *round* a . . .	RAY
racing [start]	TARTS	• spoil railway . . .	MARRY
r̲acing *start*	R	railway region	GWR, LMS, LNER, SR
racket skills	RAMPARTS	railway sorting office	RSO
radian	RAD	railway sub-office	RSO
radical	RAD, RED	r̲ailway *termini*	RY
radical [Tory]	TROY	r̲ailway *terminus*	Y

Anag [cat]; Any *; Begin IGN–; Endings –ING; eg •; Hidden /cat/; Implied add (on); Implied in (in);

Railway Traffic Officer	RTO	**ramshackle**	
railwayman	(in) B–R	[quite] ramshackle	QUIET, –TIQUE
railwaymen	NUR, RUNABOUT	*ramshackle* [huts]	SHUT, THUS
railwaymen(D)^	RUN-UP	**ran**	
rain		ran	RAN
rain	R, WATERFALL	• ran *around*	RA–N
rain fell	PELT	• ran *out*	RA–N
rain indicator	SHOWER	• [ran] *out*	ARN
[rain] *squall*	IRAN, RANI	• [ran] *riot*	ARN
[rain]*fall*	IRAN, RANI	• ran *round<*	NAR
[rain]*maker*	IRAN, RANI	• ran *round*	RA–N
[rain]*storm*	IRAN, RANI	ran	SMUGGLED
raise		• many smuggled . . .	CRAN
raise		• smuggled diamonds	RAND
indicating reversal in		• smuggled king *and* queen . . .	RANKER
Down clue(D)^:		ran all the time	RACE DAY
• *raise* boy	YOB	ran daily	EDITED
• *raise* money	NEY, NIT, RENNET	*ran riot* [in Gath]	HATING
• *raise* mug	GUM	ran weekly	EDITED
• *raise* note	RENNET		(*see also* run)
• *raise* objection	STUB, TUB	**rand**	R
• *raised* edge	MIR, PIL	**random**	
• *raised* highway	DR, EVA–, –IM, –TS	*random* [shot]	HOST, HOTS
• *raised* objection	STUB, TUB	*randomly* [cast] . . .	CATS, SCAT
raise back	REAR	**range**	
raise capital	REALISE	*free* [range]	ANGER
raise garret	LOFT	*range* [free]	REEF
[raise] *rent*	AESIR, SERAI	Rangers	QPR
raise your, *say*	RASURE, RAZURE	*ranging* [in on a] . . .	ANION
raised by	UPPER	**rank**	
raised anchor, *say*	WADE	*first* rank	R
raised capital	QUITO	rank *outsiders*	RK
raised family, *say*	BREADLINE	rank, *say*	GREYED
raised flag	KERB(STONE)	ranker, *say*	RANCOUR
raised streak, *say*	WAIL, WHALE	**ransack**	
	WHEAL, WHEEL	*ransack* [drawers]	REDRAWS, REWARDS
raises family	BEARSKIN	[room] *ransacked*	MOOR
rake		**rapid**	
rake	LOTHARIO, RIP	rapid eye movement	REM
rake's epitaph	RIP	rapidly dissipated	FAST
rallying ground	TENNIS COURT	**rare**	
ram		rare bird	RARA AVIS
female ram, *say*	BUTTRESS	*rare* [bird]	DRIB
ram	BUTTER	[rare] *disorder*	REAR
• ram vessel	BUTTERCUP	rare meat	HAMBLED
ramble		*rarely* [read]	DARE, DEAR
ramble in [field]	FILED	**rash**	
rambling [roses]	SORES	rash investigation	SPOT CHECK
rampage		*rash* [step]	PEST, PETS
rampaging [Norse] . . .	SNORE	rasher	BACON
[Huns] *on the rampage*	SHUN	**rate**	
rampant		rate	MPH
rampant [lion]	LINO	rate	SPEED
[spread] *rampantly*	DRAPES, SPARED	• rate-capping	SPEED LIMIT
rampart	LAMB, MUTTON	• rate highly	SPEEDWELL
	SHEEPSHANK	• wife *included in* rate	SPEWED

Letter replaced \c\at; Omit (a); Pointers *out*; Retain a; Split B_ED; Down (D); Backwards <or ^

rate increase	ACCELERATION, TEMPORISE	read in T/he St/rand	HEST
rate of progress	MPH	read it, *say*	RE-EDIT
rate of tax, *say*	LEVIRATE	[read] *out*	DARE, DEAR
[rate] *reform*	TARE, TEAR	*read out* banns	BANS
rating	AB	read, *say*	RED, SCARLET
	(*see also* sailor)	[reading a] *novel*	GARDENIA
rather		*reading of* [letters]	SETTLER
rather	–ISH	*reading* review	REVUE
• rather dull	BLANDISH	reads list	CONSTABLE
	(*see also* like)	[reads] *novel*	DARES, DEARS, RASED
rational number	Q	**readjust**	
rattle		*readjust* [ladies'] . . .	SAILED
rattled [dice]	DECI–, ICED	*readjustment of* [centre]	RECENT
rattle [snake]	SNEAK	**ready**	
rattling [plates]	PETALS, STAPLE	ready	CASH
raucous dog	HUSKY	• ready at this point, *say*	CASHIER
ravage		• ready *to* fight	CASH-BOX
ravage, *say*	PRAY	ready	MONEY
ravager, *say*	PRAYER	• ready *for* sea	DRINK-MONEY
ravaged [by a] . . .	BAY	• ready *to* fight	MONEY-BOX
ravaging [town]	WONT	ready to play	INSTANCE, ONSET
raw		**real**	
<u>r</u>aw *beginner*	R	real numbers	R
raw [deal]	DALE, LADE, LEAD	[real] *potential*	EARL, LEAR, RALE
raw (l)am(b)	AM	real, *say*	PUCKER, REEL
raw, *say*	CREWED, SOAR	[real son]	NEW ORLEANS
ray	X	[real] *trouble*	EARL, LEAR, RALE
razor-man	OCCAM	re(ally) *friendless*	RE
re		**realign**	
re	ABOUT	*realign* [stream]	MASTER, REMAST
• about time	RET	*realigning* [rail]	LAIR, LIAR
• ca–t *goes round* about . . .	CARET		LIRA, RIAL
• landed about . . .	LITRE	*realignment of* [lane]	LEAN
re	AGAIN	**reallocate**	
• felt pain again	REACHED	*reallocate* [letters]	SETTLER
• landed again	RELIT	*reallocation of* [grant I] . . .	GRATIN
• make further mistake	RESIN		RATING
re-		**reappear**	
many words prefixed with re-, some		*reappearance of* [players]	REPLAYS
of which follow, are used to indicate		*reappearing* [later]	ALTER, RATEL
anagrams or reversal		**reapply**	
re-arrange		*reapplication* [to let]	LOTTE
re-arrange [diary]	DAIRY	*reapplied* [his] . . .	–ISH
re-arrange [kingpin]	PINKING	**rear**	
reach		Rear Admiral	RA
reach end	DIE	*Rear* Admira<u>l</u>	L
[reach] *out*	RACHE	rear animal	BUM STEER
react		rear garden	BACKGROUND
[nuclear] *reaction*	UNCLEAR	rear of ship	STERN
react fast	REDOLENT	*rear of* ship	P
reacting to [news]	SEWN, WENS	rear post, *say*	RUMPSTEAK
reaction [to the] . . .	THINE	rear, *say*	RHEA
reactionary wets<	STEW	rear sheep	BUCKRAM
read		rear view	HINDSIGHT
read aloud	ALLOWED	reared *say*	BREAD
read *aloud*	RED, REDE, REED	rearing, *say*	RAISIN

Anag [cat]; Any *; Begin IGN–; Endings –ING; eg •; Hidden /cat/; Implied add (on); Implied in (in);

rears tree	RUMPSTEAK
rearrange	
[game] *rearranged*	MEGA–
rearrange [chairs]	CHARIS
rearrangement of [parts]	PRATS, STRAP, TRAPS
reason	
reason, *say*	CAWS
reasonable	FAIR
• king *in* reasonable . . .	FAKIR
• reasonable argument	FAIRGROUND
• reasonable method	FAIRWAY
reasonable, *say*	DESCENT
reassemble	
[Class E] *reassembled*	SCALES
reassemble [warders]	DRAWERS, REWARDS
reassure	
reassuring report	AMOK
Réaumur	R
rebel	
rebel	CADE, TYLER
rebel group	CONTRABAND
rebellious [race]	ACER, ACRE, CARE
rebels	ETA, IRA, PLO
rebuild	
rebuild most of [town]	WON, NOT, TON
rebuild [town]	WONT
rebuilding hospital	REWARDING
rebuff	
moderates *rebuffed*<	STEW
rebuff Enld<	DINE
rebut	
rebut DA's . . . <	SAD
rebut his . . .	HER
rebuttal of large . . .	SMALL
recall	
recall time<	ARE, EMIT
recalled dog<	GOD
recast	
recast [lure]	RULE
recasting [Tosca]	ASCOT, ATOCS, COATS, TACOS
recede	
receding gums<	SMUG
tide *recedes*<	EDIT
receipts	–IOUS
receive	
receive approval	incl OK
• w–e *receive* approval	WOKE
receive grant	ACCEPT
receive title, *say*	BENIGHTED
received by *	incl in *
• car *received by* Ma–y	MARRY
receiver	FENCE
• receiver's crime	OFFENCE
receiver of wreck	ABANDONEE
receives a . . .	incl A

receives *	incl *
• Ma–y *receives* car	MARRY
receiving attention	(in) H–AND
receiving deliveries	BATTING, NOT OUT
recent	
recent delivery	NEONATE, NEW YORKER
[recent] *disturbance*	CENTRE
recent friend	LATERALLY
recent graduate, *say*	PNEUMA
recent history	
–English	YESTERDAY
–French	HIER
–German	GESTRIGE TAG
–Italian	IERI
–Spanish	AYER
[recent] *novel*	CENTRE
recent race	NEWSPRINT
receptive	
receptive to a . . .	incl A
receptive to *	incl *
• w–ere *receptive to* hot . . .	WHERE
(*see also* receive)	
Rechabite	TT
recipe	
recipe	R, REC
recipe book	RB
recipe for [stew]	WEST, WETS
reciprocate	
reciprocal action	DEED
reciprocate Ben's . . . <	SNEB
reciprocating sound	TOOT
recite	
maid *reciting* . . .	MADE
recitation of ode	OWED
reckless	
reckless [action]	CATION
[throw] *recklessly*	WORTH
reclaim	
reclaimed [lost] . . .	LOTS
reclamation of [land, ie] . . .	NAILED
reclassify	
reclassification of [animal]	LAMINA, MANILA
reclassified [general] . . .	ENLARGE
reclassify [owls]	LOWS, SLOW
recollect	
[I can't] *recollect*	ANTIC
recollected [tale]	LATE, LEAT, TAEL, TELA
recommend	
recommend lawyer	ADVOCATE
recommended retail price	RRP
recondition	
recondition [frayed] . . .	DEFRAY
reconditioned [or new]	OWNER
reconditioning of [furs]	SURF
reconfigure	

Letter replaced \c\at; Omit (a); Pointers *out*; Retain a̲; Split B_ED; Down (D); Backwards <or ^

reconfiguration of [plane]	PANEL
reconfigure [shape]	HEAPS, PHASE
reconstitute	
reconstitute [meat]	MATE, TAME, TEAM
reconstituted [soup]	OPUS
reconstitution of [side]	DIES, IDES
reconstruct	
[dome] *reconstructed*	MODE
reconstruction of [Rome]	MORE
recopied	REAPED
record	
record	CD
• look *in* the record	CLOD
• nothing *in* the record	COD
record	DIARY
record	DISC
• record finished	DISCOVER
• record producing	
royalties, *say*	DISCERNING
• record time	DISCAGE
record	ENTER, ENTRY
• record it is . . .	ENTERITIS
• second record	SENTRY
record	EP
• record-carrier	EPHOD
• saint records . . .	STEPS
• we record	WEEP
record	FORTY-FIVE
record	LOG
• loud record	FLOG
• record a beat, *say*	LOGARITHM
• record *in* ship	SLOGS
record	LP
• a record in Eastern . . .	ALPINE
• he records	HELPS
record	MONO
• record container	MONOPOD
• record weight	MONOGRAM
• record the first . . .	MONOTHEIST
record	SEVENTY-EIGHT
record	SINGLE, STEREO
record	TAPE
• English record	ETAPE
• king *on* record	TAPER
• record *in* ship	STAPES
record	THIRTY-THREE
record book	ALBUM
record-*breaking*	incl EP, LOG, LP
• record-*breaking* ste–le	STEEPLE
• record-*breaking* gas . . .	CLOGS
• a–s record-*breaking* . . .	ALPS
record-*breaking*	incl in EP, LOG, LP
• Who? *French* record-*breaking* . . .	EQUIP
• win record-*breaking* . . .	LOWING
• each record-*breaking* . . .	LEAP
record-holder	ALBUM, SLEEVE

	TURNTABLE
record-*holder*	incl EP, LOG, LP
• she is hot record-*holder*	SHEEPISH
• ship is record-*holder*	SLOGS
• one in first is	
record-*holder*	ALPINIST
record-maker	ACETATE, STYLUS, VINYL
	EMI
record number	FORTY-FIVE
	SEVENTY-EIGHT, THIRTY-THREE
	SCORE
record-player	DISC JOCKEY
	NEEDLE, STYLUS
	TURNTABLE
record rebellion	FORTY-FIVE
record time	DISCAGE, MINUTE
record turnover	FLIPSIDE
recorded in Bib/le st/ory	LEST
recording band	TRACK
recording head	ARCHANGEL
recover	
recover from gra/ve il/ness	VEIL
recovered by *	incl RE
• *recovered by* th–e . . .	THREE
recovering *	incl in R–E
• *recovering* fish	RIDE
recovery ship	ARGO
recreate	
[later] *recreated*	ALTER, RATEL
recreate [theatre]	THEREAT
rectify	
rectification of [AC to] . . .	ATOC, COAT, TACO
rectify [slip]	LIPS
rector	REV(D)
recur	
recurrent moan< I . . .	NAOMI
recurrent note<	ETON
recurring decimal	OFTEN
recycle	
recycled rag<	GAR
recycled [rags in] . . .	GRAINS
recycling [centre]	RECENT
red¹	
meaning:	
angry	
• angry *carrying* silver . . .	RAGED
bloody	
• short time *in* bloody . . .	REMIND
communist, left, etc	
• anarchist deed	REDACT
• communist landlord	RED LETTER
• left study	REDDEN
• Russian sailor	RED ADMIRAL
flushed	
• flushed *in* company	CREDO
Inner Circle	

• like sanctimonious		*redistribution of* [seats]	SATES, TESSA
Inner Circle	ASPIRED	**redraft**	
owing etc	(in) R–ED	[much] *redrafting*	CHUM
• dismissed, owing . . .	ROUTED	*redraft* [letters]	SETTLER
• rower in debt	ROARED	**redraw**	
radical		[face] *redrawn*	CAFE
• radical water transport	REDRAFT	*redraw* [plans 'lim] . . .	IMPLANTS
stop		**reduce**	
• bet *on* red	BACK-STOP	reduce	GODOWN
• stop English scheme	REDEPLOY	reduce agreement	CONTRACT
red²		*reduce* agreement	YE(s)
red *and* green	RED RAW	*reduce by* a pound	omit L
Red Army man	FLAMENCO	*reduce by* a quarter	omit N, S, E, W
red *cover*	(in) R-ED	reduce fare	DIET
• red *cover for* organ	REARED	reduce friction	OIL-WELL
Red Cross	RC	reduce light	TAPER
red *flower*	DON, VOLGA	*reduced by* *	
Red Norseman	ERIC	• len(gth) *reduced by* half	LEN
Red Queen	CZARINA, TSARINA	• (of)ten *reduced by* 40%	TEN
red rag	PRAVDA	*reduced* cos(t)	COS
Red Rum	COMMUNIST SPIRIT	*reduced* [cost]	COTS, SCOT
Red Rum *turns back*<	MURDER	reduced field	GROUND
red, *say*	READ, STUDIED	reduced price	RP
red setter	SUN	*reduced* price	COS(t), (p)RICE
red suit	D, H	*reduced* responsibility	(o)NUS
redbreast, *say*	ROBBIN, ROBBING	*reduced* state	(*see* state²)
redcap	(R)MP	*reduced* ta(x)	TA
redcap	R	*reduced* t/o the r/anks	OTHER
redhead	GINGERNUT	reduces credit	CHOPSTICK
	MAO, STALIN	*reducing* velocity	V
	POPPY	*reduction of* energy	omit E
	REDNESS	*reduction of*	
redhead(D)	R	–height	H, HT
redheaded Australian	BLUE	–power	P
reddish beer	GINGER ALE	–weight	WT
reddish, *say*	RHONE	*reduction of* (h)eight	EIGHT
redstart	R	*reduction of* rat(es)	RAT
redecorate			(*see also* little², small²)
[recent] *redecoration*	CENTRE	**redundant**	
redecorate [room]	MOOR	*a redundant*	omit A
redeploy		• a *redundant* man(a)ger	MANGER
redeploy [army]	MARY, MYRA	*redundant* *	omit *
redeployment of [regiment]	METERING	• peas(ant), *redundant* worker	PEAS
redesignate		**re-edit**	
redesignate [keys]	SKYE	*re-edited* [Verne]	NEVER
redesignation of [place]	CAPEL, CAPLE	[tome] *re-edited*	MOTE
redevelop		**reel**	
redevelop [town]	WONT	reel, *say*	REAL, ROLE
redeveloping [skill]	KILLS	*reeling* [in a line]	ANILINE
redevelopment of [region]	IGNORE	[sent] *reeling*	NETS, STEN, TENS
redirect		**refashion**	
redirect [trains]	STRAIN	*refashion* [bust]	BUTS, STUB
redirecting [fire]	RIFE	[robes] *refashioned*	BORES, SOBER
redirection of [mail]	LIAM, MALI	**refer**	
redistribute		refer to drawer	RD
redistribute [wares]	SWEAR, WEARS	referee	REF

Letter replaced \c\at; Omit (a); Pointers *out*; Retain a; Split B_ED; Down (D); Backwards <or ^

reference	REF	Regency man, *say*	BONE-ASH
reference book	OED	**regenerate**	
refine		*regenerate* [Ulster's] . . .	LUSTRES, RESULTS
refine [ore]	ROE	*regeneration of* [life]	FILE, LIEF
refined [oils]	SILO, SOIL	**regiment**	
refinement of [taste]	STATE, TEATS	regiment	R(E)GT
refit		Regimental Court-Martial	RCM
refit [large] . . .	ELGAR, GLARE	Regimental Sergeant-Major	RSM
	LAGER, REGAL	**regina**	R
refitted [tyre]	TREY	**regional**	
refix		regional (=dialect)	
[parts] *refixed*	PRATS, STRAP, TRAPS	• regional farm	WICK
refix [hinge]	NEIGH	• regional network	KELL
reflect		• regional quarrel	FRATCH, WHID
reflected Don's . . . <	SNOD	Regional Seat of Government	RSG
reflection of room<	MOOR	**register**	
reflective type	ECHO, NARCISSUS	dog register	TERRIER
reflex expert	PAVLOV	register fighter	TERRIER
reform		Registered General Nurse	RGN
reform [railmen]	MINERAL	**regrade**	
reform of [penal] . . .	PANEL, PLANE	*regrade* [slope]	LOPES, POLES
Reformation [artist]	TRAITS	*regraded* [pupils]	SLIP UP
reformation of [sinner]	INNERS	**regress**	
reformat		*regression of* time<	ARE, EMIT
[later] *reformatted*	ALTER, RATEL	*regressive* way<	DR, EVA, TS, YAW
reformats [pages]	GAPES	**regret**	
reformulate		regrets, *say*	RUSE
reformulating [recipe]	PIERCE	regretted, *say*	ROOD, RUDE
reformulation of [rules]	LURES	**regroup**	
reframe		*regroup* [army]	MARY, MYRA
reframe [Lely] . . .	YELL	*regrouping* [in there]	NEITHER
reframed [oils]	SILO, SOIL	**regular**	
refreshment interval	ELEVENSES	regular	EVEN
refuge		• building *about*	
refugee	DP	regular . . .	SEVENTY
* *is refuge for*	incl in *	• regular number	EVENSONG
• church *is refuge for* prince	CRASH	• second regular . . .	SEVEN
refurbish		*regular absences of* f(o)u(r) r(a)s(h)	FURS
refurbish [snug]	GNUS, GUNS	regular habit	UNIFORM
refurbishing hospital	REWARDING	*regular ingredients of* l<u>oaf</u>	
refurbishment of [loos]	OSLO, SOLO	*of* . . .	OFF
refuse		regular soldier	ORDERLY
refusal, *say*	KNOW, NEIGH	*regularly viewed* h<u>ouse</u>	US
refuse, *say*	WAIST	troop sh<u>e</u> *regularly reviewed*	ROSE
refuse to declare	BATON	**regulate**	
refuse to *return*<	ON	*regulate* [flow]	FOWL, WOLF
refuse young . . .	LITTER	*regulation of* [credit]	TRICED
refusing *to rise*(D)^	ON	**rehabilitate**	
regal		[recent] *rehabilitation*	CENTRE
regal coin	PENNY ROYAL	*rehabilitated* [slum]	LUMS
regally	ASKING	**rehash**	
regard		*rehash* [meal]	LAME, MALE
regard drink	SAKE	*rehashed* [lamb]	BALM
regard, *say*	WRECK	**rehearsal**	SHOW-TRIAL
Regency		**reincarnate**	
Regency man	BEAU (NASH)	*reincarnating* [dead] . . .	EDDA

Anag [cat]; Any *; Begin IGN–; Endings –ING; eg •; Hidden /cat/; Implied add (on); Implied in (in);

reincarnation of [king is] . . .	SKIING
reinstate	
reinstate [teacher]	CHEATER, RETEACH
reinstated [master]	REMAST, STREAM
reinstatement order	STET
reissue	
[plays] *reissued*	SPLAY
reissue of [novels]	SLOVEN
reject	
reject a . . .	omit A
reject devil<	LIVED
reject rubbish	REFUSE
reject the article	omit A, AN, IT, THE
reject *	omit *
• fat(her) *rejects* her . . .	FAT
rejoin	
rejoin [Marines]	REMAINS, SEMINAR
[wires] *rejoined*	SWIRE
relate	
relating	REL
relating to	OF
• 500 relating to fine . . .	DOFF
• relating to iron circle	OFFERING
• relating to receiver	OFFENCE
relation	SIB
relationship	COS, PI, SINE, TAN
relative	BRER, BRO, REL, SIS
relative arrived, *say*	ANTICUM
relative article	UNCLEAN
relative atomic mass	RAM
relative, *say*	ANTI, COZEN
relative speed	GRANNY KNOT
relatively favourable	NEPOTIC
relatively *small*	BRER, BRO, REL, SIS
relatives	MASON
relatives fear, *say*	KINDRED
relative's friend	AUNT SALLY
relevant stuff	MATERIAL
relax	
relaxation of [strain]	TRAINS
relaxed (=laid *back*<)	DIAL
relaxed [rules]	LURES
relay	
relay [races]	CARES, SCARE
[tale] *relayed*	LATE, LEAT, TEAL
release	
after release [it was] . . .	WAIST, WAITS
[birds] *released*	DRIBS
release a . . .	omit a
release knight, *say*	FREEZER
release money	omit L
release *	omit *
• soldiers *released from* tor(men)t	TORT
releasing [tension]	INTONES
reliable	
reliable	SURE

• reliable cashier	SURE-FIRE
• reliable man, *say*	SHORTED
• reliable number, *say*	SHORTEN
reliable dog	SOUNDTRACK
reliable piano	UPRIGHT
reliable sort of cricketer	BRICKBAT
relief work	CAMEO, CARVING, EMBOSSING
religious	
religious	PI
• approve a religious . . .	OKAPI
• religious character	PICARD
• religious ceremony	PIRITE
• religious code	PILAW
• religious group	PILOT
• way *round* religious . . .	SPIT
religious ceremony, *say*	RIGHT, WRIGHT
religious house	CE, CH(URCH)
religious *leader*	R
religious point	SPIRE, STEEPLE
religious setting	(in) HO–LY
religious work	ALTAR PIECE
relish difficulty	PICKLE
relocate	
relocate [shop]	HOPS, POSH
relocation of [route]	OUTER, OUTRE
reluctant	
reluctant	LOTH
• 100 reluctant . . .	CLOTH
• reluctant Scot	LOTHIAN
• reluctant *to go aboard*	SLOTHS
remain	
remain at the wicket	BATON
remain indoors, *say*	STATOHM
remain unruffled	BECALM
remained at this spot, *say*	STADIA
remains	ASH
• many remains	CASH
• remains *in* the sea	MASHED
• remains of ghost, *say*	GOULASH
remains silent	SAY-SO
remake	
remake [coat]	ATOC, TACO
[when] *remade* . . .	HEWN
remarkable	
remarkable	TALL
• remarkable child	TALLBOY
• remarkable ruler	TALLER
remarkable man	COMMENTATOR
remarkable [pearl]	PALER
remarkably [paler]	PEARL
remedy	
remedial [phase]	HEAPS, SHAPE
remedied [all the] . . .	LETHAL
remedy [made]	DAME, MEAD
reminders	–IOUS

Letter replaced \c\at; Omit (a); Pointers *out*; Retain a̲; Split B_ED; Down (D); Backwards <or ^

remit
[remit]   ORDER OF MERIT
remit *by return*<   TIMER
[remit] *maybe* . . .   MERIT, MITRE, TIMER

remix
[it was] *remixed*   WAIST, WAITS
remix [paté]   PEAT, TAPE

remodel
[face] *remodelled*   CAFE
remodel [gown in] . . .   OWNING

remote
remote *ending*   E
[remote] *parts*   METEOR, –OMETER

remove
I'd *removed* . . .   omit ID
• I'd *removed from* state   FLOR(id)A
remove a . . .   omit A
remove core of a(ppl)e   AE
remove date   TAKE OUT
remove from gr/asp en/closing . . .   ASPEN
remove leader of (g)roup   ROUP
remove lid from . . .   omit 1st letter
• *remove* lid from (b)ox   OX
• *remove* lid from chest   (c)RATE
remove lock   (D)EPILATE
remove packing of pa/int
ro/ller   INTRO
remove ring   omit O
remove [stain]   SAINT, SATIN
remove tail of kit(e)   KIT
remove wrinkles   DECREASE
remove *   omit *
• (bar)ely *remove* obstruction   ELY
remove * *from*   omit *
• *remove* child *from* class   LES(son)S
removed centre, *say*   C(H)ORD
removed [van I] . . .   IVAN, VAIN
removing veins   MINING

remuster
[army] *remustered*   MARY, MYRA
remuster [cadres]   SACRED

rend
rend [open]   NOPE, PEON, PONE
rend, *say*   TARE
rending [noises]   ESSOIN
(*see also* rent)

render
render almost [secur(e)]   CURSE
render first aid   PLASTER
rendered intoxicated   PLASTERED
rendering [dues]   SUED
rendition of [song]   NOGS, SNOG
[Satchmo's] *rendition*   STOMACH

René
René's (=French)
• *René's* house   MAISON

• with *René's* . . .   AVEC
(*see also* abroad, cross[4], continental)

renegade
[he was] *renegade* . . .   HAWSE
renegade [priest]   RIPEST, STRIPE

renegotiate
renegotiate [terms I] . . .   MISTER
renegotiation of [truce]   CRUET

renew
renew [fears]   FARES, SAFER
renewal of [sub]   BUS

renounce
renounce *   omit *
• ri(sin)g to *renounce* sin   RIG

renovate
renovate [sofa]   OAFS
renovation of [table]   BLATE, BLEAT

rent
[raise] *rent*   AESIR, SERAI
rent   LET
• rent increase   LET-UP
• rented   ISLET
• rented *in* friends' . . .   PALLETS
rent   TEAR
• rent completely   TEARFULLY
• rent reduction   TEARDROP
• second rent . . .   STEAR
rent   HIRE
• rent fish . . .   HIRELING
• rent an ox, *say*   HIREABLE
• rent in ship   SHIRES
rent-a-party   TORNADO
ren(t) *reduction*   REN
rent [rise]   SIRE
rent, *say*   HIGHER, TARE
(*see also* rend)

reorder
reorder [parts]   PRATS, SPRAT, STRAP, TRAPS
reordering of [words]   SWORD

reorganise
reorganisation of [life]   FILE, LIEF
reorganise [stores]   SOREST

repack
[case] *repacked*   ACES, AESC
repack for [trips], ,   SPIRT, STRIP
repackaged [parts]   PRATS, SPRAT
STRAP, TRAPS

repair
repair   DOUP
repair   MEND
• repair ruler   MENDER
• repair *to* a large town   MENDACITY
repair porcelain, *say*   GLOOMING
repaired shoes, *say*   HEALED, SOLD
repairing [hose]   HOES, SHOE
[shoe] *repair*   HOES, HOSE

Anag [cat]; Any *; Begin IGN–; Endings –ING; eg •; Hidden /cat/; Implied add (on); Implied in (in);

repeat
repeat performance	ECHO, ENCORE
repeat performance	DODO
repeatedly volunteers	TATA
repeating decimal	OFTEN
repetition, *say*	WROTE
	(see also double, two)

repel
repel a . . .	omit A
repel one . . .	omit A, I
repel king	omit K, R
repel queen	omit ER, Q, R
repel *	omit *
• wh(it)en *to repel* it	WHEN
repellent one	GRIMACE
repellent tang<	GNAT
repelling Satan<	LIVED

repetition   *(see* repeat*)*

replace
drink *replaces* one *in* th\i\s . . .	THRUMS
replace cover	REINSURE
replace [old Rover]	OVERLORD
replace contents of c\as\k	CORK
replace New Deal	OLD HAND
replace [R with A]	WRAITH
replace weak link	REFUSE
replacement [hip]	PHI
replacement of [parts]	PRATS, SPRAT, STRAP, TRAPS
replacing locks	FORTRESSES, WIG
replacing rubber bands	RETIRING

replan
replan [estate]	TEA SET
[town] *replanned*	WONT

replant
replant [shrub]	BRUSH
[trees] *replanted*	ESTER, REEST, RESET

reply
reply	ANS
replying, *say*	ANSERINE

report
report	BANG, POP, REP(T)
report, *say*	BHANG
reported	DIT
reported you're . . .	URE
reportedly knew	GNU, NEW
reporter	GUN, REP
reporter's paper	CARTRIDGE

repose
reposing in *	incl in *
• a king *reposing in* b–ed	BARED

reposition
[castle] *repositioned*	CLEATS
reposition [lamps]	PALMS

represent
representation of [flowers]	FOWLER

representative   MP
• about a representative	CAMP
• business representative	COMP
• nothing *in* representative's . . .	MOPS

representative   REP
• representative *in* church	CREPE
• representative Indian	REPUTE
• seat representative	SITREP

representative of
–England	LION, ROSE
–Ireland	SHAMROCK
–Scotland	THISTLE, UNICORN
–Wales	DRAGON, DAFFODIL, LEEK
representative of [tribe]	BITER
representative from [Neath]	THANE
represented by [seven] . . .	EVENS
represented in [art]	RAT, TAR
represented [in art]	INTRA–, TRAIN
represented in P/aris ta/lks	ARISTA
representing [Wells]	SWELL
represents [Esher]	SHEER

reprobate expires   CADDIES

reprocess
[meat] *reprocessed*	MATE, TAME, TEAM
reprocess [oils]	SILO, SOIL

reproduce
is *reproduced*	ISIS
reproduce [much] . . .	CHUM
reproduced by [seed Vi] . . .	DEVISE
reproduced in [garden]	DANGER
reproducing dog	POMPOM
reproduction of cat	TOM-TOM
reproduction [sideboard]	BROADSIDE
reproduction of [files]	FLIES
	(see also double, two)

reprogram
reprogram [timer]	MERIT, REMIT
reprogrammed [IBM at] . . .	IMBAT

republic   REP

repulse
may *be repulsed*<	YAM
repulsed Devil<	LIVED

require
[I am] *required* . . .	AIM, MIA
requires [me to] . . .	MOTE, TOME
requiring a synonym	NEEDING

reroute
reroute [stream]	REMAST, MASTER
[road] *rerouted*	DORA

rerun
rerun [heat]	HATE, THEA
rerun time<	ARE, EMIT
rerunning [tape]	PATE, PEAT

reschedule
reschedule [planes]	PANELS
rescheduling of [tour]	ROUT

Letter replaced \c\at; Omit (a); Pointers *out*; Retain <u>a</u>; Split B_ED; Down (D); Backwards <or ^

rescue
rescue SAVE
• novice *in* rescue . . . SLAVE
• rescue husband SAVE
• rescue king SAVER
and
• rescue girl, *say* SAVANNA(H)
• rescue ox, *say* SAVEABLE
rescue from [yacht] CATHY
rescue ship (NOAH'S) ARK
rescuer NOAH, WHITE KNIGHT
resemble
resembles \G\erald HERALD
resembles [parents] PASTERN
reserve
Reserve Decoration RD
reserve BOOK
• reserve currency BOOKMARKS
• reserve seat BOOKSTALL
• reserves dance BOOKSHOP
reserve wife SPARE RIB
reserves TA, THETA
• reserve member TAMP
• reserve team TAXI
• reserves jeered TABOOED
(*see also* army)
reset
[not] *reset* TON
reset [field in] . . . INFIDEL
resettle
resettle [a tribe] BAITER
resettled in [Paris] PAIRS
reshuffle
reshuffle [cards as] . . . CSARDAS
[team] *reshuffled* MATE, MEAT, TAME
resident
Resident Medical Officer RMO
Resident Surgical Officer RSO
resident magistrate RM
residue
residue ASH
• residue of end, *say* ASHEN
• residue of reefer POTASH
• with residue WASH
resistance R
resolution
[new] *resolution* WEN
resolution of [tough] . . . OUGHT
resolve
resolve [in game] ENIGMA
resolved [to send] STONED
resort
[Alpine] *resort* NEPALI
[cheap] *resort* PEACH
resort SPA
• English resort bores, *say* ESPADRILLES

• resort finished SPADONE
• resort fish SPALING
resort [to a] . . . OAT
[the last] *resort* STEALTH
responsible
responsible for –IC
responsibilities, one
at a time CARESSINGLY
rest
re*st centre* ES
rest finished BREAKTHROUGH
rest in peace RIP
rest of the paintings EASEL
rested, *say* LADE, LANE
resting (in) B–ED, (in) CO–T
resting place BED, COT, DORM
DEN, LAIR
restaurant
restaurant bill MENU
restaurant cutlery box CANTEEN
restore
restoration of [garden] DANGER
restore [law] . . . AWL
restore revs REORDAIN
restored [stool] . . . LOOTS
restoring [much] . . . CHUM
restrain
restrain a . . . incl A
restrain * incl *
• lead *restraining* dog PROVERB
restrained by * incl in *
• dog *restrained by* lead PROVERB
restrict
restrict (i)t T
restrict stream PINCHBECK
restricted by t/he ar/my HEAR
restricted by * incl in *
• learner *restricted by* p–ay PLAY
restricted road RD
restricted (s)cope COPE
restricting a . . . incl a
restricting vie(w) VIE
restricting * incl *
• p–ay *restricting* learner PLAY
restrictive practice GAROTTING
STRANGULATION
restructure
restructure [chapter] PATCHER, REPATCH
[side] *restructured* DIES, IDES
restyle
restyle [acts] CATS, SCAT
[wigs] *restyled* SWIG
result
result of [foresight] GIFT HORSE
resulting from [state] . . . TASTE, TEATS
resume play ACTON, BATON

Anag [cat]; Any *; Begin IGN–; Endings –ING; eg •; Hidden /cat/; Implied add (on); Implied in (in);

retail

retail (=change last letter(s))	
• *retail* brea\d\	BREATH
• *retail* stor\e\	STORM
• *retailing* mea\t\	MEAD, MEAL, MEAN
retail fish, *say*	SELFISH
retail price	RP
retail price index	RPI
retail price maintenance	RPM
retailer, *say*	CELLAR

retain

retain fort	KEEP
retain the right	incl R
• state *retains* the right	CARL
retained by *	incl in *
• agent *retained by* men	MALEFACTORS
retaining a . . .	incl A
retaining *	incl *
• men *retaining* agent	MALEFACTORS
retaliate	PAY BACK, YAP

retire

retire to . . . <	OT
retired	(in) B–ED, (in) C–OT
retired	EX, RETD
retired head	omit 1st letter
• *retired head*master	(m)ASTER
retired lady<	ASSET
retired leader	omit 1st letter
• *retired leader* of (p)arty	ARTY
retired nurse<	DAV, NES
retired salesman<	PER
retirement cover	BLANKET, DUVET
	SHEET etc
retirement of sailor<	BA, RAT
retiring at ten<	NETTA
retiring member<	GEL, PM
retiring premier<	MP

retouch

[it was] *retouched*	WAIST, WAITS
retouch [snap]	NAPS, PANS

retract

not *retracted*<	TON
retract	DRAWBACK, WARD
retract No 1 tale<	ELATION

retrain

[guns] *retrained*	GNUS, SNUG
retrain [dogs]	GODS
retraining [all the] . . .	LETHAL

retreat

retreat (=go *back*<)	–OG
retreated tidily	EBBED
retreating object<	TI
retreating waters<	SLOOP

retrograde

retrograde step<	PETS
was *retrograde*<	SAW

retrospective

put *retrospective* . . . <	TUP
retrospective look<	–AL, OL

return

return flight	BACK STAIRS
return from work	INCOME, PROFIT
return game<	FLOG
return of service<	FAR
return reward<	DRAWER
return thanks<	AT
return ticket	OUTBACK
return ticket<	GAT
return to . . . <	OT
returned	RETD
Returned Letter Office	RLO
returned sweets<	STRESSED
returning learners<	SLIP-UP
returning missile	BOOMERANG
returning missile<	TRAD
returning nomad<	DAMON
returning traveller<	PER

reunion

[army] *reunion*	MARY, MYRA
reunion of [former] . . .	REFORM

rev

rev counter	ALTAR
rev indicator	DOG-COLLAR
rev up	HIGH PRIEST, SKY PILOT
rev *up*(D)^	VER

revamp

revamp [room]	MOOR
revamped [gown in] . . .	OWNING

reveal

revealed by Fren/ch art/ist	CHART
revealed in de/noumen/t	NOUMEN
revealing [hand is] . . .	DANISH
revealing performance	FAN DANCE
	STRIP-TEASE
reveals [a new] . . .	WANE, WEAN
revelation, *say*	AURICLE
Revelations	REV

revel

revel [at Lent]	LATENT, TALENT
revelling [in night]	HINTING

reverberate

[noises] *reverberating*	ESSOIN
reverberates [tin] . . .	INT–, NIT
reverberation of [steel] . . .	LEETS, STELE

revere

revere, *say*	WARSHIP
Reverend	REV(D)
	(see also rev)

reverse

Reverse Arms!<	SNUG
reverse bureaucracy	TAPERED

Letter replaced \c\at; Omit (a); Pointers *out*; Retain <u>a</u>; Split B_ED; Down (D); Backwards <or ^

reverse gear<	BRAG	**revolve**	
reverse mail chain	ARMOUR	revolve, *say*	TERN(E), WE'LL, W(H)EAL
	CHAIN-MAIL	revolver	CATHERINE WHEEL
reverse support	BACK(ING)		IRON, PIECE, ROD,
reverse tide<	EDIT		LATHE
reversible notices	SEES	revolver, *say*	PISTIL, SPINSTER
reversible parts<	STRAP	*revolving* door<	ROOD
reversible revolver	ROTOR	*revolving* [fast]	FATS
reversible uniform	LEVEL	**reward**	
review		reward, *say*	PRISE, TROPHI
[army] *review*	MARY, MYRA	reward workers	TIPSTAFF
review [all the] . . .	LETHAL	**rework**	
reviewing [novels]	SLOVEN	*rework* [sums]	MUSS
revise		*reworking of* [timber]	TIMBRE
revised	REV	**rewrite**	
revised [ice act]	ACETIC	*rewrite* [section]	NOTICES
Revised (Standard) Version	R(S)V	*rewriting* [note]	ETON, TONE
revision of [chapter]	PATCHER, REPATCH	*rewritten* [page]	GAPE
revive		**Rhodesia**	RSR
revived [sister]	RESIST	**ribonucleic acid**	RNA
revival of [play]	PALY	**rice**	
[slow] *revival*	LOWS, OWLS	rice	ARCHIE
revolt		[rice] *pudding*	CIRE, ERIC
revolting	UP	**rich**	
• 100 revolting . . .	CUP	rich	ROLLING
• revolting drunk	UPTIGHT	• rich gravy	ROLLING STOCK
• revolting players	UPCAST	• rich Irishman	PATROLLING
revolution		• self-contained and rich	SCROLLING
[counter]-*revolutionary*	RECOUNT	rich, American-style, *say*	DOLOROUS
	TROUNCE	rich entertainer	COMIC
prevent *revolutionary*<	POTS	rich man	DIVES, MIDAS
revolution	REV	**rickety**	
revolution [in art]	TRAIN	[it was] *rickety*	WAIST, WAITS
revolution in [art]	RAT, TAR	*rickety* [ladder]	RADDLE
revolutionary	CHE	**riddle**	
• artist *and* revolutionary . . .	RACHE	*riddle* [cinders]	DISCERN, RESCIND
• revolutionary directions	CHEESE	riddled, *say*	HOLY, WHOLLY
• revolutionary English		*riddling* [soil]	OILS, SILO
radical	CHEERED	**ride**	
revolutionary	RED	rider	AFTERTHOUGHT, PS
• about revolutionary . . .	CARED		GILPIN, REVERE
• revolutionary action	REDACT	riding	UP
• revolutionary movement	RED SHIFT	• *riding* engagement	UPDATE
revolutionary		• *riding* school	UPSET
–command	ABOUT FACE, ABOUT TURN	• *riding* well	UPRIGHT
–landlord	CIRCULAR LETTER	riding	(in) S–ADDLE, (on) HORSE
–movement	ABOUT FACE, ABOUT TURN	riding	(*see* astride)
–music	INTERNATIONALE	riding master	RM
–painter	TURNER	[rode]	WRONG-DOER
–period	DAY, MONTH, YEAR	**ridicule**	
–piece of equipment	LATHE	[it was] *ridiculous*	WAIST, WAITS
revolutionary [design]	SIGNED	ridicule	BOO
revolutionary part<	TRAP	• reserves ridicule . . .	TABOO
revolutionary period<	ARE, EMIT	• *ridicule and then* celebrate	BOOSING
revolutionise [all the] . . .	LETHAL	• ridicule ruler	BOOK(ING)
revolutions per minute	RPM	ridicule man	GUY

Anag [cat]; Any *; Begin IGN–; Endings –ING; eg •; Hidden /cat/; Implied add (on); Implied in (in);

ridiculed, *say*	GUIDE	• telephone right, *say*	DILATORY
ridiculous [shape]	HEAPS, PHASE	right *at the end* . . .	end with R, RT
ridiculous shape, *say*	SILICONE	right *away*	omit R, RT
ridiculous position, *say*	SILICITE	right *back<*	TR
rife		right boot	SIDEKICK
[rife]	WILDFIRE	right fish, *say*	BLUE-EYED
rifle		right *from the start*	omit initial R
Rifle Brigade	RB	• (r)ash, right *from the start*	ASH
rifle drill	GUNCOTTON, SACKCLOTH	right *ingredient*	incl R, RT
rifle fire	SACK	right *inside*	incl R, RT
rifle school	WINCHESTER	right *out of it*	omit R, RT
rift		right *outside*	(in) R–T
[cause] *rift*	SAUCE	**right²**	
rift in [lute or] . . .	ELUTOR	meaning:	
rig		off	
rig [up a net]	PEANUT	• again to off	RETORT
rigged [race]	ACER, ACRE, CARE	OK, oke	
[rig]-*out*	GIR, GRI	• OK *behind* the Post Office	PORT
right¹		lien	
right	LIEN	• has a lien *on* first . . .	ARTIST
• a right . . .	ALIEN	title	
• right *back*	NEIL	• right attendant	TITLE PAGE
• right *in* court	CLIENT	Tory	
• right, *say*	LEAN	• born Tory	BRIGHT
right	OFF	**right³**	
• 100 right . . .	COFF	right amount	NINEPENCE
• right result	OFFEND	right angle	L
• right *in* the peg	TOFFEE	right away	OFF
right	OK(E)	*right-half for* Bol<u>ton</u>	TON
• 100 right . . .	COKE	*right half of* ro<u>ad</u>	AD
• not right	NOOK	right-hand	RECTO, RH, RO
• right *in* church	COKE	right-hand man	CONSERVATIVE, TORY
right	R	right mark	TICK
• right *and* wrong	RILL	right name	TITLE
• right *at the end of* road	AVER	right of way	ROW
• right *at the start of* row	ROAR	*right of* way	Y
• right *behind* you, *say*	UR	Right Reverend	RR
• right exit	REGRESS	*right side of* road	AD, D
• right *from the start of* (r)ace	ACE	right sign	TICK
• right in Kent, *say*	RINSE	right-thinking person	CONSERVATIVE
• right lines	–RRY		TORY
• right on	ROVER	right way	CONSERVATIVE, TORY
• right round	RO–		EAST
• right time	RAGE, RT	Right Worthy	RW
• right turn	RU	[right] *wrong*	GIRTH
right	RT	**ring¹**	
• about right	CART	ring	DISC
• one *in* the right	RAT	• ring, ring . . .	DISCO
• right *at the end of*		• ring gone	DISCOVER
revolutionary . . .	CHERT	• ring rider	DISC JOCKEY
• right *round* an . . .	RANT	**ring²**	
• right *turn<*	TR	ring	O
• turn *in* right . . .	RUT	• ring Mark . . .	OSCAR
right	TORY	• ring twice	OO
• bird right . . .	MINATORY	• Ringway	–OPATH, ORD, OST
• second right	STORY	and	

Letter replaced \c\at; Omit (a); Pointers *out*; Retain <u>a</u>; Split B_ED; Down (D); Backwards <or ^

• dress ring	GARBO	ripped bird, *say*	TORMINA
• key-ring	BO, GO, SOHO, SOLO	ripped us, *say*	TAURUS
• smoke-ring	RE-ECHO	**rise**	
• tree-ring	MAYO	pay *rise*(D)^	YAP
• vice-ring	SINO–	rise, *say*	SORE
ring *in*	incl O	*rising* crime(D)^	–NIS
• ring *in* bo–th . . .	BOOTH	*rising* fury(D)^	ERI
ring *for* a . . .	substitute O for A	rising man	INSURGENT, REBEL, RIOTER
• *ring for* a d\a\te	DOTE	*rising* star(D)^	AVON, RATS
ring *from* . . .	omit O	**river¹**	
• ring *from* bo(o)th	BOTH	mythical river	ACHERON, STYX
ring *off*	omit O	poetic river	ALPH
ring *out*	omit O	river	AIRE
ringleader	start with O	• river *in* quiet delta	PAIRED
• mark ring*leader*	OSCAR	• river valley	AIREDALE
ring³		river	ALPH
ring a . . .	incl A	• river helps . . .	ALPHABETS
ring about a . . .	incl A	• river *joins* another	RALPH
ring about *	incl *	river	CAM
• w–ear *ring about* the . . .	WEATHER	• insect *covering* river	BECAME
ring *back<*	LAID, POOH	• *rising* river(D)^	MAC
ring bird	MAGPIE	• river-*side* tower	CAMSHAFT
ring container	PHONE-BOX	river	DART
ring engineer	CHIMERE	• river authority	DARTBOARD
ring fence	TELEPHONE RECEIVER	• *throw* record *in* the river	DEPART
ring journalist	BANDED	river	DEE
ring laundryman	WASHER	• River Dee	DEED
ring-*leader*	R	• river *has* vermin	DEEPEST
ring lightly, *say*	TINCAL	• river *in* India	INDEED
ring off	CLOSE CALL, HANG-UP	river	DON
ring painter	CHIMERA	• artist *on* the river	RADON
ring round bull	INNER	• River Wear	DON
ring, *say*	CYGNET, PEEL, SURCLE	• river-goddess	DONATE
ring-*side*	G	river	DOVE
ring the pub	TOLLBAR	• river bird	DOVE
ring the queen	CALLER	• river bed	DOVECOT
ring *up*(D)^	LAID, POOH	river	EXE
ring *	incl *	• river *has* attractive . . .	EXECUTE
• m–e *ringing* at . . .	MATE	• river *has* the right . . .	EXERT
ringless	NOTING	• river inspector, *say*	EXCHEQUER
riot		river	FAL
riot of [slaves]	SALVES, VALSES	• one *in* river	FAIL
rioting [tribe]	BITER, TIBER	• pertaining to the river	OFFAL
riotous [ways]	SWAY, YAWS	river	FORTH
riotous characters [in		• river appearing . . .	FORTHCOMING
street]	INTEREST	• river ceremony, *say*	FORTHRIGHT
riots	GORDON, REBECCA	river	INDUS
rip		• River Test	INDUSTRIAL
rip	TEAR	• tree *by* river, *say*	INDUSTRY
• rip off	TEARAWAY	river	ISIS
• rip sack	TEARBAG	• creditor on river	CRISIS
• second rip	STEAR	• river goddess	ISIS
[rip]-*off*	PRI–	• river islands	ISIS
rip-off [client]	LENTIC	river	OUSE
rip, *say*	TARE	• learner *on* the river	LOUSE
rip [vest]	VETS	• river-*side* (bird)	OUSEL

Anag [cat]; Any *; Begin IGN–; Endings –ING; eg •; Hidden /cat/; Implied add (on); Implied in (in);

river	PO
• river board	POTABLE
• river boards	POSTAGE
• river god	POLAR
• river insects	POLICE
river	TAY
• car *falls in* river	TARRY
• ship *goes round* river	STAYS
• South African river	SATAY
river	TEES
• place *on* river	PUTTEES
• rain *swells* river	TRAINEES
river	TEST
• boiling river	HOTTEST
• city *on a* river	LATEST
• river *on* a mountain	TESTATOR
river	TWEED
• a king *in* the river	TWEAKED
• river in front	TWEEDLED
river	URE
• quiet river	PURE
• river-insect, *say*	URETIC
river	WEAR
• River Don	WEAR
• river erosion	WEAR
• river bed	UNDERWEAR
river, *say*	HEIR, OOZE, ROAN
	TEAS(E), WARE, WHY
river²	
river	FLOWER
• bottom of river	FLOWERBED
• river engineer	FLOWER ARRANGER
• river vessel	FLOWERPOT
river	R
• East River	ER
• river animal	ROTTER
• river currents	RAMPS
• river fish	REEL, RID, RIDE
• walk *by* river	RAMBLE
river crossing, *say*	FAIRY
river king	STREAMER
	(*see also* banker, flower²)
RKII	ARCHAISE
road	
road	AVE
• hard road	HAVE
• road *and* river	AVER
• road *to the* right	AVERT
• road *up*(D)^	EVA
road	M
• road directions	MEWS
• road in America	MINUS
• road *with* no directions	MOSES
road	MI
• road *leading to* another	MIST
• road-race	MISPRINT, MITT

• road rage	MIRAGE
• road *up*(D)^	IM–
• road vehicle	MISLED
road	R
• road *back* to<	ROT
• road in London area	RINSE
• road is quiet	RISP
road	RD
• directions *on* a road	SWARD
• nothing *in* the road	ROD
• ring road	ORD
• road *round* an . . .	RAND
• road *up*(D)^	DR
road	ROAD
• road, *say*	R(H)ODE
• road to home	ROADHOUSE
• second-class road	BROAD
road	ST
• nothing *in* the road	SOT
• private road	GIST
• ring road	OST
• road *round* his . . .	SHIST
• road *up*(D)^	–TS
road	VIA
• learner *on* the road	VIAL
• road opening	VIADUCT
• test the road, *say*	TRIVIA
road block	FLAGSTONE, SETT
[road]-*builder*	DORA
[road] *construction*	DORA
Road Haulage Association	RHA
road-hog	JEHU, TOAD
road maker	TAR(MACADAM)
road, *say*	RODE, WEIGH
Road *Up!*(D)^	DR, EVA, IM–, –TS
roadman	MACADAM
roadside *verges*	RE
road*sides*	RD
[road]*works*	DORA
Roman road	VIA
	(*see also* street, way)
roam	
roaming about [in gown]	OWNING
roaming [free]	REEF
roast goat	BUTTER DISH
robin's home	SHERWOOD (FOREST)
robots	RUR
rock	
rock	DIAMOND
rock	GEM
• rock-*climbing*(D)^	MEG
rock	GIB
• rock-*climbing*(D)^	BIG
rock-adder	TOTTER
rock band(s)	STRATUM (STRATA)
rock climber	BARBARY APE

rock fracture	TORRENT	room *on* vessel	SPACECRAFT
rock [garden]	DANGER, GANDER, RANGED	**roost**	
rock group	MASSIF	*roosting in* *	incl in *
rock-music	CRADLE SONG, SWING	• bird *roosting in* h–er . . .	HOWLER
rock, *say*	BOLDER	**root**	
rock show	OUTCROP	root	RAD
rock singer	LORELEI, SIREN	root-mean-square	RMS
rock [singer]	RESIGN	*root of* evil(D)	L
rocking-[horse]	SHORE	*rootless* plan(t)(D)	PLAN
Rocky Mountain area	BC	**rope**	
rocky [shore]	HORSE	rope-dance, *say*	GUIDANCE
rocket		rope decorator	PAINTER
rocket	ARIANE, BLUE STREAK	rope, *say*	CHORD, CORED
	SATURN, VI	ropemaker	COIR, NYLON, SISAL
rocket designer	STEPHENSON	**rose**	
rocket-launcher	STEPHENSON	rose-lover	APHIS
Rod		rose, *say*	GELDER
Rod	PERCH, POLE	**Rossetti's group**	PRB
Rod in the saddle	STICK-UP	**Rossini**	
rode	(*see* ride)	Rossini *trio*	SIN
Röntgen unit	R	**rot**	
rogue		[goes] *rotten*	EGOS
rogue [male]	LAME, MEAL	rotten	OFF
rogue, *say*	NAVE	• rotten beef	BULLY OFF
roguish chief	ARCH	• rotten cargo	OFFLOAD
role		• rotten finale	OFFEND(ING)
role	HAMLET, LEAR, PART	rotten	BAD
role in T/he M/ousetrap	HEM	• man's rotten . . .	CARLSBAD
[role]-*playing*	LORE	• rotten food	BADDISH
roll		• rotten in time	BADINAGE
dog *rolling over*<	GOD	Rotten Row	RANK
rolled umbrella	BROLLY	rotten, *say*	VIAL
rolling-[pins]	NIPS, SNIP	*rotten* [tread]	RATED, TRADE
rolling ruler	PLUTOCRAT	rotting flesh, *say*	CARRY ON
rolling [stone]	NOTES, ONSET, SETON	*rotting* [meat]	MATE, TAME, TEAM
Rolling [Stones]	ONSETS, SETONS	**rotate**	
rollick		rotate flap	SPIN
[gave a] *rollicking* . . .	AGAVE	*rotate* [orb]	ROB
rollicking [song]	NOGS, SNOG	*rotate* lever<	REVEL
Roman		*rotating* [spit]	PITS, TIPS
Roman couple	II	*rotating* spit<	TIPS
• legislator *hemmed in by*		rotor arm	REVOLVER
Roman couple	IMPI	**rotund**	
Roman figures	EXCEL, VIVID, XL	rotund	O
Roman governor, *say*	PILOT	rotund character	O
Roman invasion	CAESAREAN OPERATION	[we rotund] *characters*	UNDERTOW
Roman peace, *say*	PACKS	**rough**	
Roman road	VIA	*rough and ready* [sort I] . . .	RIOTS, ROSTI
Romans	ROM	rough	COARSE
Romania	R	• rough appearance, *say*	CORSAIR
roof		• rough service, *say*	CORS(E)LET
church *roof*(D)	C	• rough times, *say*	CORSAGE
roof of house(D)	H	rough, *say*	COURSE, CREWED, RUFF
rook	R	*rough-sounding*	RUFF
room		*rough-spoken*	RUFF
room for improvement	WARD	*rough-spoken* male	MALE

Anag [cat]; Any *; Begin IGN–; Endings –ING; eg •; Hidden /cat/; Implied add (on); Implied in (in);

rough stuff	SACKCLOTH	rounded peak<	PLA–
rough [terrain]	RETRAIN, TRAINER	with * round	incl in *
roughed up [a bit]	BAIT	• church with wat–er	
roughened, say	BIRD, BURD	round	WATCHER
roughly	C, CA, CIRC, CIRCA	**roundabout**	
	(see about[1])	roundabout	OC, OCA, ORE
roughly speaking, eight	AIT, ATE, EYOT	• kings go round round	
roughly [ten]	ENT, NET	about . . .	ROCK
roughly treated [cats]	ACTS, SCAT	• learners circling roundabout	LOCAL
round[1]		• quiet roundabout	PORE, SHORE
round	CATCH	roundabout	RO–UND
• learner in round . . .	CLATCH	• square roundabout	ROTUND
• round coin	CATCHPENNY	roundabout	incl C, CA, RE
• round rod	CATCHPOLE	• lan–e roundabout	LANCE
round	LAP	• Poles' roundabout	SCAN
• many round . . .	CLAP	• hi–s roundabout	HIRES
• round on horseback	LAP UP	roundabout<	AC, ER
• roundabout<	PAL	roundabout route	ORBIT
	(see also roundabout)	roundabout [route]	OUTER, OUTRE
round	O	**rouse**	
• bread round	ROLLO	rouse prison	STIR
• girl with round . . .	MAYO	rouse [prison]	PRIONS
• round ball	–OO–	**rout**	
• whip-round	CATO	[army] routed	MARY, MYRA
and		rout [hordes]	RESHOD
• round America	–OUS	**rove**	
• round enclosure	OPEN	rove [about]	U-BOAT
• round number	ONO, OTEN	[went] roving	NEWT
• round tree	OPINE	**row**	
• round-up	OUP	Rotten Row	RANK
round off	omit O	row	ADO
round the ring	incl O	row	OAR
round[2]		• row a circuit	OARLAP
put round<	TUP	• row in ship	SOARS
round a . . .	incl A	• second-class row	BOAR
round a nut<	TUNA	row	PULL
round about	incl C, CA, RE	• circular row	RING-PULL
• particle round about . . .	ICON	• row about . . .	PULLOVER
• se–nt round about . . .	SECANT	• row with alien	PULLET
• si–n round about . . .	SIREN	row	RANK
round about	RO–UND	• loud row	FRANK
• ro–und about the start . . .	ROTUND	• quiet row	SHRANK
round house<	–IMES, –OH	• row in front	RANKLED
round mollusc	SLUG	row	TIER
round [table]	BLATE, BLEAT	• mark row	DOTTIER
round the bend	MAD	• row about note	TIGER
round the bend	incl U	• row with journalist	TIERED
round up ducks	incl OO	row about	LIN–E, RO–W, TI–ER
• doctor rounded up ducks	DOOR	row of vehicles	CARLINE
round-up<	PU	row, say	ORE, SKULL
• round up< father	PUPA	rower	BOW
round-up of [cows]	SCOW	• angry rower	CROSSBOW
round up [lost] . . .	LOTS, SLOT	• rower in front	BOWLED
round up rats(D)^	STAR	• tall rower	LONGBOW
round *	incl *	rower	STROKE
• wat–er round church	WATCHER	• rower dead	STROKED

Letter replaced \c\at; Omit (a); Pointers out; Retain a; Split B_ED; Down (D); Backwards <or ^

• rowing expert	MASTER-STROKE
• support rower	BACKSTROKE
rowing boat	EIGHT, FOUR
rowing team, *say*	AIT, ATE, EYOT
	FORE

royal¹

royal	R
• royal assent	RAY
• royal bird	REGRET
• royal worker	RANT
royal badge/insignia	ER
royal chairperson	REGIUS PROFESSOR
royal fashion	PRINCETON
royal governess	ANNA
royal horse artist	KING COBRA
royal needlewoman	CLEOPATRA
royal neighbour	BISHOP
royal supporter	LION, UNICORN
royal town	CAMELOT
royal yacht	BRITANNIA
	COURTSHIP, KINGSHIP
royalty	ER
	(see also king²*)*

royal²

Academician/Academy	RA
Academy of Music	RAM
Air Force	RAF
Artillery	RA
Australian Navy	RAN
Automobile Club	RAC
Arch Charter	RAC
Armoured Corps	RAC
Asiatic Society	RAS
Astronomical Society	RAS
Canadian Academy	RCA
College of	
–Art	RC, RCA
–Music	RCM
–Organists	RCO
–Physicians	RCP
–Preceptors	RCP
–Science	RCS
–Sculptors	RCS
Corps of	
–Signals	RCS
–Transport	RCT
Dublin Society	RDS
Engineers	RE
Exchange	RE
Flying Corps	RFC
Geographical Society	RGS
Grenadier Guards	RGG
Hibernian Academy	RHA
Highland	
–Fusiliers	RHF
–Show	RHS

Highness	RH
Historical Society	RHS
Horse	
–Artillery	RHA
–Guards	RHG
Horticultural Society	RHS
Humane Society	RHS
Institute	RI
–of Chemistry	RIC
Institution of Painters	RI
Irish	
–Academy	RIA
–Constabulary	RIC
Mail	RM
–Steamer	RMS
Marines	RM
Microscopical Society	RMS
Military	
–Academy	RMA
–Police	RMP
Naval Reserve	RNR
Navy	RN
Observer Corps	ROC
Order of Victoria and Albert	VA
Philharmonic Orchestra	RPO
Photographic Society	RPS
Radar Establishment	RRE
School of Music	RSM
Scottish	
–Academician/Academy	RSA
–Water Colour Society	RSW
Society of	
–Antiquaries	RSA
–Arts	
–British Artists	RBA
–British Sculptors	RBS
–Edinburgh	RSE
–Etchers and Engravers	RE
–Literature	RSL
–Medicine	RSM
–Painters in Water Colours	RWS
–Portrait Painters	RP
Statistical Society	RSS
Ulster Constabulary	RUC
Yacht Squadron	RYS
Yachting Association	RYA
Zoological Society	RZS
r-rower	ROAR
rub	
rub *up the wrong way*(D)^	BUR
rubber	TOWEL, ULE
rubber bands	TYRES
rubber pipe, *say*	HOES
rubbish	
rubbish devoured	ROTATE
rubbish [in hedge]	HEEDING

Anag [cat]; Any *; Begin IGN–; Endings –ING; eg •; Hidden /cat/; Implied add (on); Implied in (in);

rubbished [his] . . .	–ISH
rubbishy [sort]	ORTS, ROTS, TORS
rude	
rude *noise*	ROOD
rude [Roman]	MANOR, NORMA
rude song, *say*	CORSAIR
rudely [shaped]	PHASED
rudimentary	ABCEDARIAN
ruffle	
ruffled [lake]	KALE, LEAK
ruffling [calm I] . . .	MALIC
rugby	
Rugby	RU
• rugby building	RUSHED
• rugby craze	RUMANIA
• rugby forward	RUPERT
• rugby match	RUB-OUT
Rugby bully	FLASHMAN
Rugby Football Club	RFC
rugby player	LION
rugby player, *say*	HOOKA(H)
ruin	
[ancestral] *ruins*	LANCASTER
mother's ruin	GIN
[mother's] *ruin*	SMOTHER, THERMOS
ruin [meal]	LAME, MALE
ruin, *say*	RECK
ruination of [much] . . .	CHUM
ruined girl, *say*	RECTOR
ruined [life]	FILE, LIEF
ruins drink	SPOILSPORT
ruins of [Troy]	TORY
ruins, *say*	RECKS, REX
rule	
rule	LAW
• fine rule	FLAW
• king's rule	COLESLAW
• rule ceremony, *say*	LAURITE
[rule] out	LURE
rule, *say*	RAIN, REIN
ruler	ER
ruler	KING
• ruler is quite with it	KINGSHIP
• ruler manufacturer	KINGMAKER
• ruler of the oceans, *say*	SEEKING
rum	
rum[baba]	ABBA
rum [affair]	RAFFIA
rum chaps	ODDFELLOWS
rum child	ODDS-ON
run¹	
run	R
• run over	ROVER
• run round	RO
run *away*	omit R
run *into*	incl R
run *off*	omit R
run out	RO
run *out (of)*	omit R
run *over*(D)	start with R
• run *over* a pretty girl	RADISH
run round	RO
run *short*	omit R
runs *round*	R–R
run²	
run	RUN
run *about*	RU–N
[run] *away*	NUR, URN
[run]-off	NUR, URN
[run] *out*	NUR, URN
run *over*<	NUR
run *round*	RU–N
run *round*<	NUR
run *the wrong way*<	NUR
run-*up*(D)^	NUR
run*about*	RU–N
run*about*<	NUR
[run]*about*	NUR, URN
run³	
run	BYE
• two runs	BYE-BYE
run	DESERT
• second *in* run	DESSERT
• run away twice	DESERT RAT
run	EXTRA
• run over	EXTRA
run	FLEE
• run from anarchist	FLEERED
• run from teacher, *say*	FLEECER
• run, *say*	FLEA
run	LEGIT
• run *with* one friend	LEGITIMATE
run	MANAGE
• run, *say*	MANEGE
• run soldiers exactly . . .	MANAGEMENT
run	RAT
• quiet run	PRAT
• run *during* exercise	PRATE
• run away twice	DESERT RAT
run	SINGLE
• knight *takes* a run, *say*	SURCINGLE
• run *with* shirt	SINGLET
• run *with* weight	SINGLETON
run	TROT
• animal runs	FOXTROTS
• run *about*	TRO T
• run *about*<	TORT
• run *back*<	TORT
run⁴	
[done a] *runner*	ANODE
run	CRESTA, LADDER

run amok [in the] . . .	THINE	• g–ut *ruptured by* duck		GOUT
run-of-the-mill	RACE	*rupturing* *		incl in *
run in front	ANTELOPE	• duck *rupturing* g–ut		GOUT
run rings round	O–O	**rural**		
run riot [in the] . . .	THINE	rural automatic exchange		RAX
run straight	DIRECT	Rural Dean		RD
run twice	DOUBLE	Rural District Council		RDC
* *run into*	incl *	rural sub-office		RSO
• everyone *runs into*		**rush**		
good fortune	BALLOON	rush *around*		FLA–G, RE–ED
run[about]	U-BOAT	rush forward		SURGEON
runabout [can go] . . .	CONGA	rush job		BASKETRY, THATCHING
runaway	DISH, SPOON	rush *up*(D)^		DEER
runaway [trains]	STRAIN	*rushing* [stream]		MASTER, REMAST
runner	BEAN	**Russia**		SU, USSR
• runners speak	BEANSTALK	**Russian**		
runner	COE	Russian		BEAR
• runner *takes in* five . . .	COVE	• Russian dead, *say*		BEARDED
runner	EMU	Russian		IVAN
• strong runner-*up*(D)^	FUME	• dead Russian		DIVAN
runner	MANAGER	• many Russian . . .		DIVAN
• home runner	HOUSE MANAGER	• Russian weedkiller		IVANHOE
runner	RILL, RIVER, STREAM	Russian		RED
	(*see* river)	• Russian food		REDDISH
runner	SKI	• Russian *grabbed by* commander		CREDO
• runner *has* quiet . . .	SKIP	• Russian's family		REDSKIN
runner	SMUGGLER	Russian		RUSS
runner, *say*	STOLEN	• Russian alien		RUSSET
runner unsuited	STREAKER	Russian		SERGE
runner-up	B	• Russian cloth		SERGE
runner-up in r<u>a</u>ce	A	• Russian soldier		SERGEANT
runners *neverending* . . .	RACEME(n)	Russian capital		ROUBLE
running	ADMIN, DIRECTION	<u>R</u>ussian *capital*		R
running	(in) HAS–TE	Russian flower		VOLGA etc
running amok, [IRA men] . . .	MARINE	<u>R</u>ussian *leader*		R
running out of stock	STAMPEDE	Russian measure, *say*		VERSED
running [race]	ACER, ACRE, CARE	**rust**		
running [shoes]	HOSES	rust colour		RUSTRED
running total	CRICKET SCORE	rust on weapon, *say*		PIE-CRUST
running water	EA	*rusty* [blade]		BALED
running wild in [Penarth]	PANTHER	[sword] *rusts*		WORDS
runny [nose]	NOES, ONES	**rustic**		
runway	TRIPLANE	rustic		HIND, HOB
	(*see also* ran)	• rustic accommodation		HINDQUARTERS
runt	ANTHONY, TANTONY	• rustic skill		HOBART
rupee	R	**rustling**	STOCKTAKING, TAKING STOCK	
rupture		**rut**		LANDMARK
rupture [vein]	VINE	**rutherford**		RD
ruptured by a . . .	incl0 A	**Rwanda**		RWA
ruptured by *	incl *			

S

as, Bach's works, *bend, bob,* bridge player, dollar, entropy, es, ess, God's, has, his, *hiss,* is, *largesse, Old Bob, paragon, part of collar,* Sabbath, saint, Saturday, schilling, Schmieder, second, segno, seven, seventy (thousand), several, shilling, ship, side, siemens, sigma, singular, *sinistra, sister, snow,* society, soh, son, soprano, south, southern, spade, special, square, stokes, strangeness, succeeded, sulphur, sun, Sweden, two hundred (thousand), us

Sabbath	S
sabotage	
sabotage [plane]	PANEL
[secret] *sabotage*	RESECT
sack	
sack	FIRE
• girl sacked, *say*	MISFIRED
• sack race	FIREFLY
• sacked a representative	FIREDAMP
sack journalist	OUSTED
sack race	GOTHS, JUTES, VANDALS
sacrifice	
[lamb] *sacrificed*	BALM
sacrificed [all the] . . .	LETHAL
sad	
sad	BLUE
• sad fish, *say*	BLUE-EYED
• sad time	BLUEBIRD
• sailors *have* sad . . .	NAVY BLUE
sad	DOWN
• bird *with* sad . . .	EIDERDOWN
• lives *in* sad . . .	DISOWN
• sad team	DOWNSIDE
sad *end*	D
sad [end]	DEN, NED
sad outlook, *say*	SORICENE
sadden worker	DEPRESSANT
sadly [spoke]	POKES
safe	
safe	PETER
• safe-blower	PETER PIPER
• safe *to* criticise	PETER PAN
• sailor *has* safe, *say*	SALTPETRE
safe conduct	EARTH
safe passage	SOUND
safety catch	SHOOTING BRAKE
safety *first*	F
safety wire	EARTH
°**said**	
said he intended, *say*	SEDIMENT
said, *perhaps*	TOLLED
	(*see also* say)
sail	
sail again, *say*	RESALE
sail, *say*	SALE
sailed	SLD
sailing	(in) S–HIP
• sailors *sailing*	STARSHIP
sailing	(in) S–S
• sailor *sailing*	STARS
sailing	(on) SHIP
• master *sailing*	HEADSHIP
sailing	(on) SS
• scholar *sailing*	MASS
sailing [along]	LOGAN
sailor	
sailor	AB
• 100 sailors	CABS
• ordinary sailor	ABNORMAL
• sailor employs . . .	ABUSES
• sailors in the . . .	ABSINTHE
sailor	HAND
• sailor *has* a few . . .	HANDSOME
• sailor's drink	HAND-SALE
• support sailor	BACKHAND
sailor	HEARTY
sailor	JACK
• sailor *on* vessel	JACKPOT
• sailor's greeting	HIJACK
• sailors working	JACKSON
sailor	MATELOT, MATLO(W)
sailor	OS
• Henry the sailor	HALOS
• sailor *has* a bird	OSTEAL
• sailor is able . . .	OSCAN
sailor	SALT
• city sailors	BATH SALTS
• sailor, English Navy	SALTERN

Letter replaced \c\at; Omit (a); Pointers *out*; Retain <u>a</u>; Split B_ED; Down (D); Backwards <or ^

• unwashed sailors	SMELLING SALTS
sailor	TAR
• black sailor	COALTAR
• sailor Brown	TARTAN
• sailors	TARTAR
• sailor's *double*	TARTAR
• sailors on their knees	TARSPRAYING
• sailor's *return*<	RAT
sailor-boy	ABED, JACKSON, SALTED
sailor-boy, *say*	SALTPETRE, SEASON
sailor *has* much . . .	MATELOT
sailor-king	MARINER
sailors	CREW
• sailors notice, *say*	CRUCITE
• sailors *take* girl, *say*	CRUCIBLE
sailors	NUS
sailors	RN
• officer *with* sailors	CORN
• you and I, *say*, *in* sailors' . . .	RUIN
sailor's daughter	POP-EYED
sailor's hat	BOATER
sailor's turn	ABOUT FACE
	(see also salt, tar)

saint

saint	S
• one saint	IS–
• saint is ill	SAILING
• saint will . . .	SWILL
• saints, *without* hesitation, . . .	SUMS
saint	ST
• 51 saints	LISTS
• one saint	–IST
• saint getting old	STAGED, STAGING
• saint *takes in* city . . .	SECT
saint	PETER
• concerning a saint, *say*	REPEATER
• saint *has* false . . .	PETERSHAM
• saint *takes in* another	PESTER
saintly	NOVICES
saints	SS, STS
salacious mariner	SALT

salad

[green] *salad*	GENRE, NEGRE
salad of [greens and] . . .	ENDANGERS

salary

salary	SCREW
• international salary	UNSCREW
• salary limit	SCREW TOP

sale

sale in May, *say*	MACE–ALE
sale of	
–partitioning, *say*	STUDDINGSAIL
–wives	DUTCH AUCTION
salesman	REP
• salesman *and* consumer	REPEATER
• salesman *in* church	CREPE

• salesman *with* fish	REPROACH
sally	
Sally is efficient	SALABLE
Sally's introduction	MESAL(LY)
saloon	
saloon body	CARCASE
saloon brawl	BARROW
saloon keeper	GARAGE
salt	
salt	AB
• salt only . . .	ABALONE
• salt fish	ABIDE, ABROACH
• salt-mark	ABSTAIN
• salt on road	ABROAD
• salt solution	ABSOLUTION
salt box	SEA-CHEST
salt container	OCEAN, SEA
	SHIP
salt *in it*	incl AB, TAR
• M–el *puts* salt *in* . . .	MABEL
• saint *takes* salt *in* . . .	START
	(see also sailor, tar)
Salvation Army	SA
same	
same	DO
• same entrance	DOGATE
• same little vessel	DOMINICAN
• same money	DOCENT, DOYEN
same	ID, IDEM
• dress the same	RIGID
• same fish	IDLING
• same island	IDIOM
same place	IB
sample	
qui/te a l/arge *sample*	TEAL
sample of chee/se w/ith . . .	SEW
sanctimonious	
sanctimonious	PI
• approve a sanctimonious . . .	OKAPI
• sanctimonious people	PILOT
• saint *without* sanctimonious . . .	SPIT
sandalwood	SHOE TREE
Sandhurst	RMA
sandwich	
meat *sandwich*	(in) MEA–T
• directions *found in* meat	
sandwich	MEANEST
sandwiched in *	incl in *
• small piece	
sandwiched in p–ly	PORTLY
sandwiched, *say*	INBRED
sane	NOMAD
sap	
sap	TRENCH
sap, *say*	DEUCE
sapling, *say*	TREASON

sapper	RE
sat	
sat *out*	SA–T
[sat] *out*	AST, ATS
Satan	(*see* devil)
satisfy	
satisfied constituents	CONTENT
satisfying encounter	MEETING
Saturday	S, SAT
sauce	
sauce	CHEEK, LIP
sauce [is hot]	HOIST
saucer	PLATELET
saucier, *say*	BOULDER
saucy novel	FRESH
sauna for vagrants	TRAMP STEAMER
sausage	
contents of sa/usage/s	USAGE
sausage crate	BANGER
sausage *skin*	SE
savage	
[leader] *savaged*	DEALER, REDEAL
savage [beast]	BASTE, BEATS
savaged [lambs]	BALMS
save	
save	BUT
• save money	BUTT IN
• save *up*(D)^	TUB
save a . . .	omit A
save a Conservative, *say*	CONSERVATORY
save chopper, *say*	STORAX
save more	USELESS
save, *say*	CASH, HORDE, WHORED
save time	omit T
save *	omit *
• (k)night *saves* king	NIGHT
saving Grace	DARLING
saving weight	BUTTON
saw	
saw gun	MAXIM
saw Herb, *say*	SAUSAGE
saw joint, *say*	SAWNEY
saw off end of timber	BOAR(d), PLAN(k)
sawn-off gu(n)	GU
	(*see also* see)
say[1]	
say	EG
• say nothing	EGO
• square, say	TEG
• student, say	LEG
say	SPEAK
say	SAY
• say *about* the wife	SWAY
• says nothing and	SAY-SO
• say "Fish", *say*	SAILING
• say "Light", *say*	SALITE
• say "Row", *say*	SALINE
• say "shells", *say*	SEYCHELLES
say	UTTER
• many say	CUTTER, MUTTER
• say in paper	MUTTERS
• say more than the others	UTTERMOST
say[2]	
indicating an anagram:	
• [Germans] *say*	MANGERS
• *say* "[Quiet!]"	QUITE
• [some] *say*	MOES
indicating homophone:	
• nose, *say*	KNOWS
• *said to be* you	EWE, YEW
• *said we ten* . . .	WHEATEN
• *say* no	KNOW
• *say* Sir	NIGHT
• *saying* aloud	ALLOWED
• some *say*	SUM
indicating one of a class:	
• cat, *say*	PERSIAN
• Persian, *say*	CAT
say[3]	
said *in French*	DIT
say French . . .	DIT
say "No rubbish!"	REFUSE
say quickly	EXPRESS
says the prophet, *say*	SESELI
	(*see also* said)
scale railway	LIBRARY
scalene triangle	ALONGSIDE
scalp	
scalp	omit 1st letter
• *scalp* actor	(p)LAYER
• *scalp* (d)rummer	RUMMER
scan	
scan	PORE
• scan opening	PORE
• second scan	SPORE
• silver *found in* scan	PORAGE
scan, *say*	POOR, POUR
Scandinavian vegetable	SWEDE
scare	
scare	SHOO
• scare model	SHOOT
scare, *say*	SHOE
• scare boy off	SHOE-BOY
Scarface	AL.
Scarlatti's works	K
scatter	
scatter bedding	LITTER
scatter children	LITTER
scatter[brain]	BAIRN, BRIAN
scattered [remains]	MARINES, SEMINAR
scattered around [seaport]	ESPARTO

Letter replaced \c\at; Omit (a); Pointers *out*; Retain a̲; Split B_ED; Down (D); Backwards <or ^

scatty	
scatty [boss]	SOBS
[she is] *scatty*	SHIES
scene	
scene of action	ONSET
scene, *say*	CITE, SIGHT
scenes	ACT
scholar	
scholar	BA
• scholar *and* Marine	BARM
• scholars in charge	BASIC
• scholar's quickly . . .	BASSOON
scholar	MA
• scholar in court	MAIN-YARD
• scholars deceive	MASCON
• tidier *after* scholar . . .	MAN-EATER
	(*see also* graduate)
school[1]	
school	ETON
• British school	BRETON
• master in charge	
around school	METONIC
• school *returns<*	NOTE
school, *say*	EATEN
school	GAM
• school book	GAMB
• school *has* scholar	GAMBA, GAMMA
• school, see	GAMELY
school	SCH
• nothing *in* British school	BORSCH
• school in America	SCHINUS
• school not in	SCHOUT
school, *say*	INFORM
• Communist school	COMINFORM
• school friend	INFORMALLY
• schoolgirl, *say*	MISINFORM
school[2]	
school [bus]	SUB–
school [horses]	SHORES
school member	FISH, PORPOISE, WHALE
School Mathematics Project	SMP
school procession	TRAIN
school stage	COACH
school subject	DISCIPLINE
school teachers	NUT
school transport	COACH, TRAIN
schoolboy overdue, *say*	PUPILATE
Schubert's works	D
sciatic	HIPPY
science	
science	–OLOGY
science centre	LAB
sci*e*nce *centre*	E
science fiction	SCIFI, SF
science institution	RS
Science Research Council	SRC

scientist	FRS
scoff	
scoff	BOO
• box *enclosing* scoff	CABOOSE
• reserves scoff	TABOO
• scoff *at* monarch	BOOK(ING), BOOR
scoff	WOLF
• scoff *at* monarch	WOLFER
scoffed	–ATE
scoffed, *say*	AIT, EIGHT, EYOT
scorch	
scorch	SEAR
• scorch, *say*	CERE
• scorch them, *say*	SERUM
• scorched earth policy	SEA-ROVER
scorched earth	BURNT SIENNA
	BURNT UMBER
scorched [earth]	HATER, HEART, RATHE
score	
score	TWENTY, XX
score a goal	NETBALL
score adjuster	ARRANGER
score less than 100	EIGHTY
score *quickly*	ALLEGRO, PRESTO
score *slowly*	LENTO
score twice	FORTY
scoreless draw	O–O
scorer	COMPOSER
Scot/Scotsman	
scot	TAX
• a Scot *returns* first-class< . . .	ATAXIA
• Scot lives . . .	TAXIS
• Scotsman	TAXMAN
scot, *say*	TACKS
Scotsman	IAN
• equal with Scot	PARIAN
• Flying Scot	SWIFTIAN
• well-mannered Scot	CIVILIAN
Scotsman	JOCK
• Scot *has cut* ey(e)	JOCKEY
• Scotsman *has* a ring	JOCKO
• Scotsman's gin	JOCKSTRAP
Scotsman	MAC
• Scot in front	MACLED
• Scotsman *with a* heretic	MACARIAN
• Scottish sailor	TARMAC
Scotsman	MON
• Scotsman looked . . .	MONEYED
• Scotsman that is dead	MONIED
• Scotsman's battle	MONS
Scotsman	SANDY
Scottish	
Scottish border	SCOTIA
<u>S</u>cottish capital	S
Scottish chieftain	CLANKING
Scottish *flower*	TAY etc

Anag [cat]; Any *; Begin IGN–; Endings –ING; eg •; Hidden /cat/; Implied add (on); Implied in (in);

Scottish *leader*   S
(*see also* Caledonian)

scoundrel
scoundrel, *say*   NAVE
scoundrel's honour   KNAVE

scrag
scrag-*end*   G
scraggy [lamb]   BALM

scramble
[much] *scrambling*   CHUM
scrambled [eggs]   SEGG
scrambling [nets]   STEN, TENS

scrap
scrap dismissed . . .   RAGOUT
scrap [iron]   ROIN
scrap merchant   BOXER, PUGILIST
scrap [paper as] . . .   APPEARS
scrap vessel   JUNK
scrappy [tale]   LATE, LEAT, TEAL

scratch
scratch   PAR
• scratch golfer   PARTAKER
scratch *head*   S
scratch head   omit 1st letter
• parent *scratched* head   (m)OTHER
• (s)on *scratches* head   ON
scratch, *say*   GREYS
scratch starter   ITCH
scratch *starter*   S
scratch starter   omit 1st letter
scratched record   PALIMPSEST

scrawl
scrawling [line]   LILN, NILE
[weird] *scrawl*   WIDER, WIRED

screecher   SWIFT

screen
screen guide   CURSOR
[screen] *production*   CENSER
top of screen(D)^   S

screw steamer   SS

scribble
scribble [note]   ETON, TONE
scribbled [verse]   SERVE
scribbling [in the] . . .   THINE

scrimmage
[I made] *scrimmage*   AIMED
scrimmage [near the] . . .   EARTHEN

scripture
Scripture Union   SU
scriptures   NT, OT

scruffy
[quite] *scruffy*   QUIET, –TIQUE
scruffy [nurse]   RUNES

scrum
scrum in [field]   FILED
scrummage [for the] . . .   FOTHER

scruple   SC

scuffle
scuffle [in the] . . .   THINE
scuffling [over] . . .   ROVE

sculpture
sculpted [torso]   ROOTS, STOOR
sculpture class   FORM
sculptured   SC, SCULP(SIT)
sculptured [bust]   BUTS, STUB

scuttle
scuttled [ship]   HIPS, PISH
scuttling [along]   LOGAN, LONGA

sea¹
sea   SEA
• sea fish   SEALING
• sea king   SEAR
[sea]-*change*   ASE
sea, *say*   SEE
• sea king, *say*   SEEK(ING), SEER
• seas, *say*   SEES, SEIZE
[sea]-*trip*   ASE
sea*front*   S
[sea]*sick*   ASE
sea*side*   S, A
storm at [sea]   ASE

sea²
sea   DEEP
• sea-bed   DEEP LITTER
• sea directions   DEEPENS
• sea-ice   DEEP FREEZE
sea   DRINK
• ready for sea   DRINK-MONEY
• sea-room   DRINK-HALL
• sea-king   DRINKER
sea   MAIN
• shirt *in* sea   MATIN
• the same sea   DOMAIN
• the sea remains . . .   MAINSTAYS
sea   MED
• sea, I see   MEDIC
• sea *touching* America   MEDUSA
• seaman   MEDAL
and
• sea-fish, *say*   MEDDLING
sea   MER
• sea-lines   MERRY
• sea-song   MERCHANT
• the sea I hold back   MERISTEM

sea³
at sea [all the] . . .   LETHAL
sea, *say*   C
    DIOCESE, ELY
sea-air   SHANTY
sea-bird   WREN
sea-bird, *say*   PUFFING
sea-dog   OCEAN GREYHOUND

Letter replaced \c\at; Omit (a); Pointers *out*; Retain a̲; Split B_ED; Down (D); Backwards <or ^

sea-green	WATER COLOUR
sea power	MAIN
sea room	CABIN
Seabee	CB
seafood	BISCUIT, HARD TACK
seafront	BOW, PROM(ENADE)
seaman	(*see* sailor)
seamen	NUS
seaport	SPT
seas	CC, CS
seaside	LARBOARD, LEE, PORT
	STARBOARD, WINDWARD
seaside branch	DRIFTWOOD
seaweed, *say*	RACK
seal	
sealed in [amber]	BREAM
sealed in am/berg/ris	BERG
sealed in *	incl in *
• god *sealed in* bo–x	BORAX
seam	
seam, *say*	SEEM
	VAIN, VANE
seamstress	(*see* sempstress)
search	
search	COMB
• search one country	COMBINATION
• search round	COMBO
season	
season	FALL
season	SALT
• graduate season	BASALT
• horse *in* season	SHALT
• we *follow* the season	SALTUS
season	SPRING
• season food	SPRINGBOARD
• season well	SPRING
• well season	WELLSPRING
seasoned	
–banger	PEPPERONI
–worker, *say*	MATURANT
seat	
seat material	CARLISLE, SATIN
seat of Empire	OTTOMAN
secant	SEC
second¹	
second	B
• name a second	NAB
• second eleven	BIX
• second line	BRANK, BROW
second	BACK
• pull second . . .	DRAWBACK
• second drink	BACKDROP
• second team	BACKSIDE
second	MO
• second lake	MOLOCH
• second little dog	MOP UP

• second man	MORON, MOTED
second	S
• Second Avenue	SMALL
• second best	SCREAM, STOP
• second class	SILK
• second edition	SPRINT
• second eleven	STEAM
• second gear	SKIT
• second hand	SL, SR
	STAR
• second organ	SLIVER
• second row	STIFF
• second ship	SKETCH
• seconds *out*	omit SS
and	
• three seconds	MOSS
second	SEC
• equal second	PARSEC
• second beer	SECALE
• *broken* [into] *after*	
second . . .	SECTION
second²	
Charles II	H
second best	B
second bit of cloth	L
second character in play	L
second class	L
second dose of medicine	E
second eleven	L
second half	A
second half of game	ME
second-hand	A
second-in-command	O
second of August	U
second opinion	P
second part of play	L
second piece of cake	A
second quality	U
second rate	A
Second Test	E
second wind	I
second³	
second best	B
second character	B, EVE
second child	ABEL
second class	B
• copper *has* second-class . . .	CUB
• second-class highway	BROAD
• second-class marriage	BUNION
and	
• second-class playground	
equipment, *say*	BEESWING
• second-class team, *say*	BESIDE
second-hand	PREPOSSESSED, USED
second-hand *addition*	PAWPAW
second-hand item	CLOCK, WATCH

Anag [cat]; Any *; Begin IGN–; Endings –ING; eg •; Hidden /cat/; Implied add (on); Implied in (in);

second helping	DOUBLE TAKE	secure	SAFE
second in importance	MOMENT	• secure street	SAFEST
second mover	BLACK	• trustee *in* secure . . .	STRAFE
second person	EVE, YOU	secure locker	CHASTITY BELT
second quality	B	secure post	CHAIN MAIL
second-rate	B	secured by *	incl in *
Second Test	RESIT, RETRIAL	• organ *secured by* sh–ed	SHEARED
second thoughts	PS	*secured in* stron/g room/s	GROOM
second wedding	REMATCH	secures objective	LANDS END
secondary		*securing* a . . .	incl A
secondary	B	*securing* *	incl *
• company *has* secondary . . .	COB	• sh–ed *securing* an organ	SHEARED
• secondary road	BROAD	**see**	
• secondary school	BETON	see	C
secret		• see about	CC, CRE
secret agent	MOLE	• see girl	CLASS
• secret agent defects	MOLE-RATS	• see one	CONE
• secret agent *surrounds* artist	MORALE	• see one rear . . .	CISTERN
• secret agent's family	MOLESKIN	and	
secret drinkers	AA	• see *into* far–e	FARCE
Secret Intelligence Service	SIS	• see why, *say*	CY
secret service	CIA	• see you, *say*	COPPER, CU
secret service *leaders*	SS	see	DIOCESE
secretary		see	ELY
secretaries	CIS	• king *takes* see	RELY
secretary	SECY	• see *about* a king	EARLY
secretary	TEMP	• see water-parsnip	ELYSIUM
• secretary *to* the queen	TEMPER	see	EYE
• secretary overdue	TEMPLATE	• animal sees . . .	OX-EYES
• secretary's hair-do	TEMPTRESSES	• see ship	EYE-LINER
secrete		• see small coin	EYED
secrete	HIDE	and	
• Green secretes . . .	RAWHIDES	• sees Hell	EYE-SHADES
• secrete, *say*	HIED	• sees mineral	EYESORE
• secrete spring	HIDEBOUND	• sees retinue	EYE-STRAIN
secreting a . . .	incl A	see	LA
secreting *	incl *	• see *into* last . . .	ELAND
• ma–n *secreting* one . . .	MAIN	• see representative	LAMP
secreted by *	incl in *	• see the doctor	LAMB
• one *secreted by* ma–n	MAIN	and	
section		• see about	LAC
[inter]*section*	NITRE, TRINE	• see *about*<	AL
section of the . . .	T, H, E	see	LO
section of th/e lates/t	ELATES	• see female laugh	LOHENGRIN
secure		• see fruit	LOP-EAR
secure	BAG	• see fur	LOSABLE
• secure duct	BAGPIPE	• see nothing	LOO
• secure fruit	BAGGAGE	and	
• worker secures . . .	HANDBAGS	• see about	LOC–
secure	LOCK	• see *about*<	OL
• fine *and* secure . . .	FLOCK	see	LOOK
• gas *surrounds* secure . . .	CLOCKS	• father, see as . . .	PALOOKAS
• secures mine	LOCKSPIT	• see child	LOOKS ON
secure	NAIL	• see the queen	LOOKER
• second secure . . .	SNAIL	and	
• secure dossier	NAIL-FILE	• see twice	LOOKSEE

Letter replaced \c\at; Omit (a); Pointers *out*; Retain a; Split B_ED; Down (D); Backwards <or ^

see	NOTICE
see	SEE
• the *French* see . . .	LESSEE
• see many . . .	SEEM
• see quiet . . .	SEEP
and	
• see *about*	SE–E
• [see] *differently*	–ESE
and	
• see friends, *say*	SEPALS
• see gentleman, *say*	SET-OFF
• see girl, *say*	SENORA
and	
• see animal, *say*	SEA-DOG
• see fish, *say*	SEALING
• see ring, *say*	SEATING
and	
• see fish, *say*	CEILING
• see insect, *say*	CETIC
and	
• see Nicholas, *say*	SCENIC
and	
• see twice	LOOKSEE
see	SIGHT
• see *about* money	SLIGHT
• see *after* animal	HINDSIGHT
• see prophet	SIGHTSEER
see	SPOT
• see *about* one good . . .	SPIGOT
• see fewer . . .	SPOTLESS
• warm sea, *say*	HOTSPOT
see	SPY
• English see . . .	ESPY
• see knight, *say*	SPICER
• see state, *say*	SPICAL
and	
• saw her, *say*	SPIDER
see	V
• see flowers	VLEI
• see no married . . .	VOWED
• see one vehicle	VICAR
see	VID, VIDE
• see last one	VIDENDA
• see nothing	VIDEO
see below	ASUNDER
	(*see also* saw)
seedy	
[seem] *seedy*	MESE
seedy, *say*	CD
seem	
seems like new . . .	GNU, KNEW
seems right	RITE, WRITE
seems to be fur	FIR
seen	
[seen] *around*	–ENSE, –NESE
seen close at hand, *say*	NICENE

seen in [China]	CHAIN
seen in French town	VILLE
seen in German book	BUCH
seen in Italian hotel	ALBERGO
seen in Phi/lad/elphia	LAD
seen in Roman road	VIA
seen in Spanish house	CASA
seen in *	incl in *
• German *seen in* ship	SHUNS
seen primarily in very young	IVY
seen *talking*	CITED, SCENE, SITED
	(*see also* see, saw)
seer	
seer	EYE, OPTIC
seer, *say*	AUGER, PROFIT
	CERE, SEAR
seize	
seize claw	POUNCE
seize eggs	CLUTCH
seize her, *say*	CAESAR
seize journalist	GRIPED
seize one, *say*	CHOLERA
seize, *say*	SEAS, SEES
seize space	GRABEN
seized by *	incl in *
• king *seized by* b–east	BREAST
seizer, *say*	CAESAR
seizing a . . .	incl A
seizing *	incl *
• b–east *seizing* king	BREAST
select	
select	PICK
• select a defender	PICKABACK
• select chopper	PICKAXE
• select fish	PICKLING
and	
• select a bag, *say*	PICCADILLY
• select ceremony, *say*	PICRITE
• select speed, *say*	PICRATE
select group	IMPANEL
selected	INSIDE
selected from t/he be/st . . .	HEBE
selection from gran/d ope/ra	DOPE
selection [panel]	PLANE
Selective Employment Tax	SET
selector	ERNIE
self	
self-assured, *say*	CONFIDANT(E)
self-banking aircraft	AUTOGIRO
self-*centred*	EL
self-confessed	AM, IAM, IM
• *self-confessed* essayist	AMELIA
• *self-confessed* fool	AMASS
• *self-confessed* Scotsman	AMMON
and	
• *self-confessed* adult	IMMATURE

• self-confessed beauty	IMPEACH	sent, *say*	NOSE, SCENT
• *self-confessed* pretender	IMPOSER		TRAIL
	(*see also* admit)		(*see also* send)
self-contained	SC	**separate**	
self-description	AM, IAM, IM	separate quickly	BREAKFAST
self help	DIY	*separate parts of* <u>house</u>	HUE
self-*starter*	S	*separate parts of* [Spain]	PAINS
sell		separate way	SEVERE
sell cosh, *say*	CELL-SAP	*separated by* a . . .	incl A
sell	VEND	*separated by* *	incl *
• sell fish, *say*	VENDACE	• Poles *separated by* father	SPAN
• sell one . . .	VENDACE	*separating* *	incl in *
• sell *without* note	VENTED	• father *separating* Poles	SPAN
sell hawk	RETAIL	**September**	SEP(T)
sell-off, *say*	SAIL	**sequence**	
sell, *say*	PEDAL	*sequence from* Bib/le st/ories	LEST
seller's option	SO	*sequence in* music/al so/lo	ALSO
semester	TERMINUS	*sequence of* head/s or t/ails	SORT
seminary	SEM	**sergeant**	
semi-		*drill* [sergeant]	ESTRANGE
semi-molten	MOL, TEN	sergeant	NCO, SERG(T), SGT
[semi]-*molten*	–IMES	sergeant-at-law	SL
semi-tone	TO, NE	sergeant-major	SM
semitone	FLAT, SHARP	[sergeant's] *mess*	ESTRANGES, GREATNESS
sempstress		**series**	
sempstress	MIMI	serially, *say*	INTERN(E)
• sempstress *has* a hundred . . .	MIMIC	series	SER
• sempstress *has* to weep	MIMICRY	series, *say*	SWEET
senator	SEN	**serious matter**	GRAVEDO
send		**sermon**	SER
send car	TRANSPORT	**serve**	
[send] *letters*	DENS, ENDS	serve	
send notes to . . .	SERENADE	• former pupil serves	OBSERVES
[send] *off*	DENS, ENDS	and	
[send] *out*	DENS, ENDS	• serve many, *say*	CERVELAT
send to bed	SCUTTLE, SINK	• serve one state, *say*	CERVICAL
	(*see also* sent)	serve sentence	BEHELD
Senegal	SN	serve singer	WAIT
senior		*served up* in . . . (D)^	NI
senior	SENR, SR	*served up* [stew]	WEST, WETS
senior common room	SCR	*served up* stew(D)^	WETS
Senior Deacon	SD	**service**	
Senior Medical Officer	SMO	service	ACE
sense		• document *about* service	MACES
sense	NOUS	• service *to* king	ACER
sense of worry, *say*	GILT	• strong service	FACE
sense*less*	omit NOUS	service	LET
sensitive		• second service	BLET
sensitive	TENDER	• service he . . .	LETHE
• ban sensitive . . .	BARTENDER	• service *without* normal . . .	LENT
• sensitive back	TENDERLOIN	service	MASS
• sensitive support	TENDERFOOT	• service area	MASSACRE
sent		• service provided	MASSIF
sent boy to the bottom	SUNCLAD	• service vehicles	MASS MEDIA
sent *by* rail	SENTRY	• serviceman	MASSED
sent man, *say*	CENTRON PERFUMIER	service	RAF

Letter replaced \c\at; Omit (a); Pointers *out*; Retain <u>a</u>; Split B_ED; Down (D); Backwards <or ^

• service at this point, *say*	RAFFIA	set	GEL
• service charge	RAFFEE	• *back* in< set	NIGEL
• service *in* court	CRAFT	• set fire	GELIGNITE
service	RN	and	
• acceptable *in* service	RUN	• set *about*<	LEG
• against church service	CONCERN	• set *up*(D)^	LEG
• graduate *takes* service	BARN	• set*back*<	LEG
service area	CATHEDRAL, CHURCH	set	LAID
service book, *say*	MISSEL, MISTLE	• *about in* a set	LAIRED
service-charge	COURT MARTIAL	• quiet set	PLAID
service dress	CASSOCK, SURPLICE	• *take* one *out of* set	LA(i)D
	SD	and	
service *return*<	FAR	• set *about*<	DIAL
service tree	SORB	• set *up*(D)^	DIAL
serviceman	AIRMAN, GI	• set*back*<	DIAL
	SAILOR, SOLDIER	**set³**	
	PRIEST	*set* a *precedent*	start with A
	WAITER	• leader *sets* a *precedent*	ACID
serviceman's cap	BIRETTA, MITRE	*set* [a test]	TASTE, TEATS
servicewoman	AIRWOMAN, ATS	set *about* a	incl A
	WAAF, WREN	set *about* it	incl IT
	WAITRESS	• w–e set *about* it	WITE
serving as	QUA	set *about* it<	TI
• serving as a building	QUASHED	set *about* *	incl *
• serving as a light	QUAVERY	• w–e set *about* her	WHERE
serving girl	AIRWOMAN, ATS	*set aside* a . . .	omit A
	TENNIS PLAYER	*set free* [slave]	LAVES, VALES, VALSE
	WAAF, WREN	*set aside* money	omit D, L, P
	WAITRESS	*set aside* *	omit *
serving man	AIRMAN, GI	• (p)arish *sets aside* park	ARISH
	SAILOR, SOLDIER	*set in* a sil/ver se/a	VERSE
	TENNIS PLAYER	*set in* s/ton/e	TON
	WAITER	*set in* * . . .	incl in *
		• one *set in* he–r . . .	HEAR
set¹		set *of books*	NT, OT
set	SET	*set off* quietly	1st letter(s) P, SH
set *about* . . . <	TES	• I led *and set off* quietly	PILED
set *about*	S–ET	• journalist *set off* quietly	SHED
• s–et *about* man	SHERBET	*set off with* a . . .	1st letter A
[set] *free*	–EST, STE, TES	*set off with* king	1st letter K, R
[set] *off*	–EST, STE, TES	*set off with* student	1st letter L
set *out*	SE–T	set *out* (=start)	
• se–t *out* new . . .	SENT	• *train sets out* . . .	T
[set] *out*	–EST, TES, STE	*set out in* [bedroom]	BOREDOM
se–t *outside* a . . .	SEAT	*set out in* pla/in ter/ms	INTER
set*back*<	TES	*set up* pins(D)^	SNIP
[set]*off*	–EST, STE, TES	setter	DOG, PECTIN
[sets] *free*	TESS	*setting for* a . . .	incl A
set*up*(D)^	TES	*setting for* *	incl *
set²		• h–e *provides setting for* queen	HERE
set	PUT	[setting] *out*	TESTING
• set *about* group	PUTREFACTION	*setting* [sun I'm] . . .	MINUS
• set point	PUTS	**setback**	
and		new *setback*	WEN
• set *about*<	TUP	set*back*<	TES
• set *up*(D)^	TUP	*setback* Ben's . . .	SNEB
• set*back*<	TUP		

Anag [cat]; Any *; Begin IGN–; Endings –ING; eg •; Hidden /cat/; Implied add (on); Implied in (in);

setback for Cupid<	SORE
setback ten<	NET
settle	
settle	SAG
• settle *up*(D)^	GAS
settle down	PREEN
settle in German currency	LANDMARKS
settle on(D)	
• bird *settles on* the *French*	TITLE
settle score	BENCHMARK, COMPOSE
settle [score]	CORES
settled for [ever]	VEER
settled matter	SEDIMENT
settlement of [case]	ACES, AESC
seven	
seven	VII, S
seven Christmas presents	SWANS
seven days, *say*	WEAK
[seven] *letters*	EVENS
seven-nil	SEVENTY
seventy	
70% of hall	AUDITOR(ium)
seventy	O, OMICRON, S
seventy-eight	DISC, RECORD
seventy miles per hour	LIMIT
seventy thousand	O, OMICRON, S
seventy years	LIFESPAN
several	
several	VI, V, VI, S, TEN, X
several birds	DIVERS
several weapons, *say*	FOREARMS
several working, *say*	SUMMON
	(*see also* some[1])
severance pay	ALIMONY
sew	
sew, *say*	SO, SOW
sewer	MIMI
	SEAMSTRESS, SEMPSTRESS
	NEEDLE
sewer cover	ETUI, THIMBLE
sews, *say*	SOSO, SOWS
sex	
sex appeal	IT, SA
[sex]-*change*	EXS
sex drive, *say*	LUSTRATE
sextet	VI
Seychelles	SY
shack	QUARTER-HORSE
shade	
[acts] *shadily*	CATS, SCAT
shade doorway	HATCH
shady [deal]	DALE, LADE, LEAD
shake	
shake	ROCK
• shake sailor	ROCK-TAR
• shakes fish, *say*	ROCK-SEAL
• shakes pensioner	ROCK-SOAP
[no great] *shakes*	ETON RAG
shake [dice]	ICED
shake head	omit 1st letter
• (g)oat *shakes head*	OAT
• parent *shakes head*	(m)OTHER
• *shakes* (h)is *head*	IS
shake off a . . .	omit A
shake off *	omit *
• (M)other *shakes off* Frenchman	OTHER
shake up [bolster]	LOBSTER
shaken [by a] . . .	BAY
shaking [rattle]	TATLER
shaky condition	AGUE, PALSY
shaky notes	QUAVERS
shaky [notes]	ONSET, SETON
	STONE, TONES
sham	
[it was] *sham*	WAIST, WAITS
sham fabric	PETER
sham [satin]	STAIN
shamrock	ARTIFICIAL DIAMOND
shameful	
[acts] *shamefully*	CATS, SCAT
shameful [action]	CATION
shape	
shape insect	FORMANT
shape [of a] . . .	OAF
shape of [vase]	AVES, SAVE
shaping [ends]	DENS, SEND
share	
share allotment	ALLOWANCE
share beds	ALLOTMENT
share bill	CO-STAR
share dessert	SPLIT
share issue	SOLOMON'S JUDGEMENT
share of champ/agne s/upper	AGNES
share of m(one)y	ONE
share of profit	PR, OF, IT
share pusher	PLOUGHMAN
share, *say*	QUOTER
shared china, *say*	COMING
shared out [loot]	TOOL
[share]*out*	HARES, HEARS
	RHEAS, SHEAR
sharp	
sharp	UNNATURAL
sharp alien	BRISKET
sharp fall	ACID DROP, ACID RAIN
Sharp girl	BECKY
sharp lament	KEEN
sharp stone	BRILLIANT
sharpen, *say*	WET
sharper port	TANGIER
sharpshooter	ANNIE (OAKLEY)
	CUPID, EROS

shatter

shatter	WRECK
• second joint shattered	SHIPWRECKED
• shatter ruler, *say*	WRECKING
• shatters, *say*	RECKS, REX
and	
• shatter Conservative, *say*	RECTORY
• shattered America, *say*	RECTUS
• shattered them, *say*	RECTUM
shatter a number, *say*	RUINATE
shatter, *say*	BRAKE, RECK
shattered a street	BUSTARD
shattered [vase]	SAVE
shattering [blow]	BOWL
shatters, *say*	BRAKES

Shaw

Shaw	GBS
[Shaw] *play*	HAWS, WASH
Shaw's girl	ELIZA

she

she drowned, *say*	SEA-ADDER
She, *for one*	NOVEL
she is in debt, *say*	HEROES
she, *objectively*	HER
she will	SHE'LL
she will, *say*	SHEAL, SHEEL, SHIEL
she would	SHE'D

shed

(o)ran(g) *shed its skin*	RAN
shed a . . .	omit A
shed leaves	omit FF
shed weight	omit TON
shed will, *say*	SHACKLE
shed *	omit *
• ba(skin)g, *shedding* skin	BAG
shed [tears]	ASTER, RATES
	STARE, STEAR, TARES

sheep

sheep	RAM
• sheep and fish, *say*	RAMEAL
• sheep attendant	RAMPAGE
• sheep sheared	RAMOON, RAMSHORN
• sheep stealer	RAM RAIDER
• sheep's hobble	RAMSHACKLE
sheep-dog's kennel, *say*	COLLIERY
sheep noises	BAAS
sheep, *say*	USE, YEW(S), YOU
	WEATHER, WHETHER
sheep's family	LAMBSKIN, RAMSKIN

sheepshank

sheepshank	LEG OF LAMB
	LEG OF MUTTON
sheepshank, *say*	RAMPART

sheet

sheet	P
• sheet *missing*	omit P
sheet music	NOTEPAPER

shell

(n)ut(s) *shelled*	UT
say "shells"	SEYCHELLES
shell-(c)as(e)	AS
shell (f)ire(d)	IRE
shell of nuts	NS
shell from mortar	MR
shellfish, *say*	MUSCLE

shelter

shelter	LEE
• shelter minor	LEEWARD
• sheltered circle	LEERING
• sheltered hospital unit	LEEWARD
shelter squirrel	SKUG
sheltered by li/me tre/e	METRE
sheltered by *	incl in *
• bird *sheltered by* l–and	LOWLAND
sheltering a . . .	incl A
sheltering in c/aver/n	AVER
sheltering king	incl R
sheltering *	incl *
• l–and *sheltering* bird	LOWLAND

shenanigans

[loud] *shenanigans*	LUDO
shenanigans [in the] . . .	THINE

shield

shielded by sm/all ow/l	ALLOW
shielded by *	incl in *
• girl *shielded by* metal . . .	TANNIN
shielding a . . .	incl A
shielding *	incl *
• metal *shielding* girl	TANNIN
youn/g ash/ *shielding* . . .	GASH

shift

[gear]-*shift*	RAGE
shift [soil]	OILS, SILO
shift worker	FURNITURE REMOVER
shiftily [take] . . .	KATE, TEAK
shifting [the car]	THRACE
shifty person	NOMAD
[late] *shift*	LEAT, TALE, TEAL

shilling

shilling	BOB
• shilling animal	BOBCAT
• shilling duck	BOB
• sound shilling	PLUMB-BOB
shilling	S
• shilling *on* a horse	SHACK
• shilling *off*	omit S
shilling canopy	TESTER

shimmer

shimmering [silk 'e] . . .	LIKES
[star] *shimmers*	RATS, TARS

shine

shine	GLOW

Anag [cat]; Any *; Begin IGN–; Endings –ING; eg •; Hidden /cat/; Implied add (on); Implied in (in);

• shine a light and	GLOW LAMP
• shine *on* porcelain, *say*	GLOAMING
• shine perfectly, *say*	GLOAT
shiny, *say*	GLACIS
ship	
ship	CRAFT
• house-boat	HOMECRAFT
• ship *with* unknown . . .	CRAFTY
• shipping trade	CRAFT
• which ship, *I ask*	WITCHCRAFT
ship	HOY
• a king *in* ship	HOARY
• ship study	HOYDEN
ship	KETCH
• second ship	SKETCH
• ship to windward	KETCHUP
ship	SS
• big ship	LARGESS
• mother-ship	MASS
• ship *carrying* hot . . .	SHOTS
• the *French* ship and	LESS
• ship *has left*	omit SS
ship	LINER
• been *on* ship, *say*	BIN-LINER
• display ship	AIRLINER
• most important ship	MAINLINER
ship	MV
ship-breaker	DESTROYER
[ship]-*breaking*	HIPS, PISH
ship *docked*	LINE(r)
ship launcher	HELEN
shipboard games, *say*	DECATHLON
ship's . . .	HER
ship's name	HERN
ship's working	HERON
ship's bar	TAFFRAIL
ship's barber	CLIPPER, CUTTER
ship's bell, *say*	LUTEIN
ships' companies, *say*	CRU(I)SE
ship's company, *say*	KROO
ship's glasses	SCHOONERS
ship's orchestra	WAVEBAND
ship's side beams	PORTRAYS
ship's timber	FLEETWOOD
shipping company	LINE
shipping line	CABLE, PLIMSOLL
shipshape	SCAPHOID
[ship]*shape*	HIPS, PISH
shipworker, *say*	DECANT
[ship]*wreck*	HIPS, PISH
shirker	CUTHBERT
shirt	
shirt	T
shirt-*front*	S

shirt-*tail*	T
shirtmaker	SHIFTWORKER
shiver	
[quite] *shivery*	QUIET, –TIQUE
shivering [fits are] . . .	FAIREST
shock	
shock, *say*	HARE
shock treatment	HAIRCUT, HAIRDRESSING
shocking [case]	ACES, AESC
shocking drink	JAR
shockingly [bad]	ABD–, DAB
shoe	
shoe	LAST THING
shoe tree	SANDALWOOD
shoemaker	CRISPIN, SUTOR
	LEATHER
shoemaker, *say*	SUITOR
shoemaker's drink	COBBLER
[shoe]*making*	HOES, HOSE
shoot	
shoot	FIRE
• girl shooting, *say*	MISFIRING
• shoot a bullet	FIREBALL
• shoot a soldier and	FIREMAN
• shoot *after* uncle, *say*	SAMPHIRE
shoot	POT
• second shoot	SPOT
• shoot *at* can	POTABLE
• shoot old hen	POT-BOILER
• shoots *at* mare	POTSDAM
shoot	SNIPE
• shoot a woman, *say*	SNIPER
• shoot bird	SNIPE
shoot dog *up* . . . (D)^	GOD
[shoot]-*out*	HOOTS
shooting	(in) BU–D
shooting all over [Wales]	SWALE
shooting all over the place, [we hit], ,	WHITE
shooting box	CAMERA
shooting brake	SAFETY-CATCH
shooting break	TRUCE
shooting equipment	CAMERA
shooting-men	GUNNERS, RA
shooting star	ANNIE (OAKLEY)
shoots animals	POTSHERD
shoots sailors	FILM STARS
	(*see also* shot)
shop	
[shop] *around*	HOPS, POSH
shop laws	COUNTERACTS
shop-lifting	RUSTLING, STOCKTAKING, TAKING STOCK
shopping *centre*	PP
shopworker	COUNTERMARCHER

Letter replaced \c\at; Omit (a); Pointers *out*; Retain <u>a</u>; Split B_ED; Down (D); Backwards <or ^

shorn   DISTRESSED, UNLOCKED
short[1]
indicating abbreviation:
short answer   A, ANS
short break   HOL(S), VAC, WE
short contest   COMP
short course   PUD
short day   D, MON etc
short drink   METHS
short holiday   HOL(S), VAC, WE
short measure   FT, IMM–, IN, MM, YD
Short Metre   SM
short notice   AD(VERT)
short publication   MAG
short question   Q
short regulation   REG
short spell (=abbreviation)
 • always *has short spell*   EER
 • *short spell* of work   OP
 • *short spell* will not . . .   WON'T
short time   HR, MIN, MO, SEC, T, YR
short vacation   HOL(S), VAC, WE
short walk   PROM
short wave   SW
short work   OP
shortly I will . . .   I'LL
shortly release   DEMOB
                              (*see also* contract)

short[2]
indicating omission:
a *short* . . .   omit A
quit(e) *shortly*   QUIT
run *short*   omit R
short cut   CU(t), (l)OP, AX(e)
short *cut*   SHOR(t)
short-le(g)   LE
short-list   INVENTOR(y)
short measure   PIN(t)
short of a . . .   omit A
short of a bob   omit S
short of a bit of sugar   CUB(e)
short of energy   omit E
short of a hundred . . .   omit C
short of money   omit L, P
short of oxygen   omit O
short of space   SPA, ACE
short of time   omit AGE, T
short of *   omit *
 • b(all)et *short of* all . . .   BET
short story   (s)TORY, TAL(e)
short term   HILAR(y)
short time   (h)OUR, TIM(e)
short wal(k)   WAL
shortage of cash   CAS, ASH
shorten skir(t)   SKIR
shorter (st)ride   RIDE

shorter than you(r) . . .   YOU
shortfall in remuneration   PA(y), (s)CREW
                                            WAG(e)

short[3]
other uses:
short break   COMMA
short dance   ONE-STEP, TWO-STEP
short holiday   OFFBREAK
short illness   CURTAILMENT
short jacket, *say*   BASK
short measure   INCH, LOWELL
short of   LACK
 • second short of . . .   SLACK
 • short of a number, *say*   LACCATE
 • short of time   LACK-A-DAY
short of funds   (in) R–ED
short race   DASH, SPRINT
                                       LILLIPUTIANS
                           PIGMIES, PYGMIES
short sentence, *say*   FRAISE, FRAYS
short skirt, *say*   MINNIE
short stop   COMMA
short suit   BRIEFCASE, SINGLETON
short telephone call   RINGLET
shorten   DOCK
 • shorten *after* son had . . .   SHADDOCK
 • shorten it, *say*   DOCKET
 • shortened airport, *say*   DOCTORLY
shorten bridge   CONTRACT
shorten crossing   CONTRACT BRIDGE
shorten item   DETAIL
shortfall   SHOWER, UNDERGROWTH
shot
[moon]*shot*   MONO
shot [daring spy]   DAYSPRING
shot-wound   STAB
should
should, *say*   AUTO
 • should criticise, *say*   AUTOCARP
 • should eat, *say*   AUTODYNE
 • should marry, *say*   AUTOMATE
shout
a loud *shout*   ALLOWED, ALOUD
shout   CRY
 • shout *before* exercise   CRYPT
 • shout louder   OUTCRY
 • shout *to* child   CRY-BABY
and
 • shout "Hooter", *say*   CRINOSE
 • shout "Porcelain" *say*   CRIMING
 • shout *to* knight, *say*   CRINITE
shout in pain   CALLOW, YELLOW
[shout] out   SOUTH, THOUS
shouted, *say*   BALE, HALLOWED
shouting for meals, *say*   ROARING FORTIES
shove

shove [under a] . . .	UNREAD	**shy**	
shoving [past]	STAP, TAPS	shy bear, *say*	COYPU
show		shy writer	LOBELIA
show	AIR	**Sibyl's job**	PROPHECY
• quiet shows	PAIRS	**sick**	
• show people	AIRMEN	sick	AILING
• showboat	AIRCRAFT, AIRSHIP	• a very sick . . .	AVAILING
show a . . .	incl A	• sick king	RAILING
show *	incl *	• sick *on* a ship	ASSAILING
• lea–rn *to show* the . . .	LEATHERN	sick	ILL
show embarrassment	GORED	• saint *has* sick . . .	SILL, STILL
show-girl	EVITA	• sick head	ILLNESS
show hospitality	ENTERTAINMENT	• sick joke	ILL-HUMOUR
show-house	THEATRE	and	
show jumper	VAULTING HORSE	• sick bird, *say*	ILLEGAL
show over	CATSUP	sick person	O'NEILL
s/how/-*piece*	HOW	*sick*-[note]	ETON, TONE
show-[pieces]	SPECIE	*sick* [to her] . . .	OTHER
show-ring	MANIFESTO	*sickly* [baby 'e] . . .	ABBEY
show, *say*	SEEN	sickly child	PALETOT
show tolerance	PLAY	sickly, *say*	PICQUET
show-trial	REHEARSAL	**side**	
showboat	STAGECRAFT	side	L, R
shower	SHORTFALL	• side-*splitting* one . . .	ACRE
showing as [it was]	WAIST, WAITS	• side-*splitting* girl	LEVER, REVEL
showing in cine/ma ne/ar you	MANE	side	TEAM
shown in t/heat/re	HEAT	• second side	STEAM
shred		• side *with* journalist	TEAMED
[rag]-*shredding*	GAR	side	XI, XV
shred [papers]	SAPPER	side at sea	LARBOARD, PORT, STARBOARD
shredded [nerves]	SEVERN	[side] *at* sea	DIES, IDES
shrew	KATE, XANTIPPE	[side]-*splitting*	DIES, IDES
shrink		side to side movement	TRANSFER
shrink	omit 1st and last letters	side of	
• *shrink* (c)lot(h)	LOT	–field	LEG, OFF
• *shrunken* (c)otto(n) . . .	OTTO	–road	NEAR, OFF
shrinking violet	LET, VET, VI, VIOL	–ship	LARBOARD, PORT
shudder			STARBOARD
shuddering [when I] . . .	WHINE	side plank, *say*	WAILER, WHALER
[stop] *shuddering*	OPTS, POTS, SPOT, TOPS	side promises . . .	FACETIOUS
shuffle		side *with* friend	LEGALLY
shuffle [teams]	MATES, MEATS, STEAM	*sides of* bacon	BN
shuffling [along]	GOLAN	sides of stage	OPPOSITE PROMPT
shuffling around [town]	WONT		PROMPT SIDE
shunt		*sides of* stage	SE
shunt [engine D]	NEEDING	sidesman	BISHOP, CASTLE, ROOK
shunting [train as] . . .	ARTISAN	West *Side*	W
shut		**siemens**	S
shut in *	incl in *	**Sierra Leone**	WAL
• man *shut in* food store	PEDANTRY	**sift**	
[shut] *off*	HUTS, THUS, TUSH	[clues I] *sift* . . .	SLUICE
[shut] *out*	HUTS, THUS, TUSH	*sifting* [soil]	OILS, SILO
shut *up*(D)^	NEP	**sight**	
* *shut in*	incl *	sight, *say*	CITE, EIFFEL, SEEN, SITE
• I am *shut in* study	COIN	sight-screen	EYELID
shutter	EYELID	**sigma**	S

sign	
right sign	TICK
sign	ARIES, RAM etc
sign	MINUS, PLUS, V
sign of error	(A)CROSS, X
sign of summer	PLUS
sign of take-away	MINUS
sign of the times	DATE STAMP, X
sign, *say*	CYMBAL
sign-writing	CRYPTOGRAPHY,
	SHORTHAND
[sign]-*writing*	GINS, –INGS, SING
signing-on place	DOTTED LINE
signs of hesitation	ER(ER), UM
wrong sign	CROSS
signal	
signal "Abandon"	MAROON
signal frequency	SF
Signal Officer	SO
signal *to* workers	FLAGSTAFF
signature	SIG, SUBSCRIPTION
Sikorski's tomb	POLE VAULT
silent	
silence	GAG, SQUASH RACKET, TACE
silencer, *say*	USHER
silent	MUM, SH, ST
silent cast	DUMBFOUND
silent god	ODIN
silent picture	STILL
silks	BAR
silly	
silly	LOOPY
• silly knight, *say*	LUPINITE
• silly number, *say*	LUPININE
• silly shape, *say*	LUPIFORM
silly girl	ASSESS
silly [girl in] . . .	RILING
silly [part]	PRAT, TRAP
silly way [to put] . . .	PUTTO
silly way to put [things]	NIGHTS
silver¹	
silver	AG
• silver grass	AGREED
• silver *and* blue	AGLOW
• silver ring	AGO, AGROUND
and	
• British silver	BRAG
• hard silver	HAG
• royal silver	RAG
and	
• silver *in* hair	MANAGE
• silver *in* river	DAGON
• silver *in* warehouse	STORAGE
silver	ARGENTUM
silver-*covered*	(in) A–G
silver-*edged*	(in) A–G

silver-*lined*	incl AG
silver-*mounted*	(in) A–G
silver-*mounted*(D)^	GA
silver-*plated*	(in) A–G
silver²	
silver	PIRATE
silver pin	PEG-LEG, WOODEN LEG
silver underwear	LONG JOHNS
simple	
simple	HERB
• simple list	HERBAL
• simple man	HERB(AL)
• simple plot	HERB-GARDEN
• simple retailer	HERBALIST
• simple song	HERBARIA
simple	PLAIN
• formerly simple	EXPLAIN
• simple argument	PLAINTIFF
simple feline, *say*	MEERKAT
simple man	SIMON
simple victory	BALDWIN
simpleton	ABDERITE, GOTHAMIST
	GOTHAMITE, JOHN, SIMON
simply marsh	MERE
sin	
sin-bin, *say*	SINKAGE
sin king	VICEROY
sinning, *say*	HERRING
sincere	
sincere flatterer	IMITATOR
sincere pledge	EARNEST
sine	SIN
sing	
sing	BETRAY, GRASS, SQUEAL, TELL,
	CAROL, YODEL
sing softly, *say*	DEMISING
singer	LAYMAN
singer, *say*	BASE, TENNER
singers, *say*	QUIRE
sings [tenor]	NOTER, TRONE
singing well	INVOICE
Singapore	SGP
single	
single	A
• lady's single . . .	HERA
• single carat	ACT
single	ACE
• fine single	FACE
• paper *without* a single	MACES
• single flower	ACEROSE
single	I
• sea *has* single . . .	MERI
• single transaction	IDEAL
single	LONE
• ba–y *running round* single . . .	BALONEY
• single sailor	ABALONE

• single single and	ALONE	site of industry	HIVE
• single fish, *say*	LOAN SHARK	site of storm	TEACUP
• single word, *say*	LOAN WORD	site, *say*	CITE, PLAICE, SIGHT,
single	MONO		SEEN
• single fish, *say*	MONOCARP	**six**	
• single college	MONOPOLY	six	VI
• single man	MONODON	• 6.50	VIL
• single round	MONOCYCLE	• six die	VIPERISH
single	RUN	• six each	VIPER
• exercise *outside* single . . .	PRUNE	• six rulers	VIKINGS
• single ply	RUN	• six *to* one	VIA
single	SOLE	• six vehicles	VICARS
• 500 *on* a single	DOVER SOLE	• six wise men	VISAGES
• single artist	SOLERA	• sixpence and	VID, VIP
• single fish	SOLE	• 66 groups	VIVISECTS
• time *in* a single . . .	STOLE	six balls completed, *say*	OVERBOLD
single data converter	SDC	six-footer	ANT, BEE, INSECT
singular German	HAN(s)		HEXAMETER
singular poet	GRAVE(s)		TALLBOY
singular Scotsman	SOLOMON	six-nil	SIXTY
singular spirit	ONEGIN	six pounds, *say*	SICK SQUID
singular trade	IDEAL	six-thirty	HANDS DOWN
singularly crazy	BANANA(s)	sixpence	SICE, TANNER
Sinhalese	SINH	**sixteen**	
sinister		sixteen inches	HAND AND FOOT
sinister	LEFT	sixteenth note	SEMIQUAVER
sinister fighter	SOUTHPAW	**sixth**	
sinister trait	LEFTHANDEDNESS	sixth (music)	SEXT
sink originator	FOUNDER	sixth former	UPPER-CLASS
Sinn Fein	SF	sixth of circle	C, I, R, C, L, E,
sinuous			SEXTANT
sinuous [snake]	SNEAK	sixth-sense	ESP
sinuously [glide in]	ELIDING	**sixty**	
sir		60% of <u>crude</u>	CRU
sir	KNIGHT, SR, TEACHER	sixty	LX
Sir Ian, *say*	SERIAN, SYRIAN	sixty grains	DRAM
sister		sixty seconds	MINUTE
sister	NUN	sixty-one seconds	MINUTES
• sister, *say*	NONE	sixty-six	VIVI
• sister's hat	NUNHOOD	• sixty-six cults	VIVISECTS
sister	NURSE, S, SIS	**skate**	
sit		skating (=on ice)	
sit in *	incl in *	• pair-*skating*	PRICE
• he *sits* in s–et . . .	SHEET	• playwright *skating*	COWARDICE
[sit] *out*	–IST, ITS, TIS	**sketch**	
sit *up*(D)^	TIS	sketch	DRAW
sitter-in	PERCHERON	• accompanying sketch	WITHDRAW
sitting-bower	CELLIST	• sketch fish	DRAWLING
sitting in sha/de ne/ar . . .	DENE	• sketch game	DRAWBRIDGE
sitting, *perhaps*	NOTWITHSTANDING	**skid**	
sitting-room	COURT	[car] *skidded*	ARC
sitting, *say*	CESSION	*skid* [in road]	DORIAN
sitting tenant	SQUATTER	*skidding* [bus]	SUB
site		**skill**	
site for lavatory, *say*	LEUCITE	skilful international, *say*	HANDICAP

Letter replaced \c\at; Omit (a); Pointers *out*; Retain <u>a</u>; Split B_ED; Down (D); Backwards <or ^

skill *on* the river	FEATURE	skylight	MOON, STARS, SUN
skilled, *say*	VERST	**slack**	
skilled man	PRO	*slack* [rule]	LURE
skim		*slacken off* [ropes]	PORES, SPORE
skimmed (m)ilk	ILK	**slap**	
(t)op *skimmed*	OP	*slap-happy* [sort]	ORTS, ROTS, TORS
skin		slap-*up*(D)^	PALS
lizar<u>d</u> *skin*	LD	slapdash	SMACK
skin	HIDE	*slapdash* [sort]	ORTS, ROTS, TORS
• skin valued, *say*	HYDRATED	**slash**	
skin	PEEL	slash girl	CUTLASS
• second skin, *say*	SPIEL	*slashed* [wrist]	WRITS
• skin say	PEAL	*slashing* [rain]	IRAN, RANI
skin	PELT	**slate vessel**	PAN
• second skin	SPELT	**slattern**	
• skin a saint	PELTAST	slattern	BAG
• skin devoured	PELTATE	• betraying slattern	SHOPPING BAG
skin disease, *say*	HACKNEY	• slattern cries	BAGPIPES
skin fish	STRIPLING	• slattern killed	BAGSHOT
skin of <u>his</u> . . .	HS	**slaughter**	
skin of <u>orange</u>	OE	[animal] *slaughtered*	LAMINA, MANILA
skin off (o)rang(e)	RANG	*slaughter* [deer]	REDE, REED
skin opening	PORE	slaughter game	KILLDEER
• skin opening, *say*	POOR, POUR	**slave**	
skin <u>t</u>ight	TT	slave	SERF
<u>skin</u>*head*	S	• I *have* slaves *around*	SERIFS
skinny	DERMIC, EPIDERMAL	• slave devoured, *say*	SURFEIT
skinny monarch	THINKING	slave girl	AIDA
skins pickles	SCRAPES	**sleep**	
skip		sleep	NAP
skip a . . .	omit A	• child sleeps	KIDNAPS
skip it!	omit IT	• sleep aboard	SNAPS
skip *	omit *	• sleep *with* family	NAPKIN
skipper	LAMB	• sleep *around*<	PAN
skipping	OMITTING	sleeper	EARRING
skipping [rope]	PORE	sleeper's position	UNDERLINES
skirmish		sleeping	(in) B–ED
[men are] *skirmishing*	RENAME	• a king *sleeping*	BAKED, BARED
skirmish [in glade]	LEADING	sleeping partner ·	BEDFELLOW, BEDMATE
skirt		sleepyhead	NAPPER
skirt	MINI	<u>sleepy</u>*head*	S
skirted by *	incl in *	slept around	OUTLAY
• bend *skirted by* la–ne	LASAGNE	**slice**	
skirting <u>Southampton</u>	SOON	*slice* [loaf]	OLAF
skirting a . . .	incl A	slice of bread	TRANCHE
skirting *	incl *	*slice of* bre/ad I t/ook . . .	ADIT
• la–ne *skirting* bend	LASAGNE	*sliced* [beans]	BANES
skirts of <u>satin</u>	SN	*sliced by* *	incl in *
skit		• c–ake *sliced by* essayist	CLAMBAKE
skit on [medical] . . .	CLAIMED, DECIMAL	**slide**	
	DECLAIM	*slide back* door<	ROOD
[smart] *skit*	MARTS, TRAMS	*sliding* [panel]	PLANE
skull	HARDTOP	sliding scale	GLISSANDO
sky		**slight**	
sky	LIMIT	*slight change of* hear\t\	HEARD, HEARS
skyscrapers	TALL STORIES	*slight change of* [heart]	EARTH, HATER

Anag [cat]; Any *; Begin IGN–; Endings –ING; eg •; Hidden /cat/; Implied add (on); Implied in (in);

	RATHE
slight change of pace	PICE, PACT
slight change of [pace]	CAPE
slight fall	RAINDROP, SHOWER
slight mist, *say*	PETTIFOG
slightly mistimed	SECONDS OUT
slim	
slim (t)high(s)	HIGH
slimmers' conference	DIET
slip	
slip in front	MUFFLED
slip into *	incl in *
• I *slip into* wa–ter	WAITER
slip, *say*	LAPS
slip-*up*(D)^	RRE, PILS
slip-up when *climbing*(D)^	PUPILS
slipped [over]	ROVE
slipper	EEL
slippery one, *say*	GRECIAN
slippery, *say*	GLACIS
slippery [slope]	LOPES, POLES
slipping [into]	–TION
[slip]*knots*	LIPS
slip[knots]	STONK
slips *	omit *
• lin(net) *slips the* net	LIN
slip[stream]	MASTER, REMAST
slipshod	
slip[shod]	HODS
slipshod [sort]	ORTS, ROTS, TORS
sloppy	
sloppy [date]	–ATED
sloppy [thing]	NIGHT
sloth	AI
slough	
slough	BOG
slough skin	omit 1st and last
• (h)yen(a) *sloughs its skin*	YEN
slovenly	
slovenly, [untidy] . . .	NUDITY
[Tom is] *slovenly*	MOIST
slow	
slow deliveryman	SPIN BOWLER
slow down, *say*	BREAK
slow movement	SNAIL'S PACE
[slow] *movement*	LOWS, OWLS
slow-*spoken*	SLOE, SLOUGH
slow *start*	S
slow vehicle	BRAKE, HEARSE
slug	
slug killer	BULLET
sluggish vehicle	SLOWCOACH
slur	
slur [she 'ad]	HADES, HEADS
slurred [speech]	CHEEPS
sly	CHRISTOPHER

small¹

small	TINY
small	WEE
• shirt (small)	TWEE
• small chessman	WEEK NIGHT
• small daughter	WEED
• small letters	WEEKS, WEEPS
• small mark	WEEM
• small points	WEENS
• small type	WEEPIE
(*see also* little¹)	

small²

indicating abbreviation:

small arms ammunition	SAA
small book	B, BK, VOL
small bottle	BOT
small box	B
small branch	DEPT
small business	BIZ, CO(Y)
small capitals	SC
small change	D, –ID, IP, P
small coin	D, –ID, IP, P
small firm	CO
small girl	DI, G
small house	H, HO, COT
small illustration	FIG
small investment	P
small man	GENT, M
small marsupial	ROO
small measure	CC, EL, EM, EN
	FT, IN, MM, YD
small number	NO
small party	CON, LAB, LIB
small photograph	PIC
small point	PT
small quantity	CC
small relative	BRER, BRO, SIS
small research establishment	LAB
small section	DEPT
small volume	CC, VOL
small weight	CT, GR, OZ, WT
(*see also* little², reduce)	

small³

other uses:

small account	BILLET
small amount of fish	CARPORT
small amount of gold	CARAT, CT
small amount of gold	G
small amount off (p)rice	RICE
small audience	POORHOUSE
small beer	HALF-PINT
small blow	COUPLET
small bottle, *say*	CREWS, CRUISE, VILE
small burn	BROOK(LET), RILL
	STREAM(LET)
small car, *say*	MINNIE

small carriage, *say*	GIGLET
small cat, *say*	GIBLET
small catch	FRY, MINNOW, SARDINE
	TIDDLER
small circle	RINGLET
small coat	MATINEE
small Dickensian	(LITTLE) NELL
	(TINY) TIM
small digger	TROWEL
small family	MINIKIN
small fly, *say*	WINGLET
small fruit, *say*	BURY
small footballer	HALF, THREE-QUARTER
small hooter	OWLET
small island, *say*	EYELET
small jacket, *say*	PETTICOAT
small journalist	SHORTED
small jumper	CRICKET, FLEA
	JOEY, LEVERET
small letter	MINIM, MUTINY
small letters	MINUTE HAND
small loophole	EYELET
small luggage compartment	BOOTEE
small m	MINIM
small man	CHAPLET, MINIMAL, SHORTED
small margin	CANVAS, HEAD, NECK, NOSE
small model	BABYSITTER
small mother	MINIMA, MINIMUM
small moustache	CHARLEY, CHARLIE
small nails, *say*	TAX
small, neat ...	CALF
small part	WALK-ON
small party	DWARF, MIDGET
small piece of timber, *say*	LOGGET
small record	MINUTE
small road, *say*	LAIN
small space	EM, EN, M, N
small square	EM, EN, M, N
small-time collector	GLEANER
small turnover	CUFF, LAPEL
small witch, *say*	HAGLET
small wood, *say*	COPS
small worker	MINUTE HAND
small world	LILLIPUT
small wound	CUTLET
smaller boat	LIGHTER
smaller girl	RUTHLESS
smaller, *say*	T(A)ENIA
smallest roads	LEASTWAYS
	(*see also* little³)
smart	
smart	CHIC
• alternative in smart ...	CHORIC
• smart man	CHICKEN
• smart one	CHICANE
smart	DAPPER

• smart fisherman	DAPPER
• smart girl	DIDAPPER
smart	HIP
• leads smart ...	HEADSHIP
• smart joint	HIP
• woman *has* smart ...	WHIP
smart Alec	CLEVER DICK, KNOW-ALL
smart boy	STING-RAY
smart deal	SPRUCE
smart man	ALEC
smart *riposte*<	TRAMS
smartypants	ALEC
smash	
smash-[hit]	ITH
smash, *say*	BRAKE
smash-up of [cars]	ARCS, SCAR
smashing opportunity	LOB
smashing [vases]	SAVES
smell	
smell	BO
smell alien	WHIFFET
smell insect	ODORANT
smell your, *say*	RECURE
smelling salts	HIGH TARS
smile	
smile	GRIN
• smile *about* a ...	GRAIN
• smile *after* tea	CHAGRIN
• smile fades, *say*	GRINGOS
smithereens	(*see* in³)
smitten	
[love]*smitten*	VOLE
smitten [by a] ...	BAY
smoke	
smoke-ring	RE-ECHO
smoke screen	FILTER-TIP
smoke, *say*	WREAK
smoker	CHIMNEY, LUM
smoking hat	STOVEPIPE
smoking jacket	REEFER
smoky city	HAVANA
smooth	
smooth	DECREASE
smooth current	EVENTIDE
smooth foil	IRON CROSS
smooth metal	IRON
smooth operator	LAUNDRYMAN
smooth tree	PLANE
smoother	IRON, PLANE
smoother praise	FLATTER
smoother, *say*	PLAIN
smother	
smother a ...	incl A
smother *	incl *
• s–ores *smother* husband	SHORES
smothered in *	incl in *

Anag [cat]; Any *; Begin IGN–; Endings –ING; eg •; Hidden /cat/; Implied add (on); Implied in (in);

• husband *smothered in*	
s–ores	SHORES
smug	
smug	PI
• smug group	PILOT
• smug king (English)	PIKE
• smug novices	PILL
smuggle	
smuggle	RUN
smuggle bird	OWL
smuggled	RAN
• smuggled *in* ar–t	ARRANT
• smuggled *in* church	CRANE
• smuggled wine	RANSACK
smuggler in court	RUNNER-UP
snake	
snake	ASP
• 150 snakes	CLASPS
• angry snake	ASPIRATE
• royal snake	RASP
• snake I call . . .	ASPIRING
snake	BOA
• snake *and* dog	BOAT-RACE
• snake-bite	BOASTING
• snake *on* the road	BOARD
• snake tracks	BOAT-RACES
snake	SEPS
• snake inside	SEPSIN
• snake lives	SEPSIS
• snake, *say*	CEPS
snake	RATTLER
snake, *say*	CRATE
snap	
snap, *say*	BIGHT, BYTE
snap *up*(D)^	PANS
snapped	BIT
• bird snapped	TITBIT
• snapped bird	BITTERN
• snapped you soldiers, *say*	BITUMEN
snapper	ALLIGATOR, CROCODILE
	PHOTOGRAPHER
snare pirate	HOOK
snarl	
[quite] *snarled up*	QUIET, –TIQUE
snarl up [nets]	STEN, TENS
sneak	
sneakily [slid] . . .	LIDS
sneaking [past]	PATS, STAP, TAPS
sneaky [dealer]	LEADER, REDEAL
snooker	
snooker-ball	RED
snooker fee, *say*	CURATE
snooker manual	POCKETBOOK
snooker match, *say*	CUTEST
snoop	
snoop *around*	PR–Y

snooper	(PAUL) PRY
snow	
snow	S
• snowman	SHE
• snowplough	STILL
• snows *cover* car	SCARS
[snow] *clearing*	OWNS, SOWN
snow shifter	ADDICT
snowball	INCREASE
[snow]*drift*	OWNS, SOWN
snowdrop	AVALANCHE
snowfall	AVALANCHE
[snow]*fall*	OWNS, SOWN
[snow]*flakes*	OWNS, SOWN
snowing [in the] . . .	THINE
snowman	YETI
so	
so	AS
• so say . . .	ASSAY
• so sure	ASCERTAIN
• so *to* bed	ASCOT
so	ERGO
• so *round*<	OGRE
• so square	ERGOT
so	SIC
• graduate so . . .	BASIC
• so the man . . .	SICKEN
so	SO
• *maybe* so	SEW, SOW
• *so-called*	SEW, SOW
• so *it's* said	SEW, SOW
• so might, *say*	SOMITE
• *so they say*	SEW, SOW
• *so to speak*	SEW, SOW
• so *upset*(D)^	OS
so	THUS
• preserve *so*	CANTHUS
so as to [startle] . . .	RATTLES
so-called manor	MANNER
so to speak, a dew	ADIEU
soak	
soak	RET
• about to soak	CARET
• soak container	RETURN
• soak *up*(D)^	TER
soap	
soap	OPERA, SITCOM
soap works	OPERA
soft soap	FLANNEL
soar	
[plane] *soared* . . .	PANEL
soaring [notes]	ONSET, SETON
	STONE, TONES
soccer	
soccer blunder	OG
soccer suit	HEARTS

Letter replaced \c\at; Omit (a); Pointers *out*; Retain a; Split B_ED; Down (D); Backwards <or ^

social

social crawler	ANT
social, domestic and pleasure	SDP
social *ends*	SL
social gathering	BEE
social worker	ANT, BEE
socialist	LAB, RED
socialist *backing*<	BAL, DER
socially acceptable	U

society

society	S, SOC
Society for Psychical Research	SPR
Society member	FRIEND
Society of	
–Antiquaries	SA
–Arts	SA
–Engineers	SE
–Incorporated Accountants	SAA
–the Holy Cross	SSC

sock

socks	LOW GEAR
socks, *say*	HOES

soft¹

soft	P
• a soft fruit	APPEAR
• a soft one	APACE
• a soft spot	APPOINT
and	
• soft drink	PALE, PIT
• soft stratum	PLAYER
• soft touch	PREACH
• soft toy	PRATTLE
• softwood	PASH, PLUMBER
and	
• softwood, *say*	POKE
soft centre(d)	incl P
• *soft-centred* ro–e	ROPE
soft-*hearted*	incl P
• soft-*hearted* fellow	MAPLE
very soft	PP
• a very soft fish	APPROACH
• a very soft lotion	APPOINTMENT
• learner *has* a very soft . . .	LAPP
(*see also* gentle, quiet)	

soft²

soft	GENTLE
• soft fellow	GENTLEMAN
• soft maggot	GENTLE
• soft point	GENTLENESS
soft *centre*	OF
soft colour	MILDRED
soft drug	MELTING-POT
soft offer	TENDER

sold

sold, *I hear*	SOLED
sol(d) *short*	SOL

solder

solder [parts]	PRATS, SPRAT, STRAP
soldering-[iron]	NOIR

soldier

airborne soldier	PARA
American soldier	GI, GRUNT, JOE
• American infantry vehicle	GIBUS
• American officer	GILT
• soldier's double	GIGI
• soldier's *return*<	IG–
French soldiers	SOLDATS
German soldiers	SOLDATEN, SS
soldier	ANT
• 10 soldiers	TENANTS
• 100 soldiers	CANTS
• woman soldier	WANT
soldier	MAN
• measure soldier	FOOTMAN
• soldier *has* unknown . . .	MANX
• soldier takes exercise	MANDRILLS
soldier	PRIVATE
• soldier-king	PRIVATEER
soldier	PARA
• soldier has left, *say*	PARAGON
• soldier of the *French* . . .	PARADE
• soldier *on* horse	PARAMOUNT
soldier	TOMMY
• soldier *goes to* the pub	TOMMY-BAR
• soldier *takes* a weapon	TOMMY-GUN
soldier-surgeon	LANCER
soldiers	IMPI
soldiers	MEN
• Home Counties' soldiers	SEMEN
• soldiers take the oath	MENSWEAR
• soldiers the *German* . . .	MENDER
soldiers	OR
• *put* kit in front of soldiers	RIGOR
• soldiers *in* Maine	MORE
• soldiers rebuked	ORCHID
soldiers	RA
• soldiers in East End	RAINBOW
• soldiers offer	RABID
• soldiers watch	RASPY
soldiers	RE
• soldiers do duty	RESERVE
• soldiers in certain . . .	REINSURE
• soldiers jumped	REBOUNDED
and	
• soldiers guard, *I hear*	REGARD
soldiers	SAS
• immerse soldiers	DIPSAS
• soldiers *have* hard . . .	SASH
• soldiers in the East	SASINE
soldiers	TA
• goodbye *to* soldiers	VALETA
• soldiers *at* exercise	TAPE

• soldiers know . . .	TAKEN	some *French*	DES
soldiers dance	LANCERS	*some* idea	ID
soldier's father	CHAPLAIN, PADRE	*some* money	ONE
soldiers in France	AEF, BEF	*some of* the . . .	TH
soldiers *in France*	SOLDATS	*some of the* men	ME
soldiers *on*	add –OR, –RE	*some of* t/he m/en	HEM
• fellow soldiers *on*	DONOR	some on, *say*	SUMMON
• man soldiers *on*	HERE	*some* [quite] . . .	QUIET, –TIQUE
soldier's salute	PRESENT	some poetry	AVERSE
	(*see also* army)	some *rhymes*	BUM, COME, CRUMB,

sole

sole accompaniment	HEEL, UPPER, WELT		DRUM, DUMB, GUM, HUM,
sole expert	CHIROPODIST		LUM, MUM, SUM, TUM
sole impression	FOOTPRINT	some say (=colloquial speech)	
sole of foot(D)	T	• "Cannot", *some say*	CANT
sole protector	HOBNAIL, SOCK	• *some say* folks will . . .	FORECASTLE
sole supplier	FISHERMAN, FISHMONGER	some say (=dialect)	
	FISHWIFE	• friendly, *some say*	CADGY
sole supporter	FOOT-REST	• *some say* fine	GRADELY, GRAITHLY
sole tender	CHIROPODIST	some *say*	SUM
solemn tomb	GRAVE	*some* time	TIM
solicit		*to some extent* hap/py	
solicit support, *say*	CANVAS	re/garding . . .	PYRE
solicitor	SOL(R)	**somebody**	
Solicitor at Law	SL	*some*body	ARM, LEG
solicitor before superior court	SSC	• *some*body rented	ARMLET
Solicitor General	SG	• *some*body scoffed	LEGATE
solicitor's dress	BRIEF ATTIRE	*some*body	CHEST, TORSO etc
	LAW-SUIT	**somehow**	
Solomon's Judgement	SHARE ISSUE	[felt] *somehow* . . .	LEFT
solution		somehow [tried] . . .	TIRED
[saline] *solution*	LIANES	**somersault**	
solution	SOL	*somersault* [done at] . . .	ATONED, DONATE
solution of [clue]	LUCE	*somersault* made . . . <	EDAM
solution of [weak] . . .	WAKE	**something**	
solve		not *something like* . . .	KNOT, NOTE, NOWT
[not] *solved*	TON	*something from* comi/c ope/ra	COPE
solved [clue]	LUCE	*something like* a cow	CHOW, COWL, SCOW
some¹		**sometimes**	TEMPI
indicating numbers:		**somewhat**	
some	IV, V, VI	somewhat	–ISH
• *some* unknown	IVY	• cereal somewhat . . .	CORNISH
• *some* in square . . .	VINT	• part of fish somewhat . . .	FINISH
• *some* New Testament . . .	VINT	• *somewhat* masculine, *say*	ISHMAEL
some	PART	*some*what	HAT
• *some* allowed	PARTLET	*somewhat* hackn/eye/d	EYE
• *some* unknown	PARTY	*somewhat* minor . . .	MI
• *some*one	PARTI	somewhat sooner	RATHER
some	TEN, X	**somewhere**	
• *some* can . . .	TENABLE	somewhere else, *say*	KNOTTIER
• *some* church . . .	TENCH	**son**	
• *some* workers	TENANTS	son	S
some²		• son *and* parent	SMOTHER
other uses:		• son in church	SINCE
some ba/d apple/s	DAPPLE	• son *in* ho–t . . .	HOST
some degree of hope	HOP	• twin sons	SS
		son of	

Letter replaced \c\at; Omit (a); Pointers *out*; Retain a; Split B_ED; Down (D); Backwards <or ^

–a bitch	SOB	**sort**	
–a prostitute, *say*	HORSE-BOY	sort of bone	T
–Englishman	FITZ	sort of boy, *say*	BELL, BREECHES
–Scotsman	MAC		LIFE
–Welshman	AP	sort of fish	KINDLING
song		sort of heather	KINDLING
song		sort of horse	ARAB
–French song	CHANSON	*sort of* [horse]	SHORE
–German song	LIED	sort of shirt	T
–Italian song	CANZONE	sort of square	T
–Spanish song	CANCION	[sort] *out*	ORTS, ROTS, TORS
song	AIR	*sort* [out R's]	TOURS
• loud song	FAIR	*sorted* [letters]	SETTLER
• quiet song	PAIR	*sorted out* [main date]	ANIMATED
• song *in* company	CAIRO	*sorting out* [papers]	SAPPER
and		**soufflé**	
• songman, *say*	AIRMAIL	[lemon] *soufflé*	MELON
song	ARIA	*soufflé* [dishes]	HISSED
• song *in* Merchant Navy	MARIAN	*soufflé of* [date, cream] . . .	MACERATED
• song *in* test	PARIAH	**soul mate**	HEART
• song *with* new . . .	ARIAN	**sound**	
song	LAY	click *sound*	CLIQUE
• loud song	FLAY	great-*sounding*	GRATE
• quiet song	PLAY	sound as a bell	DING, RING, TING
• song relating to . . .	LAYABOUT	*sound as a* bell	BEL, BELLE
Song of Solomon	SOLARIA	*sound* broadcast	SEW, SO(W)
song, *say*	HIM, LEAD	*sound* heart	CORPS, HART
song tour	ROUND	*sound* men	GUISE
song-writer	SOLOMON	*sound* money	CACHE
song-writer's friend	MILKMAN	sound of bird	CHEEP, TWEET
song-writer's performing	FOSTER-SON	*sound of* bird	BURD, BURRED
songs, *say*	LEADER	sound of Davis	MILESTONE
songster, *say*	BURD, BURRED	sound of dumb-bell	NOTING
sophisticated	IN	*sound of* gong	MEDDLE
soprano	S, SOP	sound of horse	NEIGH, WHINNY
sorceress		*sound of* horse	HOARSE
sorceress	SIBYL	*Sound of* Music	HEIR
• sorceress devoured, *say*	SIBILATE	sound of pain	OUCH, OW
• sorceress *with* worker, *say*	SIBILANT	*sound of* pain	PANE
sorceress	WITCH	sound of rain	PATTER
• live sorceress	BEWITCH	*sound of* rain	REIGN, REIN
• second sorceress	SWITCH	sound of sleep	Z
and		*sound of* sleep	DOES, KNAP, WREST
• sorceress, *say*	WHICH	*sound of* the sea	C, CEE, SEE
sore		sound pleased	PURR
sore	RAW	sound properties	ACOUSTICS
• saint *with* sore . . .	STRAW	sound reproducer	GRANDFATHER
• sore head	RAWNESS		GRANDMOTHER
• sore skin	RAWHIDE	sound reproducer, *say*	HYPHAE
sore *back<*	EROS	sound sleeper	TOP
[sore] *distress*	EROS, ROES, ROSE	*sound* waves	WAIVES
s̲o̲re *head*	S	*sound* way . . .	WEIGH
sorry		*sound* wood	TIMBRE, WOULD
sorry expression	APOLOGY	*sounded* a chord	ACCORD
sorry outfit	SACKCLOTH (AND ASHES)	*sounding*-board	BORED
sorry performance	PENANCE	*soundly* based	BASTE

Anag [cat]; Any *; Begin IGN–; Endings –ING; eg •; Hidden /cat/; Implied add (on); Implied in (in);

soundly designed	–MENT
soundly educated	TAUT
soundness of limb	LIMN
sounds as if I . . .	AYE, EYE
sounds like rain	REIGN, REIN
sounds weak	WEEK
soup	
[pea] *soup*	APE
soup	DAMPCOURSE
soup [made] . . .	DAME, EDAM, MEAD
sour	
sour beer	BITTER
[sour] *disposition*	OURS
sweet-and-sour	TART
source	
source	PARENT
source of dates	PALM
source of [dates]	SATED
source of <u>d</u>ates	D
source of draughts	DISPENSARY, PHARMACY
source of <u>d</u>raughts	D
source of evidence	GRASS, WITNESS BOX
source of <u>e</u>vidence	E
source of quarrel	FLETCHER, QUIVER
source of <u>q</u>uarrel	Q
source of [stream]	MASTER, REMAST
source of stream	S
south	
south	S
south-east	SE
south *of France*	SUD
south-south-east	SSE
south-west	SW
south-south-west	SSW
South Africa	
South Africa	RSA
South Africa	SA
• South African climber	SAVINE
• South African footballer	SAPELE
• South African women	SASHES
• young Boer and	SALAD
• girl *goes to* South Africa	SALSA
• South Africans and	MENSA
• South African insect, *say*	SAMITE
• south African sheep, *say*	SALAAM
• South African ship, *say*	SALINA
South Africa	ZA
South African Airways	SAA
South African capital	RAND
<u>S</u>outh <u>A</u>frican *leaders*	SA
South African runner	ORANGE, OSTRICH
South African wine	CAPERED
South America	
South America	SA

• South American boy	SALAD
• South American gin	SATRAP
• South American girl	SABELLA
• South American shipping company	SALINE
South America	SUS, SUSA
South American girl	PERUSAL
South American runner	AMAZON NANDOO, N(H)ANDU, RHEA
South Australia	SA
South Island	SI
South Latitude	SL, SLAT
South Pole	SP
southern	
southern	S
• southern bit	SORT
• southern cape	SHORN
• southern state	SAVER
Southern Railway	SR
Southern Region	SR
sovereign	
sovereign	ER, EMPEROR, IMP K, KING, R, REX Q, QUEEN, REGINA L, POUND
sovereigns	DYNASTY, ROYALTY LL, LS, POUNDS
Soviet Union	
Soviet Union	SU, USSR
Soviet Union, *say*	RUSHER
space	
space	EM
• space complete	EMENDED
• space encountered . . .	EMMET
• space in manuscript	MENS
space	EN
• spaceship	ENS
• space shots	ENTRIES
• space suit	ENCASE
space in Fleet Street	EM, EN
space in the roof, *say*	RHEUMATIC
space traveller	ASTEROID, COMET METEOR(ITE), PLANET
spacecraft working	LEMON
spacemen	NASA
spacious, *say*	RHEUMY
spacious ship	LARGESS
spade	S
spaghetti	STRING COURSE
Spain	E
span	
span 3ft, *say*	SPANIARD
span a . . .	incl A
spanned by *	incl in *
• river *spanned by* boy	LARD
spanner	BRIDGE
spanning *	incl *

• boy *spanning* river	LARD
Spanish	
Spaniard, *say*	MANUAL
Spanish capital	EURO, PESETA
Spanish *flower*	TAGUS
Spanish fly	MOSCA
Spanish football team	SIDEREAL
Spanish leader	CID
Spanish *leader*	S
Spanish-speaking man	HOMBRE
Spanish steps	FLAMENCO, SARABANDE
spare	
spare	THIN
• spare key	THINE, THING
• spare sovereign	THINKING
spare locker	DUPLICATE KEY
spare *part*	SPAR, ARE
[spare] *parts*	PARES, PEARS, RAPES
	REAPS, SPEAR
spare ribs	HAREM
spare room	CLEARANCE, TOLERANCE
sparkle	
sparkling girl	BERYL, RUBY
sparkling [lights]	SLIGHT
sparkling plan	STARMAP
spatter	
[rain] *spattered*	IRAN, RANI
spattering [drops]	PRODS
speak	
French-speaking waiter	GARCON
German-speaking wife	FRAU
Italian-speaking girl	RAGAZZA
right *in speech*	RITE
so to speak, red	READ
Spanish-speaking teacher	MAESTRO
speak longer	UTTERMOST
speak fast	EXPRESS
speak, *say*	TORQUE
speaker	I, MOUTH
Speaker's wig	WHIG
speakers	LIPS
speaking part	LARYNX, LIPS, TONGUE
speaking to the . . .	TOOTHY
speech in chapel	ORATORY
	(*see also* spoke, spoken)
spear	
broken [spear]	PARES, PEARS
	RAPES, REAPS, SPARE
point of spear	S
spear*head*	S
[spear]*cast*	PARES, PEARS
	RAPES, REAPS, SPARE
special	
Special Air Service	SAS
Special Constable	SC
special delivery	CHINAMAN

	GOOGLY, YORKER
special drawing right(s)	SDR
special order	SO
special [care]	ACER, ACRE, RACE
special sort of [plane]	PANEL
special treatment of [steel]	LEETS
	STELE
specially-arranged [tables]	BLEATS
	STABLE
specially-shaped [canoe]	OCEAN
species	SP(P)
specify	
specific demand	EXACT
specific gravity	SG
specifically	AS
specification of [stone]	NOTES, ONSET
	SETON, TONES
specifies [whiter] . . .	WRITHE
specifying [older] . . .	DROLE
specimen	
anot/her pes/t *as specimen*	HERPES
specimen of pl/ant I c/ollected	ANTIC
spectacle	
spectacle case	FRAME
spectacle, *say*	CITE, SEEN, SITE
spectacles	OO
spectacular	incl OO
• *spectacular* mountain	MOOT
• *spectacular* woman	MOORS
	(*see also* bespectacled)
speculate	
speculated, *say*	GUEST
speculator	THEORIST
speculator	BEAR, STAG
• speculator's relative	BEARSKIN
• speculator (German)	STAGGER
speech	(*see* speak)
speed	
speed	MPH
• circles *at* speed	OOMPH
speed	RATE
• quietly speed . . .	PRATE
• speed of bowling	OVERRATE
• speed of delivery	BIRTHRATE
speed	TEMPO
• speed increase	TEMPORISE
• speed *to* meeting	TEMPORALLY
speed merchant	DRUG DEALER
speed of light	C, RUSH
speeded *up*(D)^	NAR
speedy	RAPID
• speedy ship	RAPIDS
• speedy, *say*	RABID
spell	
spell [cast] . . .	ACTS, SCAT
spell of [cool] . . .	LOCO

spelling	SP
spelling [danger]	GANDER, GARDEN
	RANGED
spelling expert	WARLOCK, WITCH, WIZARD
spelling work	SORCERY, WITCHCRAFT
sphere	
sphere of vision	EYEBALL
spherical bullet	ROUND
spice ship	SMACK
spider	
spider	WEBSTER
spiderman	BRUCE
spies	CIA
spill	
[Aintree] *spill*	TRAINEE
spill [gin]	IGN–, –ING
spilled [over]	ROVE
spilt [ale on] . . .	ALONE
spin	
spin a record	ROLL
spin [drier]	RIDER
spinner	JENNY
spinner's delivery	SPIDER'S WEB
spinning [tops]	POTS, SPOT, STOP
spinning tops<	SPOT
spun [yarn]	NARY
spirit	
spirit	RUM
• 500 spirits	DRUMS
• spirit-man	RUMAL, RUMBO
• spirits dance	RUM-SHOP
• spirited scholar	RUMBA
• spirited game	RUMMY
Spirit of America	GASOLINE, RYE
Spirit of St Louis	APPLEJACK, BOURBON
spirit photograph	BRANDY SNAP
spirit, *say*	(D)JINN, RHUMB
	SOLE
splash	
[mud she] *splashed*	MUSHED
splashing [scent]	CENTS
splatter	
[drops] *splattering*	PRODS
splattered [mud on] . . .	MOUND
splendid	
splendid	BULLY
• splendid start	BULLY-OFF
splendid	DANDY
• splendid star, *say*	DANDELION
split	
split	RENT
• shirt split	TRENT
• split gangster's . . .	RENTALS
• split twice, *say*	TORRENT
split	TORE
• second split	STORE

• split *in* ship	STORES
• split twice, *say*	TORRENT
split [atoms]	MOATS, STOMA
split by a . . .	incl A
split by *	incl *
• lo–g *split by* pin	LOPING
split from big/ger m/ass	GERM
split fruit	BANANA
split pasture	GRASS
Split personality	CROAT, SERB, YUGOSLAV
	DIVORCEE
Split tongue	SERBO-CROAT
split spice	CLOVE
splitting *	incl in *
• pin *splitting* lo–g	LOPING
spoil	
spoil	MAR
• spoil a fight	MARABOUT
• spoil drink	MARGIN
• spoil fish	MARID, MARLING
• spoils of war	MARS
and	
• soldiers spoil . . .	TAMAR
spoil [meal]	LAME, MALE
spoil plans, *say*	RECTRIX
spoiled [brat]	BART
spoiling [all the] . . .	LETHAL
spoils of [war]	RAW
spoke	
spoke from memory, *say*	RESITED
spokesman	VOICE, WHEELWRIGHT
spokesman's time	THYME
	(*see also* speak)
spoken	
spoken aloud	ALLOWED
spoken rites	RIGHTS
spoken word which it . . .	WITCHES
sponsor film	GODFATHER
sport	
[field] *sport*	FILED
sport	FA, FL, RL, RU
• sport-shirt	FAT
• first-class *in* sport	FAIL
• for example, one *in* sport	REGAL
• sports group	RUSSET
sporting a . . .	incl A
sporting [a new] . . .	WANE, WEAN
sporting animal	LION, SPRINGBOK, WALLABY
sporting bird	KIWI
sporting headgear	CAPON
sporting side	LEG, OFF, ON
sporting situation	ARENA, COURT, PITCH,
	RINK etc
	LORDS, TWICKENHAM
	WEMBLEY etc
sporting *	incl *

Letter replaced \c\at; Omit (a); Pointers *out*; Retain a; Split B_ED; Down (D); Backwards <or ^

• di–ed *sporting* medal	DIMMED
sports car	GT, ROD
sports [car]	ARC
sp<u>ort</u>s-*centre*	OR
sports club	BAT
• *put* nothing *into* sports club	BOAT
sportsman, *say*	FUNGI, FUNGUS
sportsman's column	CORINTHIAN

spot

spot	ACE
spot	DOT
• small spot	MICRODOT
• spot Henry	DOTH
• spot worker	DOTANT
spot	SEE
• spot attendant	SEEPAGE
• spot gnomes	SEE-SAWS
• spot many . . .	SEED
and	
• spot animal, *say*	SEA-BEAR
• spot insect, *say*	SEMITE
spot marked	X
spotless instrument	VIRGINAL
spots	SEES
• the *French* spots . . .	LESSEES
and	
• spots fish, *say*	SEASIDE
• spots insect, *say*	SEA-STICK
spots, *say*	FLEX
spotted	SAW
• spotted animal	SAWBUCK, SAW-HORSE
• spotted deer	SAWBUCK
spotted insect	SAWFLY
and	
• spotted Scot, *say*	SAURIAN
• spotted seabird(s), *say*	SAUTERNE(S)
spotted bananas	DOTTY
spotted bats	DOTTY
spotted cube	DI(C)E
spotted in Lon/don s/hop	DONS
spotted in *	incl in *
• dress *spotted in* Dis–s	DISROBES
spotted *outside*	SE–EN

sprawl

sprawled about [on bed]	BONED
sprawling [town]	WONT

spray

spray of flowers	HOSE, ROSE
	WATERING-CAN
spray-[tested]	DETEST
sprayed [into a] . . .	–ATION
spraying [trees]	REEST, RESET
	STERE, STEER

spread

spread *about*<	GRAM
spread [about]	U-BOAT
[spread] *about*	DRAPES, RASPED, SPARED
spread about [field]	FILED
spread container	CORSETS, CUMMERBUND
	GIRDLE, GREEN BELT
	JAR
spread [fear]	FARE
[spread] *out*	DRAPES, RASPED, SPARED
spread out [in the] . . .	THINE
spread [yarns]	SNARY
spreading [the slurs]	RUTHLESS
spreads news of fall	AIRSTRIP
spread[sheet]	THESE

spree

[go on crime] *spree*	ERGONOMIC
[A river], *Spree*	ARRIVE

spring

spring	CEE
spring	SPA
• spring about	SPARE
• spring the . . .	SPATHE
• springtime	SPAT
spring examination	MAYORAL
spring over	WELL DONE
spring publication	ISSUE
spring shrub	CAPER
spring vegetable	SPROUT
springs from [soil]	OILS, SILO
springtime	LEAP YEAR

sprinkle

sprinkle [salt]	LAST
sprinkled [over] . . .	ROVE
sprinkling of [snow]	OWNS, SOWN

sprout

sprouting	(in) BU–D
sprouting [bean]	BANE

spun (*see* spin)

spur road	DRIVE

spurn

spurn a . . .	omit A
spurn *	omit *
• (O)liver *spurns* love	LIVER

spurious

[deal] *spuriously*	DALE, LADE, LEAD
spurious [art in] . . .	TRAIN

spy

spy	AGENT, BOND, SNOOP
[spy] *out*	PSY–
spy-ring, *say*	SPIRING
spymaster	M

squadron

squadron	SQN
squadron-*leader*	S

squall

[line] *squall*	NEIL, NILE
squall [coming]	GNOMIC
squally [weather[	WREATHE

Anag [cat]; Any *; Begin IGN–; Endings –ING; eg •; Hidden /cat/; Implied add (on); Implied in (in);

squander

squander savings	BLUESTOCKING
squandered [much] . . .	CHUM
squander[mania]	ANIMA

square

square	FOUR, NINE, SIXTEEN
square	S
• all square	TOTALS
• square head	STOP
• square playing-field	SPARK
square	SQ
square	T
• main square	SEAT
• set square	PUTT, SETT
• square one	TI–
• square pipe	THOSE
square cape	TRAFALGAR
square garden	MADISON
square meal	RAVIOLI
square-root of –1	I
square seat	SETTLE

squash

[lemon] *squash*	MELON
[lime] *squash*	EMIL, MILE
[orange] *squash*	ONAGER
squash fruit	GOURD
squash racket	SILENCE
squash [racket]	RETACK, TACKER
squashed [finger]	FRINGE
squashes relative	STEPSON

squeeze

squeeze from [oranges]	ONAGERS
squeeze in a . . .	incl A
squeeze in *	incl *
• fish squeezed in pres–s	PRESIDES
squeezing *	incl in *
• pres–s *squeezing* fish	PRESIDES

squelch

squelch [about]	U-BOAT
[quite] *squelchy*	QUIET, –TIQUE

squiffy

[quite] *squiffy*	QUIET
squiffy [Scot]	COTS

squiggle

squiggle [in the] . . .	THINE
squiggly [letters]	SETTLER
[words] *squiggled*	SWORD

squirm

squirm [in anger]	EARNING, NEARING
squirming [eel]	LEE

Sri Lanka   CL

s-shed   SHUT

St Paul's

St Paul's, *for example*	WRENCH

stable

stable	STOCKHOLDER
stable at this place, *say*	STUDIER
stable closed, *say*	STUDDED
stable company	FIRM
stables, *say*	MUSE

stack wood   RICKSHAW

staff

staff appointment	MANDATE
staff character	FLAT, NATURAL, SHARP
staff claim	POST BAG
Staff College	SC
Staff Corps	SC
staff criticism	STICK
Staff Officer	SO
staff whip	POLECAT

stag party   MALEFACTION

stage

[in stage] *production*	SEATING
stage school	COACH
[stage] *make-up*	GATES
[stage] *production*	GATES

stagger

[it was] *staggering*	WAIST, WAITS
stagger *about*<	LEER
stagger [along]	LOGAN, LONGA
stagger *around*	RE–EL
stagger, *say*	REAL, ROLE
staggered [into] . . .	–TION
staggering [feat]	FATE

stain

causing [stains]	SAINTS
[stain] *remover*	SAINT
stain, *say*	DAI, DIE
stain timber, *say*	DIALOGUE

stale

stale	OFF
• 100 stale . . .	COFF
• Peg *puts* stale *in* . . .	TOFFEE
• stale buffet	OFFBEAT
stale	OLD
• 100 stale . . .	COLD
• *finest includes* stale . . .	BOLDEST
• stale fish	OLD SCHOOL
stale	
indicating old word:	
• *stale* cabbage	WORT
• *stale* jibe	BOB, GIRD
• *stale* taste	GUST
stale loaf	FLATHEAD

stamp

stamp	FRANK
stamp card	CHARACTER
stamped addressed envelope	SAE

stampede

stampede of [steers]	RESETS
stampede, *say*	BULRUSH
stampeding [herds]	SHERD, SHRED

stand

stand	TEE
• stand *astride* as . . .	TEASE
stand bats . . . (D)^	STAB
stand-in	LOCUM, REGENT
stand in church	LECTERN
stand in court	DOCK
stand-*off half*	DOFF
stand straighter	LISTLESS
standing order	SO
standing order(D)^	EBO, MO
standing up(D)^	PU
standing up as Sam . . . (D)^	MASSA
stands up, *say*	COX

standard¹

standard	FLAG
• standard length	FLAGPOLE
• Standard Time	FLAG DAY
• standard weight	FLAGSTONE
standard	NORM
• friend *follows* standard . . .	NORMALLY
• standard article	NORMA(N)
• standard man	NORMAL
standard	PAR
• standard English	PARE
• standard operation	PARENT
• standard quantity	PARAMOUNT
• standard tim(e), *almost*	PARTIM
• standard weapon	PARLANCE
standard	STOCK
• standard measure	STOCKYARD
• standard table	STOCKLIST
• standard vehicle	STOCK CAR
Standard Book Number	SBN
standard deviation	SD
Standard Serial Number	SSN
standard setter	JONES
standard temperature and pressure	STP
standard tools	HAMMER AND SICKLE

staple

staple diet	IRON RATIONS
staple food, *say*	BRED
stapling machine, *say*	TACHOMETER

star

shooting star	ANNIE OAKLEY ARCHER, SAGITTARIUS
star	LEAD
star	SUN
• former pupil *returns*< to star	BOSUN
• star goes for a swim	SUNBATHES
• starling	SUNFISH
star-gazer	NIGHTWATCHMAN
[star] *potential*	ARTS, RATS, TARS, TSAR
star professional	SOLACE

star-rating	MAGNITUDE
star *turn*<	RATS
[star] *turn*	ARTS, RATS, TARS, TSAR
starfish	PISCES
twinkling [star]	ARTS, RATS, TARS, TSAR

start

*k*ickstart	K
*r*edstart	R
start	ENTERON, GOAT
start *and* finish	OFFEND(ING)
start attack	ONSET
start attack	A
start coaching	EMBUS
start coaching	C
start of match	KICK-OFF, KO
start of match	M
start of play	ACTI
start of play	P
start of winter	FALL OVER
start of winter	W
start off . . .	O
start off (t)he . . .	HE
start off the (r)ace	ACE
start on Monday	M
start race	FOUND
start race	R
start race, *say*	SAGO
start rising *up*(D)^	SIR
start school	INSTITUTE
start school	S
start to . . .	T
start to cheer	HIP
start to cheer	C
start to disappear	omit 1st letter
• (m)any *start to disappear*	ANY
start to disappear	D
start to rain	TRAIN
start to rain	R
start to serve	WIND UP
start to serve	S
start-up	U
start up factory	FIREWORKS
start working	SETON
start working	W
starters for The Oaks	ACORNS
starters for The Oaks	TO
starting-gate	G
starting point	LINE
starting point	P
starting price	SP
starting price	P
starting price, *say*	COMMENSURATE
starting speed	FIRST RATE
starting speed	S
starts off (i)n (E)ast (b)y . . .	NASTY
starts off the race on time	TROT

Anag [cat]; Any *; Begin IGN–; Endings –ING; eg •; Hidden /cat/; Implied add (on); Implied in (in);

starts to climb	CL
starts work	TITLE PAGE
starts work(ing)	W
starvation	FAST WORK
state¹	
inter-*state*	BERRY
state	AVER
• many state number	CAVERN
• Royal states	RAVERS
• state the time	AVERAGE
and	
• states "Charged particle . . . "	AVERSION
• states "Diocese . . . "	AVERSELY
• States worker	AVERSANT
state	SAY, UTTER
state *briefly*	ARK, CAL, GA etc
	(*see* state²)
State Certificated Midwife	SCM
State Enrolled Nurse	SEN
state of collapse of [Red Inn]	DINNER
state of [the art]	HATTER, THREAT
state of vehicle	CARNATION
state *opening*	S
state ownership	CLAIM
State Registered Nurse	SRN
state support	MAINTAIN
state train	EXPRESS
state where . . .	WARE, WEAR
stately home	PILE
statement	AC
statement of identity	AM, IAM, IM
	(*see* admit, confess, declare)
states	US
• second-class states	BUS
• *states in* about . . .	RUSE
• states time	USAGE
statesman	AMERICAN, TEXAN, YANK
	EDEN, PEEL et al
stating all . . .	AWL
state²	
commonly used names:	
Alabama	AL, ALA
• good state	GAL, GALA
Arkansas	ARK
• quiet state	PARK, SHARK
California	CAL
• gold *in* state	CORAL
Colorado	COL(O)
• state *has* 500 . . .	COLD
Columbia (District)	DC
Connecticut	CT
• terrible state	DIRECT
Florida	FLA
• state *has* quiet . . .	FLAP, FLASH
• two states	FLAME
Georgia	GA
• South American state	SAGA
• state highway	–GARD, GAST
• state railway	GARY
• two states	GAGA, GALA
Illinois	ILL
• quiet state	PILL, SHILL
Indiana	IND
• Western state	WIND
Kansas	KAN, KS
• state *with* a . . .	KANA
• managed state	RANKS
• two states	KANGA
Kentucky	KEN, KY
• works *returned<* to state	SPOKEN
• spirit *returns<* to state	MURKY
Louisiana	LA
• state highway	LARD, LAST
• state representative	LAMP
• two states	LAME
Maine	ME
• state publication	MEAD
• two states	GAME, LAME
Massachusetts	MASS
• state service	MASS
Mississippi	MI, MISS
• about *to* state . . .	REMISS
• state *found in* alien . . .	EMIT
• two states	MIME
Missouri	MO
• state god	MOLAR
New York	NY
• imitator in state . . .	NAPERY
North Dakota	ND
• priest in state	NABBED
• two states	LAND, MEND
Ohio	O
Rhode Island	RI
• state vehicle	RIMINI
South Carolina	SC
• state current . . .	SCAMPS
South Dakota	SD
• dined *in* state	SATED
Tennessee	TEN(N)
• state workers	TENANTS
• state is . . .	TENNIS
Texas	TEX
• state *exactly*	TEXT
Utah	U(T)
• quiet state	PUT, SHUT
Vermont	VT
• *so* far *into* the state	VAST
Virginia	VA
• state permit	VALET
station	
station	ST
station battle	WATERLOO

Letter replaced \c\at; Omit (a); Pointers *out*; Retain a̱; Split B_ED; Down (D); Backwards <or ^

station wagon	POLICE CAR	steering group	DRIVERS, PILOTS
statuette	EMMY, OSCAR	**step**	
staunch		step on ladder, *say*	WRUNG
staunch ally	TROOPER	[step] *out*	PEST, PETS
staunch supporter	STEM	step *out*	ST–EP
stay		• ste–p *out of* the way	STEEP
"Stay hidden", *they said*	LILO	step *out*	P–ACE
stay in	BATON	• step *out of* the way	PEACE
stay out (too long)	OVERSLEEP	step-*up*(D)^	PETS
stay put	SHIFTLESS	**steradian**	SR
stay, *say*	WEIGHT	**sterling**	STER, STG
stay true	STAUNCH	**stern**	
stayed here, *say*	STADIA	stern	BACK
stays silent	SAY-SO	• sternpart	BACKBIT
steady		• stern punishment	BACKLASH
steady business	FIRM	• stern talk	BACKCHAT
steady habit	UNIFORM	stern	GRAVE
steal		• friend *has* stern . . .	PALGRAVE
she *steals some* epic . . .	SHEEP	• stern *at the finish*	ENGRAVE
steal a bit	SNAFFLE	• stern saint	GRAVEST
steal cat	WHIP	stern	GRIM
steal cattle, *say*	RUSSEL	• speaker *has* stern . . .	MEGRIM
steal cook	POACH	• stern expert	GRIMACE
steal cot	NABBED	• stern man	GRIMED
steal cutlery	POCKET KNIVES	stern accommodation	CHAIR, SEAT
steal money	TAKE NOTE	stern appearance	HINDSIGHT
steal painting	ABSTRACT	stern Athenian	DRACO
steal weapon	RIFLE	stern leader	STROKE
stealer of tarts, *say*	PITAKA	s̲tern *leader*	S
stealing, *say*	ROB(B)IN	*stern of* dinghy̲	Y
• stealing at this place, *say*	ROBINIA	stern nurse	REAR
• stealing cowl, *say*	ROBIN HOOD	stern warning	REAR-LIGHT
• stealing it, *say*	ROBINET	**Stevenson**	RLS
stole drink	WRAPS UP	**stew**	
stole, *say*	RAP	*in a stew about* [seven]	EVENS
stolen	HOT	[stew]	WILD WEST
• stolen animals	HOT-DOGS	*stew* [recipe]	PIERCE
• stolen silver	HOTPLATE	*stewed* [eels]	ELSE, SEEL
• stolen vessel	HOTPOT	*stewing*-[steak]	KEATS, SKATE
steam			STAKE, TAKES
steamer	STR	**stick**	
steaming [hot so] . . .	HOOTS, SHOOT	stick	GLUE
steamship	SS	• stick my, *say*	GLOOMY
steel drawers	MAGNETS	• stick ten, *say*	GLUTEN
steeplechasers	OVERRIDERS	• stick together, *say*	GLUON
steer		stick	GUM
steer	CON	• stick my, *say*	GUMMY
• become a steer	BEACON	• stick to second-class	
• steer boat	CONTENDER	painting	GUMBOIL
• steer *with* stick	CON-ROD	• stick *up*(D)^	MUG
steer	OX	• *sticks* to tool	GUMSHOE
• second-class steer	BOX	stick	ROD
• steer gets down, *say*	OXALITES	• stick *around*<	DOR
• steer round . . .	OXO	• stick *around* a . . .	ROAD
and		• stick-*up*(D)^	DOR
• steer I placed, *say*	OCCIPUT	• saint *takes* stick	

Anag [cat]; Any *; Begin IGN–; Endings –ING; eg •; Hidden /cat/; Implied add (on); Implied in (in);

to English . . .	STRODE
stick-figure	PASTEL
stick out	CAN–E, RO–D
[stick] *out*	TICKS
sticker	CEMENT, GLUE, GUM
sticky *end*	Y
sticky food	CELERY, RHUBARB
sticky hand	TAR
sticky sweets	ICE-LOLLY
	TOFFEE-APPLE
sticky tin, *say*	JAMAICAN
sticky wicket	PITCH
stuck in mu/d at e/bb tide	DATE
stiff	
stiff	BODY, CORPSE
stiff back	STERN
stiff examination	AUTOPSY, POST-MORTEM
stiff examiner	CORONER
stiff fabric, *say*	CANVASS
stiff paper	HARD TIMES
stiff suit	ARMOUR
stiff support(er)	BIER
stiffen signal	STAR CHAMBER
stifle	
stifled by lar/ge m/uffler	GEM
stifled by *	incl in *
• is *stifled by* ho–t . . .	HOIST
stifling a . . .	incl A
stifling *	incl *
• male *stifling* one . . .	MAIN
still	
still	PHOTO(GRAPH), SNAP(SHOT)
still employed	INFIRM
still flying	HOVERING
still single	YETI
still there	INACTIVE
stir	
stir food	BREAD AND WATER, PORRIDGE
stir-fryer, *say*	PANMIXIA
stir [soup]	OPUS
stir up [anger]	RANGE
stirred [tea]	ATE, EAT, ETA
stirring article	(TEA) SPOON
stirring [march]	CHARM
stitch	
stitch	SEW
• stitch in . . .	SEWIN
• stitch *round* shirt	STEW
and	
• stitch, *say*	SO, SOW
stitch	TACK
• second stitch	STACK
• stitch it, *say*	TACKET
• stitch *round* right	TRACK
stoa	
[stoa]	WILD OATS

stock	
stock book	RESERVE
stock car	CATTLE TRUCK
stock exchange	CATTLE MARKET
stock heroin	RACEHORSE
stocked by wi/ne st/ore	NEST
stocked by *	incl in *
• sulphur *stocked by* de–pot	DESPOT
stocked in *	incl in *
• silver *stocked in* shop	STORAGE
stockholder	CATTLEMAN, RANCHER
stocking shoe/s and s/ocks	SANDS
stocking *	incl *
• de–pot *stocking* sulphur	DESPOT
stocks drink	KEEPSAKE
stocking *	incl *
• shop *stocking* silver	STORAGE
stocktaking	RUSTLING, SHOPLIFTING
stocking	
stocking filler	(FATTED) CALF
	LEG, THIGH
stockings, *say*	HOES
stoke	
stoker	BRAM
stokes	S(T)
stolen	(*see* steal)
stomach	
be(a)st *has no stomach*	BEST
losing stomach, patient	PANT, PATENT
stone	
stone	OPAL etc
stone	PIT
• smooth stone	SANDPIT
• stone church	PITCH
• stone *found in* Home Counties	SPITE
stone	ST
• about stone	REST
• stone *found in* river	TASTY
• stone road	STAVE
stone	ROCK
• 100 stones	CROCKS
• fine stone	FROCK
• stone a goat	ROCKABILLY
and	
• stone at this place, *say*	ROCKIER
• stone it, *say*	ROCKET, ROCQUET
stone circle	ETERNITY RING
stone club	BRICKBAT
stone dam	NIOBE
stone figure	DIAMOND
stone type	EMERALD, RUBY
stone worker	LAPIDARY
stony-*hearted*	O
stony-hearted girl	OLIVE, PEACH
stop	
stop	BLOCK

• stop in Greece	BLOCKING
• stop time	BLOCKAGE
stop	COLON
stop	HO
• a total number stop . . .	TALLY-HO
• stop exercises	HOPE
• stop work	HOOP
stop	POINT
• dance *comes to* a stop	BALLPOINT
• stop *before* journalist . . .	POINTED
stop	PT
stop	STAY
• stop *after* player . . .	BACKSTAY
• stop *without* a car	STARRY
and	
• stop soldiers, *say*	STAMEN, STARE
stop advertisement	PLUG
stop *and* listen	ENDEAR
stop *at sea*	AVAST, BELAY
stop cheating	SQUASH RACKETS
stop growth	BARGAIN
stop in America	PERIOD
stop looking	PEERLESS
stop master	STEMMA
stop music	REFRAIN
stop, *say*	CHEQUE, FINNISH, SEAS, SEES, SEIZE
stop searching	CLOSE
stop short	COMMA
stop short of tow(n)	TOW
stop *talking*	SEAS, SEES, SEIZE
stopped instrument . . .	ORGAN
stopped skating	OFFICE
stopped work, *say*	WRESTED
store	
store, *say*	HORDE, WHORED
stored in *	incl in *
• one car *stored in* sh–ed	SHIRRED
storing a . . .	incl A
storing fence	HOARDING
storing *	incl *
• sh–ed *storing* one car	SHIRRED
storm	
[Desert] *Storm*	RESTED
storm damage	CHARGE
storm lantern	BLOWLAMP, BLOWTORCH
storm location	TEACUP
storm [rages]	GEARS
stormed, *say*	REI(G)NED
stormy [waters]	WASTER
story	
story	TALE
• second story	STALE
• story *about* mother	TAMALE
• story books	TALENT
and	

• story, *say*	TAIL
story in parts, *say*	CEREAL
stout	
stout carrier	PORTER
stout leader	FATHEAD
s̲tout *leader*	S
stout man	FATAL, PLUMPED
stout spar	STRONGBOX
straddle	
straddled by *	incl in A
• a horse *straddled by* J–ean	JACOBEAN
straddling a . . .	incl A
straddling river	incl R
straddling *	incl *
• J–ean *straddling* a horse	JACOBEAN
straggle	
[conifers] *straggling*	FORENSIC
straggling [line]	LIEN, NEIL, NILE
straight line	I
strain	
strain, *say*	WRETCH
strained [soup]	OPUS
straining [all the] . . .	LETHAL
strait	ST
Strand entrance	PLYMOUTH
strange	
strange	ODD
• strange child	ODDS-ON
• strange dance	ODDBALL
• strange men	ODDFELLOWS
strange	RUM
• saint *has* strange . . .	STRUM
• strange *and* quiet	RUMP
• strange manager	RUM RUNNER
and	
• strange cat, *say*	RUMPUS
strange [bird]	DRIB
strange *end*	E
strange individual	PECULIAR
s̲trange *origins*	ST
strange [thing]	NIGHT
strange [to relate]	TOLERATE
strange turn of [phrase]	SERAPH
strange way to [act]	CAT
strangely [silent]	ENLIST
stranger [saw her] . . .	HAWSER
Stravinsky	
St̲ravinsky *quintet*	RAVIN
straw	
straw	BOATER
straw cable	HAYWIRE
stray	
stray [dogs in] . . .	DOINGS
straying [over] . . .	ROVE
stream	
stream	BANKER, FLOWER

Anag [cat]; Any *; Begin IGN–; Endings –ING; eg •; Hidden /cat/; Implied add (on); Implied in (in);

stream serving mill, *say*	MILREIS
streamlining, *say*	FARING

street

street	ST
• street light	STRAY
• street needs repair	STRUTTED
• streetwarden	STRANGER
and	
• Meadow Street	LEAST
• Virginia Street	VAST
• West Fish Street	WIDEST
and	
• house *in* the street	SHOT
street *in Berlin*	STRASSE
street *in Madrid*	CALLE
street *in Paris*	RUE
street *in Rome*	STRADA
street, *say*	LAIN, RODE
streetwise bosses	LEADERSHIP

strengthen

strengthen coast	SHORE
strengthen coast, *say*	SURE

strenuous

[I tried] *strenuously*	TIDIER
strenuously [tries]	RITES, TIRES

stretch

stretch	PORRIDGE, SENTENCE
stretch	
indicating abbreviation	
to be expanded:	
• can't *stretch*	CANNOT
• *stretch* arm	ARMENIAN, ARMORIC
stretch bird	CRANE
stretch [PC30]	TRIPTYCH
stretcher	BRICK, PROCRUSTES
stretcher-bearer	HOD

stricken

stricken [by a] ...	BAY
[it was] *stricken*	WAIST, WAITS

strict

strict	STERN
• strict follower	STERN-CHASER
• strict parent	PASTERN
• strict treatment rooms	STERNWARDS
strict *limitations*	ST

strike

strike	BEAT
• strike on the head	BROWBEAT
• strike queen	BEATER
strike	BELT
• inexperienced *before*	
strike	GREEN BELT
• strike one ...	BELTANE
strike	BLOW
• strike *about* English ...	BELOW
• strike insect	BLOWFLY
strike	BUMP
• strike family	BUMPKIN
• strike Henry	BUMPH
• strike monarch	BUMPER
strike	COSH
• strike queen	COSHER
and	
• strike woman, *say*	COSHER, KOSHER
strike	HIT
• 100 strikes	CHITS
• strike woman	HITHER
• woman *on* strike	WHIT
strike	LAM
• strike a ...	LAMA
• strike a difficulty	LAMPLIGHT
• strike girl	LAMELLA
• strike victim	LAMPREY
strike	PAT
• second strike	SPAT
• strike *and* uprising	PATRIOT
• strike *in* the Home Counties	SPATE
strike	PELT
• second strike	SPELT
• strike a number, *say*	PELTATE
• strike a saint	PELTAST
strike	PUNCH
• strike a horse	PUNCH
• strike journalist	PUNCHED
• strike the ball	PUNCHBOWL
strike	RAM
• 100 *on* strike	CRAM
• strike attendant	RAMPAGE
• strike *in* iron ...	FRAME
and	
• strike *over<*	MAR
strike	RAP
• strike fish	RAPID
• strike *in* church	CRAPE
• time *to* strike	TRAP
and	
• strike *over<*	PAR
strike	SLAP
• strike rod	SLAPSTICK
• strike sailor	SLAPJACK
• strikes insect	SLAPSTICK
and	
• strike dog, *say*	SLAP-UP
• strike *over<*	PALS
strike	SOCK
• players *on* strike	WINDSOCK
• strike son	SOCKS
• strike *without* Henry	SHOCK
and	
• strike it, *say*	SOCKET
• strike woman, *say*	SOCCER
strike	TAP

• end strike	STOP-TAP		OAR, ROWER
• strike in ship	STAPS	**strong¹**	
• strike it, *say*	TAPPET, TAPPIT	strong	F
and		• strong arm	FARM
• strike *over*	PAT	• strong back	FRUMP
strike	WHIP	• strong jug	FEWER
• animal *on* strike	HORSEWHIP, WHIPCAT	and	
• strike favourite	WHIPPET	• a strong anger	AFIRE
• striking the best . . .	WHIPPING CREAM	• a strong company	AFFIRM
and		• a strong flow	AFFLUX
• strike it, *say*	WHIPPET	very strong	FF
strike	TEST MATCH	• a very strong light	AFFLUX, AFFRAY
strike *about* . . . <	MAR, PALS, PAR, PAT	• a very strong melody	AFFAIR
strike coins	MAKE READY	• a very strong No. 9	AFFIX
strike off doctor	omit DR, MO	strong	IRON
strike pest	SLUG	• drunk *in* iron . . .	ISOTRON
strike rhythm	BEAT	• strong hand	IRON DUKE
strikes fly, *say*	WAXWING	• strong slaves	IRONWORKS
striking	OUT	strong	STR
• 50 striking . . .	LOUT	**strong²**	
• afterthought *about* striking . . .	POUTS	strong-arm man	SAMSON
• striking mechanic	OUTFITTER	strong binding	STRAPPING
• striking *on* the head	OUTNESS	strong bird, *say*	TOUGHEN
• striking players	OUTCAST	strong dog	HUSKY
• striking *with* whip	OUTCROP	strong catkin	FIRMAMENT
strikebreaker	RAT, SCAB	strong current	CAMPS
strikers	MATCHES, LUCIFERS, VESTAS	strong drink	STOUT
striking redhead	MATCH, LUCIFER, VESTA	strong man	HERCULES, SAMSON, TITAN
struck on the head	BROWBEATEN	strong man, *say*	TIGHTEN, TUFTED
struck with knee, *say*	KNEAD, NEED	strong noise	SOUND
string		strong point	FORTE
string course	SPAGHETTI	• strong point, *say*	FOR TEA, FORTY
string worn	G	strong porter	STOUT
stringed instrument, *say*	LIAR, LIER	strong stem	STAUNCH
	LOOT	strong suit	ARMOUR, TRUMPS
	VIAL, VILE	strong team, *say*	MITICIDE
strings (violin)	A, D, E, G	**strontium unit**	SU
stringy bird, *say*	TOUGHEN	**struck**	(*see* strike)
strip		**structure**	
strip copy	TAKE-OFF	[plane's] *structure*	PANELS
strip off	omit ends	*structure of* [chapter]	PATCHER, REPATCH
• (a)skin(g) *to strip off*	SKIN	**struggle**	
• *strip off* (p)ain(t)	AIN	struggle forward	VIEWING
strip off	omit OFF	*struggle* to [rise]	SIRE
• *strip* off t(off)ee . . .	TEE	*struggled* [like] . . .	KIEL
strip weapon	RIFLE	*struggled with* mineral	BATTLEDORE
stripper	LOCUST, SALOME	*struggling* [up an] . . .	PUNA
stroke		**stub**	
stroke	COUP	*stub out* [a cigar]	AGARIC
stroke fawn	CRAWL	[stub] *out*	BUST, BUTS, TUBS
• stroke fish	COUPLING	stubby tail	DOG-END
stroke gander	GLANCE	**stuck**	(*see* stick)
• stroke leg	COUPON	**stud manager**	BOSS
stroke-maker	ARTIST, DECORATOR	**student**	
	PAINTBRUSH	student	L
	BATSMAN	• student in church	LINCH

Anag [cat]; Any *; Begin IGN–; Endings –ING; eg •; Hidden /cat/; Implied add (on); Implied in (in);

• student *in* rear . . .	BLACK
• student quarters	LEE, LEN, LES, LEW
• student *takes* port	LADEN
Student Christian Movement	SCM
Student of Civil Law	SCL
Student Representative Council	SRC
students	NUS
(*see also* learner)	

study

study	CON
• study dance	CONTANGO
• study music	CONSTRAIN
• study poetry	CONVERSE
and	
• studies birds family, *say*	CONSTERNATION
• studies particles	CONSORTS
study	DEN
• study gallery	DENTATE
• study weight	DENOUNCE
• the *French* study . . .	LADEN
and	
• study conurbation, *say*	DENSITY
study	READ
• study only . . .	READJUST
• study *with* one journalist	READIED
• study with *German* . . .	READMIT
study	PORE
• second study	SPORE
• study aboard	SPORES
and	
• study food, *say*	PORTABLE
• study, *say*	POOR, POUR
study	SCAN
• king *in* study	SCRAN
• study row	SCANTIER
• study square	SCANT
study French . . .	ETUDE
study of	
–chains, *say*	OROLOGY
–fish, *say*	IDEOLOGY
–Romans, *say*	VIROLOGY
–tarts, *say*	HOROLOGY
studied *speech*	RED
studies	COURSE

stuff

stuff young bird	SQUAB
stuffed into *	incl in *
• fruit *stuffed into* cleric	DAPPLED
stuffed with a . . .	incl A
stuffed with *	incl *
• cleric *stuffed with* fruit	DAPPLED

stumble

stumble[bum]	UMB–
stumbles *about*<	SPIRT
stumbles [over] . . .	ROVE
stumbles over [step]	PEST, PETS
stumbling [words]	SWORD

stumped — ST

stun

stun, *say*	DAYS
stunner	DISH, KO
stunning finale	KNOCK-OUT, KO

stunt

quit(e) *stunted*	QUIT
[quite] *stunted*	QUIET, –TIQUE
stunted tree	(l)ARCH, (t)REE

stupefy

stupefy	NUMB
• stupefy man	NUMBLES
and	
• stupefy girl, *say*	NUMMARY
• stupefy man, *say*	NUMERIC

stupid

stupid compact	DENSE
stupid team, *say*	SILICIDE
stupidly [dared]	ADDER, DREAD
[tried] *stupidly*	TIRED

sty — LITTER CONTAINER

style

style	
indicating mode of address:	
• bishop's style	GRACE
• style of prince	HIGHNESS
(*see also* address)	
style [in art]	TRAIN
stylish nightclub	HIP-JOINT
stylish [robe]	BOER, BORE, EBOR

stylite

stylite	POLE-SQUATTER
stylite's home	PERSONAL COLUMN

sub-

indicating one word written below another word or letter(D):	
• *sub*marine ruler	SEAR
• *sub*-standard colour	PARTAN
• *sub*terranean gold	LANDAU

sub-group — WOLF-PACK

subject

subject	SUB(J)
subject me . . .	I
subject of autobiography	I, ME
subject them . . .	THEY
subject to	UNDER
• subject to friction	UNDERWEAR
• subject to theft	UNDERTAKING
and	
• subject to delay, *say*	UNDERWEIGHT
• subject to proper, *say*	UNDERWRITE
subject to	
indicating one word	

written below another(D):	
• circle *subject to* queen	ERRING
• head *subject to* Russian . . .	REDPOLL
subject to error [in gold]	DOLING
subject us . . .	WE
subjunctive	SUB(J)
submarine	
submariner	LOW TAR, NEMO
submariner's gear	UNDERWEAR
submit	
submit account	RELATE, RETAIL
submit return	YIELD
subscriber trunk dialling	STD
subsequent	
subsequent	LATER
• *find* time *in* subsequent . . .	LATTER
• second *and* subsequent . . .	SLATER
• subsequent article	LATERAN
substitute	
substitute for [actor]	CROAT
substitute husband	RESERVE
substitute stableman	STANDING-ROOM
substitute train	STANDING-ROOM
subtle punishment	FINE
subtract	
subtract a . . .	omit A
subtract *	omit *
• *subtract* five *from* se(v)en	SEEN
succeed	
succeed	FAREWELL
succeed	WIN
• succeed *in* the Home Counties	SWINE
• succeed occasionally	WINSOME
• succeed *with* effort	WINTRY
• time *to* succeed	TWIN
succeed, *say*	DOWEL, WHIN
succeeded	S
succeeded	WON
• succeeded Edward	WONTED
• succeeded the *German* . . .	WONDER
• succeeded *without* the king	WORN
successful day	VE
successful dieter	LIGHTERMAN
successful singer	INVOICE
successful songwriter	HITMAN
succession, *say*	CERES
successor	HEIR
• successor appears	HEIRLOOMS
• successor *to* Portuguese noble	HEIRDOM
successor to Brand X	BRANDY
sucker	ACID DROP, STRAW
sudden stroke	SNAPSHOT
suffer	
suffer perforation, *say*	BEHOLD
suffering	(in) PA–IN
suffering [badly]	BALDY
suffering breakdown [I went] . . .	TWINE
suffering relative	AGONY AUNT
sufficient	QS
suffix	SUF(F)
sugar	
sugar beet	CUBE ROOT
sugar container	BEET, CANE
sugar daddy	TATE
sugarloaf	SWEETBREAD
sugar soap	FLATTERY
suggest	
he'll *suggest* . . .	HEAL, HEEL
suggested you will . . .	YULE
suit	
suit	C, D, H, S
suit	QUARTERDECK
suitable dance, *say*	MEATBALL
suitable for [use]	SUE
suitable head	FITNESS
suitably dressed	INVESTMENT
suitably [sited]	EDITS, TIDES
suitably prepared [meal]	LAME, MALE
suitcase	GEARBOX
sultanate	OMAN
sum of money	IMPOUNDS
summary hearing	BRIEFCASE
summer	
summer	ADDER
• many summer . . .	LADDER, MADDER
• second-rate summer	BADDER
• summer's shade	ADDERSTONE
summer	COUNTER
• summer month	COUNTERMARCH
• summer role	COUNTERPART
• summer wind	COUNTERBLAST
	COUNTERBLOW
summer job	ADDITION, ARITHMETIC
summer time	BST
summit	
international *summit*(D)	I
summit coverage	CAP, HAT, HEADGEAR
	SNOWCAP
summit of Everest(D)	E
sun¹	
sun	S
• sunbird	SCOOT, SKITE, SOWL
	STEAL, STERN
• sun dance	SHOP
• sundown	SLOW, SNOWDROPS
• sundress	SWEAR
• sunfish	SEEL, SHAKE, SIDE
	SLING, SPIKE, STENCH
• sunflower	SLILY
• sunhat	STOPPER
• sunrise	SUP
sun *comes out*	omit S

Anag [cat]; Any *; Begin IGN–; Endings –ING; eg •; Hidden /cat/; Implied add (on); Implied in (in);

sun*less*	omit S
sun²	
sun	SOL
• Indian sun, *say*	CRESOL
• sun *has* 500 . . .	SOLD
• sun *on* English . . .	SOLE
and	
sun-*up*(D)^	LOS
sun*rise*(D)^	LOS
sun³	
sun	SUN
sun*dancing*	NUS, UNS–
sunbathing	(in) SU–N
• father sunbathing	SUPAWN
sun*rise*(D)^	NUS
[sun]*set*	NUS, UNS
sun*up*(D)^	NUS
sun⁴	
sun	STAR
• sun king	STARER
• sunfish	STARLING
• sun *goes round* one . . .	SITAR
sun*rise*(D)^	RATS
sun*up*(D)^	RATS
sun⁵	
sun-god	RA, SOL
sun king	LOUIS
sunbathed, *topless*(D)	(b)ASKED
sunbather	BAKER
sunny chap	RAY
sunny, *say*	SUMMARY
sunshade	CLOUD
Sunday	S, SUN
Sunday *opening*	S
sundry	
[sent] *sundry* . . .	NETS, STEN
sundry divers	MANY
sundry [items]	EMITS, MITES, TIMES
supercilious soldier	CAVALIER
superb icing	TOPPING
superconductor	MAESTRO
superfine	SUP
superintending	–IC
superior	
superior	ARCH, OVER, U, UP
• superior head	ARCHNESS
• many superior . . .	COVER, LOVER, MOVER
• superior philosopher	USAGE
• superior group	UPSET
superior	
indicating word written	
above another (D):	
• man *is superior to* many	HELOT
• staff *with* man *in superior*	
position	HEROD
superior *American*	SWELL
Superior companion	ERIE, HURON etc
superior example	UPPER CASE
superior, *say*	HIRE
superior standing	DAIS, PLATFORM
	SOAPBOX, STAGE
superlative	SUP
supersonic transport	SST
supine	SUP
supplement	PS, SUP
supply	
supplied by hospi/tal c/linic	TALC
supplier of dope	GRASS, INFORMANT
supplies flowers	STOCKS
supply lines	PROMPT
supply material for [shop]	HOPS, POSH
support	
support	
–claim	MAINTAIN
–evil	BASE
–ruler	BOOSTER, BRAKING
–others	REST
–robbery	HOLD-UP
support	
indicating one word written	
below another word or letter(D):	
• child *supporting* mother	MASON
• mother *supported by* child	MASON
support	BACK
• boot-support	KICK-BACK
• proper support	RIGHT BACK
• support Bacon	BACKGAMMON
• support clergy	BACKCLOTH
• support team	BACKSIDE
and	
• support composer, *say*	BACH
• support relative, *say*	BACCHANTE
• support you and me, *say*	BACCHUS
support	BEAR
• miserable support	GRIZZLY BEAR
• note *in* support	BEATER
• supports family	BEARSKIN
and	
• several supports, *say*	FOR(E)BEARS
support	BRA
• county supporter	COBRA
• support church	BRACE, BRACH
• support-ship	BRASS
support	BRACE
• support *after* space . . .	EMBRACE
• support allowed . . .	BRACELET
• support son	BRACES
and	
• support woman, *say*	BRACER
support	LEG
• support friend	LEGALLY

• support one on . . .	LEGION	sure-fire	CRACK SHOT
• support queen	LEGER	sure, *say*	SHORE
support	PROP	sur(e)ly *not all* . . .	SURLY
• support no girls	PROPOSALS	**surface**	
• support queen	PROPER	slippery *surface*(D)	S
• support railway	PROPEL	*surface of* the . . . (D)	T
support	SECOND	*surface of the* moon(D)	M
• support a transport system	SECONDARY	surface-to-air missile	SAM
• support worker	SECOND-HAND	surface-to-surface missile	SSM
• supporter's gear	SECOND	**surgeon**	
support, *say*	BEFORE	surgeon	VET
supporter	FAN	• son *in* surgeons' . . .	VESTS
• supporter *has* brown . . .	FAN-TAN	• state surgeons	RIVETS
• supporter *takes* note	FAND, FANE, FANG	• surgeon in debt, *say*	VETOING
and		surgeons	RCS
• supporter notices, *say*	FANCIES	**surgery**	
• supporter has a cat, *say*	PHANTOM	[heart] *surgery*	EARTH, HATER, RATHE
supporter	BRA, BRACE, GUY, PROP,	*surgery on* [spine]	PINES
	STAY	**Suriname**	SME
supporting	PRO–	**surmount**	
• supporting position	PROPOSE	indicating one word	
• supporting the originator	PROFOUNDER	written above another	
• supporting timber	PROPINE	word or letter (D)	
supporting		• dog *surmounting* a height	CURATOR
–actress	MAE WEST	• dog *surmounting* 500 . . .	CURD
–Bill, *say*	FOUR POSTER	**surplus**	
–stocking	CARRYING, HOLDING	surplus	EXTRA
–strut, *say*	SURE	• surplus account	EXTRAVERSION
supportive		• surplus parties	EXTRADOS
–couple	BRACE	• surplus weight	EXTRACT
–member	LEG	surplus	OVER
supports	PIERS	• 500 surplus . . .	DOVER
• supports, *say*	PEERS, PIERCE	• surplus *in* credit	COVER
suppose		• surplus garment	OVERCOAT
supposed, *say*	GUEST	**surprise**	
supposing	IF	*surprising* [result]	LUSTRE
suppress		*surprisingly* [weak]	WAKE
suppress a . . .	omit A	**surrender**	
suppress *	omit *	*surrender* a . . .	omit A
• de(s)pot *suppresses* son	DEPOT	*surrender* king	omit R
suppress a	incl A	surrender profit	YIELD
suppress *	incl *	surrender, *say*	SESSION
• k–ing *suppresses* sick . . .	KILLING	*surrender* *	omit *
suppressed by m/ad dict/ator	ADDICT	• bar(ely) *surrenders* city	BAR
supra	SUP	**Surrey feature**	FRINGE
supreme		**surround**	
supreme	SUP	*surrounded by* animals	DE–ER
supreme champion	STARCH	• not *surrounded by* animals	DENOTER
supreme directors	OVERBOARD	*surrounding* a . . .	incl A
Supreme Court	SC	*surrounding* *	incl *
supreme head	ARCHNESS	• drunks *surrounding* house	SHOOTS
supreme ruler, *say*	HIKING	*surrounded by* *	incl in *
surcingle		• house *surrounded by* drunks	SHOOTS
surcingle, *say*	KNIGHT BACHELOR	**survey**	
sure		surveillance error	OVERSIGHT
sure	BOUND	survey, *say*	REVUE

surveyor	LANDSEER	• *swap* \lu\nar *leaders*	ULNAR
survive test	WEATHERPROOF	**swarm**	
suspend		[gnats] *swarming*	ANGST, STANG, TANGS
suspend	HANG	swarm, *say*	TEAM
• suspend deliveries	HANGOVER	*swarming* [flies]	FILES
• suspend *in* church	CHANGE	**sway**	
• suspend sack	HANG FIRE	*swaying* [hips]	PISH, SHIP
and		*swaying around* [a lido]	IDOLA
• suspended sentence	HANGING	**swear**	
• suspended		swearer, *say*	CURSOR
work HANGING GARDENS OF BABYLON		swearword	TETRAGRAM
suspender HANGMAN, JACK KETCH		**Sweden**	S
suspicious		**Swedish**	
[acts] *suspiciously*	CATS, SCAT	Swedish	SW
suspicious [action]	CATION	Swedish capital	KR, KRONA
sustain		Swedish *capital*	S
indicating one word written		Swedish *leader*	S
below another word or letter(D):		**sweep**	
• alien *sustaining* bird	MARTINET	sweep	GRIMES
• bird *sustained by* alien	MARTINET	*swept-up* hair styles(D)^	SNUB
swagger		**sweet**	
swaggering boaster	BOBADIL	sweet-and-sour	TART
swaggering [boaster]	BOATERS	sweet centre	BULL'S-EYE
swallow		sweet factory	ROCK PLANT
swallowed up *	incl *	sweet Fanny Adams	SFA
• it *is swallowed up in* t–he . . .	TITHE	sweet fool	GOOSEBERRY
swallowing a . . .	incl A	sweet money	LOLLY
swallowing *	incl *	sweet store	HIVE, HONEYCOMB
• s–age *swallowing* tablet	SPILLAGE	sweet toy	TRIFLE
swallowed by *	incl in *	sweetbread	SUGARLOAF
• tablet *swallowed by* s–age	SPILLAGE	sweetheart	JO(E)
swamp		sweetheart	E
swamp a . . .	incl A	sweets finished	DROPS OFF
swamp *	incl *	sweets *returned*<	STRESSED
• wat–er *swamping* church	WATCHER	**swell meal**	SPREAD
swamped by *	incl in *	**swift**	
• church *swamped by* wat–er	WATCHER	swift	SCREECHER
swan		swift father	PAPACY
swan	COB	swift horse	HOUYHNHNM
• swan *has* a high tone	COBALT	swift race	LAPUTAN
• swan painter	COBRA	swift traveller	GULLIVER
swan	PEN	**swill**	
• swan expired, *say*	PENDED	[beer]-*swilling*	BREE
• swan *on* the river	DEEPEN	*swilled* [over]	ROVE
• swan-song	PENCHANT	**swim**	
swanning around [in fine		swimmer	COD, EEL, LING etc
car]	FINANCIER	swimmer	LEANDER
young swan	CYGNET	• swimmer's plea	OLEANDER
young swan, *say*	SIGNET	swimming club	ASA
swap		*swimming in* [Lido]	IDOL
swap defenders	SWITCHBACKS	*swimming* [pool]	LOOP, POLO
swap [coins]	ICONS, SONIC	**swindle**	
swap components of [cars]	ARCS, SCAR	swindle	(BEA)CON
swap leaders		swindle	DO
• party *swaps leader*	GORY	• 51 swindles	LIDOS
• *swap leaders* \la\ter	ALTER	• swindle money	DOCENT, DOYEN

Letter replaced \c\at; Omit (a); Pointers *out*; Retain a; Split B_ED; Down (D); Backwards <or ^

• swindle people	DONATION
• swindle twice	DODO
swindle man	ROOK
swindler, *say*	CHEETAH
swindles *on* credit	FIDDLESTICK

swine

swine draw, *say*	PIGSTY
swine family	HOGSKIN, PIGSKIN
swine underfed	PIGNORATION
swinish boss	HOGSHEAD, NAPOLEON

swing

swing	ROCK
• loud swing	FROCK
• swing at this place, *say*	ROCKIER
• swing it, *say*	ROCKET
• swing sailor and	ROCK-TAR
swing [door]	ODOR, ROOD
swing door<	ROOD
swing music	CRADLE SONG, ROCK

swirl

swirl of [a skirt]	AT RISK
swirled [along]	LOGAN, LONGA
swirling [waters]	WASTER

swish

swish [cane]	–ANCE
swishing [cane isn't] . . .	INSTANCE

switch

switch *back*<	DOR
switch ends of \l\eve\r\	REVEL
switch [on light]	THOLING
switch on<	NO
switch[blade]	BALED
switched [over]	ROVE
switched over to . . . <	OT

Switzerland

Switzerland	CH
• Egypt and Switzerland . . .	ETCH
• old city *in* Switzerland's . . .	CHURCH

• Switzerland *has* no way	CHORD

swivel

swivel [gun]	GNU
swivel seat	WHEELCHAIR
swivelling [seat]	EATS, SATE, TEAS

sword

sword bearer	FROG, SCABBARD
[sword] *dance*	WORDS
sword swallower	SCABBARD

swore

swore vehemently, *say*	CUSTARD
	(*see also* swear)

swot

*start s*wotting	S
swot *up*(D)^	MARC, GUM, TOWS

swung

swung, *say*	SUEDE
	(*see also* swing)

Sydney's box	CARTON

symbol

symbol	SIGN, SYM
symbol, *say*	CYMBAL, SINE
symbol	LOGO
• symbol *and* name	LOG-ON
• symbol *with* very loud . . .	LOG-OFF
sympathetic lady	AGONY AUNT
synonym	SYN

synthesise

synthesise [ester]	REEST, RESET STEER, STERE, TREES

synthetic	
–spirit	LABRUM
–stone	SHAMROCK
syrup	SYR

system

system [made in] . . .	MAIDEN
system for [taxes]	TEXAS
system of [gears]	RAGES
Systéme Internationale	SI
SX	ESSEX

T

bandage, bar, bone, cart, cell, cloth, commence, cross(ed), group, *half-dry*, hundred and sixty (thousand), isotopic spin, it, junction, kinetic energy, model, *perfect letter*, lymphocyte, period of function, plate, rail, shirt, square, strap, surface tension, tare, tasto, tau, *te*, *tea*, *tee*, temperature, tenor, tense, tension, tera-, tesla, Thailand, the, theta, time, to, tonic, ton(ne), transitive, transmittance, trill, tritium, troy, Tuesday

3.1416	PIRATE
£1,000	IMPOUNDS
tab	BILL
little tab, *say*	BILLET
table	
table	TIMES
ta<u>b</u>le-*centre*	B
table opposite	COUNTER
table, *say*	ALTER
<u>t</u>able-*top*(D)	T
tail	
shir<u>t</u> *tail*	T
tail	BACKBIT
tail *at an* angle	DOGFISH
tai<u>l</u>-*back*	L
Tail-end Charli<u>e</u>	E
tai<u>l</u>-*ender*	L
tail-ende<u>r</u>	R
tail *first*	
• cat'\s\ *tail first*	SCAT
<u>t</u>ail *first*	T
tailless insect	LOCUS(t), MOT(h)
	WAS(p)
tailless rabbi(t)	RABBI
tail of queu<u>e</u>	E
tail of th<u>e</u> . . .	E
tail *off* th(e) . . .	TH
[tail]*spin*	–ITAL, –TIAL
[tail]*wagging*	–ITAL, –TIAL
tailing ma(n)	MA
tails <u>I</u> wi<u>n</u>	IN
tails yo<u>u</u> los<u>e</u>	–UE
top and tail (b)ean(s)	EAN
wag*tail*	G
white *tail*	E
tailor	
tailored [to his] . . .	HOIST
tailoring	HABIT-FORMING
[trews] *tailored* . . .	STREW, WREST
Taiwan	RC

take[1]	
indicating inclusion:	
take about . . .	incl RE
• mother *takes* about . . .	MARE
take in	incl IN
• support *takes* in . . .	BRAIN
take in a . . .	incl A
take in *	incl *
• w–e *take in* oars, *say*	WORSE
take it from /me, sh/e . . .	MESH
take it *to heart*	incl IT
take nothing *in*	incl O
take notice	incl AD
take on	incl ON
take part in ga/me al/though . . .	MEAL
take shelter in cast/le af/ter . . .	LEAF
take some of o/ur ge/nes	URGE
take to . . .	incl TO
• good men *take to* . . .	PIMENTO
take to heart a . . .	incl A
take to heart *	incl *
• doctors *take* boy *to heart*	MOBS
take your pick of t/he ap/ples	HEAP
taken from Lon/don s/hop	DONS
taken in by fal/se w/oman	SEW
taken in by *	incl in *
• men *taken in by* editor	EMEND
taken out of cont/ext in E/ast	EXTINE
taken to heart by *	incl in *
• boy *taken to heart by* doctors	MOBS
taking in *	incl *
• editor *taking in* men	EMEND
taking part in h/ome ga/mes	OMEGA
take[2]	
indicating omission:	
I *take leave*	omit I
head *takes leave*	omit 1st letter
take a day *off*	omit AD, D
• *Take* a day *off*, l(ad)	L

Letter replaced \c\at; Omit (a); Pointers *out*; Retain <u>a</u>; Split B_ED; Down (D); Backwards <or ^

• *Take* day *off*, (D)on	ON	take flight	SKYJACK
take a day *off*	omit MON, etc	take her in, *say*	SUCCOUR, SUCKER
• *Take* day *off*, (fri)end	END	take in	EAT
take away a . . .	omit A	take in	COD, CON, DO
take away *	omit *		(*see also* swindle)
• m(ind)ing Indian *takeaway*	MING	*take* issue	incl SON
• the *Spanish takeaway*	omit EL	• mother *takes* issue	MASON
take head *off*	omit 1st letter	take it easy, *say*	WREST
take heart from re(lat)ed . . .	REED	take it easy in this way	SOREST
take heart out of c(it)y	CY	take liberty	ENSLAVE
take lead *from*	omit 1st letter	take money from account	DRAWL
take money *from*	omit D, L, P	take notice	NB
• *take* money *from* the b(l)ind	BIND	take off	APE, COPY
take morning *off*	omit AM	take off	
take name *from*	omit N	indicating a homophone	
take no notice	omit AD	• plane *takes off*	PLAIN
take off a . . .	omit A	• *take off* for . . .	FORE, FOUR
take off first quarter	omit Q	[take] *off*	KATE, TEAK
take off (first) quarter	omit N, S, E, W	take off years	DOCKAGE
• *take off* first		*take on* a . . .	end with A
quarter of (s)wing	WING	*take on* [a new] . . .	WANE, WEAN
• *take off* second		*take out* a . . .	omit A
quarter of s(w)ing	SING	take over	BOWL
• *take off* third		*take part of* Anto/nio	
quarter of swi(n)g	SWIG	be/fore . . .	NIOBE
take off head	omit 1st letter	*take part in* h/ome ga/mes	OMEGA
take off *	omit *	take second opinion, *say*	CROSS CHEQUE
• fat(al) to *take off* a pound	FAT	take sides, *say*	BEFORE
take out a . . .	omit A	*take some*	
take out *	omit *	• he *takes some* <u>art</u>ificial . . .	HEART
• rat(her) *take out* her . . .	RAT	• *take some* litt/le the/atre	LETHE
take time *off*	omit AGE, T	*take* [steps]	PESTS
• man(age) to *take* time *off*	MAN	take turns	ROTATE
• (t)hey *take* time *off*	HEY	*take up* golf(D)^	FLOG
take top *off* (c)ream	REAM	takeaway counter	ABACUS
take * *from*	omit *	takeaway sign	MINUS
• *take* a hundred *from* (ac)count	COUNT	takeaway worker	DUSTMAN
take³		*taken aback*, Liam . . . <	MAIL
other uses:		*taken from* P/rover/bs	ROVER
[ship] *taken apart*	HIPS, PISH	*taken in*, *say*	ETON
[take] a break	KATE, TEAK	*taken orally*, spirit . . .	(D)JINN, RHUMB
take [a count]	TOUCAN	takeover operator	FERRYMAN
take a course	DINE, EAT	takes	X
take a lease here, *say*	RENTIER	• rocket *takes* measure	VIXEN
take a toss [riding]	INGRID	• chesspiece *takes* another	MANXMAN
take a turn \on\ her . . .	HERON	takes a part, *say*	AZAROLE
take ages	BELONG	*takes* [blame]	AMBLE, MABEL
take amiss, *say*	MARRY	taking a drink, *say*	WHINING
take apart	ACT	<u>tak</u>ing *heart from* . . .	AKIN
take apart [all the] . . .	LETHAL	*taking heart from* Ge(rm)an . . .	GEAN
take back from r/ecip/ient<	PICE	taking issue	ADOPTING, ADOPTION
take back note<	ETON	taking offence	RECEIVING, RUSTLING,
take command	BEHEAD		STEALING, SHOPLIFTING
take down	EAT		THEFT
take Ecstasy	TRANSPORT	*taking part in* nov/el even/ts	ELEVEN
take exercise	DOPE	taking stock	RUSTLING, SHOPLIFTING

Anag [cat]; **Any** *; Begin IGN–; Endings –ING; eg •; Hidden /cat/; Implied add (on); Implied in (in);

taking thought	ABSTRACTION
	(*see also* took)
tale	
tale of a foot	LEGEND
tale, *say*	STOREY, TAIL
tale *told*	STOREY, TAIL
tales	ANA
talent	NOUS
talk	
talk fast	EXPRESS
talk of Bonn	GERMAN
talk of Paris	FRENCH
talk of rain	REI(G)N
talk of Sidney	STRINE
talk of the Costa del Sol	SPANISH
talk of the East End	COCKNEY
talk sense	CENTS, SCENTS
talking a lot	FETE
talking bird	BUDGERIGAR, MINA,
	MYNA, PARROT, MYNAH
talking bird	CHAT
talking bird	BURD, BURRED
	MINER, MINOR
talking forbidden	BAND
talking parrot, *perhaps*	POLYGLOT
talking pictures	PICKS, PYX
tall	
tall	HIGH
• tall man	HIGHJACK
• tall stories	HIGH-RISE (FLATS)
• tall window	HIGHLIGHT
and	
• tall chimney, *say*	HILUM
• tall detective, *say*	HI-TEC,
	HIGH TECH
• tall posters, *say*	HYADS
• tall ruler, *say*	HIKING
tall, skinny person, *say*	GANGLION
tall worker	LONGHAND
taller and skinnier, *say*	GANGLIA
taller insect, *say*	TOLERANT
taller loft, *say*	HIERATIC
taller, *say*	HIRE
tallboy	SIX-FOOTER
Tamil	TAM
Tanganyika	EAK
tangent	TAN, TOUCHLINE
tangle	
[roots] *tangled*	ROOST, TORSO
tangled [webs or] . . .	BROWSE
tanner	
tanner	NATURIST, NUDIST,
	SUNBATHER, SOLARIUM,
	SUNBED, SUNLAMP
tanner	SIXPENCE, VID, VIP
Tantalus's prisoner	DECANTER
Tanzania	EAT, EAZ
tap	
[tap]-*dancing*	APT, PAT
tar	
tar	AB
• tar compound	ABSOLUTION
• tar marks	ABSTAINS
• tar *on* the highway	ABROAD
tar assessment	RATING
[tar]-*spraying*	ART, RAT
tarry rope	STAY
tarry, *say*	WEIGHT
	(*see also* sailor, tar)
taste	
taste	TANG
• taste butter	TANGRAM
• taste fish	TANGLING
• taste nothing	TANGO
tatter	
in tatters [I'd made]	DIADEM
tattered [rags]	GARS
tatty denim	MINED
tau	T
taught	
taught, *say*	TAUT
taught ten, *say*	TAUTEN
taught bird, *say*	TAUTEN
tax	
tax	IMPOST
• tax *on* gold	IMPOSTOR
• tax queen	IMPOSTER
tax	PAYE
tax	SCOT
• tax capital *return<*	SCOTIA
• tax *on* property	SCOTLAND
• tax *cut*	(s)COT
tax	TRY
• tax-*free*	omit TRY
tax	VAT
• tax *cut*	(v)AT
• tax *in* Old English . . .	OVATE
• tax *return<*	TAV
tax cut	EXCISE
tax cut	AX, TA
tax-free	ORATED
tax *haven*	R–ATE, VA–T
• the *Spanish* tax *haven*	RELATE
• the *French* tax *haven*	VALET
tax inspector	SUPERCHARGER
taxmen	IR
taxi	
taxi	CAB
taxi(D)	BACUP
Tchaikovsky	
Tchaikovsky *trio*	CHA
Tchaikovsky *quartet*	CHAI

te	T		*(see also* tore)
tea		**tear²**	
tea	CHA	[mothers] *in tears*	SMOTHER, THERMOS
• tea-boy	CHARON	tear-jerker	ONION
• tea brewed	CHAMADE	[tear]-*jerking*	RATE, TARE
• tea-money	CHAL	**tease**	
and		tease animal	BADGER
• tea-dance	CHA-CHA	tease boy	CHAFFRON
• tea for two	CHA-CHA	*tease* [listeners]	RE-ENLISTS
tea	CHAR	tease, *say*	TEAS, TEES, TS, TT
• tea *in* free . . .	RICHARD	*teasing* [dogs]	GODS
• tea-lady	CHARLOTTE, CHARWOMAN	**technology**	
• tea *with* jam	CHARLOCK	alternative technology	AT
tea	TEA	information technology	IT
• tea *at* the fête	GALATEA	technology school	CAT
• tea *with* queen	TEAR	technology institute	MIT
and		**tedious**	
• [tea] *blend*	ATE, EAT	tedious	LONG
• [tea] break	ATE, EAT	• tedious dance	LONG HOP
• [tea] *in mess*	ATE, EAT	• tedious farewell	SO LONG
• [tea] *mixture*	ATE, EAT	• tedious musical	LONG HAIR
tea, *say*	T, TEE	tedious	SLOW
teas, *say*	TEASE, TS, TT	• Henry *is in* tedious . . .	SHALLOW
teapot	BILLY	• tedious contest	SLOW MATCH
teatime	IV	• tedious trainer	SLOWCOACH
teach		**tee**	
teacher	MISS, SIR	tee	AFTERS, PEG
teachers	NUT, STAFF	tee *off*	omit T
teaches clayworker	TRAINSPOTTER	[tee] *off*	–EET, –ETE
team		tee, *say*	T, TEA
team	SIDE	[teed] *off*	–ETED
• left team	OFFSIDE	tees, *say*	TEAS(E), TS, TT
• novice *in* team	SLIDE		*(see also* teetotal)
• support team	BACKSIDE	**teenager**	UNDERSCORE
and		**teepee**	TP
• team, *say*	SIGHED	**teeter**	
team	XI, XV	*teeter* [on her] . . .	HERON
team *leader*	T	*teetering* [near the] . . .	EARTHEN, HEARTEN
team's quarters	ELEVENSES	**teetotal**	
[team]*work*	MATE, MEAT, TAME	teetotal	TT
tear		teetotal	EIGHTEEN, NINE
tear	RIP	**telegraph**	
• tear *about*<	PIR	telegram	TEL
• tear container	RIPSACK	telegram, *say*	KABUL
• tearaway	RIP-OFF	telegraph	TEL
• tearproof	CANTRIP	telegraph office	TO
tear [a T-shirt]	ATHIRST	**telepathy**	ESP
tear about	RE–NT	**telephone**	
tear [about]	U-BOAT	telephone	BLOWER
tear round	RE–NT	telephone	CALL
tear to pieces		• about *to* telephone	RECALL
[in ring at] . . .	TRAINING	• telephone you and me	CALLUS
[tear]*about*	RATE, TARE	telephone	PHONE
[tear]*away*	RATE, TARE	• telephone a number, *say*	PHONATE
tearing [about]	U-BOAT	• telephone nothing, *say*	PHONICS
[tearing] *about*	TANGIER	telephone	RING

Anag [cat]; Any *; Begin IGN–; Endings –ING; eg •; Hidden /cat/; Implied add (on); Implied in (in);

• second telephone	BRING
• telephone *about* a race	RATTING
• telephone circuit	RING
• telephone receiver	RING FENCE
• telephone rent	RINGLET
telephone	TEL
telephone kiosk	CHATTERBOX
telephone man	BELL
telephone, *say*	CAUL, FO(E)HN, WRING
teleprinter	TPR
television	
television	TV
television disconnected	OFFSET
tell	
Tell	BOWMAN
tell	INFORM
• tell friend	INFORMALLY
• tell workers	INFORMANTS
tell lies	FIB
• tell lies about	FIBRE
• tell lies *to* Returning Officer	FIBRO
tell tales	SING
• tell tales *about*	S–ING
telling tales	TAILS
tell target	APPLE
temper	
[lose] *temper*	SLOE, SOLE
temperance group	AA
temperate area	CONTINENT
tempered [steel]	LEETS, SLEET, STELE
temporary	
temporary	
accommodation	BRIDGING LOAN
temporary accommodation	TENT
• king *in* temporary	
accommodation	TRENT
• in temporary accommodation	INTENT
• temporary accommodation	
in the river	DETENTE
temporary darn	STOPGAP
temporary site *by* a river	CAMPANILE
ten	
pertaining to ten	OFTEN
ten	CHI
• ten about . . .	CHIC
• ten quiet . . .	CHIP
• ten-ten	CHICHI
ten	CROSS
• doublecross	TWENTY
• ten above . . .	CROSSOVER
• ten land . . .	CROSS COUNTRY
ten	IO
• spoil ten . . .	MARIO
• stroke ten . . .	PATIO
• ten reserves	IOTA
ten	TEN

• 10SE	TENNESSEE
• [ten] *letters*	ENT, NET
ten	X
• monkey *has* ten . . .	APEX
• ten *behind* the Post Office	POX
• ten *drunk*	AXLE
• ten pence	–XP–
Ten Commandments	HOLY ORDERS
ten days	SEP, TEM, BER
ten-nil	HUNDRED
ten-nil *reversed<*	LINNET
tenanted	ISLET
tend	
tend	NURSE
tender	NURSE
• tender shark	NURSE
tender	OFFER
• 100 tender . . .	COFFER
• tender monarch	OFFERER
• tender politician	OFFERTORY
tender	SHEPHERD
tender words	OFFER, QUOTATION
Tennessee	
Tennessee	TEN(N)
Tennessee transport	DESIRE, STREETCAR
Tennessee Valley Authority	TVA
tenor	T, TEN
tense	
tenor, *say*	TENNER
tense	T
tense finish	PERFECT
tense, *say*	QUAYED, TAUGHT
tense over . . .	PAST
tent	
in tent	TEN–T, T–ENT
• English men *in* ten–t	TENEMENT
• gangster *in* t–ent	TALENT
tent-maker	PAUL
tent, *say*	TP
(*see also* temporary accommodation)
tentative	
[smile] *tentatively*	LIMES, MILES
tentative [plan I] . . .	PLAIN
terminal	
terminal	POLE
terminal illness	S
terminally ill	L
terminate	
terminate lease	E
termination of tenancy	Y
termini of railway	RY
terrace	TER(R)
terrible	
[Ivan] *the Terrible*	VAIN
terrible [heat]	HATE, THEA
terrible man	IVAN

Letter replaced \c\at; Omit (a); Pointers *out*; Retain a; Split B_ED; Down (D); Backwards <or ^

terrible skin	FELL
terrible way	DIREST
terribly [cruel]	LUCRE
t(erribl)y *heartless*	TY

terriers

terriers	TA
• crossed terriers	TAX
• Terriers gave blood	TABLED
• Terriers I led	TAILED

(*see also* army, reserve, territorials)

terrify

[quite] *terrified*	QUIET, –TIQUE
terrifying [ascent]	SECANT

territorials

Territorials	TA
Territorial Decoration	TD
Territorial Force (Reserve)	TF(R)

(*see also* army, reserve, terriers)

territory	TER(R)

terrorist

terrorists	ETA
• *almost all of* th(e) terrorists . . .	THETA
• *return*, for example<, *after* terrorists . . .	ETAGE
• terrorist exercise	ETAPE
terrorists	IRA
• terrorists *found in* p<u>ira</u>te . . .	IRA
• terrorists *in* five long . . .	VIRAL
• terrorists, note	IRATE
terrorists	PLO
• terrorist branch	PLOWING
• terrorists *have* 500 . . .	PLOD
• terrorists *take* square	PLOT
terrorists	PROVOS
tesla	T

test

test	MOT
• nothing *in* test	MOOT
• test I have . . .	MOTIVE
• test *in* the Home Counties	SMOTE
test	ORAL
• 100 tests	CORALS
• Spring test	MAYORAL
• test finished	PASTORAL
test	TRY
• cars test . . .	MINISTRY
• test the road and	TRYST
• test fish, *say*	TRIANGLE
• test-paper, *say*	TRIREME
test case	MATCHBOX
test centre	LORDS, OVAL
te<u>st</u> *centre*	ES
test match	CHECKMATE
	STRIKE A LIGHT

	TRIAL MARRIAGE
test playing	AUDITION
[test] *playing*	SETT, STET
testy fellow	EXAMINER
tethers donkey	CHAINSMOKE
text	MS
texturised vegetable protein	TVP
Thailand	T
Thames boatman	HARRIS

thank

thank you letter	COLLINS
thanks	TA
• thanks, man	TAMALE
• thanks members	TAMPS
• thanks the *French* . . .	TALE(S)
thank*less*	omit TA

that

that church	THATCH
that *French* . . .	CELA
that is	IE
• swamp that is . . .	BOGIE
• that's *about* right	IRE
• that's right	–IER
that is	SC
• that is current . . .	SCAMP
• that is *in* the e–ar	ESCAR
• that is torn, *I hear*	SCRIPT
that man	HIM
that man, *say*	HYMN
that old . . .	YT
that place	THERE
that place, *say*	THEIR
that Roman . . .	ID
that woman	HER
that you cause to know	SCI FA
	SCIRE FACIAS
that's *been stolen*	omit IE, SC
that's *missing*	omit IE, SC
that's not right	LEFT, LARBOARD, PORT
that's *not* right	omit R
• F(r)ee? That's *not* right!	FEE
that's right	STARBOARD
that's *the end*	end with IE
• measure that's *the end* . . .	GILLIE
• *That's the end of* i<u>t</u>, That's *the end*	TIE

the¹ — THE

the¹	THE
he *leaves* t(he)	T
part of the . . .	T, TH, H, HE, E
some of the . . .	T, TH, H, HE, E
the bar	THEBAN
<u>the</u> *beginning*	T
<u>the</u> *border* of . . .	T
<u>the</u> *borders* of . . .	TE
<u>the</u> *boundaries* . . .	TE
th(e) *detailed* . . .	TH

the *edges*	TE
the embargo	THEBAN
the *central* . . .	H
the *central* . . .	incl THE
• use the *Central* fo–r . . .	FOTHER
the *centre*	H
the check	THEREIN
the Circle Line	THEORY
the *climbing* . . . (D)^	EHT
the *contents*	incl THE
• wea–r the *contents* . . .	WEATHER
the *contents*	incl in TH–E
• about th–e *contents* . . .	THREE
the *core*	H
the course	THEE, THEN, THEW
the directions	THESE, THEWS
[the] *drunk(en)*	ETH, HET
the *end*	E
the *entrant*	incl THE
• see–s the *entrant*	SEETHES
the *entrant*	T
the *extremes*	TE
the *finish*	E
the first	THEIST
the *first* . . .	T
the *first slice of* apple	TAP
th(e) *footloose*(D) . . .	TH
the *front end*	T
the Globe Circle	THEORBO
(t)he *headless* . . .	HE
t(h)e *heartless* . . .	TE
• t(h)e *heartless* man	TEAL
• t(h)e *heartless* woman	TENANCY
• t(h)e *heartless* US agent	TEGMAN
the *initial*	T
the *initiative*	T
"The *Insider*"	H
the *last* . . .	E
the *last comes first*	start with E
the *latter*	E
the *leader*	T
[the] *mixture*	ETH, HET
[the] *mobile* . . .	ETH, HET
the *most*	TH
t(he) *non-male*	T
the *Northern(er's)* . . .	T
• the *northern* end	TEND
• the *Northern* Line	TROW
• the *northerner's* drink	TALE
[the] *novel* . . .	ETH, HET
the offender	THERAPIST
the old	YE
• the old shirt	YET
• the old soldiers	YEMEN
the others	REST
• graduate *with* the others	BAREST
• the others scoffed	RESTATE
the others, *say*	WREST
• the others went in front, *say*	WRESTLED
the *outside*	TH–E
• queen *with* th–e *outside* . . .	THERE
"The *Outsiders*"	TE
the *penultimate* . . .	H
the place in question	WHERE
the place in question, *say*	WARE, WEAR
the point	THEE, THEN, THEW
the *point*	T
th(e) *pointless* . . .	TH
the reserves	THETA
the *second* . . .	H
th(e) *short* . . .	TH
the *summit*(D)	T
the ten of us, *say*	WHEATEN
the thing in question	WHICH
the thing in question, *say*	WITCH
the *third* . . .	E
[the] *Twist*	ETH, HET
th(e) *Unfinished* . . .	TH
the woman	HER
• the woman has expired, *say*	HERDED
• the woman spoke, *say*	HERSED
• the woman was in front, *say*	HURLED
[the] *wrong* . . .	ETH, HET
[the] *wrong way*	ETH, HET

the²

alien (=foreign)

the *alien* . . .	AL, DAS, DER, DIE, EL, IL, LE, LA, LAS, LES, LOS
the *Arabic* . . .	AL
• drink *with* the *Arabic* . . .	TOTAL
• the *Arabic in* m–e	MALE
• the *Arabic* lily	ALARUM
the *Camptown* . . .	DE
• the *Camptown* drink	DECIDER, DEPORT
• the *Camptown* money	DECENT
• the *Camptown* trail	DESCENT
the *foreign* . . .	(*see* alien *above*)
the *French (style)* . . .	LA, LE, LES
• circle the *French* . . .	HOOPLA
• the *French-style* bird	LAMINA
• the *French in* F–red and	FLARED
• require the *French* . . .	NEEDLE
• the *French* gentleman	LET-OFF
• the *French in* need, *say* and	KNEELED
• bird *without* the *French* . . .	COOLEST
• hit the *French* . . .	COUPLES
• the *French* boy	LESSON
the *French/English* . . .	LATHE, LETHE
the *French/German* . . .	UNDER

the *German* . . .   DAS, DER, DIE
• Russian king with the *German*   CZARDAS
• the *German with* horse   DASH
• unknown *in* the *German* . . .   DAYS
and
• gained the *German* . . .   WONDER
• state *in* the *German* . . .   DRIER
• the *German* near . . .   DERBY
and
• the *German caught in* a mist   HARDIER
• the *German* died   DIED
• king *in* the *German* . . .   DIRE
the *Italian* . . .   IL, LA, LE, LO
• the *Italian* has one bill   ILIAC
• the *Italian* street   LAST
• master the *Italian* . . .   MALE
• the *Italian* honour   LOOM
the *old (style)* . . .   YE
• the *old* people   YEMEN
• the *old* record-editor   YELPED
• the *old-style* students   YELL
the *Spanish* . . .   EL, LA, LAS, LOS
• drink the *Spanish* . . .   LAPEL
• the *Spanish* alcove   ELAPSE
• the *Spanish in* transport   RELY
and
• firm *with* the Spanish . . .   COLA
• the *Spanish* hut   LASHED
• the *Spanish in* Cyprus   CLAY
and
• knock out the *Spanish* . . .   KOLAS
• the *Spanish in* Communist Party   CLASP
• the *Spanish* vehicles   LASCARS
and
• guns the *Spanish* . . .   HALOS
• the *Spanish* can . . .   LOSABLE
• the *Spanish in* church   CLOSE
the *Spanish/French* . . .   ELLA
the *Spanish/German* . . .   ELDER

the³
the beginning of life   L
the bitter end   R
the borders of France   FE
the centre of Paris   R
the end of it   T
the final straw   W
the finish of play   Y
the first ball   B
the first slice of apple   AP
the footloose tram(p)(D)   TRAM
the initial gesture   G
the last of winter   R
the leader of Russian . . .   R
The Lion's *Head*   L

the⁴
the boy's . . .   HIS

the girl's . . .   HER
the lady's . . .   HER
[the last] *resort*   STEALTH
the man's . . .   HIS
the old   AGED
the others   EM, DEM, THEIR, THEM
[the rate] *of exchange*   THEATRE, THEREAT
the same   DITTO, DO
the subject   IT
the writer   I, ME

theatre
theatre company   PLAYGROUP
theatre company   REP
• Oriental theatre   REPINE
• theatre atmosphere   REPAIR
• theatre is not . . .   REPAINT
• theatre royal   REPR–
• theatre scoffer   REPEATER
• theatre *with* Indian . . .   REPUTE
theatre director   STAGECOACH
    SURGEON
theatre designer   PLASTIC SURGEON
theatre-goer   GLOBETROTTER
theatre in the round   GLOBE
[theatre] *movement*   THEREAT
theatre part   SHOWPIECE
theatre performer   SURGEON
theatre producer   EMPIRE-BUILDER
theatre strike   CAST OUT, OUTCAST
theatre tour   CASTAWAY
theatrical number   ANAESTHETIC, ETHER
theatrical part   BOX, GODS, PART
    PROSCENIUM
    STAGE, WINGS
theatrical [part]   PRAT, RAPT, TRAP
theatrical performance   OPERATION
    SURGERY

their
Their Majesties   MM
their opponents   US
Their Royal Highnesses   TRH
their, *say*   THERE
them   EM, NOTUS
theme   EGO, I
theologian   ANSELM, BEDE, ORIGEN et al
    BD, DD
there
there *in France*   LA
there, *say*   THEIR
these
[these] *characters*   SHEET
these days   AD
these *in France*   CES
they
they *initially*   T
they object   THEM

Anag [cat]; Any *; Begin IGN–; Endings –ING; eg •; Hidden /cat/; Implied add (on); Implied in (in);

they say	
indicating a homophone:	
• "No", *they say*	KNOW
• *they say* not	KNOT
• *they say* we'll . . .	WEAL, WHEEL
thick	
thick	FAT
• learner *in* thick . . .	FLAT
• thick head	FATNESS
• thick soup	FATSTOCK
thick slice, *say*	STAKE
thief	AUTOLYCUS, MAGPIE
thin	
thin	LEAN
• 100 thin . . .	CLEAN
• thin ruler	LEANER
• thin shirt	LEANT
thin	SPARE
• key *found in* thin . . .	SPARGE
• thin bone	SPARE RIB
• thin tycoon	SPARE WHEEL
thin copy	FLIMSY
thin letter	MUSLIM
thin metal sword	FOIL
thin note	SHARP
thin porcelain	SLIMMING
thin shirt	LEANT
thinner	ACETONE, TURPENTINE
think	
think *about*	MUS–E
thin(k) king *is lost*	THIN
third	
third	C
third half	SIXTH
third man	ABEL, LIME
third of August	AU, GU, ST
third of August	G
third out of four	U
third party	R
third place in race	C
third-rate	C
thirteen	
thirteen	BAKER'S DOZEN
	TEAM
	UNLUCKY (NUMBER)
thirteen witches	COVEN
thirteenth loaf	MAKEWEIGHT
thirty	
thirty	L, LA(M)BDA
thirty seconds,	MIN, UTE
thirty-three	DISC, LP, RECORD
thirty-nine	BOOKS, STEPS
this	
this bird, *say*	DISPARATE
this country	UK
this era	AD
this evening, *say*	TONITE
this *foreign* . . .	CE, CET, CETTE
this *French* . . .	CE, CET, CETTE
this *in* France	CE, CET, CETTE
this *in* Rome	HIC
th(is) is *missing*	TH
this month	INST(ANT)
• queen *in* this month's . . .	INSERT
• this month's record	INSTEP
• this month's worker	INSTANT
this *Roman* . . .	HIC
this time	AD
this way	SO
• mountain this way	TORSO
• this way is legal	SOLICIT
• this way over	SOON
this way	THUS
this year	HA
this way [leads]	DALES, DEALS
	LADES, SLADE
Thomas	THO(S)
T(h)orah	PENTATEUCH
those	
those killed in combat	WARDED
[those] *parts*	ETHOS
though	
though *brief* . . .	THO
th–ough run *in* . . .	THROUGH
though square . . .	THOUGHT
thoroughfare	COMPLETE MEAL
thousand	
one *and* a half thousand	ID
thousand	CHILIAD
thousand(s)	G(G)
• a thousand English . . .	AGE
• one in a thousand	UNITING
• silver *in* thousands	GAGS
thousand	K
• managed a thousand . . .	RANK
• thousand English records	KELPS
• thousand *in* cash	MONKEY
thousand(s)	M(M)
• a thousand drill	AMBIT
• one *in* thousands	MAM
• thousand refuse	MASH
and	
• thousand *and* one	MA, MACE, MAN, MI
• thousand *and* two	IMPAIR
• thousand pounds	IMPOUNDS
thousand	THOU
thousand	X
thousandth	THOU
thrash	
thrash idler	LAYABOUT
thrash worker	WHIPHAND
thrashed out ['is ideas]	DAISIES

thread of story	YARN	through the agency of	PP
threat		throughout	PE–R
[threat]	MAD HATTER	throughout	OU–T
three		*throughout* *	incl in *
three	CROWD, GAMMA	• sleep *throughout* ship	SNAPS
three articles	ANTHEA, LAUNDER	*through*put	PU–T
three blind mic(e)	MIC	**throw**	
three boys	PATERNAL, PATRONAL	throw	CAST
[three-card] *trick*	CHARTERED	• girl *takes* a throw	DICAST
three Christmas presents	FRENCH HENS	• throw a fight	CAST ABOUT
three drinks	CHA-CHA-CHA	• throw *over* ring	COAST
three figures	LID	throw	LOB
three-foot coppers	YARD	• second throw	SLOB
three foreign articles	LAUNDER	• throw *into* ship	SLOBS
three girls	VIVALDI	• throw *to* essayist	LOBELIA
three-handed murderer	CUT-THROAT	throw	PITCH
three keys	DECAY	• throw *at* queen	PITCHER
three-legged race	MANX	• throw tar	PITCH
three-man	TRIAL	• throw tool	PITCHFORK
three men	PATERNAL, PATRONAL	throw	SHY
Three Men in a Boat	COXED PAIR	• spoil throw	MARSHY
three-nil	THIRTY	• throw *around* in . . .	SHINY
three notes	ABE, BEG etc	• throw joint, *say*	SHINY
	DOTED, MIMIC etc	*throw around* on< . . .	NO
three of <u>hearts</u>	HEA	*throw around* [on her] . . .	HERON
three parts <u>wine</u>	WIN	*throw away* a . . .	omit A
three people	BETRAYAL	*throw away* money	omit D, L, P
three points	ESCAPE, NEEDLESS	*throw away* *	omit *
	NEW, SEN, SEW, WEN	• h(old)er *threw away* old . . .	HER
three rings	OOSPHERE	*throw* [caution] *to the winds*	AUCTION
threefold voice	TREBLE	throw drink	SLING
thresh		*throw* [grenade]	DERANGE
thresh grain	BEATRICE	*throw in* a . . .	incl A
threshing [grain in] . . .	RAINING	*throw in* *	incl *
threw		• two hundred *thrown into* o–ur . . .	OCCUR
threw, *say*	THROUGH	*throw out* a . . .	omit A
threw [stones]	ONSETS, SETONS	throw out beetle	PROJECT
	(*see also* throw)	*throw out* [man or] . . .	ROMAN
throb		*throw out* * . . .	omit *
[heart]*throb*	EARTH, HATER, RATHE	• *throw* fool *out of* cl(ass)	CL
throbbing [beat]	BATE	*throw over* [regime]	EMIGRE
throe		*throw over* bows<	SWOB
[death] *throes*	HATED	*throw over* *	incl *
throe, *say*	THROW	• *throw* h–er *over* high . . .	HALTER
through		*throw* [pie]	EPI–
through	PER	*throw* [rope]	PORE
• about through	CAPER	throw *up*(D)^	BOL
• through one building	PERISHED	*throw up* bat(D)^	TAB
• through the tower	PERSPIRE	*throwback*<	BOL
through	VIA	*throwback* part<	TRAP
• sun *gets in* through . . .	VISA	thrower, *say*	CHUKKA, CHUKKUR
• through *in* a–n . . .	AVIAN	throwing disc, *say*	DISCUSS
• through passage	VIADUCT	*throwing* [darts]	STRAD
through, *say*	THREW	*thrown* [at me]	MATE, MEAT, TAME, TEAM
through *	incl in *	**thrust ahead**	(see also throw)
• run *through* exercises	PRUNE		RAMON

thunder		timber *frame*	TR
Thunderer	THOR, TIMES	timber measure	STERE
thundering [past]	PATS, STAP, TAPS	timber measure, *say*	STEARE, STEER
Thursday	TH(UR)	timber-merchant	ALDERMAN
thus		timber, *say*	TIMBRE, WOULD
thus	SIC	**time[1]**	
• the graduate thus . . .	BASIC	time	AGE
• thus the king . . .	SICK	• quiet time	PAGE
thus	SO	• time away from work	OUTAGE
• thus copied	SOAPED	• time *in* ship	SAGES
• thus the painter . . .	SOLELY	time	EON
tickertape	CARDIOGRAM	• model *in* time	ETON
tide		• student *has* time . . .	LEON
tide	EBB, FLOW	• swelling *before* time	GALLEON
tide *over<*	EDIT, WOLF	time	ERA
tidy		• time *in* fine library	FERAL
tidy	NEAT	• time *to* celebrate	ERASING
• tidy cattle	NEAT	• victory time	VERA
• tidy sum	NEAT FIGURE	and	
tidy up [a mess]	MESAS	• time *after* time	ERAT
tidying [a tress]	ASSERT	• time *and* time *again*	ERAT
tie		time	HR
tie	X	• time *in* t–ough . . .	THROUGH
[tie]-*break*	–ITE	time	MO
tie-breaker	DIVORCEE	• soldiers *take* time . . .	GISMO
tie design	DRAW	• time *in* a–n . . .	AMON
[tie] *design*	–ITE	• time *flying*	MOWING
tie fastener, *say*	TYPE IN	and	
tie game	DRAWBRIDGE, TIEPOLO	• time *after* time	MOT
tie-*up*(D)^	EIT, ROOM, WARD	• time *and* time *again*	MOT
tie up, *say*	MORE	• time to run	MOTOR
tie up Moroccan	MOOR	time	SEC
[tied] *in knots*	DIET, EDIT, TIDE	• equal time	PARSEC
tied [ropes]	PORES, SPORE	• time *in* part . : .	BISECT
tied, *say*	TIDE	• worker *behind* time	SECANT
tied [Tory] *in knots*	RYOT, TROY	and	
tying again	RECORDING	• time *after* time	SECT
tight		• time *and* time *again*	SECT
tight	DRUNK, INEBRIATED	and	
tight finish	CLOSE	• time to support	SECOND
tight, *say*	TAUGHT	time	T
tight space	TAUTEN	• leave *before* time	GOT
Tiller girls	LAND ARMY	• time *after* time	TT
tilting object	WINDMILL	• time *and* time *again*	TT
timber		• time *to* die	TEND
replace end of timbe\r\	TIMBRE	• time *to* leave	GOT
rotten [timber]	TIMBRE	and	
split [timber]	TIMBRE	• time *off*	omit T
timber	DEAL	• time *to* leave	omit T
• 100 *in* timber . . .	DECAL	• time *out*	omit T
• *put* timber *before* ruler	DEALER	• time-*wasting*	omit T
• timber trade	DEAL	• time*less*	omit T
timber	LOG	time	TIME
• timber in ship	SLOGS	• time *of backwardness<*	EMIT
• timber record	LOG	• [time] *off*	EMIT, MITE
• timber reserve	LOGBOOK	• [time]-*out*	EMIT, MITE

Letter replaced \c\at; Omit (a); Pointers *out*; Retain <u>a</u>; Split B_ED; Down (D); Backwards <or ^

• _time_piece	TIM
• time's _up_(D)^	EMIT
• time-_sharing_	EM–IT, IM–TE, M–ITE
• time _to get up_(D)^	EMIT
• [time] _warp_	EMIT, MITE
• tim(e) _without end_	TIM
• [times] _change_	EMITS, MITES, SMITE
time	YR
• time's _up_(D)^	–RY
time	TEMPO
• time to get up	TEMPORISE
• The Times	TEMPI
time	(THE) ENEMY
time _limits_	TE
time²	
time _and_ money	TIDEMARK
time of arrival	ETA
time-server	CONVICT
timely strike	CHIME
times	X
Times factor	NEWSAGENT
Times _leader_	T
Times Educational Supplement	TES
Times Literary Supplement	TLS
Times past	THUNDERER
Timothy	
Timothy	TIM
Timothy's _origin_	T
Timothy's origin	GRASS ROOTS
tin	
tin	CAN
• large tin	MAJORCAN
• tin man	CANAL, CANED, CANTED
• tin monkey	CANAPE
tin	MONEY
• potassium _in_ tin	MONKEY
• tin container	MONEY-BAG, MONEY-BELT
	MONEY-BOX, WALLET
tin	SN
• nothing _in_ tin	SON
• tin fish	SNIDE
• tin mineral	SNORE
and	
• tin-_plated_	(in) S–N
tin fish	TORPEDO
tin-opener	T
tin plate	TERNE
tin plate, _say_	TERN, TURN
tinned	(in) CA–N, (in) TI–N
• no _canned_ . . .	CANON
• _tinned_ beef	TOXIN
tinker	
tinker	SLY
• tinker _about_	S–LY
tinker _about_<	REKNIT
tinker _with_ Rod's . . .	FIDDLESTICKS

tint	CANT
tip	
asparagus _tip_	A
good _tip_	G
new tip on \c\ue	HUE, RUE, SUE
tip _backwards_<	PIT
tip backward<	DRAW
tip from (t)out	OUT
tip of iceberg	I
tip of foil	BUTTON
tip of foil<	F
tip-off	POINTLESS
tip _off_ (s)pike	PIKE
tip out of bed	DEBUNK
tip [over]	ROVE
tip over jar<	RAJ
tip over [vase]	SAVE
tip _up_(D)^	PIT
tip up pots(D)^	STOP
tip stew<	WETS
tip _w_inner	W
tips off (s)pie(s)	PIE
tiptop	PEAK
tip[top]	OPT, POT
_tip_top(D)	T
_tip_top<	POT
tiptop accommodation	ATTIC,
	GARRET, LOFT
tiptop wear	(C)OVERALL
_v_aluable _tip_	V
tipsy	
[leer] _tipsily_	REEL
tipsy [state]	TASTE, TEATS
tire	
[tired]	TRIED OUT
tired fellow	STALEMATE
[tired] _out_	DETRI–, TRIED
tired period	BEAT TIME
[tires] _out_	RESIT, RITES, TRIES
tiresome child	SMALL BORE
tissue	
tissue of [lies]	LEIS, SILE
tissue [papers]	SAPPER
Titus	TIT
to¹	TO
to east	TOE
to flower	TOASTER
to left	TOL, TOLT
to north	TON
to one side	TOL(T), TOR(T), TOWING
to plant	TOASTER
to right	TOR(T)
to the Home Counties	TOSE
to _turn_ to<	OTTO
to Tyneside	TONE
to understand	TOKEN

Anag [cat]; Any *; Begin IGN–; Endings –ING; eg •; Hidden /cat/; Implied add (on); Implied in (in);

to west	TOW
to your, *say*	TOOTHY
to²	
indicating foreign language:	
• give *to Italian*	DARE
• road *to German* . . .	STRASSE
• say *to Spaniard*	DECIR, RECITAR
• walk *to French* . . .	MARCHER
and	
• send *to Jose*	ENVIAR, REMITIR
• sing *to Luciano*	CANTARE
• speak *to Pierre*	PARLER
• write *to Hans*	SCHREIBEN
to the *French* . . .	ALA, AU, AUX
• to the *French* doctor	ALAMO
• o the *French* spirit	AURUM
• to the *French* in . . .	AUXIN
to the *Italian* . . .	AL
• add lard to the *Italian* . . .	FATAL
• to the *Italian* group	ALLOT
• to the *Italian* in b–ed	BALED
to³	
look *to-and-fro*	PEEP
to a large extent th(e) . . .	TH
to-and-fro action	DEED
to be heard	
• intended *to be heard*	–MENT
• *to be heard* when . . .	WEN
to do with	RE
	(*see* about²)
to infinity	AD INF(INITUM)
to London	UP
to no purpose	(in) VA–IN
to some degree	(in) PAR–T
• quarters, *to some degree*	PARENT
to some extent go/od in/side, ,	ODIN
to start with, <u>c</u>heese <u>on</u> toast	COT
to take leave	PPC, TTL
to the beginning	AD INIT(IUM)
to the end	AD FINEM
to the ear, airs . . .	HEIRS
to the fore in <u>n</u>early <u>e</u>very <u>w</u>ay	NEW
to windward	UP
toady	JENKINS
toast	
British toast	CHEERS
French toast	BON SANTE
German toast	GESUNDHEIT
Irish toast	SLAINTE
Roman toast	BENE VOBIS
Scandinavian toast	SKO(A)L
very thin toast	MELBA
tobacco-bird	SHAG
today	AD
toe	
broken [toe]	–OTE
toe	LEGEND
[toe]-*tapping*	OTE
twiddling [toes]	TOSE
Togo	TG
toilet	
toilet	LOO
• soldier *returns*< *to* toilet	IGLOO
• toilet *has* directions . . .	LOOSE
• toilet-master	LOOKING
and	
• toilet training, *say*	LUCENCE
told	
perhaps told	TOLLED
[told] *off*	DOLT
Toledo housing	SCABBARD
Tom	
Tom's tongue	CLAPPER
tom-tom	CATS
Tommy	SOLDIER
Tommy's father	CHAPLAIN, PADRE
tome	TOM(US)
ton	
ton	T, TONNE
ton-*up*(D)^	NOT
too	
too	
indicating palindrome:	
• served *up, too*(D)	DID
• send *back, too*	REFER
too fat	OS
too fine	OVERGROUND
t(o)o *heartless*	TO
too long for man	MANE, MANY
too much	OTT
too much m/one/y	ONE
too short to spa(n)	SPA
too small for arm(y)	ARM
too unprofessional	OVERLAY
took	
took advantage, *say*	MAYDAY
took afternoon meal, *say*	EIGHTY
took amiss	MARRIED
took courses	ATE, DINED
took it easy, *say*	WRESTED
	(*see also* take)
tool	
[garden] *tool*	DANGER, GANDER
tool, *say*	ADDS, SPAYED
tool thief, *say*	PICNICKER
tooled [letters]	SETTLER
tooth	
tooth	FANG
• tooth in front	FANGLED
top	
<u>B</u>ig *Top*(D)	B
top	APEX

Letter replaced \c\at; Omit (a); Pointers *out*; Retain <u>a</u>; Split B_ED; Down (D); Backwards <or ^

top	BEST	top man	CO, KING
• learner *in* top . . .	BLEST	*top* man(D)	M
• top Irish . . .	BESTIR	*top* (m)an	AN
• top mount	BESTRIDE	top mark	A, ALPHA
top	CAP	*top* mark	M
• top cereal	CAPRICE	*top* (m)ark(D)	ARK
• top *in* London area	SCAPE	top musician	SUPERCONDUCTOR
• top mount	CAPTOR	*top* musician(D)	M
top	HEAD	*top* musician	(d)RUMMER
• top branch	HEAD OFFICE	top needle manufacturer, *say*	PINKING
• top brands	HEADLINES	*top*-notch(D)	N
• top orchestra	HEADBAND	top note	G
top(D)	omit 1st letter	*top* note(D)	N
• *top* (t)able	ABLE	top note(D) start with A, B, C, D, E, F, G	
• *top* table	(l)IST	start with DO, RE etc	
top and bottom of the . . . (D)	TE	• hundred *top* notes	MIMIC
top and bottom of the matter(D)	MR	• man *takes top* note	REAL
top and tail (t)wi(g)	WI	• *top* note is not . . .	FAINT
top artist	PRA, RAKING	top notes, *say*	HIGH SEAS
top artist(D)	A	top of head	VERTEX
top artist	(l)ELY	*top of* head(D)	H
top barman	QC, SILK	*top of* the . . . (D)	T
top cat	CHIEF WHIP	*top of* the chart(D)	C
top cat(D)	C	top of the chart	(TRUE) NORTH
top (c)at	AT	*top off* (t)he . . .	HE
top class	U	*top off* the (c)hart	HART
top class(D)	C	top of the hill	CAPTOR
top (c)lass	LASS	*top of* the hill(D)	H
top company man	MD	*top off* the (h)ill	ILL
top confectioner, *say*	BUNKING	top players	HEADBAND
top dog	WINNER	*top* players(D)	P
top dog(D)	D	*top* (p)layers	LAYERS
top (d)og	OG	top race(D)	CROWN DERBY
top drawer	FAST GUN, GUNSLINGER	*top* race	R
	DEGAS, LEONARDO et al	*top* (r)ace	ACE
	PRA	top specialist	HAIRDRESSER
	U		TRICHOLOGIST
top drawer(D)	D	top trophy	GOLD, SCALP
top (d)rawer	RAWER	top *up*(D)^	POT
top dressing	BRILLIANTINE,	topless dress	SHOW JUMPERS
	SHAMPOO, WIG	*topless* (g)own(D)	OWN
	OVERCOAT	topper	EXECUTIONER
	LIME, MULCH	topping place	GIBBET, SCAFFOLD
top dressing(D)	D	*topping* (p)lan(D)	LAN
top figure	NUMERATOR	**topple**	
top floor	ATTIC	dog *topples over*<	GOD
top floor(D)	F	topple mountain	FELL
top (f)loor	LOOR	*toppling over* step<	PETS
top floor, *say*	GAROTTE	**topsy-turvy**	
top gear	HAT	[it was] *topsy-turvy*	WAIST, WAITS
top gear(D)	G	*topsy-turvy* [reasons]	SENORAS
top (g)ear	EAR	**tore**	
top grade	A	tore	RIPPED
top-heavy(D)	H	• 100 tore, *say*	CRYPT
top honours	A, ACE, K, KING	• tore fish, *say*	RIPTIDE
top lawyer, *say*	BARKING	(*see also* tear)	

Anag [cat]; Any *; Begin IGN–; Endings –ING; eg •; Hidden /cat/; Implied add (on); Implied in (in);

tore up [papers]	SAPPER
torn	RENT
• shirt torn	TRENT
• torn at this point, *say*	RENTIER
• torn volume	RENT BOOK
torn [towel]	OWLET
torn up [papers]	SAPPER
	(see also tear*)*
torment	
[devil] *tormented* . . .	LIVED
torment animal	BADGER
torment *say*	PANE
tormented [animal]	LAMINA, MANILA
torn	
torn	RENT
• shirt torn	TRENT
• torn at this point, *say*	RENTIER
	(see also tear, tore*)*
torpedo-boat	
torpedo-boat	MTB, TB
torpedo-boat destroyer	TBD
tortuous	
tortuous [lane]	LEAN
[writhe] *tortuously*	WITHER
torture	
torture machine, *say*	WRACK
tortured by [fire]	RIFE
torturing [slave]	SALVE, VALSE
Tory	
Tory	BLUE
• sad Tory	BLUE
• Tory high-flier	BLUEBIRD
Tory	C
• it *is back<* to Tory . . .	TIC
• Tory *has* many	CLOT
Tory	CON
• Tory *backing<*	NOC
• Tory in charge	CONIC
Tory	RIGHT
• second-class Tory	BRIGHT
• strong Tory . . .	FRIGHT
Tory, *say*	WIG
toss	
[ship] *tossed about*	HIPS, PISH
toss head	SHYNESS
toss tool	PITCHFORK
toss *up*(D)^	NIPS
toss up Ben's . . . (D)^	SNEB
toss up [coin]	ICON
tossed [caber]	ACERB, BRACE
tossed about [in the] . . .	THINE
tossed out [into an] . . .	NATION
Tosti's song	TATA
total	
total	ALL
• 100 total . . .	CALL

• b–et *about* total . . .	BALLET
• total disrepute	ALLODIUM
• totally dependent	ALLOWING
and	
• credit total, *say*	CRAWL
total	SUM
• total account	SUMAC
• total, *say*	SOME
• total with *German* . . .	SUMMIT
total	WHOLE
• total *and* more	WHOLESOME
• total, *say*	HOLE
• totally *say*	HOL(E)Y
total number	GENERAL
	ANAESTHETIC
	GROSS
total *speaking*	SOME
totter	
tottered [into] . . .	–TION
tottered, *say*	SUEDE
tottering [steps]	PESTS
touch	
touch	FEEL
• touch fish, *say*	FEELING
• touching sympathy	FEELING
touch	PAT
• second touch	SPAT
• touch a number	PATTEN
• touch bird	PATTERN
touch coin	FINGERMARK
touch fish	DAB
touch lightly, *say*	GRAYS, GREYS
touch of garlic	G
touched	FELT
• touched cloth	FELT
• touched journalist	FELTED
touching	ANENT
touching	RE
• touching song	RELIED
• try touching . . .	GORE
touchingly written	TYPED
touchline	TANGENT
tough	
tough	HARD
• tough course	HARD TACK
• tough defender	HARDBACK
• tough guy, *say*	HARD-WON
• tough joint	HARD SHOULDER
• tough ship	HARDLINER
tough bird, *say*	TOUGHEN
tough blades	ESPARTO
tough lawman	DRACO
tough Scot, *say*	RUFFIAN
tough worker	NUTANT
toughen	ANNEAL
toughen, *say*	ANNELE

Letter replaced \c\at; Omit (a); Pointers *out*; Retain a̲; Split B_ED; Down (D); Backwards <or ^

tour

on tour [in the] . . .	THINE
Tour de France	EIFFEL (TOWER)
tour of [Rome}	MORE
toured by *	incl in *
• north *toured by* bu–s	BUNS
touring car	GT
touring [car]	ARC
touring a . . .	incl A
touring *	incl *
• bu–s *touring* north	BUNS
tourist *centre*	R
Tourist Trophy	TT

towards

towards boy	TOKEN
towards dog	TOP-UP
towards Sussex	DOWNWARDS

tower

tower block(s)	TALL STORIES
tower in Paris, *say*	EYEFUL, TOUR
tower maintenance	KEEP
Tower of London	BARBICAN, CENTRE POINT
tower (of strength)	CARTHORSE, SHIRE
	TRACTOR, TUG

town

town	
indicating origins:	
• car *in* Boston	AUTO
• house *in* Essen	HAUS
• *Paris-style* hat	CHAPEAU
• *Roman* boy	RAGAZZO
	(*see also* from³)
town	TN
• I am *in* town	TIN
• nothing *in* town	TON
town ahead	BURGLED
town *centre*	(l)OUT(h), (n)EAT(h) etc
to*wn-centre*	OW
town crier, *say*	BAULKING
town house	HANOVER, LANCASTER
	WINDSOR, YORK etc
Town Planning Institute	TPI
town sub-office	TSO
townsman, *say*	BURGER

toy

toy	DOLL
• toy instruments, *say*	DOLDRUMS
• toy *with* unknown . . .	DOLLY
• toyboy, *say*	DOLMAN
toy revolver	CAROUSEL, (PEG-)TOP
	ROUNDABOUT, WHIRLIGIG
toy sweet	TRIFLE
toyed with [soup]	OPUS

track

tracked vehicle	CAT, TANK
tracks	R(L)Y

trade

trade centre	MALL, MART
tr*a*de *centre*	A
trade name	TN
trade union	TU
trademark	TM
trader	INDIAMAN, MERCHANTMAN
Trades Union Congress	TUC
• Trade Unionists	CUTBACK
tradesmen	TU
tradesmen's *entrance*	T
trading [coins]	ICONS, SONIC

traditional

indicating old words:

• *traditional* hero	EORL
• *traditionally* excellent	EXIMIOUS

traffic

traffic light	CAT'S-EYE
	AMBER, GREEN, RED
traffic sign	TRADEMARK
traffic signal	GO, STOP

tragic

tragic [Latin hero]	LIONHEART
tragic woman	ELECTRA, HECUBA,
	MEROPE et al
tragically [dead]	EDDA

train

train	APT
train fish	SCHOOL
train line	REARRANGE
train reserves	EXERCISE BOOKS
train, *say*	SWEET
train [seals]	SALES
trained as [nurse]	RUNES
trained [guns]	GNUS, SNUG, SUNG
trainee	L
training	PE, PT
training centre	STATION
	WATERLOO etc
trai*ning centre*	IN
training [centre]	RECENT
training manual	EXERCISE BOOK
training [ship]	HIPS, PISH
Training within Industry	TWI
trains	BR, RY
train[spotter]	POTTERS

tramp

tramp	HOBO, STEAMER
tramp steamer	DRIFTER

tramples

tramples	STEPSON

transactions

transactions	TR
transactions [in grain]	RAINING

transatlantic

	US
	(*see also* America)

transcendental meditation	TM

transcribe

transcribe [older] . . .	DROLE
transcribing nearly	
all [Chines(e)]	INCHES
transcription of [trio]	RIOT

transfer

transfer	PASS
• reserves *involved in* transfer	PASTAS
• transfer help, *say*	PASSADE
• transfer I have . . .	PASSIVE
transfer [a winger]	WEARING
transference of [coins]	ICONS, SONIC

transfigure

transfigured [sinner]	INNERS
transfiguration of [devil]	LIVED

transform

transform [my pet]	EMPTY
transformation of [stage] . . .	GATES
transforming [into] . . .	–TION

transfuse

transfusion of [saline] . . .	LIANES
[weak] *transfusion*	WAKE

transgress

transgress again	RESIN
transgress before nine, *say*	SCINTILLATE
transgress [laws]	AWLS, SLAW
transgression of [rules]	LURES

translate

translate	
–*French* word	MOT
–*German* word	WORT
–*Italian* word	PAROLA
–*Latin* word	VERBUM
–*Spanish* word	PALABRA
translate	
–*French* book	LIVRE
–*German* book	BUCH
–*Italian* book	LIBRO
–*Latin* book	LIBER
–*Spanish* book	LIBRO
translate	
–from *French*	DE
–from *German*	VON
–from *Italian*	DA
–from *Latin*	AB
–from *Spanish*	DE
–from the *French*	DELA, DES, DU
translate	
–into *French*	EN, ENTRE
–into *Italian*	DENTRO
–into *Latin*	INTRO
–into *Spanish*	EN, ENTRE
translate	
–the *French* . . .	LA, LE, LES
–the *German* . . .	DAS, DER, DIE
–the *Italian* . . .	GLI, IL, LA, LO, LE
–the *Spanish* . . .	EL, LA, LAS, LOS
translated [verse]	SERVE, SEVER
translation	CRIB, TR
translation of [Norse]	SENOR, SNORE
translator	TR

transmute

[may be] *transmuted*	BEAMY
transmutation of [silver]	LIVERS, SLIVER
transmute [lead]	DALE, DEAL, LADE

transplant

transplant [shrub]	BRUSH
transplantation of [tree]	RETE
transplanted [heart]	EARTH, HATER
	RATHE
transplanted heart of m\a\in . . .	MINA

transport

transport	BR
• transport expert	BRACE
• transport school	BRETON
• transport worker	BRANT
transport	BUS
• about transport	REBUS
• transport army *by* road	BUSTARD
• transport sheep	BUST-UP
transport	CAB
• transport fish	CABLING
• transport *in* front	CABLED
• transport *on* the *French*	
road	CABLEWAY
transport	CAR
• six transport . . .	VICAR
• transport *in* ship	SCARS
• transport *to* harbour	CARPORT
transport	ENTRANCE
transport	RLY
• man *in* transport	RALLY
• mother *has* transport	MARLY
transport	RY
• everybody *in* transport	RALLY
• mother *has* transport	MARY
transport	TRAM
• transport a man . . .	TRAMMEL
• transport *has* quiet . . .	TRAMP
Transport Officer	TO
transport opening	ENTRANCE
transport worker	SHIRE (HORSE)
transported [in car]	CAIRN

transpose

transpose [result]	LUSTRE, ULSTER
transpose reviled . . . <	DELIVER

transvestite

transvestite, *say*	DRAGSTER
transvestites	DRAG-RACE

Transworld Airlines | TWA

trap

trap	GIN

Letter replaced \c\at; Omit (a); Pointers *out*; Retain a̲; Split B_ED; Down (D); Backwards <or ^

• a trap *has* good . . .	AGING	*travelling* [crane]	NACRE
• live trap	BEGIN	travelling light	HEADLAMP
• trapnet	GINNET	travelling players, *say*	ROADSIDE, TROOP
and		**treacherous**	
• trap dog, *say*	JINKER	[act] *treacherously*	CAT
• trap, *say*	(D)JINN	treacherous guy	BURGESS
trap	MOUTH	*treacherous* [reef]	FEER, FERE, FREE
trap	NET	**treacle**	
• 50 in a trap	LINNET	[treacle] *pudding*	ELECTRA
• trap a spirit	NETRUM	*spread* [treacle]	ELECTRA
• trap a woman	NETHER	**treasury**	
trap European	CATCHPOLE	treasury keeper	DRAGON
trapped by Fren/ch arm/y	CHARM	treasury note, *say*	TENOR
trapped by *	incl in *	**treat**	
• one *trapped by* m–en	MIEN	[hormone] *treatment*	MOORHEN
trapped in ca/ve al/l . . .	VEAL	[painless] *treatment*	SPANIELS
trapped spirit	SNARE DRUM	[medical] *treatment*	CLAIMED, DECIMAL,
trapping a . . .	incl A		DECLAIM
trapping *	incl *	treat timber	DEAL
• m–en *trapping* one	MIEN	*treated* [timber]	TIMBRE
trash		*treating* [flu]	–FUL
[it was] *trashed*	WAIST, WAITS	*treatment of* [yaws]	SWAY, WAYS
trashed [all the] . . .	LETHAL	**tree**	
travel		tree	ALDER
travel	GO	• black tree	BALDER
• travel *by* rail	GORY	• tree joint, *say*	ALDERNEY
• travel *in* al–l . . .	ALGOL	• tree *on* island	ALDERMAN
• travel *with* wife	GO DUTCH	tree	ASH
and		• hard tree	HASH
• travel east *and* south	GOES	• tree-god	ASHLAR
• travel north-east	GONE	• tree *in* China	MASHING
• travel west *and* north	GOWN	tree	FIR
travel	TO	• king *has* a tree	KAFIR
• travel north	TON	• saint *hid behind* tree	FIRST
• travel north-east	TONE	• tree-ring	FIRRING
• travel west	TOW	tree	MAY
travel agency	CARRIAGE	• girl's tree	DISMAY
travel guide	SIGNPOST	• king *hidden in* tree	MARY
travel [in car]	CAIRN	• tree-ring	MAYO
travel West		tree	OAK
• dog *travels West<*	GOD	• second tree	SOAK
travelled	RODE	• tree unknown	OAKY
• travelled *by* Circle	RODEO	• tree *used in* ship	SOAKS
• travelled on pig, *say*	ROAD-HOG	tree	PALM
• travelled to this place, *say*	ROE-DEER	• goat *behind* tree	PALM-BUTTER
traveller	REP	• North American tree	NAPALM
• traveller in the East	REPINE	• tree in Greece	PALMING
• traveller isn't . . .	REPAINT	tree *climbing*(D)^	EMIL, YAM
• traveller wandered	REPROVED	tree expert	GENEALOGIST
• traveller's *return<*	PER	tree-house	ORANGE
• traveller's tales	REPLIES	tree list, *say*	TREATABLE
traveller's fare	PASSENGER	tree maintenance	SERVICE
travelling bag	CARCASE	Tree, *perhaps*	ACTOR, TRAGEDIAN
travelling-case	OUT-PATIENT	tree, *say*	BEACH, EWE, FUR, OKE
travelling-[case]	ACES, AESC		PLAIN, SEEDER, YOU
travelling companion	CARPET	tree, *say*	–TERY, –TRY

• criticise tree	PANTRY	tried	
• half-standard tree	CEMETERY	[tried]	TIRED OUT
• osier	BASKETRY	[tried] *out*	TIRED
• river tree	INDUSTRY		*(see also* try)
• saucepan rack	PANTRY	trifle	
• smelly tree	MUSKETRY	a trifle depressed	WHITLOW
• twisted tree	BANDITRY	*trifling with* [meal]	LAME, MALE
tree worship	SERVICE	trim	
treeless	OPINES	*trim* [ends]	DENS, SEND
trees *with* everything	FORESTALL	*trim* (h)air	AIR
treetops, *say*	BEACHHEADS	*trim* t/he len/gth	HELEN
tremble		trim tree	SPRUCE
[leaf] *trembling*	FLEA	*trimmed both ends of* (s)car(f)	CAR
trembling [lips]	PILS, SLIP	trimmer ship	CLIPPER, CUTTER
tremulous		trinity	
[speak] *tremulously*	PEAKS, SPAKE	Trinity College, Dublin	TCD
tremolo [notes]	ONSET, SETON	Trinity College of Music	TCM
	STONE, TONES	trio	
tremulous [speech]	CHEEPS	Beethoven's *first trio*	BEE
trench digger	JCB, RE, SAPPER	Mozart's *second trio*	ART
trendy		*trio from* Rossini	SIN
trendy	IN	trip	
• ask trendy . . .	BEGIN	trip over	JOURNEY'S END
• trendy *in* ways	NINE, SINE, SINS	*trip* [over]	ROVE
	WINE, WINS	*trip over* [step]	PEST, PETS
• trendy people	INSET	*trip over* step<	PETS
Trent Bridge	NE	*trip* [to Mars]	STROMA
trial		triumph	
trial	TEST	triumph	V
• large trial	FATTEST	triumphant cry	IO
• trial marriage	TEST MATCH	trivial sum	ID, IP
• trial TV	TEST-TUBE	troop	
trial marriage	PRACTICE MATCH	troop	TP
trial shot, *say*	CITER	troops *on* jetty	RAPIER
triangular	DELTA	tropic disease	CANCER
tribe		trot	
tribe	DAN, GAD	*trot* [past]	PATS, SPAT, STAP, TAPS
tribe	SEPT	*trotting* [race]	ACER, ACRE, CARE
• beyond the tribe	TRANSEPT	trouble	
• tribe *has a* . . .	SEPTA	[real] *trouble*	LEAR
• tribe in charge	SEPTIC	[take] *trouble*	KATE, TEAK
tribute	CAIN	trouble	ADO, AIL
trick		trouble afoot	BUNION, CORN, VERRUCA
[quite] *tricky*	QUIET, –TIQUE	trouble (and strife)	WIFE
trick	CON	*trouble in* [Iran]	RAIN, RANI
• one trick	ICON	trouble maker	GREMLIN
• trick *in* the Home Counties	SCONE	*troubled* [times]	ITEMS, MITES, SMITE
• trick questions	CONTESTS	[trouble]*maker*	BOULTER
trick of [fate]	FEAT	*troublesome* [priest]	RIPEST, STRIPE
trick, *say*	FAINT, RUES, WHILE		TRIPES
tricky achievement	GRAND SLAM	trounce	
tricky command	ABRACADABRA	*trounced* [team]	MATE, MEAT, META–, TAME
	HEY PASS, HEY PRESTO	*trouncing* [best] . . .	BETS
	OPEN SESAME	true	
tricky contest	BRIDGE, WHIST	true blue	RIGHT
tricky [part]	PRAT, RAPT, TRAP	true height	REALTOR

[true or] *false*	ROUTER, TOURER
[true] *to form*	–TURE
true, *say*	REEL, STRAIT
trumpeter	ARMSTRONG, JAMES
	ELEPHANT
	JOSHUA
trunk	
trunk, *say*	BOWL
trunk service	STD
trust	
trusted friend	ACHATES
trustee	TR
trustee *said . . .*	TRUSTY
Trustee Savings Bank	TSB
trusty pilot	SAFE CONDUCT
truth	
truth-drug, *say*	LIGHTEST
try	
try	GO
• to go *after* graduate	TOBAGO
• try *covered by* wager	BEGOT
• try publicity	GOAD
try	HEAR
• second try	SHEAR
• try the Home Counties	HEARSE
• try *to capture* note and	HEATER
• try and try again and	HEAR-HEAR
• try excessively, *say*	HERETO
• try, *say*	HERE
try	TEST
• city tries . . .	LATESTS
• try a peg	TESTATEE
• try *about* everything and	TALLEST
• try at this place, *say*	TESTIER
try-*out*	T–EST, TR–Y
[try]-*out*	TYR
try *to contain . . .*	T–EST, TR–Y
try to fish	CASTANET
TT	
TT	DOUBLET
TT	DRY
• old *and* dry	OTT
TT	RACE
• one *in* race	TAT, TIT
t-take in	TEAT
tub	
tub	BATH, BOAT
tubby fellow	DIOGENES
tubby trio	BAKER, BUTCHER
	CANDLESTICK MAKER
tube	UNDERLINE
French tube	METRO
tube fare	MACARONI

Tube Investments	TI
tube traveller	TORPEDO
tuber	MURPHY, POTATO, SPUD
tuberculosis	TB
TUC	
TUC(D)	CUT UP, NOTCH UP
TUC *rises*(D)^	CUT
tuck	
tuck, *say*	FRIAR
tucked in *	incl in *
• tyro *tucked in* s–acks	SLACKS
tucked into	ATE
tucked into mea/l at e/ight	LATE
tucked into sin/gle be/d	GLEBE
tucked into *	incl in *
• airman *tucked into* me–at	MEERKAT
tucked round a . . .	incl A
tucked round *	incl *
• s–acks *tucked round* tyro	SLACKS
Tuesday	T, TU, TUES
tumble	
tumble [drier]	DIRER
tumble [dryer]	DERRY
tumbled [into Po]	OPTION, POTION
tumbled over step<	PETS
tumbled over [step]	PEST, PETS
tumbledown [shack]	HACKS
tumbler	JILL
tumbler-maker	ACROBAT, LOCKSMITH
tumult	
tumult [in the] . . .	THINE
tumultuous [riot]	TRIO
tune	
[fine]-*tuning*	NIFE
tune, *say*	HEIR, REAL
tuned [a sitar]	TIARAS
Tunisia	TN
tuppence	DD, PP
turbulent	
[act] *turbulently*	CAT
[air] *turbulence*	RIA
turbulent [priest]	RIPEST, STRIPE
	TRIPES
turf	
turf out	DIVOT
turf study	SODDEN
Turkey	TR
turmoil	
[much] *turmoil*	CHUM
turmoil [in great] . . .	INGRATE, TEARING
turn¹	
turn	ACT
• space *to* turn	ENACT
• transport turns . . .	BRACTS
• turn gold	ACTOR
• turns book	ACTS

Anag [cat]; Any *; Begin IGN–; Endings –ING; eg •; Hidden /cat/; Implied add (on); Implied in (in);

turn | GO
• a turn *to* the north | AGON
• turn *and* throw | GOSLING
• turn sheep | GOT UP
• turn *to* latest . . . | GONE WEST
• turn *to* publicity | GOAD
and
• turn *back*< | OG
• turn *over*< | OG
• turn *up*(D)^ | OG
turn | S
• turn *in* | incl S
• turn *into* | incl S
• turn *out* | omit S
turn | SPIN
• one *in* a turn | SPAIN
• turn a number | SPINAL
• turn alien . . . | SPINET
and
• turn *back*< | NIPS
• turn *over*< | NIPS
• turn *up*(D)^ | NIPS
turn | U
• turn about | URE
• turn *in* church | CUE
• turn round | UO
• turn ship | U-BOAT
and
• turn *in* | incl U
• turn *into* | incl U
• turn *out* | omit U
turn | WHEEL
• turn a hair | WHEEL LOCK
• turn *behind* the vehicle | CARTWHEEL
• turning circle | STEERING WHEEL
and
• turn, *say* | WEAL, WE'LL, WHEAL
turn | WIND
• turn girl | WINDLASS
• turn *to* hospital wing | WINDWARDS
• turn *round* English . . . | WINED
• turn here, *say* | WINDIER

turn²
turn
indicating anagram:
• *turn* [into] . . . | –TION
• *turn* [into a] . . . | –ATION
• *turn* into [street] | SETTER, TESTER
• *turn* [it on] | INTO, –TION
• *turn* of [phrase] | SERAPH, SHERPA
• [turn] *out* | RUNT
• *turn* out [the guard] | DAUGHTER
• *turn* over [a bit] | BAIT
• *turn* [over a bit] | ABORTIVE
• *turn* [sour] | OURS
• *turn* [tables] | BLEATS, STABLE

• *turned out* [fine] | NIFE
• *turned out to be* [a dry] . . . | DRAY, YARD
• *turn*[coats] | ASCOT, ATOCS, COAST, TOSCA
turn
indicating reversal:
• *turn* about< | ER, AC
• *turn* again< | ER
• turn *back*< | NIPS
• *turn* Communist< | DER
• *turn* green< | WAR
• *turn* in< | NI
• *turn* it< on | –TION
• *turn* it *over*< | TI
• *turn* it *up*(D)^ | TI
• *turn* on< | NO
• *turn* over to< . . . | OT
• *turn* red< | DER
• *turn* round but . . . < | TUB
• *turn* to . . . < | OT
• *turn* up< | PU
• *turn* up parts(D)^ | STRAP
• *turning* tide< | EDIT
• *turnover* made . . . < | EDAM
• *turn*spit< | TIPS

turn³
turn again | ENCORE
turn left | BEND SINISTER
turn on | SWITCH
turn out fine | omit F
turn over | TO
turn quickly | VS
turn ring | ROLLCALL
turn round | SCREWBALL, UO
turn *tail*
• Boc\r\ *turns tail* | BORE
• *turn tail of* lin\e\ | LIEN
turncoat feature | LAPEL
turned out fine | omit F
turner | LATHE, SPIT, WHEEL
 | PAINTER
turning force, *say* | TALK, TORC
 | (*see also* twist)

Turnberry
Turnberry *they say* . . . | SINTER
Turnberry's first | T, TEE
tweak
tweak [ear] | ARE, ERA
tweaked [nose] | NOES, ONES
twelve
Glorious Twelfth | AUGUST
twelve | DOZ(EN), HANDS UP, XII
twelve Christmas presents | DRUMMERS
twelve hours | AM, PM
twelve houses | ZODIAC
twelve hundred | MCC
twelve inches | AFOOT

Letter replaced \c\at; Omit (a); Pointers *out*; Retain a̲; Split B_ED; Down (D); Backwards <or ^

twelve jobs	LABOURS OF HERCULES
twelve men	JURY
twelve tribes	ISRAELITES

twenty

20	DOUBLE CROSS, XX
21	KEY OF THE DOOR, MAJORITY
22	CATCH, TWO-BY-TWO
24	BLACKBIRDS
25 pounds (£25)	PONY
25% *off* bee(f)	BEE
25% price *cut*	COS(t)
27 books	NT
28 grams	OZONE
Twentieth Century Dictionary	TCD
twenty	SCORE
• twenty directors	SCOREBOARD
• twenty *plus* 500	SCORED
• twenty ties	SCORE DRAWS
twenty thousand	K
twenty-twenty	VISION

twice

twice blessed	BB

(*see also* double, doubly, two³)

Twickenham game   RU, RUGBY

twiddle

[stop] *twiddling!*	OPTS, POST, POTS, SPOT
twiddle [toes]	TOSE

twin

twin	CASTOR, POLLUX
twin daughters	DD
twin sons	SS

(*see also* two³)

twine

[liane] *twined* . . .	ANILE
twining [arms]	MARS, RAMS

twinkle

[in a] *twinkling*	AIN, IAN
twinkling [star]	ARTS, RATS, TARS, TSAR

twirl

twirl knob<	BONK
twirling [stick]	TICKS

twist

twist a number, *say*	TERNATE
twist alien	CRICKET
twist road	WARPLANE
twist-ring	SCREWBALL
twist, *say*	REST, RING, TERN
twist verse	SPINODE
twisted [a leg]	GALE, GAEL
twisted injury	WOUND
twisted, *say*	RESTED, RUNG, RYE
twisted sheep, *say*	WRITE-UP
twisted you and me, *say*	RICTUS
twisting [client]	LENTIC
twists nut	RICKSHAW

(*see also* turn)

twitch

twitch [nose]	NOES, ONES
twitching [nerves]	SEVERN

two¹

two	COMPANY
two	COUPLE
• one *French with* two . . .	UNCOUPLE
• two *plus* 500	COUPLED
• two shirts	COUPLETS
two	II
two	PAIR, PR
• 1000 couples	IMPAIRS
• about two	REPAIR
• I am two . . .	IMPAIR
• two soldiers	REPAIR
two-by-two	FOUR
two-*by*-two	TWENTY-TWO
two Christmas presents	TURTLEDOVES
two-dimensional figure	FLATTEN
two holding hands	EN, NS, WE etc
two hundred	CC
two hundred thousand	S, SIGMA
two in song	LILLYWHITE BOYS
two-nil	TWENTY
two spades	SP
two, *say*	BRAYS, PARE, PEAR
two, *say*	TO, TOO, TOU, TU
• two names	TONS
• two shirts	TOOTS
• two tins	TOUCANS
• two extra	TUMOUR
two score, *say*	FOR TEA, FORTE
two thousand	MM, Z
two-way names	LEON, NOEL
two-way transport	KAYAK
writer or two	TWAIN

(*see also* pair)

two²

actions	SUITCASE
advertisements	BILLPOSTER
animals	BUCKRAM, BULL-PUP,
	BULLDOG, FOXHOUND
	RAMCAT, SHEEPDOG
	WOLFRAM
animals, *say*	RAMBLE
arguments	SPARROW
articles	AIL, ALA, LATHE
	LETHE, THEA, UNDER
bases	BEDEVIL
beds	CRIBBED
Biblical characters	JOB LOT
birds	COCKCROW, RAVENDUCK
	TITLARK, TITREE
black things	NIGHTCLUB
blows	SMASH HIT
blues	ROYAL NAVY

Anag [cat]; Any *; Begin IGN–; Endings –ING; eg •; Hidden /cat/; Implied add (on); Implied in (in);

boys	ALBERT, ALFRED, ARTHURIAN	finals	TAIL-END
	BASILDON, BASILIAN, BENTHOS	fish	CODLING, IDLING
	DONJON, DENTED, EDWARDIAN,		NURSELING, RUDDLING
	FRANKED, GLENGARRY, GREGORIAN	fish, *say*	DABBLING
	GUYED, HALBERT, HALTED,	flavours	PEPPERMINT
	HERBAL	foods	BREADFRUIT, CHEESECAKE
	JACKAL, JACKED, MALTED,		JELLYBEAN, JELLYFISH
	MARKED		PEANUT, SWEETMEAT
	NICKED, NORMAL, NORMANDY,	forms of transport	CARRY
	PATRON,	friends	PALMATE
	PATTED, PETERED, REGAL,ROYAL,	fruits, *say*	PLUMBERY
	RUSSIAN, SAMIAN, SIDED, SIDLES,	games	PONTOON BRIDGE
	TOMBOY, TIMED, VICTIM,	garments	BRAVEST
	VICTORIAN	generations	DAMSON, MASON
boys and a girl	BETRAYAL	Germans	HUNGER
buildings	HUTCH	girls	BELLADONNA, CLARABELLA
cans	POTABLE		DISALLY, DIVI, GALENA
card games	PONTOON BRIDGE		MILLIGAL, PATELLA, PATINA
cards	TENACE		ROSEMARY, SALINA, TESSELLA
cats	TOMALLEY	girls *with* a Scotsman	SALMONELLA
celestial bodies	EARTHSTAR	glances	LOOK-SEE
characters	(*see* letters)	goddesses	DEVIATE
chiefs	HEADFIRST	graves	STERN-CHASE
children	–DS	Greek letters	PIETA
churches	ROMANCE	groups of officers	COSMOS
circles	DISCO	hands	–RL
cities	ROMANY	headdresses	CROWN DERBY
clubs	IRONWOOD	heads	BLUFFNESS, ONION DOME
colours	OLIVETAN	homes	HONEST
containers	BASKET CASE, CHAMBERTIN	in family	DAMSON, MASON
	PAN-JUG, POT BOILER	insects, *say*	NATANT
	TINPOT, TUNDISH	inspections	LOOK-SEE
coppers	CUD, CUP, DD, DP, PD, PP	instruments	HORNPIPE
	PENNYFARTHING	journalists	CUBED
cots	CRIBBED	keys	BORA, CORA, DORA
courses	JELLYFISH, SWEETMEAT		BORD, CORD, FORD
court calls	LET OUT		BORE, CORE, FORE, GORE
creatures	CLAMANT	kings	EDWARD LEAR, GRANDER, GROG
cuts	HACK-SAW	languages	FRENCH POLISH
dances	FOOTBALL, FOOTSTEP	lashers	WHIPCAT
defects	DESERT RAT	learners	TYROL
dioceses	ELYSEE	letter girl	ELLA, ELLEN, EMMA
directions	EN, WE etc	letters	BANDY, CANDY, DANDY
	WANDS		MANDY, PANDA, RANDY
disputes	SPARROW		SANDY, TANDEM
doctors, *say*	PARADOX	letters, *say*	TEPEE
dogs	CURTAIL	lots of coins	BITS AND PIECES
dots	COLON	maidens	MALICE, MANNA
drinks	ALEVIN, SUPPORTER	means of transport	CARAVAN, MOTORBOAT,
drugs	CRACKPOT, TEAPOT		TRAMCAR
enclosures	DAMPEN, HEMPEN	measures	FOOTSTEP, ELLEN
expressions of surprise	HOOCH	men	ALBERT, CHAPMAN, DESMAN
fabrics	REPLACE		GENTLES, GILBERTIAN
fathers	PAPAW		HE-MAN, HEAL, HELEN, HEROD
favourites	PUPPET		HERON, LANCE-JACK, MACRON
fells	DOWNHILL		MANAL, MELTED

Letter replaced \c\at; Omit (a); Pointers *out*; Retain a̲; Split B_ED; Down (D); Backwards <or ^

	(see also boys above)
men and a woman	BETRAYAL, HELEN
months	DECOCT
mothers	DAMPEN, MADAM, MAMMA
movements	SPRING ROLL
natural products	FURORE
negatives	NONARY
notes	DOME, DOTE, LATE, MERE, METE, MIRE, REDO, SOFA, REME, SITE, SOLE, SOME, TIME
novices	TYROL
numbers, say	TOFORE
odd fellows	CRANKCASE
old elements	FIREWATER
paces	JOG-TROT
paper sizes	CROWN IMPERIAL
parts of goal	BARNET
people	DAWNED, DIAL, DIED, VIAL, VIED
periods	ADAGE
pieces	BIT PART
–of timber	LOGWOOD
pins	PEG-LEG
pints, say	QUARTZ
placards	BILLPOSTER
poets, say	HARDIHOOD
points	NIBS, SNIB, NEEDLESS, PEAKS, SPEAK, TINES
political parties	CLEFT
politicians, say	LABORATORY
pounds	LIQUID
presents	NOWHERE
pronouns	USHER
records	LOGBOOK
reduced	LOWDOWN
regiments	RARE
relations	MASON, SISKIN
remarks in court	OUTLET
resins	GUMLAC
rings	DINGO, DISCO
rivers	AIRER, DEER, RALPH, ROUSE, RURAL
roads	AVER, MIST, PATHWAY, RAILROAD, STANDARD, STAVE
rows	RANK AND FILE
Scots	CAMERONIAN
scraps	SPARROW
seamen	MERCHANTABLE
seas	SEAMED
seater bicycle (tandem)	TM
sentences	LIFE AND DEATH
sets of cards	DECKHAND
short periods	MOHR
sides	OFF AND ON, ON AND OFF
sleeping places	CRIBBED
sources of water	WELLSPRING
spoons	NECK AND NECK
states	FLAME, GALA, LAVA, MEMO, NYALA, PENNILL, RIME
streets	(see roads above)
sticky things	TARGUM
strikes	SMASH HIT
surprised reactions	JUMP-START
tennis shots	SMASH HIT
things	
–naturally produced	FURORE
–to eat	(see courses, foods above)
timepieces	WATCH (THE) CLOCK
torches	LAMPLIGHT
traps	GINNET
trees	BOX ELDER, BOXTHORN, OAK APPLE, PINEAPPLE
undergarments	BRAVEST
vehicles	CARAVAN, TRAMCAR
violent people	GO THROUGH
water sources	WELLSPRING
ways	EN, WE, etc, MODEST
–to go	(see roads above)
weapons	BOMBSHELL
whiskies	PAIR OF SHORTS
wines	RED ROSE, WHITE ROSE
women	LADYBIRD, MADAM, MADONNA, MALADY, VIDAME

two³

adverts	PUFF-PUFF
agreements	DADA
animals in…	ASSASSIN
armies	TATA
army men	GIGI
basic subjects	RR
bears	POOH-POOH
berries	HAW-HAW
black queens	BERBER
blows	CHOP-CHOP
boys	TOM-TOM, WILLY-WILLY
cats	TOM-TOM
chants	SING-SING
cheers	HEAR-HEAR
coats	FURFUR
coins	DD, PP, SS
companies	COCO
containers	JUG-JUG
cuts	CHOP-CHOP
daughters	DD
days	DD
detectives, say	DIK-DIK
digits	TOETOE
discounts	DIVI-DIVI

Anag [cat]; Any *; Begin IGN–; Endings –ING; eg •; Hidden /cat/; Implied add (on); Implied in (in);

dogs	POMPOM	pounds	LL
drinks	CHA-CHA	presents, *say*	HEAR-HEAR, NOW-NOW
essays	GOGO	prisons	CAN-CAN
extras	BYE-BYE	quiet . . .	HUSH-HUSH
fathers	PAPA	ravines	NULLANULLA
features	CHIN-CHIN	refusals	NEVER-NEVER
feet	PAWPAW	roads	MIMI, MM
firms	COCO	Romany women	CHICHI
French words	MOT-MOT	runs	BYE-BYE
friends	PALPAL	sailors	TARTAR
fruits	HAW-HAW, HIP-HIP	seconds	SS
fruits, *say*	BERI-BERI	shillings	SS
girls	LILLIL	soldiers	GIGI
girls, *say*	SOOSOO	sounds	HUMHUM
graduates	BABA, MAMA	starting points	TEE-TEE
grasses	SING SING	starting points, *say*	TITI
halves of <u>mi</u>ld	MIMI	states	GAGA
hands	PAWPAW	stomachs	TUM-TUM
hats	TAM-TAM	supports	TEE-TEE
hundred	CC	supports, *say*	TITI
Israelites, *say*	JU-JU	teas	CHA-CHA
jeers	BOOBOO	tests	MOT-MOT
kicks	TOETOE	thousand	MM
learners	LL	tins	CAN-CAN
letters	CHICHI	tree trunks	LOG-LOG
lots of		tries	GOGO, HEAR-HEAR
–hair	FURFUR	volcanic rocks	LAVA-LAVA
–salt	TARTAR	votes for	AYE-AYE
male birds	TOM-TOM	water sources	WELL WELL
meals, *say*	TEE-TEE, TITI	(*see also* double[2])	
men	PP, TOMTOM	**Tyneside**	
mothers	MAMA	Tyneside	NE
motorways	MIMI, MM	• about Tyneside	CANE
noises	DIN-DIN	• arrive *in* Tyneside	NARRE
notes	DODO, MIMI, SO-SO	• Tyneside entrance	NEGATE
oaths, *say*	C(O)USC(O)US, KHUSKHUS	Tynesider	GEORDIE
officers	COCO	**tying**	(*see* tie)
parents	MAMA, PAPA	**type**	
parties	DODO	type	KIND
pawns	PP	• type in front	KINDLED
peers	SEESEE	• type queen's letters	KINDER
pegs	TEE-TEE	• type "Red"	KINDRED
pegs, *say*	TITI	typical measure	ELITE, PICA
pence	DD, PP		EM, EN, POINT
pieces	PP	typical traveller	REPRESENTATIVE
pieces of		**tyro**	L
–meat	CHOP-CHOP	(*see also* learner)	
–timber	LOG-LOG		

U

acceptable, *aristocratic*, bend, boat, bolt, *educational establishment*, ewe, *film*, *high-class*, *posh*, *superior*, title of respect, trap, tube, turn, union, Unionist, united, universal, universe, university, upper-class, upsilon, uranium, Uruguay, Utah

U-boat	SUB	umpire's announcement	OUTCRY
U-turn		**un**[1]	A, AN, I
U-turn was . . . <	SAW	**un-**[2]	
new *U-turn*<	WEN	many words with the prefix	
Uganda	EAU	un-, some of which follow,	
ugly		are used to indicate anagrams	
ugly	PLAIN	**un-English**	omit E
• Penny *has* ugly, *say*	PENEPLAIN	**unable**	
• ugly quarrel	PLAINTIFF	unable	CANT
• ugly queen	PLAINER	unable (=having no . . .)	O
ugly, *say*	PLAIN	• unable to fly	OWING
ugly [mug]	GUM	• unable to stretch	OGIVE
ugly sister	GORGON	• unable to write	OPEN
ugly truth	PLAIN FACTS	**unacceptable**	
Ulster		unacceptable	NON-U
Ulster	NI	unacceptable	OUT
Ulster		• unacceptable habit, *say*	OUTWEIGH
–Defence Association	UDA	• unacceptable job	OUTPOST
–Defence Regiment	UDR	• unacceptable players	OUTCAST
–Freedom Fighters	UFF	**unaccompanied**	ALLA BREVE
–Unionists	UU		A(LLA) CAPELLA
–Volunteer Force	UVF	**unaffected by reversal**	
ultimate		indicating a palindrome:	
th**e** *ultimate* . . .	E	• boat *unaffected by reversal*	KAYAK
the ultimate deterren**t**	T	• woman *unaffected by reversal*	AVA, EVE
ultimate letter	OMEGA, Z, ZED, ZEE		MADAM
ultimate outcom**e**	E	**unauthorised**	NOOK
ultimately	(in) EN–D	**unavailable**	
• can *ultimately* . . .	ENABLED	money *unavailable*	omit D, L, P
• prison *ultimately* . . .	ENCAGED	father *unavailable*	omit PA
• *ultimately* prosecute	ENSUED	* *unavailable*	omit *
ultimately wen**t** t**o** German**y**	TOY	unavailing, *say*	VANE, VEIN
ultra		**unbalanced**	
ultra high frequency	UHF	[quite] *unbalanced*	QUIET, –TIQUE
ultrashort wave	USW	*unbalanced* [German I] . . .	REAMING
ultrasonic waves	USW	*unbalanced* [scale]	LACES
ultra-violet	UV	**unbelievable female**	CASSANDRA
umbrella	BROLLY, MUSH	**unbounded**	
umpire		(j)o(y) *unbounded*	O
umpire	REF	*unbounded* (p)lain(s)	LAIN
• umpire allowed	REFLET	**unbowed**	PIZZICATO
• umpire has hurt his leg	REFLAME	**unbridled**	
• umpire not well	REFILL	[horse] *unbridled*	HOERS, SHORE

Anag [cat]; Any *; Begin IGN–; Endings –ING; eg •; Hidden /cat/; Implied add (on); Implied in (in);

unbridled [greed]	EDGER
unbroken past	SOLIDAGO
unceasing	FORAY
uncertain	
uncertain [sort]	ORTS, ROTS, TORS
uncertainty [as to] . . .	OATS
unchanged	
unchanged	SIC
[un]*changed*	NU
uncharged particle	NOTION
uncle	
uncle	PAWNBROKER
• uncle's place	PAWNSHOP
uncle	SAM
Uncle Sam (=America)	
• *Uncle Sam's* braces	SUSPENDERS
• *Uncle Sam's* lift	ELEVATOR
• *Uncle Sam's* marines	LEATHERNECKS
uncle	BOB, TOM
unclosed	
back-(d)*oor< unclosed*	ROO
unclosed cove(r)	COVE
unclothed	
unclothed	OUT OF GEAR
unclothed (=with nothing on)	
• *father unclothed*	DADU
• *unclothed* drivers	RACOON
	(*see also nothing³*)
uncomfortable	
uncomfortable [seat]	EATS, SATE, TEAS
uncomfortably [seated]	TEASED
uncommon	
uncommon coin	NOBLE
uncommon person	NOBLE
uncommonly [silent]	ENLIST, LISTEN
uncompleted	
stag(e) *uncompleted* . . .	STAG
uncompleted book	LEDGE(r), TOM(e)
uncompleted bus(t)	BUS
unconscious	
unconscious	COLD
• son unconscious	SCOLD
• unconscious queen	COLDER
unconscious	OUT
• 150 unconscious . . .	CLOUT
• unconscious players	OUTCAST
unconscious	UNDER
• second unconscious . . .	SUNDER
• unconscious boxer	UNDERDOG
unconstrained	
unconstrained [by a] . . .	BAY
[it was] *unconstrained*	WAIST, WAITS
uncontrolled	
[quite] *uncontrolled*	QUIET, -TIQUE
uncontrollable [rage]	GARE, GEAR
uncontrolled [anger]	RANGE

unconventional	
[acted] *unconventionally*	CADET
unconventional [ways]	SWAY, YAWS
uncoordinated	
[a bit] *uncoordinated*	BAIT
uncoordinated [action]	CATION
uncouth	
[spoke] *uncouthly*	POKES
uncouth actors	ROUGHCAST
uncouth [Huns]	SHUN
uncover	
un*cover*	incl UN
• un*covered by* note	TUNE
un*cover* *	U–N
• un*covering* right . . .	URN
uncovered	OLID
uncovered (c)ache(D)	ACHE
uncurl	
[rope] *uncurls*	PORE
uncurl [coil C]	COLIC
undecided	
[he is] *undecided*	HIES
undecided [voter]	TROVE
undecorated	NOTICED
under¹	
many words beginning with under,	
some of which follow, are used	
to indicate a word or letter written	
underneath another in Down clues	
under²	
indicating implied inclusion:	
under canvas	(in) TEN-T
under control	(in) H–AND
under cover	(in) HA–T
	(in) TEN-T
under the blankets	(in) BE–D
	(in) CO–T
under³	
indicating a word or letter	
written under another(D):	
• exercise *under*lines	RYPE
• free *under*current	ACRID
• good *under*study	CONFINE
• I am *under*study	DENIM
• I have some *under*wear	WEARISOME
• or *under*sea . . .	MAINOR
• piece *under* 1 metre	IMPART
• row *under*way	STRANGE
• Scot *under*cooks	FRIESIAN
• son is *under*graduate	MASON
• space *under* the table	BOARD ROOM
• the French *under*garment	GARBLE
• *under* five beers	VALES
• *under*go a(n) . . .	GOA(N)
• *under*write church	PENCE
	(*see also* underwater, underwrite)

Letter replaced \c\at; Omit (a); Pointers *out*; Retain <u>a</u>; Split B_ED; Down (D); Backwards <or ^

under⁴
  other uses:
  under consideration   SUBJUDICE
  under cover   INSURED, INTENT
  under forty   FOR, FORT
  under-secretary   US
  under seven   SIX
  under (s)even   EVEN
  under stress [arch] . . .   CHAR
  under tension [rope] . . .   PORE
  under that heading   VV
  under the rose   SUB ROSA
  under the table   DRUNK
  under the word   SV
  under this word   SH
underarm bowler   LOBSTER
underclothes   LOW GEAR
undercooked
  undercook, *say*   BAKELITE
  undercooked   RARE
  [under]*cooked*   RUNED
undercurrent   ACHERON, LETHE, STYX etc
undercut
  undercut side of stream   BAN(k)
  [under]*cut*   RUNED
underdone
  bee(f) *underdone*   BEE
  underdone   RARE
  underdone lam(b)   LAM
undergarment
  undergarment   BRA
  • undergarment at
    the laundry   BRAINWASH
  • undergarment in
    wash-basin   BRAINPAN
  • undergarments *and* hose   BRASSOCK
  and
  • firm undergarment   COBRA
  • undergarments   BRAVEST
undergo
  undergoing instruction   INTUITION
undergraduate   ONE UP
underground
  underground   METRO, SUBSOIL
  underground   TUBE
  • underground plant   TUBEROSE
  • underground ruler   TUBER
  underground spring   VAULT
  underground stem, *say*   ROUTE
  underground vault   LANDGRAVE
  underground worker   (EARTH)WORM, MINER
  underground worker, *say*   MINOR
underlined   UL
underneath   (*see* under³)
underpinned   ONE-LEGGED
underscore   TEENAGER

undersea   IN THE MAIN
understand
  understand   DIG
  • understand it   DIGIT
  understand, *say*   NO
  understand trick   TAKE IN
  understands measures   FATHOMS
  understands, *say*   NOES, NOSE
  understood   –MENT, ROGER
  understood by
  foreigners (=foreign language)
  • language *understood by*
    foreigners   LANGUE
  • verse *understood by*
    foreigners   STANZA
  • word *understood by*
    foreigners   PALABRA
  understood, *say*   GNU, NEW
  understood vessel   TACITURN
understood   (*see* understand)
understudy
undertaker
  undertakers'
    business   GRAVE CONCERN
  undertakers' magazine   GRAVE NEWS
  undertaking, *say*   DYE-WORK
underwater
  indicating one word or letter
  written underneath the name of
  a river, lake, etc(D):
  • boy *under*water   MEDIAN
  • child *under*water   SEASON
  • clever *under*water   EXECUTE
  • *under*water *and* [into a] . . .   TARNATION
  • *under*water fleas   POLICE
  • *under*water object   TEETHING
underwear
  underwear   LOW GEAR
  underwear, *say*   NICKERS
       (*see also* undergarment)
underworld
  underworld   ABADDON
  underworld   DIS
  • underworld class   DISORDER
  • underworld character   DISCARD
  • underworld makes . . .   DISUSES
  underworld   EREBUS, HADES, HELL
       PIT, TARTARUS
underwrite
  underwrite
  indicating one word or letter
  written below another(D):
  • church *has underwritten* it   ITCH
  • reserves *used to*
    underwrite the . . .   THETA
  • Times *underwriting* bond   BONDAGES

Anag [cat]; Any *; Begin IGN–; Endings –ING; eg •; Hidden /cat/; Implied add (on); Implied in (in);

underwriter   SUBSCRIBER
(*see also* under³)

undeveloped country   GREENLAND
undisciplined
  undisciplined [form]   FROM
  undisciplined career   WILDLIFE
undivided   ONE
undo
  [I am] *undone*   AIM
  undoing [clasp]   CLAPS
  un[done]   NODE
undressed   OUT OF GEAR
(*see also* unclothed)

uneasy
  [toss] *uneasily*   SOTS
  uneasy [sleep]   PEELS
unemployed
  unemployed   OUSE
  unemployed man   FREE-HAND
unending
  unending journey   TRI(p)
  unending rout(e)   ROUT
uneven
  uneven [road]   DORA
  unevenly [laid]   DIAL
unexpected
  [quite] *unexpected*   QUIET, –TIQUE
  unexpected [snag]   NAGS, SANG
unfair   BRUNETTE, DARK
unfamiliar
  unfamiliar [taste]   ETATS, STATE, TEATS
  unfamiliarity of [route]   OUTER, OUTRE
unfashionable
  unfashionable   OUT
  • afterthought *about*
    unfashionable . . .   POUTS
  • road *has* unfashionable . . .   STOUT
  • unfashionable clothes   OUTWEAR
  unfashionable   SQUARE
  • model *has* unfashionable . . .   T-SQUARE
  • unfashionable food   SQUARE MEAL
     SQUARE ROOTS
  unfashionable   omit IN
  • *unfashionable* material   SAT(in)
  unfashionable   omit U
  • *unfashionable* ca(u)se   CASE
unfavourable aspect   N
unfinished
  unfinished business   FIR(m)
  unfinished tas(k)   TAS
unfeeling
  unfeeling   NUMB
  unfeeling, *say*   NUM–
  • unfeeling girl, *say*   NUMMARY
  • unfeeling man, *say*   NUMBLES, NUMERIC
     REGNUM

unfit
  ['e felt] *unfit*   FLEET
  unfit [to plead]   TADPOLE
unfixed
  [rates] *unfixed*   ASTER, STARE, TARES
     TEARS,
  unfixed [latches]   SATCHEL
unfold
  unfold [a tale]   ALATE
  unfolding [arms]   MARS, RAMS
unfortunate
  unfortunate [end]   DEN, NED
  unfortunately [not her] . . .   THRONE
unfrozen   NOTICE(D)
unfulfilled
  MP *unfulfilled*   TOR(y)
  unfulfilled need   NEE(d), LAC(k), WAN(t)
unfurl
  [tops'l] *unfurled*   PLOTS
  unfurl [sails]   SILAS
ungainly
  [Len is] *ungainly*   LIENS, LINES
  ungainly [stride]   DIREST
ungrammatical
  ungrammatical introduction   SMEE
  ungrammatical refusal   WONT
unhappy
  unhappily [married]   ADMIRER
  unhappy [feeling]   FLEEING
unhealthy
  unhealthy   SICK
  • unhealthy horse   SICK-BAY
  • unhealthy man   SICKLES
unhesitating
  unhesitating(ly)   omit ER, UM, UR
  • moth(er) *unhesitating* . . .   MOTH
  • s(um)s *unhesitatingly*   SS
  • *unhesitating* co(ur)se   COSE
unidentified
  unidentified   NU
  unidentified flying object   UFO
unilateral
  unilateral (=one-sided)
  • *unilateral* help   LAID, RAID
  • *unilateral* states   RUSA
  Unilateral Declaration of Independence   UDI
unimaginative   NON-FICTION
uninhibited
  uninhibited (p)layer(s)   LAYER
  uninhibited [when it] . . .   WHITEN
uninspired footman   PEDESTRIAN
union
  union   MARRIAGE
  • union charter   MARRIAGE LICENCE
  • union convenor   MARRIAGE BROKER
  • union meeting   MARRIAGE, WEDDING

union	NUS, NUT etc	Universal Postal Union	UPU
• number *in* union	NUNS	universal set	E
• union row	NUTTIER	Universal Time	UT
union	RUSSIA	**university**	U, UNIV
union	TU	at university	UP
• union *has* second-class . . .	TUB	combined universities	OXBRIDGE
• union inspection	TUSCAN	Open University	OU
union	U	• Open University man	OUTED
• union representative	–UMP	university drop-out	omit U
union agreement	BETHROTHAL	University Grants Committee	UGC
	ENGAGEMENT	university man	BA, MA
union attendant	BEST MAN, BRIDESMAID		DON, PROF
	MATRON OF HONOUR	university press	CUP, OUP
union colleague	BRO	university sinecure	EASY CHAIR
	JOINER, WELDER	university student	UL
union issue	CHILD(REN)	university study	READING
union leader	SHERMAN	university teachers	UAT
Union *leader*	U	**unkempt**	
union measure	LEAGUE	[man is] *unkempt*	MAINS
union member	BRIDE, GROOM	*unkempt* [beard]	BARED, BREAD
	HUSBAND, WIFE	**unknown**	
union negotiator	MARRIAGE BROKER	unknown	X, Y, Z
	MATCHMAKER	• unknown man	X-RAY
union of man or . . .	MANOR	• unknown quarter	YEAST
union trouble	DIVORCE	• unknown river	ZAIRE
	SEVEN YEAR ITCH	unknown number	N
Unionist	U	unknown private	SECRET
unique		**unladen**	
unique	ONE, SOLE	unladen (=with nothing on)	
unique fish	SOLE	• *unladen* tree	MAYO
unique *sound*	SOUL, WON	• *unladen* wagon	CARTOON
unit		*(see also* unload)	
unit	A, I	**unlikely**	TALL
unit of the Marines	THERM	[not] *unlikely*	TON
units	SI	*unlikely* [tale]	LATE, LEAT, TEAL
united[1]		**unlimited**	
united you and me, *say*	LINCTUS	(c)rim(e) *unlimited*	RIM
united, *say*	TIDE	*unlimited* liability	(r)IS(k)
united[2]		*unlimited* (m)one(y)	ONE
United Arab Republic	UAR	**unlined**	
United Dominions Trust	UDT	*unlined*	omit BR
United Free Church	UF	• *unlined* (b)owe(r)	OWE
United Kingdom	UK	*unlined*	omit centre
United Nations Association	UNA	• t(h)e *unlined* . . .	TE
United Nations (Organisation)	UNO	• *unlined* s(kir)t	ST
United Presbyterian	UP	*unlined*	omit L
United Press	UP	• *uniined* ki(l)t	KIT
United States	US, USA	*unlined*	omit RY
–Army	USA	• *unlined* fine(ry)	FINE
–(Army) Air Force	US(A)AF	**unload**	
–Navy	USN	*unload contents*	omit middle
–Ship	USS	• *unload contents of* l(orr)y	–LY
universal		unload fish	DUMPLING
universal	U	*(see also* unladen)	
Universal Decimal Classification	UDC	**unlock**	
universal organisation	UN	unlock	DISTRESS

Anag [cat]; Any *; Begin IGN–; Endings –ING; eg •; Hidden /cat/; Implied add (on); Implied in (in);

unlocked	BALD, DISTRESSED, SHORN
unlocking	HAIRCUT

unloved

unloved	omit O
• b(o)re *unloved by* journalist	BREED
• *unloved* t(o)y	–TY

unmanned

unmanned	omit HE
• *unmanned* Jew	(he)BREW
unmanned	omit MAN
• smuggled *unmanned* Ger(man)	RANGER

unmarried

unmarried	MATCHLESS
unmarried	omit M
• *unmarried* (m)other	OTHER
unmarried heavyweight	SINGLETON

unmasked

unmasked [US spy]	PUSSY
unmasking [German] . . .	MANGER

unnamed

unnamed	omit N
• Germ(an) *without* a name	GERM
• *unnamed* male	MA(n)
• *unnamed* ma(n)	MA

unnatural

unnatural	FLAT, SHARP
unnatural [desire]	RESIDE
unnaturally [created]	REACTED

unnumbered

unnumbered	omit C, D, L, M, V etc
• *unnumbered* (c)hair	HAIR
• *unnumbered* car(d)	CAR
• *unnumbered* p(layer)	PAYER
• *unnumbered* roo(m)	ROO
• *unnumbered* (v)erse	ERSE

unoccupied

o(fte)n *unoccupied*	ON
unoccupied h(ous)e	HE

unofficial

unofficial [rule]	LURE
unofficially [agreed]	GEARED

unopened

(c)rate *unopened*	RATE
unopened (c)ask	ASK

unorthodox

[most] *unorthodox*	MOTS
unorthodox [means]	MANES, NAMES

unpaid

unpaid	HON
• *unpaid in* Kent	SHONE
• *unpaid* monarch	HONKING
unpaid account	BILLOWED, BILLOWING

unplaced

unplaced	FOURTH
unplaced, *say*	FORTH

unpopular doctor   FELL

unpredictable

unpredictable [weather]	WREATHE
unpredictably [threw a] . . .	WREATH

unpreferred girl   BRUNETTE

unqualified

unqualified	LAY
• mother *takes* unqualified . . .	MALAY
• unknown *in* qualified . . .	LAZY
and	
• *unqualified* fellow, *say*	LAID-ON
unqualified	TOTAL(LY)
unqualified person	L, NOTABLE

unravel

[test case] *unravelled*	CASSETTE
unravelled [a scarf]	FRACAS
unravels, say	FRAISE, PHRASE

unreasonable

unreasonable [fear]	FARE
unreasonably [demand] . . .	DAMNED

unrecognised

unrecognised [danger]	GANDER
	GARDEN, RANGED
unrecognisable [faces]	CAFES

unrefined actors   ROUGHCAST

unreliable

[he is] *unreliably* . . .	HIES
unreliable [man is] . . .	MAINS

unrest

[much] *unrest*	CHUM
unrest in [Yemen]	ENEMY

unrestrained

unrestrained [anger]	RANGE
[Australian]	
unrestrained	SATURNALIA

unruly

[she was] *unruly*	WASHES
unruly [kids]	SKID

unsafe

[plane] *is unsafe*	PANEL
unsafe [car]	ARC

unscramble

unscramble [atom's cipher]	ATMOSPHERIC
unscrambling [data man] . . .	ADAMANT

unseen companion   GUIDE DOG

unsettled

[score] *unsettled*	CORES
unsettled	NOMADIC
	OWED, OWING
unsettled [weather]	WREATHE

unskilled   NOTABLE

unsnarl

unsnarled [ropes]	PORES, SPORE
unsnarling [tape]	PATE, PEAT

unsound

[parts] *unsound*	PRATS, STRAP, SPRAT
unsound [wares]	SWEAR, WEARS

unstable	
[land is] *unstable*	ISLAND
unstable [site]	–ITES, TIES
unsteady	
unsteady [steps]	PESTS
unsteadily [rise]	SIRE
unstuck	
[came] *unstuck*	MACE
[tape] *came unstuck*	PATE, PEAT
unstuck [when I] . . .	WHINE
unsuccessful	
unsuccessful fisherman	NONET(S)
unsuccessful oilman	NOWELL
unsuccessful suitor	NOWED
unsuccessful vocalist	NOSING
unsuited	
unsuited	BARE, NAKED, NUDE
unsuited runner	STREAKER
untangle	
untangle [threads]	HARDEST
untangling [nets]	TENS, SENT, STEN
untaxed	ORATED
untearable	CANTRIP
untidy	
untidy [heaps]	PHASE, SHAPE
[wraps] *untidily*	WARPS
untied	
untie [knots]	STONK
untied [rope]	PORE
untimed	
untimed	omit AGE, T
• *untimed* communication	MESS(age)
• *untimed* (t)rip	RIP
untreated wood	RAW DEAL
untrue	
[it was] *untrue*	WAIST, WAITS
untrue [tales]	LEATS, STEAL
	SLATE, TEALS
untutored saint	RUDEST
unusual	
unusual	ODD
• unusual *in* bashful . . .	SHODDY
• unusual man	ODDFELLOW
• unusual people	ODDFELLOWS
unusual	RARE
• copper *with* unusual . . .	CURARE
• unusual choice	RARE
• unusual coin	RAREBIT
unusual athlete	RUM RUNNER
unusual [fate]	FEAT
unusual production of [Tosca]	ASCOT, ATOCS
	COATS
unusually [fat]	AFT
unused	
unused *	omit *
• *entrance to* (t)own *unused*	OWN

• *unused* money in b(l)ack . . .	BACK
unwanted	
unwanted fruit	GOOSEBERRY
unwanted *	omit *
• man *unwanted in* t(he)re	TRE–
• (was)her was *unwanted*	HER
unwieldy	
unwieldy [tool]	LOOT
[it was] *unwieldy*	WAIST, WAITS
unwilling	INTESTATE
unwind	
unwind [hose]	HOES, SHOE
unwinding [yarn]	NARY
unwound [reel]	LEER
unwrap	
unwrap (g)if(t)	IF
unwrap [parcel]	PLACER
unwrapping (s)hoe(s)	HOE
unwrapping [T-shirt]	THIRST
up¹	

many words beginning with up, some of which
follow, are used to indicate words written
backwards in Down clues

up²

indicating words written
backwards in down clues (D)^:

• *up*-beat	NAT, PAR
• *up*-country	MAIS, MASSA
• *up* late	MANET
• *up*-market	TRAM
• *up* the mountain	ANTE, ROT
• *upped* the ante	ETNA

up³

meaning:
ahead

• *leading* firm	UPTIGHT
• time *ahead*	TUP

at university

• 100 *at university*	CUP

in court

• in court *with* a group	UPSET

riding

• child *riding*	TOT UP

to windward

• ship *to windward*	KETCHUP

up⁴

up *front*	start with UP
• actors up *front*	UPCAST
• hurry up *front*	UPRUSH
• wild animal up *front*	UPBEAR

up North
indicating use of
Scottish words:

• go *up North*	GANG
• *up North*, only . . .	ANERLY
• useful *up North*	WAKERIFE

Anag [cat]; Any *; Begin IGN–; Endings –ING; eg •; Hidden /cat/; Implied add (on); Implied in (in);

up⁵

up in arms	RAMPANT
up the creek [in an] . . .	NAIN
up with the lark	(in) S–KY
upper	AMPHETAMINE, SPEED
upper case	CAPS, CAPITALS
upper class	A, SIXTH FORM, U
upper classes	AB–
upper house	ATTIC, GARRET, LOFT
Upper House	LORDS
Upper House, *say*	LAUDS
upper limit	CEILING
upper limit, *say*	SEALING
upper set	DENTURE, TEETH

upbringing

poor *upbringing*(D)^	ROOP
upbringing of Eros(D)^	SORE

upcoming

upcoming supporter(D)^	ARB–, GEL
was *upcoming*(D)^	SAW

upfront

<u>m</u>oney *upfront*	M
<u>u</u>pfront	U

upheaval

[great] *upheaval*	GRATE
upheaval [in her] . . .	RHINE

uphill

uphill(D)^	ROT
trot *uphill*(D)^	TORT

upholding

up-*holding*	U–P
upholding	
indicating reversal and	
inclusion in Down clues:	
• l–aw *upholding* learner(D)^	WALL

uplift

uplift	BUST-UP
uplift spirits(D)^	SNIG
uplifting art (D)^	TRA–

upon

indicating one word written	
above another word or letter(D):	
• live *upon* state	BEAVER
• look *upon* American	GAZEBO
• man *is upon* the *Spanish* . . .	HEEL
indicating one word written	
backwards above another(D):	
• act *upon* our . . .	ODOUR
• live *upon* on(e) *almost* . . .	EBON
• sit *upon* girl	TISSUE
indicating one word written	
backwards above 'on'(D):	
• honour *upon* . . .	MOON
• man *upon* . . .	LEMON
• works *upon* . . .	SPOON

upper

(*see* up⁵)

uppity

[act] *uppity*	CAT
uppity boy(D)^	YOB

upright¹

upright	I
• upright board	IDEAL
• *upright* man	IRON
• *upright* one	IAN
upright	PI
• *upright* attendant	PIPAGE
• *upright* friend	PIPAL
• *upright* girl	PIANINA
upright	POST
• upright character	POSTCARD
• upright monarch	POSTER
• upright person	POSTAL, POSTMAN
upright player	PIANO
upright reputation	STANDING
upright type	ROMAN

upright²

upright(D)^	TR
upright bat(D)^	TAB

uprising

some con/tinu/ous *uprising*(D)^	UNIT
up*rising*(D)^	PU
uprising at . . . (D)^	TA

upriver

indicating name of river	
written backwards, usually	
in Down clues:	
• look *upriver*	LOOP
• *upriver with* man	MACRON
• run *upriver*	REED
• sun unknown *upriver*	SYNOD

uproot

uproot yew(D)^	WEY
uprooting [yew]	WEY, WYE

upset

upset(D)^	TES
upset class(D)^	SLIP-UP
upset gin	RATTLETRAP
upset [master]	REMAST, STREAM
upset no-one(D)^	–ION
upset revel<	LEVER
upset shed	SPILL
upset [timer]	MITRE, REMIT
upset timer(D)^	REMIT
upset Tom	TIPCAT

upshot

CHIP, LOB

upside

upside down(D)^	
• draw *upside down*	WARD
• put *upside down*	TUP
• was *upside down*	SAW

upstairs lighting

LANDING

upstanding

be *upstanding* on . . .(D)^	EBON	used by man/y es/timators	YES
upstanding part(D)^	TRAP	used car dealer	AUTO-CHANGER
upstart		used *in* pa/in k/illers	INK
u̲pstart	U	used in poetry	(*see* poetic)
upstart	start with UP	used to be	EX
• killed up*start*	UPSHOT		(*see also* old²)
• up*start* making loud noises	UPROARS	useful card	PRACTICAL JOKER
• when up*starts* . . .	UPAS	useful headgear	HANDICAP
upstream		useless	DUFF
up*stream*(D)^	EDIT	• fruit *has* useless . . .	PLUM DUFF
upsurge		• useless journalist	DUFFED
upsurge of sap(D)^	PAS	• useless ruler	DUFFER
up-to-date business	NEWMARKET	useless	US
upturn		use*less*	omit USE
up*turn*<	PU	• use*less* ho(use)	HO
• up*turn*< about . . .	PURE	*useless* [tool]	LOOT
• up*turn*< *for* animals	PUMICE	*using part of* h/er go/od . . .	ERGO
• up*turn*< *for* friend	PUPAL	*using some* ne/w ide/eas	WIDE
upturn of . . . (D)^	FO	*using* [tools]	LOOTS, STOOL
upward		**usher**	
up*ward*(D)^	DRAW	*usher in* a . . .	incl A
upward step(D)^	PETS	*usher in* *	incl *
upwardly mobile way . . . (D)^	YAW	• bu–tler *ushers in* son	BUSTLER
Urban District Council	UDC	usher, *say*	GUYED, SILENCER
urge		*ushered in by* *	incl in *
urge	SPUR	• son *ushered in by* bu–tler	BUSTLER
• violent urge	HOTSPUR	usherette	GIRL GUIDE
• urge Communist . . .	SPURRED	**usual**	
• urge Edward	SPURTED	usual colour	STANDARD
urge crowd	PRESS	usual flag	STANDARD
urges insects	EGG-SLICE	usually	USU
urgent		**usurp**	OUSTER
urgent	BABYLONIAN	**utilise**	
urgent mood	IMPERATIVE	[other] *characters utilised*	THROE
ursine group	BEARSKIN	*utilised* [tool]	LOOT
Uruguay		**utmost**	
Uruguay	ROU, U, URU	*utmost ends of* th̲e eart̲h	EH
capital of Uruguay	PESO	*utmost* urgenc̲y	Y
capital of U̲ruguay	U	**utter**	
US(A)	(*see* America)	utter	
use		indicating a homophone:	
buil/d ark/ *using* . . .	DARK	• not *utterly*	KNOT
[not] *used*	TON	• *utter* rot	WROUGHT
usable as [a bed]	BADE, BEAD	• *utter* some . . .	SUM
use [a pen]	NAPE, NEAP, PANE, PEAN	• *utterance of* boy	BUOY
use drill	DOPE, EXERCISE	• *utterance of* a girl	ALAS
[use] *guile*	SUE	• *uttered* word	WHIRRED
use, *say*	EWES, US, UU	• *uttering* rhyme	RIME
	YOUSE, YEWS	• *utterly* cruel	CREWEL
used abroad (=foreign language)		utter cry	CALLOW, YELLOW
• cup *used abroad*	TAZZA	*uttermost ends of* th̲e eart̲h	EH
• hat *used abroad*	CHAPEAU	*uttermost parts of* C̲hina	CA
• shawl *used abroad*	MANTILLA	**u-upset**	URILE
	(*see also* abroad)		
used as [part] . . .	PRAT, TRAP		

Anag [cat]; Any *; Begin IGN–; Endings –ING; eg •; Hidden /cat/; Implied add (on); Implied in (in);

V

against, agent, bomb, chevron, chip, day, electric potential difference, **five**, **five thousand**, **frequency**, **thousand**, *look*, neck, *neckline*, *notch*, *nu*, *see*, shape, sign, valve, vanadium, Vatican, vatu, vee, velocity, verb, verse(d), verso, versus, very, victory, vide, violin, voice, volt, volume, win

vacant

vacancy	O
vacant	VAC
vacant h(ous)e	HE
vacant job	FREE POST
vacant (=nothing in it)	incl O
• co–t *is vacant*	COOT
• *vacant* lo–t	LOOT
• *vacant* church	COE
vacation	VAC

vacillate

vacillating [priest]	STRIPE, TRIPES
vacillation [by a] . . .	BAY
vacillated [when I] . . .	WHINE

vacuous

t(otall)y *vacuous*	TY
vacuous i(dio)t	IT

vagrant

vagrant	TRAMP
• vagrant in front	TRAMPLED
• vagrant in Germany	TRAMPING
vagrant [airs]	SAIR, SARI
vagrant *American*	HOBO

vague

vague [noises]	ESSOIN
vaguely [hears] . . .	HARES, SHARE, SHEAR

vale

vale (=goodbye)	
vale *in England*	FAREWELL, GOODBYE
vale *in France*	A BIENTOT, ADIEU
vale *in Germany*	AUF WIEDERSEHEN
vale *in Italy*	ADDIO, ARRIVEDERCI
vale *in Spain*	ADIOS, HASTA LA VISTA
valiant Indian	BRAVE

value

valuable coat	GOLDEN FLEECE
value	PH, RATE, VAL
Value-added Tax	VAT
value of function	PIRATE
value of soil	PH
value*less*	ORATED, OVAL
valuer's statement	IRATE
valuing at 3.14	PIRATING

vandal

[louts] *vandalise* . . .	LOTUS
vandalised [parks]	SPARK

vanguard

fleet *vanguard*	F
vanguard of army	A
vanity case	EGO(T)IST

vapour

vapour caused corrosion	MISTRUSTED
vapour density	VD
vapour pressure	VP
variable	(*see* vary)
varslty	U

vary

variable [gear]	RAGE
variant	VAR
variations of Elgar . . .	GLARE, LAGER
	LARGE, REGAL
varies in [shape]	HEAPS, PHASE
variegated [tints]	STINT
varietal	VAR
varieties of [meat]	TEAM-MATE
variety	VAR
variety	
indicating origins:	
• *German variety* with . . .	MIT
• *Italian variety of* wine	VINO
• one *Scottish variety*	ANE
• the *French variety*	LA, LE, LES
• this *Latin variety*	HAEC, HIC, HOC
variety [show]	HOWS, WHOS
variety of [crocus]	OCCURS
various dates	VD
various years	VY
various [items]	EMITS, SMITE, TIMES
variously prescribed	
[doses a] . . .	ODESSA
vary [rate]	TARE, TEAR
vary, *say*	ALTAR
varying [all the] . . .	LETHAL

vast

not really [vast]	VATS
vast *majority*	VAS

Letter replaced \c\at; Omit (a); Pointers *out*; Retain a; Split B_ED; Down (D); Backwards <or ^

VAT-free	ORATED	**Venerable**	VEN
Vatican	V, VAT	**venereal disease**	VD
vault		**Venetian**	
vault, *say*	CELLA, SELLA, SELLER	Venetian	OTHELLO
vault working	CRYPTON	Venetian leader	DOGE
vaulting horse	SHOW JUMPER	Venetian *leader*	V
vaulting [horse]	SHORE	Venetian merchant	ANTONIO, POLO
vee	V	**Venezuela**	YV
vegetable		**ventilate**	
vegetable	BEET	ventilate	AIR
• run *in* vegetable . . .	BERET	• ventilates *inside* saint's . . .	STAIRS
• vegetable first	BEETLED	• ventilate liner	AIRSHIP
vegetable	PEA	• ventilates *after* Henry . . .	HAIRS
• vegetable competes	PEAVIES	ventilate	SUNDRY
• vegetables *with* fish	PEALING, PEASCOD	**verb**	
• vegetables *have* worker . . .	PEASANT	verb	V, VB
and		verb intransitive	VI
• vegetable *with* fish, *say*	PEELING	verb transitive	VT
vegetable	VEG	verbal	
vegetables, *say*	CHARRED, LEAK, SALARY	indicating a homophone:	
vegetarian		• *verbal* refusal	KNOW, NEIGH
indicates word 'eating'		• *verbally* made an . . .	MAIDEN
a vegetable:		• *verbally* not . . .	KNOT
• vegetarian animal(AP–E)	APPEASE	verbal reasoning quotient	VRQ
vehicle		verbally	BY-WORD
vehicle	CAB	verbally, *say*	AURALLY
• run-*in* vehicle	CRAB	**verge**	
• vehicle container	CABURN	highway *verges*	HY
• vehicle *in front of*		*verges* of *road*	RD
obstruction	CABLET	**vermouth**	IT
vehicle	CAR	**Verne**	
• vehicle number	CARD, CARL	[Verne] *work*	NEVER
• vehicle speeding	CARAPACE	*rehash* [Verne's] . . .	SEVERN
• vehicle weight	CARTON	**versatile**	
vehicle	CART	[quite] *versatile*	QUIET, –TIQUE
• vehicle *on* high ground	CARTRIDGE	*versatile* [actor]	CROAT
• vehicle working	CARTON	**version**	
vehicle	TRAM	[new] *version*	WEN
• vehicle goes inside	TRAMLINES	*version* [of a] . . .	OAF
• vehicle park	TRAMP	*version* of [Tuscan's] . . .	SANCTUS
vehicle application	DILIGENCE	**versus**	V
vehicle corrosion	CARROT	**vertical**	
vehicle cover	BONNET	vertical, *say*	PLUM
	CARPORT, GARAGE	vertical take-off	VTO
	INSURANCE	vertical take-off and landing	VTOL
	VANGUARD	**very**	
vehicle entrance	TRANSPORT	very	V
vehicle for a . . .	incl A	• very close	VEND
vehicle for *	incl *	• very offhand	VAIRY
• rotten *vehicle for* learner	BALD	• very spry	VAGILE
vehicle traffic	TRUCK	very black	BB
vehicle was blue	MOPED	very cheerful	JOLLY
vein		very *French*	TRES
vein joint	SEAM	very good	VG
vein, *say*	LAIR, LOAD, SEEM, VAIN, VANE	very green	EXTRAVERT
velocity	MPH, MV, V, VEL	very hesitant	–ERER

Anag [cat]; Any *; Begin IGN–; Endings –ING; eg •; Hidden /cat/; Implied add (on); Implied in (in);

very high frequency	VHF	**vibrate**	
very large	OS	[rich, deep] *vibrato*	DECIPHER
very low frequency	VLF	*vibrating* [noises]	ESSOIN
very hard	HH	*vibration of* [plane]	PANEL
very late	STONE DEAD	**vicar**	
very little	WEE	vicar	REV(D), VIC
very loud	FF	Vicar Apostolic	VA
very *much like* Leeds	LEADS	Vicar-General	VG
very *musical*	ASSAI, MOLTO	vicarage	VIC
very *nearly*	ERY, VER	**vice**	
very quiet	PP	Vice-Chancellor	VC
very *Scottish*	UNCO	Vice-Consul	VC
very short	INSTALL	Vice-President	VP
very *short*	V, VER(y)	**Vichy water**	EAU
very short distance	IMM–	**vicious**	
very small European	TADPOLE	[snap] *viciously*	PANS, SPAN
very soft	PP	*vicious* [circle]	CLERIC
very soft *centre*	incl PP	**Victoria**	
• apple *with* very soft *centre*	PIPPIN	Victoria Cross	VC
• co–in *with* very soft *centre*	COPPIN	Victoria Medal of Honour	VMH
very sore	REDRAW	**victory**	
very strong	FF	victory	V
very young	ONE OR TWO	• victory in Asia	VINE
vessel		• victory shout	VOUCH
vessel	MV, SHIP, SS, SUB	• victory sign	VINDICATION
vessel	EWER	victory	VE
• fine vessel	FEWER	• 51 victories	LIVES
• second king *has a* vessel	SKEWER	• victory in . . .	VEIN
vessel	POT	• victory *to the Italian* . . .	VEIL
• one vessel *inside* another	SPOTS	victory	VJ
• second vessel	SPOT	victory day	VE, VJ
• vessel is warm	POTSHOT	victory race	MARATHON
vessel	URN	**vide**	V
• graduate *in* vessel	URBAN	**video**	
• second-class vessel	BURN	video cassette recorder	VCR
• vessel *in* garden	BURNED	video frequency	VF
vessel	VASE	video tape recorder	VTR
• 51 *in* vessel	VALISE	**Vietnam**	
• vessel *has* pedigree	VASELINE	Vietnam	VN
	(*see also* ship)	Vietnamese	BOAT RACE
Vesta's home	MATCHBOX	**view**	
veteran		view	SCAPE
veteran		view	SEE
indicating old words:		• normal view	PARSEE
• *veteran's* friend	INGLE	• view Parliament	SEETHING
	(*see also* old [3])	• view *round* royal . . .	SERE
veteran actor	OLDHAM	• view twice	LOOK-SEE
veteran car	CHARIOT	and	
veterinary		• view fifty, *say*	SEAL
veterinary	VET	view America	PROSPECTUS
veterinary surgeon	VET, VS	view the king of	
vex		beasts, *say*	SEA-LION, SELION
[act] *vexatiously*	CAT	view, *say*	CITE, SEEN, SITE
[most] *vexing*	MOTS, TOMS	viewed, *say*	SCENE
vexation, *say*	PEAK	viewer	EYE
vexed [teacher]	CHEATER, RECHEAT	views always . . .	SIGHTSEER

Letter replaced \c\at; Omit (a); Pointers *out*; Retain <u>a</u>; Split B_ED; Down (D); Backwards <or ^

vigorous	
vigorous fight	STRONG-BOX
vigorously [defend]	FENDED
vile	
[acted] *vilely*	CADET
vile [deed Tom] . . .	DEMOTED
vile *outsiders*	VE
village	
village	HAMLET, VIL(L)
village drama	HAMLET
village hero	HAMLET
vintage	
vintage car	OLD BEAN
vintage poet	GRAVES
violate	
violate at this spot, *say*	RAPIER
violated [rules]	LURES
violation of [code I get] . . .	GEODETIC
violent	
[shove] *violently*	HOVES
violent players	ROUGHCAST
violent [push to] . . .	UPSHOT
violin	
old violin	GJO, GJU, GU(E)
violin	AMATI, STRAD, V
violin lessons	STRING COURSE
violin strings	A, D, E, G
violin swindle	FIDDLE
virtual	
virtual [space]	CAPES
virtually al(l)	AL
virtually identical	SAM(e)
virtually [real]	LEAR, RALE
virtuous	
virtuous	NOVICES
virtuous amateur	NOVICE
viscount	
viscount	VIS
viscount's son	HON
visible	
visible	INSIGHT
visible in h/er e/yes	ERE
visible inside t/he ro/om	HERO
visible, *say*	INSIGHT
visit	
visit	SEE
• visit many . . .	SEED
• the *French* visit	LESSEE
and	
• visit boy, *say*	SEASON
• visit Egypt, *say*	SENILE
• visit the sea, *say*	SEAMED, SEAMER
visited by a . . .	incl A
visited by *	incl *
• county *visited by* queen	YORKERS
visited frequently	CAMELOT

visitor, *say*	CHOLER, COLLAR
	GUESSED
visits *	incl in *
• queen *visits* county	YORKERS
visual	
visual aid	CONTACT LENS, MICROSCOPE
	MONOCLE, SPECTACLES
	TELESCOPE
visual display unit	VDU
vital	
vital ingredient of fre/sh e/ggs	SHE
vital part of en/gin/e	GIN
vital part perishes	ORGANDIES
vital timber	KEYBOARD
vital to Briti/sh in/terests	SHIN
vital to Britis/h int/erests	HINT
vitamin	A, B, C, D, E, F, G, H
	K, I, M, P, X
vivisection	
[detest] *vivisection*	TESTED
vivisection of [rat]	ART, TAR
vocal	
plain *vocal style*	PLANE
vocal number	AIT, ATE, EYOT
	FOR(E), TO(O), WON
vocal style of tenor	TENNER
vocal turn	TERN(E)
vocalising all . . .	AWL
vocalist's statement, *say*	ICING
vocally rough	RUFF
vocally, *say*	ALLOWED
vocative	VOC
voguish	IN
voice	
[it was] *voiced*	WAIST, WAITS
voice-box	BOCKS
voice frequency	VF
voiced [all the] . . .	LETHAL
volatile	
volatile [oils]	SILO, SOIL
volatility of [gas]	SAG
volcanic	
volcanic rock	LAVA
• two lumps of volcanic	
rock	LAVA-LAVA
• volcanic rock, right?	LAVATORY
• volcanic rock, time and	
time again . . .	LAVATERA
volcanic rock	MOYA
volcanic rock	TUFF
• son *has* volcanic rock	STUFF
• volcanic rock, *say*	TOUGH
volcanic [tremors]	STORMER
volt	V
volt-amp	VA
volt-ampere-reactive	VAR

volume

volume	BOOK
• volume of income	PAYBOOK
• volume of money	CASHBOOK
• volume of	
small . . .	MINUTE BOOK
volume	TOM, TOME, TOMUS
	V, VOL

volunteer

Voluntary Aid Detachment	VAD
Voluntary Defence Corps	VDC
Volunteer (Officers') Decoration	VD
Volunteer Reserve Decoration	VRD
Voluntary Service Overseas	VSO
voluntary work	ORGAN RECITAL
volunteer	VOL
volunteers	TA, THETA
• volunteers 49 . . .	TAIL
• volunteers blood	TAGORE
• volunteers *to* a man	TAKEN, TALES
	(*see also* army, reserve, terrier)

vote

vote	CROSS
• vote on . . .	CROSS OVER
• vote twice	DOUBLE CROSS
• vote *with* lawyers	CROSS-BAR
vote	PUT ACROSS
vote	X
• a vote the *French* . . .	AXLE
• copy vote	APEX
• vote counter, *say*	EXCHEQUER
vote against	BEANO

voyage

voyage, *say*	CREWS, CRUSE
voyaging [in the] . . .	THINE
[went] *voyaging*	NEWT

vulgar

are not *vulgarly* . . .	AINT
vulgar	VUL(G)
vulgar (h)at	AT
Vulgate	VUL(G)
v-ventilated	VAIRY

W

boson, bridge player, complex cube root, particle, tungsten, watt, weak, Wednesday, week, weight, Welsh, west, western, whole numbers, wicket, wide, width, wife, William, winter, with, wolfram, woman, women, won

W8	WEIGHT
wacky	
wackiness [of a] . . .	OAF
wacky [ideas]	AIDES, ASIDE, SADIE
Wacky [Races]	ACERS, CARES, SCARE
wader	HERON
wag	
wag [finger]	FRINGE
wagging [dog]	GOD
wag*tail*	G
wag[tail in a] . . .	ITALIAN
wager	
wager	BET, BETON
• wager *on Cockney* horse	BETOSS
• wager *on* fish	BETIDE, BETRAY
• wager on unknown . . .	BETONY
wager, *say*	STEAK
waggle	
waggle [rear]	RARE
waggling [hips]	PISH, SHIP
Wagner's work	RING
wait	
waiters	QUEUE
waiters, *say*	CUE, KEW
waitress, *say*	MADE
Wales	CYMRU
walk	
walk	FOOT
• walk *to* dance	FOOTBALL
• walks the plank	FOOTSLOG
• warm walk	HOTFOOT
walk	LEGIT
walk *about*	TREA–D
walk *about*<	MAOR
walk in front	TRAMPLED
walk [on beside]	EBONISED
walk over	WO
walk *over*<	MAOR
walk, *say*	GATE
walk straight	LEGIT
walk *then* run	MARCH HARE
walk through water, *say*	WEIGHED
walked	RODEO
walker	JAY, PED
walking	(on) FOOT
• bird *walking*	CROWFOOT, GOOSEFOOT
• Negro *walking*	BLACKFOOT
• *walking to* dance	FOOTBALL
walking [along]	GOLAN
walking-on part	FOOT, HEEL, SOLE
wall	
wall builder	HADRIAN
wall *in* France	MUR
(w)all *with no opening*	ALL
wall's make-up	ROUGHCAST
walled city	BERLIN, JERICHO
Walloon	WAL
walrus	MORSE
wan	
wan	PALE
• claim to be wan	IMPALE
• wan child	PALETOT
• wan race, English	PALETTE
wan, *say*	PAIL
wander	
[Ezra] *the wanderer*	RAZE
wander about [in the] . . .	THINE
wander around	MOON
[wander] *around*	WARNED
wander round the hospital, *say*	ROMEWARDS
wandering eyes, *say*	ROMANISE
wandering [stream]	MASTER, REMAST
want	
want fish	NEEDLING
want, *say*	KNEAD, KNEED
want spinster	MISS
wants a . . .	incl A
wants *	incl *
• *wants* everything *in* p–et	PALLET
wanted	(in) NE–ED
• saint *wanted*	NESTED
wanting a . . .	omit a
wanting *	omit *
• ma(n) *wanting* new . . .	MA
• (p)arty *wanting* leader	ARTY
wanton	
[act] *wantonly*	CAT

Anag [cat]; Any *; Begin IGN–; Endings –ING; eg •; Hidden /cat/; Implied add (on); Implied in (in);

wanton [waste]	SWEAT, TAWSE	warmly dressed	(in) FU–R
wantonly [drive] . . .	DIVER	warmly dressed, *say*	INFER
war		**warning**	
at war [over] . . .	ROVE	warning	AMBER
spoils of war	MARS	• 51 warnings	CLAMBERS
spoils of [war]	RAW	warning	FORE
[total class] *war*	AT ALL COSTS	• warning *to* man	FORECASTLE
war	WAR	• warning *to* prop	FORESHORE
• war at sea	WARMED, WARMER	warning card	CAUTION
• wartime	WART	warning cry	CAVE, FORE
and		warning light	AMBER, RED
• [war] *dance*	RAW	**warp**	
• war *over<*	RAW	*warp* [into an] . . .	NATION
• *spoils of* [war]	RAW	*warped* [door]	ODOR, ROOD
war artist	ACTION PAINTER	**Warrant Officer**	WO
war *at* sea	WARMED, WARMER	**Warsaw Pact**	WP
war club	WADDY	**was**	
war club, *say*	WADI	was not loud	WASP
war criminal	HESS	was painful	DIDACHE
war of [words]	SWORD	was *raised*(D)^	DEVIL, SAW
War Office	WO	[was] *wrong*	SAW
war record	LILI MARLENE, SCRAPBOOK	**wash**	
war, *say*	WORE	wash comb	SCOUR
warhead	W	[wash]-out	HAWS, SHAW
warhorse, *say*	HORS DE COMBAT	**Washington**	DC
warlike poet	MARTIAL	**waste**	
warlike, *say*	MARSHAL	[waste] *disposal*	SWEAT, TAWSE
warlord	KITCHENER	waste food	FRITTER
warmonger	SCRAP MERCHANT	waste nothing	USEFULLY
warring [tribes]	BITERS	waste of water	OCEAN
warship *returns<*	POOLS	waste of time	SPILLAGE
wartime act	DORA	waste-paper basket	WPB
wartime *leader*	W	*waste* [time]	EMIT
ward		*waste* time	omit T
ward*<*	DRAWBACK, PULLOVER	waste wool, *say*	PHLOX
warder *returns<*	REDRAW	*wasted* [life]	FILE, LIEF
warder's salary	SCREW	*wasting* [asset]	TASSE, TESSA
warm		*wasting away*	omit *
warm	HEAT	• b(adl)y *wasting away*	BY
• sun *has* warm, hard . . .	SHEATH	• ca(usi)ng *wasting away*	CANG
• warm bird	HEATHEN	**watch**	
• warms kettle	HEATSPOT	watch	BEHOLD
warm	HOT	• watch points	BEHOLDEN
• sun *has* everybody *in* warm . . .	SHALLOT	• watch queen	BEHOLDER
• warm lugs	EARSHOT	watch	EYE
• warm rifles	GUNSHOT	• watches note	EYESTONE
and		watch cover	SENTRY BOX
• warm kitchen, *say*	GALLIOT	watch horse	HUNTER
warm coat	BLAZER	watch organ	TICKER
warm drink	CORDIAL, TOAST	watchchain	ALBERT
warm *environment*	(in) HO–T	watcher	ARGUS, EYE
• son *in* warm *environment*	HOST	watches crop	TURNIPS
warm *front*	W	watchful people	SPIES, SWISS
warm-hearted	CENTRALLY HEATED	watching cricket	ATTEST
warm-*hearted*	AR	watching slip	OVERSIGHT
warming up	OFFICE	watchman	ALBERT

Letter replaced \c\at; Omit (a); Pointers *out*; Retain a; Split B_ED; Down (D); Backwards <or ^

watchword	HUNTER, OMEGA, TURNIP	• way *to* beginner's . . .	VIAL
water		way out	omit N, S, E, W
water	ADAM'S ALE, ADAM'S WINE	• fi(n)d way *out*	FID
	AQ, EA, H–O	• (s)hoot out *out*	HOOT
water	NOTICE	ways *out*	omit NE, NW, SE, SW, etc
water at 0ºC	JUSTICE	• fi(n)d(s) ways *out*	FID
water carrier	AQUEDUCT	• (sw)itch ways *out*	ITCH
	BUCKET	ways *out*	incl in N–E etc
	TEAR-DUCT	• all ways *out*	WALLS
water colour	LAKE, SEA-GREEN	• four ways *out*	WIVES
water pipe	HOOKAH, MAIN	**way³**	
water pipe, *say*	HOOKER, MANE	indicating highway:	
water rate	KNOT(S)	by the way	incl RD, ST
waterfall	EBB-TIDE, RAIN	• *by the* way, *the French* . . .	LARD
*water*front	W		LAST, LEST
Waterloo	ROUT, WC	• company, *by the* way, . . .	CORD
waterman	BARGEE, SAILOR		CEST
watermen	NAVY, RN	way	AVE, MALL, RD, ST
*water*side	W	• quiet way	PAVE
watersports champion	SURFACE	• Southern way is hard	SMALLISH
waterway	CANAL, RIVER	• he is *on* a way	HEARD
water(way)		• a way *to divide* h–en	HARDEN, HASTEN
indicating name of river,		way *back*<	DR, EVA, TS
sea, etc:		way *off*	omit RD, ST
• free *in* waterway	DERIDE	• report way *off*	HANSA(rd)
• learner *on* water	LOUSE	• fir(st) way *off*	FIR
• nine *in* water	MIXED	way *out*	omit RD, ST
watery [soup]	OPUS	• co(rd)on the way *out*	COON
watt	W	• way *out of* (St)afford	AFFORD
wave		way out	(in) R–D, S–T
[arm]-*waving*	MAR, RAM	• first-class way *out*	RAID
wave, *say*	WAIVE	• very small way *out*	SWEET
wave *to* sailor	FLAP-JACK		(*see also* street)
waving [to me]	MOTE	**way⁴**	
waver		indicating permanent way:	
waver [over sin]	VERSION	way	RLY, RY
wavering [voter]	OVERT, TROVE	• fellow *has* first-class way . . .	FAIRLY
way¹		• standard way	PARRY
way *back*<	YAW	**way⁵**	
way *out*	WA–Y	other uses:	
• right way *out*	WARY, WARTY	the way	HOW
[way]-*out*	YAW	way home	ROADHOUSE
way²		way of working	MO
indicating direction:		way *to* assess	MODERATE
way	L, R	*way to* [Paris]	PAIRS
• my way	MYR–	way out	EGRESS, EXIT
• no-way	NOR	*way-out* [design]	DEIGNS, SIGNED
• one way *and* another	LR, RL	way, *say*	WEIGH
• way above	LOVER, ROVER	way-out name	EGRESS, EXIT
way	N, S, E, W	*way-out* [name]	MANE, MEAN
• do *in* many ways	ENDOWS	*wayward* [boy]	YOB
• way *in* t–o . . .	TWO	**we**	
• ways *to* wrap . . .	ENFOLD	we	WE
way	VIA	• we are, *say*	WEIR, WERE
• a way *to* the hill	AVIATOR	• we had, *say*	WEED
• way *into* Sha–n . . .	SHAVIAN	• we have, *say*	WEAVE

Anag [cat]; Any *; Begin IGN–; Endings –ING; eg •; Hidden /cat/; Implied add (on); Implied in (in);

• we sell, *say*	WEASEL	wears out overalls	FATIGUES
• we, *say*	OUI, WEE		(*see also* worn)
• we shall grow old, *say*	WHEELAGE	**weary**	
• we shall impose levy, *say*	WHEEL-TAX	wearied	BORED
• we *take* grave . . .	WESTERN	• fish wearied, *say*	SKATEBOARD
• we understood, *say*	WEAKENED	• wearied her, *say*	BOARDER
• we will, *say*	WEAL, WELL,	• wearied him, *say*	BORDMAN
	WHEAL, WHEEL	weary	BORE
• we would, *say*	WED, WEED	weary	FLAG
we *hear* talk	TORQUE	• no weary . . .	OFLAG
we object	US	• weary ensign	FLAG
weak		• weary workers	FLAGSTAFF
weak	LIMP	weary band	TIRE
• b . . . . . weak	BLIMP	weary, *say*	BOAR, BOER
• weak alien	LIMPET	**weather**	
• weak ruler	LIMPER	weather permitting	WP
weak	W	weatherstation	STANDPOINT
• no weak . . .	NOW	weather*talk*	WETHER, WHETHER
• weak beer	WALE	weathercock, *say*	VAIN, VEIN
• weak member	WARM	**weave**	
weak	WET	*weave* [satin]	STAIN
• everybody *in* weak . . .	WALLET	weave, *say*	BRAYED, NIT, WE'VE
• Henry *is in* weak . . .	WHET	weaver	BOTTOM
• weak man	WETTED	weaver-bird	WHIDAH, WHYDAH
weak acts	POOR LAWS	weaver-bird, *say*	WIDER
weak monarch	THINKING	*woven* [lace if] . . .	FACILE
weak, *say*	FEINT, PORE, POUR, WEEK	**wedding**	
weapon		wedding	UNION (MEETING)
weapon carrier	FROG, HOLSTER	wedding fixer	SHOTGUN
	SCABBARD, SHEATH	**Wednesday**	W, WED
weapon search	RIFLE	**weed**	
weapon-training school	COLLEGE OF ARMS	weed, *say*	TEAR
wear		weedkiller	HOE
[wear] *out*	WARE	weeds	SACKCLOTH
wear out donkey, *say*	TIRASSE	weeds, *say*	HOSE, TEARS
wearing	IN	**week**	
• wearing cooler hat	INFANTILE	week	WK
• wearing dog's . . .	INCURS	week-end	WE
• wearing tight . . .	INTENSE	wee<u>k</u>-*end*	K
• wearing undershirt	INVEST	**weeper**	CROCODILE, NIOBE
• wearing uniform	INHABIT	**weigh**	
wearing hat	CAPON	weigh down, *say*	ESCALATOR
wearing headgear	(in) HA–T		STAIRCASE
wearing long hair	(in) MAN–E	weigh joint, *say*	WANEY
wearing spots	(in) RA–SH	weigh up, *say*	ESCALATOR
wearing stockings	(in) HOS–E		STAIRCASE
wearing undershirt	(in) V–EST	weight	CT, G, GR, OZ, ST
wearing vest	SINGLETON		TON(NE), WT
wearing vest	(in) V–EST	weight-lifter	ATLAS
wearing waistcoat	(in) V–EST		CRANE, JACK
wearing waterproof	MACON	weight-*lifting*(D)^	NOT
wearing women's clothes	DRAGON	weight*less* package	CAR(ton)
wearing *	incl in *	weighty harvest	STONECROP
• devil *wearing* hat	LIMPID	weighty rollers	STONES
• he *is wearing* c–ap	CHEAP	**weird**	
• learner *wearing* ha–t	HALT	weird sister	WITCH

Letter replaced \c\at; Omit (a); Pointers *out*; Retain <u>a</u>; Split B_ED; Down (D); Backwards <or ^

weird [sister]	RESIST, RESISTS
weird sisters	COVEN
weird [sisters]	RESISTS
well	
well (=not ill)	
• m(ill)et *well* . . .	MET
• *Well*, B(ill)y, . . .	BY
well	SPA
• well in . . .	SPAIN
• Well, 500 English . . .	SPADE
• well-run	SPAR
[well] *blended*	LLEW
well-blended [wines]	SINEW, SWINE
well-built structure	STAIRCASE
well content	TREACLE
well covered	CAPON
well drilled	INSTEP
well-earned money	PETRO-DOLLARS
well-favoured	IN
well-informed expert	WISECRACK
well-maintained road, *say*	TIDIEST
well-off	(SOUND) ASLEEP
well-placed	DROWNED
well-placed fluid	INK
well-produced material	GAS, OIL, WATER
well protected flight	STAIRCASE
well-provided area	OILFIELD
well qualified	BA, MA
well-run	SPAR
• state *has* well-run . . .	GASPAR
• English *in* well-run	SPEAR
• well-run brown . . .	SPARTAN
well-used equipment	(DRILLING) RIG
welsh	LEVANT, RAT
Welsh	
Welsh	CAMBRIAN, CYMRIC
Welsh	W
• no Welsh . . .	NOW
• Welsh language, *say*	WORSE
• Welsh member	WARM
Welsh girl	MEGAN
*W*elsh *leader*	W
Welshman	DAI
• Welshman's platform and	DAIS
• Welshman, *say*	DIE, DYE
Wembley game	FA, FOOTBALL
went	
went about in . . . <	NI
went, *say*	HIDE
[went] *wrong*	NEWT
went wrong [there]	ETHER, THREE
Wesleyan chapel	WC
west	
west	W
• West Country	WOMAN

• West has a very . . .	WAVERY
• West has no study	WODEN
• West in church	WINCE, WINCH
• west *to* east	WE
West Africa	WA
West Brom(wich Albion)	WBA
West Country	WOMAN
West Country trip	FLORAL DANCE
Wes*t End*	T
west end of town	T
West Indies	WI
west-north-west	WNW
West Side girl	MARIA
west-south-west	WSW
western	W
• western aid	WHELP
• western art	WART
• western side	WEDGE
Western Australia	WA
Western Central	WC
Western European Union	WEU
*W*estern *Front*	W
Western Region	WR
Western Samoa	SS
Westminster	WI
Westminster district	SW(I)
westwards	TOW
wet	
wet fat	DRIPPING
wet practice	BAPTISM
wet suit	BATHING COSTUME
	BIKINI
whack	QUARTER-HORSE
whale food	JONAH
	KRILL, PLANKTON
what	
what *did you say*	WATT, WOT
what *French* . . .	QUE
what *German* . . .	WAS
what *Italian* . . .	CHE
what *Spanish* . . .	CHE
what's-his-name, *say*	TYLER, WAT(T)
[What's] *new?*	SWATH, THAWS
What's the matter?	SUBSTANCE
wheel	
wheel rim, *say*	FELLOW
wheel round Eton<	NOTE
wheel spin<	NIPS
wheel [spin]	NIPS, PINS
wheeling [about]	U-BOAT
wheeling bats<	STAB
wheelwright	SPOKESMAN
when	
when	AS
• British when . . .	BRAS
• when alone	ASPERSE

Anag [cat]; Any *; Begin IGN–; Endings –ING; eg •; Hidden /cat/; Implied add (on); Implied in (in);

• when *in* church	CASE, CASH
• when put in order	ASSORTED
• when *short* film . . .	ASPIC
[when] *ordered*	HEWN
when, *say*	WEN
when speaking aloud	ALLOWED
when *speaking aloud*	WEN
when talking, Scandinavians . . .	LAPSE
where	
where *in ancient Rome*	UBI
where *in France*	OU
where *in Germany*	WO
where *in Italy*	DOVE
where *in Spain*	DONDE
where the sun rises	(in) EAS–T
where the sun sets	(in) W–EST
wherein w/e lan/guish	ELAN
which	
which is	QE
which *said*	WITCH
which see	QV
which was to be done	QEF
which was to be found	QEI
which was to be proved	QED
whichever way	
indicating palindrome:	
• a lady, *whichever way* . . .	MADAM
• grass *whichever way you look*	MARRAM
• *whichever way* it goes, boat . . .	KAYAK
whip	
whip	CAT
• whip a hairdresser	CATACOMB
• whip his mother	CATHISMA
• whip-round	CATO
whip cream	BEST
whip [cream]	CRAME, MACER
whip *round*	CA–T, LA–SH
• he *has* whip-*round*	CHEAT
• six *have* whip-*round*	LAVISH
whip *round*<	GOLF, TAC
whip, *say*	NOWT
whip soldiers, *say*	FLAMEN
whirl	
whirl [bone]	EBON
whirled [about]	U-BOAT
whirled about [in anger]	EARNING
	NEARING
*whirl*igig	GIGI
whirling [dervish]	SHRIVED
whirl[pool]	LOOP, POLO
*whirl*pool<	LOOP
whirlwind [romance]	CREMONA
whisk	
whisked [eggs]	SEGG
whisking [flies]	FILES
whistler	REF
white	
white	PALE
• white baby	PALETOT
• whiter doctor	PALERMO
white bowl	JACK
white charger	RHINO(CEROS)
white flower	NILE
white horse	BREAKER, WAVE
white lie	GROUND FROST
white rose bowl	YORK
whittle	
whittle down lis(t)	LIS
whittle down (s)tick	TICK
whittling [stick]	TICKS
who	
who	
–*French*	QUI
–*German*	WER
–*Italian*	CHI, CHE
–*Spanish*	QUIENE
who, *say*	HOO
• who do . . . ?	HOODOO
• who expired?	HOODED
• who *has* the ruler?	HOOKING
whole	
the whole gamut	A–Z
whole numbers	W
whole *speech*	HOLE
wholly *observed in* . . .	incl ALL
• wholly *observed in* sh–ow	SHALLOW
wholly *sound*	HOLEY, HOLY
	MOTH-EATEN
why	
why answer	BECAUSE
why, *say*	
• why examine?	WHITEST
• why solicit?	WHITE-OUT
• why that number?	WHITEN
and	
• why make faces?	WIPE-OUT
• why no . . . ?	WINO
• why reel?	WIRE HEEL
• why stained?	WIDE-EYED
• why that flower?	WILILY
why, *say*	WYE, Y
whys, *say*	WISE, YS, YY
wicked	
wicked graduate	BASINFUL
wicked ruler	SINKING
wicked sister	REGAN
wicked thing	CANDLE
wicket	
wicket	W
wicket-keeper	BAILSMAN
	DOORMAN, GATEMAN
wicket, *say*	GAIT

Letter replaced \c\at; Omit (a); Pointers *out*; Retain a̲; Split B_ED; Down (D); Backwards <or ^

wide

wide	BROAD
• a wide . . .	ABROAD
• wide characters	BROADCAST
• wide letter	BROADEN
• wide shed	BROADCAST
wide	THICK
• wide head	THICKNESS
• wide ruler	THICKER
• wide space	THICKEN
wide	W
wide clearing	SWEEPING
wide lid	SOMBRERO
wide *mouth*	W
wider, *say*	WHIDAH, WHYDAH

widespread

[it was] *widespread*	WAIST, WAITS
[wide]*spread*	DEWI
widespread [tales]	LEATS, SLATE, TEALS, STALE

widow

widow married, *say*	WIDOWED
widow's coin, *say*	MIGHT

wield

wielding [guns]	GNUS, SNUG
[that seer] *wielded*	THEATRES

wife

wife	BRIDE, DUTCH
wife	RIB
• 100 wives	CRIBS
• wife *takes* directions	RIBES
• wife's weight	RIBSTON
wife	UX
wife	W
• no wife	NOW
• pass *over* wife	COWL
• wife sick	WAILS, WILL
wife beater	PUNCH
wife of	
–Billy	NANNY
–Punch	JUDY

wigmaker   LOCKSMITH

wild

go wild [over]	ROVE
[region] *is wild*	IGNORE
wild abuse of [all the] . . .	LETHAL
wild *and free*	MADRID
wild [animal]	LAMINA, MANILA
wild [beast]	BASTE, BATES, BEATS
wild *flower*	RAPIDS, TORRENT
wild [flower]	FOWLER
wild [oats]	STOA
wild river	MANICURE
wild state of [garden]	DANGER
	GANDER, RANGED
Wild West (=America)	
• *Wild West* saloon	SEDAN

Wild [West]	STEW, WETS
wild[cat]	ACT
wildcat [strike]	TRIKES
wild[fowl]	FLOW, WOLF
wilder plant	MADDER
wilder [than ripe] . . .	PERIANTH
wild[fire]	RIFE
wild[life]	FILE, LIEF
wildlife sanctuary	NOAH'S ARK
wildly [rage]	GEAR
wilds of [Burma]	RUMBA

will[1]

will	
abbreviated to 'LL' or 'LE':	
• he will	HELL
• she will	SHELL
• we will	WELL
and	
• bat will, *say*	BATTLE
• cat will, *say*	CATTLE
• rat will, *say*	RATTLE
will Edward, *say*	WILTED
willing man	BARKIS
willing to take a job, *say*	WOODWORK
willingly, *say*	FANE, FEIGN

will[2]

willing	TESTATE
willing person	TESTATOR
willing recipient	TESTATEE
willing woman	TESTATRIX
Will's appendix	CODICIL

William

William	BILL
• William of Occam	RAZORBILL
William	WM
• gold *in* William's . . .	WORMS

willy-nilly

[went] *willy-nilly*	NEWT
willy-nilly [into an] . . .	NATION

wily

[men are] *wily*	MEANER
wily [stoat]	TOAST

win

win	GAIN
• prohibit winning . . .	BARGAINING
• win for example	GAINSAY
• wins support	GAINSAID
win	V
win five points	WINTRY
win gold	SUCCESSOR
winner	ACE
• 50 winners	LACES
• winner got up	ACEROSE

wind

wind	BLOW
wind	GALE

• wind eroded . . .	GALEATE
• wind, *say*	GAEL
wind	WRAP
• wind, *say*	RAP
• wind through . . .	WRAPPER
wind circle	GUSTO
wind-sock	BLOW
wind [up an] . . .	PUNA
wind up an . . . (D)^	NA
winder, *say*	QUAY
winding lever<	REVEL
winding [stream]	MASTER, REMAST
windjammer	ANORAK, CAGOULE, PARKA
window	
window *doesn't open*	(d)ORMER, (o)RIEL
w<u>i</u>ndow *opening*	W
wine	
wine	ASTI
• compere *drinks* wine	MASTIC
• run *after* wine	ASTIR
• wine *in* company	PLASTIC
wine	HOCK
• a vessel *included in* the wine . . .	HASSOCK
• *son takes* wine	SHOCK
• wine aboard	SHOCKS
wine	PORT
• drink wine	SUPPORT
• *put* wine *before* the queen	PORTER
• ship *carrying* wine	SPORTS
• wine can	PORTABLE
• wine *vintage*	PORTAGE
w<u>i</u>ne	ROSE
• put *nothing in* wine	ROOSE
• soft wine	PROSE
• wine bowl	ROSEWOOD
• wine *goes by* rail	ROSERY
wine	TENT
• directions *about* wine	ENTENTE
• *put* wine *before* the queen	TENTER
• wine-grower	TENT-MAKER
• wine *without* an . . .	TENANT
wine container	SACK
wine, *say*	BONE, ROAN, WHINE
wine store, *say*	CELLA, SELLA, SELLER
winebearer	GANYMEDE
winebearer	HEBE
• winebearer ate, *say*	HEBETUDE
wing	
w<u>ide</u> *wings*	WE
wingless	OWING
wingless, *say*	KNOWING
wings	ALA
wings of <u>s</u>ong	SG
wings off (r)oo(k)	OO
w<u>i</u>ngtip	W
wire gauge	WG

wise	
wise	SAGE
• father's wise . . .	PASSAGE
• wise Herb	SAGE
• wise saint	SAGEST
wise judge	DANIEL, SOLOMON
wise man	BALTHAZAR, GASPAR, MELCHIOR
	MAGUS, SAGE
	SOLON
Wise Men	MAGI
wise, *say*	WHYS, YS, YY
wit	
wit's *end*	T
wit*less*	omit WIT
• wit*less* bird	T(wit)E
witch	
witch	CIRCE
witch	HAG
• second witch	SHAG
• witch *has* protector, *say*	HAGGARD
witches	COVEN
• witches attempt . . .	COVENTRY
• witches *have* worker . . .	COVENANT
witchcraft	BROOMSTICK
Witchville	SALEM
with¹	
with	W
• *contend* with	VIEW
• with a bird	WHEN
with *French*	AVEC
with *German*	MIT
• with *German backing*<	TIM
• with *German* Communist	MITRED
• woman with *German* . . .	HERMIT
with *Italian*	CON
• graduate with *Italian* . . .	BACON
• with *Italian* kind	CONSORT
• with *Italian* sailors	CONCREW
with Latin	CUM
• *put* learner *in* with *Latin* . . .	CULM
• with *Latin*, GBS . . .	CUMSHAW
• with *Latin in* . . .	CUMIN
with *Spanish*	CON
• mother's with Spanish . . .	MASCON
• with *Spanish and*	
Italian leader	CONDUCE
• with *Spanish* in charge	CONIC
with²	
indicating addition:	
with hesitation	add ER
• two *with* hesitation	BOTHER
with much hesitation	add ERER
• two *with* much hesitation	BOTHERER
with nothing (on)	–O
• father *with* nothing	DADO
• Prince *with* nothing	HALO

Letter replaced \c\at; Omit (a); Pointers *out*; Retain <u>a</u>; Split B_ED; Down (D); Backwards <or ^

• surgeon *with* nothing	VETO
with nothing on	–OON
• dance *with* nothing on	BALLOON
• girl *with* nothing on	GOON
• many *with* nothing on	LOON, MOON

with³

indicating inclusion:

with a . . .	incl A
with *a hole in*	incl O
with a name	incl AN
with *	incl *
• wea–r *with* the . . .	WEATHER
with an overdraft	(in) RE–D
with hesitation	incl ER
with love	incl O
• c–at *with* love . . .	COAT
with no . . .	incl O
with nothing *in*	incl O

with⁴

indicating omission:

with a *loss*	omit A
with a *missing* . . .	omit A
with *no* aspiration	omit H
with no sides	omit end letters
• (c)rat(e) *with no sides*	RAT
with nothing *in it*	omit centre
• c(rat)e *with nothing in it*	CE

with⁵

other uses:

[dance] *with abandon*	CANED
with a [grin]	RING
with a tenant	LET
with *difficulty* [masters]	REMASTS, STREAMS
with it	HIP
with love for a . . .	substitute O for A
• c\a\t *with love for* a . . .	COT
with one leg	-ION
• cat *with* one leg	CATION
with praise	CL
with string	CORDON

withdraw

withdraw	ATTRACTIVE
withdraw a . . .	omit A
withdraw money	omit L
withdraw part . . . <	TRAP
withdraw *	omit *
• in (cr)ash, *withdraw* credit	ASH
withdrawn from du/ty ro/ster	TYRO

withhold

withhold a . . .	omit A
withhold money	omit L
withhold *	omit *
• *withhold* everything from sh(all)ow . . .	SHOW
with*holding*	W–ITH
• with*holding* note	WIDTH, WITCH

within

call *within earshot*	CAUL
not *within hearing*	KNOT
within	incl IN
• mother *within*	MAIN
within 24 hours	(in) DA–Y
within bounds of Ol/d En/glish . . .	DEN
within call	R–ING
within earshot, hail	HALE
within his rights	R–R
• Is 'e *within his* rights?	RISER
within n̲ormal *limits*	N–L
within range, *say*	INCITE
within the limits of d̲ecency̲	D–Y
within t̲hese *limits*	T–E
within the/se w/alls	SEW
within limits, mo/st em/ployers	STEM
within view, *say*	INCITE
within *	incl in *
• learner *within* s–ight	SLIGHT

without¹   SIN, SINE

without a day fixed	SD, SINE DIE
without children	SINE PROLE, SP
without date	SA, SINE ANNO
without doubt	SINE DUBIO
without issue	SP, SINE PROLE

without²

indicating inclusion:

without a . . .	incl A
without hesitation	incl ER, UM
without money	incl L
without permission	incl OK
• *without* permission, ten . . .	TOKEN
without *	incl *
• w–e *without* her	WHERE

without³

indicating omission:

chips *without* fish	(carp)ENTER
without a . . .	omit A
without a head	omit 1st letter
without a key	omit A, B, C, D, E, F, G
• box *without* a key	(b)OX, (c)HEST (c)OFFER, (c)RATE
• *gat(e) without* a key	GAT
without a lead(er)	omit 1st letter
• (c)how *without a lead*	HOW
• (p)arty *without* a leader	ARTY
without a name	omit AN
without a penny	omit D, P
without a starter	omit 1st letter
• meal *without a starter*	(d)INNER (s)UPPER
without aspiration	omit H
without back	omit last letter
• sea(t) *without back*	SEA
without capital	omit 1st letter

Anag [cat]; Any *; Begin IGN–; Endings –ING; eg •; Hidden /cat/; Implied add (on); Implied in (in);

without copyright	omit C
without direction	omit N, S, E, W
without end	omit last letter
• boo(k) *without* end	BOO
• composition *without* end	CONCERT(o)
without energy	omit E
without eyes, *say*	omit IS, ISE
without finalising agreement	TREAT(y)
without heart	
• was *without* heart	LI(v)ED
• without heart, Pe(t)er	PEER
without hesitation	omit ER
without honour	omit CH, OBE, OM
• *without* honour, (ch)eat	EAT
• fairy king *without* honour	(Obe)RON
• s(om)e *without* honour	SE
without introduction	omit 1st letter
• *without* introduction, actor	(p)LAYER
• *without* introduction, (m)aster	ASTER
without king	omit ER, GR, R etc
without love	omit O
without money	omit L
without my . . .	omit MY
• *without* my fa(m)il(y)	FAIL
without name	omit N
without nothing	omit O
without notice	omit AD
• m(ad)e *without* notice	ME
without one . . .	omit A, I
without opening	omit 1st letter
• (w)all *without* opening	ALL
• window *without* opening	(o)RIEL
without oxygen	omit O
without passion	omit IRE
without rating	omit AB, TAR
• overseas *without* rating	(ab)ROAD
• s(tar)ting *without* rating	STING
without reaching a	
conclusion	omit last letter
without royal . . .	omit KING, R
• (r)ule(r) *without* royal . . .	ULE
• win(king) *without* royal . . .	WIN
without tail	omit last letter
• do(g) *without* tail	DO
without (t)he *initiative*	HE
without the initiative to (s)tart	TART
without the queen	omit ER
without victory	omit V
without⁴	
without (=having no)	
• noiseless	NOBEL
• without a parliament	NOTHING
• without ceremony	NORITE
• without furniture	NOTABLE
• without papers	–NOID
• without water	NOWELL

• without water, *say*	NOEL
and	
• without topping	NOTICED
• without the ability	NOTABLE
and	
• cannot fly	OPINIONS, OWING
• friendless	OPAL(S)
• noiseless	OBANG, ODIN
• unable to write	OPEN
without (=*with* out)	
• 150 *without*	CLOUT
• leaving *without*	OUTGOING
• sailor *without* . . .	ABOUT
without	–LESS
• without Lords	COUNTLESS, PEERLESS
• without proposals	MOTIONLESS
• without weapons	ARMLESS
and	
• without a jetty, *say*	PEERLESS
• without children, *say*	(H)AIRLESS
• without understanding, *say*	NOSE LESS
without⁵	
other uses:	
without a synonym	EXTERNAL, OUTSIDE
without end	ETERNAL, INFINITE
without *end*	T
without fully ap/pear/ing	PEAR
without punctuation	NON-STOP
without rank	NOTWITHSTANDING
withstanding	RESPECTED
witness	
witness	SEE
• witness *in* re–d	RESEED
• witness many . . .	SEED, SEEL, SEEM
• witness twice	LOOK-SEE
witnessed	SAW
• orchestra witnessed	BANDSAW
• witnessed fight	SAWMILL
• witnessed your, *say*	SAWYER
witty	
witty girl	SALLY
witty rhyme	BITTY, CITY
	DITTY, PITY
witty, *say*	WHITE
wizened	
wizened [hag sat] . . .	AGHAST
[skin is] *wizened*	SISKIN
wobble	
wobble boulder	ROCK
wobbling [chin]	INCH
wobbly dog	LURCHER
wobbly [dog]	GOD
wobbly note	QUAVER
wobbly [note]	ETON, TONE
woeful	
[plead] *woefully*	PALED

Letter replaced \c\at; Omit (a); Pointers *out*; Retain a̲; Split B_ED; Down (D); Backwards <or ^

woeful [plea]	LEAP, PALE, PEAL
wolf	
[wolf]	WILDFOWL
wolf pack	SUB-GROUP
wolf *returns*<	FLOW
wolfing, *say*	GOBLIN
woman[1]	
woman	ADA
• woman *follows* learner	LADA
• woman *with* child	ADAMITE
• woman *surrounded by*	
Frenchmen	MADAM
woman	EVE
• woman *is given* directions	EVENS
• woman *is neutral*	LEVER
• woman n(o)t *heartless*	EVENT
woman	F
• woman is hot	FISH
• woman or man	FORM
• woman *with* one aim	FIEND
woman	HER
• strike woman	HITHER
• tie *back*< woman . . .	EITHER
• woman with *German* . . .	HERMIT
woman	LADY
• woman is with it	LADYSHIP
• woman's joint	LADYSHIP
• woman's story, *say*	LADYSMITH
woman	RIB
• about a woman	CARIB
• b–e *without* a woman	BRIBE
• woman *with* good *French*	RIBBON
woman	SHE
• woman *has* a red . . .	SHEARED
• woman *is given* directions	SHEWN
• woman *with* learners	SHELL
woman	W
• woman *has* all . . .	WALL
• woman is queen	WISER
• woman's crew	WEIGHT
woman's	HER
• woman's age	HEREON
• woman's husband *and* father	HERMANDAD
• woman's working	HERON
and	
• woman's glove, *say*	HERMIT
• woman's outlook, *say*	HIRCINE
• woman's suit, *say*	HIRSUTE
	(*see also* girl[1, 2])
woman[2]	
Australian woman	ADELAIDE, SHEILA
Dutch woman	FROW, VROUW
Egyptian woman	BINT
French woman	FEMME
German woman	FRAU
Italian woman	DONNA

Spanish woman	MUJER
tragic woman	ELECTRA, HECUBA, MEROPE
woman[3]	
headless (w)oman	OMAN
short (w)omen	OMEN
woman *has* a kiss	THORAX
woman *losing her head*	(m)ARIA, (w)OMAN
woman *losing* her *head*	BET(h)
woman *with* man	EVADES, MANGAL
	SALTED, VIAL etc
woman's angle	NORMAL
woman's army	ATS
women excluded, *say*	FOREMAN
women *losing* their head	(w)OMEN
Women's	
–Institute	WI
–Land Army	WLA
–Liberal Federation	WLF
–Rural Institute	WRI
–Voluntary Service	WVS
women's extra	WX
women's magazine	POWDER ROOM
won't	
I *won't be there*	omit I
* *won't be there*	omit *
• p(r)ay king *won't be there*	PAY
wood	
wood	ASH, DEAL, FIR
• wooden measure	ASHEN
• wooden square	DEALT
• wooden saint	FIRST
wood	BOWL, JACK
wood processor	LATHE, TERMITE
wood, *say*	BOLE, TIMBRE, WOULD
woodcraft	ELDERSHIP
woodcut(ter)	SAW
woodcutter, *say*	FELLAH
wooden-faced	VENEERED
wooden junk	LUMBER
wooden vessel, *say*	TREPAN
Woodwork	EAST LYNNE
wool	
woollen fabric, *say*	RUSTLE
wooll [aphis]	SPAHI
woolly creature	GUERNSEY, JERSEY
woolly jumper	LAMB
word	
word of mouth news	GNUS
word processing	WP
word processor	ETYMOLOGIST, WP
word *sound*	WHIRRED
words per minute	WPM
wordsmith	PUNGENT
work	
work	ERG
• second-class work	BERG

Anag [cat]; Any *; Begin IGN–; Endings –ING; eg •; Hidden /cat/; Implied add (on); Implied in (in);

• work *in* an–y, *say*	ENERGY
• work *with* no . . .	ERGO
work	OP(US)
• church work	CHOP
• quiet work	SHOP
• see work	LOOP
• stop work	HOOP
• work a long time	OPERA
• work *at* laundry	OPPRESSING
• work *at* newspaper	OPPRESS
• work *by* painter, *say*	OPTICIAN
• work-force	OPPRESS
• work hard	OPH–
• work *over*<	PO
• work *overtime*(D)	OPERA, OPT
• work problems	OPPOSERS
• work-time	OPERA
• work together	COOP
• workman	OPAL
work	PLY
• admit *to* work	IMPLY
• work *after* the morning . . .	AMPLY
• work *with* timber	PLYWOOD
and	
• work about, *say*	PLICA
• work class, *say*	PLIFORM
• work well, *say*	PLIABLY
work *at* it, *say*	TOILET
work into [shape]	HEAPS, PHASE
wor(k) *not finished*	WOR
work on [road]	DORA
work out [sums]	MUSS
work record	BOOK OF JOB
worked out [in gym]	MINGY
worked [over]	ROVE
working	AT
working	ON
• girl working	SALON
• spacecraft working	LEMON
• vehicle working	CARTON
• working in hospital	ONWARDS
working	(in) HAR–NESS
• girl *working*	HARDINESS
working	INFIRM
working [men are] . . .	MEANER, RENAME
working [models]	SELDOM
working pupils	EYEING, LOOKING, SEEING
working well	INFORM
workman	GRAFTED
workout [when I] . . .	WHINE
work[rate]	TARE, TEAR
workshop striker	HAMMER, MALLET
worker	
worker	ANT
• defame worker	MALIGNANT
• ditch worker	TRENCHANT
• school worker	INFORMANT
• worker in charge	ANTIC
• worker *in* afterthought	PANTS
• worker's child	SONANT
worker	BEE
• worker *at* church	BEECH
• worker for each . . .	BEEPER
• worker on railway	BEERY
worker	HAND
• pack-worker	DECK-HAND
• worker *has* a few . . .	HANDSOME
• worker *on strike*	HANDOUT
worker	MAN
• worker and *French* . . .	MANET
• worker *is given* directions	MANSE
• worker *has* unknown . . .	MANY
worker	TEMP
• worker *has* one . . .	TEMPI
• worker is *French*	TEMPEST
• worker *with* nothing . . .	TEMPO
worker in force	OPERATIVE
worker writing	HAND
Workers' Education Association	WEA
workers' group	BEE, TU
workers' store	HONEYCOMB
world	
world	EARTH
World	
–Bank	BIS
–Boxing Association	WBA
–Boxing Council	WBC
–Championship Tennis	WCT
–Council of Churches	WCC
–Health Organisation	WHO
–Meteorological Organisation	WMO
–Wildlife Fund	WWF
world, *say*	WHIRLED
world terminal	EARTH
worldwide	MONDIAL
worm catcher	EARLY BIRD
worn	
worn by	incl A
worn by *	incl *
• ha–t *worn by* learner	HALT
worn-down (m)at	AT
worn foundations	BRA(SSIERE)
	CORSETS, PANTS, VEST
	(*see also* wear)
worn-out horse	SHORE
worn [shoe]	HOES, HOSE
worry	
worried [mien]	MINE
worry badger, *say*	BAIT, HARASS
worry [over]	ROVE
worrying [sheep]	PHESE
Worshipful	WP

Letter replaced \c\at; Omit (a); Pointers *out*; Retain a; Split B_ED; Down (D); Backwards <or ^

worst	
[Coat] *Worsted*?	ATOC, CATO, TACO
worsted	BESTED
worsted [a Red] . . .	DARE, DEAR
	RADE, READ
worthless ship	JUNK
would	
would-be queen	PAWN
would he, *say*	WOODY
would *you say*	WOOD
would you say 'No'?	KNOW
would you say so?	SEW, SOW
wound	
wound	SCAR
• wound an insect	SCARABEE
• wound inflamed	SCARRED
• wound sailor	SCARAB
• wound stripe	SCAR
wound fly	WING
wound man with knife	STABLES
wounded	BULLETIN
wounded [deer that's] . . .	SHATTERED
woven	(*see* weave)
wrap	
wrapped in pa/per for	
m/y . . .	PERFORM
wrapped in *	incl in *
• is *wrapped in* hide	SISKIN
wrapping a . . .	incl A
wrapping *	incl A
• hide *wrapping* is . . .	SISKIN
wreathe	
[it was] *wreathed in* . . .	WAIST, WAITS
wreathed in [smoke]	MOKES
wreck	
wreckage of [yacht]	CATHY
wrecked [ship]	HIPS
Wren church	WRENCH
wrestle	
[arm]-*wrestling*	MAR, RAM
wrestling [ring is] . . .	RISING
wretched	
[lived] *wretchedly*	DEVIL
wretched [life]	FILE, LIEF
wriggle	
[eels] *wriggling*	ELSE, SEEL
wriggling [past]	PATS, SPAT, STAP
wriggly [adder]	DREAD
wring	
wring [neck or] . . .	RECKON
wring out [sheet]	THESE
wring [withers]	WRITHES
wringer, *say*	MANGEL
wrinkle	
wrinkle, *say*	PUKKA
wrinkled [skin]	INKS, SINK

wrinkles	HEADLINES
write[1]	
write	PEN
• mother writes	DAMPENS
• write a number . . .	PENNINE
• write songs	PENCHANTS
• write *to* Edward	PENNED
• write *to* Gotham	PENNY
and	
• write a little, *say*	PENSUM
• write riddle, *say*	PENSIVE
• write *to* a number, *say*	PENNATE
• write *to* worker, *say*	PENNANT
• writing material, *say*	PENTACLE
and	
• write *back*<	NEP
write-*up*(D)^	NEP
• write-*up* Greek letter	NEPETA
• write-*up* in i–t	INEPT
• write-*up* song	NEPTUNE
	(*see also* writer)
write[2]	
good writing	BIBLE, NT, OT
	SCRIPTURE(S)
write off [car]	ARC
write, *say*	INDICT, RITE, (W)RIGHT
write up notes(D)^	SETON
writing	HAND
• second writing	BACKHAND
• writing report	HANDCLAP
• writing *with* unknown . . .	HANDY
writing	MS
• he *has* writing	HEMS
• writing up . . . (D)^	SM
writing a synonym	INSCRIBING
writing cards	HAND
writing out [the list]	THISTLE
written about a . . .	incl A
written about *	incl *
• wor–ds *written about*	
out[set]	WORSTEDS
written in full	
• is *written in full*	ISLAND
• *written in full*, it . . .	ITALIAN
written in [prose]	PORES, POSER, SPORE
written in S/pan/ish	PAN
written in(to) *	incl in *
• out[set] *written in* wor–ds	WORSTEDS
	(*see also* wrote)
writer	
writer	ELIA
writer	NIB
• writer aboard	SNIBS
• writer beats . . .	NIBLICKS
• writer lost blood	NIBBLED
writer	I, ME

writer	PEN	*wrong way* to VIP<	PIVOT
• lower writer	COW-PEN	*wrong way* up(D)^	PU
• writer *has* no *French*	PENNON	*wrong* [ways]	SWAY, YAWS
• writer *with* some . . .	PENNINE	*wrong, [wrong]*	GROWN
	(see also write[1])	*wrong*[doer]	ODER, RODE
writer	BUCHAN, POE, WELLS et al	*wrong*[doing]	DINGO
• writer present, *say*	BUCCANEER	*wrongfully* [the law] . . .	WEALTH
• writer *exactly* . . .	POET	*wrongly constructed* [arch]	CHAR
• writer *after* 500 . . .	DWELLS	*wrongly executed* [turn]	RUNT
writer or two	TWAIN	**wrote**	
Writer to the Signet	WS	[wrote] *off*	TOWER
writer's block	PAD	*wrote off* [cars]	ARCS, SCAR
wrong		[wrote] *novel*	TOWER
wrong	TORT	[wrote] *out*	TOWER
• girl's wrong . . .	DISTORT	wrote, *say*	PEND
• when wrong	ASSORT	• wrote in Greece	PENDING
• wrong river	TORTOISE	• wrote *to* hospital department	PENDENT
• wrong *turning*<	TROT	• wrote *to* worker	PENDANT
wrong again	SECOND SLIP	wrote, *say*	ROTE
wrong fount	WF		*(see also* write)
wrong letters	TYPOS	**wrought**	
wrong [letters]	SETTLER	[over]*wrought*	ROVE
[wrong] *letters*	GROWN	*wrought* [iron panel]	NONPAREIL
wrong mark	(A)CROSS, X	**wry**	
[wrong] *parts*	GROWN	[spoke] *wryly*	POKES
wrong [parts]	PRATS, SPRAT, STRAP	*wry* [smile]	LIMES, MILES, SLIME
wrong sign	(A)CROSS, X	**w-worker**	WANT
wrong version of [song]	SNOG	**Wye**	
wrong way<	DR, EVA, TS	Wye, *say*	WHY, Y
	YAW	Wyeville	ROSS

X

across, axis, body, chi, Christ, chromosome, craft, cross, draw, ex, Exe, factor, film, generation, height, *illiterate's sign*, kiss, particle, *PM's address*, ray, reactance, *sign of the times*, spot marked, takes, ten, ten thousand, times, unknown, variable, vitamin, vote, *wrong sign*, xi, Xian, Xmas

X		X-ray	CROSS-BEAM
X		Xantippe	SHREW
• related to x	TEN	Xeres	SHERRY
• x + 1	OFTEN	XLNC	EXCELLENCY
• x-square	TENACE	XPDNC	EXPEDIENCY
x + 1	TENT		
	XI		

Y

axis, alloy, chromosome, factor, level, moth, one hundred and fifty (thousand), track, unknown, variable, *why*, *Wye*, yard, year, yen, yes, yocto-, young, yttrium

y	
Y-*front*	start with Y
• our Y-*front*	YOUR
Y, *say*	WHY, WYE
yacht	
[yacht]-*building*	CATHY
yacht's *bow*	Y
yacht's *stern*	T
yap	
yap	PAY BACK, RETALIATE
yapping, *say*	BARKHAN
yard	
yard	CID, Y, YD
yard measure	AREA
year	
year	A(NNUS), Y, YR
year of reign	AR
year *off*	omit Y
• man(y) *take* year *off*	MAN
[year] *off*	YARE
yearly	PA
• yearly call	PARING
• yearly employment	PAUSE
• yearly expense	PARENTAL
yearly meeting	AGM
yellow	
yellow	OR
• yellow *in* m–e	MORE
• yellow metal	ORAL
• yellow timber	ORDEAL
yellow bird	CHICKEN
yellow invertebrate	SPINELESS
yellow plate	CHROME
yellow polish	BUFF
yen	YN
yeomanry	YEO
yes	
yes	AY, AYE
–*French*	OUI
–*French/German*	OUIJA
–*German*	JA
–*Italian*	SI
–*Russian*	DA
–*Spanish*	SI

yew	
yew, *say*	EU, EWE, U, YOU
yews, *say*	EUS, EWES, US, USE, UU, YOUSE
yield	
yield from [shares]	SHEARS
yield, *say*	SEED
yielding [oil]	OLI–
yielding, *say*	SEEDING
yields [much] . . .	CHUM
Yorkshire	
Yorkshire town, *say*	ARROGATE
Yorkshire town, *say*	LEADS
• Yorkshire beauty queen, *say*	MISLEADS
Yorkshireman	TYKE
you	
you	THOU
• you *on* the beach	THOUSANDS
you	YE
• you *exactly*	YET
• you *note*	YETI
• you soldiers	YEMEN
you are very generous, *say*	BEGONIA
you are, *say*	UR, YORE, YOUR
you can get [wet in] . . .	TWINE
you can *hear*	YUKON
you can hear a noise	ANNOYS
you can see so/me ant/s . . .	MEANT
you desert	THOUSAND
you *in France*	TU, VOUS
you *in Germany*	DU, DICH, SIE
you *in Italy*	LEI, TU, VOI
you *in Spain*	TU, USTED, VOSOTROS
y*ou in the middle*	O
you may have [to shout]	OUTSHOT
you might say we . . .	OUI, WEE
you *no longer*	THEE, THOU, YE
you *once*	THEE, THOU, YE
you queue	UQ
you queue *up*(D)^	QU
you, *say*	EU
• a girl *with* you	ADIEU
• you are a sham	EUPHONY
• you are from the East	EURASIAN
• you dog!	EUCHRE

Letter replaced \c\at; Omit (a); Pointers *out*; Retain <u>a</u>; Split B_ED; Down (D); Backwards <or ^

you, *say*	EWE	young runner	ERRAND BOY
• you were	EWER	young sailor	SEASON
• you *in* telephone system	STEWED	young salmon, *say*	GRILL(E)S
you, *say*	U	young swan, *say*	SIGNET
• you fool!	UNIT	young swimmer	ELVER
• you get better	URALI	younger	YR
• you *have* a case	UKASE	younger brother	ABEL
• you make tidy	UNEATEN	youngest son	BENJAMIN
you, *say*	YEW	youngster	MINOR
you say no	KNOW	**your**	
you see, *say*	UC	your	YR
you *sound* . . .	EU, EWE, U, YEW	your *head*	Y
you will, *say*	YULE	Your Holiness	SV
• you will record	YULE-LOG	your *opposite*	MY
young		your *predecessor*	THY
young actress, *say*	MISLEAD(ING)	your room is No, 8, *say*	URINATE
young bird lost blood	SQUABBLED	your, *say*	THIGH, YORE
young bird, *say*	CHEAPER	your uncle	BOB
young bounder	JOEY, LAMB, LEVERET	yours	NOTOUR
young Conservative	BLUE BABY	yours truly	I, ME
young cook	FRY	**youth**	
young feller	WASHINGTON	youth	MINOR
young gangster	BOYHOOD	Youth Hosteller, *say*	CAMPANOLOGIST
young insect	LITTERBUG	youth leader	GUIDER
young lad *after* money	DOUGHBOY	youth *leader*	Y
young learner	BABEL	youth *leaders*	WISE, YS
young male fish	LADLING	youth *leaders*	YO
young male worker, *say*	BUOYANT	youth, *say*	BUOYAGE
young pi-dog, *say*	PIPE UP	**Yule log**	HOLLYWOOD
young refuse . . .	LITTER		

Anag [cat]; Any *; Begin IGN–; Endings –ING; eg •; Hidden /cat/; Implied add (on); Implied in (in);

Z

atomic number, axis, bar, bend, boson, cedilla, contraction-mark, DNA, factor, impedance, integers, izzard, *last character*, last letter, omega, particle, proton number, two thousand, seven, seven thousand, two million, *sound of sleep*, unknown, variable, Zambia, zed, zee, zenith, zepto-, zero, zeta, zetta, zone

Zaire	ZR	zero *fall-out*	omit O
Zambia	Z	• bor(o)n *has* zero *fall-out*	BORN
Zamenhof's language	ESPERANTO	zero population growth	ZPG
Zantippe(Zentippe)	SHREW		
zero			*(see also* no², nothing*)*
zero	DUCK, LOVE	**zig-zag**	
	NIL, NO	*zig-zag* [line]	LIEN, NEIL, NILE
	NOTHING, NOUGHT	*zig-zagging* [about]	U-BOAT
zero	O	**Zone Standard Time**	ZST
• zero hour	OH	**zoo**	
• zero mark	OSCAR	zoo-keeper	NOAH
• zero-rated	ORATED	zoo-keeper's assistant	HAM, JAPHET
zero	OUGHT		SHEM